Volume III.

The Sermons of John Donne

John Egerton, first Earl of Bridgewater
From the portrait at Mertoun, Roxburghshire, in the
possession of the Earl of Ellesmere.

THE
SERMONS
OF
JOHN DONNE

Edited,
with Introductions
and Critical Apparatus, by
GEORGE R. POTTER
and
EVELYN M. SIMPSON

In Ten Volumes

III.

UNIVERSITY OF CALIFORNIA PRESS
BERKELEY AND LOS ANGELES
1957

Table of Contents

Volume III

List of Illustrations

Volume III

Prefatory Note

BEFORE his untimely death George Potter had done a considerable amount of work on the text of this volume, but he left no material for the Introduction. I have supplied this, and have collected and revised the textual notes. I wish to express my gratitude to the friends who have helped me, and in particular to Mrs. Mary Holtby and Miss Elizabeth Wade White. Miss Helen Gardner, Reader in English Literature in the University of Oxford, has given me valuable advice on some special points. My thanks are due to His Grace the Duke of Bedford for permission to reproduce the portrait at Woburn Abbey of Donne's patroness, Lucy, Countess of Bedford, before whom one of the sermons in this volume was preached; and to the Delegates of the Clarendon Press for kindly allowing us to make use of their photograph of this portrait, which appeared in Volume VIII of *The Works of Ben Jonson,* edited by C. H. Hereford and Percy and Evelyn Simpson. I am also much indebted to the Right Honorable the Earl of Ellesmere for his kindness in allowing me to reproduce the fine portrait at Mertoun, St. Boswells, of his ancestor the first Earl of Bridgewater.

E. M. S.

Introduction

THIS volume continues the series of sermons preached by Donne at Lincoln's Inn and Whitehall, and at the close of it we reach his appointment to the Deanery of St. Paul's Cathedral, and his subsequent relinquishment of his office as Reader in Divinity at Lincoln's Inn. It covers the period from the beginning of April, 1620, to the middle of February, 1621/2.

In the first eight sermons we see Donne in a mood of frustration and perplexity. This is particularly strong in Sermons 1, 6, 7, and 8, where he repeats the cry of the Preacher in *Ecclesiastes,* "Vanity of vanities, all is vanity," and later echoes Christ's warning, "Woe unto the world because of offences." In the latter part of the volume his mood gradually changes. His melancholy disappears, and in a number of fine sermons[1] he concentrates his thoughts on God made manifest in Christ, the Light of the World. Such an alternation of mood is frequent in Donne's experience, but it is not readily perceived in the sermons until these have been arranged in the order in which they were delivered, since the arrangement of the Folios is planned according to the ecclesiastical seasons or according to the place at which the sermons were preached.

There is, of course, no contradiction between the first and second parts of the volume. All the sermons are soundly based on the Christian Faith, but there is a difference of mood and emphasis. In the first part Donne shows us that he is acutely aware of the human predicament, and that he is himself involved in it. Something of this may be due to personal disappointment or to a spell of poor health, but in Sermons 6, 7, and 8 Donne shows himself troubled by the political situation in Europe and the disasters which overcame the Elector's cause. His continental travels in Doncaster's embassy in 1619 had brought him into close touch with the Elector and his wife, the Princess Elizabeth. He must have seen for himself how great were the

---

[1] The latter part of the volume is not uniformly fine. Sermon 10 is elaborate but not very interesting, and Sermon 18 is short and disappointing, inferior in quality to several of the sermons in the earlier part.

dangers which threatened the Protestant cause in Europe, and must have realized that the impending war would bring disaster to millions of Catholics and Protestants alike. King James had hoped that the embassy would help to keep the peace, but his effort had failed, and the miseries of the Thirty Years' War began.

Sermon 1 was preached at Whitehall on April 2, 1620. It begins with a theme to which we have already alluded—the vanity of vanities, the vexation and weariness, the sense of frustration in worldly things. Donne admits the greatness of the universe: "all the world together, hath amazing greatness, and an amazing glory in it, for the order and harmony, and continuance of it"—but yet the world is not eternal, it will pass away. "Therefore *Solomon* shakes the world in peeces, he dissects it, and cuts it up before thee, that so thou mayest the better see, how poor a thing, that particular is, whatsoever it be, that thou sets thy love upon in this world. He threads a string of the best stones, of the best Jewels in this world, knowledge in the first Chapter, delicacies in the second, long life in the third, Ambition, Riches, Fame, strength in the rest, and then he shows you an Ice, a flaw, a cloud in all these stones, he layes this infamy upon them all, *vanity, and vexation of spirit."*[2]

The main body of the sermon is concerned with the danger of riches to the soul. "Some sins we have done, because we are rich; but many more because we would be rich; And this is a spiritual harm, the riches do their owners. . . . Summe up the diseases that voluptuousness by the ministery of riches imprints in the body; the battery that malice, by the provocation of riches, layes to the fortune; the sins that confidence in our riches, heaps upon our souls; and we shall see, that though riches be reserved to their owners, yet it is to their harm."[3]

The sermon is not, however, an indiscriminate attack on wealth of all kinds. Donne distinguishes between money acquired by trade which enriches the community, and money acquired by usury: "And this good use is not, when thou makest good use of thy Money, but when the Common-wealth, where God hath given thee thy station, makes use of it: The Common-wealth must suck upon it by trade, not it upon the Common-wealth, by usury. Nurses that give suck to

---

[2] P. 48.
[3] P. 54–55.

children, maintain themselves by it too; but both must be done; thou must be enriched so, by thy money, as that the state be not impoverished."[4]

The close of the sermon is sombre. Donne describes the death of the wicked rich man: "The substance of the ungodly shall be dryed up like a river; and they shall make a sound like a thunder, in rain. It shall perish, and it shall be *in Parabolam,* it shall be the wonder, and the discourse of the time. . . . he shall hear, or he shall whisper to himself that voice: O fool, This night they will fetch away thy soul; he must go under the imputation of a fool, where the wisdome of this generation, (which was all the wisdome he had) will do him no good; he must go like a fool. His soul must be fetch'd away; he hath not his *In manus tuas,* his willing surrender of his Soul ready; It must be fetch'd in the night of ignorance, when he knows not his own spiritual state; It must be fetch'd in the night of darkness, in the night of solitude, no sence of the assistance of the communion of Saints in the Triumphant, nor in the Militant Church; in the night of *disconsolatenes,* no comfort in that seal, Absolution, . . . and it must be fetch'd this night, the night is already upon him, before he thought of it."[5]

We have printed this sermon as one, though the reader will see that on p. 60 there is a heading "The Second Sermon Preached at White-Hall upon *Ecclesiastes* 5.12, & 13." Our reasons for so doing will be found at the beginning of the Textual Notes for this volume.

The next sermon (No. 2) was preached at Whitehall four weeks later. Donne gave his hearers a discourse which was evidently more to their taste than the sombre attack on riches which had preceded it. It has been preserved in four manuscripts (*D, L, M, P*) as well as in the Folio of 1640, which appears to give us a slightly revised form of the manuscript text.[6] In this sermon Donne considered the national blessings for which the psalmist prayed, and transferred the application from Israel to his own nation. The blessings mentioned in the psalm were first of a temporal kind—victory, plenty, and health—and secondly spiritual, allegiance to the true God. Donne spent an

---

[4] P. 65.

[5] Pp. 70–71.

[6] See the textual notes on lines 137, 222 of this sermon, and also Vol. I, pp. 69–70, n. 44.

unnecessary amount of time in considering the comments of those Fathers who debated whether temporal blessings would be considered blessings at all, but he finally decided that peace, plenty, and health were seals and testimonies of God's blessing. He converted the psalmist's prayer for victory into a eulogy of peace, and made an adroit compliment to King James in "an acknowledgement of blessed-nesse, that we are borne in a Christian Church, in a Reformed Church, in a Monarchy, in a Monarchy composed of Monarchies, and in the time of such a Monarch, as is a Peace-maker, and a peace-preserver both at home and abroad; ..."[7]

"For the first temporall blessing of peace, we may consider the love-linesse, the amiablenesse of that, if we looke upon the horror and gastlinesse of warre: either *in Effigie,* in that picture of warre, which is drawn in every leafe of our own Chronicles, in the blood of so many Princes, and noble families, or if we looke upon warre it selfe, at that distance where it cannot hurt us, as God had formerly kindled it amongst our neighbours, and as he hath transferred it now to remoter Nations, whilest we enjoy yet a Goshen in the midst of all those Egypts."[8]

In speaking of the blessing of plenty, Donne makes the same lament that was made by Ben Jonson, that so many families had left the land for the City, or rather, "have brought their lands into the City, they have brought all their Evidences into Scriveners shops, and changed all their renewing of leases every seaven yeares, into renewing of bonds every six moneths."[9] On the subject of health Donne has some heartfelt words to say. "What is all the peace of the world to me, if I have the rebellions and earth-quakes of shaking and burning Feavers in my body? What is all the plenty of the world to me, if I have a languishing consumption in my blood, and in my marrow? ... All temporall blessings are insipid and tastlesse, without health."[10]

The nation is not truly blessed, unless these blessings are lasting, for the people of the text are a living organism renewed from one generation to another. "Nay, the people are not blessed, if these bless-ings be not permanent; for, it is not onely they that are alive now, that are the people; but the people is the succession." And the term

---

[7] P. 80.

[8] P. 81.

[9] P. 82.

[10] Pp. 82–83.

people includes the King as well as his subjects; the King must join his subjects in blessing God, and the people must see that the King partakes in the blessings given by God.[11]

Finally Donne comes to the spiritual blessing of the text—"Blessed are the people whose God is the Lord." "In which, first wee must propose a *God,* that there is one, and then appropriate this God to our selves, that he be *our God,* and lastly, be sure that we have the right God, that *our God be the Lord.*"[12] Donne points out that there are many professing Christians who are practically atheists. "He that enterprises any thing, seeks any thing, possesses any thing without recourse to God, without acknowledging God in that action, he is, for that particular, an Atheist, he is without God in that; and if hee doe so in most of his actions, he is for the most part an Atheist. If he be an Atheist every where, but in his Catechisme, if onely then he confesse a God when hee is asked, Doest thou beleeve that there is a God, and never confesse him, never consider him in his actions, it shall do him no good, to say at the last day, that he was no speculative Atheist, he never thought in his heart, that there was no God, if hee lived a practique Atheist, proceeded in all his actions without any considera-tion of him."[13] But to those who recognize God not only in their words, but in their actions, and who accustom themselves to a per-petual sense of the presence of God, He manifests Himself as their God, and each one can speak of Him as *Deus meus* and *Deus noster,* my God and our God. "It is a wise and a provident part, to ask more of him, whose store is inexhaustible; So if I feele God, as hee is *Deus meus,* as his Spirit works in me, and thankfully acknowledge that, *Non sum ingratus;* But if I derive this Pipe from the Cistern, this *Deus meus,* from *Deus noster,* my knowledge and sense of God, from that knowledge which is communicated by his Church, in the preach-ing of his Word, in the administration of his Sacraments, in those other meanes which he hath instituted in his Church, for the assist-ance and reparation of my soule that way, *Non ero vacuus,* I shall have a fuller satisfaction, a more abundant refection then if I rely upon my private inspirations: for there he is *Deus noster.*"[14]

---

[11] P. 84.
[12] P. 86.
[13] Pp. 86–87.
[14] P. 88.

The two sermons which we have placed as Nos. 3 and 4 were preached at Lincoln's Inn, probably in the Easter Term, which this year must have begun rather late, for Easter Day itself, which was always in the vacation, was celebrated on April 16. These two sermons are placed in *Fifty Sermons* immediately after the sermons on *John* 5.22 and 8.15, which we printed as Sermons 15 and 16 of Volume II of our edition. There Donne took two texts which appeared to contradict each other, and showed that there was no real discrepancy when the true sense of both was understood. He remarked that he thought it "a usefull and acceptable labour, ... to employ for a time those Evening exercises to reconcile some such places of Scripture, as may at first sight seem to differ from one another."[15] Careful examination of the present sermons shows that these two must belong to the same course, for they are similarly complementary to each other.[16] In Sermon 3 Donne took as his text the words of *Job* 19.26: "And though, after my skin, worms destroy this body, yet in my flesh shall I see God," while the text of Sermon 4 was, "Now this I say, brethren, that flesh and blood cannot inherit the kingdom of God." At the close of this latter sermon Donne remarks:

Adde we but this, by way of recollecting this which hath been said now, upon these words, and that which hath been formerly said upon those words of *Job,* which may seem to differ from these, (*In my flesh I shall see God*) *Omne verum omni vero consentiens,* whatsoever is true in it selfe agrees with every other truth. Because that which *Iob* says, and that which *Saint Paul* says, agree with the truth, they agree with one another. For, as *Saint Paul* says, *Non omnis caro eadem caro, there is one flesh of man, another of beasts,* so there is one flesh of *Job,* another of *Saint Paul;* And *Jobs* flesh can see God, and *Pauls* cannot; because the flesh that *Job* speakes of hath overcome the destruction of skin and body by wormes in the grave, and so is mellowed and prepared for the sight of God in heaven; And *Pauls* flesh is overcome by the world. . . . *Jobs* argument is but this, *some* flesh shall see God, (*Mortified* men here, *Glorified* men there shall) *Pauls* argument is this, *All* flesh *shall not* see God, (*Carnall* men here, *Impenitent* men there, shall not.)[17]

---

[15] Vol. II, p. 325.

[16] In Vol. II, Introduction, p. 41, we unwisely stated, "If he [Donne] did actually go on to preach such a series, the other sermons in it are lost to us." We had read these present sermons, but had not then realized the full implications of the evidence given below.

[17] Pp. 132–133.

It is therefore a fair conclusion that these two sermons were preached not many weeks later than the two earlier ones, which we know to have been preached one in the morning and one in the evening of January 30, 1619/20. Since these present sermons deal with death and resurrection, the season of Easter is the most likely period for them, though we do not exclude the possibility that they may have been preached during Lent.[18]

Sermon 3 shows Donne's obsession with the physical aspects of death—the disintegration, the corruption, the skeleton, the worms. We are familiar with these in his poems, but here in prose they are more distasteful. From the contemplation of these horrors Donne passes on to the lessons of resurrection which can be learnt from Nature.

And yet as *Solomon* sends us to creatures, and to creatures of a low rank and station, to Ants and Spiders, for instruction, so Saint *Gregory* sends us to creatures, to learne the Resurrection. . . . That glorious creature, that first creature, the light, dyes every day, and every day hath a resurrection . . . ; from the Cedar of *Libanus,* to the Hyssop upon the wall, every leafe dyes every yeare, and every yeare hath a Resurrection. . . . Doe all kindes of earth regenerate, and shall onely the Churchyard degenerate? Is there a yearely Resurrection of every other thing, and never of men? . . . All other things are preserved, and continued by dying; . . . And canst thou, O man, suspect of thy selfe, that the end of thy dying is an end of thee? Fall as low as thou canst, corrupt and putrefie as desperately as thou canst, . . . thinke thy selfe nothing; . . . even that nothing is as much in his power, as the world which he made of nothing; And, as he called thee when thou wast not, as if thou hadst been, so will he call thee againe, when thou art ignorant of that being which thou hast in the grave, and give thee againe thy former, and glorifie it with a better being.[19]

This, however, is only an analogy, not an argument, and Donne turns to Scripture for stronger proof. Even the Old Testament bears witness to "a generall, though not an explicite knowledge of the resurrection." Christ referred the Sadducees to the words of God to Moses, *I am the God of Abraham, the God of Isaac, and the God of*

---

[18] We have here followed our usual practice of assigning to the later rather than the earlier probable date those sermons for the date of which we have only conjectural evidence. We know from Donne's own statement (Vol. II, p. 325) that his courses of sermons did not necessarily end with the term, but might be extended over a longer period.

[19] Pp. 97–98.

Jacob. And Donne takes his stand with the majority of expositors of his day in interpreting the words of Job, in the text which he had chosen, as a reference to the resurrection. He interrupts his sermon, however, with an interesting aside, to arrest his hearers' attention:

I am not all here, I am here now preaching upon this text, and I am at home in my Library considering whether *S. Gregory,* or *S. Hierome,* have said best of this text, before. I am here speaking to you, and yet I consider by the way, in the same instant, what it is likely you will say to one another, when I have done. You are not all here neither; you are here now, hearing me, and yet you are thinking that you have heard a better Sermon somewhere else, of this text before; you are here, and yet you think you could have heard some other doctrine of down-right *Predestination,* and *Reprobation* roundly delivered somewhere else with more edification to you; you are here, and you remember your selves that now yee think of it, this had been the fittest time, now, when every body else is at Church, to have made such and such a private visit; and because you would bee there, you are there.[20]

Donne continues in a loftier strain to deal with the concluding words of the text—"I shall see God":

Ego, I, the same person; *Ego videbo,* I shall see; I have had no looking-glasse in my grave, to see how my body looks in the dissolution; I know not how. I have had no houre-glasse in my grave to see how my time passes; I know not when: for, when my eylids are closed in my death-bed, *the Angel hath said to me, That time shall be no more;* Till I see eternity, the ancient of days, I shall see no more; but then I shall....

No man ever saw God and liv'd; and yet, I shall not live till I see God; and when I have seen him I shall never dye.... As he that fears God, fears nothing else, so, he that sees God, sees every thing else: when we shall see God, *Sicuti est,* as he is, we shall see all things *Sicuti sunt,* as they are; for that's their Essence, as they conduce to his glory. We shall be no more deluded with outward appearances: for, when this sight, which we intend here comes, there will be no delusory thing to be seen. All that we have made as though we saw, in this world, will be vanished, and I shall see nothing but God, and what is in him; ...[21]

Sermon 4 is less interesting than its predecessor. Donne gives us a long discussion, first of what various heretical sects had conjectured about the resurrection of the body, and secondly, of what St. Jerome, Melanchthon, Musculus, and the Schoolmen had said of the Trans-

[20] P. 110.
[21] Pp. 110–112.

figuration of Christ, which was a prefiguration of the resurrection body. After this second discussion Donne gives his own summary of the points in which the Transfiguration may be taken to anticipate the future glory of the saints:

Let us modestly take that which is expressed in it, and not search over-curiously farther into that which is signifyed, and represented by it; which is, the state of glory in the Resurrection. First, his face shin'd as the Sunne, says that Gospell, he could not take a higher comparison, for our Information, and for our admiration in this world, then the Sunne. And then, the Saints of God in their glorifyed state are admitted to the same comparison. *The righteous shall shine out as the Sunne in the Kingdome of the Father;* the Sunne of the firmament which should be their compari-son, will be gone; But the Sun of grace and of glory, the Son of God shall remain;[22] and they shall shine as he; that is, in his righteousnesse.

In this transfiguration, *his clothes were white,* says the text; ... *As white as snow,* and *as white as light,* says that Gospel. Light implies an active power, Light is operative, and works upon others. The bodies of the Saints of God, shall receive all impressions of glory in themselves, and they shall doe all that is to bee done, for the glory of God there. There, they shall stand in his service, and they shall kneel in his worship, and they shall fall in his reverence, and they shall sing in his glory, they shall glorifie him in all positions of the body; They shall be glorified in themselves passively, and they shall glorify God actively, *sicut Nix, sicut Lux,* their *beeing,* their *doing* shall be all for him ....[23]

After some controversial matter against the Church of Rome, Donne goes on to interpret his text in a secondary sense, that is, of the kingdom of God in this world. In this interpretation he is following the example of Tertullian, whom he quotes on the subject. It enables him to preach at some length on the claim of the Church to represent the divine kingdom:

You see then, what this Kingdome of God is; It is, when he comes, and is welcome, when he comes in his *Sacraments,* and speaks in his *Word;* when he speaks and is answered; knocks and is received, (he knocks in his *Ordinances,* and is received in our *Obedience* to them, he knocks in his *example,* and most holy conversation, and is received in our *conformity,* and imitation.) So have you seen what the *Inheritance* of this Kingdome

---

[22] Here we have the pun on *Sun* and *Son* which Donne makes in the *Hymne to God the Father,* lines 15–16, and in his Christmas sermon on *Isaiah* 7.14 (Vol. VI of the present edition, p. 173, lines 199–200).

[23] Pp. 120–121.

is, it is a Having, and Holding of the Gospel, a present, and a permanent possession, a holding fast, lest another (another Nation, another Church) take our Crown.[24]

Sermon 5 was preached at Lincoln's Inn on Trinity Sunday, 1620. Like all Donne's sermons it is worthy of study, and it is clearly and carefully planned. From the story of the appearance of three men to Abraham before the destruction of Sodom, Donne drew many practical lessons. Abraham showed hospitality and charity to these strangers, whom he took to be ordinary wayfarers though they proved to be the messengers of God.

Now here is our copie, but who writes after this copie? *Abraham* is *pater multitudinis,* A father of large posterity, but he is dead without issue, or his race is failed; for, who hath this hospitall care of relieving distressed persons now? Thou seest a needy person, and thou turnest away thine eye; but it is the Prince of Darknesse that casts this mist upon thee; Thou stoppest thy nose at his sores, but they are thine own incompassionate bowels that stinke within thee; Thou tellest him, he troubles thee, and thinkest thou hast chidden him into a silence; but he whispers still to God, and he shall trouble thee worse at last, when he shall tell thee, in the mouth of Christ Jesus, *I was hungry and ye fed me not:* ... Give really, and give gently; Doe kindly, and speake kindly too, for that is Bread, and Hony.[25]

On the whole, however, the sermon is somewhat disappointing. It has little of Donne's peculiar power of showing us truth by lightning flashes of insight.

Sermons 6 and 7, which were preached at Lincoln's Inn, are closely connected, for they both take as their text *Matthew* 18.7, and No. 7 is evidently a continuation of No. 6. They cannot belong to the course preached during the first half of 1620, for which we have already had four sermons, in which the second of each pair is preached on a text which had to be reconciled with the text of the first sermon. The general tone of these two sermons indicates that they were preached in the winter of 1620, probably soon after November 24, 1620, when the first news of the defeat of the Elector Palatine reached London. There was great agitation in the city, and soon there arose a demand that King James should intervene in support of the Protestant cause on

---

[24] P. 130.
[25] P. 137.

the Continent.[26] There are passages in Sermon 7 which indicate that Donne was inculcating in his hearers a policy of patience in avoiding rash criticism of the King and his ministers. Donne himself had taken part as chaplain in the embassy which James had sent to the Continent and he had preached before the Prince and Princess Palatine (Vol. II, Sermon 12). He was a strong admirer of the Princess, who was Elizabeth, only daughter of King James, and he sent her copies of his Devotions and also two of his sermons.[27] But mobs who clamour for immediate war are often in the wrong. Whatever we may think of James's vacillating policy, we can recognize that Donne was probably right in recommending abstention from violent criticism.

Speaking of the man who is easily scandalized, Donne says:

Hee stays not to give men their Law, to give Princes, and States time to consider, whether it may not be fit for them to come to leagues, and alliances, and declarations for the assistance of the Cause of Religion next year, though not this. But *continuò scandalizatur,* as soon as a *Catholique army* hath given a blow, and got a victory of any of our forces, or friends, or as soon as a *crafty Jesuit* hath forged a Relation, that that Army hath given such a blow, or that such an Army there is, (for many times they intimidate weake men, when they shoote nothing but Paper, when they are onely *Paper-Armies,* and *Pamphlet-Victories,* and no such in truth) *Illico scandalizatur,* yet with these forged rumours, presently hee is scandalized . . .[28]

A little later he observes:

Not to mourn under the sense of evils, that may fall upon us, is a stony disposition; Nay, the hardest stone, marble, will weep towards foul weather. But, to make all *Possible* things *Necessary,* (this may fall upon us, therefore it must fall upon us) and to make contingent, and accidentall things, to be the effects of counsels, (this is fallen upon us, therefore it is fallen by *their practise* that have the government in their hands) this is a vexation of spirit in our selves, and a defacing, a casting of durt in the face of Gods image, of that representation, and resemblance of God, which

---

[26] See S. R. Gardiner, *History of England, 1603–1642,* Vol. III, p. 385: "It was easy to see that, in their hearts, the citizens laid the blame of all that had taken place upon the King. Not a few took refuge in incredulity. The story, it was said, had come through Brussels, and had probably been invented by the Papists. Many days passed before the unwelcome news was accepted."

[27] See Vol. VII of the present edition, pp. 5–6.

[28] P. 179.

he hath imprinted in them, of whom hee hath sayd, *They are Gods*. In divine matters there is principally exercise of our *faith,* That which we understand not, we beleeve. In civill affairs, that are above us, matters of State, there is exercise of our *Hope;* Those ways which we see not, wee hope are directed to good ends. In Civill actions amongst our selves, there is exercise of our *Charity,* Those hearts which we see not, let us charitably beleeve to bee disposed to Gods service.... It is well for us, if, though we be put to take in our sayls, and to take down our masts, yet we can hull it out; that is, if in storms of contradiction, or persecution, the Church, or State, though they be put to accept worse conditions then before, and to depart with some of their outward splendor, be yet able to subsist and swimme above water, and reserve it selfe for Gods farther glory, after the storm is past; onely Christ could becalm the storme; He is a good Christian that can ride out, or board out, or hull out a storme, that by industry, as long as he can, and by patience, when he can do no more, over-lives a storm, and does not forsake his ship for it, that is not scandalized with that State, nor that Church, of which he is a member, for those abuses that are in it.[29]

There is a sense of sadness in these two sermons, which is expressed in Donne's choice of a text: "Woe unto the world, because of offences." We feel in them Donne's unhappiness in the troubles and misfortunes of the times, and his deeper and more persistent sense of the sins and miseries of the world. He recalls that the Old Testament prophets lamented the judgements which they had to pronounce, and that Christ wept bitterly over Jerusalem. Christ is twice recorded to have shed tears of compassion, once for a private grief, the death of Lazarus, and once for "his glorious and beloved City." He implores his hearers to refrain from those sins which grieve God and dishonour the Church in which they have been brought up.

Grieve not then the holy Spirit of God, says the Apostle; extort not from him those Judgements, which he cannot in justice forbear, and yet is grieved to inflict. How often doe we use that motive, to divert young men from some ill actions, and ill courses, How will this trouble your friends, how will this grieve your Mother, this will kill your Father? ... Our sins have grieved our Mother; that is, made the Church ashamed, and blush that she hath washed us, and clothed us, in the whiteness and innocency of Christ Jesus in our baptisme, and given us his bloud to drinke in the other Sacrament. Our sins have made our mother the Church ashamed

[29] Pp. 183–185. Here *to hull* is to lie a-hull or drift to the wind with sails furled, and *to board* is to tack, to sail athwart the wind on alternate sides.

in her selfe, (we have scandalized and offended the Congregation) and our sinnes have defamed and dishonoured our mother abroad, that is, imprinted an opinion in others, that that cannot be a good Church, in which we live so dissolutely, so falsely to our first faith, and contract, and stipulation with God in Baptisme. Wee have grieved our brethren, the Angels, our mother, the Church, and we have killed our *Father: God is the father of us all;* and we have killed him; for *God hath purchased a Church with his bloud,* says Saint *Paul.* And, oh, how much more is God grieved now, that we will make no benefit of that bloud which is shed for us, then he was for the very shedding of that bloud![30]

Helen Gardner in her admirable edition of Donne's *Divine Poems* makes a strong case for assigning the Holy Sonnet "Show me deare Christ, thy spouse, so bright and cleare" to the winter of 1620.[31] The Church which "laments and mournes in Germany and here" is described as "rob'd and tore"—a description which would hardly apply to it in 1617, the date which Gosse ascribed to the poem, but which was fitting enough after the disaster which overtook the Elector's cause late in 1620. The whole poem should be read carefully as an expression of Donne's dismay and bewilderment parallel to that found in the sermons of this period.

This tone of melancholy continues in the next dated sermon (Sermon 8), which was preached before the Countess of Bedford on January 7, 1620/21. Lucy, daughter of John Harington, first Baron Harington of Exton, was married to Edward, third Earl of Bedford, in 1594. She was the most brilliant figure at Court during the early years of James's reign, and she took part in several of the masques of Ben Jonson as well as in Daniel's *Vision of the Twelve Goddesses.* She was the centre of a group of scholars and poets, and she be-

---

[30] Pp. 161–162.

[31] *Divine Poems,* ed. Gardner (1952), pp. 124–125: "I would suggest that Donne has seen a parallel between the captivity of Israel and the total collapse of the Protestants after the defeat of the Elector in the battle of the White Mountain, outside Prague, on October 29, 1620. The news of the defeat reached London on November 24 and caused consternation.... The opening lines [of the sonnet] are an expression of distress at the spectacle Christendom presented at the beginning of the Thirty Years' War. Where is the promised bride? On the one hand there is a figure more like the Babylonish woman of the Apocalypse; on the other, one like the desolate Virgin of Zion, once beloved, now, for her sins, abandoned by her Lord and left to be the prey of her enemies."

friended Drayton, Daniel, Jonson, and Donne, who all in turn sang her praises. Between 1608 and 1614 Donne wrote to her a number of verse epistles. These all emphasize her piety and learning as well as her beauty. Thus in a poem which begins with the line "Reason is our Soules left hand, Faith her right," Donne continues:

> In every thing there naturally growes
> A *Balsamum* to keepe it fresh, and new,
> If 'twere not injur'd by extrinsique blowes;
> Your birth and beauty are this Balme in you.
>
> But you of learning and religion,
> And vertue, and such ingredients, have made
> A methridate, whose operation
> Keepes off, or cures what can be done or said.
>
> Yet, this is not your physicke, but your food,
> A dyet fit for you; for you are here
> The first good Angell, since the worlds frame stood
> That ever did in womans shape appeare.[32]

In the winter of 1612–13 the Countess had a serious illness, in which she was attended by Dr. Burges, an Anglican clergyman of strong Puritan convictions, who in 1604 after preaching before the King was imprisoned for a short time, and then studied medicine at Leyden. After some years he returned to England and built up a practice at Isleworth. His influence with the Countess seems to have been hostile to Donne, who wrote to Goodyer in 1614 that he was afraid that some suspicions of himself had arisen in her mind "rather from some ill impression taken from D. Burges, then that they grow in her self."[33] On August 1, 1613, Chamberlain wrote to Carleton: "Dr. Burges (who is turned phisician) was much about her in her sicknes, and did her more good with his spirituall counsaile, then with naturall phisike."

When the Countess returned to Court it was noted that her dress was much more sober than before, and that she had given up painting her face. Her father died in 1613, and her brother, the second

---

[32] *Poems,* ed. Grierson, I, 189–190.

[33] *Letters* (1651), p. 218. The information about Burges in this paragraph is taken from an article by P. Thomson, "John Donne and the Countess of Bedford," *Modern Language Review,* XLIV (1949), 329–340.

Lord Harington, in February, 1614. On the latter Donne wrote an elegy of 258 lines which he presented to Lady Bedford. After these two bereavements she seems to have worn mourning for some time. There are portraits of her in a black dress with black jewellery and a golden coronet at Woburn Abbey, the seat of the Duke of Bedford, at Alloa Castle in Scotland, and in the Town Hall of Stow-on-the-Wold. The Alloa portrait has the date 1620, and Thomas Pennant in his *Tour of Scotland,* 1776 (II, 219–220) describes it as having been painted by Cornelius Jansen.

The Countess continued to attend on the Queen until the latter's death in 1619. She and her husband were usually in debt, like most of the Jacobean aristocracy, and she was obliged to sell two of the Harington estates which had been left her by her brother. In 1622 she left London and withdrew to Moor Park, Hertfordshire, where she lived till her death in 1627.

The sermon has a melancholy tinge, for Donne took as his text the words of Job, *Loe, though he slay me, yet will I trust in him.* His theme is the transitoriness of life, the certainty of death, and the need for a constant trust in God.

Our whole life is but a *parenthesis,* our *receiving* of our soule, and *delivering* it back againe, makes up the perfect sentence; Christ is *Alpha* and *Omega,* and our *Alpha* and *Omega* is all we are to consider.... This world then is but an *Occasionall* world, a world onely to be us'd; and that but so, *as though we us'd it not:* The next world is the world to be *enjoy'd,* and that so, as that we may *joy* in nothing by the way, but as it directs and conduces to that end; Nay, though we have no Joy at al, though God deny us all conveniences here, *Etiamsi occiderit,* though he end a weary life, with a painefull death, as there is no other hope, but in him, so there needs no other, for that alone is both abundant, and infallible in it selfe.[34]

The whole frame of the world is mortall, *Heaven and earth passe away:* and upon us all, there is an irrecoverable Decree past, *statutum est, It is appointed to all men, that they shall once dye.* But when? quickly;... If thou see a cloud in the aire, aske St. *James* his question, *what is your life?* and give St. *James* his answer, *It is a vapour that appeareth and vanisheth away....* Looke upon the *water,* and we are as that, and as that spilt upon the ground: Looke to the *earth,* and we are not like that, but we are earth it self: At our Tables we feed upon the dead, and in the Temple we tread

---

[34] Pp. 188–189.

LUCY, COUNTESS OF BEDFORD
From the portrait at Woburn Abbey, in the collection of the Duke of
Bedford, reproduced from a photograph in the possession
of the Clarendon Press, Oxford.

upon the dead: and when we meet in a Church, God hath made many *echoes,* many testimonies of our death, in the walls, and in the windowes, and he onely knowes, whether he will not make another testimony of our mortality, of the youngest amongst us, before we part, and make the very *place of our buriall,* our *deathbed.*[35]

Yet Donne's melancholy always stops short of despair. There is a spring of hope within him, for this world and for the next too. He turns to his text, and draws from it the lesson that, whatever might befall, Job based his hope and trust on God.

It is an ill affection to say, I look for nothing at the worlds hands, nor at Gods neither. God onely hath all, and God hath made us capable of all his gifts; and therefore we must neither hope for them, any where else, nor give over our hope of them, from him, by intermitting our *prayers,* or our *industry* in a lawfull calling; for we are bound to suck at those breasts which God puts out to us, and to draw at those springs, which flow from him to us; ... *Job* trusted not in the *meanes,* as in the *fountaine,* but yet *speravit,* he doubted not, but God, who is the *fountaine,* would, by those meanes, derive his blessings, temporall and spirituall, upon him.

Hee Hoped; now *Hope* is onely, or principally of invisible things, for *Hope that is seen, is not hope,* says the Apostle. And therefore, though we may hope for *temporall* things, for health, wealth, strength, and liberty, and victory where Gods enemies oppresse the Church, ... yet our *Hope* is principally directed upon the *invisible* part, and invisible office of those visible and temporall things; which is, that by them, we may be the better able to performe religious duties to God, and duties of assistance to the world. ... And therefore every Christian hope being especially upon spirituall things, is properly, and purposely grounded upon these stones; that it be ... a hope of *pardon,* for that which is past, and then ... a hope of *Grace,* to establish me in that state with God, in which, his pardon hath placed mee, and lastly ... a hope that this *pardon,* and this *grace,* shall lead me to that everlasting *glory,* which shall admit no night, no eclipse, no cloud.[36]

Sermon 9 was preached before the King at Whitehall on February 16, the first Friday in Lent, 1620/21. Donne took as his text a verse from the *First Epistle to Timothy* in which a brief summary of the Christian Faith is given. He opened with an arresting sentence: "This is no Text for an Houre-glasse: if God would afford me *Ezekiahs* signe, *Ut revertatur umbra,* that the shadow might go backward upon the Dial; or *Joshuah*'s signe, *Ut sistat Sol,* that the Sun might stand

[35] P. 202.
[36] Pp. 196–197.

still all the day, this were text enough to employ all the day, and all the dayes of our life. The *Lent,* which we begin now, is a full Tythe of the year; but the houre which we begin now, is not a full tythe of this day, and therefore we should not grudge all that."

The sermon is divided into two main parts, the first dealing with mystery, "the mystery of Godlinesse," the second with the manifestation of Christ. "Here is the compass, that the essential Word of God, the Son of God, *Christ Jesus,* went: He was God, *humbled in the flesh;* he was Man, *received into glory.* Here is the compasse that the written Word of God, *went,* the Bible; that begun in *Moses,* in darknesse, in the *Chaos;* and it ends in Saint *John,* in clearnesse, in a Revelation. Here is the compass of all time, as time was distributed in the Creation, *Vespere & mane;* darknesse, and then light: the Evening and Morning made the Day; Mystery and Manifestation make the Text."[37]

Donne had evidently taken great pains with this sermon, and it is written throughout in a style full of paradox and antithesis. Of Christ's Incarnation he says:

Now, when he was *manifested in the flesh,* it behooved him to be *justified in the spirit;* for he came *in similitudinem carnis peccati:* they took him for a sinner, and they saw him converse with sinners: for any thing they could see, it might have been *Caro peccati,* sinfull flesh; and they saw enough to make them sure that it was *Caro mortis,* mortall flesh. Though he were *Panis de cœlo,* Bread from Heaven, yet himself was hungry; and though he were *fons perennis,* an everlasting spring, yet himself was thirsty; though he were *Deus totius consolationis,* the God of all comfort, yet his soul was heavy unto death; and though he were *Dominus vitæ,* the Lord of Life, yet Death had dominion over him.[38]

Donne defends the Church of England on the ground that it holds the great doctrine of the Apostles' Creed—faith in God the Father, the Creator, faith in God the Son, the Redeemer, and faith in the Holy Spirit—and that it ministers the Word and Sacraments.

... no Scripture is of private interpretation. I see not this mystery by the eye of Nature, of Learning, of State, of mine own private sence; but I see it by the eye of the Church, by the light of Faith, that's true; but yet organically, instrumentally, by the eye of the Church. And this Church is

[37] P. 206.
[38] Pp. 213–214.

that which proposes to me all that is necessary to my salvation, in the Word, and seals all to me in the Sacraments. If another man see, or think he sees more then I; if by the help of his Optick glasses, or perchance but by his imagination, he see a star or two more in any constellation then I do; yet that starre becomes none of the constellation; it addes no limb, no member to the constellation, that was perfect before: so, if other men see that some additional and traditional things may adde to the dignity of the Church, let them say it conduces to the well-being, not to the very being; to the existence, not to the essence of the Church; for that's onely things necessary to salvation. And this mystery is, Faith in a pure conscience: for that's the same thing that is called Godliness in this text: and it is to profess the Gospel of Christ Jesus sincerely, and intirely; to have a conscience testifying to himself, that he hath contributed nothing to the diminution of it, that he labours to live by it, that he hopes to die in it, that he feares not to die for it.[39]

Sermon 10 was preached at Whitehall on April 8, 1621. Donne chose a curious text from the book of *Proverbs,* and the sermon is not particularly interesting, though it has some shrewd passages on the insatiable nature of ambition and covetousness. But the sermon is spoilt by Donne's too evident desire to be learned and ingenious.

No. 11 is a much more eloquent and interesting sermon. In the Folio it is described merely as "Preached at a mariage," without any indication of date, place, and occasion, but through the help of the manuscripts, and of the marriage register of St. Clement Danes Church, London, we are able to present it as affording a most interesting link between Donne and the Washington family. The Ellesmere manuscript (*E*) describes it as preached "By M^r D^r D at ye mariage of M^ris Washington,"[40] and this information is repeated in the list of contents at the beginning of the volume. The Merton manuscript (*M*) describes it as "a Sermon preach'd at St Clements danes by D: Dunn at Mr Washingtons mariage," and the St. Paul's Cathedral manuscript (*P*), which is derived from the same source as *M,* has a similar note, except that the word "danes" is omitted after "Clements." The register of St. Clement Danes, for the possible years, contains no mention of the marriage of a male Washington; the accuracy of the reading "M^ris Washington" in *E* is confirmed, however, by an entry in the register for May 30, 1621, "Margaret

---

[39] P. 210.

[40] See our account of this manuscript in Vol. II, App. A, pp. 365, 369–370.

Washington: Robert Sands." We have found no record of any previous friendship between Donne and the Washington family, but a link is provided by a letter written by Chamberlain to Carleton on June 2, 1621: "The Lady of Doncaster set forward yesterday toward the Spaa having on Wensday maried her fine woman Washington to a younger son of Sir Miles Sandes and gieven her a thousand pound to her portion, besides much more in presents from the King, Prince, and all the great ones about the towne."[41] Evidently Donne preached this sermon at the request of Lord and Lady Doncaster, who were well known for their generosity and extravagant hospitality. Doncaster had much appreciated Donne's sermons during the German tour in 1619, and in the years which followed he did many acts of kindness to Donne, which the latter repaid in his own way.[42]

It should be noted that when John Donne junior printed this sermon in the *Fifty Sermons* of 1649 he suppressed the information given in the manuscripts about the name of the bride and the church where the marriage was celebrated, just as in printing the sermon preached at the marriage of Sir Francis Nethersole with Lucy Goodyer (Vol. II, No. 17) he suppressed the name of Nethersole, which was given in the Merton MS. On the other hand, he gave a long and full title to the sermon preached at the marriage of Lord Herbert's

---

[41] *Letters of John Chamberlain,* ed. McClure, II, 379–380. In a footnote the editor describes the lady as Alice Washington, but this is an error, as is proved by the St. Clement Danes register. Margaret Washington belonged to the famous family from which George Washington was descended. She was the daughter of Lawrence Washington of Sulgrave and Brington, who died in 1616. Her eldest brother, Sir William Washington, married a half sister of the Duke of Buckingham, and one of her younger brothers was a page to Prince Charles and died in Spain in 1623. There is a Latin elegy on his death with the initials "J. D." in MS.

The bridegroom, Robert Sandys, was a younger son of Sir Miles Sandys of Wilburton, Cambs, and a nephew of Sir Edwin Sandys, co-founder of Virginia.

For much of the information in this note we are indebted to Professor R. C. Bald of the University of Chicago.

[42] Donne preached an undated sermon at Essex House, "at the Churching of the Lady Doncaster," another "to the Earl of Carlile, and his Company, at Sion" after Doncaster had been created Earl of Carlisle, and a third "at Hanworth, to my Lord of Carlile, and his company, . . . Aug. 25. 1622."

son to the daughter of the Earl of Bridgewater (Vol. VIII, No. 3). The difference in treatment which the younger Donne accorded to these three marriage sermons is clearly due to political reasons. In 1649 he was courting the favour of the Parliamentarian chiefs. He did not wish to remind them of any connection which the sermons might have had with the now hated name of Buckingham, and Sir Francis Nethersole had been a royalist whose name would be no recommendation. On the other hand, Lord Herbert of Cherbury had made his peace with Parliament before he died in 1648, and he was the kinsman of the powerful Philip, Earl of Pembroke and Montgomery, a strong Parliamentarian, while the Earl of Bridgewater took no part in the Civil War after 1643, when he retired to his house at Ashridge in Hertfordshire. So the volume of *Fifty Sermons* paraded the names of Herbert and Bridgewater, while the two other wedding sermons were headed merely "Preached at a marriage."

This sermon is certainly the finest of the few marriage sermons preached by Donne which are still extant. It is based on a text from *Hosea* in which Donne has deliberately chosen the reading of the Geneva version, "And I will marry thee unto me for ever," instead of that of the Authorized Version, "And I will betroth thee unto me for ever."

In his first sentence he explains that the Hebrew word which he transliterates as *Erash* "signifies not onely a betrothing, as our later Translation hath it, but a mariage . . . so our former Translation had it, and so we accept it, and so shall handle it." He continues, in a plain but vigorous style:

The first mariage that was made, God made, and he made it in Paradise: And of that mariage I have had the like occasion as this[43] to speak before, in the presence of many honourable persons in this company. The last mariage which shall be made, God shall make too, and in Paradise too; in the Kingdome of heaven: and at that mariage, I hope in him that shall make it, to meet, not some, but all this company. The mariage in this Text hath relation to both those mariages: It is it self the spirituall and mysticall mariage of Christ Jesus to the Church, and to every mariage-able soule in the Church: And it hath a retrospect, it looks back to the first

---

[43] This seems to be an allusion to the sermon on *Genesis* 2.18 (Vol. II, No. 17) at the marriage of Sir Francis Nethersole. Nethersole had been Lord Doncaster's secretary on the German embassy.

mariage; for to that the first word carries us, because from thence God takes his metaphor, and comparison, *sponsabo, I will mary; ..."*

The first part of the sermon, in which Donne instructs his hearers in the duties of married life, is clear and outspoken in its demand for the mutual faithfulness of husband and wife, and for their willingness to produce children who shall be brought up in the Christian faith. This is followed by a discussion of the spiritual marriage between Christ and the Christian soul. Here Donne's style at once changes, and becomes more eloquent and impassioned. In the following passage an elaborate pattern is discernible:

... in this spirituall mariage we consider first Christ and his Church, for the Persons, but more particularly Christ and my soul. And can these persons meet? in such a distance, and in such a disparagement can these persons meet? the Son of God and the son of man? When I consider Christ to be *Germen Jehovæ,* the bud and blossome, the fruit and off-spring of Jehovah, Jehovah himself, and my self before he took me in hand, to be, not a Potters vessell of earth, but that earth of which the Potter might make a vessel if he would, and break it if he would when he had made it: When I consider Christ to have been from before all beginnings, and to be still the Image of the Father, the same stamp upon the same metall, and my self a peece of rusty copper, in which those lines of the Image of God which were imprinted in me in my Creation are defaced and worn, and washed and burnt, and ground away, by my many, and many, and many sins: When I consider Christ in his Circle, in glory with his Father, before he came into this world, establishing a glorious Church when he was in this world, and glorifying that Church with that glory which himself had before, when he went out of this world; and then consider my self in my circle, I came into this world washed in mine own tears, and either out of compunction for my self or compassion for others, I passe through this world as through a valley of tears, where tears settle and swell, and when I passe out of this world I leave their eyes whose hands close mine, full of tears too, can these persons, this Image of God, this God himself, this glorious God, and this vessell of earth, this earth it self, this inglorious worm of the earth, meet without disparagement?[44]

Here we have Donne the consummate craftsman, the poet and artist, at work. In the first half of the sermon he had faithfully done his duty as a Christian priest in instructing the couple before him, and the congregation as a whole, in the duties of married life. For this purpose his speech had been plain and practical. Something more,

[44] Pp. 250–251.

however, than a homily on the lines of the Anglican Prayer Book was expected from a well-known preacher on such an occasion, and Donne was able in the second half of his sermon to let the mystical signification of marriage kindle his imagination and inspire his rhetoric. The long sentence beginning "When I consider Christ..." in the passage just quoted is most carefully wrought. It contains three consecutive pairs of parallel clauses, of which each set is a comparison between "Christ...[and]...my self," and these are followed by a final question, in which the dignity of Christ is summed up in three phrases rising in a crescendo, "this Image of God, this God himself, this glorious God," and the inferiority of Donne himself, as a typical human being, is expressed in three phrases sinking in a diminuendo, "this vessell of earth, this earth it self, this inglorious worm of the earth," and the question is asked "can these persons...meet in such a disparagement?" to be met in the next sentence with the triumphant answer, "They doe meet and make a mariage; because I am not a body onely, but a body and soul, there is a mariage, and Christ maries me."

Throughout the passage Donne obtains much of his effect by alliteration and antithesis, and by the repetition of certain key words in slightly different positions and with differing emphasis. Thus we find "*dist*ance and *dis*paragement," "*b*ud and *b*lossome," "*com*punction for my self or *com*passion for others," and the key words "Potters vessel," "vessel of earth," "Image of God," "glory...glorious...glorifying... glory," "Circle," "tears." We are not to suppose that Donne deliberately hunted for alliterative words or consciously employed elaborate artifices. The passage is in its own kind a parallel to a piece of music in which the composer has a central theme which is worked out in different musical phrases. One set of notes suggests another, and the composer's fancy plays round his theme and embellishes it, but he never loses sight of the central motive, and the whole passage moves on to its triumphant climax.

Donne distinguishes between the "spiritual marriage," which belongs to this life, and the "eternal marriage," which is consummated in the life hereafter. He views the spiritual marriage as sacramental rather than mystical, in the sense in which those who are technically described as mystics use the word. Thus he says, "woe unto that single man that is not maried to Christ in the Sacraments of the Church; and ... woe unto them that are barren after this spirituall mariage," and he speaks of baptism in a church as "a Parish mariage." He is distressingly literal and prosaic in his description of the effects of this spiritual marriage. When, however, he reaches the subject of the eternal marriage in the Kingdom of Heaven, his eloquence soars again. He bases the final passages of the sermon on that favourite book of his, the *Revelation of St. John the Divine: "The mariage of the Lamb is come, and blessed are they that are called to the mariage Supper of the Lamb,* says S. *John* speaking of our state in the generall Resurrection. That Lamb who was *brought to the slaughter and opened not his mouth,* and I who have opened my mouth and poured out imprecations and curses upon men, and execrations and blasphemies against God upon every occasion; That Lamb who *was slain from the beginning,* and I who was slain by him who *was a murderer from the beginning;* That *Lamb which took away the sins of the world,* and I who brought more sins into the world, then any sacrifice but the blood of this Lamb could take away: This Lamb and I (these are the Persons) shall meet and mary; there is the Action."[45]

There is a dramatic vividness in Donne's description of the penitent and redeemed soul standing with all its sins laid bare in the great congregation of God's saints. The blessed virgins see its uncleanness, the Martyrs see its cowardice, the Confessors see its double dealings in God's cause. Abraham, the Father of the faithful, sees its lack of faith in God's promises. Job, the exemplar of patience, sees its impatience at God's corrections. Lazarus, the beggar who went to Abraham's bosom, sees its hardness of heart in giving to the poor. All these, and all the congregation, look at the two—the Lamb and the trembling soul—and they look at one another, as though they would forbid the banns, and say to one another, "Will this Lamb have any thing to doe with this soule?" and yet "there and then this Lamb shall mary me, and mary me *In æternum,* for ever?"

He concludes the sermon with a passage in which the apocalyptic imagery of *Revelation* is woven into the fabric of his own prose:

I shall see all the beauty, and all the glory of all the Saints of God, and love them all, and know that the Lamb loves them too, without jealousie,

---

[45] P. 253.

on his part, or theirs, or mine, and so be maried *in æternum,* for ever, without interruption, or diminution, or change of affections. I shall see the Sunne black as sackcloth of hair, and the Moon become as blood, and the Starres fall as a Figge-tree casts her untimely Figges, and the heavens roll'd up together as a Scroll. I shall see a divorce between Princes and their Prerogatives, between nature and all her elements, between the spheres, and all their intelligences, between matter it self, and all her forms, and my mariage shall be, *in æternum,* for ever. I shall see an end of faith, nothing to be beleeved that I doe not know; and an end of hope, nothing to be wisht that I doe not enjoy, but no end of that love in which I am maried to the Lamb for ever. . . . There, where the Angels, which cannot die, could not live, this very body which cannot choose but die, shall live, and live as long as that God of life that made it. Lighten our darkness, we beseech thee, ô Lord, that in thy light we may see light: Illustrate our understandings, kindle our affections, pour oyle to our zeale, that we may come to the mariage of this Lamb, and that this Lamb may come quickly to this mariage: And in the mean time bless these thy servants, with making this secular mariage a type of the spirituall, and the spirituall an earnest of that eternall, which they and we, by thy mercy, shall have in the Kingdome which thy Son our Saviour hath purchased with the inestimable price of his incorruptible blood.[46]

The whole of this last passage is worthy of the most careful study. In it Donne has given us a vision of the "last things," of the final Judgement and of the dissolution of the world order, which is highly characteristic of his genius. It is based on Scripture and tradition, and is an embodiment of the belief of Christendom for many centuries, but it is thrown into a new and arresting form by his shaping imagination. He would have been the first to admit that his vision of the soul undergoing judgement in Heaven was symbolic. It was an attempt to dramatise that which is in reality beyond the wit of man

---

[46] Pp. 254–255. Throughout this passage Donne uses the first person singular, which gives an arresting quality to the description. Here, however, as in many similar passages, it is used where we should say "one" or "the soul." Donne certainly includes himself as hoping to be one of the redeemed souls, but it is not an egotistic description of his own hope for triumph, after an exposure of his sins. Though the charges of uncleanness and double dealing and impatience might well apply to his earlier conduct, the charge of "hardness of heart in distributing Gods blessings to the poore" could hardly be brought against him, in view of what Walton tells us of his generosity to the poor. The picture is a composite one, in which "I," that is, the penitent soul, represents a number of types of sinners.

to conceive, and for which no words are adequate. Elsewhere Donne expounds his conviction that Heaven is a state rather than a place, and that to be in the presence of God and in union with Him is the meaning of final blessedness. But, as the medieval artists portrayed the Last Judgement in vivid colours and bold outlines in their frescoes on the church walls, so Donne used his imagination to shadow forth truths beyond expression. For the moment he sets aside one time-honoured set of symbols derived from the book of *Revelation,* that of the judgement assize and the books in which all the deeds of the soul are recorded, and replaces it by another set derived from a different chapter of the same book, and more suitable to the occasion on which he is speaking. This is a marriage in which the soul is lowlier than a beggar maid, and the bridegroom is none other than the King of Heaven, all around is the vast congregation of the Blessed, and here we may note the link with Donne's poem *The Litanie,* written some fourteen or fifteen years earlier, before Donne took orders. There he had enumerated, in his "particular mention of the blessed Triumphers in heaven," the Virgin Mary (or "our Lady," as in his first manuscript draft) and other blessed virgins, the Angels, the Patriarchs, the Prophets, the Apostles, the Martyrs, the Confessors, and the Doctors. In the sermon we have the blessed Virgins, the Martyrs, the Confessors, with Abraham representing the Patriarchs, and Job the Prophets, with allusions to the Angels and the Apostles. There is an agonizing moment in which the shrinking soul sees all its sins laid bare before the eyes of the assembly and, feeling itself utterly unworthy of its high destiny, imagines that it is despised by the whole vast congregation, and then the Bridegroom steps forward and claims his bride forever.

We come now to four undated sermons (Nos. 12–15) which are described in the Folio as "Preached on Trinity Sunday" without any indication of place or date. It seems evident, however, from a passage in the first of the four, that the sermons were not preached on four Trinity Sundays in successive years, but that they formed part of a course preached by Donne on successive Sundays in the Trinity Term at Lincoln's Inn in one particular year. He says:

...I have bent my meditations, for those dayes, which this Terme will afford, upon that, which is the character and mark of all Christians in generall, The Trinity, the three Persons in one God; not by way of subtile disputation, as to persons that doubted, but by way of godly declaration, as to persons disposed to make use of it; not as though I feared your faith needed it, nor as though I hoped I could make your reason comprehend it, but because I presume, that the consideration of God the Father, and his Power, and the sins directed against God, in that notion, as the Father; and the consideration of God the Son, and his Wisedome, and the sins against God, in that apprehension, the Son; and the consideration of God the Holy Ghost, and his Goodnesse, and the sins against God, in that acceptation, may conduce, as much, at least, to our edification, as any Doctrine, more controverted.[47]

The second sermon supports this view, for it opens with the words:

You may remember, that I proposed to exercise your devotions and religious meditations in these exercises, with words which might present to you, first the severall persons in the Trinity, and the benefits which we receive, in receiving God in those distinct notions of Father, Son, and holy Ghost; And then with other words which might present those sins, and the danger of those sins which are most particularly opposed against those severall persons. Of the first, concerning the person of the Father, we spoke last, and of the other, concerning sins against the Father, these words will occasion us to speak now.

It was only at Lincoln's Inn that Donne was likely to have mentioned "those dayes, which this Terme will afford," as he did in the first passage which we have quoted. At St. Paul's or St. Dunstan's the phrase would have had little meaning.[48] It seems probable that Donne marked the four sermons as "Preached in Trinity Terme," and that his son, who was a careless and hasty editor, finding that he had only three sermons marked as belonging to Trinity Sunday, added these to the packet, so that the list of sermons for Trinity Sunday might bear some proportion to the lists for Christmas, Lent, Easter, and Whitsunday.

---

[47] P. 257. This passage was quoted, and the present argument was developed, rather more briefly, by one of the present editors, E. M. Simpson, as early as 1924, in the first edition of her *Study of the Prose Works of John Donne*, p. 350.

[48] Our argument does not rest solely on the use of the word "Terme," but also on the fact that it was only at Lincoln's Inn that Donne preached these compact courses of six or more sermons which were closely connected in pairs. See pp. 6–7 of the present volume.

The course must have contained six sermons, but the two on the Holy Ghost are missing. Donne did not attempt to preserve copies of all the series of sermons which he preached at Lincoln's Inn, but apparently he kept specimens of each course. As for the year in which these Trinity Term sermons were preached, we have no certain evidence, but 1621 is the latest date possible, for Donne gave up his readership at Lincoln's Inn in February, 1622. The tone of the sermons has some affinity with that of the sermon preached by Donne at St. Paul's on Christmas Day, 1621, and 1621 seems a likely year, for without these sermons we should have only five sermons for the year. We do not, however, exclude the possibility that they may have been preached in the Trinity Term of 1620. We think that they can hardly be earlier than that, for they have a maturity of thought and a richness of tone which we do not find in the earlier Lincoln's Inn sermons.

In the two sermons which are devoted to God the Father, Donne has many wise things to say. For the first (No. 12) he takes as his text the words of St. Paul, "Blessed be God, even the Father of our Lord Jesus Christ, the Father of mercies, and the God of all comfort." On these words he gives a short exposition: "The duty required of a Christian, is *Blessing,* Praise, Thanksgiving; To whom? To *God,* to God onely, to the onely God. There is but one; But this one God is such a tree, as hath divers boughs to shadow and refresh thee, divers branches to shed fruit upon thee, divers armes to spread out, and reach, and imbrace thee. And here he visits thee as a *Father:* From all eternity a *Father of Christ Iesus,* and now thy Father in him, in that which thou needest most, *A Father of mercy,* when thou wast in misery; And a *God of comfort,* when thou foundest no comfort in this world, And a *God of all comfort,* even of spirituall comfort, in the anguishes, and distresses of thy conscience."[40]

In this sermon and in that which succeeds it Donne expresses his sense of the immanence of God in creation, and His revelation of Himself throughout the whole of Nature: "There is an elder booke in the World then the Scriptures; It is not well said, in the World, for it is the World it selfe, the whole booke of Creatures; And indeed the Scriptures are but a paraphrase, but a comment, but an illustration

---

[40] P. 258.

of that booke of Creatures.... He is therefore inexcusable, that considers not God in the Creature, that comming into a faire Garden, sayes onely, Here is a good Gardiner, and not, Here is a good God."[50]

This is an echo of the passage in *Essays in Divinity* in which Donne quotes "Sebundus" (Raymond of Sabund) to the effect that the Book of Creatures "cannot be forgotten, requires no books, needs no witnesses, and in this, is safer then the Bible it self, that it cannot be falsified by Hereticks."[51]

The relation of God to the world and all that is in it is not merely that of a Maker, but of a Father, and this fatherhood extends even to what we sometimes call the inanimate creation. "By that impression of God, which is in the very beeing of every creature, God, that is, the whole Trinity, is the Father of every creature, as in *Iob, Quis pluviæ Pater? Hath the raine a Father? or who hath begotten the drops of dew?* And so in the Prophet, *Have we not all one Father? hath not one God created us?*"[52]

This is expressed more fully in the second sermon, where Donne describes God as the

Father of lights, of all kinds of lights, *Lux lucifica,* as S. *Augustine* expresses it, The light from which all the lights which we have, whether of nature, or grace, or glory, have their emanation. Take these *Lights* of which God is said to be *the Father,* to be the Angels ... Or take these *Lights* to be those faithfull servants of God, who have received an illustration in themselves, and a coruscation towards others, who by having lived in the presence of God, in the houshold of his faithfull, in the true Church, are become, as *Iohn Baptist* was, *burning and shining lamps* ... Or take this *light* to be a fainter light then that, (and yet that which S. *Iames* doth most literally intend in that place) The light of naturall understanding, That which *Plinie* calls *serenitatem animi,* when the mind of man, dis-encumbred of all Eclipses, and all clouds of passion, or inordinate love of earthly things, is enlightned so far, as to discerne God in nature; Or take this *light* to be but the light of a shadow, (for *umbræ non sunt tenebræ, sed densior lux,* shadows are not darknesses, shadows are but

---

[50] P. 264.

[51] *Essays in Divinity,* ed. Simpson, 1952, p. 7. Donne remarks a little later: "Howsoever, he may be too abundant in affirming, that *in libro creaturarum* there is enough to teach us all particularities of Christian religion, ... yet St. Paul clears it thus far [*Rom.* 1.19.20] that there is enough to make us inexcusable, if we search not further."

[52] P. 266.

a grosser kind of light) Take it to be that shadow, that designe, that delineation, that obumbration of God, which the creatures of God exhibit to us, that which *Plinie* calls *Cœli lætitiam,* when the heavens, and all that they imbrace, in an opennesse and cheerefulnesse of countenance, manifest God unto us; Take these *Lights* of which S. *Iames* speaks, in any apprehension, any way, Angels of heaven who are ministring spirits, Angels of the Church, who are spirituall Ministers, Take it for the light of faith from hearing, the light of reason from discoursing, or the light flowing from the creature to us, by contemplation, and observation of nature, Every way, by every light we see, that he is *Pater luminum, the Father of lights;* all these lights are from him, and by all these lights we see that he is A Father, and Our Father.[53]

Donne insists on the Unity of God. In contrast to the many pagan gods he quotes the words of *Deuteronomy:* "Heare O Israel, the Lord thy God is one God." The doctrine of the Trinity exhibits to us the one God in three aspects:

And though he be in his nature incomprehensible, and inaccessible in his light, yet this is his infinite largenesse, that being thus infinitely One, he hath manifested himselfe to us in three Persons, to be the more easily discerned by us, and the more closely and effectually applied to us. Now these notions that we have of God, as a Father, as a Son, as a Holy Ghost, as a Spirit working in us, are so many handles by which we may take

[53] Pp. 276–277. This passage should be compared with one in a later sermon, that preached at Paul's Cross on May 6, 1627 (Vol. VII, p. 417), where Donne again calls God the Father of all creatures, even of the rain, and the Father of lights. "From that inglorious drop of raine, that falls into the dust, and rises no more, to those glorious Saints who shall rise from the dust, and fall no more, . . . all are the children of God, and all alike of kin to us." Donne often writes of God as the Father of lights (*James* 1.17), and for the gradation of lights which he traces in this present sermon he may perhaps have taken some hints from the treatise *Liber de Lumine* of the Italian Platonist Ficino. On the question of light symbolism Professor D. C. Allen writes: "Ficino expands the theories of the Middle Ages, perceiving many analogies between light itself and the Father of Lights, . . . Ficino thinks that it is almost as difficult for mortals to comprehend the true nature of light as it is for them to know the symbolic Divine Light. It exists through itself and incorporeally in itself, but as it descends from the fountain of light, it assumes materiality, it becomes clouded and shadowy. Hence we see light through a blurring window as a scale of opacities. The same is true of the *lumen divina,* but here we may rise by a ladder of light to an almost complete comprehension of its real source." *The Harmonious Vision* (1954), p. 101.

hold of God, and so many breasts, by which we may suck such a knowledge of God, as that by it wee may grow up into him. And as wee cannot
take hold of a torch by the light, but by the staffe we may; so though we
cannot take hold of God, as God, who is incomprehensible, and inapprehensible, yet as a Father, as a Son, as a Spirit, dwelling in us, we can.[54]

In Sermons 14 and 15 Donne makes it clear that he is continuing
his course, and that he is speaking not as a theological professor but
as a pastor of souls. "I take it [his text, *I Cor.* 16.22] now, when in my
course proposed, I am to speak of the second Person in the Trinity;
but, (as I said of the first Person, the Father) not as in the Schoole,
but in the Church, not in a Chaire, but in a Pulpit, not to a Congregation that required proofe, in a thing doubted, but edification, upon a
foundation received."[55]

Donne speaks of the union of the two natures, God and Man, in
Christ. He follows St. John Damascen, a Greek Father whom he read
in a Latin translation.

The name of *Christ* denotes one person, but not one nature: neither is
Christ so composed of those two natures, as a man is composed of Elements; for man is thereby made a third thing, and is not now any of
those Elements; ... But Christ is so made of God and Man, as that he is
Man still, for all the glory of the Deity, and God still, for all the infirmity
of the manhood: ... In this one Christ, both appear; The Godhead bursts
out, as the Sun out of a cloud, and shines forth gloriously in miracles,
even the raysing of the dead, and the humane nature is submitted to contempt and to torment, even to the admitting of death in his own bosome;
sed tamen ipsius sunt tum miracula, tum supplicia, but still, both he that
rayses the dead, and he that dyes himself, is one Christ, his is the glory of
the Miracles, and the contempt and torment is his too.[56]

The words of the text furnish Donne with an analysis of the aspects
under which the Son of God is to be loved, but he soon moves on to a
more personal and impassioned expression of his love for the Saviour
who died on the cross.

Love him then, as he is presented to thee here; Love the *Lord,* love
Christ, love *Iesus.* If when thou lookest upon him as the *Lord,* thou findest
frowns and wrinkles in his face, apprehensions of him, as of a Judge, and
occasions of feare, doe not run away from him, in that apprehension; look

[54] P. 263.
[55] Pp. 292–293.
[56] P. 299.

upon him in that angle, in that line awhile, and that feare shall bring thee to love; and as he is *Lord*, thou shalt see him in the beauty and love-linesse of his creatures, in the order and succession of causes, and effects, and in that harmony and musique of the peace between him, and thy soule: As he is *the Lord*, thou wilt feare him, but no man feares God truly, but that that feare ends in love.

Love him as he is the *Lord*, that would have nothing perish, that he hath made; And love him as he is *Christ*, that hath made himselfe man too, that thou mightest not perish: Love him as the *Lord* that could shew mercy; and love him as *Christ*, who is that way of mercy, which the Lord hath chosen. Returne againe, and againe, to that mysterious person, *Christ*; . . .

I love my Saviour as he is *The Lord*, He that studies my salvation; And as *Christ*, made a person able to work my salvation; but when I see him in the third notion, *Iesus*, accomplishing my salvation, by an actuall death, I see those hands stretched out, that stretched out the heavens,[57] and those feet racked, to which they that racked them are foot-stooles; I heare him, from whom his nearest friends fled, pray for his enemies, and him, whom his Father forsooke, not forsake his brethren; I see him that cloathes this body with his creatures, or else it would wither, and cloathes this soule with his Righteousnesse, or else it would perish, hang naked upon the Crosse; And him that hath, him that is, *the Fountaine of the water of life*, cry out, *He thirsts*, when that voyce overtakes me, in my crosse wayes in the world, *Is it nothing to you, all you that passe by? Behold, and see, if there be any sorrow, like unto my sorrow, which is done unto me, where-with the Lord hath afflicted me, in the day of his fierce anger*; When I conceit, when I contemplate my Saviour thus, I love the *Lord*, and there is a reverent adoration in that love, I love *Christ*, and there is a mysterious admiration in that love, but I love *Iesus*, and there is a tender compassion in that love, and I am content to suffer with him, and to suffer for him, rather then see any diminution of his glory, by my prevarication.[58]

---

[57] This passage on the Crucifixion should be compared with Donne's poem *Goodfriday, 1613* (*Poems*, ed. Grierson, I, 336), which treats the same subject, especially lines 21–28:

> Could I behold those hands which span the Poles,
> And turne all spheares at once, peirc'd with those holes?
> Could I behold that endless height which is
> Zenith to us, and our Antipodes,
> Humbled below us? or that blood which is
> The seat of all our Soules, if not of his,
> Made durt of dust, or that fleshe which was worne
> By God, for his apparell, rag'd and torne?

[58] Pp. 306–308.

Here we feel the truth of Coleridge's words in comparing Donne with Jeremy Taylor: "The cross of Christ is dimly seen in Taylor's works. Compare him in this respect with Donne, and you will feel the difference in a moment."[59] The same love of Christ is expressed in Sermon 15, which has as its text "Kisse the Son, lest he be angry":

Compare the Prophets with the Son, and even the promises of God, in them, are faint and dilute things. . . . In the Old Testament, at first, God kissed man, and so breathed the breath of life, and made him a man; In the New Testament Christ kissed man, he breathed the breath of ever-lasting life, the holy Ghost, into his Apostles, and so made the man a blessed man. *Love is as strong as death;* As in death there is a transmigra-tion of the soule, so in this spirituall love, and this expressing of it, by this kisse, there is a transfusion of the soule too: . . . In this kisse, where *Right-eousnesse and peace have kissed each other,* In this person, where the Divine and the humane nature have kissed each other, In this Christian Church, where Grace and Sacraments, visible and invisible meanes of salva-tion, have kissed each other, *Love is as strong as death;* my soule is united to my Saviour, now in my life, as in death, and I am already made *one spirit with him:* and whatsoever death can doe, this kisse, this union can doe, that is, give me a present, an immediate possession of the kingdome of heaven: And as the most mountainous parts of this kingdome are as well within the kingdome as a garden, so in the midst of the calamities and incommodities of this life, I am still in the kingdome of heaven.[60]

Sermon 16 was preached at Lincoln's Inn, but it is undated, and it gives no clear indication of the occasion on which it was preached. The opening sentence might seem to indicate that it formed part of the course which Donne preached on texts which had been misapplied by the Roman Church,[61] but he goes on to say: "But this is a doctrine which I have had occasion heretofore in this place to handle; And a doctrine which indeed deserves not the dignity to be too diligently disputed against; And as we will not stop upon the disproving of the doctrine, so we need not stay long, nor insist upon the vindicating of these words, from that wresting and detortion of theirs, in using them for the proofe of that doctrine." All that we can say, therefore, is that it was preached before February 11, 1621/2, and that it is not likely to have been preached as early as 1616 or 1617.

[59] *Table Talk* (1835), I, 168.
[60] Pp. 320–321.
[61] See Vol. II, pp. 40, 325.

Donne has a sharp rap at those who wish to be always hearing sermons on predestination:

Now God hath delivered us in a great measure ... from this penury in preaching, we need not preach others Sermons, nor feed upon cold meat, in Homilies, but wee are fallen upon such times too, as that men doe not thinke themselves Christians, except they can tell what God meant to doe with them before he meant they should bee Christians; for we can be intended to be Christians, but from Christ; and wee must needs seek a Predestination, without any relation to Christ; a decree in God for salvation, and damnation, before any decree for the reparation of mankind, by Christ. Every Common-placer will adventure to teach, and every artificer will pretend to understand the purpose, yea, and the order too, and method of Gods eternall and unrevealed decree.[62]

The main theme, however, is that of joy through suffering, and in particular the joy which St. Paul felt in suffering for Christ. The text is taken from St. Paul's letter to the Colossians, and Donne devotes some time to reminding his hearers of the greatness of this his favourite saint.[63] The finest parts of the sermon deal with joy, "which when it is true, and truly placed, is the nearest representation of heaven it selfe to this world." The joy of heaven begins in this life, and continues and expands till it reaches its final fulfillment hereafter.

... As that man must never look to walk with the Lamb wheresoever he goes in heaven, that ranne away from the Lamb whensoever he came towards him, in this life; so he shall never possesse the joyes of heaven hereafter, that feels no joy here; ... For heaven and salvation is not a Creation, but a Multiplication; it begins not when wee dye, but it increases and dilates it self infinitely then; ... *When thou goest to receive that bread, of which whosoever eates shall never dye,* the bread of life in the Land of life, Christ shall consider what joy thou broughtest with thee out of this world, and he shall extend and multiply that joy unexpressibly; but if thou carry none from hence, thou shalt find none there. Hee that were to travell into a far country, would study before, somewhat the map, and the manners, and the language of the Country; Hee that looks for the fulnesse of the joyes of heaven hereafter, will have a taste, an insight in them before he goe: And as it is not enough for him that would

---

[62] P. 338.

[63] We deduce that St. Paul was Donne's favourite saint, partly because he tells us that the Epistles of St. Paul were his favourite books in the New Testament, and partly because he preached more sermons on the Conversion of St. Paul than on the festival of any other saint.

travail, to study any language indifferently (were it not an impertinent thing for him that went to lye in France, to study Dutch?) So if wee pretend to make the joys of heaven our residence, it is a madnesse to study the joys of the world; *The Kingdome of heaven is righteousnesse, and peace, and joy in the Holy Ghost,* says Saint *Paul;* And this Kingdome of heaven is *Intra nos,* says Christ, it is in us, and it is joy that is in us; but every joy is not this Kingdome, and therefore says the same Apostle, *Rejoyce in the Lord.*[64]

We now come to the point at which Donne entered upon a new and fruitful field of work in his appointment to the Deanery of St. Paul's. For more than a year and a half there had been rumours of ecclesiastical changes which might include some preferment for him. As early as March 20, 1619/20, Chamberlain had written to Sir Dudley Carleton: "Dr. Fotherbie bishop of Salisberie died some eight dayes since, and his bishopricke bestowed on the Dean of Westminster, to whom one Williams deane of Salisberie succeeds, and Dr. Bowles (who pretends a promise of Westminster) must content himself with the deanrie of Salisberie: in the meane time poore Dr. Dun is cast behind hand and fallen from his hopes."[65] This shows that on his return from the Continent Donne had hoped for some piece of preferment, perhaps through the influence of Doncaster.[66] It was indeed time that King James should redeem his earlier promises to Donne, but he was growing old and slothful, and all through 1620 and the first half of 1621, changes went on in dioceses and deaneries, and still Donne remained at Lincoln's Inn. However, in the middle of 1621 three bishoprics fell vacant, and there was a grand series of ecclesiastical promotions. Through the influence of Buckingham and Lord Hunsdon, Valentine Cary, Dean of St. Paul's, was appointed by the King to the bishopric of Exeter on September 14, 1621, to fill the place of Bishop Cotton, who had died on August 26. Cary does

---

[64] Pp. 339–340.

[65] Chamberlain, *Letters,* II, 296.

[66] Doncaster was on very friendly terms with Buckingham, who now arranged all ecclesiastical preferments. It was Doncaster who in 1622 wrote to Donne advising him to preface the sermon preached at Paul's Cross by an epistle to Buckingham (Tobie Matthew, *Letters,* 1660, p. 303). Donne himself addressed two letters to Buckingham in August and September, 1621 (Historical Manuscripts Commission, *Report* II, Appendix, p. 59; *Cabala,* 1654, pp. 314–315).

not seem to have been a man of any particular distinction, either as Dean of St. Paul's or as Bishop of Exeter. He left behind him no published works, and he managed to quarrel with the Mayor and Corporation of Exeter almost as soon as he took up residence in his see. Hacket describes him as "a prudent courtly man," and we may leave him at that.

There was a delay over the consecration of Cary and of two other new bishops, because Archbishop Abbot, who should have consecrated them, had committed involuntary homicide by shooting a keeper by mistake in Lord Zouch's park, and a Commission had been appointed to inquire into his case. However, the King let it be known that as soon as the Deanery of St. Paul's should be vacant, Donne would be appointed to it. Walton's account of Donne's receipt of the news runs thus:

> Dr. *Cary* was made Bishop of *Exeter,* and by his removal the Deanry of St. *Pauls* being vacant, the King sent to Dr. Donne, and appointed him to attend him at dinner the next day. When his Majesty was sate down, before he had eat any meat, he said after his pleasant manner, *Dr. Donne, I have invited you to Dinner; and, though you sit not down with me, yet I will carve to you of a dish that I know you love well; for knowing you love London, I do therefore make you Dean of Paul's; and when I have dined, then do you take your beloved dish home to your study; say grace there to your self, and much good may it do you.*[67]

Finally Cary was consecrated Bishop on November 18, and on November 19 the King sent his message to the Chapter of St. Paul's, requiring them to elect Donne as their new Dean, which was immediately done. The Dean was required to preach on Christmas Day, Easter Sunday, and Whitsunday, and he could, as he chose, preach also on other occasions. The first of Donne's sermons as Dean was preached on Christmas Day, 1621. This is Sermon 17 of the present volume, and it is a magnificent discourse, which demands the closest attention from the reader.

This first sermon at St. Paul's was a proclamation of the truth which was to be Donne's central theme during his years as Dean. It was not merely the first of a series of remarkable sermons—it was a

---

[67] Walton, Life of Donne, in *Lives* (1670), pp. 45–46.

manifesto in which he stated his position. He chose his text from the great prologue to the *Gospel of St. John,* which seems to have been his favourite of the four Gospels. This prologue describes Christ as the incarnate Word, the Logos, the Light of the World. Donne found such riches of thought in the single verse which he selected that he made it the text of three sermons at St. Paul's: this Christmas sermon, one on the feast of St. John Baptist, June 24, 1622, and one a few months later. It described Christ as "that light," the essential Light, the inner light which lightens every man coming into the world. The sermon is a profound affirmation of Donne's belief in God manifest in the flesh, and also of his belief in the immanence of God in the world and in the soul of man. Some of Donne's sermons may seem to lay too much stress on the doctrine of God's transcendence, on God as the King and the Judge, but the doctrines of transcendence and immanence are not contradictory, they are complementary to each other.

The symbolism of light which Donne used here was particularly suitable for a Christmas sermon. Soon after the winter solstice, when the sun seems to have sunk to its lowest point, the Church keeps the feast of the birth of the Sun of Righteousness, who rises with healing in his wings. At Christmas the London of Donne's day was plunged for nearly sixteen hours out of the twenty-four[68] into a darkness which cannot be realized by modern city-dwellers for whom night is turned into day by the brilliance of electric standards and flashing neon lights. Oil lamps, candles, and torches were the sole means of lighting the houses and streets. In the narrow lanes the height of the overhanging houses almost blocked out the sky, so that even the light of moon and stars on a clear night could hardly penetrate the murky darkness. Londoners hailed with joy the first faint indications that the sun was beginning to regain its strength. Donne saw in the coming of Christ into the world the dawn of hope, the promise that what he calls in this sermon "the long and frozen winter nights of sinne, and of the works of darkness" would be dispersed by the eternal Light. His message from the pulpit of St. Paul's was to be that Christ is the source and fountain of life and light. From him proceed the light of

[68] It should be remembered that London is in the latitude of Labrador, and that the sun rises at 8:08 A.M. and sets at 3:45 P.M. on the shortest day.

nature and the light of reason, the light of grace and the light of glory.[69]

The first two or three pages of the sermon are rather halting, but Donne warms to his subject, as soon as he has cleared away preliminary difficulties:

Light therefore, is in all this Chapter fitliest understood of *Christ;* who is noted here, with that distinctive article, *Illa lux, that light.* For, ... Christ is not so called *Light,* as he is called a *Rock,* or a *Cornerstone;* not by a metaphor, but truly, and properly.[70] It is true that the Apostles are said to be *light,* and that with an article, *the light;* but yet with a limitation and restriction, *the light of the world,* that is, set up to convey light to the world. It is true that *John Baptist* himselfe was called *light,* and with large additions, *Lucerna ardens, a burning and a shining lampe,* to denote both his own *burning zeale,* and the *communicating* of this his light to others. It is true, that *all the faithfull* are said to be *light in the Lord;* but all this is but to signifie that they had been in darknesse before; they had been beclouded, but were now illustrated; they were light, but light by *reflexion,* by illustration of a greater light.... But Christ himselfe, and hee onely, is *Illa lux, vera lux; that light, the true light.* Not so opposed to those other lights, as though the *Apostles,* or *John Baptist,* or the *faithfull,* who are called *lights,* were *false* lights; but that they were *weake* lights. But Christ was *fons lucis,* the fountaine of all their light; light so, as no body else was so; so, as that hee was nothing but light.... All other men, by occasion of this flesh, have darke *clouds,* yea *nights,* yea long and frozen winter nights of *sinne,* and of the *works of darknesse.* Christ was incapable of any such nights, or any such clouds, any approaches towards *sinne;* but yet Christ admitted some *shadowes,* some such degrees of *humane infirmity,* as by *them,* he was willing to show, that the nature of man, in the best perfection thereof, is not *vera lux, tota lux,* true light, all light, which he declared in that *Si possibile,* and that *Transeat calix, If it bee possible, let this cup passe;* words, to which himselfe was pleased to allow so much of a retractation, and a correction, *Veruntamen, yet Father,* whatsoever the sadnesse of my soule have made mee say, *yet, not my will but thine be done; not mine, but thine.*[71]

The sermon is considerably longer than the Lincoln's Inn sermons had been, and it contains a few weak passages, which Donne might well have excised, but it has many excellent short remarks on the

---

[69] Pp. 353–354 of the present sermon should be compared with the passage in Sermon 13 which has already been quoted on pp. 29–30 of this Introduction.

[70] Donne is here quoting St. Augustine, as he indicates in the margin.

[71] Pp. 353–354.

place of reason in religion. "We may search so far, and reason so long of *faith* and *grace,* as that we may lose not onely *them,* but even our reason too, and sooner become *mad* then *good.* Not that we are bound to believe any thing *against reason,* that is, to believe, we know not why. It is but a slacke opinion, it is not *Beliefe,* that is not grounded upon reason."[72]

Donne presents a slightly ironical picture of a zealous missionary confronting "a Heathen man" and telling him, "Thou shalt burn in fire and brimstone eternally, except thou believe *a Trinitie of Persons, in an unitie of one God,"* followed by a summary of the Incarnation, the Virgin Birth, and the death of Christ. Such a missionary, says Donne, would be "so farre from working any spirituall cure upon this poore soule, as that he should rather bring Christian Mysteries into scorne, then *him* to a beliefe. For, that man, if you proceed so, Believe all, or you burne in Hell, would finde an easie, an obvious way to escape all; that is, first not to believe *Hell* it selfe, and then nothing could binde him to believe the rest."[73]

Donne then briefly outlines the way in which the light of nature and the light of reason may lead man to see that the universe, "a frame of so much harmony, so much concinnitie and conveniencie, and such a correspondence, and subordination in the parts thereof, must necessarily have had a workeman, for nothing can make it selfe." The Maker of such a world must still retain the administration of "a frame, and worke, of so much Majestie," and sustain it by his "watchfull Providence." He must reveal himself to man, not only in the universe which he has made, but by a more definite revelation in which his will is made known. Donne is not attempting to construct a severely logical proof. He is addressing Christians, and is urging them to see that the religion which they profess is not a set of arbitrary dogmas enforced by a threat of hell fire, but a faith which is consonant with the deepest instincts of their nature.

For let no man thinke that *God* hath given him so much ease here, as to save him by believing he knoweth not what, or why. *Knowledge* cannot save us, but we cannot be saved without Knowledge; Faith is not on this side Knowledge, but beyond it; we must necessarily come to *Knowledge* first, though we must not stay at it, when we are come thither.... Divers

[72] P. 357.
[73] Pp. 357–358.

men may walk by the Sea side, and the same beames of the Sunne giving light to them all, one gathereth by the benefit of that light pebles, or speckled shells, for curious vanitie, and another gathers precious Pearle, or medicinall Ambar, by the same light. So the common light of reason illumins us all; but one imployes this light upon the searching of impertinent vanities, another by a better use of the same light, finds out the Mysteries of Religion; and when he hath found them, loves them, not for the lights sake, but for the naturall and true worth of the thing it self.

Donne goes on to show how by the light of reason men have found out inventions useful to the whole world, such as the art of printing, or, on the other hand, that they have used their reason to make money by profiting by another man's weakness, or to gain high place in court.

But when they have gone all these wayes by the benefit of this light, they have got no further, then to have walked by a tempestuous Sea, and to have gathered pebles, and speckled cockle shells. . . . But, if thou canst take this light of reason that is in thee, this poore snuffe, that is almost out in thee, thy faint and dimme knowledge of God, that riseth out of this light of nature, if thou canst in those embers, those cold ashes, finde out one small coale, and wilt take the paines to kneell downe, and blowe that coale with thy devout *Prayers,* and light thee a *little candle,* (a *desire* to read that Booke, which they call the Scriptures, and the Gospell, and the Word of God;) If with that little candle thou canst creep humbly into low and poore places, if thou canst finde thy Saviour in a *Manger,* and in his *swathing clouts,* . . . if thou canst follow him to the place of his scourging, and to his crucifying, and provide thee some of that balme, which must cure thy soule; . . . thou shalt never envy the lustre and glory of the great lights of worldly men, . . . but thou shalt finde, that howsoever they magnifie their lights, their wit, their learning, their industry, their fortune, their favour, and *sacrifice to their own nets,* yet thou shalt see, that thou by thy small light hast gathered *Pearle* and *Amber,* and they by their great lights nothing but shels and pebles; they have determined the light of nature, upon the booke of nature, this world, and thou hast carried the light of nature higher, thy naturall reason, and even *humane arguments,* have brought thee to reade the Scriptures, and to that *love,* God hath set to the seale of *faith.*[74]

It was only when Donne moved from the pulpit of Lincoln's Inn to that of St. Paul's Cathedral that he was able to show to the world his full greatness as a preacher. Lincoln's Inn had been a training ground for him. He had learnt confidence there through the feeling

---

[74] Pp. 359–362.

that he was among friends, with many of whom he had been acquainted for years before his ordination. But there were drawbacks about preaching to so limited a circle, all of them studying or practising law, men of keen intellect but without much knowledge of life outside the law courts. There were no women, no citizens, no courtiers, no poor people in such an audience. The great development that we notice in Donne as a preacher is not a development in intellect, for his powers had reached their maturity before he was ordained, but a development in human sympathy and in imaginative grasp of the problems of his audience as men and women. The Lincoln's Inn sermons are limited in their range. They show learning and ingenuity, they are full of legal metaphors and similes, they are clear in construction, and appeal to the logical faculty of the hearers. But at St. Paul's Donne had a large audience drawn from both sexes and from all ranks and sections of the population. Like all great orators, Donne was stimulated by the presence of a large audience, some members of which were keenly interested, while others were critical and censorious, and yet others were frankly bored by the church service which they had to attend willy-nilly, on pain of a fine or imprisonment. They presented a challenge to the preacher, and Donne rose to the occasion, convincing men by his evident sincerity, by his passion for the truths which he proclaimed.

We have assigned to 1621/2 the sermon on *Romans* 12.20, which in the Folio is headed "Preached upon Candlemas Day" because it opens with the words:

It falls out, I know not how, but, I take it, from the instinct of the Holy Ghost, and from the Propheticall spirit residing in the Church of God, that those Scriptures which are appointed to be read in the Church, all these dayes, (for I take no other this Terme) doe evermore afford, and offer us Texts, that direct us to patience, as though these times had especial need of those instructions. And truly so they have; for though God have so farre spared us as yet, as to give us no exercise of patience in any afflictions, inflicted upon our selves, yet, as the heart akes if the head doe, ... so all that professe the name of Christ Jesus aright, making up but one body, we are but dead members of that body, if we be not affected with the distempers of the most remote parts thereof.... Our patience therefore being actually exercised in the miseries of our brethren round about us, and probably threatned in the aimes and plots of our adversaries upon us, though I hunt not after them, yet I decline not such Texts, as may direct our thoughts upon duties of that kinde.[75]

This indicates that Donne was preaching in the week of the third Sunday after Epiphany, in the Epistle for which day his text occurs. The only years during Donne's ministry in which Candlemas Day fell in this week were 1621/2 and 1627/8. The general tenor of the sermon, with its references to "the miseries of our brethren round about us" and "the aimes and plots of our adversaries upon us," makes 1621/2 much the more probable year.

It is not easy to decide whether the sermon was preached at Lincoln's Inn or at St. Paul's, for during the short period between November 20, 1621, and February 11, 1621/2, Donne had a duty towards both places. He probably gave notice of his intended resignation of his office at Lincoln's Inn as soon as he had been elected Dean of St. Paul's, but by that time the Michaelmas Term had ended, and no new Divinity Reader could be elected in time for the Hilary Term. It would be quite in accordance with the friendly relations which Donne had always had with the Benchers that he should go on preaching there during the very short term, and his words in the paragraph which we have quoted above, "I take no other this Terme," seem to suggest that the place was Lincoln's Inn. On the other hand, we have no evidence that the Divinity Reader was required to preach on Candlemas Day if it fell during the week, as it did in February, 1621/2, while it was customary on that day for the Lord Mayor of London to go in procession with torches to St. Paul's for service.[76] We have four other Candlemas sermons which were preached by Donne, almost certainly at St. Paul's, and in the last winter of his life he wrote[77] expressing his hope that he would be able to preach on

[75] Pp. 376–377.

[76] See Chamberlain, *Letters* (ed. McClure), II, 602–603: "Indeed your magnifico of Venice doth *star sopra di se* and sends you great newes of his reception as much as yf I should dilate to you the Lord Mayors going to Powles with his torches on Candlemas day."

[77] On January 15, 1630/31, Donne wrote to Mrs. Cokain: ". . . I purpose, God willing, to be at *London,* within a fortnight after your receit of this, as well because I am under the obligation of preaching at *Pauls* upon Candlemas day, as because I know nothing to the contrary, but that I may be called to Court, for Lent service." (*Letters,* 1651, p. 317; Gosse, *Life and Letters,* II, 270.)

Candlemas Day—a hope which he was not well enough to fulfil. It seems therefore more likely that this sermon was delivered at St. Paul's, and that we have no sermon preserved which Donne preached during these last weeks at Lincoln's Inn.

On February 11, 1621/2, the Council of Lincoln's Inn accepted Donne's formal resignation with an expression of deep gratitude to him for his services. "With one voice and assent" they ordered that Donne should "continue his chamber in this House which he nowe hath as a Bencher of this House, with such priviledges touching the same as the Masters of the Bench nowe have and ought to have for their severall and respective chambers in this House."[78] Donne for his part presented to the Benchers a handsome copy of the Vulgate in six volumes with the commentary of Nicholas de Lyra, which is still preserved in the Library of Lincoln's Inn. Thus happily the period of Donne's Readership came to an end, though he returned in May, 1623, to preach the "Encænia" sermon at the dedication of the new chapel, in the building of which he had taken so much interest.

---

[78] The relevant document is printed in Vol. II, pp. 2–3, of the present edition.

The Sermons

Number 1.

A Sermon Preached at White-Hall, April 2. 1620.

ECCLES. 5.[13 and 14]. *THERE IS AN EVIL SICK-NESS THAT I HAVE SEEN UNDER THE SUN: RICHES RESERVED TO THE OWNERS THERE-OF, FOR THEIR EVILL. AND THESE RICHES PERISH BY EVIL TRAVAIL: AND HE BEGET-TETH A SON, AND IN HIS HAND IS NOTHING.*

Ver. 12. and 13. in Edit. I. In alia 13. and 14.

THE KINGDOM of heaven is a feast; to get you a Stomach to that, we have preached abstinence. The kingdom of heaven is a treasure too, and to make you capable of that, we would bring you to a just valuation of this world. He that hath his hands full of dirt, cannot take up Amber; if they be full of Counters, he cannot take up gold. This is the Book, which St. *Hierome* chose to expound to *Blesilla* at *Rome,* when his purpose was to draw her to heaven, by making her to understand this world; It was the book fittest for that particular way: and it is the Book which St. *Ambrose* calls *Bonum* ¹⁰ *ad omnia magistrum;* A good Master to correct us in this world, a good Master to direct us to the next. For though *Solomon* had asked at Gods hand, onely the wisdom fit for Government, yet since he had bent his wishes upon so good a thing as wisdom, and in his wishes, even of the best thing, had been so moderate, God abounded in his grant, and gave him all kinds, Naturall and Civil, and heavenly wisdom. And therefore when the Fathers and the latter Authours in the *Roman* Church, exercise their considerations, whether *Solomon* were wiser, then *Adam,* then *Moses,* then the Prophets, then the

Hierome

Ambros.

[1 Kings 3.9–12]

August.

47

Apostles, they needed not to have been so tender, as to except onely
²⁰ the Virgin *Mary,* for though she had such a fulness of heavenly
wisdom, as brought her to rest in his bosome, in heaven, who had
rested in hers upon earth, yet she was never proposed for an example
of natural, or of civil knowledge. *Solomon* was of all; and therefore
St. *Austin* sayes of him; *Prophetavit in omnibus Libris suis, Solomon*
prophesied in all his books; and though in this book his principal
scope be moral, and practique wisdom, yet in this there are also
mysteries, and prophecies, and many places concerning our eternal
happiness, after this life.

But because there is no third object for mans love, this world, and
³⁰ the next, are all that he can consider, as he hath but two eyes, so he
hath but two objects, and then *Primus actus voluntatis est Amor,*
Mans love is never idle, it is ever directed upon somthing, if our
love might be drawn from this world, *Solomon* thought it a direct
way to convay it upon the next: And therefore consider *Solomons*
method, and wisdom in pursuing this way: because all the world
together, hath amazing greatness, and an amazing glory in it, for the
order and harmony, and continuance of it (for if a man have many
Manors, he thinks himself a great Lord, and if a Man have many
Lords under him, he is a great King, and if he have Kings under
⁴⁰ him, he is a great Emperor:) and yet what profit were it, *to get all*
the world and loose thy soule? Therefore *Solomon* shakes the world
in peeces, he dissects it, and cuts it up before thee, that so thou mayest
the better see, how poor a thing, that particular is, whatsoever it be,
that thou sets thy love upon in this world. He threads a string of the
best stones, of the best Jewels in this world, knowledge in the first
Chapter, delicacies in the second, long life in the third, Ambition,
Riches, Fame, strength in the rest, and then he shows you an Ice, a
flaw, a cloud in all these stones, he layes this infamy upon them all,
vanity, and vexation of spirit.

⁵⁰ Which two words, *vanity and vexation,* because they go through
all, to every thing *Solomon* applies one of them; they are the inseparable Leaven, that sowers all, and therefore are intended as well
of this Text, as of the other text; we shall by the way make a little
stop upon those two words; first, how could the wisedome of *Solomon*
and of the Holy Ghost, avile and abase this world more, then by this

Aquinas

[Mat. 16.26;
Mark 8.36]

[Eccles.
1.14; 2.11]
Vanitas

annihilating of it in the name of vanity, for what is that? It is not enough to receive a definition; it is so absolutely nothing, as that we cannot tell you, what it is. Let Saint *Bernard* do it; *vanum est, quod nec confert plenitudinem continenti;* for who amongst you hath not
60 room for another bagg, or amongst us for another benefice; *nec fulcimentum innitenti,* for who stands fast upon that, which is not fast it self? and the world passeth, and the lusts thereof; *Nec fructum laboranti,* for you have sowen much, and bring in little, *yee eat, but have not enough, yee drink but are not filled, yee are cloth'd, but wax not warm, and he that earneth wages, puts it into a bagg with holes,* midsummer runs out at *Michalmas,* and at years end he hath nothing.

Agg. 1.6

And such a vanity is this world. Least it were not enough, to call it vanity alone, simply vanity, though that language in which *Solomon,* and the Holy Ghost spoke, have no degrees of comparison, no
70 superlative, (they cannot say *vanissimum,* the greatest vanity,) yet *Solomon* hath found a way to expresse the height of it, another way conformable to that language, when he calls it, *vanitatem vanitatum,* for so doth it (*Canticum Canticorum,* The Song of Songs; *Deus Deorum,* the God of gods; *Dominus dominantium,* The Lord of Lords; *Cœli Cœlorum,* The Heaven of Heavens) alwaies signifie the superlative, and highest degree of those things; vanity of vanities is the deepest vanity, the emptiest vanity, the veriest vanity that can be conceived. Saint *Augustin* apprehended somewhat more in it, but upon a mistaking; for accustoming himself to a Latin copy of the
80 Scriptures, and so lighting upon copies, that had been miswritten, he reads that, *vanitas vanitantum:* O the vanity of those men that delight in vanity; he puts this lowness, this annihilation not only in the thing, but in the Men themselves too. And so certainly he might safely do; for though, as he saies, in his Retractations, his Copies misled him, yet that which he collected even by that errour, was true, they that trust in vain things are as vain, as the things themselves. If Saint *Augustin* had not his warrant to say so from *Solomon* here, yet he had it from his Father before, who did not stop at that, when he had said *Man is like to vanity,* but proceeds farther; *surely,* that is,
90 without all contradiction, *every Man,* that is, without all exception, *in his best state,* that is, without any declination, *is altogether vanity.* Let no man grudge to acknowledge it of himself; The second man

[Eccles. 1.2; Cant. 1.1; Deut. 10.17; Deut. 10.14]

Aug. Retract.

Psal. 144.4 39.5

that ever was begot and born into this world, (and then there was world enough before him to make him great) and the first good man, had his name from vanity; *Cain,* the first man, had his name from possession; but the second, *Habel,* had his name from vacuity, from vanity, from vanishing; for it is the very word, that *Solomon* uses here still for vanity. Because his parents reposed no confidence in *Habel,* for they thought that *Cain* was the Messias, they called
¹⁰⁰ him vanity. Because God knew that *Habel* had no long term in this world, he directed them, he suffered them to call him vanity. But therefore principally was he, and so may we be content with the name of vanity, that so acknowledging our selves to be but vanity, we may turn, for all our being, and all our well being, for our essence, and existence, and subsistence, upon God *in whom onely we live and move and have our being;* for take us at our best, make every one an *Abel,* and yet that is but *Evanescentia in nihilum,* a vanishing, an evapourating. When the Prophets are said to speak the motions, and notions, the visions of their own heart, and not out of the mouth of
¹¹⁰ the Lord, then because that was indeed nothing, (for a lye is nothing) they are said (in this very word) to speak vanity. And still where the Prophets have that phrase, in the person of God, *provocaverunt me vanitatibus, They have provoked God with their vanities,* the *Chaldee* Paraphrase ever expresseth it, *Idolis,* with their Idols; and *Idolum nihil est,* an Idol, that is vanity, is nothing. Man therefore can have no deeper discouragement, from enclining to the things of this world, then to be taught that they are nothing, nor higher encouragement, to cleave to God for the next, then to know that himself is nothing too. This last of our selves, is St. *Pauls* hu-
¹²⁰ mility, *I am nothing;* The first of other Creatures, is the Prophet *Isaiahs* instruction, *The nations are as a drop of the bucket, as the dust of the ballance, the Isles are as a little dust:* This was little enough; but, *all nations are before him as nothing;* that was much less; for the disproportion between the least thing, and nothing, is more infinite then between the least thing, and the whole world. But there is a diminution of that too, *they are all less then nothing;* and what's that, *vanity;* in that place, *Nihilum, & inane,* and that's as low as *Solomon* carries them.

But because all the imaginations of the thoughts of mans heart, are

[Gen. 4.1]

[Acts 17.28]

Jer. 23.16

[Deut. 32.21] 1 Cor. 8.4

2 Cor. 12.11 Esay 40.15

[Isa. 40.17]

Vexatio

¹³⁰ onely evil continually, as *Moses* heightens the Corruption of man, and therefore men are not so much affrighted with this returning to nothing, for they could be content to vanish at last and turn to nothing, there appears no harm to them in that, that the world comes to nothing; what care they, when they have no more use of it? and there appears an ease to them, if their souls might come to nothing too; therefore *Solomon* calls this world not onely nothing, vanity, but affliction, and vexation of spirit. Tell a natural voluptuous man, of two sorts of torments in hell, *Pœna damni,* and *Pœna sensus,* one of privation, he shall not see God, and the other of reall Torments, ¹⁴⁰ he shall be actually tormented; the loss of the sight of God will not so much affect him, for he never saw him in his life; not in the marking of his grace, not in the glass of his creatures, and he thinks it will not much trouble him there to lack his sight, whom he never saw here; But when he comes to think of reall Torments, he sees some examples of them here in this life upon himself. And if he have but the toothach, he will think, that if that were to last eternally, it were an unsufferable thing. And therefore *Solomon* affects us with that sensible addition, love not this world; why? It is vanity, it will come to nothing: I care not for that; I will love it, as long as it is ¹⁵⁰ something; do not so, for it is not onely vanity, but affliction, vexation too. It will be nothing at last, it ends; but it is vexation too, that shall never end. The love of the world, is but a smoke, there's the vanity; but such a one, as putts out our eyes, there's the vexation; we do not see God here, we shall not see God hereafter.

These two words then, as to all the other parts in *Solomons* Anatomy, and cutting up of the world, so they do belong to that particular disposition, in this Text; This reserving of Riches to the owner, for his evill, and that which follows, is vanity, and vexation; But now we have passed that generall consideration, there is thus much more ¹⁶⁰ to be considered. First an imputation laid upon the reserving, the gathering of Riches: though Riches be not in themselves ill, yet we are to be abstinent from an over-studious heaping of them, because naturally they are mingled with that danger, that they may be for the owners evil: And therefore because it may come to that, It is a sickness to gather Riches; and it is an evil sickness, for all sickness is not so: and it was no imaginary, but a true sickness, it was seen, it was under the sun; for that death it self, which is not seen, spiritual death in the torments of hell, is not so much thought of; this is seen; but it was the part of a wise man to see it, *Solomon* saw it, *there is an* ¹⁷⁰ *evil sickness, that I have seen under the Sun : Riches reserved to the owners thereof, for their evill.* There follows a dangerous, and deadly Symptome of this sickness, that the riches perish. *And those Riches perish by evil travail: And he begetteth a son; and in his hand is nothing.* But that will not fall into this exercise.

Imputatio

First then, the imputation that is generally laid upon riches, appears most in those difficulties, which in the Gospels are so often said to lye in the rich mans way to heaven: Particularly, where it is said

[Mat. 19.24]

to be, *as hard for a rich man to enter into heaven, as for a Camel to passe a needels eye;* God can do this; but if a rich man shall stay for ¹⁸⁰ his salvation, till God do draw a *Camel* through a needels eye, he may perchance stay, till all be served, and all the places of the Angels filled.

Epist. 160.7.1

St. *Hierom* made it not a proverb, but he found it one, and so he cites it, *Dives, aut iniquus est, aut iniqui hæres:* A rich man is dishonest himself, or, at least he succeeds a dishonest predecessor: Proverbs have their limits, and rules have exceptions; but yet the proverb, and the rule laies a shrewd imputation, *ut plurimum,* for the most part it is so. It is not alwaies so; we have a better proverb, against that

Prov. 22.4

proverb, The reward of humility, and the fear of God is Riches, and glory, and life; If we were able to digest, and concoct these temporal ¹⁹⁰ things into good nourishment, Gods natural way is, and would be, to convay to us the testimony of his spiritual graces in outward and temporal benefits; as he did to the Iews in abundance of wine, and honey, and milk, and oyl, and the like. ⁺He had rather we were Rich, because we might advance his glory the more: At least they are equal: and any great measure of either, either of Riches, or of Pov-

Bernard

erty, are equal in their danger too.⁺ *Et quæ mulcent, et quæ molestant, timeo;* Poverty, as well as Riches, may put us from our Christian constancie; and therefore they are both praied against, *Divitias et*

Prov. 30.[8]

paupertates ne dederis; How Riches are to be esteemed when they ²⁰⁰ are compared with Poverty, is another question; but how compared with heaven, is no question: We may see that by the place from whence they are said to come.

Christ is presented there in the person of wisdome; and there it is

said, length of daies, that is Eternity, is in her right hand, and in her
left hand Riches, and Glory: *Nolite sitire sinistram;* presse not too
much upon Gods left hand for Riches here, least that custome imprint a Bias in you, and turn you on the left hand here, and bring
thee to Gods left hand in heaven too. Briefly they have an imputation
upon them, they have an ill name, as hindrances to the next life, and
210 they have it also as Traitors to their Masters, That they are reserved
to the hurt of their owners in this life; And then, if that *Væ,* be well
placed, *Wo be unto you, that are rich, for you have received your*
consolation, what a wofull thing is it, to have received no consolation
in them, but to have had harm here by them?

　　To proceed then, riches may do harm to their owners. It is no easie
matter for a rich man, to finde out the true owners of all his riches.
Thou art not owner of all, that the right owner cannot recover of
thee; that all that is his by law, should be his. Certainly no rich Man
hath dealt much in this world, but he hath something, of which him-
220 self knows not the right owner, when he receives usury for his money,
that interest is not his money, but when he receives usury again for
that, there neither the interest, nor principal was his own money; he
takes usury for that money of which himself was not the owner,
because it was ill gotten: If thou do truly know the owner, restore it
to him; if after a diligent examination of thy self, thou do not know
the particular owner, yet thou knowest it is none of thine, and therefore give it him, whose it was at first; both before thou hadst it, and
before he from whom thou gottest it corruptly, had it; give it to God,
in giving it to his poor, and afflicted members; give it him, and give
230 it willingly, and give it now, for that that thou givest at thy death
thou dost but leave by thy last will, thou dost not give; he onely gives
that might keep, thou givest unwillingly; howsoever they have it, by
thy will, yet it is against thy will that they have it, thou givest then,
but art sorry, that they to whom thou givest, that which thou givest,
came so soon to it. And then *sæpe infirmitatis servi efficimur,* we become slaves to our last sickness often; oftentimes Apoplexies stupifie
us and we are dull, and Fevers enrage us and we are mad; we are
in a slavery to the disease, *Et servi non testantur,* says the law, slaves
have no power to make a Will; *Testare Liber,* make thy Will, and
240 make it to be thy Will, give it the effect, and execute thy Will whilest

[Prov. 3.16]
Bernard

Luke 6.24

Owners

Bernard

Idem

thou art a free man, in state of health; restore that which is not thine; for even that of which thou art true owner may be reserved to thy harm, much more that, which is none of thine.

Harm   Every man may finde in himself, that he hath done some sinnes, which he would not have done, if he had not been so rich: for there goes some cost to the most sins; his wantonness in wealth makes him do some; his wealth hath given him a confidence, that that fault would not be lookt into, or that it would be bought out, if it were. Some sins we have done, because we are rich; but many more be-
250 cause we would be rich; And this is a spiritual harm, the riches do their owners. And for temporal harm, if it were hard to finde in our own times, examples of men, which have incurr'd great displeasure, undergone heavy calamities, perished in unrecoverable shipwrack, all which they had escaped, if they had not been eminently, and enormously rich; we might in ancient history both profane and holy, finde such precedents enough, as *Naboth* was; who if he had had no such vineyard, as lay convenient for so much greater a person, might have passed for an honest and religious Man to God, and a good subject to the King, without any indictment of blasphemy against either,

1 Reg. 21   260 and never have been stoned to death. The rich Merchant at Sea, is afraid that every fisherman is a Pyrat, and the fisherman fears not him. And if we should survay the body of our penal Laws, whensoever the abuse of them, makes them snares and springes to entangle men, we should see that they were principally directed upon rich men; neither can rich men comfort themselves in it, that though they be subject to more storms then other men, yet they have better ground tackling, they are better able to ride it out then other men; for it goes more to the heart of that rich Merchant, which we spoke of, to cast his goods over-board, then it does to the fisherman to loose

Bernard 270 his boat: and perchance his life. *Sudat pauper foris;* It is true the
Idem   poor mans brow sweats without; *Laborat intus dives,* the rich mans heart bleeds within; and the poor man can sooner wipe his face, then the rich man his heart; *Gravius fastidio, quam ille inedia cruciatur;* the rich man is worse troubled to get a stomach, then the cruor man to satisfie his: and his loathing to meat, is more wearisome, then the others desire of it. Summe up the diseases that voluptuousness by the ministery of riches imprints in the body; the battery that malice,

by the provocation of riches, layes to the fortune; the sins that confidence in our riches, heaps upon our souls; and we shall see, that
280 though riches be reserved to their owners, yet it is to their harm.

As then the burden of that song in the furnace, where all creatures
were called upon to blesse the Lord, was still, *praise the Lord, and
magnifie him for ever;* And as the burden of that Psalm of thanksgiving, where so many of Gods miracles are recorded, is this, *for his
mercy endureth for ever;* so the burden of *Solomons* exclamation
against worldly things, is still in all these Chapters, *vanity,* and *vanity
of vanities, and vexation of spirit;* so he addes thus much more to this
particular distemper of reserving Riches, naturally disposed to do us
harm; That it is a sickness. Now, *Sanitas naturalis;* Nature abhors
290 sickness, and therefore this is an unnatural desire. For whether we
take this phrase of *Solomon,* for a Metaphor and comparison, that
this desire of Riches, is like a sickness, that it hath the pains, and the
discomforts, and the dangers of a sickness, or whether we take it literally, that it is a disordering, a discomposing, a distemper of the
mind, and so truely, and really a sickness, and that this sickness in-
duceth nothing but eternal death, nothing should make us more
afraid then this sickness, (for, the root of all evil is the desire of
money.) And then if it be truely a sickness all the way, and *Morbus
complicatus,* (a dropsie, and a consumption too) we seem great, but
300 it is but a swelling, for our soul is lean; what a sad condition will
there be, when their last bodily sickness, and this spiritual sickness
meet together; a sick body, and a sick soul, will be but ignorant
Physitians, and miserable comforters to one another.

It is a sickness, and an evil sickness; and there is a weight added
in that addition; for though all sickness have *rationem mali,* some
degrees of the evil of punishment in it, yet sometimes the good purpose of God, in inflicting a sickness, and the good use of man, in
mending by a sickness, overcome and weigh down that little dram,
and wash away the pale tincture of evil, which is in it. There is a
310 wholsome sickness, *Et est sanitas, quæ viaticum ad peccatum,* health
sometimes victuals us, and fuels us, and armes us for a sin, and we
do those sins, which, if we were sick, we could not do: And then,
Mala sanitas carnis, quæ ducit ad infirmitatem animæ. It is an un-
wholsome health of the body, that occasions the sickness of the soul.

Sickness
[Song of the
Three Holy
Children]
[Psal. 136]

Bernard

[1 Tim.
6.10]

Evil

Basil

Bernard

Bernard

It is true, that in bodily Sickness, *Tua dimicant contra te arma.* It is a discomfortable war, when thou fightest against thy self; *in ipso gemis, in quo peccasti,* that that flesh in which thou hast sinned, comes to vex, and anguish thee; that thy body is become but a bottle of rheum, thy Sinews but a bundle of thornes, and thy bones but a ³²⁰ furnace of vehement ashes. But if thou canst hear God, as St. *Au-*

Augustin
[2 Cor.
12.9]
2 Cor. 12.10

gustin did, *Ego novi unde ægrotes, Ego novi unde saneris,* I know thy disease, and I know thy cure, *Gratia mea sufficit,* my grace shall serve thy turn, Thou shalt come to that disposition of the Apostle too; *Therefore I take pleasure in infirmities, because when I am weak, then am I strong:* when thou art come to an apprehension of thy own weakness, thou comest also to a recourse to him, in whom onely is thy saving health and recovery. But this Sickness of gathering those riches which are reserved for our evil, comes not to that; it comes to the Sickness, but not to the physick. In small diseases ³³⁰ (saith St. *Basil,*) we go to the Physitians house; in greater diseases, we send for the Physitian to our house; but in violent diseases, in the stupefaction of an Apoplexy, in the damp of a letargy, in the furnace of a Pleurisie, we have no sence, no desire of a Physitian at all. When this inordinate love of Riches begins in us, we have some tenderness of Conscience, and we consult with Gods Ministers: After we admit the reprehensions of Gods Ministers when they speak to our Consciences; but at last, the habit of our sin hath seared us up, and we never find that it is we, that the Preacher means; we find that he touches others, but not us. Our wit, and our malice is awake, but ³⁴⁰ our conscience is asleep; we can make a Sermon a libel against others, and cannot find a Sermon in a Sermon, to our selves. It is a sickness, and an evil sickness.

Visibilis

Now this is not such a sickness, as we have onely read of, and no more. It concernes us not onely so, as the memory of the sweat, of which we do rather wonder at the report, then consider the manner, or the remedies against it. Those divers plagues which God inflicted upon *Pharaoh,* for withholding his people; That devouring Pesti-

[2 Sam. 24]
[2 Kings
19]

lence, which God stroke *Davids* kingdom with for numbring his people; That destruction which God kindled in *Sennacheribs* army ³⁵⁰ for oppressing his people; These, because God hath represented them, in so clear, and so true a glass as his word, we do in a manner see

them. Things in other stories we do but hear; things in the Scriptures
we see: The Scriptures are as a room wainscotted with looking-glass,
we see all at once. But this evil sickness of reserving riches to our
own evil, is plainer to be seen; because it is daily round about us,
dayly within us, and in our consciences, and experiences. There are
sins, that are not evident, not easily discerned; and therefore *David*
annexes a Scedule to his prayer after all, *Ab occultis meis munda me,*
saith *David*. There are sins, which the difference of religion, makes
360 a sin, or no sin; we know it to be a sin, to abstain from coming to
Church, our adversaries are made beleeve it is a sinne to come. There
are middle-men, that when our Church appoints coming, and receiving, and another Church forbids both, they will do half of both;
they will come, and not receive; and so be friends with both. There
are sins recorded in the Scriptures, in which it is hard, for any to find
the name, and the nature, what the sin was; how doth the School
vex it self, to find out what was the nature of the sin of the Angels,
or what was the name of the sin of *Adam?* There are actions recorded in the Scriptures, in which by Gods subsequent punishment,
370 there appears sin to have been committed, and yet to have considered
the action alone, without the testimony of Gods displeasure upon it,
a natural man would not easily find out a sin. *Balaam* was solicited
to come, and curse Gods people; he refused, he consulted with God:
God bids him go, but follow such instructions as he should give him
after; And yet the wrath of God was kindled, because he went.
Moses seems to have pursued Gods commandement exactly, in drawing water out of the Rock, and yet God sayes, Because you believed
me not, you shall not bring this congregation into that land of
promise. There are sins hard to be seen, out of the nature of Man,
380 because Man naturally is not watchful upon his particular actions,
for if he were so, he would escape great sins; when we see sand, we
are not much afraid of a stone; when a Man sees his small sins, there
is not so much danger of great. But some sins we see not out of a
natural blindness in our selves, some we see not out of a natural dim-
ness in the sin it self. But this sickly sin, this sinful sickness, of gathering Riches, is so obvious, so manifest to every mans apprehension,
as that the books of Moral men, and Philosophers are as full of it as
the Bible. But yet the Holy Ghost, (as he doth alwaies, even in

[Psal.
19.12]

Numb. 22

Numb.
20.[1–12]

moral Counsels) exceeds the Philosophers; for whereas they place
390 this sickness in gathering unnecessary riches injuriously; the Holy
Ghost in this place extends it further, to a reserving of those riches;
that when we have sinn'd in the getting of them, we sin still in the
not restoring of them. But to thee, who shouldest repent the ill getting; *Veniet tempus, quo non dispensasse, pænitebit,* there will come
a time when thou shalt repent the having kept them: *Hoc certum*

Basil   *est, Ego sum sponsor,* of this I dare be the surety (saith St. *Basil*);
But we can leave St. *Basil* out of the bond; we have a better surety
and undertaker, the Holy Ghost in *Solomon;* So that this evil sickness may be easily seen, it is made manifest enough to us all, by prece-

Solomon   400 dent from God, by example of others, by experience in our selves.

To see this then, is an easie, a natural thing; but to see it so, as to
condemn it, and avoid it, this is a wisemans slight; this was *Solomons*
slight. The wiseman seeth the plague, and shunneth it; therein con-

Psal. 50.18 sists the wisedome. But for the fool, when he sees a theif, he runneth
with him; when he sees others thrive by ill getting, and ill keeping,
he runs with them, he takes the same course as they do. Beloved, it
is not intended, that true and heavenly wisedome may not consist
with riches: *Iob,* and the Patriarchs abounded with both; And our
pattern in this place, *Solomon* himself, saith of himself; That he was

Eccles. 2.9 410 great, and increased above all that were before him in *Ierusalem,* and
yet his wisdome remained with him. The poor man and the rich are
in heaven together; and to show us how the rich should use the poor;

[Luk.   *Lazarus* is in *Abrahams* bosome; The rich should succour and re-
16.23]   leive, and defend the poor in their bosomes. But when our Saviour
declares a wisdome belonging to Riches, (as in the parable of the

Luk.   unjust Steward) he places not this wisedome, in the getting, nor in
16.[1-9]   the holding of Riches, but onely in the using of them; make you
friends of your Riches, that they may receive you into everlasting
habitations. There's no Simony in heaven, that a man can buy so
420 much as a door-keepers place in the Triumphant Church: There's

Gen.   no bribery there, to fee Ushers for accesse; But God holds that ladder
28.[12]   there, whose foot stands upon the earth here, and all those good
works, which are put upon the lowest step of that Ladder here, that
is, that are done in contemplation of him, they ascend to him, and

descend again to us. Heaven and earth are as a musical Instrument; if
you touch a string below, the motion goes to the top: any good done
to Christs poor members upon earth, affects him in heaven; And as
he said, *Quid me persequeris, Saul Saul, why persecutest thou me?*
So he will say, *Venite benedicti, pavistis me, visitastis me.* This is the
430 wisedome of their use; but the wisedome of their getting and keeping,
is to see, that it is an evil sickness to get too laboriously, or to reserve
too gripingly, things which tend naturally to the owners evil: For,
therefore in that parable doth Christ call all their Riches generally,
universally, *Mammonas iniquitatis,* Riches of iniquity, not that all
that they had was ill got (that's not likely in so great a company)
but that whatsoever, and howsoever they had got it, and were become true owners of it, yet they were Riches of iniquity; because that
is one iniquity to possess much, and not distribute to the poor; and
it is another iniquity to call those things riches, which are onely
440 temporal, and so to defraud heavenly graces, and spiritual treasure
of that name, that belongs onely to them; And the greatest iniquity
of all is towards our selves; To take those riches to our heart, which
Christ calls the thornes that choak the good seeds, and the Apostle
calls tentations, and snares, and foolish, and noysome lusts, which
drown men in perdition, and in destruction, and which the wise
man hath seen, and hath shewed us here, *to be reserved to the owners
for their evil.* To return to our beginning, and make an end; Heaven
is a feast, and Heaven is a treasure: If ye prepare not for his feast,
by being worthy guests at his table, if you embrace not his treasure,
450 by being such Merchants as give all for his pearl; another feast, and
another treasure are expressed, and heightned in two such words, as
never any tongue of any Author, but the Holy Ghost himself spoke;
Inebriabit absinthio, there's the feast, you shall be drunk with wormwood, you shall tast nothing but bitter affliction, and that shall make
you reel, for you shall find in your affliction no rest for your souls.
And for the treasure, *Thesaurizabis iram dei;* you shall treasure up
wrath against the day of wrath; and this will be an exchequor ever
open, and never exhausted. But use the creatures of God, as creatures,
and not as God, with a confidence in them, and you shall find *juge*
460 *convivium,* in a good conscience, and *Thesauros absconditos,* all the

[Acts 9.4]
[Mat. 25.
34–36]

Mat. 13.22
1 Tim. 6.9

[Mat.
13.45–46]

[Lam. 3.15]

Rom. 2.5

[Prov.
15.15]
Col. 2.3

hid treasures of wisedome and knowledge; you shall know how to be rich in this world by an honest getting of riches, and how to be rich in the next world by a christianly use of those riches here.

The Second Sermon Preached at White-Hall upon Eccles. 5. 12, & 13.

THERE IS AN EVIL SICKNESS THAT I HAVE SEEN UNDER THE SUN: RICHES RESERVED TO THE OWNERS THEREOF, FOR THEIR EVILL. AND THESE RICHES PERISH BY EVIL TRAVAIL: AND HE BEGETTETH A SON, AND IN HIS HAND IS NOTHING.

THAT then which was intended in the former verse, That Riches were hurtful even to the owners, St. *Augustin* hath well and fully expressed, *Eris præda hominum, qui jam es diaboli;* The devil hath preyed upon thee already, by knowing what thou wouldst have, and great Men will prey upon thee hereafter, by knowing what thou hast. But because the rich man thinks himself hard enough for both, for the devil, and for great men, if he may keep his riches; therefore here is that, which seems to him a greater calamity inflicted; first, his riches shall perish; and secondly those riches, those which he hath ¹⁰ laboured and travailed for; And thirdly, they shall perish in travail, and labor, and affliction. And then not onely all his present comfort shall perish, but that which was his future hope: The son, which he hath begot, shall have nothing in his hand.

He that increaseth his riches by usury and interest, gathereth them

Aug. in
Psal. 131.
[sect. 25]

Divisio

2 Part

for him that will be merciful to the poor, says *Solomon*. Is there a
discomfort in this? There is. It is presented there for an affliction,
and vexation to a rich Man, to be told, that his money shall be imployed in any other way, not onely then he gathered it for, but then
he gathered it by. It would grieve him to know, that his heir would
²⁰ purchase land, or buy an office with his money; for all other means
of profit then himself hath tried, he esteems unthriftiness, casuall, and
hazardous; difference of seasons may change the value of his land,
affections of Men may change the value of an office; but whether
the year be good or bad, a year it must be, and nothing can lengthen,
or shorten his two harvests in the year, from six moneths to six. All
ways, but his own, displease him in his heir; but if his heir will be
giving to the poor (as *Solomon* says) then here are two mischiefs
met together, that he could never abide the poor, and giving; and
therefore such a contemplation is a double vexation to him; but much
³⁰ more must it be so, to hear that his riches shall perish, that they shall
come to nothing; for though, if we consider it aright, it is truly all
one, whether a covetous mans wealth do perish, or no, for so much,
as he hoards up, and hides, and puts to no use; it is all one whether
that thousand pound be in his chest or no, if he never see it; yet since
he hath made his gold his God, he hath so much devilish Religion
in him as to be loath that his God should perish. And this, that is
threatned here is an absolute perishing, an absolute annihilation; It
is the same word, by which *David* expresses the abolition, and perishing of the wicked, *The way of the wicked shall perish;* and which
⁴⁰ *Moses* repeats with vehemency twice together *pereundo peribitis;*
I pronounce unto you this day you shall surely perish. So *Judas* and
his mony perished. The mony that *Judas* had taken, he was weary
of keeping it, and they who had given it, would none of it neither.
Se primum mulctavit pecunia, deinde vita. First he fin'd himselfe, and
then he hang'd himselfe; first he cast back the mony, and then he cast
himselfe head-long and burst: often times the mony perishes, and
the man too: yea it is not here only that they shall perish, in the
future; that were a repreive; it were a stalling of a debt; but (as
both our Translations have it) they do perish, they are always melt-
⁵⁰ ing; yea as the Original hath it, *vadit et periit,* They are already
perished, they were born dead; ill gotten riches, bring with them

Perish
Prov. 28.8

Psal. 1.6

Deut. 30.18

Aug.
[Mat.
27.3–5]

from the beginning a Contagion that works upon themselves, and their Masters.

The riches shall perish, though they be his, though his title to them be good, if he put his trust in them; And those riches, those which he hath got by his travail, Those which he hath reserved by his parsimony, and frugallity. There is somtimes a greater reverence in us towards our ancient inheritance, towards those goods, which are devolved upon us, by succession; There is another affection expressed
60 towards those things, which dying friends have left us, for they preserve their memories; another towards Jewells, or other Testimonies of an acceptation of our services from the Prince: but still we love those things most, which we have got with our own labour, and industrey. When a man comes to say with *Jacob,* with my staffe

Gen. 32.10

came I over *Iordan,* and now have I gotten two bands, with this Staffe came I to *London,* with this staffe came I to Court, and now am thus and thus increased, a man loves those additions, which his owne Industry hath made to his fortune. There are some ungratefull Natures that love other men the worse, for having bound them by
70 benefits, and good turns to them: but that were a new ingratitude, not to be thankful to our selves, not to love those things, which we our selves have compassed. We have our reason to do so, in our great example, Christ Jesus, who loves us most, as we are his purchase, as he hath bought us with his bloud; And therefore, though he hath expressed a love too, to the Angels, in their confirmation, yet he cannot be said to love the Angels, as he doth us, because his death hath wrought nothing upon them, which were fallen before; and for us, so he came principally to save sinners: the whole body and band of Angels, are not his purchase, as all mankind is. This affection
80 is in worldly men too; they love their own gettings; and those shall

Lam. 1.11

perish. *They have given their pleasant things for meat, to refresh their souls:* whatsoever they placed their heart upon, whatsoever they delighted in most, whatsoever they were loath to part withal, it shall perish; and the measure of their love to it and the desire of it shall be the measure of Gods judgement upon it; that which they love most, shall perish first.

*In occu-
patione*

Those riches then, those best beloved riches shall perish, and that, saith the text, *by evil travail;* which is a word, that in the original

signifies both *Occupationem, Negotiationem,* labour and Travail,
90 and *afflictionem, vexationem;* affliction, and vexation: They shall
perish *in occupatione,* then when thou art labouring, and travailing
in thy calling, then when thou art harkening after a purchase, and
a bargain, then when thy neighbors can impute no negligence, thou
wast not negligent in gathering, nay no vice to thee, thou wast not
dissolute in scattering, then when thou risest early, lyest down late, [Psal.
and eatest the bread of sorrow, then shalt thou find, not onely that 127.2]
that prospers not, which thou goest about, and pretendest to, but
that that which thou haddest before, decaies, and molders away. If
we consider well in what abundance God satisfied the children of
100 Israel with Quails, and how that ended, we shall see example enough
of this: You shall eat, saith God, not one nor two daies, nor five, nor Num. 11.19
ten, nor twenty, but a whole moneth, until it come out at your nostrils, and be loathsome unto you; here was the promise, and it was
performed for the plenty, that quailes fell a daies journey round ver. 31
about the Camp, and they were two cubits thick upon the earth; The
people fell to their labour, and they arose, and gathered all that day, 32
and all that night, and all the next day, saith the Text; and he that
gathered least, gathered ten Gomers full; But as the promise was
performed in the plenty, so it was in the course too; *whilest the flesh* ver. 33
110 *was yet between their teeth before it was chewed, even the wrath of*
the Lord was kindled against the people, and he smote them with
an exceeding great plague. Even whilest your money is under your
fingers, whilest it is in your purposes determined, and digested for
such, and such a purpose, whilest you have put it in a ship in Mer-
chandice, to win more to it; whilest you have sow'd it in the land of
borrowers, to multiply, and grow upon Mortgages, and usury, even
when you are in the mid'st of your travail, stormes at Sea, theeves
at land, enviers at court, informations at *Westminster,* whilest the
meat is in your mouthes, shall cast the wrath of God upon your
120 riches, and they shall perish, *In occupatione,* then, when you travail [Num.
to increase them. The Children of *Israel* are said in that place, onely 11.4, 13]
to have wept to *Moses,* out of a lust, and a grief, for want of flesh.
God punished not that weeping; it is a tenderness, a disposition,
that God loves; but a weeping for worldly things, and things not
necessary to them (for *Manna* might have served them) a weeping

for not having, or for loosing such things of this world, is alwaies
accompanied with a murmuring; God shall cause thy riches to perish
in thy travail, not because he denies thee riches, nor because he would
not have thee travail, but because an inordinate love, an overstudious,
130 and an intemperate, and overlaborious pursuite of riches, is alwaies
accompanied with a diffidence in Gods providence, and a confidence
in our own riches.

To give the wicked a better sense of this, God proceeds often the
same way with the righteous too; but with the wicked, because they
do, with the righteous, least they should trust in their own riches. We
[Job 1]   see in *Iobs* case, It was not onely his Sons, and daughters, who were
banquetting, nor onely his asses, and sheep, and camels that were
feeding, that were destroyed; but upon his Oxen, that were plough-
ing, upon his servants, which were doing their particular duties, the
140 *Sabæans* came, and destruction in their sword; His Oxen, and his
servants perished, *in occupatione,* in their labour, in their travail,
when they were doing that, which they should do. And if God do
thus to his children, to humble them beforehand, that they do not
[Hab. 1.16]   sacrifice to their own nets, not trust in their own industry, nor in
their own riches, how much more vehemently shall his judgments
burn upon them, whose purpose in gathering Riches, was principally,
that they might stand of themselves, and not need God. There are
beasts that labour not, but yet furnish us, with their wool alive, and
with their flesh, when they are dead; as sheep; there are men, that
150 desire riches, and though they do no other good, they are content to
keep good houses, and that their Heire should do so, when they are
dead; There are beasts that labour, and are meat at their death, but
yield no other help in their life, and these are Oxen; there are men
that labour to be rich, and do no good with it, till their death; There
are beasts that onely labour, and yield nothing else in life, nor death,
as horses: and there are some, that do neither, but onely prey upon
others, as Lyons, and others such; we need not apply particularly;
there are all bestial natures in rich men; and God knows how to
meet with them all; and much more will he punish them, which do
160 no good, in life, nor death, nay that labor not for their riches, but
surfet upon the sweat of other men, since even the riches of those,
that trust in riches, shall perish *in Occupatione,* in the very labor, and

in the very travail, which (if it were not done with a confidence in the riches, when they are got,) were allowable, and acceptable to God.

You may have a good Embleme of such a rich man, whose riches perish in his travail, if you take into your memorie, and thoughts, a Spunge that is overfilled; If you presse it down with your little finger, the water comes out of it; Nay, if you lift it up, there comes water out of it; If you remove it out of his place, though to the right hand
170 as well as to the left, it poures out water; Nay if it lye still quiet in his place, yet it wets the place, and drops out his moisture. Such is an overfull, and spungy covetous person: he must pour out, as well as he hath suck't in; if the least weight of disgrace, or danger lye upon him, he bleeds out his money; Nay, if he be raised up, if he be prefer'd, he hath no way to it, but by money, and he shall be rais'd, whether he will or no, for it. If he be stirr'd from one place to another, if he be suffered to settle where he is, and would be, still these two incommodities lye upon him; that he is loathest to part with his money, of any thing, and yet he can do nothing without it. He labours for
180 riches, and still he is but a bagg, for other men: *Pereunt in occupatione,* as fast as he gather by labour, God raises some occasion of drawing them from him again. It is not then with Riches in a family, as it is with a nail in a wall, that the hard beating of it in, makes it the faster. It is not the hard and laborious getting of money, the fixing of that in a strong wall, the laying it upon lands, and such things as are vulgarly distinguished from moveables, (as though the world, and we were not moveables) nor the beating that nail hard, the binding it with Entailes, of Iron, and Adamant, and perpetuities of eternity, that makes riches permanent, and sure; but it is the good
190 purpose in the getting, and the good use in the having. And this good use is not, when thou makest good use of thy Money, but when the Common-wealth, where God hath given thee thy station, makes use of it: The Common-wealth must suck upon it by trade, not it upon the Common-wealth, by usury. Nurses that give suck to children, maintain themselves by it too; but both must be done; thou must be enriched so, by thy money, as that the state be not impoverished. This is the good use in having it; and the good purpose in getting it, is, that God may be glorified in it. Some errours in using of Riches, are not so dangerous; for some imploying of them in excesses, and

²⁰⁰ superfluities, this is a rust without, it will be fil'd off with good
counsel, or it will be worn off in time; in time we come to see the
vanity of it: and when we leave looking at other mens cloaths, or
thinking them the better men for their cloaths, why should we think,
that others like us the better for our cloaths; those desires will decay
in us. But an ill purpose in getting of them, that we might stand of
our selves, and rely upon our Riches, this is a rust, a cancer at the
heart, and is incurable. And therefore, if as the course, and progress
of money hath been in the world from the beginning, (the observation is St. *Augustins,* but it is obvious to every man acquainted with
²¹⁰ history) That first the world used Iron money, and then Silver money,
and last of all, Gold; If thy first purpose in getting, have been for
Iron, (that thou have intended thy money to be thy strength, and
defence in all calamities) And then for silver, (to provide thee
abundance, and ornaments, and excesses) And then for gold, to hord,
and treasure up in a little room; *Thesaurizasti iram,* thou hast
treasured up the anger of God, against the day of anger.

Rom. 2.5

Go the same way still; account Riches Iron, (naturally apt to receive those rusts which we spoke of, in getting, and using) account
them silver, (naturally intended to provide thee of things necessary)
²²⁰ but at last come to account them gold, naturally disposed to make
thee a treasure in heaven, in the right use of them.

Psal.
127.[1]

This is the true value of them; and except thou value them thus,
Nisi Dominus edificaverit nisi Dominus custodierit, Except the Lord
build, except the Lord watch, the house, and city perish; so except the
Lord and his glory, be in thy travail, it is not said thou shalt not get
by thy travail, *Sed pereunt in occupatione,* Even in the mid'st of thy
travail, that which thou gettest, shall perish.

And then that which makes this loss the more insupportable is, (as
we noted the words to signifie too) *pereunt in afflictione,* they shall
²³⁰ perish then, when thou art in affliction, and shouldst have most use of
them, most benefit by them, most content in them. If the disfavour
of great persons lye heavy upon me abroad, *mihi plaudo domi,* I may
have health, and wealth, and I can enjoy those at home, and make
my self happy in them; if I have not all that, but that sickness lye
heavy upon me, yet gold is cordial: that can provide all helps, that
may be had, for my recovery, and it gives me that comfort to my

mind, that I shall lack no attendance, no means of reparation. But if I suffer, under the judgement of the Law, under the anger of the Prince, under the vehemency of sickness, and then hear, that I am
240 begged for some offence, hear of fines, and confiscations, and extents, hear of tempests and ship-wracks, hear of Mens breaking, in whose hands my estate was, This is the wrath of Gods anger, in this signification of the word, *pereunt in afflictione.* Those riches perish then, when nothing, but they, could be of use to thee.

And all this hath one step lower yet, They perish in evill Travail, and in evil affliction. Now travail did not begin in that curse, *In sudore vultus;* for *Adam* was appointed to dress paradise, and to keep paradise before; and that implied a travail. But then became his travail to be evil travail, when seeing that he could not get bread
250 without travail, still that refreshed to him the guiltiness of that sin, which had dejected him to that misery. Then doth the rich Man see, That his riches perish by evil travail, when he calls himselfe to account, and findes that he trusted wholly to his own travail, and not to the blessings of God. So also every affliction is not evil: it is rather evil to have none; if ye be without correction, you are bastards, and not sons. Gods own and onely essential Son, Christ Jesus, suffered most; and his adopted sons, must fulfill his sufferings in their flesh; we are born Gods sons, and heirs, in his purpose at first, and we are declared to be so, in our second birth of Baptisme, but yet we are not
260 come to years, not come to a tryal, how we can govern our selves, till we suffer afflictions; but then doth this affliction become evil, when that which God intended for physick, we turn into poyson: when God hearkens after this affliction, to hear what voice it produces, and when he looks for repentance, he hears a murmuring, and repining, when he bends down his ear, for a *Tibi peccavi,* he hears a *Quare non mortuus?* Why dyed I not in my birth? When he hearkens after a *Domine ne statuas,* Lord lay not this sin to their charge, a prayer for our persecutors, he hears a *Redde eis vicem,* Give them a recompence O Lord, according to their work, Give them
270 a sorrow of heart, thy curse to them; as it is there, (though there, not by way of murmuring, but by way of foresight, and Prophesie, that God would do so.) But to end this part, then when the Rich man can make no good use of his affliction, when he finds *Nullam ansam,* no

Mala
[Gen. 3.19]
[Gen. 2.15]

[Heb. 12.8]

[Psal. 41.4]
Iob 3.11
Act. 7.[60]
Lam. 3.64

handle in it, to take hold of God by, when he can find no comfort
in the next world, he shall loose all here too. And his Riches, Those
Riches, which his labour hath made dear unto him, shall not onely
be taken from him, and he put to his recovery, but they shall perish,
and they shall perish in the midd'st of those labours, which are evil,
and eat him up, and macerate him. And they shall perish in these
280 afflictions which are evil too, which shall not work, nor conduce to
his good.

2 Part   We come now to the second part: which respects more the future;
He begetteth a Son. First that may seem to give him some ease; every
body desires it. And secondly, It may seem to give him some excuse
of his gathering, because having children, he was bound to provide
for them. But such is Gods indignation for the getting of Riches with
a confidence in them, that he looses all, all comfort in his Son, all
excuse in himself, for in the hands of his Son shall be nothing. First
then, for the having of children, and the testimony of Gods love in
290 that blessing, this diminishes nothing the honour due to the first
chastity, the chastity of virginity. There is a chastity in Marriage:
But the chastity of virginity, is the proper, and principal chastity.
Barrenness, amongst the Iews was an ignominious thing; but it was
considered onely in them which did marry, and were barren: God
hath given us Marriage for Physick; but it is an unwholsom wantonness to take Physick before we need it: Marriage, In Gods institution
at first, had but two ends; *In prolem,* and *in adjutorium;* After man
was fallen sick, then another was added, *In remedium.* Marriage is
properly according to Gods institution, when all these concurr: where
300 none do it is scarce a Marriage. When we have taken the Physick, yet
we are not come to the state of strength, and health, which is intended
in Marriage, till we have Children to be the staff of our age; Be-
Psal. 127.3   hold Children are the inheritance of the Lord, and the fruit of the
womb his reward; He gives Marriage for Physick; but Children are
a reall blessing, in it self, and reserved to him. And therefore, when
God hath given us that use of Marriage, (we are married) he is at an
end of his Physick; he doth not appoint us to take Physick again for
children: he does not forbid us to take phisick, to preserve our
bodyes in a good, and healthy constitution; but drugs, and broths,
310 and baths, purposely for children, come not out of his shop; they are

not his ingredients. It is his own work, the gift of children: And therefore when *Rachel* came to say to *Jacob; Give me children, or else I die, Jacobs* anger was kindled against her, *Anne ego pro Deo:* Am I a God to do this? And therefore it is not inconveniently noted, that as the first man *Cain,* was called *Acquisitus a Domino,* he was possessed from the Lord; so after, so very many names in the Scriptures, held that way of testifying the guift to come from God, that as *Samuel,* which is, *postulatus a Deo,* so all the names that have that termination, *El,* have such a signification in them; And so in the
320 declining of the Jews state, *Matheus,* is *Domini Dei,* and *Johanes,* is *gratia Dei;* and in the beginning of the Christian Church, every where they abounded with, *Deo date, Deus dedit,* and *quod vult Deus,* and such names, as were acknowledgements, that children were the immediate gift of God. And therefore when God said to *Abraham; I will be thine exceeding great reward,* and *Abraham* said, *O Lord God what wilt thou give me, seeing I am childlesse?* God comes to particulars with him first in that, that he would give him children: And therefore, as to all men, so to this rich man, in our text, it may be naturally admitted for a comfort, that he had a Son.
330 Now as it was a just comfort, to have children, so it was a just excuse, a just encouragement to provide for them; If there be any that provideth not for his own, he denieth the faith, (that is, in his actions, and works of faith,) and he is worse then an Infidel; for Infidels do provide for their own. *Christianismi famam negligit,* he betraies the honour, and dignity of the Christian Religion, if he neglect his children; and he hath opened a large gate of Scandal to the Gentils. And therefore saith St. *Augustin, quicunque vult,* Whosoever will disinherit his Sons, though it be upon pretext of doing good service, by building, or endowing a Church, or making the
340 Church his heir, *Quærat alterum qui suscipiat, non Augustinum, Immo, Deo propitio, neminem inveniet:* Let him find another that will accept his offer; for *Augustin* will not; nor, by Gods grace any other. The tye, the obligation of providing for our Children, binds us strictly; for it is, *secunda, post Deum fœderatio;* next to the band of Religion, next to our service to God, our first duty is to provide for them.

But yet, *Dic obsecro, cum liberos a Deo petiisti;* when thou did'st

Gen. 30.1

[Gen. 4.1]

[1 Sam. 1.20]

Gen. 15.1

1 Tim. 5.8

Chrysost.

Augu.

Hier. epist. 47

Chrysost.

pray to God to give thee Children, did'st thou add this clause to thy prayer, *Da liberos,* give me Children, that I may thereby have an ³⁵⁰ excuse, of my covetousness, of my breach of thy Commandement, of my prophaning thy Sabaths, of my usury, of my perjury; was this in thy prayer, saith he. If it were, the Childe shall surely dye, as *Nathan* said to *David;* God will punish thee, in taking those children from thee, which were the colours of thy sin: The children of the ungodly, shall not obtain many branches; not extend to many generations; If they do, if his children be in great number, the sword shall destroy them; His remnant shall be buried in death, and his widows shall not weep. Howsoever, as the words of the text stand, the Holy Ghost hath left us at our liberty, to observe one degree of misery ³⁶⁰ more in this corrupt man; That he is said, to have begot his Son, after those Riches are perished. He had a discomfort in evil travail, and in evil affliction before; he hath another now, that when all is gone, then he hath children, the foresight of whose misery must needs be a continual affliction unto him. For St. *Augustin* reports it, not as a leading Case, likely to be followed, but as a singular Case, likely to stand alone; that when a rich man, who had no childe, nor hope of any, had given his Estate to *Aurelius* Bishop of *Carthage,* and after, beyond all expectation came to have children, that good Bishop unconstrained by any law, or intent in the donor, gave him back his ³⁷⁰ Estate again. God, when he will punish ill getting, will take to himself that which was rob'd from him, and then, if he give Children, he will not be bound to restitution.

But if this rich man have his riches, and his Son together, the Son may have come from God, and the riches from the devil, and God will not joyn them together. Howsoever he may in his mercy provide for the son otherwise, yet he will not make him heir of his fathers estate. The substance of the ungodly shall be dryed up like a river; and they shall make a sound like a thunder, in rain. It shall perish, and it shall be *in Parabolam,* it shall be the wonder, and the discourse ³⁸⁰ of the time. If they be not wasted in his own time, yet he shall be an ill, but a true prophet upon himself; he shall have impressions, and sensible apprehensions of a future wast, as soon as he is gone: he shall hear, or he shall whisper to himself that voice: O fool, This night they will fetch away thy soul; he must go under the imputation

[2 Sam.
12.14]

Ecclus.
40.15
Iob 27.14

Augustin.

Ecclus.
40.[13]

of a fool, where the wisdome of this generation, (which was all the
wisdome he had) will do him no good; he must go like a fool. His
soul must be fetch'd away; he hath not his *In manus tuas,* his willing
surrender of his soul ready; It must be fetch'd in the night of ignorance, when he knows not his own spiritual state; It must be
390 fetch'd in the night of darkness, in the night of solitude, no sence of
the assistance of the communion of Saints in the Triumphant, nor
in the Militant Church; in the night of *disconsolatenes,* no comfort
in that seal, Absolution, which by the power committed to them,
Gods Ministers, comes to the penitent, *In the name of the Father, the
Son, and the holy Ghost;* and it must be fetched this night, the night
is already upon him, before he thought of it. All this, that the soul of
this fool shall be fetched away this night, is presented for certain, and
inevitable; all this admits no question; but the *Quæ parasti, cujus
erunt,* there's the doubt; Then, whose shall those things be, which
400 thou hast provided? If he say, they shall be his Sons, God saith here,
In his hand shall be nothing; for, though God may spare him, that
his riches be not perished before his death, though God have not discovered his iniquity, by that manner of punishment, yet, *Quod in
radice celatur, in ramis declaratur;* God will show that in the bough
which was hid in the root, the iniquity of the father in the penury of
the son. And therefore, To conclude all, since riches are naturally
conditioned so, as that they are to the owners harm, either testimonies
of his former hard dealing in the world, or tentation to future sins, or
provocations to other mens malice; since that though thou may have
410 repented the ill getting of those riches, yet thou maiest have omitted
restitution, and so there hovers an invisible owner over thy riches,
which may carry them away at last; since though thou maiest have
repented, and restored, and possess thy riches, that are left, with a
good Conscience, yet as we said before, from *Nathans* mouth, the
Child may die; God, that hath many waies of expressing his mercies,
may take this one way of expressing his judgment, that yet thy son
shall have nothing of all that in his hand; put something else into his
hand; put a book, put a sword, put a ship, put a plough, put a trade,
put a course of life, a calling, into his hand; And put something into
420 his head, the wisdome, and discretion, and understanding of a serpent,
necessary for those courses, and callings. But principally, put some-

thing into his heart, a religious fear, and reverence of his Maker, a religious apprehension, and application of his Saviour, a religious sense, and acceptation of the comforts of the Holy Spirit; that so, if he feel, that for his fathers hard dealing, God hath removed the possession from him, he doth not doubt therefore of Gods mercy to his father, nor dishonor his fathers memory, but behave himself so in his course, as that the like judgement may not fall upon his son; but that his riches increasing, by his good travail, they may still 430 remain in the hands of his son, whom he hath begotten.

Number 2.

Preached at White-hall, the 30. Aprill 1620.

PSAL. 144.15. BEING THE FIRST PSALME FOR THE DAY.

BLESSED ARE THE PEOPLE THAT BE SO; YEA
BLESSED ARE THE PEOPLE, WHOSE GOD IS
THE LORD.

THE FIRST part of this Text hath relation to temporall blessings, *Blessed is the people that be so:* The second part to spirituall, *Yea blessed is the people, whose God is the Lord. His left hand is under my head,* saith the Spouse; That sustaines me from falling into murmuring, or diffidence of his Providence, because out of his left hand he hath given me a competency of his temporall blessings; *But his right hand doth embrace mee,* saith the Spouse there; His spirituall blessings fill me, possesse me, so that no rebellious fire breaks out within me, no outward tentation breaks in upon me. [10] So also sayes *Solomon* againe, *In her left hand is riches and glory,* (temporall blessings) *and in her right hand length of dayes,* all that accomplishes and fulfils the eternall joyes of the Saints of heaven. The person to whom *Solomon* attributes this right and left hand is Wisedome; And a wise man may reach out his right and left hand, to receive the blessings of both sorts. And the person whom *Solomon* represents by Wisedome there, is Christ himselfe. So that not onely a worldly wiseman, but a Christian wiseman may reach out both hands, to both kinds of blessings, right and left, spirituall and temporall. And therefore, *Interrogo vos, filios regni cœlorum,* saith S. [20] *Augustine,* Let mee ask you, who are sonnes and heires of the Kingdome of Heaven, *Progeniem Resurrectionis in æternum,* You that are the off-spring of the Resurrection of Christ Jesus, and have your resurrection in his, *Membra Christi, Templa Spiritus Sancti,* You that are the very body of Christ, you that are the very temples of the

Cant. 2.6

Prov. 3.16

73

Holy Ghost, *Interrogo vos,* Let me ask you, for all your great reversion hereafter, for all that present possession which you have of it, in an apprehensive faith, and in a holy conversation in this life, for all that blessednesse, *Non est ista fœlicitas?* Is there not a blessednesse in enjoying Gods temporall blessings here too? *Sit licet, sed sinistra,*
30 saith that Father; It is certainely a blessednesse, but a left handed blessednesse, a weaker, a more imperfect blessednesse, then spirituall blessings are.

As then there is *dextra,* and *sinistra beatitudo,* a right handed, and a left handed blessednesse in the Text: so there is *dextra* and *sinistra Interpretatio,* a right and a left Exposition of the Text. And as both these blessednesses, temporall and spirituall, are seales and testimonies of Gods love, though not both of equall strength, and equall evidence; so both the Interpretations of these words are usefull for our edification, though they bee not both of equall authority. That which we
40 call *Sinistram Interpretationem,* is that sense of these words, which arises from the first Translators of the Bible, the *Septuagint,* and those Fathers which followed them; which, though it bee not an ill way, is not the best, because it is not according to the letter; and then, that which we call *Dextram Interpretationem,* is that sense which arises pregnantly, and evidently, liquidly, and manifestly out of the Originall Text it selfe.

The Authors and followers of the first sense reade not these words as we doe, *Beatus populus,* That people is blessed, but *Beatum dixerunt 'populum,* That people was esteemed blessed; and so they
50 referre this and all the temporall blessings mentioned in the three former Verses to a popular error, to a generall mistaking, to the opinions, and words of wicked and worldly men, that onely they desire these temporall things, onely they taste a sweetnesse, and apprehend a blessednesse in them; whereas they who have truely their conversation in heaven, are swallowed up with the contemplation of that blessednesse, without any reflection upon earth or earthly things. But the Author of the second sense, which is God himselfe, and his direct word, presents it thus, *Beatus populus,* That people is truely blessed, there is a true blessednesse in temporall things; but
60 yet, this is but *sinistra 'beatitudo,* a lesse perfect blessednesse; For the followers of both Interpretations, and all Translators, and all Exposi-

tors meet in this, That the perfect, the accomplishing, the consummatory blessednesse is onely in this, *That our God be the Lord.*

First then, to make our best use of the first sense, That temporall
things conduce not at all to blessednesse, S. *Cyprians* wonder is just,
Deum nobis solis contentum esse, nobis non sufficere Deum; That
God should think man enough for him, and man should not bee
satisfied with God; That God should be content with *Fili da mihi
cor, My sonne give me thy heart,* and man should not be content with
70 *Pater da mihi Spiritum,* My God, my Father, grant me thy Spirit,
but must have temporall additions too. *Non est castum cor,* saith S.
Augustine, si Deum ad mercedem colit; as he saith in another place,
Non est casta uxor, quæ amat quia dives, She is never the honester
woman, nor the lovinger wife, that loves her husband in contemplation of her future joynture, or in fruition of her present abundancies; so hee sayes here, *Non est castum cor,* That man hath not
a chast, a sincere heart towards God, that loves him by the measure
and proportion of his temporall blessings. The Devill had so much
colour for that argument, that in prosperity there can bee no triall,
80 whether a man love God or no, as that he presses it even to God himselfe, in *Iobs* case: *Doth Iob serve God for nought? hast not thou
hedged him in, and blessed the works of his hands, and encreased his
substance?* How canst thou tell whether he will love thee, or feare
thee, if thou shouldst take away all this from him? thou hast had no
triall yet. And this argument descended from that father to his
children, from the Devill there, to those followers of his whom the
Prophet *Malachy* reprehends for saying, *It is in vaine to serve God,
for what profit is it, that wee have kept his commandements?* When
men are willing to prefer their friends, we heare them often give
90 these testimonies of a man; He hath good parts, and you need not
be ashamed to speake for him; hee hath money in his purse, and you
need not be sorry to speak for him; he understands the world, he
knowes how things passe, and he hath a discreet, a supple, and an
appliable disposition, and hee may make a fit instrument for all your
purposes, and you need not be afraid to speake for him. But who ever
casts into this scale and valuation of a man, that waight, that he hath
a religious heart, that hee feares God? what profit is there in that,
if wee consider this world onely?

[1.] *Inter-
pretatio*

Iob 1.[9, 10]

Mal. 3.14

[Mar. 8.36]

But *what profits it a man, if he get all the world, and lose his owne*
¹⁰⁰ *soule?* And therefore that opinion, That there was no profit at all, no
degree towards blessednesse in those temporall things, prevailed so
farre, as that it is easie to observe in their Expositions upon the Lords
Prayer, that the greatest part of the Fathers doe ever interpret that

[Mat. 6.11]

Petition, *Da nobis hodie, Give us this day our daily bread,* to be
intended onely of spirituall blessings, and not of temporall; So S.
Hierome saith, when we ask that bread, *Illum petimus, qui panis
vivus est, & descendit de cœlo;* we make our petition for him, who is
the bread of life, and descended from the bosome of the Father; and
so he refers it to Christ, and in him, to the whole mystery of our
¹¹⁰ Redemption. And *Athanasius* and S. *Augustine* too (and not they
two alone) refer it to the Sacramentall bread; That in that Petition,
wee desire such an application of the bread of life, as wee have in
the participation of the body and blood of Christ Jesus in that Communion. S. *Cyprian* insists upon the word *Nostrum, Our bread;* For,
saith he, temporall blessings cannot properly bee called Ours, because
they are common to the Saints, and to the reprobates; but in a prayer
ordained by Christ for the faithfull, the petition is for such things as
are proper, and peculiar to the faithfull, and that is for spirituall
blessings onely. If any man shall say, *Ideo quærenda, quia necessaria,*
¹²⁰ We must pray, and we must labour for temporall things, because
they are necessary for us, we cannot be without them, *Ideo non
quærenda quia necessaria,* sayes S. *Chrysostome,* so much of them, as
is necessary for our best state, God will give us, without this laborious
anxiety, and without eating the bread of sorrow in this life, *Non
sperandum de superfluis, non desperandum de necessariis,* sayes the
same Father; It is a suspicious thing to doubt or distrust God in
necessary things, and it is an unmannerly thing to presse him in
superfluous things. They are not necessary before, and they are not
ours after: for those things onely are ours, which no body can take
¹³⁰ from us: and for temporall things, *Auferre potest inimicus homo,
invito:* Let the *inimicus homo* be the devill, and remember *Iobs* case,
Let the *inimicus homo* be any envious and powerfull man, who hath
a minde to that that thou hast, and remember *Naboths* case, and this
envious man can take any temporall thing from thee against thy will.
But spirituall blessings cannot bee taken so, *Fidem nemo perdidit,*

nisi qui spreverit, sayes S. *Augustin,* No man ever lost his faith, but
he that thought it not worth the keeping.

But for *Iobs* temporall estate, sayes S. *Augustine,* all was lost. And
lest any man should say, *Vxor relicta erat, Iob* had not lost all, be-
140 cause his Wife was left, *Misericordem putatis diabolum,* saies that
Father, *qui ei reliquit Vxorem?* doe you thinke that *Iob* lighted upon
a mercifull and good natur'd devill, that the devill did this out of
pity and compassion to *Iob,* or that *Iob* was beholding to the devill
for this, that he left him his Wife? *Noverat per quam deceperat
Adam,* sayes he, The devill knew by what instrument he had deceived the first man, and by the same instrument he practices upon
Iob; Suam reliquit adjutricem, non mariti consolatricem, He left *Iob* a
helper, but a helper for his owne ends, but for her Husband a miserable comforter. *Caro conjux,* sayes the same Father in another place,
150 This flesh, this sensuall part of ours, is our wife: and when these
temporall things by any occasion are taken from us, that wife, that
flesh, that sensuality is left to murmure and repine at Gods corrections, and that is all the benefit we have by that wife, and all the
portion we have with that wife.

Though therefore S. *Hierom,* who understood the Originall Language, the best of his time, in his Translation of the Psalmes, doe give
the true, the right sense of this place, yet in his owne Commentaries
upon the Psalmes, he takes this first sense, and beats upon that
doctrine, that it is but a popular error, a generall mistaking, to make
160 worldly blessings any degree of happinesse: he saw so good use of
that doctrine, as that he would not see the right interpretation of the
words: he saw well enough, that according to the letter of the text,
temporall things were blessings, yet because they were but left-
handed blessings, remembring the story in the booke of Judges, of   Iudg. 20.16
700. left-handed Benjamites, that would sling stones at a haires
breadth, and were better mark-men then the right-handed, and considering the left-handed men of this world, those who pursue temporall blessings onely, went with most earnestnesse, and best successe
to their works, to correct that generall distemper, that generall vehe-
170 mence upon temporall things, S. *Hierom,* and so many of the Fathers
as accompany him in that interpretation, were content to embrace
that sense, which is not truly the literall sense of this place, that it

should be only *Beatum dixerunt,* and not *Beatus populus,* a popular error, and not a truth, that any man, or any people, were blessed in temporall things; and so we have done with the first sense of these words, and the reason why so many follow it.

2. *Inter-
pretatio*

We are come now to the second Interpretation: where there is not *Beatitudo falsa* and *vera,* for both are true, but there is *dextra* and *sinistra,* a right-handed and left-handed blessednesse; there is *In-*
¹⁸⁰ *choativa* and *perfectiva,* there is an introductory, and a consummatory blessednesse: and in the first of these, in the left-handed, in the lesse perfect blessednesse, we must consider three things. First, *Beatitudinem ipsam,* That there is a blessednesse proposed: and secondly, *In quibus,* in what that blessednesse is placed in this text, *Quibus sic,* blessed are they *that are so,* that is, so, as is mentioned in the three former verses: and thirdly, another *In quibus,* not in what things, but in what persons this first blessednesse is placed, *Beatus populus,* It is when all *the people,* the whole body, and not some ranks of men, nor some particular men in those ranks, but when all the people
¹⁹⁰ participate of these blessings.

Beatitudo

Now first, for this first blessedness, As no Philosophers could ever tell us amongst the Gentiles, what true blessedness was, so no Grammarian amongst the Jews, amongst the Hebrews, could ever tell us, what the right signification of this word is, in which *David* expresses blessedness here; whether *Asherei,* which is the word, be a plurall Noune, and signifie *Beatitudines,* Blessednesses in the plurall, and intimate thus much, that blessedness consists not in any one thing, but in a harmony and consent of many; or whether this *Asherei* be an Adverbe, and signifie *beatè,* and so be an acclamation, O how
²⁰⁰ happily, how blessedly are such men provided for that are so; they cannot tell. Whatsoever it bee, it is the very first word, with which *David* begins his booke of Psalmes; *Beatus vir:* as the last word of that booke is, *Laudate Dominum;* to shew, that all that passes betweene God and man, from first to last, is blessings from God to man, and praises from man to God; and that the first degree of blessednesse is, to finde the print of the hand of God, even in his temporall blessednesse, and to praise and glorifie him for them, in the right use of them.

A man that hath no land to hold by it, nor title to recover by it, is

²¹⁰ never the better, for finding, or buying, or having a faire peece of evidence, a faire instrument, fairely written, duly sealed, authentically testified; A man that hath not the grace of God, and spirituall blessings too, is never the neerer happinesse, for all his abundances of temporall blessednesse. Evidences are evidences to them who have title. Temporall blessings are evidences to them, who have a testimony of Gods spirituall blessings in the temporall. Otherwise as in his hands, who hath no Title, it is a suspicious thing to finde evidences, and he will be thought to have embeazeled and purloyned them, he will bee thought to have forged and counterfaited them, ²²⁰ and he will be called to an account for them, how he came to them, and what he meant to doe with them: so to them, who have temporall blessings without spirituall, they are but uselesse blessings, they are but counterfait blessings, they shall not purchase a minutes peace of conscience here, nor a minutes refreshing to the soule hereafter; and there must be a heavy account made for them, both how they were got, and how they were employed.

But when a man hath a good title to Heaven, then these are good evidences: for, *Godlinesse hath a promise of the life to come, and of the life that now is;* and if we spend any thing in maintenance of ²³⁰ that title, give, or lose any thing for his glory and making sure this salvation, *We shall inherit everlasting life,* sayes the best surety in the world; but we shall not stay so long for our bill of charge, we shall have *A hundred fold in this life.* S. *Augustine* seemes loath to take Christ at that large word, he seemes to thinke it too great usury, to take a hundred fold for that which we have laid out for Christ: And therefore he reads that place, *Accipiet septies tantum,* He shall receive seven times as much, in this life. But in both the Euangelists, *Matthew* and *Marke,* the overflowing bounty and retribution of God is so expressed, *Centuplum accipiet.* God repaired *Iob* so, as he had ²⁴⁰ beene impaired; God recompenced him *in specie,* in the same kinde as he had beene damnified. And Christ testifies of himselfe, that his comming to us is not onely, *Vt vitam habeatis, sed ut habeatis abundantiùs;* More abundantly; that is, as diverse of the Fathers interpret it, that you might have eternall life sealed to you, in the prosperity and abundancies of this life. *I am the doore,* sayes Christ, in the same Chapter: we must not thinke to flye over wals, by sudden

1 Tim. 4.8

Mat. 19.29

Iohn 10.10

Iohn 10.9

and undeserved preferments, nor to sap and undermine, and supplant others; wee must enter at that doore, by faire and Christian meanes: And then, *By me if any man enter,* sayes Christ there, *he shall be* 250 *saved;* there is a rich and blessed inheritance; but before he come to that salvation, *He shall goe in and out, and finde pasture,* sayes that text. Now, in Heaven there is no going in and out; but in his way to Heaven, in this life, he shall finde his interest in the next, conveied and sealed to him in temporall blessings here.

If *Plato* found and acknowledged a happinesse in that, *Quòd natus homo,* that he was borne a man, and not a beast, (*Lactantius* adds in *Platoes* behalfe, when he cites that place out of him, *Quòd natus vir,* that he was borne a man and not a woman) if he found a farther happinesse, *Quòd Græcus,* that he was borne a Grecian, and not a 260 Barbarian; *quòd Atheniensis,* that he was borne in the Towne which was the receptacle, and dwelling of all wisdome; and *quòd tempore Socratis,* and that he was borne in *Socrates* his time, that so he might have a good example, as well as a good rule for his life: As all we owe to God an acknowledgement of blessednesse, that we are borne in a Christian Church, in a Reformed Church, in a Monarchy, in a Monarchy composed of Monarchies, and in the time of such a Monarch, as is a Peace-maker, and a peace-preserver both at home and abroad; so let all them who are borne of Nobility, or borne up to Nobility upon the two faire wings of merit and of favour, all that 270 are borne to riches, and born up and born out by their riches, all whom their industry, and wisedome, and usefulnesse to the State, hath or may any way preferre, take heed of separating the Author and the meanes; of separating God and the King, in the wayes of favour; of separating God and their riches, in the wayes of purchase; of separating God and their wisedome, in the wayes of preferment; but let them alwayes discerne, and alwayes acknowledge, the hand of God, the Author, in directing and prospering the hand of his instrument in all these temporall things, and then, these temporall things are truly blessings unto them, and they are truly blessed in 280 them.

In quibus This was our first Consideration, our first branch in this part, that temporall things were seales and testimonies of blessednesse; The second is, to what particular evidence this seale is annexed in this text,

upon what things this blessednesse is placed here; which are all involved in this one little particle, this monosyllable *So, Blessed are they*
that are so; that is, so, as a prayer is made in the three former verses,
that they might be. Now as the maledictions which were threatned
to *David,* were presented to him by the Prophet in three formes, of
warre, of famine, of pestilence; so these blessings which are com-
290 prized in those three verses, may well be reduced to three things
contrary to those three maledictions; To the blessing of peace, contrary to *Davids* warre, *That there may be no invasion;* To the blessing   Ver. 14
of plenty, contrary to *Davids* famine, *That our barnes may abound*   Ver. 13
with all sorts of Corne; To the blessing of health, contrary to *Davids*
destroying sicknesse, *That our sonnes may grow up as plants in their*   Ver. 12
youth.

For the first temporall blessing of peace, we may consider the   *Pax*
lovelinesse, the amiablenesse of that, if we looke upon the horror and
gastlinesse of warre: either *in Effigie,* in that picture of warre, which
300 is drawn in every leafe of our own Chronicles, in the blood of so
many Princes, and noble families, or if we look upon warre it selfe,
at that distance where it cannot hurt us, as God had formerly kindled
it amongst our neighbours, and as he hath transferred it now to
remoter Nations, whilest we enjoy yet a Goshen in the midst of all
those Egypts. In all Cities, disorderly and facinorous men, covet to
draw themselves into the skirts and suburbs of those Cities, that so
they may be the nearer the spoyle, which they make upon passengers.
In all Kingdomes that border upon other Kingdomes, and in Islands
which have no other border but the Sea, particular men, who by
310 dwelling in those skirts and borders, may make their profit of spoile,
delight in hostility, and have an adversenesse and detestation of
peace: but it is not so within: they who till the earth, and breed up
cattell, and imploy their industry upon Gods creatures, according to
Gods ordinance, feele the benefit and apprehend the sweetnesse, and
pray for the continuance of peace.

This is the blessing, in which God so very very often expresses his   *Copia*
gracious purpose upon his people, that he would give them peace;
and peace with plenty; *O that my people had hearkned unto me!*   Psal. 81.13
sayes God, *I would soone have humbled their enemies,* (there is their   and ult.
320 peace) *And I would have fed them with the fat of wheat, and with*

the honey out of the Rocke, and there is their plenty. Persons who are preferred for service in the warre, prove often suspicious to the Prince. *Ioabs* confidence in his own merit and service, made him insolent towards the King, and the King jealous of him. But no man was more suddenly nor more safely preferred then *Ioseph,* for his counsell to resist penury, and to preserve plenty and abundance within the Land. St. *Basil* in an Homily which he made in a time of dearth and drought, in which he expresses himselfe with as much elegancy, as any where, (and every where I thinke with as much as any man)

330 where he sayes, there was in the skie, *Tristis serenitas et ipsa puritate molesta,* That the ayre was the worse for being so good, and the fouler for being so faire; and where he inverts the words of our Saviour,

Luk. 10.2   *Messis magna, operarii pauci,* sayes Christ, Here is a great harvest, but few workmen; but *Operarii multi, messis parva,* sayes *Basil,* Here are workmen enow, but no harvest to gather; in that Homily he notes a barrennesse in that which used to be fruitfull, and a fruitfulnesse in that which used to be barren; *Terra sterilis & aurum fœcundum,* He prophecyed of our times; when not onely so many families have left the Country for the City, in their persons, but have brought their

340 lands into the City, they have brought all their Evidences into Scriveners shops, and changed all their renewing of leases every seaven yeares, into renewing of bonds every six moneths: They have taken a way to inflict a barrennesse upon land, and to extort a fruitfulnesse from gold by usury. Monsters may be got by unnaturall mixtures, but there is no race, no propagation of monsters: money may be raised by this kinde of use; but, *Non hærebit,* It is the sweat of other men, and it will not stick to thine heire. Nay, commonly it brings not that outward blessing of plenty with it; for, for the most part, we see no men live more penuriously, more sordidly, then these

350 men doe.

Sanitas   The third of these temporall blessings is health, without which both the other are no more to any man, then the Rainbow was to him who was ready to drowne; *Quid mihi, si peream ego?* sayes he, what am I the better, that God hath past his word, and set to his seale in the heavens, that he will drowne the world no more, if I be drowned my selfe? What is all the peace of the world to me, if I have the rebellions and earth-quakes of shaking and burning Feavers in my

body? What is all the plenty of the world to me, if I have a languishing consumption in my blood, and in my marrow? The Heathens
360 had a goddesse, to whom they attributed the care of the body, *deam Carnam:* And we that are Christians, acknowledge, that Gods first care of man, was his body, he made that first; and his last care is reserved for the body too, at the Resurrection, which is principally for the benefit of the body. There is a care belongs to the health, and comelinesse of the body. When the Romans canonized *Pallorem* and *Febrim,* Palenesse and Fevers, and made them gods, they would as faine have made them Devills, if they durst; they worshipped them onely, because they stood in feare of them. Sicknesse is a sword of Gods, and health is his blessing. For when *Ezechias* had assurance
370 enough, that he should recover and live, yet he had still a sense of misery, in that he should not have a perfect state of health. *What shall I say,* says he, *I shall walke weakly all my yeares, in the bitternesse of my soule.* All temporall blessings are insipid and tastlesse, without health.

Esay 38.15

Now the third branch of this part, is the other *In quibus,* not the things, but the persons, in whom these three blessings are here placed: And it is *Beatus populus,* when this blessednesse reaches to all, dilates it selfe over all. When *David* places blessednesse in one particular man, as he does in the beginning of the first Psalme, *Beatus vir,*
380 *Blessed is that man,* there he pronounces that man blessed, *If he neither walke in the counsell of the wicked, nor stand in the way of sinners, nor sit in the seate of the scornfull.* If he doe not all, *walke,* and *stand,* and *sit* in the presence and feare of God, he is not blessed. So, if these temporall blessings fall not upon all, in their proportions, the people is not blessed. The City may be blessed in the increase of accesse; And the Lawyer may be blessed in the increase of suits; and the Merchant may be blessed in the increase of meanes of getting, if he be come to get as well by taking, as by trading; but if all be not blessed, the people is not blessed: yea, if these temporall blessings
390 reach not to the Prince himselfe, the people is not blessed. For *in favorabilibus Princeps è populo,* is a good rule in the Law; in things beneficiall, the King is one of the people. When God sayes by *David, Let all the people blesse the Lord,* God does not exempt Kings from that duty; and when God sayes by him too, *God shall blesse all the*

Populus

people, God does not exempt, not exclude Kings from that benefit; And therfore where such things as conduce to the beeing, and the well-beeing, to the substance and state, to the ceremony and majesty of the Prince, be not chearfully supplied, and seasonably administred, there that blessing is not fully faln upon them, *Blessed is that people*
⁴⁰⁰ *that are so;* for the people are not so, if the Prince be not so.

Nay, the people are not blessed, if these blessings be not permanent; for, it is not onely they that are alive now, that are the people; but the people is the succession. If we could imagine a blessing of health without permanency, we might call an intermitting ague, a good day in a fever, health. If we could imagine a blessing of plenty without permanency, we might call a full stomach, and a surfet, though in a time of dearth, plenty. If we could imagine a blessing of peace without permanency, we might call a nights sleepe, though in the midst of an Army, peace; but it is onely provision for the permanency and con-
⁴¹⁰ tinuance, that makes these blessings blessings. To thinke of, to provide against famine, and sicknesse, and warre, that is the blessing of plenty, and health, and peace. One of Christs principall titles was,

Esay 9.[6]
[Mat. 10.34]

that he was *Princeps pacis,* and yet this Prince of peace sayes, *Non veni mittere pacem,* I came not to bring you peace, not such a peace as should bring them security against all warre. If a Ship take fire, though in the midst of the Sea, it consumes sooner, and more irrecoverably, then a thatched house upon Land: If God cast a fire-brand of warre, upon a State accustomed to peace, it burnes the more desperately, by their former security.

⁴²⁰   But here in our Text we have a religious King, *David,* that first prayes for these blessings, (for the three former Verses are a prayer) and then praises God in the acknowledgement of them; for this Text is an acclamatory, a gratulatory glorifying of God for them. And when these two meet in the consideration of temporall blessings, a religious care for them, a religious confessing of them, prayer to God for the getting, praise to God for the having, *Blessed is that people,* that is, Head and members, Prince and subjects, present and future people, *that are so;* So blessed, so thankefull for their blessings.

2 Part   We come now, *Ad dextram dextræ,* to the right blessedness, in the
⁴³⁰ right sense and interpretation of these words, to spirituall blessedness,

1 Cor. 9.9

to the blessedness of the soule. *Estne Deo cura de bobus?* is the

Apostles question, and his answer is pregnantly implied, God hath care of beasts: But yet God cared more for one soule then for those two thousand hogges which he suffered to perish in the Sea, when that man was dispossessed. A dram of spirituall is worth infinite talents of temporall. Here then in this spirituall blessedness (as we did in the former) wee shall looke first, *Quid beatitudo,* what it is; and then, *In quibus,* in what it is placed here, *Vt Deus eorum sit Dominus,* That their God bee the Lord; And lastly, the extent of it, 440 That all the people bee made partakers of this spirituall blessedness.

This blessedness then, you see is placed last in the Text; not that it cannot be had till our end, till the next life; In this case, the *Nemo ante obitum* failes, for it is in this life, that we must find our God to be the Lord, or else, if we know not that here, we shall meet his *Nescio vos,* he will not know us; But it is placed last, because it is the waightiest, and the uttermost degree of blessedness, which can be had, *To have the Lord for our God.* Consider the making up of a naturall man, and you shall see that hee is a convenient Type of a spirituall man too.

450 First, in a naturall man wee conceive there is a soule of vegetation and of growth; and secondly, a soule of motion and of sense; and then thirdly, a soule of reason and understanding, an immortall soule. And the two first soules of vegetation, and of sense, wee conceive to arise out of the temperament, and good disposition of the substance of which that man is made, they arise out of man himselfe; But the last soule, the perfect and immortall soule, that is immediatly infused by God. Consider the blessedness of this Text, in such degrees, in such proportions. First, God blesses a man with riches, there is his soule of vegetation and growth, by that hee growes in estimation, and 460 in one kinde of true ability to produce good fruits, for he hath where-withall. And then, God gives this rich man the blessing of under-standing his riches, how to employ them according to those morall and civill duties, which appertaine unto him, and there is his soule of sense; for many rich men have not this sense, many rich men understand their owne riches no more then the Oaks of the Forrest doe their owne Akorns. But last of all, God gives him the blessing of discerning the mercy, and the purpose of God in giving him these temporall blessings, and there is his immortall soule. Now for the

riches themselves, (which is his first soule) he may have them *ex*
470 *traduce,* by devolution from his parents; and the civill wisedome,
how to governe his riches, where to purchase, where to sell, where to
give, where to take, (which is his second soule) this he may have by
his owne acquisition, and experience, and conversation; But the immortall soule, that is, the discerning of Gods image in every piece,
and of the seale of Gods love in every temporall blessing, this is
infused from God alone, and arises neither from Parents, nor the
wisedome of this world, how worldly wise so ever wee bee in the
governing of our estate.

And this the Prophet may very well seeme to have intimated, when
Psal. 112.2 480 he saith, *The generation of the righteous shall be blessed;* Here is a
permanent blessedness, to the generation. Wherein is it expressed?
thus; *Riches and treasure shall bee in his house, and his righteousnesse
endureth for ever.* Hee doth not say, that Simony, or Usury, or Extortion shall bee in his house; for riches got so are not treasure; Nor he
doth not say, that Riches well got, and which are truely a blessing,
shall endure for ever, but *his righteousnesse shall endure for ever.*
The last soule, the immortall soule endures for ever. The blessedness
of having studied, and learnt, and practised the knowledge of Gods
purpose in temporall blessings, this blessedness shall endure for ever;
490 When thou shalt turne from the left to the right side, upon thy death
bed, from all the honours, and riches of this world, to breathe thy
soule into his hands that gave it, this righteousness, this good conscience shall endure then, and then accompany thee: And when thine
eyes are closed, and in the twinckling of his eye that closed thine, thy
soule shall be gone an infinite way from this honour, and these riches,
this righteousness, this good conscience shall endure then, and meet
thee in the gates of heaven. And this is so much of that righteousness,
as is expressed in this Text, (because this is the root of all) *That our
God be the Lord.*

In quibus 500 In which, first wee must propose a *God,* that there is one, and then
appropriate this God to our selves, that he be *our God,* and lastly, be
sure that we have the right God, that *our God be the Lord.* For, for
the first, he that enterprises any thing, seeks any thing, possesses any
thing without recourse to God, without acknowledging God in that
action, he is, for that particular, an Atheist, he is without God in that;

and if hee doe so in most of his actions, he is for the most part an
Atheist. If he be an Atheist every where, but in his Catechisme, if
onely then he confesse a God when hee is asked, Doest thou beleeve
that there is a God, and never confesse him, never consider him in
510 his actions, it shall do him no good, to say at the last day, that he was
no speculative Atheist, he never thought in his heart, that there was no
God, if hee lived a practique Atheist, proceeded in all his actions without any consideration of him. But accustome thy selfe to find the
presence of God in all thy gettings, in all thy preferments, in all thy
studies, and he will be abundantly sufficient to thee for all. *Quantum-
libet sis avarus,* saith S. *Augustine, sufficit tibi Deus,* Be as covetous
as thou wilt, bee as ambitious as thou canst, the more the better; God
is treasure, God is honour enough for thee. *Avaritia terram quærit,*
saith the same Father, *adde & Cælum;* wouldst thou have all this
520 world? wouldst thou have all the next world too? *Plus est, qui fecit
cælum & terram,* He that made heaven and earth is more then all
that, and thou mayest have all him.

And this appropriates him so neare to us, as that hee is thereby *Noster*
Deus noster. For, it is not enough to finde *Deum,* a God; a great and
incomprehensible power, that sits *in luce,* in light, but *in luce inaccessibili,* in light that we cannot comprehend. A God that enjoyes his
owne eternity, his owne peace, his owne blessedness, but respects not
us, reflects not upon us, communicates nothing to us. But it is a God,
that is *Deus noster;* Ours, as we are his creatures; ours, as we are like
530 him, made to his image; ours, as he is like us, in assuming our
nature; ours, as he hath descended to us in his Incarnation; and ours,
as we are ascended with him in his glorification: So that wee doe not
consider God, as our God, except we come to the consideration of
God in Christ, God and man. It is not enough to find *Deum,* a God
in generall, nor to find *Deum meum,* a God so particularly my God,
as that he is a God of my making: That I should seeke God by any
other motions, or know God by any other notions, or worship God
in any other fashions, then the true Church of God doth, for there
he is *Deus noster,* as hee is received in the unanime consent of the
540 Catholique Church. Sects are not bodies, they are but rotten boughes,
gangrened limmes, fragmentary chips, blowne off by their owne
spirit of turbulency, fallen off by the waight of their owne pride, or

hewen off by the Excommunications and censures of the Church. Sects are no bodies, for there is *Nihil nostrum,* nothing in common amongst them, nothing that goes through them all; all is singular, all is *meum* and *tuum,* my spirit and thy spirit, my opinion and thy opinion, my God and thy God; no such apprehension, no such worship of God, as the whole Church hath evermore been acquainted withall, and contented with.

550   It is true, that every man must appropriate God so narrowly, as to find him to be *Deum suum,* his God; that all the promises of the Prophets, and all the performances of the Gospell, all that Christ Jesus said, and did, and suffered, belongs to him and his soule; but yet God is *Deus meus,* as he is *Deus noster,* my God, as he is our God, as I am a part of that Church, with which he hath promised to be till the end of the world, and as I am an obedient sonne of that Mother, who is the Spouse of Christ Jesus: For as S. *Augustine* saith of that Petition, *Give us this day our daily bread, Vnde dicimus Da nostrum?* How come we to ask that which is ours, *Quomodo nostrum,*
560 *quomodo da?* if we be put to ask it, why doe wee call it ours? and then answers himselfe, *Tuum confitendo, non eris ingratus,* It is a thankfull part to confesse that thou hast some, that thou hast received some blessings; and then, *Ab illo petendo, non eris vacuus,* It is a wise and a provident part, to ask more of him, whose store is inexhaustible; So if I feele God, as hee is *Deus meus,* as his Spirit works in me, and thankfully acknowledge that, *Non sum ingratus;* But if I derive this Pipe from the Cistern, this *Deus Meus,* from *Deus noster,* my knowledge and sense of God, from that knowledge which is communicated by his Church, in the preaching of his Word, in the administration
570 of his Sacraments, in those other meanes which he hath instituted in his Church, for the assistance and reparation of my soule that way, *Non ero vacuus,* I shall have a fuller satisfaction, a more abundant refection then if I rely upon my private inspirations: for there he is *Deus noster.*

Dominus   Now, as we are thus to acknowledge a God, and thus to appropriate that God; so we must be sure to confer this honour upon the right God, upon him who is *the Lord.* Now this name of God, which is translated *the Lord* here, is not the name of God, which presents him with relation to his Creatures: for so it is a problematicall, a dis-

580 putable thing, Whether God could be called *the Lord,* before there were any Creatures. *Tertullian* denies absolutely that he could be called Lord till then; S. *Augustin* is more modest, he sayes, *Non audeo dicere,* I dare not say that he was not; but he does not affirme that he was; Howsoever the name here, is not the name of Relation, but it is the name of his Essence, of his Eternity, that name, which of late hath beene ordinarily called *Iehovah.* So that we are not to trust in those Lords, *Whose breath is in their nostrils,* as the Prophet sayes, *For, wherein are they to be esteemed?* sayes he; we are lesse to trust in them, whose breath was never in their nostrils, such imaginary

Esay 2. ult.

590 Saints, as are so far from hearing us in Heaven, as that they are not there: and so far from being there, as that they were never here: so farre from being Saints, as that they were never men, but are either fabulous illusions, or at least, but symbolicall and allegoricall allusions. Our Lord is the Lord of life and being, who gave us not onely a well-being in this life, (for that, other Lords can pretend to doe, and doe indeed, by preferments here) nor a beginning of a temporary being in this life, (for that our Parents pretend, and pretend truly to have done) nor onely an enlarging of our being in this life, (for that the King can doe by a Pardon, and the Physitians by a Cordiall) but

600 he hath given us an immortall being, which neither our Parents began in us, nor great persons can advance for us, nor any Prince can take from us. This is *the Lord* in this place, this is *Iehova,* and *Germen Iehovæ,* The Lord, and the off-spring of the Lord; and none is the off-spring of God, but God, that is, the Son, and the Holy Ghost. So that this perfect blessednesse consists in this, the true knowledge and worship of the Trinity.

Esay 4.2

And this blessing, that is, the true Religion and profession of Christ Jesus, is to be upon all the people; which is our last Consideration. *Blessed is the Nation, whose God is the Lord, and the people whom*

Populus

610 *he hath chosen for his Inheritance.* And here againe (as in the former Consideration of temporall blessednesse) The people includes both Prince and people; and then, the blessing consists in this, that both Prince and people be sincerely affected to the true Religion; And then, the people includes all the people; and so, the blessing consists in this, that there be an unanimitie, a consent in all, in matter of Religion; And lastly, the people includes the future people; and

Psal. 33.12

there, the blessing consists in this, that our posterity may enjoy the
same purity of Religion that we doe. The first tentation that fell
amongst the Apostles carried away one of them: *Iudas* was transported
⁶²⁰ with the tentation of money; and how much? For thirty peeces, and
in all likelihood he might have made more profit then that, out of the
privy purse; The first tentation carried one, but the first persecution
carried away nine, when Christ was apprehended, none was left but
two, and of one of those two, S. *Hierom* saies, *Vtinam fugisset & non
negasset Christum,* I would *Peter* had fled too, and not scandalized
the cause more by his stay, in denying his Master: for, a man may
stay in the outward profession of the true Religion, with such purposes, and to such ends, as he may thereby damnifie the cause more,
and damnifie his owne soule more, then if he went away to that
⁶³⁰ Religion, to which his conscience (though ill rectified) directs him.
Now, though when such tentations, and such persecutions doe come,
the words of our Saviour Christ will alwayes be true, *Feare not little*
flocke, for it is Gods pleasure to give you the Kingdome, though God
can lay up his seed-corne in any little corner, yet the blessing intended
here, is not in that little seed-corne, nor in the corner, but in the
plenty, when all the people are blessed, and the blessed Spirit blowes
where he will, and no doore nor window is shut against him.

And therefore let all us blesse God, for that great blessing to us, in
giving us such Princes, as make it their care, *Ne bona caduca sint, ne*
⁶⁴⁰ *mala recidiva,* That that blessednesse which we enjoy by them, may
never depart from us, that those miseries which wee felt before them,
may never returne to us. Almighty God make alwaies to us all,
Prince and people, these temporall blessings which we enjoy now,
Peace, and Plenty, and Health, seales of his spirituall blessings, and
that spirituall blessednesse which we enjoy now, the profession of the
onely true Religion, a seale of it selfe, and a seale of those eternall
blessings, which the Lord the righteous Judge hath laid up for his, in
that Kingdome which his Son, our Saviour hath purchased for us,
with the inestimable price of his incorruptible blood. In which glori-
⁶⁵⁰ ous Son of God, &c.

Luke 12.32

Number 3.

Preached at Lincolns Inne.

JOB 19.26. *AND THOUGH, AFTER MY SKIN, WORMES DESTROY THIS BODY, YET IN MY FLESH SHALL I SEE GOD.*

AMONGST those *Articles,* in which our Church hath explain'd, and declar'd her faith, this is the *eight* Article, that the three Creeds, (that of the councell of *Nice,* that of *Athanasius,* and that which is commonly known by the name of the *Apostles Creed*) ought throughly to be received, and embrac'd. The meaning of the Church is not, that onely that should be beleev'd in which those *three Creeds agree;* (for, the *Nicen Creed* mentions no Article after that of the *holy Ghost,* not the Catholique Church, not the Communion of Saints, not the Resurrection of the flesh; *Athanasius*
¹⁰ his Creed does mention the Resurrection, but not the Catholique Church, nor the communion of Saints,) but that *all* should be beleev'd, which is in any of them, all which is summ'd up in the Apostles Creed. Now, the reason expressed in that Article of our Church, why all this is to be beleeved, is; *Because all this may be prov'd by most certaine warrants of holy Scriptures.* The Article does not insist upon particular places of Scripture; not so much as point to them. But, they who have enlarged the Articles, by way of explanation, have done that. And when they come to cite those places of Scripture, which prove the Article of the Resurrection, I observe that amongst
²⁰ those places they forbeare this text; so that it may seem, that in their opinion, this Scripture doth not concerne the *Resurrection.* It will not therefore be impertinent, to make it a first part of this exercise, whether this Scripture be to be understood of the Resurrection, or no; And then, to make the particular handling of the words, a second part. In the first, we shall see, that the *Jews* always had, and have

still, a persuasion of the Resurrection. We shall look after, by *what light* they saw that; whether by the light of *naturall reason;* And, if not by that, by what light given in other places of Scripture; and then, we shall shut up this inquisition with a unanime consent, (so
30 unanime, as I can remember but *one* that denies it, and he but faintly) that in this text, the doctrine of the resurrection is established. In the second part, the doctrine it selfe comprised in the words of the text, (*And though after my skin, wormes destroy this body, yet in my flesh shall I see God*) we shall see first, that the *Saints* of God themselves, are not priviledged from the common corruption and dissolu-

Gen. 3.14

[Gen. 3.19]

tion of the body; After that curse upon the Serpent, *super pectus gradieris,* upon thy belly shalt thou goe, we shall as soon see a Serpent goe upright, and not craule, as, after that Judgment, *In pulverem revertêris,* to dust thou shalt returne, see a man, that shall
40 not see death, and corruption in death. Corruption upon our *skin,* says the text, (our outward beauty;) corruption upon our *body,* (our whole strength, and constitution.) And, this corruption, not a green palenesse, not a yellow jaundise, not a blue lividnesse, not a black morpheu upon our skin, not a bony leannesse, not a sweaty faintnesse, not an ungratious decrepitnesse upon our body, but a destruction, a destruction to both, *After my skin my body shall be destroyed.* Though not destroyed by being resolved to ashes in the fire, (perchance I shall not be burnt) not destroyed by being washed to slime, in the sea, (perchance I shall not be drowned) but destroyed con-
50 temptibly, by those whom I breed, and feed, by wormes; (*After my skin wormes shall destroy my body.*) And thus farre our case is equall; one event to the good and bad; wormes shall destroy all in them all. And farther then this, their case is equall too, for, they shall both rise againe from this destruction. But in this lies the future glory, in this lies the present comfort of the Saints of God, that, *after all this,* (so that this is not my last act, to dye, nor my last scene, to lie in the grave, nor my last *exit,* to goe out of the grave) *after,* says *Job;* And indefinitely, *After,* I know not how soone, nor how late, I presse not into Gods secrets for that; but, *after all this, Ego,* I, I that
60 speak now, and shall not speak then, silenced in the grave, I that see now, and shall not see then, *ego videbo,* I shall see, (I shall have a new *faculty*) *videbo Deum,* I shall see *God* (I shall have a new

object) and, *In carne*, I shall see him in the *flesh*, (I shall have a new *organ*, and a new *medium*) and, *In carne mea*, that flesh shall be *my flesh*, (I shall have a new propriety in that flesh) this flesh which I have now, is not *mine*, but the wormes; but that flesh shall be so mine, as I shall never *devest it more*, but *In my flesh I shall see God for ever.*

    In the first part then, which is an inquiry, whether this text con-
70 cerne the Resurrection, or no, we take knowledge of a *Crediderunt*, and of a *Credunt* in the *Jews*, that the *Jews* did beleeve a Resurrection, and that they doe beleeve it still. That they doe so now, appears out of the doctrine of their *Talmud*, where we find, that *onely the Jews* shall rise againe, but all the Gentiles shall perish, body and soule together, as *Korah, Dathan,* and *Abiram* were swallowed all at once, body, and soule into hell. And to this purpose, (for the first part thereof, that the *Jews* shall rise) they abuse that place of *Esay, Thy dead men shall live; awake and sing, yee that dwell in the dust.* And, for the second part, that the Gentiles shall not rise, they apply the
80 words of the same Prophet before, *They are dead, they shall not live, they are deceased, they shall not rise.* The *Jews* onely, say they shall rise; but, *not all they;* but onely the *righteous* amongst them. And, to that purpose, they abuse that place of the Prophet *Zachary, two parts shall be cut off, and dye, but the third shall be left therein, and I will bring that third part, through the fire, and will refine them, as silver is refined, and try them, as gold is tried.* The *Jews* onely of all men, the good *Jews* onely of all *Jews,* and of these good *Jews,* onely they who were buried in the land of promise shall have this present, and immediate resurrection; And to that purpose they force that place
90 in *Genesis* where *Jacob,* upon his deathbed, advised his sonne *Joseph,* to bury him in *Canaan,* and not in *Egypt,* and to that purpose, they detort also, that place of *Ieremy,* where the Prophet lays that curse upon *Pashur, That he should dye in Babylon, and be buried there.* For, though the *Jews* doe not absolutely say, that all that are buried out of *Canaan,* shall be without a resurrection, yet, they say, that even those good and righteous *Jews,* which are not buried in that great Churchyard, the land of promise, must, at the day of judgment, be brought through the hollow parts of the earth, into the land of promise at that time, and only in that place, receive their resurrec-

1 Part

Iudæi credunt

Numb.
16.32
[Isa.] 26.19

14

13.8

47.29

20.6

¹⁰⁰ tion, wheresoever they were buried. But yet, though none but *Jews,* none but righteous *Jews,* none but righteous *Jews* in that place, must be partakers of the Resurrection, yet still a Resurrection there is in their doctrine.

Crediderunt

Iohn 11.23

Luke 14.14

Mar. 6.14

Iohn 20.9

Mat. 16.22

It is so now; it was so always. We see, in that time, when *Christ* walked upon the earth, when he came to the raising of *Lazarus,* and said to his sister *Martha, Thy brother shall rise againe,* she replies to Christ, *Alas, I know he shall rise againe, at the Resurrection of the last day,* I make no doubt of that, we all know that. So also, when Christ put forth that parable, that in placing of benefits, we ¹¹⁰ should rather choose such persons, as were able to make no recompense, he gives that reason, *Thou shalt be recompensed at the resurrection of the just.* The Resurrection was a vulgar doctrine, well knowne to the *Jews* then, and always. For, even *Herod,* when Christ preached and did miracles, was apt to say, *Iohn Baptist is risen from the dead;* And when it is said of those two great *Apostles,* (the loving, and the beloved Apostle, *Peter,* and *Iohn*) that as yet they knew not the Scripture, that *Christ must rise from the dead,* this argues no more, but that as *Peters* compassion before Christs death, made him disswade Christ from going up to *Jerusalem,* to suffer, so their ¹²⁰ extreme passion after Christs death, made them the lesse attentively to consider those particular Scriptures, which spoke of the Resurrection. For, the *Jews* in generall, (much more, they) had always an apprehension, and an acknowledgment of the Resurrection of the dead. By what light they saw this, and how they came to this knowledge, is our next consideration.

An ex
ratione

Had they this by the common notions of other men, out of naturall *Reason? Melancthon,* (who is no bold, nor rash, nor dangerous expressor of himselfe) says well, *Articulus resurrectionis propria Ecclesiæ vox;* It is the Christian Church, that hath delivered to us the ¹³⁰ article of the resurrection. Nature says it not, Philosophy says it not; it is the language and the Idiotisme of the Church of God, that the resurrection is to be beleeved as an article of faith. For, though articles of faith be not *facta Ecclesiæ,* they are *dicta Ecclesiæ,* though the Church doe not *make* articles, yet she *declares* them. In the Creation, the way was, *Dixit & facta sunt,* God spake, and so things were made; In the Gospell, the way is, *Fecit, & dicta sunt,* God makes articles

of faith, and the Church utters them, presents them. That's *mani-festè verum,* evidently, undeniably true, that Nature, and Philosophy say nothing of articles of faith. But, even in Nature, and in Philos-
140 ophy, there is some preparation *A priore,* and much illustration *A posteriore,* of the Resurrection. For, first, we know by naturall reason, that it is no such thing, as God cannot doe; It implies no contradiction in it selfe, as that new article of *Transubstantiation* does; It implies no defectivenesse in God, as that new article, *The necessity of a perpetuall Vicar upon earth,* does. For, things contradictory in themselves, (which necessarily imply a falshood) things arguing a defectivenesse in God, (which implies necessarily a derogation, to his nature, to his naturall goodnesse, to that which we may justly call even *the God of God,* that which makes him God to us, *his*
150 *mercy*) such things God himselfe cannot doe, not things which make him an unmercifull, a cruell, a precondemning God. But, excepting onely such things, God, who is that, *Quod cum dicitur, non potest dici,* whom if you name you cannot give him halfe his name; for, if you call him God, he hath not his Christen name, for he is Christ as well as God, a Saviour, as well as a Creator; *Quod cum æstimatur, non potest æstimari,* If you value God, weigh God, you cannot give him halfe his weight; for, you can put nothing into the balance, to weigh him withall, but all this world; and, there is no single sand in the sea, no single dust upon the earth, no single atome in the ayre,
160 that is not likelyer to weigh down all the world, then all the world is to counterpose God; *What is the whole world to a soule?* says Christ; but what are all the soules of the world, to God? *What is man, that God should be mindefull of him,* that God should ever thinke of him, and not forget that there is such a thing, such a nothing? *Quod cum definitur, ipsa definitione crescit,* says the same Father; If you limit God with any definition, hee growes larger by that definition; for even by that definition you discerne presently that he is something else then that definition comprehends: That God, *Quem omnia nesciunt, & metuendo sciunt,* whom no man
170 knows perfectly, yet every man knows so well, as to stand in feare of him, this incomprehensible God, I say, *that works, and who shall let it?* can raise our bodies again from the dead, because, to doe so, implies no derogation to himselfe, no contradiction to his word.

Greg.
Nazianz.

Mar. 8.36

Psal. 8.4

Idem

Esay 43.13

An velit

Our reason tells us, he *can* doe it; doth our reason tell us as much of his *will,* that he will doe it? Our reason tells us, that he will doe, whatsoever is most convenient for the Creature, whom, because he hath made him, he loves, and for his owne glory. Now this dignity afforded to the dead body of man, cannot be conceived, but, as a great addition to him. Nor can it be such a diminution to God, to take
180 man into heaven, as it was for God to descend, and to take mans nature upon him, upon Earth. A King does not diminish himselfe so much, by taking an inferior person into his bosome at Court, as he should doe by going to live with that person, in the Countrey, or City; and this God did, in the incarnation of his Sonne. It cannot be thought inconvenient, it cannot be thought hard. Our reason tells us, that in all Gods works, in all his materiall works, still his latter works are easier then his former. The *Creation,* which was the first, and was a meer production out of nothing, was the hardest of all. The *specification* of Creatures, and the disposing of them, into their
190 severall kinds, the making of that which was made something of nothing before, a particular thing, a beast, a fowle, a fish, a plant, a man, a Sun or Moon, was not so hard, as the first production out of nothing. And then, the *conservation* of all these, in that order in which they are first created, and then distinguished, the Administration of these creatures by a constant working of second causes, which naturally produce their effects, is not so hard as that. And so, accordingly, and in that proportion, the last worke is easiest of all; Distinction and specification easier then creation, conservation and administration easier then that distinction, and restitution by resurrection,

Tertull.   200 easiest of all. *Tertullian* hath expressed it well, *Plus est fecisse quam refecisse, & dedisse quam reddidisse;* It is a harder worke to make, then to mend, and, to give thee that which was mine, then to restore thee that which was thine. *Et institutio carnis quàm destitutio;* It is a lesse matter to recover a sicke man, then to make a whole man.

Just. Mart.
Athenago.

Does this trouble thee, says *Justin Martyr,* (and *Athenagoras* proceeds in the same way of argumentation too, in his Apology) does this trouble thee, *Quòd homo à piscibus, & piscis ab homine comeditur,* that one man is devoured by a fish, and then another man that eats the flesh of that fish, eats, and becomes the other man? *Id nec ho-*
210 *minem resolvit in piscem, nec piscem in hominem,* that first man

did not become that fish that eate him, nor that fish become that second man, that eate it; *sed utriusque resolutio fit in elementa,* both that man, and that fish are resolved into their owne elements, of which they were made at first. Howsoever it be, if thine imagination could carry thee so low, as to thinke, not onely that thou wert become some other thing, a fish, or a dogge that had fed upon thee, and so, thou couldst not have thine owne body, but therewithall must have his body too, but that thou wert infinitely farther gone, that thou wert annihilated, become nothing, canst thou chuse but thinke God
220 as perfect now, at least as he was at first, and can hee not as easily make thee up againe of nothing, as he made thee of nothing at first? *Recogita quid fueris, antequam esses;* Thinke over thy selfe; what wast thou before thou wast any thing? *Meminisses utique, si fuisses;* If thou hadst been any thing then, surely thou wouldst remember it now. *Qui non eras, factus es; Cum iterum non eris, fies;* Thou that wast once nothing, wast made this that thou art now; and when thou shalt be nothing againe, thou shalt be made better then thou art yet. And, *Redde rationem quâ factus es, & ego reddam rationem quâ fies;* Doe thou tell me, how thou wast made then, and I will tell
230 thee how thou shalt be made hereafter. And yet as *Solomon* sends us to creatures, and to creatures of a low rank and station, to Ants and Spiders, for instruction, so Saint *Gregory* sends us to creatures, to learne the Resurrection. *Lux quotidie moritur, & quotidie resurgit;* That glorious creature, that first creature, the light, dyes every day, and every day hath a resurrection. *In arbustis folia resurrectione erumpunt;* from the Cedar of *Libanus,* to the Hyssop upon the wall, every leafe dyes every yeare, and every yeare hath a Resurrection. *Vbi in brevitate seminis, tam immensa arbor latuit?* (as he pursues that meditation.) If thou hadst seen the bodies of men rise out of the
240 grave, at Christs Resurrection, could that be a stranger thing to thee, then, (if thou hadst never seen, nor hard, nor imagined it before) to see an Oake that spreads so farre, rise out of an Akorne? Or if Churchyards did vent themselves every spring, and that there were such a Resurrection of bodies every yeare, when thou hadst seen as many Resurrections as years, the Resurrection would be no stranger to thee, then the spring is. And thus, this, and many other good and reverend men, and so the *holy Ghost* himselfe sends us to *Reason,*

Tertull.

[Prov. 6.6;
30.25, 28]
Greg.

and to the *Creature,* for the doctrine of the Resurrection; *Saint Paul*

1 Cor. 15.36

allowes him not the reason of a man, that proceeds not so; *Thou fool,*
²⁵⁰ says he, *that which thou sowest, is not quickned except it dye;* but
then it is. It is truly harder to conceive a translation of the body into

Ambr.

heaven, then a Resurrection of the body from the earth. *Num in
hominibus terra degenerat, quæ omnia regenerare consuevit?* Doe
all kinds of earth regenerate, and shall onely the Churchyard degenerate? Is there a yearely Resurrection of every other thing, and never

Tertull.

of men? *Omnia pereundo servantur,* All other things are preserved,
and continued by dying; *Tu homo solus ad hoc morieris, ut pereas?*
And canst thou, O man, suspect of thy selfe, that the end of thy
dying is an end of thee? Fall as low as thou canst, corrupt and putre-
²⁶⁰ fie as desperately as thou canst, *sis nihil,* thinke thy selfe nothing;

Idem

Ejus est nihilum ipsum cujus est totum, even that nothing is as much
in his power, as the world which he made of nothing; And, as he
called thee when thou wast not, as if thou hadst been, so will he call
thee againe, when thou art ignorant of that being which thou hast
in the grave, and give thee againe thy former, and glorifie it with a
better being.

*An ex
Scripturis*

The *Jews* then, if they had no other helpes, might have, (as naturall men may) preparations *à Priore,* and illustrations *à Posteriore,*
for the doctrine of the Resurrection. The *Jews* had seen resuscitations
²⁷⁰ from the dead in particular persons, and they had seen miraculous
cures done by their Prophets. And *Gregory Nyssen* says well, that

Greg. Nyss.

those miraculous cures which Christ wrought, with a *Tolle grabatum,*
and an *Esto sanus,* and no more, they were *præludia resurrectionis,*
halfe-resurrections, prologues, and inducements to the doctrine of
the resurrection, which shall be transacted with a *Surgite mortui,*
and no more. So these naturall helps in the consideration of the creature, are *præludia resurrectionis,* they are halfe-resurrections, and
these naturall resurrections carry us halfe way to the miraculous
resurrection. But certainely, the *Jews,* who had that, which the Gen-
²⁸⁰ tiles wanted, *The Scriptures,* had from them, a generall, though not
an explicite knowledge of the resurrection. That they had it, we see

2 Macab.
12.43

by that practise of *Judas the Maccabee,* in gathering a contribution
to send to *Jerusalem,* which is therefore commended, because he was
therein mindefull of the Resurrection. Neither doth Christ find any

that opposed the doctrine of the Resurrection, but those, who though they were tolerated in the State, because they were otherwise great persons, were absolute *Heretiques,* even amongst the *Jews, The Sadduces.* And *Saint Paul,* when, finding himselfe to bee oppressed in Judgement, hee used his Christian wisedome, and to draw a strong
290 party to himselfe, protested himselfe to bee of the sect of the *Pharisees,* and that, as they, and all the rest, in generall, did, he maintained the Resurrection, he knew it would seem a strange injury, and an oppression, to be called in question for that, that they all beleeved; Though therefore our Saviour Christ, who disputed then, onely against the Sadduces, argued for the doctrine of the Resurrection, onely from that place of the Scripture, which those Sadduces acknowledged to be Scripture, (for they denied all but the *bookes of Moses*) and so insisted upon those words, *I am the God of Abraham, the God of Isaac, and the God of Jacob,* yet certainely the *Jews* had
300 established that doctrine, upon other places too, though to the Sadduces who accepted *Moses* onely, *Moses* were the best evidence. It is evident enough in that particular place of *Daniel, Many of them that sleep in the dust of the earth, shall awake, some to everlasting life, and some to shame, and everlasting contempt.* And in *Daniel,* that word *many,* must not be restrained to lesse then all; *Daniel* intends by that many, that how many soever they are, they shall all arise; as Saint *Paul* does, when he says, By one mans disobedience, *many* were made sinners; that is, *All;* for, death passed over *all men;* for all have sinned. And Christ doth but paraphrase that place of *Daniel,*
310 who says, *Multi,* many, when he says, *Omnes,* all; *All that are in the grave shall heare his voyce and shall come forth;* They that have done good, unto the resurrection of life, and they that have done evill to the resurrection of damnation. This then being thus far settled, that the *Jews understood* the resurrection, and more then that, they *beleeved* it, and therefore, as they had light in nature, they had assurance in Scripture, come we now, to that which was our last purpose in this first part, whether in *this* text, in these words of *Iob,* (*though after my skin, wormes destroy my body*) there be any such light of the Resurrection given.
320 It is true, that in the new Testament, where the doctrine of the resurrection is more evidently, more liquidly delivered, then in the

Act. 23.6

Luke 20.37
Exod. 3.6

12.2

Rom. 5.19
12

John 5.28

An ex hâc Scriptura

old, (though it be delivered in the old too) there is no place cited out of the book of *Iob,* for the resurrection; and so, this is not. But it is no marvaile; both upon that reason which we noted before, that they who were to be convinced, were such as received onely the *books* of *Moses,* and therefore all citations from this booke of *Iob,* or any other had been impertinently and frivolously employed, and, because in the new Testament, there is but one place of this booke of *Iob* cited at all. To the *Corinthians* the Apostle makes use of those ³³⁰ words in *Iob, God taketh the wise in their owne craft;* And more then this one place, is not, (I thinke) cited out of this booke of *Iob* in the new Testament. But, the authority of *Iob* is established in another place; *you have heard of the patience of Iob, and you have seen the end of the Lord,* says Saint *Iames.* As you have seen this, so you have heard that; seen and heard one way, out of the Scripture; you have hard that out of the booke of *Iob,* you have seen this out of the Gospell. And further then this, there is no naming of *Iobs* person, or his booke in the new Testament. Saint *Hierome* confesses, that both the Greeke, and Latine Copies of this booke, were so defective ³⁴⁰ in his time, that seven or eight hundred verses of the originall were wanting in the booke. And, for the originall it selfe, he says, *Obliquus totus liber fertur, & lubricus,* it is an uncertaine and slippery book. But this is onely for the sense of some places of the book; And that made the authority of this book, to be longer suspended in the Church, and oftner called into question by particular men, then any other book of the Bible. But, in those who have, for many ages, received this book for Canonicall, there is an unanime acknowledgement, (at least, tacitely) that this peece of it, this text, (*When, after my skin, wormes shall destroy my body, yet in my flesh I shall see* ³⁵⁰ *God*) does establish the Resurrection.

Divide the expositors into three branches; (for, so, the world will needs divide them) The first, the Roman Church will call theirs; though they have no other title to them, but that they received the same translation that they doe. And all they use this text for the resurrection. *Verba viri in gentilitate positi erubescamus;* It is a shame for us, who have the word of God it selfe, (which *Iob* had not) and have had such a commentary, such an exposition upon al the former word of God, as the reall, and actuall, and visible resur-

Marginal notes:

1 [Cor.]
3.19
[Job] 5.13

[Jas.] 5.11

Præfat.
in Iob

Partes

Greg.

rection of Christ himselfe, *Erubescamus verba viri in gentilitate*
360 *positi,* let us be ashamed and confounded, if *Iob,* a person that lived
not within the light of the covenant, saw the resurrection more
clearly, and professed it more constantly then we doe. And, as this
Gregory of *Rome,* so *Gregory Nyssen* understood *Iob* too. For, he
considers *Iobs* case thus; God promised *Iob twofold* of all that he had
lost; And in his sheep and camels, and oxen, and asses, which were
utterly destroyed, and brought to nothing, God performes it punc-
tually, he had all in a double proportion. But *Iob* had seven sonnes,
and three daughters before, and God gives him but seven sonnes,
and three daughters againe; And yet *Iob* had *twofold* of these too;
370 for, *Postnati cum prioribus numerantur, quia omnes deo vivunt;*
Those which were gone, and those which were new given, lived all
one life, because they lived all in God; *Nec quicquam aliud est mors,
nisi vitiositatis expiatio;* Death is nothing else, but a devesting of
those defects, which made us lesse fit for God. And therefore, agreeably to this purpose, says Saint *Cyprian, Scimus non amitti, sed
præmitti;* thy dead are not lost, but lent. *Non recedere, sed præcedere;*
They are not gone into any other wombe, then we shall follow them
into; *nec acquirendæ atræ vestes, pro iis qui albis induuntur,* neither
should we put on *blacks,* for them that are clothed in white, nor
380 mourne for them, that are entred into their Masters joy. We can
enlarge our selfes no farther in this consideration of the first branch
of expositors, but that all the *ancients* tooke occasion from this text
to argue for the resurrection.

Take into your Consideration the other two branches of moderne
expositors, (whom others sometimes contumeliously, and themselves
sometimes perversly have call'd *Lutherans* and *Calvinists*) and you
may know, that in the first ranke, *Osiander,* and with him, all his
[followers] interpret these words so; And in the other ranke, *Tremellius,* and *Pellicanus,* heretofore, *Polanus* lately, and *Piscator,* for
390 the present; All these, and all the Translators into the vulgar tongues
of all our neighbours of Europe, do all establish the doctrine of the
Resurrection by these words, this place of *Job.* And therefore, though
one, (and truly for any thing I know, but one) though one, to whom
we all owe much, for the interpretation of the Scriptures, do think
that *Job* intends no other resurrection in this place, but that, when he

Marginal notes:
Greg. Nyss.
42.10

13

Cyprian

Lutheran
Calvinist

Calvin

shall be reduc'd to the miserablest estate that can bee in this life, still
he will look upon God, and trust in him for his restitution, and reparation in this life; let us with the whole Christian Church, embrace
and magnifie this Holy and Heroicall Spirit of *Iob; Scio,* says he; I
⁴⁰⁰ know it, ·(which is more in him, then the *Credo* is in us, more to
know it then, in that state, then to *believe* it now, after it hath been so
evidently declar'd, not onely to be a certain truth, but to be an article
of faith) *Scio Redemptorem,* says he; I know not onely a Creator, but
a Redeemer; And, *Redemptorem meum,* My Redeemer, which implies a confidence, and a personall application of that Redemption to
himself. *Scio vivere,* says he; I know that he lives; I know that hee
begunne not in his Incarnation, I know he ended not in his death, but
it always was, and is now, and shall for ever be true, *Vivit,* that he
lives still. And then, *Scio venturum,* says he too; I know hee shall
⁴¹⁰ stand at the last day to Judge me and all the world; And after that,
and *after my skinne and body is destroyed by worms, yet in my flesh
I shall see God.* And so have you as much as we proposed for our
first part; That the Jews do now, that they always did believe a
Resurrection; That as naturall men, and by naturall reason they
might know it, both in the possibility of the thing, and in the purpose of God, that they had better helpes then naturall reason, for
they had divers places of their Scripture, and that this place of Scripture, which is our text, hath evermore been received for a proof of
the Resurrection. Proceed we now, to those particulars which con-
⁴²⁰ stitute our second part, such instructions concerning the Resurrection,
as arise out of these words, *Though after my skinne, worms destroy
my body, yet in my flesh I shall see God.*

2 Part   In this second part, the first thing that was propos'd, was, That
Sancti non   the Saints of God, are not priviledg'd from this, which fell upon
eximuntur   *Job,* This Death, this dissolution after death. Upon the *Morte morieris,* that double death, interminated by God upon *Adam,* there is
a *Non obstante; Revertere,* turn to God, and thou shalt not dy the
death, not the second death. But upon that part of the sentence, *In
pulverem revertêris, To dust thou shalt return,* there is no *Non ob-*
⁴³⁰ *stante;* though thou turn to God, thou must turn into the grave;
for, hee that redeem'd thee from the other death, redeem'd not himself from this. Carry this consideration to the last minute of the

world, when we that remain shall bee caught up in the clouds, yet 1 Thes. 4.17
even that last fire may be our fever, those clouds our winding sheets,
that rapture our dissolution; and so, with *Saint Augustine,* most of
the ancients, most of the latter men think, that there shall be a sudden
dissolution of body and soul, which is death, and a sudden re-uniting
of both, which is resurrection, in that instant; *Quis Homo,* is *Davids* Psal. 89.48
question; *What man is he that liveth and shall not see death?* Let us
440 adde, *Quis Deorum?* What god is he amongst the Gentiles, that hath
not seen death? Which of their three hundred *Jupiters,* which of
their thousands of other gods, have not seen death? *Mortibus moriuntur;* we may adde to that double death in Gods mouth, another death;
The gods of the Gentiles have dyed *thrice;* In body, in soul, and in
fame; for, though they have been glorified with a Deification, not
one of all those old gods, is, at this day, worshipt, in any part of the
world, but all those temporary, and transitory Gods, are worn out,
and dead in all senses. Those gods, who were but men, fall under
Davids question, *Quis Homo?* And that man who was truly God,
450 fals under it too, Christ Jesus; He saw death, though he saw not the
death of this text, *Corruption.* And, if we consider the effusion of his
precious blood, the contusion of his sacred flesh, the extension of
those sinews, and ligaments which tyed heaven, and earth together,
in a reconciliation, the departing of that Intelligence from that sphear,
of that high Priest from that Temple, of that Dove from that Arke,
of that soul from that body, that dissolution (which, as an ordinary
man he should have had in the grave, but that the decree of God,
declar'd in the infallibility of the manifold prophesies, preserv'd him
from it) had been but a slumber, in respect of these tortures, which
460 he did suffer; The *Godhead* staid with him in the grave, and so he
did not corrupt, but, though our souls be gone up to God, our bodies
shall.

Corruption in the skin, says *Iob;* In the outward beauty, These be *In pelle*
the Records of velim, these be the parchmins, the endictments, and
the evidences that shall condemn many of us, at the last day, our
own skins; we have the book of God, the Law, written in our own
hearts; we have the image of God imprinted in our own souls; wee
have the character, and seal of God stamped in us, in our baptism;
and, all this is bound up in this velim, in this parchmin, in this skin

⁴⁷⁰ of ours, and we neglect book, and image, and character, and seal, and all for the covering. It is not a clear case, if we consider the

2 Reg. 9.30

originall words properly, That *Iesabel did paint;* and yet all translators, and expositors have taken a just occasion, out of the ambiguity of those words, to cry down that abomination of painting. It is not a

2 Sam. 18.9

clear case, if we consider the propriety of the words, That *Absolon was hanged by the hair of the head;* and yet the Fathers and others have made use of that indifferency, and verisimilitude, to explode that abomination, of cherishing and curling haire, to the enveagling, and ensnaring, and entangling of others; *Iudicium patietur æternum,*

Hieron.

⁴⁸⁰ says *Saint Hierome,* Thou art guilty of a murder, though no body die; *Quia vinum attulisti, si fuisset qui bibisset;* Thou hast poyson'd a cup, if any would drink, thou hast prepar'd a tentation, if any

Tertul.

would swallow it. *Tertullian* thought he had done enough, when he had writ his book *De Habitu muliebri,* against the excesse of women in clothes, but he was fain to adde another with more vehemence, *De cultu fœminarum,* that went beyond their clothes to their skin. And he concludes, *Illud ambitionis crimen,* there's vain-glory in their excesse of clothes, but, *Hoc prostitutionis,* there's prostitution in drawing the eye to the skin. *Pliny* says, that when their thin silke stuffes ⁴⁹⁰ were first invented at Rome, *Excogitatum ad fœminas denudandas;* It was but an invention that women might go naked in clothes, for their skins might bee seen through those clothes, those thinne stuffes: Our women are not so carefull, but they expose their nakednesse professedly, and paint it, to cast bird-lime for the passengers eye. Beloved, good dyet makes the best Complexion, and a good Conscience is a continuall feast; A cheerfull heart makes the best blood, and peace with God is the true cheerfulnesse of heart. Thy Saviour neglected his skin so much, as that at last, hee scarse had any; all was torn with the whips, and scourges; and thy skin shall come to ⁵⁰⁰ that absolute corruption, as that, though a hundred years after thou art buryed, one may find thy bones, and say, this was a *tall* man, this was a *strong* man, yet we shall soon be past saying, upon any relique of thy skinne, This was a *fair* man; Corruption seises the skinne, all outward beauty quickly, and so it does the body, the whole frame and constitution, which is another consideration; *After my skinne, my Body.*

If the whole body were an eye, or an ear, where were the body, *In corpore*
says Saint *Paul;* but, when of the whole body there is neither eye 1 Cor. 12.17
nor ear, nor any member left, where is the body? And what should
510 an eye do there, where there is nothing to be seen but loathsomnesse;
or a nose there, where there is nothing to be smelt, but putrefaction;
or an ear, where in the grave they doe not praise God? Doth not
that body that boasted but yesterday of that priviledge above all creatures, that it onely could goe upright, lie to day as flat upon the earth
as the body of a horse, or of a dogge? And doth it not to morrow
lose his other priviledge, of looking up to heaven? Is it not farther
remov'd from the eye of heaven, the Sunne, then any dogge, or
horse, by being cover'd with the earth, which they are not? Painters
have presented to us with some horrour, the *sceleton,* the frame of
520 the bones of a mans body; but the state of a body, in the dissolution
of the grave, no pencil can present to us. Between that excrementall
jelly that thy body is made of at first, and that jelly which thy body
dissolves to at last; there is not so noysome, so putrid a thing in nature. This skinne, (this outward beauty) this body, (this whole constitution) must be destroy'd, says *Iob,* in the next place.

The word is well chosen, by which all this is expressed, in this text, Destroyed
Nakaph, which is a word of as heavy a signification, to expresse an
utter abolition, and annihilation, as perchance can be found in all
the Scriptures. *Tremellius* hath mollifyed it in his translation; there
530 it is but *Confodere,* to pierce. And yet it is such a piercing, such a
sapping, such an undermining, such a demolishing of a fort or Castle,
as may justly remove us from any high valuation, or any great confidence, in that skinne, and in that body, upon which this *Con-
foderint* must fall. But, in the great Bible it is *Contriverint,* Thy
skinne, and thy *body* shall be *ground* away, trod away upon the
ground. Aske where that iron is that is ground off of a knife, or axe;
Aske that marble that is worn off of the threshold in the Church-
porch by continuall treading, and with that iron, and with that
marble, thou mayst finde thy Fathers skinne, and body; *Contrita*
540 *sunt,* The knife, the marble, the skinne, the body are ground away,
trod away, they are destroy'd, who knows the revolutions of dust?
Dust upon the Kings high-way, and dust upon the Kings grave, are
both, or neither, Dust Royall, and may change places; who knows

the revolutions of dust? Even in the dead body of Christ Jesus himself, one dram of the decree of his Father, one sheet, one sentence of
the prediction of the Prophets preserv'd his body from corruption,
and incineration, more then all *Iosephs* new tombs, and fine linnen,
and great proportion of spices could have done. O, who can expresse
this inexpressible mystery? The soul of Christ Jesus, which took no
550 harm by him, contracted no Originall sin, in coming to him, was
guilty of no more sin, when it went out, then when it came from the
breath and bosome of God; yet this soul left this body in death. And
the Divinity, the Godhead, incomparably better then that soul, which
soul was incomparably better then all the Saints, and Angels in
heaven, that Divinity, that God-head did not forsake the body,
though it were dead. If we might compare things infinite in themselves, it was nothing so much, that God did assume mans nature,
as that God did still cleave to that man, then when he was no man,
in the separation of body and soul, in the grave. But fall we from
560 incomprehensible mysteries; for, there is mortification enough, (and
mortification is vivification, and ædification) in this obvious consideration; *skinne and body,* beauty and substance must be destroy'd;
And, *Destroyed by wormes,* which is another descent in this humiliation, and exinanition of man, in death; *After my skinne, wormes
shall destroy this body.*

Vermes

21.26

24.20

I will not insist long upon this, because it is not in the Originall;
In the Originall there is no mention of *wormes.* But because in other
places of *Iob* there is, (*They shal lye down alike in the dust, and the
worms shall cover them*) (*The womb shal forget them, and the*
570 *worm shal feed sweetly on them*) and because the word *Destroying*
is presented in that form and number, *Contriverint,* when *they* shall
destroy, *they* and no other persons, no other creatures named; both
our later translations, (for indeed, our first translation hath no mention of *wormes*) and so very many others, even *Tremellius* that ad-
heres most to the letter of the Hebrew, have filled up this place, with
that addition, *Destroyed by worms.* It makes the destruction the more
contemptible; Thou that wouldest not admit the beames of the Sunne
upon thy skinne, and yet hast admitted the pollutions of sinne; Thou
that wouldst not admit the breath of the ayre upon thy skinne, and
580 yet hast admitted the spirit of lust, and unchast solicitations to breath

upon thee, in execrable oathes, and blasphemies, to vicious purposes;
Thou, whose body hath (as farre as it can) putrefyed and corrupted
even the body of thy Saviour, in an unworthy receiving thereof, in
this *skinne,* in this *body,* must be the food of worms, the prey of
destroying worms. After a low birth thou mayst passe an honourable
life, after a sentence of an ignominious death, thou mayst have an
honourable end; But, in the grave canst thou make these worms silke
worms? They were bold and early worms that eat up *Herod* before
he dyed; They are bold and everlasting worms, which after thy
590 skinne and body is destroyed, shall remain as long as God remains,
in an eternall gnawing of thy conscience; long, long after the destroying of skinne and body, by bodily worms.

Thus farre then to the *destroying of skinne and body by worms,*
all men are equall; Thus farre all's *Common law,* and no *Prerogative,*
so is it also in the next step too; The Resurrection is common to all:
The Prerogative lies not in the Rising, but in the rising to the fruition
of the sight of God; in which consideration, the first beam of comfort is the *Postquam, After all this,* destruction before by worms;
ruinous misery before; but there is something else to be done upon
600 me after. God leaves no state without comfort. God leaves some inhabitants of the earth, under longer nights then others, but none
under an everlasting night; and, those, whom he leaves under those
long nights, he recompenses with as long days, after. I were miserable, if there were not an *Antequam* in my behalfe; if before I had
done well or ill actually in this world, God had not wrapped me up,
in his *good purpose* upon me. And I were miserable againe, if there
were not a *Postquam* in my behalfe; If, after my sinne had cast me
into the grave, there were not a lowd trumpet to call me up, and a
gracious countenance to looke upon me, when I were risen. Nay,
610 let my life have been as religious, as the infirmities of this life can
admit, yet, *If in this life onely we have hope in Christ, we are, of all*
men, most miserable. For, for the worldly things of this life, first, the
children of God have them in the least proportions of any; and, besides that, those children of God, which have them in larger proportion, do yet make the least use of them, of any others, because
the children of the world, are not so tender conscienced, nor so much
afraid, lest those worldly things should become snares, and occasions

Acts 12.23

Post

1 Cor. 15.19

of tentation to them, if they open themselves to a full enjoying
thereof, as the children of God are. And therefore, after my wanting
⁶²⁰ of many worldly things, (after a penurious life) and, after my not
daring to use those things that I have, so freely as others doe, after
that holy and conscientious forbearing of those things that other
men afford themselves, after my leaving all these absolutely behind
me here, and my skin and body in destruction in the grave, After
all, there remaines something else for me. *After;* but *how long
after?* That's next.

Quando?

Mar. 13.32

When Christ was in the body of that flesh, which we are in, now,
(sinne onely excepted) he said, in that state that he was in then, *Of
that day and houre, no man knoweth, not the Angels, not the Sonne.*
⁶³⁰ Then, in that state, he excludes himselfe. And when Christ was risen
againe, in an uncorruptible body, he said, even to his nearest followers, *Non est vestrum,* it is not for you, to know times, and seasons.
Before in his state of mortality, *seipsum annumeravit ignorantibus,*
he pretended to know no more of this, then they that knew nothing.
After, when he had invested immortality, *per sui exceptionem,* (says
that Father) he excepts none but himselfe; all the rest, even the
Apostles, were left ignorant thereof. For this *non est vestrum,* (it is
not for you) is part of the last sentence that ever Christ spake to them.
If it be a convenient answer to say, Christ knew it not, as man, how
⁶⁴⁰ bold is that man that will pretend to know it? And, if it be a convenient interpretation of Christs words, that he knew it not, that is,
knew it not so, as that he might tell it them, how indiscreet are they,
who, though they may seem to know it, will publish it? For, thereby
they fill other men with scruples, and vexations, and they open themselves to scorne and reproach, when their predictions prove false, as
Saint *Augustine* observed in his time, and every age hath given
examples since, of confident men that have failed in these conjec-
tures. It is a poore pretence to say, this intimation, this impression
of a certaine time, prepares men with better dispositions. For, they
⁶⁵⁰ have so often been found false, that it rather weakens the credit of
the thing it selfe. In the old world they knew exactly the time of the
destruction of the world; that there should be an hundred and twenty
years, before the flood came; And yet, upon how few, did that prediction, though from the mouth of God himselfe, work to repent-

Acts 1.7

Basil

Gen. 6.3

ance? *Noah* found grace in Gods eyes; but it was not because he mended his life upon that prediction, but he was gratious in Gods sight before. At the day of our death, we write *Pridie resurrectionis,* the day before the resurrection; It is *Vigilia resurrectionis;* Our Easter Eve. *Adveniat regnum tuum,* possesse my soule of thy kingdome
660 then: And, *Fiat voluntas tua,* my body shall arise after, but how soon after, or how late after, thy will bee done then, by thy selfe, and thy will bee knowne, till then, to thy selfe.

We passe on. As in *Massa damnata,* the whole lump of mankind is under the condemnation of *Adams* sinne, and yet the good purpose of God severs some men from that condemnation, so, at the resurrection, all shall rise; but not all to glory. But, amongst them, that doe, *Ego,* says *Iob,* I shall. I, as I am the same man, made up of the same body, and the same soule. Shall I imagine a difficulty in my body, because I have lost an Arme in the East, and a leg in the West?
670 because I have left some bloud in the North, and some bones in the South? Doe but remember, with what ease you have sate in the chaire, casting an account, and made a shilling on one hand, a pound on the other, or five shillings below, ten above, because all these lay easily within your reach. Consider how much lesse, all this earth is to him, that sits in heaven, and spans all this world, and reunites in an instant armes, and legs, bloud, and bones, in what corners so ever they be scattered. The greater work may seem to be in reducing the soul; That that soule which sped so ill in that body, last time it came to it, as that it contracted *Originall sinne* then, and was put to the
680 slavery to serve that body, and to serve it in the ways of sinne, not for an Apprentiship of seven, but seventy years after, that that soul after it hath once got loose by death, and liv'd God knows how many thousands of years, free from that body, that abus'd it so before, and in the sight and fruition of that God, where it was in no danger, should willingly, nay desirously, ambitiously seek this scattered body, this Eastern, and Western, and Northern, and Southern body, this is the most inconsiderable consideration; and yet, *Ego,* I, I the same body, and the same soul, shall be recompact again, and be identically, numerically, individually the same man. The same integrity of body,
690 and soul, and the same integrity in the Organs of my body, and in the faculties of my soul too; I shall be all there, my body, and my

Ego

soul, and all my body, and all my soul. I am not all here, I am here now preaching upon this text, and I am at home in my Library considering whether *S. Gregory,* or *S. Hierome,* have said best of this text, before. I am here speaking to you, and yet I consider by the way, in the same instant, what it is likely you will say to one another, when I have done. You are not all here neither; you are here now, hearing me, and yet you are thinking that you have heard a better Sermon somewhere else, of this text before; you are here, and ⁷⁰⁰ yet you think you could have heard some other doctrine of downright *Predestination,* and *Reprobation* roundly delivered somewhere else with more edification to you; you are here, and you remember your selves that now yee think of it, this had been the fittest time, now, when every body else is at Church, to have made such and such a private visit; and because you would bee there, you are there. I cannot say, you cannot say so perfectly, so entirely now, as at the Resurrection, *Ego,* I am here; I, body and soul; I, soul and faculties;

[Mat.
14.27]

as Christ sayd to *Peter, Noli timere, Ego sum, Fear nothing, it is I;* so I say to my selfe, *Noli timere;* My soul, why art thou so sad, my ⁷¹⁰ body, why dost thou languish? *Ego,* I, body and soul, soul and faculties, shall say to Christ Jesus, *Ego sum,* Lord, it is I, and hee shall not say, *Nescio te, I know thee not,* but avow me, and place me at his

Lam. 3.1
1 Pet. 5.4

right hand. *Ego sum, I am the man that hath seen affliction, by the rod of his wrath; Ego sum,* and I the same man, shall receive the crown of glory which shall not fade.

Videbo

Ego, I, the same person; *Ego videbo,* I shall see; I have had no looking-glasse in my grave, to see how my body looks in the dissolution; I know not how. I have had no houre-glasse in my grave to see how my time passes; I know not when: for, when my eylids are

Apoc. 10.6
Dan. 7.9

⁷²⁰ closed in my death-bed, *the Angel hath said to me, That time shall be no more;* Till I see eternity, the ancient of days, I shall see no more; but then I shall. Now, why is *Job* gladder of the use of this sense of seeing, then of any of the other? He is not; He is glad of seeing, but not of the sense, but of the Object. It is true that is said

Aquin. sup.
q. 82 ar. 4

in the School, *Vicinius se habent potentiæ sensitivæ ad animam quàm corpus;* Our sensitive faculties have more relation to the soul, then to the body; but yet to some purpose, and in some measure, *all* the senses shall be in our glorifyed bodies, *In actu,* or *in potentiâ,* say

they; so as that wee shall use them, or so as that we might. But this
730 sight that *Job* speaks of, is onely the fruition of the presence of God,
in which consists eternall blessednesse. Here, in this world, we see
God *per speculum,* says the Apostle, by reflection, upon a glasse; $\qquad$ 1 Cor. 13.12
we see a creature; and from that there arises an assurance that there
is a Creator; we see him *in ænigmate,* says he; which is not ill rendred
in the margin, in a *Riddle;* we see him in the Church, but men have
made it a riddle, which is the Church; we see him in the Sacrament,
but men have made it a riddle, by what light, and at what window:
Doe I see him at the window of bread and wine; Is he in that; or
doe I see him by the window of faith; and is he onely in that? still
740 it is in a riddle. Doe I see him *à Priore,* (I see that I am elected, and
therefore I cannot sinne to death?) Or doe I see him *à Posteriore,*
(because I see my selfe carefull not to sin to death, therefore I am
elected?) I shall see all problematicall things come to be dogmaticall,
I shall see all these rocks in Divinity, come to bee smooth alleys; I
shall see Prophesies untyed, Riddles dissolved, controversies reconciled; but I shall never see that, till I come to this sight which follows
in our text, *Videbo Deum, I shall see God.*

No man ever saw God and liv'd; and yet, I shall not live till I see $\qquad$ *Deum*
God; and when I have seen him I shall never dye. What have I ever
750 seen in this world, that hath been truly the same thing that it seemed
to me? I have seen marble buildings, and a chip, a crust, a plaster, a
face of marble hath pilld off, and I see brick-bowels within. I have
seen beauty, and a strong breath from another, tels me, that that
complexion is from without, not from a sound constitution within.
I have seen the state of Princes, and all that is but ceremony; and,
I would be loath to put a *Master of ceremonies* to define *ceremony,*
and tell me what it is, and to include so various a thing as ceremony,
in so constant a thing, as a Definition. I see a great Officer, and I see
a man of mine own profession, of great revenues, and I see not the
760 interest of the money, that was paid for it, I see not the pensions,
nor the Annuities, that are charged upon that Office, or that Church.
As he that fears God, fears nothing else, so, he that sees God, sees
every thing else: when we shall see God, *Sicuti est,* as he is, we shall
see all things *Sicuti sunt,* as they are; for that's their Essence, as they $\qquad$ 1 Iohn 3.2
conduce to his glory. We shall be no more deluded with outward

appearances: for, when this sight, which we intend here comes, there will be no delusory thing to be seen. All that we have made as though we saw, in this world, will be vanished, and I shall see nothing but God, and what is in him; and him I shall see *In carne, in* 770 *the flesh,* which is another degree of Exaltation in mine Exinanition.

In carne   I shall see him, *In carne suâ, in his flesh:* And this was one branch in *Saint Augustines* great wish, That he might have seen Rome in her state, That he might have heard S. *Paul* preach, That he might have seen Christ in the flesh: *Saint Augustine* hath seen Christ in the flesh one thousand two hundred yeares; in Christs glorifyed flesh; but, it is with the eyes of his understanding, and in his soul. Our flesh, even in the Resurrection, cannot be a spectacle, a perspective glasse to our soul. We shall see the Humanity of Christ with our bodily eyes, then glorifyed; but, that flesh, though glorifyed, 780 cannot make us see God better, nor clearer, then the soul alone hath done, all the time, from our death, to our resurrection. But as an indulgent Father, or as a tender mother, when they go to see the King in any Solemnity, or any other thing of observation, and curiosity, delights to carry their child, which is flesh of their flesh, and bone of their bone, with them, and though the child cannot comprehend it as well as they, they are as glad that the child sees it, as that they see it themselves; such a gladnesse shall my soul have, that this flesh, (which she will no longer call her prison, nor her tempter, but her friend, her companion, her wife) that this flesh, that is, I, in the 790 re-union, and redintegration of both parts, shall see God; for then, one principall clause in her rejoycing, and acclamation, shall be, that this flesh is her flesh; *In carne meâ, in my flesh I shall see God.*

Mea   It was the flesh of every wanton object here, that would allure it in the petulancy of mine eye. It was the flesh of every Satyricall Libeller, and defamer, and calumniator of other men, that would call upon it, and tickle mine ear with aspersions and slanders of persons in authority. And in the grave, it is the flesh of the worm; the possession is transfer'd to him. But, in heaven, it is *Caro mea, My flesh,* my souls flesh, my Saviours flesh. As my meat is assimilated to 800 my flesh, and made one flesh with it; as my soul is assimilated to my
2 Pet. 1.4   God, and *made partaker of the divine nature,* and *Idem Spiritus,*
1 Cor. 6.17   the same Spirit with it; so, there my flesh shall be assimilated to the

flesh of my Saviour, and made the same flesh with him too. *Verbum* Athanas.
caro factum, ut caro resurgeret; Therefore the Word was made flesh,
therefore God was made man, that that union might exalt the flesh
of man to the right hand of God. That's spoken of the flesh of Christ;
and then to facilitate the passage for us, *Reformat ad immortalitatem* Cyril
suam participes sui; those who are worthy receivers of his flesh here,
are the same flesh with him; And, *God shall quicken your mortall* Rom. 8.11
810 *bodies, by his Spirit that dwelleth in you.* But this is not in consummation, in full accomplishment, till this resurrection, when it shall
be *Caro mea,* my flesh, so, as that nothing can draw it from the allegiance of my God; and *Caro mea, My flesh,* so, as that nothing can
devest me of it. Here a bullet will aske a man, where's your arme;
and a Wolf wil ask a woman, where's your breast? A sentence in
the Star-chamber will aske him, where's your ear, and a months close
prison will aske him, where's your flesh? a fever will aske him,
where's your Red, and a morphew will aske him, where's your white?
But when after all this, when *after my skinne worms shall destroy*
820 *my body, I shall see God,* I shall see him in my flesh, which shall be
mine as inseparably, (in the *effect,* though not in the *manner*) as the
Hypostaticall union of God, and man, in Christ, makes our nature
and the Godhead one person in him. My flesh shall no more be none
of mine, then Christ shall not be man, as well as God.

Number 4.

Preached at Lincolns Inne.

I Cor. 15.50. *NOW THIS I SAY BRETHREN, THAT FLESH AND BLOOD CANNOT INHERIT THE KINGDOME OF GOD.*

Moral. 14.29

SAINT GREGORY hath delivered this story; That *Eutychius,* who was Bishop of Constantinople, having written a book of the Resurrection, and therein maintained that errour, That the body of Christ had not, that our bodies, in the Resurrection should not have any of the qualities of a *naturall body,* but that those bodies were, *in subtilitatem redacta,* so rarifyed, so refined, so attenuated, and reduced to a thinnesse, and subtlenesse, that they were *aery bodies,* and not bodies of flesh and blood; this error made a great noise, and raised a great dust, till the Emperour, to avoid scandall, (which for
¹⁰ the most part arises out of publick conferences) was pleased to hear *Eutychius,* and *Gregory* dispute this point privately before himself, and a small company; And, that upon conference, the Emperour was so well satisfyed, that hee commanded *Eutychius* his books to bee burnt. That after this, both *Gregory* and *Eutychius* fell sicke; but *Eutychius* dyed; and dyed with this protestation, *In hâc carne,* in this flesh, (taking up the flesh of his hand in the presence of them that were there) in this flesh, I acknowledge, that I, and all men shall arise at the day of Judgement. Now, the principall place of Scripture, which in his book, and in that conference *Eutychius* stood
²⁰ upon, was this Text, these words of *Saint Paul;* (*This I say brethren, that flesh and blood cannot inherit the Kingdome of God.*) And the directest answer that *Gregory* gave to it was, *Caro secundum culpam non regnabit, sed Caro secundum naturam;* sinfull flesh shall not, but naturall flesh; that is, flesh indued with all qualities of flesh, all such qualities as imply no defect, no corruption, (for there was *flesh* be-

fore there was *sin*) such flesh, and such blood shall inherit the Kingdome of God.

As there have been more Heresies about the *Humanity* of Christ, then about his *Divinity,* so there have been more heresies about the
30 Resurrection of his body, and consequently of ours, then about any other particular article, that concerns his Humiliation, or Exaltation. *Simon Magus* strook deepest at first, to the root; That there was no Resurrection at all; The Gnosticks, (who took their name from *knowledge,* as though they knew all, and no body else any thing, which is a pride transferr'd through all Heretickes: for, as that sect in the Roman Church, which call themselves *Ignorantes,* and seem to pretend to no knowledge, doe yet believe that they know a better way to heaven, then all other men doe, so that sect amongst them, which called themselves *Nullanos,* Nothings, thought themselves
40 greater in the Kingdome of God, then either of the other two sects of diminution, the *Minorits,* or the *Minims* did) These Gnosticks acknowledged a Resurrection, but they said it was of the *soul* onely, and not of the body, for they thought that the soul lay dead (at least, in a dead sleep) till the Resurrection. Those Heretickes that are called the *Arabians,* did (as the Gnosticks did) affirm a temporary death of the soul, as well as of the body, but then they allowed a Resurrection to both soul, and body, after that death, which the Gnostickes did not, but to the soul onely. *Hymeneus* and *Philetus,* (of whom *Saint Paul* speakes) they restrained the Resurrection to   2 Tim. 2.18
50 the soule, but then they restrained this Resurrection of the soule to this life, and that in those who were baptized, the Resurrection was accomplished already. *Eutychius,* (whom wee mentioned before) enlarged the Resurrection to the body, as well as to the soul, but enlarged the qualities of the body so far, as that it was scarce a body. The *Armenian* hereticks said, that it was not onely *Corpus humanum,* but *Corpus masculinum,* That all should rise in the perfecter sex, and none, as *women. Origen* allowed a Resurrection, and allowed the Body to be a naturall body; but he contracted the time; he said, that when we rose we should enjoy the benefits of the resur-
60 rection, even in *bodily pleasures,* for a *thousand years,* and then be annihilated, or absorpted and swallowed up into the nature, and essence of God himselfe; (for, it will be hard to state *Origens* opinion

in this point; *Origen* was not, herein, well understood in his owne
time; nor doe we understand him now, (for the most part) but by
his accusers, and those that have written against him.) Divers of
these Heretiques, for the maintenance of their severall heresies, perverted this Scripture, (*Flesh and bloud cannot inherit the kingdome of
God*) and that occasioned those *Fathers* who opposed those heresies, so
diverse from one another, to interpret these words diversly, according
⁷⁰ to the heresie they opposed. All agree, that they are an argument for the
resurrection, though they seem at first, to oppose it. For, this Chapter
hath three generall parts; first, *Resurrectionem esse,* that there shall be
a Resurrection, which the Apostle proves by many and various arguments to the *thirty fifth verse*. And then *Quali corpore,* the body shall
rise, but some will say, *How are the dead raised, and with what body,
doe they come?* in that *thirty fifth verse:* And lastly, *Quid de supersti-
tibus,* what whall become of them, who shall be found alive, at that
day? *We shall all be changed, verse fifty one.* Now, this text is the knot,
and corollary of all the second part, concerning the qualities of the
⁸⁰ bodies in the resurrection; *Now,* says the Apostle, now that I have said
enough to prove that a resurrection there is, now, now that I have said
enough what kind of bodies shall arise, now, I show you as much in
the Negative as I have done in the Affirmative, now I teach you what
to avoid, as well as I have done what to affect, *now this I say brethren,
that flesh and bloud cannot inherit the kingdome of God.*

Now, though those words be primarily, principally intended of
the *last* Resurrection, yet in a secondary respect, they are appliable
in themselves, and very often applied by the ancients, to the *first*
Resurrection, our resurrection in this life. *Tertullian* hath intimated,
⁹⁰ and presented both together, elegantly, when he says of God, *Nobis
arrhabonem spiritus reliquit & arrhabonem à nobis accepit,* God hath
given us his earnest, and a pawn from him upon earth, in giving us
the holy Ghost, and he hath received our earnest, and a pawn from
us into heaven, by receiving our nature, in the body of Christ Jesus
there. Flesh and bloud, when it is conformed to the flesh and bloud
of Christ now *glorified,* and made like his, by our *resurrection,* may
inherite the kingdome of God, in heaven. Yea flesh and bloud being
conformed to Christ by the *sanctification* of the *holy Ghost,* here, in
this world, may inherit the kingdome of God, here upon earth; for,

Tertull.

[100] God hath a kingdome here; and there is a Communion in *Armes,* as well as a communion in *Triumph.* Leaving then that acceptation of flesh and bloud, which many thinke to be intended in this text, that is, *Animalis caro,* flesh and bloud that must be maintained by eating, and drinking, and preserved by propagation and generation, that flesh, and that bloud cannot inherit heaven, where there is no marying, nor giving in mariage, but *Erimus sicut Angeli,* we shall be as the Angels, (though such a heaven, in part, *Mahomet* hath proposed to his followers, a heaven that should abound with worldly delights, and such a heaven the Disciples of *Origen,* and the *Mil-* [110] *lenarians,* that look for one thousand years of all temporall felicity, proposed to themselves; And, though amongst our latter men, *Cajetan* doe thinke, that the Apostle in this text, bent himselfe upon that doctrine, *non caro, non Animalis caro,* flesh and bloud, that is, no carnall, no worldly delights are to be looked for, in heaven,) leaving that sense, as too narrow, and too shallow for the holy Ghost, in this place, in which he hath a higher reach, we shall determine our selves at this time, in these two acceptations of this phrase of speech; first, *non caro,* that is, *non caro corrupta,* flesh and bloud cannot, sinfull flesh, corrupt flesh, flesh not discharged of sinfull corruption [120] here, by repentance, and Sanctification, and the operation of Gods spirit, such flesh cannot inherit the kingdome of God here. Secondly, *non caro,* is *non caro corruptibilis,* flesh and bloud cannot, that is, flesh that is yet subject to corruption, and dissolution, and naturall passions and impressions, tending to defectivenesse, flesh that is still subject to any punishment that God lays upon flesh, for sinne, such flesh cannot inherit the kingdome of God hereafter; for our present possession of the kingdome of God here, our *corrupt* flesh must be purged by *Sanctification* here, for the future kingdome, our naturall *Corruptiblenesse* must be purged by *glorification* there. We will make [130] the last part first, as this flesh, and this bloud, by devesting the corruptiblenesse it suffers here, by that glorification, shall inherit that kingdome; and, not stay long upon it neither. For, of that we have spoken conveniently before, of the resurrection it selfe. Now we shall looke a little into *the qualities* of *bodies* in *the resurrection;* and that, not in the intricacies, and subtilties of the Schoole, but onely in that one patterne, which hath been given us of that glory, upon earth,

Divisio

which is the *Transfiguration* of Christ; for, that Transfiguration of his, was a representation of a glorified body in a glorified state. And then in the second place, we shall come to our first part, what that
[140] flesh and bloud is that is denied to be capable of the inheritance of that kingdome here, that is, that earnest of heaven, and that inchoation of heaven which may be had in this world; and, in that part we shall see, what this inheritance, what this title to heaven here, and what this kingdome of God, that heaven which is proposed to us here, is.

1 Part
Melancthon

First then, for the first acceptation, (which is of the *later* resurrection) no man denies that which *Melancthon* hath collected and established to be the summe of this text, *Statuit resurrectionem in corpore, sed non quale jam corpus est;* The Apostle establishes a resurrection
[150] of the body, but yet not such a body as this is. It is the *same* body, and yet not *such* a body; which is a mysterious consideration, that it is the *same* body, and yet not *such* as it selfe, nor like any other body of the same substance. But, what kind of body then? We content

Musculus

ourselves with that, *Transfiguratio specimen appositissimum Resurrectionis,* the Transfiguration of Christ, is the best glasse to see this resurrection, and state of glory in. But how was that transfiguration

Hierom.

wrought? We content our selves with Saint *Hieromes* expressing of it, *non pristinam amisit veritatem, vel formam corporis;* Christ had still the same true, and reall body, and he had the same forme, and
[160] proportion, and lineaments, and dimensions of his body, in it selfe. *Transfiguratio non faciem subtraxit, sed splendorem addidit,* sayes he; It gave him not another face, but it super-immitted such a light, such an illustration upon him, as, by that irradiation, that coruscation, the beames of their eys were scattered, and disgregated, dissipated so, as that they could not collect them, as at other times, nor constantly, and confidently discerne him. *Moses* had a measure, a

Exod. 34.29

proportion of this; but yet when *Moses* came down with his shining face, though they were not able to looke long upon him, they knew him to be *Moses.* When Christ was transfigured in the presence of

Mat.
17.[1, 2]

[170] *Peter, James* and *John,* yet they knew him to be Christ. Transfiguration did not so change him, nor shall glorification so change us, as that we shall not be *known.* There is nothing to convince a man of error, nothing in nature, nothing in Scriptures, if he beleeve that he shall

know those persons in heaven, whom he knew upon earth; and, if
he conceive soberly, that it were a lesse degree of blessednesse, *not*
to know them, then to know them, he is bound to beleeve that he
shall know them, for he is bound to beleeve, that all that conduces
to blessednes shall be given him. The School resolves, that at the
Judgement, all the *sins* of all, shall be manifested to all; even those
¹⁸⁰ secret sinfull *thoughts* that never came out of the heart. And, when
any in the School differs or departs from this common opinion, they
say onely, that those sins which have been, *in particular, repented,*
shall not be manifested: all others shall. And therefore it is a deep
uncharitablenes, to reproach any man, of sins formerly repented; and
a deep uncharitablenesse, not to beleeve, that he whom thou seest at
the *Communion,* hath repented his former sins; Reproach no man,
after thou hast seen him *receive,* with last years sins; except thou have
good evidence of his *Hypocrisie* then, or of his *Relapsing* after; For,
in those two cases, a man remaines, or becomes againe guilty of his
¹⁹⁰ former sinnes. Now, if in heaven they shall know the hearts of one
another, whose faces they never knew before, there is lesse difficulty
in knowing them, whom we did know before. From this transfiguration of Christ, in which, the mortall eye of the Apostles, did see that
representation of the glory of Christ, the Schooles make a good argument, that in heaven we shall doe it much more. And though in this
case of the Transfiguration, in which the eyes of mortall men could
have no proportion with that glory of heaven, this may bee well said
to have been done, either *Moderando lumen,* (that God abated that
light of glory) or *Confortando visum,* (that God exalted their sense
²⁰⁰ of seeing supernaturally) no such distinctions, or modifications will
bee needfull in heaven, because how highly soever the body of my
Father, or of my friend shall bee glorifyed there, mine eyes shall be
glorifyed as much, and we are both kept in the same proportion there,
as wee had towards one another here; here my naturall eye could see
his naturall face, and there mine eye is as much mended, as his body
is, and my sense as much exalted as mine object; And as well, as I
may know, that I am I; I may know, that He is He; for, I shall not
know my selfe, nor that state of glory which I am then in, by any
light of Nature which I brought thither, but by that light of Glory
²¹⁰ which I shall receive there. When therefore a man finds, that this

Aquin.

Lombar.

consideration does him good in his conversation, and retards him towards some sinnes; how shall I stand then, when all the world shall see, that my solicitation hath brought such a woman to the stews, to the Hospitall, to hell, who had scap'd all this, if I had not corrupted her at first, (which no man in the world knew before, and all shall know then)? Or that my whispering, and my calumny hath overthrown such a man in his place, in his reputation, in his fortune, ·(which he himself knew not before, and all shall know then)? Or, that my counsell, or my example hath been a furtherance to any
220 mans spirituall edification here? He that in rectified reason, and a rectified conscience finds this, in Gods name let him beleeve; yea, for Gods sake let him take heed of not beleeving that we shall know one another, *Actions* and *Persons,* in the Resurrection, as the Apostles did know Christ at the Transfiguration, which was a Type of it.

*Trans-
figuratio*
Hierom.

This Transfiguration then upon earth, was the same glory, which Christ had after, in heaven. *Qualis venturus, talis apparuit;* such as all eyes shall see him to be, when he comes in glory at last, those Apostles saw him then, but of the particular circumstances, even of this transfiguration upon earth, there is but little said to us. Let us
230 modestly take that which is expressed in it, and not search over-curiously farther into that which is signifyed, and represented by it; which is, the state of glory in the Resurrection. First, his face

Sol
Mat. 17.2

shin'd as the *Sunne,* says that Gospell, he could not take a higher comparison, for our Information, and for our admiration in this world, then the Sunne. And then, the Saints of God in their glorifyed

13.43

state are admitted to the same comparison. *The righteous shall shine out as the Sunne in the Kingdome of the Father;* the Sunne of the firmament which should be their comparison, will be gone; But the Sun of grace and of glory, the Son of God shall remain; and they
240 shall shine as he; that is, in his righteousnesse.

Nix
[Mark] 9.3
[Mat. 17.2]

In this transfiguration, *his clothes were white,* says the text; but how white, the holy Ghost does not tell us at once, *as white as snow,* says Saint *Mark, as white as light,* says Saint *Matthew.* Let the garments of the glorifyed Saints of God be their bodies, and then, their bodies are as white as snow, as snow that fall's from heaven, and hath toucht no pollution of the earth. For, though our bodies have been upon earth, and have touched pitch, and have been defiled, yet

that will not lye in proof, nor be given in evidence; Though he that
drew me, and I that was drawn too, know, in what unclean places,
²⁵⁰ and what unclean actions, this body of mine hath been, yet it lyes
not in proof, it shall not be given in evidence, for, *Accusator fratrum,*   Apoc. 12.10
The accuser of the brethren is cast down, the Devill shall find nothing
against me; And if I had *spontaneum Dæmonem,* as Saint *Chrys-*
ostome speaks, a bosome Devill, and could *tempt* my self, though
there had been no other tempter in this world, so I have *spontaneum*
Dæmonem, a bosome accuser, a conscience that would accuse me
there, if I accuse my self there, I reproach the mercy of God, who
hath seal'd my pardon, and made even my body, what sins soever had
discoloured it, *as white as snow.*

²⁶⁰ *As white as snow,* and *as white as light,* says that Gospel. Light   *Lux*
implies an active power, Light is operative, and works upon others.
The bodies of the Saints of God, shall receive all impressions of glory
in themselves, and they shall doe all that is to bee done, for the glory
of God there. There, they shall stand in his service, and they shall
kneel in his worship, and they shall fall in his reverence, and they
shall sing in his glory, they shall glorifie him in all positions of the
body; They shall be glorified in themselves passively, and they shall
glorifie God actively, *sicut Nix, sicut Lux,* their *beeing,* their *doing*
shall be all for him; Thus they shall shine as the Sun; Thus their
²⁷⁰ garments shall be *white,* white as *snow,* in being glorified in their
own bodies, white as *light,* in glorifying God in all the actions of
those bodies.

Now, there is thus much more considerable, and applyable to our   *Societas*
present purpose, in this transfiguration of Christ, that there was *com-*
pany with them. Be not apt to think heaven is an *Ermitage,* or a
Monastery, or the way to heaven a sullen *melancholy;* Heaven, and
the way to it, is a *Communion of Saints,* in a holy cheerfulnesse. Get
thou thither; make sure thine *own salvation;* but be not too hasty to
think, *that no body* gets thither, except he go thy way in all opinions,
²⁸⁰ and all actions.

There was company in the transfiguration; but no other company   *Quæ*
then *Moses,* and *Elias,* and Christ, and the Apostles; none but they,   *societas*
to whom God had manifested himself otherwise then to a meer
naturall man, otherwise then as a generall God. For, in the *Law,*

and in the *Pædagogie,* and Schoolmastership, and instruction thereof, God had manifested himself particularly by *Moses.* In *Elias* and the Prophets, whom God sent in a continuall succession, to refresh that manifestation which he had given of himself in the *Law,* before, in the example of these rules, in *him,* who was the consummation of the
²⁹⁰ Law, and the Prophets, *Christ Jesus;* And then, in the *Application* of all this, by the Apostles, and by the Church established by them, God had more particularly manifested himself, then to *naturall* men. *Moses, Elias,* Christ, and the Apostles, make up the houshold of the faithfull; and none have interest in the Resurrection, but in, and by these; These, to whom, and by whom, God hath exhibited himself, to his Church, by other notions, then as one universall God; For, nothing will save a man, but to believe in God; so as God hath proposed himself, in *his Son,* in his Scriptures, in his Christ.

*Communi-
catio*
          These were with him in the transfiguration, and they *talked with*
³⁰⁰ *him,* says that text. As there is a *Communion* of Saints, so there is a *Communication* of Saints. Think not heaven a Charter-house, where men, who onely of all creatures, are enabled by God to *speak,* must not speak to one another. The Lord of heaven is *Verbum,* The word, and his servants there talk of us here, and pray to him for us.

*Quæ com-
municatio*
Luke 9.31
          They *talked* with him; but of what? *They talked of his Decease,* (says the text there) which he should accomplish at Jerusalem, all that they talked of, was of his Passion. All that we shall say, and sing in heaven, will be of his Passion, accomplished at Jerusalem, in that
Apoc.
5.9, 12 Hymn, *This Lamb hath redeemed us to God, by his blood; Worthy*
³¹⁰ *is the Lamb that was slaine, to receive power, and riches, and wisdome, and strength, and honour and glory, and blessing, Amen.* Even our glory in heaven, at last, is not principally for our selves, but to contribute to the glory of Christ Jesus. If we inquire further then this, into the state of our glorifyed bodies, remember that in this *reall Parable,* in this Type of the Resurrection, the transfiguration of
Mar. 9.6
Mat. 17.9 Christ, it is said, that *even Peter himself wist not what to say;* and remember too, That even Christ himself forbad them to say any thing at all of it, till his Resurrection. Till our Resurrection, we cannot know clearly, we should not speak *boldly,* of the glory of the Saints of
³²⁰ God, nor of our blessed endowments in that state.

Tertull.
          The summe of all is, *Fiducia Christianorum est resurrectio mor-*

tuorum; My faith directs it self first upon that which Christ hath done, he is dead, he is risen; and my *hope* directs it selfe upon that which *shall bee done,* I shall rise again. And yet says *Luther, Papa, Cardinales & primarii viri,* I know the Pope, the Cardinals, the Bishops are *Ingenio, doctrinâ, ratione, prudentiâ excellentes,* they abound in naturall parts, in reading, in experience, in civill wisdome: yet says he, *si tres sunt, qui hunc articulum indubitanter credunt,* If there be three amongst them, that do faithfully and undoubtedly be-
330 lieve this article of the Resurrection of the body, three are more then I look for amongst them. Beloved, as no things are liker one another, then *Court* and *Court,* the same ambitions, the same underminings in one Court as in another, so *Church* and *Church* is alike too; All persecuted Churches are religious, all peaceable Churches are dis-solute; when *Luther* said that of the Church of Rome, (That few of them believed the Resurrection) the Roman Church wallowed in all abundances, and dissolutenesse, and scarce a man, (in respect) opened his mouth against her, otherwise then that the holy Ghost, to make his *continuall claime,* and to interrupt their prescription, in every age
340 raised up some to declare their impieties and usurpations. But then, when they bent all their thoughts entirely, and prosperously upon possessing this *world,* they thought they might spare the Resurrection well enough; As hee that hath a plentifull fortune in Europe, cares not much though there be no land of perfumes in the East, nor of gold, in the West-Indies; God in our days, hath given us, and our Church, the fat of the glory of this world too, and we also neglect the other: But when men of a different religion from them, (for they will needs call a differing from their errours, a different Religion, as though all their religion were errours, for (excepting errours) we
350 differ in no point) when, I say, such men came to enquire into them, to discover them, and to induce or to attempt in divers parts of their government a reformation, then they shut themselves up closer, then they grew more carefull of their manners, and did reform themselves somewhat, though not thoroughly, and are the better for that ref-ormation which was offered to them, and wrought more effectually upon others. As we say in the School, that even the Devill is some-what the better for the death of Christ, so the Roman Church is somewhat the better for the Reformation. Our assiduity of *preaching*

Luther

hath brought them to another manner of frequency in preaching,
360 then before the Reformation they were accustomed to, and our answers
to their books have brought them to a more reserved manner of
writing, then they used before. Let us therefore by their example,
make as good use of our enemies, as our enemies have done of us.
For, though we have no military enmity, no hostility with any nation,
though we must all, and doe, out of a true sense of our duty to God,
pray ever for the continuance of peace amongst Christian Princes, and
to withhold the effusion of Christian blood, yet to that intendment,
and in that capacity as they were our enemies in 88. when they
provoked by their *Excommunications,* dangerous invasions, and in
370 that capacity as they were our enemies in 1605. when they bent their
malice even against that place, where the Laws for the maintenance
of our religion were enacted, so they are our enemies still, if we be
still of the same religion. He that by Gods mercy to us, leads us, is
as sure that the *Pope* is *Antichrist,* now, as he was *then;* and we that
are blessedly led by him, are as sure, that their doctrine is the doctrine
of *Devils,* now, as we were then. Let us therefore make use of those
enemies, and of their aery insolences, and their frothy confidences,
as thereby to be the firmer in our selves, and the carefuller of our
children, and servants, that we send not for such a Physitian as brings
380 a *Roman Priest* for his *Apothecary,* nor entertain such a School-
master, as brings a *Roman Priest* for his *Usher,* nor such a *Mercer,*
as brings a Priest for his *Tayler;* (for, in these shapes they have, and
will appear.) But in true *faith* to God, true *Allegiance* to our Prince,
true obedience to the Church, *true dealing* with all men, make our
selves sure of the Resurrection in the next life; *In carne incorruptibili,*
in flesh that shall bee capable of no corruption, by having that resurrection in this life, *in carne incorruptâ,* in devesting or correcting the
corruptions which cleave to our flesh here, that we bee not corrupted
spiritually, (not disputed out of our Religion, nor jeasted out, nor
390 threatened out, nor bought out, nor beat out of the truth of God) nor
corrupted *carnally* by the *pleasures* or *profits* of this world, but that
wee may conforme our selves to the purity of Christ Jesus, in that
measure, which wee are able to attain to, which is our spirituall Resurrection, and constitutes our second part, That Kingdome of God,
which flesh and blood may inherit in this life.

From the beginning we setled that, That the primary purpose of
the Apostle in these words, was to establish the doctrine of the last
Resurrection. But in *Tertullians* exposition, *Arrabonem dedit, & arrabonem accepit;* That God hath left us the earnest of his Spirit upon
400 earth, and hath taken the earnest of our flesh into heaven, it grew
indifferent, of which Resurrection, spirituall, or bodily, first, or last,
it be accepted. But take *Tertullian* in another place, upon the verse
immediately preceding our Text (*Sicut portavimus, portemus,* (for
so *Tertullian* reads that place, and so does the Vulgate) *As we have*
born the image of the earthly, so let us beare the Image of the
heavenly) there from *Tertullian* it must necessarily be referred to the
first Resurrection, the Resurrection by grace in this life; for, says he
there, *Non refertur ad substantiam resurrectionis, sed ad præsentis
temporis disciplinam;* the Apostle does not speak of our glorious
410 resurrection at last, but of our religious resurrection now. *Portemus,
non portabimus, Let us bear his image,* says the Apostle; Let us *now,*
not that we shall bear it at the last day. *Præceptivè dictum, non
promissivè;* The Apostle delivers it as a duty, that we must, not as a
reward, that wee shall bear that image. And therefore in *Tertullians*
construction, it is not onely indifferent, and probable, but necessary
to refer this Text to the first Resurrection in this life; where it will
be fittest, to pursue that order, which we proposed at first, first to
consider *Quid regnum,* what Kingdome it is, that is pretended to;
And then, *Quid hæreditas,* what estate and term is to be had in it:
420 It is an *Inheritance.* And lastly, *Quid caro, & sanguis,* what flesh and
blood it is, that is excluded out of this Kingdome. *Flesh and blood
cannot inherit the Kingdome of* God.

First, for this kingdome of God in this world, let us be glad that
is is a *kingdome,* that it is so *much,* that the government is taken out
of the hands of *Saints,* and *Angels* and re-united, re-annexed to the
Crown, restored to *God,* to whom we may come immediately, and be
accepted. Let us be glad that it is a kingdome, so much, and let us
be glad that it is *but* a kingdome, and *no more,* not a *Tyranny;* That
we come not to a *God* that *will damne* us, because he *will* damne us,
430 but a God that proposes *Conditions,* and enables us to performe those
conditions, in such a measure as he will vouchsafe to accept from us;
A *God* that governs us by his *word,* for in his word is truth, and by

his *law,* for in his law is clearnesse. Will you aske what this kingdome of God is? What did you take it to be, or what did you mean
by it, when, even now, you said with me, in the *Lords prayer, Thy
kingdome come?* Did you deliberately, and determinately pray for
the day of Judgment, and for his comming in the kingdome of *glory,*
then? Were you all ready for that, when you said so? *Puræ con-*

Hierom.

scientiæ, & grandis audaciæ est, It is a very great confidence, and (if
440 it be not grounded upon a very pure conscience) it must have a
worse name, *Regnum Dei postulare, & judicium non timere;* To call
upon God for the day of Judgment, upon confidence of our own
righteousnesse, is a shrewd distemper; To say, *Veni Domine Jesu,*
come Lord Jesu, come and take us, as thou findst us, is a dangerous
issue. But *Adveniat regnum,* and then *veniat Rex,* let his kingdome
of *grace* come upon us, in this life, and then let himselfe come too, in
his good time, and when his good pleasure shall be, in the kingdome

Augustin.

of *Glory: Sive velimus sive nolimus, regnum Dei utique veniet;* what
need we hasten him, provoke him? says Saint *Augustine;* whether
450 we will or no, his kingdome, his Judgment will come. Nay, before
we called for it, even his kingdome of *grace* was come. Christ said to

Mar. 12.34
Luke 17.21

the *Scribe, Non longè, Thou art not far from the kingdome of God;*
And to the *Pharisees* themselves he said, *Intra vos, the kingdome of
God is among you, within you.* But, where there is a whole *Hospitall*
of *three hundred* blinde men together, (as there is at *Paris*) there is
as much *light,* amongst *them* there, as amongst us here, and yet *all
they have no light,* so this kingdome of *God* is amongst us all, and
yet God knows whether we see it, or no. And therefore *Adveniat ut*

Augustin.

manifestetur Deus, says S. *Augustine,* his kingdom come, that we
460 may *discerne* it is come, that we may see that God offers it to us; and,
Adveniat regnum, ut manefestemur Deo, his kingdome come so, that
he may *discern us* in our reception of that Kingdom, and our obedience to it. He comes when we see him, and he comes again, when we

Idem

receive him; *Quid est, Regnum ejus veniat, quàm ut nos bonos
inveniat?* Then his Kingdome comes, when he finds us willing to be
Subjects to that Kingdome. God is a King in his own right. By
Creation, by Redemption, by many titles, and many undoubted

Chrys.

claimes. But, *Aliud est Regem esse, aliud regnare,* It is one thing to
be a King, another to have Subjects in obedience; A King is not the

⁴⁷⁰ lesse a King, for a Rebellion; But, *Verè justum regnum est,* (says that Father) *quando & Rex vult homines habere sub se, & cupiunt homines esse sub eo,* when the King would wish no other Subjects, nor the Subjects other King, then is that Kingdom come, come to a durable, and happy state. When God hath shewed himself in calling us, and wee have shewed our willingnesse to come, when God shewes his desire to preserve us, and we adhere onely to him, when there is a *Dominus regnat, Lætetur terra,* When our whole Land is in posses-   Psal. 97.1
sion of peace, and plenty, and the whole Church in possession of the Word and Sacraments, when the Land rejoyces because the Lord
⁴⁸⁰ reigns; and when there is a *Dominus regnat, Lætentur Insulæ,* Be-cause the Lord reigneth, every Island doth rejoice; that is, every man; that every man that is encompassed within a Sea of calamities in his estate, with a Sea of diseases in his body, with a Sea of scruples in his understanding, with a Sea of transgressions in his conscience, with a Sea of sinking and swallowing in the sadnesse of spirit, may yet open his eyes above water, and find a place in the Arke above all these, a recourse to God, and joy in him, in the Ordinances of a well estab-lished, and well governed Church, this is truly *Regnum Dei,* the Kingdome of God here; God is willing to be present with us, (that
⁴⁹⁰ he declares in the preservation of his Church) And we are sensible of his presence, and residence with us, and that wee declare in our frequent recourses to him hither, and in our practise of those things which we have learnt here, when we are gone hence.

This then is the blessed state that wee pretend to, in the Kingdome   *Hæreditas*
of God in this life; Peace in the State, peace in the Church, peace in our Conscience: In this, that wee answer the motions of his blessed Spirit here in his Ordinance, and endevour a conformity to him, in our life, and conversation; In this, hee is our King, and wee are his Subjects, and this is this Kingdome of God, the Kingdome of Grace.
⁵⁰⁰ Now the title, by which we make claim to this Kingdome, is in our text *Inheritance:* Who can, and who cannot inherit this Kingdome of God. I cannot have it by purchase, by mine own merits and good works; It is neither my former good disposition, nor Gods fore-sight of my future cooperation with him, that is the cause of his giving mee his grace. I cannot have this by Covenant, or by the gift, or by bequeath-ing of another, by works of *Supererogation,* (that a Martyr of the

primitive Church should send mee a violl of his blood, a splinter of his bone, a Collop of his flesh, wrapped up in a halfe sheet of paper, in an imaginary six-penny Indulgence from Rome, and bid mee re-
510 ceive grace, and peace of Conscience in that.) I cannot have it by purchase, I cannot have it by gift, I cannot have it by Curtesie, in the right of my wife, That if I will let her live in the obedience of the Roman Church, and let her bring up my children so, for my selfe, I may have leave to try a Court, or a worldly fortune, and bee secure in that, that I have a Catholique wife, or a Catholique child to pray, and merit for mee; I have no title to this Kingdome of God, but *Inheritance,* whence growes mine Inheritance? *Ex semine Dei;* be-cause I am propagated of the *seed of God,* I inherit this peace. *Who-*
1 Ioh. 3.9 *soever is born of God doth not commit sinne; for, his seed remaineth*
520 *in him, and hee cannot sinne, because hee is born of God:* That is, hee cannot desire to sinne; Hee cannot *antidate* a sinne, by delighting in the hope of a future sin, and sin in a præfruition of his sinne, before the act; Hee cannot post-date a sinne, delight in the memory of a past-sinne, and sin it over againe, in a post-fruition of that sinne; Hee cannot boast himself of sinne, much lesse bely himself in glorying in sinnes, never done; Hee cannot take sinnes dyet, therefore, that hee may bee able to sinne againe next Spring; Hee cannot hunger and thirst, and then digest and sleepe quietly after a sinne; and to this purpose, and in this sense Saint *Bernard* says, *Prædestinati non pos-*
530 *sunt peccare,* That the Elect cannot sinne; And in this also, That when the sinnes of the Elect, are brought to tryall, and to judgement, there their sinnes are no sinnes; not because they are none in them-selves; but because the blood of Jesus covering them, they are *none in the eyes of God.* I am Heir then as I am the Son of God, born of the seed of God. But, what is that seed? *Verbum Dei,* the seed is the
Iames 1.18 word of God, *Of his own will begat he us,* (says that Apostle) with the *word of truth;* And our Saviour himselfe speaks very clearly in
Luke 8.11 expounding the Parable; *The seed is the word of God.* We have this Kingdome of God; as we have an inheritance, as we are Heirs; we
540 are Heirs as we are Sons; we are Sons as we have the seed, and *the seed is the Word.* So that all ends in this; We inherit not this King-dome if we possesse not the *preaching* of the Word; if we professe not the true *religion* still: for, the word of this text which we translate

to *inherit,* for the most part, in the translation of the *Septuagint,* answers the *Hebrew* word, *Nachal;* and *Nachal* is *Hæreditas cum possessione;* not an inheritance in reversion, but in possession. *Take us O Lord for thine inheritance,* says *Moses; Et possideas nos,* as Saint *Hierome* translates that very place; *Inherit us,* and *Possesse us; Et erimus tibi,* whatsoever we are, we will bee thine, says the *Septuagint.*

Exod. 34.9
Hier.

550 You see then how much goes to the making up of this *Inheritance* of the Kingdome of God in this world, First, *Vt habeamus verbum,* That we have this *seed* of God, his *word;* (In the Roman Church they have it not; not that that Church hath it not, not that it is not there; but they, the people have it not) and then, *Vt possideamus,* That we possesse it, or rather that it possesse us; that we make the Word the *onely rule* of our faith, and of our actions; (In the *Roman Church* they do not so, they have not pure wheat, but *mestlin,* other things joyned with this good seed, the word of God) and lastly, *Vt simus Deo,* that we be his, that we be so *still,* that we doe not begin with God, and 560 give over, but that this seed of God, of which we are born, may (as Saint *Peter* says) *be incorruptible,* and abide for ever; that wee may be his so entirely, and so constantly, as that we had rather have no *beeing,* then for any time of suspension, or for any part of his fundamentall truth, be without it, and this the *Roman* Church cannot be said to do, that expunges and interlines articles of faith, upon *Reason of State,* and emergent occasions. *God hath made you one,* says the Prophet, who bee the parties whom God hath maryed together, and made *One,* in that place? you and your religion; (as our expositors interpret that place.) And why *One,* says the Prophet there; *That God might have a godly seed,* 570 says he, that is, a continuation, a propagation, a race, a posterity of the same religion; Therefore says he, *Let none deal treacherously against the wife of his youth.* Let none divorce himself from that religion, and that worship of God, which God put into his armes, and which he embraced in his Baptism. Except there be errour in *fundamentall* points, such as make that Church no Church, let no man depart from that Church, and that religion, in which he delivered himself to the service of God at first. Wo be unto us, if we deliver not over our religion to our posterity, in the same sincerity, and the same totality in which our Fathers have delivered it us; for that, that continuation, is that, that makes 580 it an inheritance: for, (to conclude this) every man hath an inheritance

1 [Pet.] 1.23

Mal. 2.15
Ribera

in the *Law,* and yet if he be hanged, he is hanged *by the Law,* in which hee had his inheritance: so wee have our inheritance in the Word of God, and yet, if wee bee damned, we are damned by that Word; *If thy heart turn away, so as that thou worship other Gods, I denounce unto you this day, that you shall surely perish.* So then, wee have an inheritance in this Kingdome, if we preserve it, and we incurre a forfeiture of it, if wee have not *this seed,* (The Word, the truth of Religion) so as that we *possesse* it; that is, conform our selves to him, whose Word it is, by it, and possesse it so, as that we persevere in the ⁵⁹⁰ true profession of it, to our end; for, *Perseverance,* as well as *Possession,* enters into our title, and inheritance to this Kingdome.

You see then, what this Kingdome of God is; It is, when he comes, and is welcome, when he comes in his *Sacraments,* and speaks in his *Word;* when he speaks and is answered; knocks and is received, (he knocks in his *Ordinances,* and is received in our *Obedience* to them, he knocks in his *example,* and most holy conversation, and is received in our *conformity,* and imitation.) So have you seen what the *Inheritance* of this Kingdome is, it is a Having, and Holding of the Gospel, a present, and a permanent possession, a holding fast, lest ⁶⁰⁰ another (another Nation, another Church) take our Crown. There remains onely that you see, upon whom the exclusion fals; and for the clearing of that, *This I say brethren, that flesh and blood cannot inherit the Kingdome of God.*

It is fully express'd by Saint *Paul, The carnall mind is enmity against God.* It is not a coldnesse, a slacknesse, an omission, a preterition of some duties towards God, but it is *Enmity,* and that's an exclusion out of the Kingdome; for, (says the Apostle there) it is not *subject to the Law of God;* and no subjection, no Kingdome; it is not, says hee, neither can it be; *It is not,* that excludes the *present; It* ⁶¹⁰ *cannot be,* that excludes the *future;* so that it is onely this incorrigible, this desperate state that constitutes this flesh, and blood, that cannot inherit the Kingdome of God; for this implies *impenitiblenesse,* which is the sin against the holy Ghost. Take the word *flesh,* so literally, as that it be either the *adorning* of my flesh in pride, or the *polluting* of my flesh in *wantonnes,* whether it be a *pampering* of my flesh with voluptuous provocations, or a withering, a shriveling of my flesh with *superstitious* and *meritorious* fastings, or other macerations, and lacera-

Deut. 30.
[17,] 18

Caro &
sanguis

Apoc. 3.11

Rom. 8.7

tions by inhumane violence upon my body; Take the word *Bloud*
so literally, as that it be either an admiring and adoring of honourable
620 blood, in a servile flattering of great persons, or an insinuating of
false and *adulterous* blood, in a *bastardizing* a race, by supposititious
children, whether it bee the inflaming the blood of young persons by
lascivious discourse, or *shedding* the blood of another in a murderous
quarrell, whether it be in *blaspheming* the blood of my Saviour, in
execrable oathes, or the prophaning of his blood in an *unworthy*
receiving thereof, all these ways, and all such, doth this flesh and
blood exclude from the Kingdome of God; It is summarily, all those
works which proceed meerly out of the nature of man, without the
regeneration of the Spirit of God; all that is *flesh and blood,* and
630 *enmity* against God, says the Apostle in that place.

But in another place, that Apostle leads us into other considerations; to the *Galatians* he says, *The works of the flesh are manifest:*   Gal. 5.19
And amongst those manifest works of the flesh, he reckons not onely
sins of wantonnesse, and sins of anger, not onely sins *in concupiscibili,*
and *in irascibili,* but *in intelligibili,* sins and errours in the understanding, particularly *Heresie,* and *Idolatry* are *works of the flesh,* in Saint
Pauls inventory, in that place, *Heresie* and *Idolatry,* are *that flesh and*
blood which shall not inherit the Kingdome of God. Bring wee this
consideration home to our selves. The Church of Rome does not
640 charge us with affirming any *Heresie,* nor does she charge us with any
Idolatry in our practise. So far we are discharged from the works of
the flesh. If they charge us with Doctrine of *flesh and blood* because
we prefer Mariage before Chastity, it is a charge ill laid, for Mariage
and Chastity consist well together; *The bed undefiled is chastity.* If
they charge us that wee prefer Mariage before Continency, they
charge us unjustly, for we do not so: Let them contain that can, and
blesse God for that heavenly gift of Continency, and let them that
cannot, mary, and serve God, and blesse him for affording them that
Physick for that infirmity. As Mariage was ordained at first, for those
650 two uses, *Procreation of children,* and *mutuall assistance of man, and*
wife, so Continency was not preferr'd before Mariage. As there was a
third use of Mariage added after the fall, by way of *Remedy,* so
Mariage may well be said to be inferiour to continency, as physick
is in respect of health. If they charge us with it, because our Priests

mary, they doe it frivolously, and impertinently, because they deny
that wee are Priests. We charge them with *Heresie* in the whole *new
Creed* of the *Councell of Trent*, (for, if all the particular doctrines be
not *Hereticall*, yet, the doctrine of inducing new Articles of faith is
Hereticall, and that doctrine runs through all the Articles, for else
⁶⁶⁰ they could not be Articles.) And we charge them with *Idolatry*, in
the *peoples practise*, (and that practise is never controld by them)
in the greatest mystery of all their Religion, in the *Adoration* of the
Sacrament; And *Heresie* and *Idolatry* are manifest works of the
flesh. Our kingdome is the Gospel; our Inheritance is our holding
that; our exclusion is *flesh and blood, Heresie* and *Idolatry*. And

Gal. 1.16   therefore let us be able to say with the Apostle, *when God had called
us, and separated us, immediately we conferred not with flesh and
blood.* Since God hath brought us into a fair prospect, let us have no
retrospect back; In Canaan, let us not look towards Ægypt, nor
⁶⁷⁰ towards *Sodom* being got to the Mountain; since God hath setled us
in a true Church, let us have no kind of byas, and declination towards
a false; for that is one of Saint *Pauls* manifest works of the flesh, and
I shall lose all the benefit of the flesh and bloud of Christ Jesus, if I
doe so, for *flesh and bloud cannot inherite the kingdome of God.*

    We have done; Adde we but this, by way of recollecting this which
hath been said now, upon these words, and that which hath been
formerly said upon those words of *Job,* which may seem to differ

19.26   from these, (*In my flesh I shall see God*) *Omne verum omni vero
consentiens,* whatsoever is true in it selfe agrees with every other
⁶⁸⁰ truth. Because that which *Iob* says, and that which *Saint Paul* says,
agree with the truth, they agree with one another. For, as *Saint Paul*

1 Cor. 15.39   says, *Non omnis caro eadem caro, there is one flesh of man, another
of beasts,* so there is one flesh of *Job,* another of *Saint Paul;* And *Jobs*
flesh can see God, and *Pauls* cannot; because the flesh that *Job*
speaks of hath overcome the destruction of skin and body by wormes
in the grave, and so is mellowed and prepared for the sight of God in
heaven; And *Pauls* flesh is overcome by the world. *Jobs* flesh triumphes over *Satan,* and hath made a victorious use of Gods corrections, *Pauls* flesh is still subject to tentations, and *carnalities. Jobs*
⁶⁹⁰ argument is but this, *some* flesh shall see God, (*Mortified* men here,
Glorified men there shall) *Pauls* argument is this, *All* flesh *shall not*

see God, (*Carnall* men here, *Impenitent* men there, shall not.) And therefore, that as our texts answer one another, so your resurrections may answer one another too; as at the last resurrection, all that heare the sound of the Trumpet, shall rise in one instant, though they have passed thousands of years between their burialls, so doe all ye, who are now called, by a lower and infirmer voice, rise together in this resurrection of grace. Let him that hath been buried *sixty* years, *forty* years, *twenty* years, in covetousnesse, in uncleannesse, in indevotion, 700 rise now, now *this minute,* and then, as *Adam* that dyed *five thousand* before, shall be no sooner in heaven, in his body, then you, so *Abel* that dyed *for God,* so long before you, shall be no better, that is, no fuller of the glory of heaven, then you that dye *in God,* when it shall be his pleasure to take you to him.

Number 5.

Preached at Lincolns Inne upon
Trinity-Sunday. 1620.

GEN. 18.25. *SHALL NOT THE IUDGE OF ALL*
THE EARTH DO RIGHT?

[Joh. 8.58]

Luk. 11.11

THESE WORDS are the entrance into that prayer and expostulation, which *Abraham* made to and with God, in the behalfe
of Sodome, and the other Cities. He that is, before *Abraham*
was, Christ Jesus himselfe, in that prayer, which he hath proposed to
us, hath laid such a foundation, as this is, such a religious insinuation
into him, to whom we make that prayer; Before we aske any thing,
we say, *Our Father, which art in heaven:* If he be our Father, A
Father when his sonne asks bread, will not give him a stone; God
hath a fatherly disposition towards us; And if he be our Father in
¹⁰ Heaven, *If evill fathers know how to give good things unto their*
children, how much more shall your heavenly Father give the Spirit
to them that aske him? Shall your Father, which is in heaven, deny
you any good thing? sayes Christ there; It is impossible: *Shall not the*
Iudge of all the Earth do right? sayes *Abraham* here; It is as impossible.

The history which occasioned and induced these words, I know
you know. The Holy Ghost by *Moses* hath expressed plainly, and
your meditations have paraphrased to your selves this history, That
God appeared to *Abraham,* in the plaine of Mamre, in the persons of
²⁰ three men; three men so glorious, as that *Abraham* gave them a great
respect: That *Abraham* spoke to those three, as to one person: That
he exhibited all offices of humanity and hospitality unto them: That
after they had executed the first part of their Commission, which was
to ratifie, and to reduce to a more certainty of time, the promise of
Isaac, and consequently of the Messias, though *Abraham* and *Sara*

were past hope in one another; that they imparted to *Abraham,* upon
their departure, the indignation that God had conceived against the
sins of Sodome, and consequently the imminent destruction of that
City; That this awakened *Abrahams* compassion, and put him into
30 a zeale, and vehemence; for, all the while, he is said, *to have been
with him that spoke to him,* and yet, now it is said, *Abraham drew
near,* he came up close to God, and he sayes, Peradventure, (I am
not sure of it) but peradventure, there may be some righteous in
the City, and if there should be so, it should be absolutely unjust to
destroy them; but, since it may be so, it is too soone to come to a
present execution; *Absit à te,* sayes *Abraham, Be that far from thee;*
And he repeats it twice; And upon the reason in our text, *Shall not
the Iudge of all the Earth do right?*

First then, The person who is *the Iudge of all the Earth,* submits
40 us to a necessity of seeking, who it is that *Abraham* speaks to; and
so, who they were that appeared to him: whether they were three
men, or three Angels, or two Angels, and the third, to whom *Abraham* especially addressed himselfe, were Christ: Or whether in these
three persons, whatsoever they were, there were any intimation, any
insinuation given, or any apprehension taken by *Abraham,* of the
three blessed Persons of the glorious Trinity. And then, in the second
part, in the expostulation it selfe, we shall see, first, The descent, and
easinesse of God, that he vouchsafes to admit an expostulation, an
admonition from his servant, He is content that *Abraham* remember
50 him, of his office: And the Expostulation lyes in this, That he is a
Iudge, And *shall not a Iudge do right?* But more in this, That he is
Iudge of all the Earth, and, if he do wrong, there is no Appeal from
him, And *shall not the Iudge of all the Earth do right?* And from
thence we shall fall upon this consideration, What was that *Right,*
which *Abraham* presses upon God here: And we shall finde it two-
fold: for, first, he thinks it unjust, that God should wrap up just and
unjust, righteous and unrighteous, all in one condemnation, in one
destruction, *Absit, be this far from God:* And then, he hath a farther
ayme then that, That God for the righteous sake, should spare the
60 unrighteous, and so forbeare the whole City. And though this Judge
of the whole Earth, might have done right, though he had destroyed
the most righteous persons amongst them, much more, though he

Ver. 23
24

Divisio

had not spared the unrighteous, for the righteous sake, yet we shall
see at last, the abundant measure of Gods overflowing mercy to have
declared it selfe so far, as if there had been any righteous, he had
spared the whole City. Our parts then are but two: but two such, as
are high parts, and yet growing rich, and yet emproving, so far, as
that the first is above Man, and the extent of his Reason, The Mystery
of the Trinity; And the other is above God so, as that it is above all
70 his works, The infinitenes of his Mercy.

1 Part
An viri

To come to the severall branches of these two maine parts, first,
in the first, we aske, *An viri,* whether these three that appeared to
Abraham, were men or no. Now, between *Abrahams* apprehension,
who saw this done, and ours, who know it was done, because we
read it here in *Moses* relation, there is a great difference. *Moses* who
informes us now, what was done then, sayes expresly, *Apparuit
Dominus, The Lord appeared,* and therefore we know they were
more then ordinary men; But when *Moses* tels us how *Abraham*
apprehended it, *Ecce tres viri, He lift up his eyes, and he saw three
80 men,* he took them to be but men, and therefore exhibited to them
all offices of humanity and curtesie: Where we note also, that even
by the Saints of God, civill behaviour, and faire language is conveniently exercised: A man does not therefore meane ill, because he
speaks well: A man must not therefore be suspected to performe
nothing, because he promises much: Such phrases of humilitie, and
diminution, and undervaluing of himselfe, as *David* utters to *Saul;*
such phrases of magnifying, and glorifying the Prince, as *Daniel*
uses to the King, perchance no secular story, perchance no moderne

1 Sam. 25

Court will afford; Neither shall you finde in those places, more of
90 that which we call Complement, then in *Abigails* accesse to *David,*
in the behalfe of her foolish husband, when she comes to intercede
for him, and to deprecate his fault. Harshnesse, and morosity in behaviour, rusticity, and coorsenesse of language, are no arguments in
themselves, of a plaine, and a direct meaning, and of a simple heart.
Abraham was an hundred yeares old, and that might, in the generall, indispose him; And it was soone after his Circumcision, which
also might be a particular disabling; He was *sitting* still, and so not
onely enjoying his bodily ease, but his Meditation, (for his eyes were
cast downe) But as soon as *he lift up his eyes,* and had occasion pre-

¹⁰⁰ sented him to doe a curtesie, for all his age, and infirmity, and
possession of rest, he *runs* to them, and he *bowes* himselfe to them,
and *salutes* them, with words not onely of curtesie, but of reverence:
Explorat itinera, sayes S. *Ambrose,* he searches and inquires into their
journey, that he might direct them, or accompany, or accommodate
them; *Adest non quærentibus,* He prevents them, and offers before
they aske; *Rapit prætergressuros,* when they pretended to goe farther, he forced them, by the irresistible violence of curtesie, to stay
with him, and he calls them, (or one amongst them) *Dominum,*
Lord, and professes himselfe their *servant.* But *Abraham* did not
¹¹⁰ determine his curtesie in words, and no more: We must not think,
that because onely man of all creatures can speak, that therefore the
onely duty of man is to speake; faire Apparell makes some shew in
a wardrobe, but not halfe so good as when it is upon a body: faire
language does ever well, but never so well as when it apparels a reall
curtesie: *Abraham* entreated them faire, and entertained them well:
he spoke kindly, and kindly performed all offices of ease, and refo-
cillation to these way-faring strangers.

Now here is our copie, but who writes after this copie? *Abraham*
is *pater multitudinis,* A father of large posterity, but he is dead without
¹²⁰ issue, or his race is failed; for, who hath this hospitall care of relieving distressed persons now? Thou seest a needy person, and thou
turnest away thine eye; but it is the Prince of Darknesse that casts
this mist upon thee; Thou stoppest thy nose at his sores, but they
are thine owne incompassionate bowels that stinke within thee; Thou
tellest him, he troubles thee, and thinkest thou hast chidden him into
a silence; but he whispers still to God, and he shall trouble thee worse
at last, when he shall tell thee, in the mouth of Christ Jesus, *I was*   [Mat.
hungry and ye fed me not: Still thou sayest to the poore, I have not   25.42]
for you, when God knowes, a great part of that which thou hast,
¹³⁰ thou hast for them, if thou wouldst execute Gods commission, and
dispense it accordingly, as God hath made thee his steward for the
poore. Give really, and give gently; Doe kindly, and speake kindly
too, for that is Bread, and Hony.

Abraham then tooke these for men, and offered curtesies proper   *An Angeli*
for men: for though hee called him, to whom hee spoke, *Dominum,*
Lord, yet it is not that name of the *Lord,* which implyes his Divinity,

it is not *Iehovah,* but *Adonai;* it is the same name, and the same word, which his wife *Sara,* after, gives him. And *Mary Magdalen* when she was at Christs Sepulchre, speaks of Christ, and speaks to the Gardiner (as she thought) in one and the same word: *Tulerunt Dominum,* she sayes of Christ, *They have taken away my Lord,* And to the Gardiner she sayes, *Domine, si sustulisti:* for Κύριος, which is the word in both places, was but a name of civill curtesie, and is well enough translated by our men, in that later place, *Sir, Sir if you have taken him away, &c. Abraham* then, at their first appearing, had no evidence that they were other then men; but we have; for that place of the Apostle, *Be not forgetfull to entertaine strangers, for thereby some have entertained Angels unawares,* hath evermore, by all Expositors, had reference to this action of *Abrahams;* which proves both these first branches, That he knew it not, and That they were Angels. The Apostles principall purpose there is, to recommend to us Hospitality, but limited to such hospitality as might in likelihood, or in possibility, be an occasion of entertaining Angels, that is, of Angelicall men, good and holy men. Hospitality is a vertue, more recommended by the Writers in the Primitive Church, then any other vertue: but upon this reason, That the poore flock of Christ Jesus, being by persecution then scattered upon the face of the earth, men were necessarily to be excited, with much vehemence, to succour and relieve them, and to receive them into their houses, as they travailed.

Tertullian sayes well, That the whole Church of God is one houshold: He sayes every particular Church is *Ecclesia Apostolica, quia soboles Apostolicarum,* An Apostolicall Church, if it be an off-spring of the Apostolicall Churches: He does not say, *quia soboles Apostolicæ,* because that Church is the off-spring of the Apostolicall Church, as though there were but one such, which must be the mother of all: for, sayes he, *Omnes primæ, & omnes Apostolicæ,* Every Church is a supreme Church, and every Church is an Apostolicall Church, *dum omnes unam probant unitatem,* as long as they agree in the unity of that doctrine which the Apostles taught, and adhere to the supreme head of the whole Church, Christ Jesus. Which S. *Cyprian* expresses more clearly, *Episcopatus unus est,* The whole Church is but one Bishoprick, *Cujus, à singulis, in solidum pars*

tenetur, Every Bishop is Bishop of the whole Church, and no one more then another. The Church then was, and should be, as one houshold; And in this houshold, sayes *Tertullian* there, there was first *Communicatio pacis,* a peaceable disposition, a charitable interpretation of one anothers actions: And then there was *Appellatio fraternitatis,* sayes he; That if they did differ in some things, yet they
180 esteemed themselves sons of one Father, of God, and by one Mother, the Catholique Church, and did not break the band of Brotherhood, nor separate from one another for every difference in opinion; And lastly, sayes he, There was *Contesseratio Hospitalitatis,* A warrant for their reception and entertainment in one anothers houses, wheresoever they travailed. Now, because for the benefit and advantage of this ease, and accommodation in travailing, men conterfeited themselves to be Christians that were not, the Councel of Nice made such provision as was possible; (though that also were deluded after) which was, That there should be *literæ formatæ,* (as they called
190 them) certaine testimoniall letters, subscribed with foure characters, denoting Father, Son, and holy Ghost; and those letters should be *contesseratio hospitalitatis,* a warrant for their entertainment wheresoever they came. Still there was a care of hospitality, but such, as Angels, that is, Angelicall, good and religious men, and truly Christians, might be received.

Beloved, Baptisme in the name of the Father, Son, and holy Ghost, is this Contesseration; all that are truly baptized are of this houshold, and should be relieved and received: But certainly, there is a race that have not this Contesseration, not these testimoniall letters, not
200 this outward Baptisme: Amongst those herds of vagabonds, and incorrigible rogues, that fill porches, and barnes in the Countrey, a very great part of them was never baptized: people of a promiscuous generation, and of a mischievous education; ill brought into the world, and never brought into the Church. No man receives an Angel unawares, for receiving or harbouring any of these; neither have these any interest in the houshold of God, for they have not their first Contesseration: And as there are *sins* which we are not bid *to pray for,* so there are beggers which we are not bid to give to. God appeared by Angels in the Old Testament, and he appeares by
210 Angels in the New, in his Messengers, in his Ministers, in his Serv-

ants: And that Hospitality, and those feasts which cannot receive
such Angels, those Ministers and Messengers of God, where by reason
of excesse and drunkennesse, by reason of scurril and licentious discourse, by reason of wanton and unchast provocations, by reason
of execrable and blasphemous oathes these Angels of God cannot
be present, but they must either offend the company by reprehension, or prevaricate and betray the cause of God by their silence, this
is not *Abrahams* hospitality, whose commendation was, *that he received Angels.*

220   Those Angels came, and *stood before Abraham,* but till he *lift
up his eyes,* and *ran forth to them,* they came not to him: The Angels of the Gospel come within their distance, but if you will not
receive them, they can break open no doores, nor save you against

Revel. 3.20

your will: The Angel does, as he that sends him, *Stand at the doore,
and knock, if the doore be opened, he comes in, and sups with him;*
What gets he by that? This; *He sups with me* too, sayes Christ
there; He brings his dish with him; he feeds his Host, more then
his Host him. This is true Hospitality, and entertainment of Angels,
both when thou feedest Christ, in his poore members abroad, or
230 when thou feedest thine owne soule at home, with the company and
conversation of true and religious Christians at thy table, for these
are Angels.

An Christus

Abraham then, took these three for men, and no more, when as
they were Angels: But were they all Angels, and no more? was not
that one, to whom more particularly *Abraham* addressed himselfe,
and called him *Lord,* The Son of God, Christ Jesus? This very many,
very learned amongst the Ancients, did not onely aske by way of
Probleme, and disputation, but affirme Doctrinally, by way of resolution. *Irenæus* thought it, and expressed it so elegantly, as it is al-
240 most pity, if it be not true; *Inseminatus est ubique in Scripturis,
Filius Dei,* sayes he: The Son of God is sowed in every furrow, in
every place of the Scripture, you may see him grow up; and he gives
an example out of this place, *Cum Abraham loquens, cum Abraham
comesurus,* Christ talked with *Abraham,* and he dined with him.
And they will say, that whereas it is said in that place to the *He-
brewes, That Abraham received Angels,* the word *Angel* must not
be too precisely taken: For sometimes, *Angel* in the Scriptures, sig-

nifies lesse then Angel, (as *Iohn,* and *Malachy* are called *Angels*)
and sometimes *Angel* signifies more then Angel, as Christ himselfe
250 is called *The Angel of the great Councell,* according to the *Sep-*   Esay 9.[6]
tuagint: So therefore, they will say, That though Christ were there,
Christ himselfe might be called so, *An Angel;* Or it may be justly
said by S. *Paul, That Abraham did receive Angels,* because there
were two, that were, without question, Angels. This led *Hilary* to a
direct, and a present resolution, that *Abraham* saw Christ, and to
exclaime gratulatorily in his behalfe, *Quanta fidei vis, ut in indis-*
creta assistentium specie, Christum internosceret! What a perspicacy
had *Abrahams* faith, who, where they were all alike, could discerne
one to be above them all!

260   Make this then the question, whether Christ ever appeared to men
upon earth, before his Incarnation; and the Scriptures not determin-
ing this question at all, if the Fathers shall be called to judge it, it
will still be a perplexed case, for they will be equall in number, and
in waight. S. *Augustine* (who is one of them that deny it) sayes
first, for the generall, the greatest worke of all, the promulgation
of the Law, was done by Angels alone, without concurrence of the
Son; and for this particular, sayes he, concerning *Abraham,* they
who thinke that Christ appeared to *Abraham,* ground themselves
but upon this reason, That *Abraham* speakes to all, in the singular
270 number, as to one person; And then, sayes that Father, they may
also observe, that when this one Person, whom they conclude to be
Christ, was departed from the other two, and that the other two
went up to *Sodome,* there *Lot* speakes to those two, in the singular   Gen. 19.18
number, as to one person, as *Abraham* did before. From this argumentation of S. *Augustines,* this may well be raised, That when the
Scriptures may be interpreted, and Gods actions well understood,
by an ordinary way, it is never necessary, seldome safe to induce
an extraordinary. It was then an ordinary, and familiar way for God,
to proceed with those his servants by Angels; but by his Son, so
280 extraordinary, as that it is not cleare, that ever it was done; and
therefore it needs not be said, nor admitted in this place.

    In this place, this falls properly to be noted, that even in these
three glorious Angels of God, there was an eminent difference; One
of them seemed to *Abraham,* to bee the principall man in the Com-

mission, and to that one, he addressed himselfe. Amongst the other Angels, which are the Ministers in Gods Church, one may have better abilities, better faculties then another, and it is no errour, no weaknesse in a man to desire to conferre with one rather then with another, or to heare one rather then another. But *Abraham* did not ²⁹⁰ so apply himselfe to one of the three, that he neglected the other two: No man must be so cherished, so followed, as that any other be thereby either defrauded of their due maintenance, or dis-heartened for want of due incouragement. Wee have not the greatest use of the greatest Starres; but wee have more benefit of the Moone, which is lesse then they, because she is nearer to us. It is not the depth, nor the wit, nor the eloquence of the Preacher that pierces us, but his nearenesse; that hee speaks to my conscience, as though he had been behinde the hangings when I sinned, and as though he had read the book of the day of Judgement already. Something ³⁰⁰ *Abraham* saw in this Angel above the rest, which drew him, which *Moses* does not expresse; Something a man finds in one Preacher above another, which he cannot expresse, and he may very lawfully make his spirituall benefit of that, so that that be no occasion of neglecting due respects to others.

An Trinitas   This being then thus fixed, that *Abraham* received them as men, that they were in truth no other then Angels, there remaines, for the shutting up of this Part, this Consideration, whether after *Abraham* came to the knowledge that they were Angels, he apprehended not an intimation of the three Persons of the Trinity, by these three ³¹⁰ Angels. Whether Gods appearing to *Abraham* (which *Moses* speaks

Ver. 13   of in the first verse) were manifested to him, when *Sarah* laughed in her selfe, and yet they knew that she laughed; Or whether it were

Ver. 17   manifested, when they imparted their purpose, concerning *Sodome;* (for, in both these places, they are called neither men nor Angels, but by that name, *The Lord,* and that Lord which is Jehovah) whether, I say, when *Abraham* discerned them to be such Angels, as God appeared in them, and spoke and wrought by them, whether then, as he discerned the Divinity, he discerned the Trinity in them too, is the question. I know the explicite Doctrine of the Trinity ³²⁰ was not easie to be apprehended then; as it is not easie to be expressed now. It is a bold thing in servants, to inquire curiously into

their Masters Pedigree, whether he be well descended, or well allied: It is a bold thing too, to inquire too curiously into the eternall generation of Christ Jesus, or the eternall procession of the Holy Ghost. When *Gregory Nazianzen* was pressed by one, to assigne a difference between those words, *Begotten,* and *Proceeding, Dic tu mihi,* sayes he, *quid sit Generatio, & ego dicam tibi, quid sit Processio, ut ambo insaniamus:* Doe thou tell me, what this *Begetting* is, and then I will tell thee, what this *Proceeding* is; and all the world
330 will finde us both mad, for going about to expresse inexpressible things.

And as every manner of phrase in expressing, or every comparison, does not manifest the Trinity; so every place of Scripture, which the Fathers, and later man have applied to that purpose, does not prove the Trinity. And therefore, those men in the Church, who have cryed downe that way of proceeding, to goe about to prove the Trinity, out of the first words of *Genesis, Creavit Dii,* That because God in the plurall is there joyned to a Verb in the singular, therefore there is a Trinity in Unity; or to prove the Trinity out of this
340 place, that because God, who is but one, appeared to *Abraham* in three Persons, therefore there are three Persons in the God-head; those men, I say, who have cryed downe such manner of arguments, have reason on their side, when these arguments are imployed against the Jews, for, for the most part, the Jews have pertinent, and sufficient answers to those arguments. But yet, betweene them, who make this place, a distinct, and a literall, and a concluding argument, to prove the Trinity, and them who cry out against it, that it hath no relation to the Trinity, our Church hath gone a middle, and a moderate way, when by appointing this Scripture for this day, when we
350 celebrate the Trinity, it declares that to us, who have been baptized, and catechised in the name and faith of the Trinity, it is a refreshing, it is a cherishing, it is an awakening of that former knowledge which we had of the Trinity, to heare that our onely God thus manifested himselfe to *Abraham* in three Persons.

Luther sayes well upon this text, If there were no other proofe of the Trinity but this, I should not believe the Trinity; but yet sayes he, This is *Singulare testimonium de articulo Trinitatis,* Though it be not a concluding argument, yet it is a great testimony of the Trinity. *Fateor,* saies he, *historico sensu nihil concludi præter hospitalitatem,* I confesse, in the literall sense, there is nothing but a recommendation of hospitality, and therefore, to the Jews, I would urge no more out of this place: *Sed non sic agendum cum auditoribus, ac cum adversariis,* We must not proceed alike with friends and with enemies. There are places of Scriptures for direct proofes, and there are places to exercise our meditation, and devotion in things, for which we need not, nor aske not any new proofe. And for exercise, sayes Luther, *Rudi ligno ad formam gladii utimur,* We content our selves with a foyle, or with a stick, and we require not a sharpe sword. To cut off the enemies of the Trinity, we have two-edged swords, that is, undeniable arguments: but to exercise our owne devotions, we are content with similitudinary, and comparative reasons. He pursues it farther, to good use: The story doth not teach us, That

Gal. 4.24

Sarah is the *Christian Church,* and *Hagar* the *Synagogue;* But S. *Paul* proves that, from that story; he proves it from thence, though he call it but an *Allegory.* It is true that S. *Augustine* sayes, *Figura nihil probat,* A figure, an Allegory proves nothing; yet, sayes he, *addit lucem, & ornat,* It makes that which is true in it selfe, more evident and more acceptable.

And therefore it is a lovely and a religious thing, to finde out *Vestigia Trinitatis,* Impressions of the Trinity, in as many things as we can; and it is a reverent obedience to embrace the wisdome of our Church, in renewing the Trinity to our Contemplation, by the reading of this Scripture, this day, for, even out of this Scripture, *Philo Iudæus,* (although hee knew not the true Trinity aright) found a threefold manifestation of God to man, in this appearing of God to *Abraham:* for, as he is called in this Story, *Iehova,* he considers him, *Fontem Essentiæ,* To be the fountaine of all Being; As hee is called *Deus, God,* he considers him, in the administration of his Creatures, in his providence; As he is called *Dominus, Lord,* and *King,* he considers him in the judgement, glorifying, and rejecting according to their merits: So, though hee found not a Trinity of Persons, he found a Trinity of Actions in the Text, Creation, Providence, and Judgement. If he, who knew no Trinity, could finde one, shall not we, who know the true one, meditate the more effectually upon that, by occasion of this story? Let us therefore, with S. *Bernard,*

consider *Trinitatem Creatricem,* and *Trinitatem Creatam,* A Creating, and a Created Trinity; A Trinity, which the Trinity in Heaven,
Father, Son, and Holy Ghost, hath created in our soules, Reason,
Memory, and Will; and that we have super-created, added another
400 Trinity, Suggestion, and Consent, and Delight in sin; And that God,
after all this infuses another Trinity, Faith, Hope, and Charity, by
which we returne to our first; for so far, that Father of Meditation,
S. *Bernard,* carries this consideration of the Trinity. Since therefore
the confession of a Trinity is that which distinguishes us from Jews,
and Turks, and al other professions, let us discerne that beame of
the Trinity, which the Church hath shewed us, in this text, and with
the words of the Church, conclude this part, *O holy, blessed, and*   [Book of
glorious Trinity, three Persons, and one God, have mercy upon us   Common
miserable sinners.   Prayer]

410   We are descended now to our second part, what past between God   2 Part
and *Abraham,* after he had thus manifested himselfe unto him;   *Expostulatio*
Where we noted first, That God admits, even expostulation, from
his servants; almost rebukes and chidings from his servants. We need
not wonder at *Iobs* humility, that he did not despise his man, nor   Iob 31.13
his mayd, when they contended with him, for God does not despise
that in us. God would have gone from *Iacob* when he *wrestled,* and
Iacob would not let him go, and that prevailed with God. If we have   Gen. 32.26
an apprehension when we beginne to pray, that God doth not heare
us, not regard us, God is content that in the fervor of that prayer, we   [Psa.
420 say with *David, Evigila Domine,* and *Surge Domine, Awake O Lord,*   44.23]
and *Arise O Lord;* God is content to be told, that he was in bed, and   [Psa. 132.8]
asleepe, when he should heare us. If we have not a present deliverance
from our enemies, God is content that we proceed with *David, Eripe*   [Psa. 74.11]
manum de sinu, Pluck out thy hand out of thy bosome; God is content to be told, that he is slack and dilatory when he should deliver
us. If we have not the same estimation in the world, that the children
of this world have, God is content that we say with *Amos, Pauperem*   Amos. 2.6
pro calceamentis, that *we are sold for a paire of shooes;* And with
S. *Paul,* that *we are the off-scouring of the world:* God is content to   [1 Cor.
430 be told, that he is unthrifty, and prodigall of his servants lives, and   4.13]
honours, and fortunes. Now, *Offer this to one of your Princes,* says   [Mal. 1.8]
the Prophet, *and see whether he will take it.* Bring a petition to any

earthly Prince, and say to him, *Evigila,* and *Surge,* would your Majesty would awake, and reade this petition, and so insimulate him of a former drowsinesse in his government; say unto him, *Eripe manum,* pull thy hand out of thy bosome, and execute Justice, and so insimulate him of a former manacling and slumbring of the Lawes; say unto him, we are become as old shooes, and as off-scourings, and so insimulate him of a diminution, and dis-estimation
440 faln upon the Nation by him, what Prince would not (and justly) conceive an indignation against such a petitioner? which of us that heard him, would not pronounce him to be mad, to ease him of a heavier imputation? And yet our long-suffering, and our patient God, (must we say, our humble and obedient God?) endures all this: He endures more; for, when *Abraham* came to this expostulation, *Shall not the Iudge of all the earth do right?* God had said never a word, of any purpose to destroy Sodom, but he said only, *He would go see, whether they had done altogether, according to that cry, which was come up against them;* and *Abraham* comes
450 presently to this vehemency: And might not the Supreme Ordinary, God himselfe, goe this visitation? might not the supreme Judge, God himselfe, go this Circuit? But as long as *Abraham* kept himselfe upon this foundation, *It is impossible, that the Iudge of all the earth should not do right,* God mis-interpreted nothing at *Abrahams* hand, but received even his Expostulations, and heard him out, to the sixt petition.

Almost such an Expostulation as this, *Moses* uses towards God; He asks God a reason of his anger, *Lord, why doth thy wrath waxe hot against thy people?* He tels him a reason, why he should not doe
460 so, *For thou hast brought them forth with a great power, and with a mighty hand:* And he tels him the inconveniences that might follow, *The Egyptians will say, He brought them out for mischiefe, to slay them in the mountaine:* He imputes even perjury to God himselfe, and breach of Covenant, to *Abraham, Isaac,* and *Iacob,* which were Feffees in trust, betweene God and his people, and he sayes, *Thou sware'st to them, by thine owne selfe, that thou wouldst not deale thus with them;* And therefore he concludes all with that vehemence, *Turne from thy fierce wrath, and repent this evill purpose against them.* But we finde a prayer, or expostulation, of much more

⁴⁷⁰ exorbitant vehemence, in the stories of the Roman Church, towards the blessed Virgin, (towards whom, they use to bee more mannerly and respective then towards her Son, or his Father) when at a siege of Constantinople, they came to her statue, with this protestation, Looke you to the drowning of our Enemies ships, or we will drowne you: *Si vis ut imaginem tuam non mergamus in mari, merge illos.* The farthest that *Abraham* goes in this place, is, That God is a *Iudge,* and therefore must *doe right:* for, *Far be wickednesse from God, and iniquity from the Almighty; surely God will not do wickedly, neither will the Almighty pervert judgement.* An Usurer, an Extortioner, ⁴⁸⁰ an Oppressor, a Libeller, a Thiefe, and Adulterer, yea a Traytor, makes shift to finde some excuse, some flattery to his Conscience; they say to themselves; the Law is open, and if any be grieved, they may take their remedy, and I must endure it, and there is an end. But, since nothing holds of this oppressor, and manifold malefactor, but the sentence of the Judge, shall not the Judge doe right? how must this necessarily shake the frame of all? An Arbitrator or a Chancellor, that judges by submission of parties, or according to the Dictates of his owne understanding, may have some excuse, He did as his Conscience led him: But shall not a *Iudge,* that hath a certaine ⁴⁹⁰ Law to judge by, *do right?* Especially if he be such a Judge, as is *Iudge of the whole earth?* which is the next step in *Abrahams* expostulation.

Iob 34.10

Now, as long as there lies a Certiorari from a higher Court, or an Appeale to a higher Court, the case is not so desperate, if the Judge doe not right, for there is a future remedy to be hoped: If the whole State be incensed against me, yet I can finde an escape to another Country; If all the World persecute me, yet, if I be an honest man, I have a supreame Court in my selfe, and I am at peace, in being acquitted in mine owne Conscience. But God is the Judge of all the ⁵⁰⁰ earth; of this which I tread, and this earth which I carry about me; and when he judges me, my Conscience turnes on his side, and confesses his judgement to be right. And therefore S. *Pauls* argument, seconds, and ratifies *Abrahams* expostulation; *Is God unrighteous? God forbid;* for then, says the Apostle, *how shall God judge the World?* The Pope may erre, but then a Councell may rectifie him: The King may erre; but then, God, in whose hands the Kings heart

Omnem terram

Rom. 3.6

is, can rectifie him. But if God, that judges all the earth, judge thee, there is no error to be assigned in his judgement, no appeale from God not throughly informed, to God better informed, for hee al-
510 waies knowes all evidence, before it be given. And therefore the larger the jurisdiction, and the higher the Court is, the more carefull ought the Judge to be of wrong judgement; for *Abrahams* expostulation reaches in a measure to them, *Shall not the Iudge of all* (or of a great part of the earth) *do right?*

Now what is the wrong, which *Abraham* disswaded, and deprecated here? first, *Ne justi cum impiis,* That God would not destroy the Just with the unjust, not make both their cases alike. This is an injustice, which never any bloody men upon earth, but those, who exceeded all, in their infamous purposes, the Authors, and Actors
520 in the Powder treason, did ever deliberately and advisedly, upon debate whether it should be so, or no, resolve, that all of both Religions should perish promiscuously in the blowing up of that house. Here the Devill would be Gods Ape; and as God had presented to S. *Peter,* a sheete of all sorts of Creatures, cleane and uncleane, and bad him take his choice, kill and eate; So the Devill would make S. *Peter,* in his imaginary Successor, or his instruments, present God a sacrifice of cleane and uncleane, Catholiques and Heretiques, (in their denomination) and bid him take his choyce: which action, whosoever forgets so, as that he forgets what was intended in it,
530 forgets his Religion, and whosoever forgets it so, as that he forgets what they would doe againe, if they had power, forgets his reason. But this is not the way of Gods justice; God is a God of harmony, and consent, and in a musicall instrument, if some strings be out of tune, wee doe not presently breake all the strings, but reduce and tune those, which are out of tune.

As gold whilest it is in the mine, in the bowels of the earth, is good for nothing, and when it is out, and beaten to the thinnesse of leaf-gold, it is wasted, and blown away, and quickly comes to nothing; But when it is tempered with such allay, as it may receive a stamp
540 and impression, then it is currant and usefull: So whilest Gods Justice lyes in the bowels of his own decree and purpose, and is not executed at all, we take no knowledge that there is any such thing; And when Gods Justice is dilated to such an expansion, as it overflowes all alike,

whole Armies with the sword, whole Cities with the plague, whole Countryes with famine, oftentimes we lose the consideration of Gods Justice, and fall upon some naturall causes, because the calamity is faln so indifferently upon just and unjust, as that, we thinke, it could not be the act of God: but when Gods Justice is so allayd with his wisedome, as that we see he keeps a Goshen in Ægypt, and saves his
550 servants in the destruction of his enemies, then we come to a rich and profitable use of his Justice. And therefore *Abraham* presses this, with that vehement word, *Chalilah, Absit: Abraham* serves a Prohibition upon God, as S. *Peter* would have done upon Christ, when he was going up to Jerusalem to suffer, *Absit,* sayes he, *Thou shalt not* [Mat. *do this.* But the word signifies more properly *prophanationem, pol-* 16.22] *lutionem: Abraham* intends, that God should know, that it would be a prophaning of his holy honour, and an occasion of having his Name blasphemed amongst the Nations, if God should proceed so, as to wrap up just and unjust, righteous and unrighteous, all in one
560 condemnation, and one execution; *Absit, Be this far from thee.*

But *Abrahams* zeale extended farther then this; his desire and his *Ut parcat* hope was, That for the righteous sake, the unrighteous might be *Impiis* spared, and reserved to a time of repentance. This therefore ministers a provocation to every man, to be as good as he can, not onely for his own sake, but for others too. This made S. *Ambrose* say, *Quantus murus patriæ, vir bonus?* An honest and religious man, is a wall to a whole City, a sea to a whole Iland. When our Saviour Christ observed, that they would presse him with that Proverb, *Medice, cura* Luk. 4.23 *teipsum, Physitian, heal thy selfe,* we see there, that himselfe was not
570 his person, but his Country was himselfe; for that is it that they intend by that Proverb, *Heal thy selfe,* take care of them that are near thee, do that which thou doest here in Capernaum, at home; Preach these Sermons there; do these miracles there: cure thy Country, and that is curing thy selfe. Live so, that thy example may be a precedent to others; live so, that for thy sake, God may spare others; and then, and not till then, thou hast done thy duty. God spares sometimes, *ob commixtionem sanguinis,* for kindreds sake, and for alliance; and therefore it behoves us to take care of our allyances, and planting our children in religious families. How many judgements do we escape,
580 because we are of the seed of *Abraham,* and made partakers of the

Covenant, which the Gentils, who are not so, are overwhelmed under? God spares sometimes, *Ob cohabitationem,* for good neighbourhood; he will not bring the fire near a good mans house: As here, in our Text, he would have done in Sodome, and as he did save many, onely because they were in the same Ship with S. *Paul.* And therefore, as in the other Religion, the Jews have streets of their own, and the Stews have streets of their own; so let us choose to make our dwellings, and our conversation of our own, and not affect the neighbourhood, nor the commerce of them who are of evill com-
590 munication. Be good then, that thou mayest communicate thy goodnesse to others; and consort with the good, that thou mayest participate of their goodnesse. *Omnis sapiens stulti est redemptio,* is excellently said by *Philo,* A wise man is the saviour and redeemer of a foole: And, (as the same man says) though a Physitian when he is called, discerne that the patient cannot be recovered, yet he will prescribe something, *Ne ob ejus negligentiam periisse videatur,* lest the world should think he dyed by his negligence; How incurable, how incorrigible soever the world be, be thou a religious honest man, lest some childe in thy house, or some servant of thine be damned,
600 which might have been saved, if thou hadst given good example. Gods ordinary way is to save man by man; and *Abraham* thought it not out of Gods way, to save man for man, to save the unjust for the just, the unrighteous for the righteous sake.

Si nolit But if God do not take this way, if he do wrap up the just and the
Deus unjust in the same Judgement, is God therefore unjust? God forbid.
Eccles. 9.2 *All things come alike to all,* sayes *Solomon; One event to the righteous, and to the wicked, to the cleane, and to the uncleane, to him that sacrificeth, and to him that sacrificeth not; as is the good, so is the sinner, and he that sweareth, as he that feareth an Oath. There*
610 *is one event of all,* sayes he; but, sayes he, *This is an evill,* that it is so: But what kinde of evill? An evill of vexation; because the weake are sometimes scandalized that it is so, and the glory of God seems for a time to be obscured, when it is so, because the good are not discerned from the evill. But yet God, who knowes best how to repayre his own honour, suffers it, nay appoints it to be so, that just and unjust are wrapped up in the same Judgement. The Corne is as much beaten in the threshing, as the straw is; The just are as much

Act. 27

punished here as the unjust. Because God of his infinite goodnesse, hath elected me from the beginning, therefore must he provide that [620] I have another manner of birth, or another manner of death, then the Reprobate have? Must he provide, that I be borne into the world, without originall sin, of a Virgin, as his Son was, or that I go out of the world, by being taken away, as *Enoch* was, or as *Elias?* And though we have that one example of such a comming into the world, and a few examples of such a going out of the world, yet we have no example (not in the Son of God himselfe) of passing through this world, without taking part of the miseries and calamities of the world, common to just and unjust, to the righteous and unrighteous. If *Abraham* therefore should have intended onely temporall destruc- [630] tion, his argument might have been defective: for *Ezekiel,* and *Daniel,* and other just men, were carried into Captivity, as well as the unjust, and yet God not unrighteous: God does it, and avowes it, and professes that he will do it, and do it justly; *Occidam in te justum & injustum, I will cut off the righteous and unrighteous to-gether.* There is no man so righteous, upon whom God might not justly inflict as heavy judgements, in this world, as upon the most unrighteous; Though he have wrapped him up in the righteousnesse of Christ Jesus himselfe, for the next world, yet he may justly wrap him up in any common calamity falling upon the unrighteous here. [640] But the difference is onely in spirituall destruction. *Abraham* might justly apprehend a feare, that a sudden and unprepared death might endanger them for their future state; And therefore he does not pray, that they might be severed from that judgement, because, if they dyed with the unrighteous, they dyed as the unrighteous, if they passed the same way as they, out of this world, they therefore passed into the same state as they, in the next world, *Abraham* could not conclude so, but because the best men do alwayes need all meanes of making them better, *Abraham* prayes, that God would not cut them off, by a sudden destruction, from a considering, and contem- [650] plating the wayes of his proceeding, and so a preparing themselves to a willing and to a thankfull embracing of any way, which they should so discerne to be his way. The wicked are suddenly destroyed, and do not see what hand is upon them, till that hand bury them in hell; The godly may die as suddenly, but yet he sees and knows it

Ezek. 21.3

to be the hand of God, and takes hold of that hand, and by it is carried up to heaven.

Now, if God be still just, though he punish the just with the unjust, in this life, much more may he be so, though he do not spare the unjust for the righteous sake, which is the principall drift of 660 *Abrahams* expostulation, or deprecation. God can preserve still, so as he did in Ægypt. God hath the same Receipts, and the same Antidotes which he had, to repell the flames of burning furnaces, to binde or stupifie the jawes of hungry Lyons, to blunt the edge of Swords,

and overflowing Armyes, as he had heretofore. Christ was invisible to his enemies, when he would scape away; And he was impregnable to his enemies, when in his manifestation of himself, (*I am he*) they fell downe before him; And he was invulnerable, and immortall to his enemies, as long as he would be so, for if he had not opened himselfe to their violence, no man could have taken away his soule; 670 And where God sees such deliverances conduce more to his honour then our suffering does, he will deliver us so in the times of persecution. So that God hath another way, and he had another answer for *Abrahams* petition; he might have said, There is no ill construction, no hard conclusion to be made, if I should take away the just with the unjust, neither is there any necessity, that I should spare the wicked for the righteous: I can destroy Sodome, and yet save the righteous; I can destroy the righteous, and yet make death an advantage to them; which way soever I take, I can do nothing unjustly.

But yet, though God do not binde himselfe to spare the wicked 680 for the righteous, yet he descends to do so at *Abrahams* request. The jaw-bone of an Asse, in the hand of *Samson,* was a devouring sword. The words of man, in the mouth of a faithfull man, of *Abraham,* are a Canon against God himselfe, and batter down all his severe and heavy purposes for Judgements. Yet, this comes not, God knows, out of the weight or force of our words, but out of the easinesse of God. God puts himselfe into the way of a shot, he meets a weak prayer, and is graciously pleased to be wounded by that: God sets up a light, that we direct the shot upon him, he enlightens us with a knowledge, how, and when, and what to pray for; yea, God charges, 690 and discharges the Canon himself upon himselfe; He fils us with good and religious thoughts, and appoints and leaves the Holy Ghost,

to discharge them upon him, in prayer, for it is the Holy Ghost him-
selfe that prayes in us. *Mauzzim,* which is, *The God of forces,* is not   Dan. 11.38
the name of our God, but of an Idoll; Our God is the God of peace,
and of sweetnesse; spirituall peace, spirituall honey to our souls; His
name is *Deus optimus maximus;* He is both; He is all Greatnesse,
but he is All Goodnesse first: He comes to shew his Greatnesse at
last, but yet his Goodnesse begins his Name, and can never be worne
out in his Nature. He made the whole world in six dayes, but he was
⁷⁰⁰ seaven in destroying one City, Jericho. God threatens *Adam, If thou*   [Gen. 2.17]
eate that fruit, in that day, Morte morieris, Thou shalt dye the death;
Here is a double Death interminated in one Day: Now, one of these
Deaths is spirituall Death, and *Adam* never dyed that Death; And
for the other Death, the bodily Death, which might have been executed that day, *Adam* was reprieved above nine hundred yeares. To
lead all to our present purpose, Gods descending to *Abrahams* petition, to spare the wicked for a few just, is first and principally to advance his mercy, That sometimes in abundant mercy, he does so;
but it is also to declare, that there is none just and righteous. *Run to*   Jerem. 5.1
⁷¹⁰ *and fro through the streets of Ierusalem,* (sayes God in the Prophet)
and seeke in the broad places, If yee can finde a man, if there be any
that executeth Iudgement, that seeketh Truth, and I will pardon it.
Where God does not intimate, that he were unjust, if he did not
spare those that were unjust, but he declares the generall flood and
inundation of unrighteousnesse upon Earth, That upon Earth there
is not a righteous man to be found. If God had gone no farther in
his promise to man, then that, if there were one righteous man, he
would save all, this, in effect, had been nothing, for there was never
any man righteous, in that sense and acceptation; He promised and
⁷²⁰ sent one who was absolutely righteous, and for his sake hath saved us.
　　To collect all, and bind up all in one bundle, and bring it home to   *Conclusio*
your own bosomes, remember, That though he appeared in men, it
was God that appeared to *Abraham;* Though men preach, though
men remit sins, though men absolve, God himself speakes, and God
works, and God seales in those men. Remember that nothing appeared to *Abrahams* apprehension but men, yet Angels were in his
presence; Though we binde you not to a necessity of beleeving that
every man hath a particular Angel to assist him, (enjoy your Chris-

tian liberty in that, and think in that point so as you shall find your
730 devotion most exalted, by thinking that it is, or is not so) yet know,
that you do all that you doe, in the presence of Gods Angels; And
though it be in it selfe, and should be so to us, a stronger bridle, to
consider that we doe all in the presence of God, (who sees clearer
then they, for he sees secret thoughts, and can strike immediately,
which they cannot do, without commission from him) yet since the
presence of a Magistrate, or a Preacher, or a father, or a husband,
keeps men often from ill actions, let this prevaile something with
thee, to that purpose, That the Angels of God are alwayes present,
though thou discerne them not. Remember, that though Christ him-
740 self were not amongst the three Angels, yet *Abraham* apprehended
a greater dignity, and gave a greater respect to one then to the rest;
but yet without neglecting the rest too: Apply thy selfe to such Ministers of God, and such Physitians of thy soule, as thine owne conscience tels thee doe most good upon thee; but yet let no particular
affection to one, defraud another in his duties, nor empaire another
in his estimation. And remember too, That though Gods appearing
thus in three persons, be no irrefragable argument to prove the Trinity against the Jews, yet it is a convenient illustration of the Trinity
to thee that art a Christian: And therefore be not too curious in search-
750 ing reasons, and demonstrations of the Trinity, but yet accustome thy
selfe to meditations upon the Trinity, in all occasions, and finde
impressions of the Trinity, in the three faculties of thine owne soule,
Thy Reason, thy Will, and thy Memory; and seeke a reparation of
that thy Trinity, by a new Trinity, by faith in Christ Jesus, by hope
of him, and by a charitable delivering him to others, in a holy and
exemplar life.

Descend thou into thy selfe, as *Abraham* ascended to God, and
admit thine owne expostulations, as God did his. Let thine own
conscience tell thee not onely thy open and evident rebellions against
760 God, but even the immoralities, and incivilities that thou dost
towards men, in scandalizing them, by thy sins; And the absurdities
that thou committest against thy selfe, in sinning against thine owne
reason; And the uncleannesses, and consequently the treachery that
thou committest against thine owne body; and thou shalt see, that
thou hadst been not onely in better peace, but in better state, and

better health, and in better reputation, a better friend, and better company, if thou hadst sinned lesse; because some of thy sins have been such as have violated the band of friendship; and some such as have made thy company and conversation dangerous, either for ten-
⁷⁷⁰ tation, or at least for defamation. Tell thy selfe that thou art the Judge, as *Abraham* told God that he was, and that if thou wilt judge thy selfe, thou shalt scape a severer judgement. He told God that he was Judge of all the earth; Judge all that earth that thou art; Judge both thy kingdomes, thy soule and thy body; Judge all the Provinces of both kingdomes, all the senses of thy body, and all the faculties of thy soule, and thou shalt leave nothing for the last Judgement. Mingle not the just and the unjust together; God did not so; Doe not thinke good and bad all one; Doe not think alike of thy sins, and of thy good deeds, as though when Gods grace had quickned
⁷⁸⁰ them, still thy good works were nothing, thy prayers nothing, thine almes nothing in the sight and acceptation of God: But yet spare not the wicked for the just, continue not in thy beloved sin, because thou makest God amends some other way. And when all is done, as in God towards *Abraham,* his mercy was above all, so after all, *Miserere animæ tuæ,* Be mercifull to thine owne soule; And when the effectuall Spirit of God hath spoken peace and comfort, and sealed a reconciliation to God, to thy soule, rest in that blessed peace, and enter into no such new judgement with thy selfe againe, as should overcome thine own Mercy, with new distractions, or new suspitions
⁷⁹⁰ that thy Repentance was not accepted, or God not fully reconciled unto thee. God, because he judges all the earth, cannot doe wrong; If thou judge thy earth and earthly affections so, as that thou ex-amine clearly, and judge truly, thou dost not doe right, if thou extend not Mercy to thy selfe, if thou receive not, and apply not cheerfully and confidently to thy soul, that pardon and remission of all thy sins, which the holy Ghost, in that blessed state, hath given thee com-mission to pronounce to thine owne soul, and to seale with his seale.

[Ecclus. 30.24 Vulg.]

Number 6.

Preached at Lincolns Inne.

MATTH. 18.7. *WO UNTO THE WORLD, BECAUSE OF OFFENCES.*

THE *Man Moses was very meeke, above all the men which were upon the face of the Earth.* The man *Moses* was so; but the *Child Jesus* was meeker then he. Compare *Moses* with men, and *Moses* will scarce be parallel'd; Compare him with him, who being so much more then man, as that he was God too, was made so much lesse then man, as that he was a worme and no man, and *Moses* will not be admitted. If you consider *Moses* his highest expression, what he would have parted with for his brethren, in his *Dele me, Pardon them, or blot my name out of thy book,* yet Saint ¹⁰ *Pauls* zeale will enter into the balance, and come into comparison with *Moses* in his *Anathema pro fratribus,* in that he wished himselfe to be separated from Christ, rather then his brethren should be. But what comparison hath a sodaine, a passionate, and indigested vehemence of love, expressed in a phrase that tasts of *zeale,* but is not done, (*Moses* was not blotted out of the book of life, nor Saint *Paul* was not separated from Christ for his brethren) what comparison hath such a love, that was but *said,* and perchance *should* not have been said (for, we can scarce excuse *Moses,* or Saint *Paul,* of all excesse and inordinatenesse, in that that they said) with a deliberate ²⁰ and an eternall purpose in Christ Jesus conceived as soon as we can conceive God to have knowen that *Adam* would fall, to come into this world, and dye for man, and then actually and really, in the fulnesse of time, to do so; he did come, and he did dye. The man *Moses* was very meeke, the child Jesus meeker then hee. *Moses* his meeknesse had a determination, (at least an interruption, a discontinuance) when hee revenged the wrong of another upon that *Egyp-*

156

Numb. 12.3

[Exod. 32.32]
[Rom. 9.3]

Exod. 2.12

tian whom he slew. But a *bruised* reed might have stood unbroken, and *smoking flax* might have lien unquenched for ever, for all Christ. And therefore though Christ send his Disciples to School, to the
30 Scribes and Pharisees, because they sate in *Moses* seat, for other lessons, yet for this, hee was their School-master himselfe, *Discite à me, learne of mee, for I am meek.* In this Chapter hee gives them three lessons in this doctrine of meeknesse; Hee gives them foundations, and upperbuildings, The *Text,* and a *Comment,* all the Elements of true instruction, *Rule* and *Example.* First, hee findes them contending for *place, Quis maximus,* who should be greatest in the kingdome of heaven. The disease which they were sick of, was truly an ignorance what this kingdome was; For, though they were never ignorant that there should bee an eternall kingdome in heaven, yet
40 they thought not that the kingdome of Christ here should onely be a spirituall kingdome, but they looked for a temporall inchoation of that kingdome here. That was their disease, and a dangerous one. But as Physitians are forced to doe sometimes, to turne upon the present cure of some vehement symptome, and accident, and leave the consideration of the maine disease for a time, so Christ leaves the doctrine of the kingdome for the present, and does not rectifie them in that *yet,* but for this pestilent symptome, this malignant accident of precedency, and ambition of place, he corrects that first, and to that purpose gives them the example *of a little child,* and tells
50 them, that except they become as humble, as gentle, as supple, as simple, as seely, as tractable, as ductile, as carelesse of place, as negligent of precedency, as that little child, they could not onely not be great, but they could not at all enter into the kingdome of heaven. He gives them a second lesson in this doctrine of meeknesse against scandals, and offences, against an easinesse in *giving* or an easinesse in *taking* offences. For, how well soever we may seeme to be in our selves, we are not well, if we forbear not that company, and abstaine not from that conversation, which by ill example may make us worse, or if wee forbear not such things, as, though they bee indifferent in
60 themselves, and can do us no harme, yet our example may make weaker persons then we are, worse, because they may come to doe as we do, and not proceed upon so good ground as we doe; They may sin in doing those things by our example, in which we did not sinne,

Esay 42.3

Mat. 23.2

11.29

ver. 1

[Mat. 18.4]

because we knew them to be indifferent things, and therefore did
them, and they did them though they thought them to bee sinnes.
And for this Doctrine, Christ takes an example very near to them,
vers. 8 *If thy hand, or foot, or eye offend thee, cut it off, pull it out.* His third
lesson in this doctrine of meeknes is against hardnesse of heart,
against a loathnesse, a wearinesse in forgiving the offences of other
vers. 21 70 men, against us, occasioned by *Peters* question, *Quoties remittam,*
How oft shall my brother sinne against me, and I forgive him? and
the example in this rule Christ hath wrapped up in a parable, The
Master forgave his servant ten thousand Talents, (more money then
vers. 28 perchance any private man is worth) and that servant took his fellow
by the throat, and cast him into prison, because he did not presently
pay an hundred pence, perchance fifty shillings, not three pound of
our money: in such a proportion was Christ pleased to expresse the
Masters inexhaustible largenesse and bounty, (which is himselfe,)
and the servants inexcusable cruelty, and penuriousnesse, (which is
80 every one of us.) The root of all Christian duties is *Humility,* meeknesse, that's violated in an ambitious precedency, for that implyes an
over-estimation of our selves, and an undervalue of others; And it is
violated in *scandals,* and *offences,* for that implies an unsetlednesse
and irresolution in our selves, that we can bee so easily shaked, or a
neglecting of weaker persons, of whom Christ neglected none; and
it is violated in an *unmercifulnesse,* and *inexorablenesse,* for that implies an *indocilenesse,* that we will not learn by Christs doctrine; and
an *ungratefulnesse,* that we will not apply his example, and do to his
servants, as he, our Master, hath done to us: And so have you some
90 Paraphrase of the whole Chapter, as it consists of Rules and Examples
in this Doctrine of meeknes, endangered by pride, by scandall, by uncharitablenes. But of those two, pride and uncharitablenes (though
they deserve to be often spoken of,) I shal have no occasion from
these words of my text, to speak, for into the second of these three
parts, *The Doctrine of scandals,* our text fals, and it is a Doctrine
very necessary, and seldome touched upon.

Divisio   As the words of our Text are, our parts must be three. First, that
heavy word *Væ,* woe; Secondly, that generall word, *Mundo, Woe*
be unto the world; And lastly, that mischievous word, *A scandalis,*
100 *Woe bee unto the world because of scandals,* of offences. Each of

these three words wil receive a twofold consideration; for the first, *Væ*, is first *Vox dolentis,* a voice of condoling and lamenting, Christ laments the miseries imminent upon the world, *because of scandals,* and then it is *Vox minantis,* a voice of threatning, and intermination, Christ threatens, he interminates heavy judgements upon them, who occasion and induce these miseries by these scandals; This one *Væ* denotes both these; sorrow, and yet infallibility; They always go together in God; God is loath to doe it, and yet God will certainly inflict these judgements. The second word, *Mundo, Woe be unto the*
110 *world,* lookes two ways too; *Væ malis,* woe unto evill men that raise scandals, *væ bonis,* woe unto them who are otherwise good in themselves, if they be so various, as to be easily shaked and seduced by scandals. And then upon the last word *A scandalis, Woe be unto the world, because of scandals,* of *offences,* wee must look two ways also; first, as it denotes *Scandalum activum,* a scandall given by another, and then, as it denotes *Scandalum passivum,* a scandal taken by another.

First then, our first word, in the first acceptation thereof, is *Væ*   1 Part
dolentis, the voice of condoling and lamentation; God laments the
120 necessity that he is reduced to, and those judgements which the sinnes of men have made inevitable. In the person of the Prophets which denounced the judgements of God, it is expressed so, *Onus Baby-*   [Isa. 13.1;
lonis, Onus Egypti, Onus Damasci; O the burthen of Damascus, the   19.1; 17.1]
burthen of Egypt, the burthen of Babylon; And not only so, but
Onus visionis, Not onely that that judgment would be a heavy bur-   [Isa. 22.1]
then, when it fell upon that Nation, but that the very pre-contemplation, and pre-denunciation of that judgement upon that people, was a burthen and a distastfull bitternesse, to the Prophet himself, that was sent upon that message. In reading of an *Act of Parliament,* or
130 of any Law that inflicts the heaviest punishment that can be imagined upon a delinquent, and transgressour of that Law, a man is not often much affected, because hee needs not, when he does but read that law, consider that any particular man is fallen under the penalty, and bitternesse thereof. But if upon evidence and verdict he be put to give judgement upon a particular man that stands before him, at the bar, according to that Law, That that man that stands there that day, must that day be no man; that that breath breathed in by God, to

glorify him, must be suffocated and strangled with a halter, or evaporated with an Axe, he must be hanged or beheaded, that those limbs
[140] which make up a Cabinet for that precious Jewell, the image of God,
to be kept in, must be cut into quarters, or torne with horses; that that
body which is a consecrated Temple of the Holy Ghost, must be
chained to a stake, and burnt to ashes, hee that is not affected in
giving such a judgment, upon such a man, hath no part in the bowels
of Christ Jesus, that melt in compassion, when our sinnes draw and
extort his Judgements upon us in the mouth of those Prophets, those
men whom God sends, it is so, and it is so in the mouth of God himself that sends them. *Heu vindicabor,* (says God) *Alas, I will revenge
mee of mine enemies; Alas, I will,* is *Alas, I must,* his glory compels
[150] him to doe it, the good of his Church, and the sustentation of his
Saints compell him to it, and yet he comes to it with a condolency,
with a compassion, *Heu vindicabor, Alas, I will revenge mee of mine
enemies:* so also in another Prophet, *Heu abominationes, Alas for all
the evill abominations of the house of Israel;* for (as it is added there)
they shall fall, (that is, *they will fall*) by the *sword,* by *famine,* by
pestilence, and (as it follows) *I will accomplish my fury upon them;*
Though it were come to that height, fury, and accomplishment, consummation of fury, yet it comes with a condolency, and compassion,
*Heu abominationes, Alas for all the evill abominations of the house
[160] of Israel,* I would they were not so ill, that I might be better to them.
Men sent by God do so, so does God that sends those men, and he
that is both God and man, Christ Jesus does so too: We have but two
clear records in the Scriptures of Christs weeping, and both in compassion for others; when *Mary* wept for her dead brother *Lazarus,*
and the Jews that were with her wept too, *Jesus also wept, and he
groan'd in the spirit, and was troubled.* This was but for the discomfort of one family, (it was not a mortality over the whole
Country) It was but for one person in that family, (it was not a
contagion that had swept, or did threaten the whole house) it was
[170] but for such a person in that family, as he meant forthwith to restore
to life again, and yet *Iesus wept,* and *groaned in the Spirit, & was
trobled;* he would not lose that opportunity of shewing his tendernesse, and compassion in the behalf of others. How vehement, how
passionate then, must we beleeve his other weeping to have been,

Esa. 1.24

Ezech. 6.11

Ioh. 11.33

when hee had his glorious and beloved City Jerusalem in his sight, Luke 19.41
and wept over that City, and with that stream of tears powred out that
Sea, that tempestuous Sea, those heavy judgements, which, (though
he wept in doing it) he denounced upon that City, that glorious, that
beloved City, which City (though Christ charge, to have stoned them Mat. 23.34
180 that were sent to her, and to bee guilty of all the righteous blood shed
upon the earth) the holy Ghost cals the holy City for all that, not
onely at the beginning of Christs appearance, (*The Devill took him* 4.5
up into the holy City) (for at that time she was not the unholyer for
any thing that shee had done upon the person of Christ,) but when
they had exercised all their cruelty, even to death, the death of the
Crosse upon Christ himselfe, the Holy Ghost calls still the holy City; Mat. 27.53
Many bodies of Saints, which slept, arose, and went into the *holy*
City. When the Fathers take into their contemplation and discourse,
that passionate exclamation of our Saviour upon the Crosse, *My God,* [Mat.
190 *my God, why hast thou forsaken me?* those blessed Fathers, that 27.46]
never thought of any such sense of that place, that Christ was, at that
time, actually in the *reall torments of hell,* assign no fitter sense of
those words, then that the foresight of those insupportable, and inevitable, and imminent judgements upon his City, and his people,
occasioned that passionate exclamation, *My God, my God, why hast*
thou forsaken me? That as, after he was ascended into heaven, he said
to *Saul, Cur me persequeris?* He called *Sauls* persecuting of his Acts 9.4
Church, a persecuting of him, so when hee considered that God had
forsaken his people, his Citie, his Jerusalem, he cryed out, that God
200 had forsaken him. God that sent the Prophets; the Prophets that were
sent; Christ who was both, the person sent, and the sender, came to
the inflicting and denouncing of judgements, with this *Væ dolentis,*
a heart, and voice of condoling and lamentation.

Grieve not then the holy Spirit of God, says the Apostle; extort not Eph. 4.30
from him those Judgements, which he cannot in justice forbear, and
yet is grieved to inflict. How often doe we use that motive, to divert
young men from some ill actions, and ill courses, How will this
trouble your friends, how will this grieve your Mother, this will kill
your Father? The Angels of heaven who are of a friendship and
210 family with us, as they rejoyce at our conversion, so are they sorry
and troubled at our aversion from God. Our sins have grieved our

Mother; that is, made the Church ashamed, and blush that she hath washed us, and clothed us, in the whitenesse and innocency of Christ Jesus in our baptisme, and given us his bloud to drinke in the other Sacrament. Our sins have made our mother the Church ashamed in her selfe, (we have scandalized and offended the Congregation) and our sinnes have defamed and dishonoured our mother abroad, that is, imprinted an opinion in others, that that cannot be a good Church, in which we live so dissolutely, so falsely to our first faith, and contract,
220 and stipulation with God in Baptisme. Wee have grieved our brethren, the Angels, our mother, the Church, and we have killed our *Father: God is the father of us all;* and we have killed him; for *God hath purchased a Church with his bloud,* says Saint *Paul.* And, oh, how much more is God grieved now, that we will make no benefit of that bloud which is shed for us, then he was for the very shedding of that bloud! We take it not so ill, (pardon so low a comparison in so high a mystery; for, since our blessed Saviour was pleased to assume that metaphor, and to call his passion a *Cup,* and his death a *drinking,* we may be admitted to that Comparison of drinking too)
230 we take it not so ill, that a man go down into our Cellar, and draw, and drinke his fill, as that he goe in, and pierce the vessells, and let them runne out, in a wastfull wantonnesse. To satisfie the thirst of our soules, there was a necessity that the bloud of Christ Jesus, should be shed; To satisfie Christs own *sitio,* that thirst which was upon him, when he was upon the Crosse, there was a necessity too, that Christ should bleed to death. On our part there was an absolute and a primary necessity; God in his justice requiring a satisfaction, nothing could redeem us, by way of satisfaction, but the bloud of his Sonne. And though there were never act more voluntary, more spontaneous,
240 then Christs dying for man, nor freer from all coaction, and necessity of that kind, yet after Christ had submitted himselfe to that *Decree* and *contract* that passed between him, and his Father, that he, by shedding his bloud, should redeem Mankind, there lay a necessity upon Christ himselfe to shed his bloud, as himselfe says first to his Disciples that went with him to *Emaus, Nonne oportuit,* ought not Christ to suffer all these things? do ye not find by the prophets that he was bound to do it? and then to his Apostles at *Jerusalem, Sic oportuit, Thus it behoved Christ to suffer.* There was then an absolute

Mal. 2.10
Act. 20.28

Mat. 20.22

[Joh. 19.28]

Luke 24.26

verse 46

necessity upon us, an obedientiall necessity upon Christ, that his
²⁵⁰ bloud must be shed; But to let him dye in a wantonnesse, to let out
all that precious liquor, and taste no drop of it, to draw out all that
immaculate and unvaluable bloud, and make no *balsamum,* no antidote, no plaister, no fomentation in the application of that bloud, to
labour still under a burning fever of lust, and ambition, and presumption, and finde no cooling *julips* there, in the application of that bloud,
to labour under a cold damp of indevotion, and under heartlesse
desperation, and find no warming *Cordialls* there, to be still as farre
under judgements and executions for sinne, as if there had been no
Messias sent, no ransome given, no satisfaction made, not to apply
²⁶⁰ this bloud thus shed for us, by those meanes which God in his Church
presents to us, this puts Christ to his wofull Interjection, to cast out
this *wo* upon us, (which he had rather have left out) *wo be unto the*
world, which, though it begin in a *væ dolentis,* a voice of condoling
and lamenting, yet it is also *væ minantis,* a voice of threatning, and
intermination, denoting the infallibility of Judgements, and that's
our next consideration.

    I thinke we find no words in Christs mouth so often, as *væ,* and
Amen. Each of them hath two significations; as almost all Christs
words, and actions have; consolation, and commination. For, as this
²⁷⁰ *væ* signifies (as before) a sorrow, (wo, that is, *wo is me,* for this *will*
fall upon you) and signifies also a Judgment inevitable and infallible,
(wo, that is, *wo be unto you,* for this Judgement *shall* fall upon you)
so *Amen* is sometimes *vox Asserentis,* and signifies *verè,* verily, *Verily*
I say unto you, when Christ would confirm, and establish a beleefe in
some doctrine, or promise of his, (as when he says *Amen, Amen,*
verily verily I say unto you, he that beleeveth on me, the works that
I doe, shall he doe also, and greater works then these shall he doe)
so it is *vox Asserentis,* a word of assertion, and it is also *vox Deserentis,*
a word of desertion, when God denounces an infallibility, an un-
²⁸⁰ avoydablenesse, an inevitablenesse in his judgements, *Amen dico,*
verily I say unto thee, thou shalt by no meanes come out thence till
thou hast paid the uttermost farthing; so this *Amen* signifies *Fiat,* this
shall certainly be thus done. And this seale, this Amen, as Amen is
Fiat, is always set to his *væ,* as his *væ* is *vox minantis;* whensoever
God threatens any Judgement, he meanes to execute that Judgement

Væ
minantis

Iohn 14.12

Mat. 5.26

as farre as he threatens it; God threatens nothing *in terrorem* onely, onely to frighten us; every *væ* hath his *Amen,* every Judgement denounced, a purpose of execution. This then is our wofull case; every man may find upon record, in the Scriptures, a *væ* denounced upon 290 that sinne, which he knows to be his sinne; and if there be a *væ,* there is an *Amen* too, if God have said it shall, it shall be executed, so that this is not an execution of a few condemned persons, but a Massacre of all: It is not a *Decimation,* as in a rebellion, to spare nine, and hang the tenth, but it is a washing, a sweeping away of all: every man may find a Judgement upon record against him. It doth not acquit him that he hath not committed an *adultery;* and yet, is he sure of that? He may have done that in a *looke,* in a *letter,* in a *word,* in a *wish:* It doth not acquit him, that he hath not done a *murder;* and yet, is he sure of that? He may have killed a man, in not defend- 300 ing him from the oppression of another, if he have power in his hand, and he may have killed in not relieving, if he have a plentifull fortune. He may have killed in not reprehending him who was under his charge, when he saw him kil himself in the sinful ways of death.

Ardoinus   As they that write of Poysons, and of those creatures that naturally maligne and would destroy man, do name the *Flea,* as well as the *Viper,* because the Flea sucks as much bloud as he can, so that man is a murderer that stabs as deep as he can, though it be but with his tongue, with his pen, with his frowne; for a man may kill with a frowne, in withdrawing his countenance from that man, that lives 310 upon so low a pasture as his countenance, nay he may kill with a smile, with a good looke, if he afford that good looke with a purpose to delude him. And, beloved, how many dye of this disease; how many dye laughing, dye of a tickling; how many are overjoyed with the good looks, and with the familiarity of greater persons then themselves, and led on by hopes of getting more, wast that they have? An adultery, a murder may be done in a *dreame,* if that dreame were an effect of a murderous, or an adulterous thought conceived

1 Cor. 4.4   before. The Apostle says, *I know nothing by my selfe, yet am I not thereby justified,* we sinne some sinnes, that all the world sees, and 320 yet we see not, but then, how many more, which none in the world sees but our selves? Scarce any man scapes all degrees of any sinne; scarce any man some great degree of some great sinne; no man

escapes so, but that he may find upon record, in the Scriptures, a *væ,* and an *Amen,* a Judgment denounced, and an execution sealed against him. And, if that be our case, where is there any roome for this milder signification of these two words, *væ,* and *Amen,* which we spoke of before, as they are words of *Consolation?* If because God hath said *Stipendium peccati mors est, the wages of sinne is death,* because I have sinned, I must dye, what can I doe in a *Prayer?* can

330 I flatter God? what can I doe in an *Almes?* Can I bribe God, or frustrate his purpose? Can I put an *Euge* upon his *væ,* a *vacat* upon his *Fiat,* a *Non obstante* upon his *Amen?* God is not man; not a false man that he can lie, nor a weake man that he can repent. Where then is the restorative, the consolatory nature of these words? In this, beloved, consists our comfort, that all Gods *væ's* and *Amens,* all judgments, and all his executions are *Conditionall;* There is a *Crede & vives,* Beleeve and thou shalt live; there is a *Fac hoc & vives,* doe this and thou shalt live; If thou have done otherwise, there is a *Converte & vives,* turne unto the Lord and thou shalt live; If thou have done so,

340 and fallen off, there is a *Revertere & vives,* returne againe unto the Lord, and thou shalt live. How heavy so ever any of Gods judgements be, yet there is always roome for *Davids* question, *Quis scit,* who can tell whether God will be gracious unto mee? What better assurance could one have, then *David* had? The Prophet *Nathan* had told *David* immediately from the mouth of God, *this child shall surely dye,* and ratified it by that reason, *because thou hast given occasion to the enemies of the Lord to blaspheme,* this child shall surely dye, yet *David* fasted, and wept, and said, *who can tell whether the Lord will be gratious unto me, that the child may live?* There is always

350 roome for *Davids* question, *Quis scit, who can tell?* Nay there is no roome for it, as it is a question of diffidence and distrust; every man may and must know, that whatsoever any Prophet have denounced against any sinne of his, yet there are conditions, upon which the Lord will be gracious and thy soule shall live. But if the first condition, that is *Innocency,* and the second, that is *Repentance,* be rebelliously broken, then every man hath his *væ,* and every *væ* hath his *Amen,* the judgements are denounced against him; and upon him they shall bee executed; for God threatens not to fright children; but the Mountains melt, and Powers, and Thrones, and Principalities

[Rom. 6.23]

[Num. 23.19]

[Luke 10.28]

[Ezek. 18.32]
2 Sam. 12.22

³⁶⁰ tremble at his threatning. And so have you the doubled signification of the first word *væ*, as it is *vox Dolentis*, and as it is *Vox minantis*, God is loath, but God will infallibly execute his judgement, and we proceed to the extension of this *væ*, over all, *væ mundo*, woe unto the world, and the double signification of that word.

I have wondred sometimes that that great Author, and Bishop in the Roman Church, *Abulensis*, is so free, as to confesse that some Expositors amongst them, have taken this word in our Text, *Mundo, adjectivè,* not to signify the world, but a clean person, a free man, that it should be *væ immuni,* woe unto him that is free from offences, that ³⁷⁰ hath had no offences; perchance they mean from crosses. And so, though it be a most absurd, and illiterate, and ungrammaticall construction of the place that they make, yet there is a doctrine to bee raised from thence, of good use. As God brought light out of darknesse, and raises glory out of sin, so we may raise good Divinity out of their ill Grammar; for *væ mundo,* indeed, *væ immuni,* woe be unto him that hath had no crosses. There cannot be so great a crosse as to have none. I lack one loaf of that dayly bread that I pray for, if I have no crosse; for afflictions are our spirituall nourishment; I lacke one limb of that body I must grow into, which is the body of ³⁸⁰ Christ Jesus, if I have no crosses; for, my conformity to Christ, (and that's my being made up into his body) must be accomplished in my

fulfilling his sufferings in his flesh. So that, though our adversaries out of their ignorance mislead us in a wrong sense of the place; the Holy Ghost leads us into a true, and right use thereof. But there is another good use of their error too, another good doctrine out of their ill Grammar; Take the word *mundo, adjectivè,* for an adjective, and *væ mundo, væ immuni,* wo unto him that is so free from all offences, as to take offence at nothing; to be indifferent to any thing, to any Religion, to any Discipline, to any form of Gods service; That from ³⁹⁰ a glorious Masse to a sordid *Conventicle,* all's one to him; all one to him, whether that religion, in which they meet, and light candles at Noon; or that, in which they meet, and put out candles at midnight; what innovations, what alterations, what tolerations of false, what extirpations of true Religion soever come, it shall never trouble, never offend him; 'Tis true, *Væ mundo* indeed, wo unto him that is so free, so unsensible, so unaffected with any thing in this kinde; for, as to

bee too inquisitive into the proceedings of the State, and the Church, out of a jealousie and suspicion that any such alterations, or tolerations in Religion are intended or prepared, is a seditious disaffection
⁴⁰⁰ to the government, and a disloyall aspersion upon the persons of our Superiours, to suspect without cause, so, not to be sensible that the Catterpillars of the Roman Church, doe eat up our tender fruit, that the Jesuites, and other enginiers of that Church, doe seduce our forwardest and best spirits, not to be watchfull in our own families, that our wives and children and servants be not corrupted by them, for the *Pastor* to slacken in his duty, (not to be earnest in the Pulpit) for the Magistrate to slacken in his, (not to be vigilant in the execution of those Laws as are left in his power) *væ mundo, væ immuni,* woe unto him that is unsensible of offences. Jealously, suspiciously to
⁴¹⁰ mis-interpret the actions of our Superiours, is inexcusable, but so is it also not to feel how the adversary gains upon us, and not to wish that it were, and not to pray that is may be otherwise; *væ mundo, væ immuni,* wo to him that is un-offended, unsensible, thus. But as I have wondred that that Bishop would so easily confesse, that some of their Expositors were so very unlearned, so barbarously ignorant, so enormously stupid, as to take this *væ mundo adjectivè,* so doe I wonder more, that after such confessions, and acknowledgements of such ignorances and stupidities amongst them, they will not remedy it in the cause, but still continue so rigid, so severe in the maintenance
⁴²⁰ of their own Translation, their Vulgate Edition, as in places, and cases of doubt, not to admit recourse to the Originall, as to the Supreme Judge, nor to other Translations: for, by either of those ways, it would have appeared, that this *væ mundo* could not be taken *adjectivè,* but is a cloud cast upon the whole world, a woe upon all, no place, no person, no calling free from these scandals, and offences, from tentations, and tribulations; when there was a *væ Sodom,* that God raigned fire and brimstone upon *Sodom,* yet there was a *Zoar,* were Lot might be safe. When there was a *væ Ægypto,* wo and wo upon wo upon Egypt, there was a *Goshen,* a Sanctuary for the chil-
⁴³⁰ dren of God in Egypt. When there is a *væ inhabitantibus,* a persecution in any place, there is a *Fuge in aliam,* leave to fly into another City. But in such an extension, such an expansion, such an exaltation, such an inundation of woe, as this in our text, *Væ mundo,* woe to the

Gen. 19.
[23, 24]
[Exod.
9.26]
[Mat.
10.23]

world, to all the world, a tide, a flood without any ebbe, a Sea without any shoare, a darke skie without any Horizon; That though I doe withdraw my selfe from the wofull uncertainties, and irresolutions and indeterminations of the Court, and from the snares and circumventions of the City; Though I would devest, and shake off the woes and offences of Europe in Afrique, or of Asia in America, I cannot, 440 since wheresoever, or howsoever I live, these woes, and scandals, and offences, tentations, and tribulations will pursue mee, who can expresse the wretched condition, the miserable station, and prostration of man in this world? *væ mundo.*

Ioh. 17.9

Take the word, *World,* in as ill a sense as you will, as ill as when Christ says, *I pray not for the world,* (and they are very ill, for whom Christ Jesus who prayed for them that crucifyed him, would not pray:) Take the word *world,* in as good a sense as you will, as good as when Christ says, *I give my flesh for the life of the world,* (and they are very good that are elemented, made up with his flesh, and 450 alimented and nursed with his blood:) Take it for the *Elect,* take it for the *Reprobate,* the Reprobate and the Elect too are under this *væ,* wo to the world, from tentations, and tribulations, scandals, and offences.

6.51

1 Ioh. 2.18

So it is if the world be *persons,* and it is so also, if it be *times;* Take the world for the times wee live in *now,* and it is *Novissima hora,* this is the last time, and the Apostle hath told us, that the last times are the worst. Take the world for the *Old* world, *Originalis mundus,* as *Saint Peter* call's it; the *Originall world,* of which, this world, since the flood, is but a copy, and God spared not the Old world, says that 460 Apostle. Take it for an elder world then that, the world in Paradise, when one *Adam,* the Son of God, and one *Eve* produced by God, from him, made up the world: or take it for an elder world then that, the world in heaven, when onely the Angels, and no other creatures made up the world; Take it any of these ways, we in this latter world do, *Noah* in the old world did, so did *Adam* in the world in Paradise, and so did the Angels in the oldest world of all, find these *woes* from offences, and scandals, tentations, and tribulations.

2 [Pet.] 2.5

So it is in all persons, in all men, so it is in all times, in all ages, and so it is in all places too; for hee that retires into a Monastery upon 470 pretence of avoiding tentations, and offences in this world, he brings

them thither, and he meets them there; Hee sees them *intramittendo,* and *extramittendo,* he is scandalized by others, and others are scandalized by him. That part of the world that sweats in continuall labour in severall vocations, is scandalized with their laziness, and their riches, to see them anoint themselves with other mens sweat, and lard themselves with other mens fat; and then these retired and cloistrall men are scandalized with all the world, that is out of their walls. There is no sort of men more exercised with contentious and scandalous wranglings, then they are: for, first, with all eager ani-
480 mosity they prefer their Monasticall life before all other secular callings, yea, before those Priests, whom they call *Secular Priests,* such as have care of souls, in particular parishes, (as though it were a Diminution, and an inferiour state to have *care of souls,* and study and labour the salvation of others.) And then as they undervalue all secular callings, (Mechaniques, and Merchants, and Magistrates too) in respect of any *Regular order,* (as they call them) so with the same animosity doe they prefer their own Order, before any other Order. A Carthusian is but a man of fish, for one Element, to dwell still in a Pond, in his Cell alone, but a Jesuit is a usefull *ubiquitary,* and his
490 Scene is the Court, as well as the Cloister. And howsoever they pretend to bee gone out of the world, they are never the farther from the Exchange for all their Cloister; they buy, and sell, and purchase in their Cloister. They are never the farther from *Westminster* in their Cloister, they occasion and they maintain suits from their Cloister; and there are the Courts of Justice noted to abound most with suits, where Monasteries abound most. Nay, they are never the farther from the field for all their Cloister; for they give occasions of *armies,* they raise armies, they direct armies, they pay armies from their Cloister. Men should not retire from the mutuall duties of this world, to avoid
500 offences, tentations, tribulations, neither doe they at all avoid them, that retire thus, upon that pretence.

Shall we say then, as the Disciples said to Christ; *If the case of the man be so with his wife, it is not good to mary?* If the world be nothing but a bed of Adders, a quiver of poysoned arrows, from every person, every time, every place, woes by occasion of offences, and scandals, it had been better God had made no world, better that I had never been born into the world, better, if by any meanes I could get

Mat. 19.10

out of the world quickly, shall we say so? God forbid. As long as *Job*
charged not God foolishly, it is said, *in all this Job sinned not;* but
when he came to curse his birth, and to loath his life, then *Job*
charged God foolishly. When one Prophet (*Eliah*) comes to proportion God the measure of his corrections, *Satis est, Lord, this is enough;*
Thou hast done enough, I have suffered enough, now take away my
life. When another Prophet comes to wish his own death in anger,
and to justify his anger, and dispute it out with God himselfe, for not
proceeding with the *Ninivites,* as he would have had him doe; nay
for the withering of his gourd that shadowed him, in all these, they
did, in all such, we doe charge God foolishly; And shall we that are
but wormes, but *silke-wormes,* but *glow-wormes* at best, chide God
that hee hath made *slow-wormes,* and other venimous creeping
things? shall we that are nothing but boxes of poyson in our selves,
reprove God for making Toads and Spiders in the world? shall we
that are all discord, quarrell the harmony of his Creation, or his
providence? Can an Apothecary make a Soveraign triacle of Vipers,
and other poysons, and cannot God admit offences, and scandals
into his physick? scandals, and offences, tentations, and tribulations,
are our leaven that ferment us, and our lees that preserve us. Use them
to Gods glory, and to thine own establishing, and then thou shall be a
particular exception to that generall Rule, the *Væ mundo à scandalis,*
shall be an *Euge tibi à scandalis,* thou shalt see that it was well for
thee, that there were scandals and offences in the world, for they shall
have exercised thy patience, they shall have occasioned thy victory,
they shall have assured thy triumph.

[Job] 1.22

1 Reg. 19.4

Ion.
4.[3–11]

Number 7.

Preached at Lincolns Inne.
The Second Sermon on Matth. 18.7.

WO UNTO THE WORLD, BECAUSE OF OFFENCES.

WEE HAVE seen in the first word the *væ,* as it is *vox Dolentis,* the voice of condoling and lamenting, that it is accompanyed with a *Heu;* Gods judgments come against his will, he had rather they might be forborn, he had rather those easie conditions had been performed; And as it is *vox minantis,* a voice of threatning and intermination, it is accompanyed with an *Amen;* if conditions be rebelliously broken, Gods judgements doe come infallibly, inevitably; And we have seen in the second word, *væ mundo,* and the twofold signification of that, that these offences, and scandals fall upon
10 all the world; the wicked embrace tentations, and are glad of them, and sorry when they are but weak; the godly meet tentations, and wrastle with them, and sometimes doe overcome them, and are sometimes overcome by them; but all have them, and yet we must not break out of the world by a retired life, nor break out of the world by a violent death, but take Gods ways, and stay Gods leasure. In this our third part, we are to consider the *root* from which this overspreading *væ,* this woe proceeds, *A scandalis,* from scandals, from offences, and the double signification of that word, first, *Scandalum activum,* the active scandall, which is a malice, or at least an indiscre-
20 tion in *giving* offence, and *Scandalum passivum,* the passive scandall, which is a forwardnesse, at least an easinesse in taking offence; To know the nature of the thing, look we to the derivation, the extraction, the Origination of the word. The word from which scandall is derived (*scazein*) signifies *claudicare,* to halt; and thence, a scandall

is any trap, or Engin, any occasion of stumbling, and laming, hid in the way that I must goe, by another person; and as it is transferred to a spirituall use, appropriated to an Ecclesiasticall sense, it is an occasion of sinning. It hath many branches; too many to bee so much as named; but some fruits from some of them we shall gather, and

Activum   30 present you. First, in our first, the Active Scandall, to doe any thing that is naturally ill, formally sin, whereby another may be occasioned or encouraged by my example to do the like, this is the active scandall most evidently, and most directly, and this is *morbus complicatus,* a disease that carries another disease in it, a fever exalted to a frenzy; It is *Peccatum prægnans, peccatum gravidum,* a spauning sin, a sin of multiplication, to sinne purposely, to lead another into tentation. But there is a lesse degree then this, and it is an active scandall too; To doe any thing that in it selfe is *indifferent,* (and so no sin in mee, that do it) in the sight of another that thinks it not indifferent, but un-
40 lawfull, and yet because he hath a reall, or a reverentiall dependence upon me, (my Son, my Servant, my Tenant) and thinks I would be displeased if he did it not, does it against his conscience by my example, though the sinne be formally his, radically it is mine, because I gave the occasion; And there is a lower degree then this, and yet is an active scandall. If I doe an indifferent thing in the sight and knowledge of another, that thinks it unlawfull, though he doe not come to doe it, out of my example, by any dependence upon me, yet if he come to think uncharitably of me, or to condemn me for doing it, though this uncharitablenesse in him bee his sinne, yet the root
50 grew in me, and I gave the scandall. And there is a lower degree then this, and yet is an Active scandall too. *Origen* hath expressed it thus, *Scandalum est quo scandentium pedes offenduntur;* To hinder the feet of another, that would goe farther, or climbe higher in the ways of godlinesse, but for me; to say to any man, What need you be so pure, so devout, so godly, so zealous, will this make you rich, will this bring you to preferment? this is an active scandall in me, though hee that I speak to, be not damnified by me. Of which kind of scandall, there is an evident, and an illustrious example, between

Mat. 16.23   Saint *Peter* and Christ; Christ cals *Peter* a scandall unto him; when
60 *Peter* rebuked Christ for offering to goe up to Jerusalem in a time of danger. Christ was to accomplish the work of our salvation at Jeru-

salem, by dying, and *Peter* disswades, discounsels that journey; and
for this, Christ lays that heavy name upon his indiscreet zeal, and that
heavy name upon his person, *Vade retro,* Get thee behind me Satan,
thou art a scandall unto me. This is *Scandalum oppositionis,* the
scandall of opposing, disswading, discounselling, discountenancing,
and consequently the frustrating of Gods purpose in man; This is but
by word, and yet there is a lesse then this, which is *Scandalum timoris,*
when he that hath power in his hand, in a family, in a parish, in a
70 City, in a Court, intimidates them who depend upon him, (though
nothing bee expressely done or said that way) and so slackens them
in their religious duties to God; and in their constancy in Religion it
selfe; And *væ illis,* woe unto them that doe so, and *væ mundo ab
illis;* woe unto the world, because there are so many that doe so. And
yet there is another scandall which seems lesse then this, *Scandalum
amoris,* the scandall of love; as *Saul* gave *David* his daughter *Michol,*   1 Sam. 18.21
ut esset ei in scandalum, that she might be a snare unto him; that is,
that *David* being over-uxorious, and over-indulgent to his wife, might
thereby lye the more open to *Sauls* mischievous purposes upon him,
80 and *væ illis,* woe unto them that doe so; and *væ mundo ab illis,* woe
unto the world, because there are so many that doe so, that study the
affections, and dispositions, and inclinations of men, and then,
minister those things to them, that affect them most, which is the way
of the instruments of the Roman Church, to promise preferments to
discontented persons, and is indeed, his way, whose instrument the
Roman Church is, *The Devill;* for this is all that the Devill is able to
doe, in the ways of tentation, *Applicare passivis activa,* To finde out
what will work upon a man, and to work by that. The Devill did not
create me, nor bring materials to my creation; The Devill did not
90 infuse into mee, that choler, that makes me ignorantly and indis-
creetly zealous, nor that flegm that choakes mee with a stupid indevotion; Hee did not infuse into mee that bloud, that inflames mee in
licentiousnesse, nor that melancholy that dampes me in a jealousie
and suspicion, a diffidence and distrust in God. The Devill had no
hand in composing me in my constitution. But the Devill knows,
which of these govern, and prevail in me, and ministers such tentations, as are most acceptable to me, and this is *Scandalum amoris,* the
scandall of Love.

So have ye then the Name, and Nature, and extent of the Active
[100] Scandall; against which, the inhibition given in this Text is generall,
wee are forbidden to scandalize any person by any of these ways, The
scandall of Example, or the scandall of Perswasion, The scandall of
Fear, or the scandall of Love. For, there is scarce any so free to himselfe, so entirely his own, so independent upon others, but that
Example, or Perswasion, or Fear, or Love may scandalize him, that
is, *Lead him into tentation,* and make him doe some things against
his own mind. Our Saviour Christ had spoken, *De pusillis,* of little
children, of weak persons, easie to be scandalized, before this Text,
and he returns, *ad pusillos,* to the consideration of little children, per-

ver. 10   [110] sons easie to bee scandalized again; this Text is not of *them,* or not of
them onely, but of *all;* say not thou of any man, *ætatem habet,* he is
old enough, let him look to himselfe, he hath reason as other men
have, he hath had a learned and a religious education, ill example can
doe him no harm; but give no ill example to any, study the setling,
and the establishing of all; for, scarce is there any so strong, but may
bee shaked by some of these scandals, Example, Perswasion, Fear, or
Love. And hee that employs his gift of wit, and Counsell to seduce
and mislead men, or his gift of Power, and Authority to intimidate,
and affright men, or his gift of other graces, lovelinesse of person,
[120] agreeablenesse of Conversation, powerfulnesse of speech, to ensnare
and entangle men by any of these scandals, may draw others into
perdition, but he falls also with them, and shall not be left out by
God in the punishments inflicted upon them that fall by his occasion.

The Commandement is generall, scandalize none, scarce any but
may bee overthrown, by some of these ways; And then the Apostles

2 Cor. 6.3   practise was generall too, we give no occasion of offence in *any thing.*
As he requires that wee should eat and drinke to the glory of God, so

1 Cor. 10.31   hee would have us study to avoid scandalizing of others, even in our

8.13   eating and drinking; *If meat make my brother to offend,* (offend
[130] either in eating against his own conscience, or offend in an uncharitable mis-interpretation of my eating) *In æternum,* says the Apostle

Rom. 14.15   there, *I will eat no flesh while the world standeth;* Nor, *destroy my
brother with my meat, for whom Christ dyed.* That's the Apostles
tendernesse in things; (He would give no occasion of offence in *any
thing*) And it is as generall in contemplation of persons, he would

1 Cor. 10.32

have no offence given, neither to the *Iew,* nor to the *Grecian,* nor to
the Church of God: He was as carefull not to scandalize, not to give
just occasion of offence to Jew, nor Gentile, as not to the Church of
God; so must we be towards them of a superstitious religion amongst
140 us, as carefull as towards one another, not to give any scandall, any
just cause of offence. But what is to be called a just cause of offence
towards those men? Good ends, and good ways, plain, and direct,
and manifest proceedings, these can be called no scandall, no just
cause of offence, to Jew, nor Gentile, to Turk, nor Papist; nor does
Saint *Paul* intend that we should forbear essentiall and necessary
things, for fear of displeasing perverse and peevish men. To maintain
the *doctrinall truths* of our religion, by conferences, by disputations,
by writing, by preaching. to avow, and to prove our religion to be
the same, that Christ Jesus and his Apostles proposed at beginning,
150 the same that the generall Councels established after, the same that
the blessed Fathers of those times, unanimely, and dogmatically delivered, the same that those glorious Martyrs quickned by their death,
and carryed over all the world in the rivers, in the seas of their blood,
to avow our religion by writing, and preaching, to be the same religion, and then to preserve and protect that religion which God hath
put into our hearts, by all such meanes as hee hath put into our hands,
in the due execution of *just Laws;* this is no scandall, no just cause
of offence to Jew nor Gentile, Turke nor Papists. But when leaving
fundamentall things, and necessary truths, we wrangle uncharitably
160 about Collaterall impertinencies, when wee will refuse to doe such
things as conduce to the exaltation of Devotion, or to the order, and
peace of the Church, not for any harme in the things, but onely therefore because the Papists doe them, when, because they kneel in the
worship of the bread in the Sacrament, wee will not kneel in *Thanksgiving* to God for the Sacrament; when because they pray to Saints,
we will reproach the Saints, or not *name* the Saints, when because
they abuse the Crosse, we will abhor the Crosse; This is that that
Saint *Paul* protests against, and in that protestation Catechizes us, that
as he would give no just occasion of offence to the true Church of
170 God, so neither would hee doe it to a false or infirme Church. He
would not scandalize the true Church of God, by any modifications,
any inclinations towards the false; nor hee would not scandalize the

false and infirme Church, by refusing to communicate with them, in the practise of such things, as might exalt our Devotion, and did not endanger nor shake any foundation of religion: which was the wisdome of our Church, in the beginning of the Reformation, when the *Injunctions* of our Princes forbad us to call one another by the odious names of *Papist,* or *Pápisticall Heretique,* or *Schismatique,* or *Sacramentary,* or such *convitious* (as the word of the Injunction is) and
180 *reproachfull names;* but cleaving always intirely, and inseparably to the fundamentall truths of our own religion, as farre as it is possible

[Rom.
12.18]

we should *live peaceably with all men.* Saint *Paul* would give no offence to the true Church of God, he would not *prevaricate,* nor to the Jew nor Gentile neither, he would not *exasperate.* And this may bee enough to have been said of the *active scandall;* and passe we now, in our order, to the *Passive.*

Passivum

It is no wonder to see them who put all the world, into differences, (the Jesuits) to differ sometimes amongst themselves. And therefore though the Jesuit *Maldonat* say of this Text, That Christ did not here
190 intend to warne, or to arm his Disciples against scandals, as scandals are occasions of sin, but onely from offering injury to one another, That scandall in this text is nothing but *wrong,* yet another Jesuit, (*Vincentius Rhegius*) is not onely of another opinion himselfe, but thinks that opinion (as he calls it) absurd; It is absurd, says he, to interpret it so; for, can a mans own hand or foot, or eye, be said to injure him? And yet, in this place, they are often said to scandalize him, to offend him. The interpretation that *Maldonat* departs from, himselfe acknowledges to be the interpretation of Saint *Chrysostome,* of *Euthymius,* of *Theophylact,* of others of the Fathers; and, by the
200 councell of Trent, he is bound to interpret Scriptures according to the Fathers; and he is angry with us, if at any time we doe not so; and here he departs from them, where, not onely his reverence to them, but the frame, and the evidence of the place should have kept them to him; for here Christ utters his *væ,* as it is *væ Dolentis,* as he laments their miseries, and as it is *væ Minantis,* as he threatens his judgements, not onely upon them that offend and scandalize others, but upon them also that are easily scandalized by others, and put from their religion, and Christian constancy with every rumour. *Parum*

Hierom.

distat scandalizare, & scandalizari; It is almost as great a sin to be

²¹⁰ shaked by a scandall given, as to give it. Christ intends both in this Text; the *Active,* and the *Passive* scandall; but the latter, *melius quadrat,* says a later Divine, worthy to be compared to the *Ancients,* for the exposition of Scriptures, it fits the scope and purpose of Christ best, to accept and interpret this *væ,* (*Woe be unto the world*) of the *Passive* scandall, the scandall taken.

In that, we consider the working of this *Væ,* three ways; first, *væ quia illusiones fortes,* woe unto the world because these scandals and offences, tentations, and tribulations are so strong in their nature; and then *væ quia infirmi vos,* woe because you are so weak in your ²²⁰ nature; and again, *væ quia Prævaricatores,* woe because wee prevaricate in our own case, and make our selves weaker then we are, and are scandalized with things which are not in their nature scandalous, nor were scandalously intended. The two first, are woe because we shall be scandalized, for scandals are truly strong, and you are truly weak; The other is woe because ye will bee scandalized, when, and where you might easily unentangle the snare, and devest the scruple. First, for the vehemence, the violence, the unavoydablenesse and impetuousnesse of these scandals, tentations, and tribulations under which wee all suffer in this world, it may bee enough to ²³⁰ consider that one saying of our Saviours, *They shall seduce, Si possibile, even the elect,* where (by the way) it is not meerly, not altogether, as we have translated it, *If it were possible,* for that sounds, as if Christ had positively, and dogmatically determined, that it is not possible for the elect to be seduced; but Christ says onely, *Si possibile,* if it be possible, as being willing to leave it in doubt, and in suspense how farre, in so great scandals, so very great tentations, even the elect might bee seduced. *Ista Dominici sermonis dubitatio, trepidationem mentis in electis relinquit;* this doubtfulnesse in Christs speech, makes the very elect stand in fear of falling, in the midst of ²⁴⁰ such tentations, for, howsoever the elect shall rise again, the elect may fall by these scandals, and though they may be reduced, they may be seduced. We are to consider men, as they are delivered in the approbation, and testimony of the Church, that judges *secundum allegata & probata,* according to the evidence that she sees and heares, and not as they are wrapped up in the infallible knowledge of God; and so, our election admits an outward tryall, that is, *Sanctification:*

Calvin

Mat. 24.24

Gregor.

1 Pet. 1.1 so S. *Peter* writes, *to the strangers elect through sanctification.* They were *strangers,* strangers to the *Covenant,* and yet *Elect;* for, as all of the houshold, all within the Covenant, all children of the faithfull, ²⁵⁰ are not elect, (for to be born of *Christian parents* within the Covenant, gives us a *title to the Sacrament of Baptism,* so as that we may claim it, and the Church cannot deny it us; but this birth doth not give us *that title to heaven,* which Baptism it self does) so all *strangers,* all that are without the Covenant, are not excluded in the election. S. *Peter* admits *strangers* to election, but yet no otherwise then *through sanctification;* when we are come to that hill, to *sanctification,* we have a fair prospect to see our *election* in: so, God hath *elected*

2 Thes. 2.13 *you to salvation,* says S. *Paul,* to the *Thessalonians;* but how? *To salvation through sanctification;* that's your hill, there opens your pros-

2 Ioh. 1.1 ²⁶⁰ pect. Agreeably to these two great Apostles, says the *beloved Apostle,* the Elder unto the elect Lady, and her children; but still, how elect?

verse 6 as he tels you, *elect if she walk in the Commandements of God, elect if she lose not her former good works, that she may receive a full*

verse 9 reward; *elect, if she abide in the doctrine of Christ.* Always from that mount of *sanctification* arises our prospect to *election;* and *sanctification* were *glorification,* if it were impossible to fall from it. If a tentation of mony made *Iudas* an Apostle fall from his Master, how easily will such a tentation make men fall with their Master, that is, run into dangerous and ruinous actions with them? How easily will ²⁷⁰ our children, our servants, our tenants fall from the truth of God, if they have both the example of their superiors to countenance them, and their purse to reward them for it? That scandal, that tentation

[1 Sam.
17.7] is a Giant, and an armed Gyant, a *Goliah,* and a *Goliah with a speare like a weavers beame,* that marches upon those two leggs, *Example* to doe it, and *Preferment* for doing it.

*Quia
infirmi* This is the *væ,* in the consideration of the *passive* scandal, as it arises out of the vehemence of the scandal, and tentation, *Quia illusiones fortes,* because they are so strong in themselves. It arises also out of our weaknesse, *Quia infirmi nos,* because we are so weak, even ²⁸⁰ the strongest of us. And for this, it may also be enough to consider

Mat. 13.21 those words of our Saviour; That a man may *receive* the word, and receive it with *joy,* and yet, *Temporalis est,* says Christ, it *may bee but for a while,* hee may be but a time-server, for, assoon as persecu-

tion comes, *Illico continuò scandalizatur,* by and by, instantly, forthwith hee is scandalized and shaked. Hee stays not to give God his
leasure, whether God will succour his cause to morrow, though not
to day. Hee stays not to give men their Law, to give Princes, and
States time to consider, whether it may not be fit for them to come
to leagues, and alliances, and declarations for the assistance of the
290 Cause of Religion next year, though not this. But *continuò scandalizatur,* as soon as a *Catholique army* hath given a blow, and got a
victory of any of our forces, or friends, or as soon as a *crafty Jesuit*
hath forged a Relation, that that Army hath given such a blow, or
that such an Army there is, (for many times they intimidate weake
men, when they shoote nothing but Paper, when they are onely
Paper-Armies, and *Pamphlet-Victories,* and no such in truth) *Illico
scandalizatur,* yet with these forged rumours, presently hee is scandalized, and hee comes apace to those dangerous conclusions, *Non
potens Deus,* (for any thing I see, God is not so powerfull a God, as
300 they make him, for his enemies Armies prevaile against his) *Non
sapiens Deus,* (for any thing I see, God does not take so wise courses
for his glory, of which hee talkes so much, and pretends to bee so
jealous, for his enemies Counsels prevaile against his;) And hee
comes at last to the *Non est Deus,* to labour to over-rule his own
Conscience, and make himselfe beleeve, or (at least) to wish, though
hee cannot beleeve it, that there were no God.

Now to correct, or to repair this weaknesse, you see our Saviours
physique here; *If thy foot, thy hand, thine eye, scandalize thee, offend
thee, abscinde & projice, erue & projice, Cut it off, pull it out,* and
310 then cast it away. You see Christs method in his physique; It determines not in a preparative, that does but stirre the humours, (for
every remorse, and every compunction, and every sense that a man
hath, that such, and such company leades him into tentation, does
that, it workes in the nature of such a preparative, as stirres the humours, affects the soul,) Christs physique determines not in a blood-
letting, no not in cutting off the gangren'd part, for it is not onely
Cut off, and *pull out,* but, *Cast away,* it is an absolute evacuation
and purging out of the peccant humour. It is not a halting with the
foot, nor a shifting with the hand, it is not a winking with the eye,
320 but *abscinde,* and *erue, Cut off, pull out;* and, after that, Though

hee bee the foot upon which thou standest, thy Master, thy Patron, thy Benefactor; Though hee be thy hand by which thou gettest thy living, thy meanes, the instrument of thy maintenance, or preferment; Though hee bee thine eye, the man from whom thou receivest all thy Light, and upon whose learning thou engagest thy Religion, *abscindatur, & projice,* if hee scandalize thee, shake thee in thy Religion at the heart, or in the ways of godlinesse in thine actions, Cut him off; that is, cut off thy selfe from that conversation, and *cast him away,* returne no more within distance of that tentation: for, as sinne
330 hath that quality of a worm, that it gnawes, (it gnawes the conscience) so hath it also that quality of a worm, that if you cut it into pieces, yet if those pieces come together again, they will re-unite again; sinne, though discontinued, will finde his old pieces, if they keep not farre asunder. And since it is said of God himself by *David,*

Psalm
18.[26]

Cum perverso perverteris, That God will grow froward with the froward, and since God says of himselfe, *That with them that goe crookedly, hee will goe crookedly too,* that the behaviour of other men are said to make impressions upon God himselfe, consider the slipperinesse of our corrupt nature, how easily the vices of other men
340 insinuate and infuse themselves into us, and how much need wee have of all Christs physique, *abscinde, erue, projice, Cut off, pull out, and cast away.*

But to come to our last note, Besides the woe arising from the strength of the scandall, and the woe from the corruptnesse of our weak nature, there is a woe upon our wilfulnesse, upon our easinesse in being scandalized by an over-jealousie, and suspicious mis-interpretations of the actions of other men. And for this, in the highest consideration, as it hath relation to our Saviour himselfe, and his Gospell, it may be enough to consider that which himselfe says,

Mat. 11.6

350 *Blessed is hee, whosoever shall not be offended in me.* But, *Quis homo,* What man is hee that is not offended in him, and his Gospel? *Qui non erubescit, aut timet,* what man is he that is not ashamed of the Gospel, or afraid of it; that does not desire that the religion that he professes, were a religion of more liberty and of less threatnings? We see, that though the Cross of Christ, that is, Christ crucified, were daily represented to the Jews in their sacrifices, and preached to them in the succession of their Prophets, yet this Crosse of Christ

was *Scandalum Judæis,* a scandal to the Jews; It was, (as the Apostle says there) *Stultitia Græcis,* to the Gentiles, that had no such prep-
360 aration to the Gospel, as the Jews had in their Law, and Sacrifices, the Gospel was meer foolishnes, a religion unconformable to nature, and to reason, but even to the Jews themselves, it was a scandal, a stumbling block; they grudged that that religion left them so narrow a way open to *pleasure,* and to *profit,* and that it referred all to a spirituall Kingdome, whereas the Jews looked for a temporall King-dome in their Messias. And so truly Christ and his Gospel will be a scandal to all them that will needs set Christ a price, at which hee shall sell his Gospel. If Tithes, or some small matter in lieu of Tithes, will serve his turn, and now and then a groat to a Brief, and some-
370 times an extraordinary contribution, when extraordinary knowledge may bee taken of it, if this will serve his turn hee shall have it. But if it must come to a *Non pacem,* that Christ profess hee comes not to settle peace, but to kindle a warre, if wee must maintain armies for his Gospel, if it come to an *Odisse vitam,* to hate Father, and Mother, and Wife, and Children, and our owne lifes for his Gospel, this is too high a price, *Nolumus hunc regnare,* now the Gospell growes a Tyran, and wee will not be under a tyrannous government; If hee will govern by his Law, that hee be content with our coming to Church every Sunday, and our receiving every Easter, wee will
380 live under his Law; but if he come to *exercise his Prerogative,* and presse us to extraordinary duties, in watching all our particular ac-tions, and calling our selves to an account, for words and thoughts, then Christ and his Gospell become a scandall, a stumbling block unto us, and lye in our way, and retard our ends, our pleasures, and our profits. But if we can overcome this one scandall of the Gospell, that we be not ashamed nor afraid of that, (that is, well satisfied in the sufficiency of that Gospel for our salvation, and then content to suffer for that Gospel) if we can devest this scandall, no other shall trouble us. *Great peace have they which love thy Law,* says
390 *David;* To love it, is to prefer it before all things; and great peace have they that doe so, says he; Wherein consists this peace? In this, *Et non est illis scandalum, Great peace have they that love thy Law, for they have no scandals;* nothing shall offend them. *There shall no evill happen to the just,* says his Son *Solomon;* not that the just shall

1 Cor. 1.23

[Mat. 10.34]

[Luke 19.14]

Psal. 119.165

Prov. 12.21

feel no worldly misery, but that that misery shall not make them miserable; how evill so ever it be in it self, it shall not be evill to them, but *Omnia in bonum, All things work together for good, to them that love God. Who is he that will harme you, if you be followers of God?* says Saint *Peter,* The wicked will not follow you in [400] that strange Country; their conversation is not in heaven; if yours be, they will not follow you thither. They will doe, as he, whose instruments they are, does, the Devill; and *Resist the Devill, and he will flee from you.* A religious constancy blunts the edge of any sword, dampes the spirits of any counsel, benums the strength of any arme, opens the corners of any Labyrinth, and brings the subtilest plots against God and his servants, not onely to an invalidnesse, an ineffectualnesse, but to a derision; not onely to a *Dimicatum de cœlis,* that the world shall see, that the Lord fights for his servants from heaven, but to an *Irridebit in cœlis,* that he that sits in heaven, [410] shall laugh them to scorn; he shall ruine them, and ruine them in contempt. That prayer that *David* makes, *Libera me Domine ab homine malo, deliver me O Lord, from the evill man,* is a large, an extensive, an indefinite prayer; for, there is an evill man (occasion of tentation) in every man, in every woman, in every action; there is *Coluber in via,* a snake in every path, danger in every calling. But Saint *Augustine* contracts that prayer, and fixes it, *Liberet te Deus à temet, noli tibi esse malus; God blesse me from my selfe, that I be not that evill man to my selfe,* that I lead not my selfe into tentation, and nothing shall scandalize me. To which purpose it concerns us [420] to devest that naturall, but corrupt easinesse of uncharitable misconstruing that which other men doe, especially those whom God hath placed in his own place, for government over us; that we doe not come to think that there is nothing done, if all bee not done; that no abuses are corrected, if all be not removed; that there's an end of all Protestants, if any Papists bee left in the world. Upon those words of our Saviour, speaking of the last day of Judgement, *The son of man shall send forth his Angels, and they shall gather out of his Kingdome, Omnia scandala, All things that might offend: Calvin* says learnedly and wisely, *Qui ad extirpandum quicquid displicet* [430] *præpostere festinant,* They that make too much haste to mend all at once, *antevertunt Christi judicium, & ereptum Angelis officium*

Rom. 8.28

1 [Pet.]
3.13

[Phil 3.20]

Jacob. 4.7

Iudg. 5.20

Psal. 2.4

[Psa. 140.1]

Mat. 13.41

sibi temere usurpant, They prevent Christs judgment, and rashly, and sacrilegiously they usurp the Angels office. Christ hath reserved the cleansing and removing of all scandals, all offences to the last day; the Angels of the Church, the Minister, the Angels of the State, the Magistrate, cannot doe it; nor the Angels of heaven themselves, till the day of judgement. All scandals cannot be removed in this life; but a great many more might be then are, if men were not so apt to suspect, and mis-constru, and imprint the name of scandall
440 upon every action, of which they see not the end, nor the way; for from this jealousie and suspicion, and mis-construction of the Angels of Church and State (our Superiours in those sphears) wee shall become jealous, and suspicious of God himselfe, that he hath neg-lected us, abandoned us, if he do not deliver us, and establish us, at those times, and by those means, which we prescribe him; we shall come to argue thus against God himselfe, Surely, if God meant any good to us, he would not put us into their hands, who doe us no good. Reduce all to the precious mediocrity; To be unsensible of any declination, of any diminution of the glory of God, or his true
450 worship and religion, is an irreligious stupidity; But to bee so om-bragious, so startling, so apprehensive, so suspicious, as to think every thing that is done, is done to that end; this is a seditious jealousie, a Satyr in the heart, and an *unwritten Libell;* and God hath a Star-chamber, to punish unwritten Libels before they are published; Libels against that Law, *Curse not, or speak not ill of the King, no not in thy thought.* Not to mourn under the sense of evils, that may fall upon us, is a stony disposition; Nay, the hardest stone, marble, will weep towards foul weather. But, to make all *Possible* things *Necessary,* (this may fall upon us, therefore it must fall
460 upon us,) and to make contingent, and accidentall things, to be the effects of counsels, (this is fallen upon us, therefore it is fallen by *their practise* that have the government in their hands) this is a vexation of spirit in our selves, and a defacing, a casting of durt in the face of Gods image, of that representation, and resemblance of God, which he hath imprinted in them, of whom hee hath sayd, *They are Gods.* In divine matters there is principally exercise of our *faith,* That which we understand not, we beleeve. In civill affairs, that are above us, matters of State, there is exercise of our *Hope;* Those

Eccles.
10.20

[Psa. 82.6]

ways which we see not, wee hope are directed to good ends. In Civill
470 actions amongst our selves, there is exercise of our *Charity,* Those
hearts which we see not, let us charitably beleeve to bee disposed to
Gods service. That when as Christ hath shut up his *woe* onely in
those two, *Væ quia fortes illusiones, Woe because scandals and offences are so strong in their nature;* and *Væ quia infirmi vos, woe
because you are so weak in yours,* we doe not create a third *woe, Væ
quia prævaricatores,* in an uncharitable jealousie, and mis-interpretation of him, (that we are not in his care) nor of his *Ministers* (that
they doe not execute his purposes,) nor of one another; that when
as God hath placed us in a Land, where there are *no wolfes,* we doe
480 not think *Hominem homini Lupum,* imagine every man to be a wolf
to us, or to intend our destruction. But as in the *Arke* there were
Lions, but the Lion shut his mouth, and clincht his paw, (the Lion
hurt nothing in the Arke) and in the Arke there were Vipers and
Scorpions, but the Viper shewed no teeth, nor the Scorpion no taile,
(the Viper bit none, the Scorpion stung none in the Arke) (for, if
they had occasioned any disorder there, their escape could have been
but into the Sea, into irreparable ruine) so, in every State, (though
that State be an Arke of peace, and preservation) there will be some
kind of oppression in some Lions, some that will abuse their power;
490 but *Væ si scandalizemur,* woe unto us if we be scandalized with
that, and seditiously lay aspersions upon the State and Government,
because there are some such in every Church, (though that Church
bee an Arke, for integrity and sincerity) there will bee some Vipers,
Vipers that will gnaw at their Mothers belly, men that will shake the
articles of Religion; But *Væ si scandalizemur,* woe if we be so scandalized at that, as to defame that Church, or separate our selves
from that Church which hath given us our Baptism, for that. It is
the chafing of the Lion, and the stirring of the Viper, that aggravates the danger; The first blow makes the wrong, but the second
500 makes the fray; and they that will endure no kind of abuse in State
or Church, are many times more dangerous then that abuse which
they oppose. It was only Christ Jesus himself that could say to the
Tempest, *Tace, obmutesce,* peace, be still, not a blast, not a sob more;
onely he could becalm a Tempest at once. It is well with us, if we
can ride out a storm at anchour; that is, lie still and expect, and

Mar. 4.39

surrender our selves to God, and anchor in that confidence, till the storm blow over. It is well for us if we can beat out a storm at sea, with boarding to and again; that is, maintain and preserve our pres-ent condition in Church, and State, though we encrease not, that
510 though we gain no way, yet wee lose no way whilst the storm lasts. It is well for us, if, though we be put to take in our sayls, and to take down our masts, yet we can hull it out; that is, if in storms of contra-diction, or persecution, the Church, or State, though they be put to accept worse conditions then before, and to depart with some of their outward splendor, be yet able to subsist and swimme above water, and reserve it selfe for Gods farther glory, after the storme is past; onely Christ could becalm the storme; He is a good Christian that can ride out, or board out, or hull out a storme, that by industry, as long as he can, and by patience, when he can do no more, over-lives
520 a storm, and does not forsake his ship for it, that is not scandalized with that State, nor that Church, of which he is a member, for those abuses that are in it. The Arke is peace, peace is good dispositions to one another, good interpretations of one another; for, if our im-patience put us from our peace, and so out of the Arke, all without the Arke is sea; The bottomlesse and boundlesse Sea of Rome, will hope to swallow us, if we dis-unite our selves, in uncharitable mis-interpretations of one another; The peace of God is the *peace that*   Phil. 4.7
passeth all understanding; That men should subdue and captivate even their understanding to the love of this peace, that when in their
530 understanding they see no reason why this or this thing should be thus or thus done, or so and so suffered, the peace of God, that is, charity, *may passe their understanding,* and goe above it; for, how-soever the affections of men, or the vicissitudes and changes of af-fairs may vary, or apply those two great axiomes, and aphorisms of ancient Rome, *Salus populi suprema lex esto,* The good of the people is above all Law, and then, *Quod Principi placet, lex esto,* The pleasure of the Prince is above all Law, howsoever I say, various occasions may vary their Laws, adhere we to that Rule of the Law, which the Apostle prescribes, that we always make *Finem præcepti charitatem,*   1 Tim. 1.5
540 *The end of the Commandement charity:* for, no Commandement, (no not those of the first Table) is kept, if, upon pretence of keeping that Commandement, or of the service of God, I come to an un-

Ephes. 3.17

1 Pet. 1.2

1 Thes. 3.12

charitable opinion of other men. That so first, *Fundemur & radice-mur in charitate,* that wee be planted, and take root in that ground, in charity, (so wee are, by being planted in that Church, that thinks charitably even of that Church, that uncharitably condemns us) And then, *Vt multiplicemur, That Grace and peace may be multiplyed in us,* (so it is, if to our outward peace, God adde the inward peace of conscience in our own bosomes) and lastly, *Vt abundemus,* that
550 we may not onely *encrease,* (as the Apostle says there) but (as he adds) *abound in charity* towards one another, and towards all men, for this abundant and overflowing charity, (as long as we can, to beleeve well, for the present, and where we cannot do so, to hope well of the future) is the best preservative and antidote against the *woe* of this Text, *Woe unto the world because of scandals and offences;* which, though it be spoken of the *Active,* is more especially intended of the *Passive* scandal; and though it be pressed upon us, first, *Quia Illusiones fortes,* because those scandals are so strong, and then, *Quia infirmi nos,* because we are so weak, doe yet endanger us
560 most, in that respect, *Quia prævaricatores,* because we open our selves, nay offer our selves to the vexation of scandals, by an easie, a jealous, a suspicious, an uncharitable interpreting of others.

Number 8.

Preached to the Countesse of Bedford,
then at Harrington house.
January 7. 1620.

Job 13.15. *LOE, THOUGH HE SLAY ME, YET WILL I TRUST IN HIM.*

THE NAME, by which God notified himselfe, to all the world, at first, was, *Qui sum, I am;* this was his style, in the Commission, that he gave to *Moses* to *Pharaoh;* say, *that he whose name is, I am, hath sent thee,* for there, God would have it made known, that all *Essence,* all *Beeing,* all things, that fall out, in any time, past, or present, or future, had their dependence upon *him,* their derivation from *him,* their subsistence in *him.* But then, when God contracts himselfe into a narrower consideration, not to be considered *as God,* which implies the *whole Trinity,* but *as Christ,* which

10 is onely *the second Person,* and when he does not so much notifie himselfe to the *whole world,* as to the *Christian Church,* then he contracts his name too, from that spacious and extensive *Qui sum, I am,* which includes all time, to *Alpha and Omega, first* and *last,* which are peeces of time, as we see, in severall places of the *Revelation,* he styles himselfe: when God speaks to the *whole world,* his name is, *Qui sum, I am,* that all the world may confesse, that all that is, is nothing, but with relation to him; when he speaks to *a Christian,* his name is *Alpha* and *Omega, first* and *last,* that a Christian may, in the very name of God, fixe his thoughts upon his *be-*

20 *ginning,* and upon his *end,* and ever remember, that as a few years since, in his *Cradle,* he had no sense of that honour, those riches, those pleasures, which possess his time now, so, God knowes how few days hence, in his grave, he shall have no sense, no memory of

Exod. 3.14

[Rev. 1.11]

[Rev. 21.6]

them. Our whole life is but a *parenthesis,* our *receiving* of our soule, and *delivering* it back againe, makes up the perfect sentence; Christ is *Alpha* and *Omega,* and our *Alpha* and *Omega* is all we are to consider.

Now, for all the *letters* in this *Alphabet* of our life, that is, for all the various accidents in the course thereof, we cannot study a better 30 booke, then the person of *Iob.* His first letter, his *Alpha,* we know not, we know not his *Birth;* His last letter, his *Omega,* we know not, we know not his *Death:* But all his other letters, His *Children,* and his *riches,* we read over and over againe, How he *had* them, how he *lost* them, and how he *recovered* them. By which though it appeare that those temporall things doe also belong to the care and provision of a godly man, yet it appears too, that neither his first care, nor his last care appertaines to the things of this world, but that there is a *Primùm*
[Mat. 6.33]   *quærite,* something to be sought for before, The *kingdome* of God; And there is a *Memorare novissima,* something to be thought on 40 after, The *Joyes of heaven;* And then, *Cætera adjicientur,* says Christ, All other cares are allowable by way of *Accessary,* but not as *principall.* And therefore, though this History of *Iob,* may seeme to spend it selfe, upon the relation of *Iobs* temporall passages, of his *wealth,* and *poverty,* of his *sicknesse,* and *recovery,* yet, if we consider the *Alpha* and *Omega* of the booke it selfe, the first beginning, and the later end thereof, we shall see in both places, a care of the *Holy ghost,* to shew us first *Iobs righteousnesse,* and then his *riches,* first his *Goodnesse,* and then his *Goods;* in both places, there is a *Catechisme,* a *Confession* of his *faith* before, and then an *Inventory,* and *Cata-* 50 *logue* of his *wealth;* for, in the first place, it is sayd, *He was an up-*
[Job 1.1]   *right and just man, and feared God, and eschewed evill,* and then, his Children, and his substance follow; And in the last place, it is
[Job 42.8]   said, *That Iob was accepted by God, and that he prayed for those friends, which had vext him,* and then it is, that his *former substance was doubled* unto him.

This world then is but an *Occasionall* world, a world onely to be us'd; and that but so, *as though we us'd it not:* The next world is the world to be *enjoy'd,* and that so, as that we may *joy* in nothing by the way, but as it directs and conduces to that end; Nay, though 60 we have no Joy at al, though God deny us all conveniencies here,

Etiamsi occiderit, though he end a weary life, with a painefull death, as there is no other hope, but in him, so there needs no other, for that alone is both abundant, and infallible in it selfe.

Now, as no History is more various, then *Iobs fortune,* so is no phrase, no style, more ambiguous, then that in which *Iobs history* is written; very many words so expressed, very many phrases so conceived, as that they admit a diverse, a *contrary* sense; for such an ambiguity in a *single word,* there is an example in the beginning, in *Iobs* wife; we know not (from the word it selfe) whether it be
70 *Benedicas,* or *maledicas,* whether she sayd *Blesse God, and die* or *Curse God:* And for such an ambiguity, in an *intire sentence,* the words of this text are a pregnant, and evident example, for they may be directly, and properly thus rendered out of the Hebrew, *Behold he will kill me, I will not hope;* and this seemes to differ much from our reading, *Behold, though he kill me, yet will I trust in him.* And therefore to make up that sense, which our translation hath, (which is truely the true sense of the place) we must first make this paraphrase, *Behold he will kill me,* I make account he will kill me, I looke not for life at his hands, his will be done upon me for that;
80 And then, the rest of the sentence (*I will not hope*) (as we read it in the *Hebrew,*) must be supplyed, or rectified rather, with an *Interrogation,* which that language wants, and the translators use to add it, where they see the sense require it: And so reading it with an *Interrogation,* the Originall, and our translation will constitute one and the same thing; It will be all one sense to say, with the Originall, *Behold he will kill me,* (that is, let him kill me) *yet shall not I hope in him?* and to say with our translation, *Behold though he kill me, yet will I hope in him:* And this sense of the words, both the *Chaldee paraphrase,* and all translations (*excepting* onely the *Septuagint*) do
90 unanimously establish.

So then, the sense of the words being thus fixed, we shall not distract your understandings, or load your memories, with more then two parts: Those, for your ease, and to make the better impression, we will call *propositum,* and *præpositum;* first, the purpose, the resolution of a godly man, which is, to rely upon God; and then the consideration, the inducement, the debatement of this beforehand. That no Danger can present it selfe, which he had not thought of

[Job 2.9]

Divisio

before, He hath carried his thoughts to the last period, he hath stirred
the *potion* to the last scruple of *Rheubarb,* and *Wormewod,* which is
¹⁰⁰ in it, he hath digested the worst, he hath considered *Death* it selfe,
and therefore his resolution stands unshak'd, *Etiamsi occiderit,
Though he dy for it, yet he will trust in God.*

1 Part   In the first then, The Resolution, the purpose it selfe, we shall
consider, *Quem,* and *Quid;* The *Person,* and the *Affection:* To *whom*

Quis   *Iob* will beare so great, and so reverent a respect; and then, *what*
this respect is, *I will trust in him.* I would not stay you, upon the first
branch, upon the *person,* as upon a particular consideration (though
even that, The person upon whom, in all cases, we are to rely, be
entertainement sufficient for the meditation of our whole life) but
¹¹⁰ that there arises an usefull observation, out of that *name,* by which
Iob delivers that person, to us, in this place: *Iob* says, *though He kill
me, yet he will trust in him;* but he tells us not in this verse, *who
this He is.* And though we know, by the frame, and context, that this
is *God,* yet we must have recourse to the *third* verse, to see, in what
apprehension, and what notion, in what Character, and what Contemplation, in what *name,* and what nature, what *Attribute,* and
what Capacity, *Iob* conceived and proposed *God* to himselfe, when

[Deut. 4.24]   he fix'd his resolution so intirely to rely upon him; for, as *God is a
jealous God,* I am sure I have given him occasion of jealousy, and

Ezek.   ¹²⁰ suspicion, *I have multiplied my fornications, and yet am not satisfied,*

16.[29]   as the prophet speaks: As God is a *Consuming fire,* I have made my
selfe fuell for the fire, and I have brought the fires of *lust,* and of

[Exod.   *ambition,* to kindle that fire: As *God visits the sinnes of fathers upon*

20.5]   *Children,* I know not what sinnes my fathers and grandfathers have
layd up in the treasure of Gods indignation: As God comes to my

[Heb.   notion, in these formes, *Horrendum,* it were *a fearefull thing* to

10.31]   flesh and bloud, to deliver ones selfe over to him, as he is a jealous
God, and a Consuming fire; But in that third verse, *Iob* sets before
him, that God, whom he conceives to be *Shaddai,* that is, *Omnip-*
¹³⁰ *otens, Allmighty; I will speake to the Allmighty, and I desire to
dispute with God.* Now, if we propose God to our selves, in that
name, as he is *Shaddai,* we shall find that word in so many significations in the scriptures, as that no *misery* or *calamity,* no *prosperity* or
happinesse can fall upon us, but we shall still see it (of what kinde

so ever it be) descend from God, in this acceptation, as God is *Shaddai*. For, first, this word signifies *Dishonor*, as the *Septuagint* translate it in the Proverbs, *He that Dishonoreth his parents, is a*   19.26 *shamelesse child;* There's this word; *Shaddai* is the name of *God,* and yet *Shaddai* signifies *Dishonor*. In the prophet *Esay* it signifies *Depre-*   33.1
140 *dation*, a forcible and violent taking away of our *goods; væ prædanti,* says God in that place, *woe to thee that spoyledst, and wast not spoyled; Shaddai* is the name of *God,* and yet *Shaddai* is *spoyle,* and *violence* and *depredation*. In the prophet *Ieremy*, the word is carried   4.13 farther, there it signifies *Destruction*, and an utter *Devastation, De-vastati sumus,* says he, *wo unto us, for we are Destroy'd;* The word is *Shaddai*, and is *Destruction*, though *Shaddai* be the name of *God :* yea, the word reaches to a more *spirituall affection*, it extends to the *under-standing,* and *error* in that, and to the *Conscience,* and *sinne* in that; for so the *Septuagint* makes use of this word in the Proverbs, *To deceive,*   Prov. 24.15
150 and to *ly;* and in one place of the Psalmes, they interpret the word,   Psal. 91 of the *Devil* himselfe. So that, (recollecting all these heavy significa-tions of the word) *Dishonor* and *Disreputation, force* and *Depreda-tion, Ruine* and *Devestation, Error* and *Illusion,* the *Devill* and his *Tentations,* are presented to us, in the same word, as the name and power of God is, that, when so ever any of these doe fall upon us, in the same instant when we see and consider the name and quality of this calamity that falls, we may see and consider the power and the purpose of God which inflicts that Calamity; I cannot call the calam-ity by a name, but in that name, I name *God;* I cannot feel an afflic-
160 tion, but in that very affliction I feel the hand (and, if I will, the medicinall hand) of my *God*. If therefore our *Honor* and *Reputation* decay, all honor was a beame of *him,* and if he have sucked that beame into himselfe, let us follow it home, let us labor to be honorable in him, glorified in him, and our honor is not extinguished in this world, but growne too glorious for this world to comprehend. If spoyle and *Depredation* come upon us, that we be covered with wrath, and persecuted, slaine and not spared, That those *that fed delicately*   [Lam. 4.5] *perish in the streets, and they that were brought up in scarlet embrace the Dunghill,* and that the hands of pitifull women have sodden
170 their owne children, as the prophet complains in the *Lamentations;*   [Lam. 4.10] if there be such an irreparable *Devastation* upon us, as that we be

[Isa. 30.14]
broken as an Earthen vessell, in the breaking whereof there remaines not a sheard to fetch fire from the hearth, nor water from the pit, That our *estate* be ruined so, as that there is nothing left, not onely for future *posterity,* but not for the present *family,* yet still God and the calamity are together, God does not *send* it, but bring it, he is there as soone as the calamity is there, and calling that calamity by his owne name, *Shaddai,* he would make that very calamity a candle to thee, by which thou mightst see him; that, if thou wert not so
180 puffed up before, as that thou forgotst to say, *Dominus dedit, It was*

[Job 1.21]
the Lord that gave all, thou shouldst not be so dejected, so rebellious now, as not to say *Dominus tulit,* It is the Lord that hath taken, and committed to some better steward, those treasures of his, which he saw, thou dost employ to thine owne danger.

Yea, if those *spirituall afflictions,* which reach to the *understanding,* and are intimated and involved in this word, in this name of God,

Lam. 1.19
doe fall upon us, *That we call for our lovers, and they deceive us* (as we told you, the word did signifie *deceit*) that is, we come to see how much we mistooke the matter, when we fell in love with worldly
190 things, (as certainely, *once* in our lives, though it be but upon our *Death beds,* we doe come to discover that *deceit*) yea, when the deceit is so spirituall, as that it reaches not onely to the *understanding,* but to the *Conscience,* that that have been deceived either with *security* at one time, or with *anxieties,* and unnecessary *scruples,* and impertinent *perplexities* at another; if this spirituall deceit have gone so high, as that wee came to thinke our selves to be amongst them, of

Ier. 4.10
whom the prophet sayes, *Ah Lord God, surely thou hast deceived thy people, and Jerusalem,* that we come to suspect, that *God* hath misled us in a *false religion* all this while, and that there is a better then this,
200 if we would looke to it; if God to punish our negligence, and surfet

Ier. 5.31
of his word, should suffer *the prophet to prophecy lyes, That the*
Hose. 9.7
prophet should be a foole, and *the spirituall man mad,* (that is, as *Saint Hierom* reads that place, *Arreptitius,* possessed, possessed with the spirit of *ambition,* and *flattery,* and *temporizing,* to preach to their appetites, who governe the times, and not to his instructions, who sent them to preach) yea, where this word is carried the highest of all, that this word, which is the name of *God,* is used for the

Lam. 2.2
Devill, (as we noted before, out of the Psalmes) That *Satan was let*

loose, and polluted the kingdome, and the princes thereof, with false
210 *worships,* yet to what height so ever, this *violence,* or this *deceit,* or
this *tentation* should come, God comes with it; and, *with God, there*
is strength and wisdome, He discerns our Distresses, and is able to
succour us in them; And, (as it is added there) *He that is deceived,*
and he that deceives are his; The deceiver is his, because *he catcheth*
the crafty in their owne nets, and the deceived are his, that he may
rectifie and unbeguile them. So then the children of God, are the
Marble, and the *Ivory,* upon which he workes; In them his purpose
is, to re-engrave, and restore his Image; and affliction, and the *malig-*
nity of man, and the *deceits of Heretiques,* and the *tentations of the*
220 *Devill* him selfe, are but his instruments, his tools, to make his Image
more discernible, and more durable in us. *Iob* will *speake to God,*
hee will *dispute with God,* he will *trust in God,* therefore, because he
is *Shaddai,* because neither *dishonor,* nor *Devastation,* of *fortune,* or
understanding, or *Conscience,* by *deceit* of treacherous *friends,* by
backsliding of false *teachers,* by illusion of the *Devill* himselfe, can be
presented him, but the name and power of God accompanies that
calamity, and he sees that they came from *God,* and therefore he
should be patient in them, and how impatient so ever he be, he sees
he must beare them, because they came from *him.*

230 But *Iob* hath another hold too, another assurance, for his Confidence in God, from this name *Shaddai;* It is not onely because all
Calamity comes from him, and therefore should be borne, or therefore
must be borne; but all *Restitution,* all Reparation of temporall, or
spirituall detriment, is included in that name too, for *Shaddai* is
Omnipotens, Almighty, He *can do all* things; And the consolation is
brought nearer then so, in one place, it is *Omnia faciens,* That, not
onely for the *future he can,* but for *the present, he does* study, and he
does accomplish my good; even then, when his hand is upon me, in a
calamity, his hand is under me, to raise me up againe; as he that
240 flings *a ball* to the ground, or to a wall, intends in that action, that that
ball should returne back, so even now, when God does throw me
down, it is the way that he hath chosen to returne me to himselfe.
Since therefore this name *Shaddai* assured *Iob,* that all which we call
Good, and all which we call *Evill,* that is, *prosperity,* and *adversity,*
proceed from God; that God (who in the signification of this name)

Iob 12.16

Iob 8.3

is able to shatter, and scatter, to devastate and depopulate, not onely
our *estate,* but our *Conscience,* in an instant, with the horror of his
Judgements; and then is able to binde up, and consolidate all this
againe, with his *temporall,* and *spirituall Comforts,* since he can

[John 2.19] ²⁵⁰ *destroy* in an *instant that Temple,* which was so long in building,
that is, overthrow that *fortune,* which employed the industry of man,
the favor of princes, and the ruine and supplantations of other men,
for many yeares, to the making thereof, and then *can raise this ruin'd
Temple,* this overthrowne man, *in three dayes,* or hours, or minutes,
as it pleaseth him, to measure his owne purposes, since *good* and
bad, peace and *anguish, life* and *death* proceed from him, who is
Shaddai, the Almighty God, *Iob* had good reasons, *to trust in him,* in
that God, though *hee,* that God, should *kill him;* which Emphaticall,
and applyable significations of the *name,* hath occasion'd me (though
²⁶⁰ it be obvious and present to every apprehension, that God is the person, who in this text, is to be relied upon) to insist upon this, as a
particular part or branch; And so we passe to that, which we proposed
for a second branch, from the *person,* (*God,* and God in this notion,
Shaddai, Almighty) to the *respect,* which he promises, *Trust, Though
hee kill me, yet will I trust in him.*

Quid   It is a higher degree of Reverence and Confidence, to *trust in one,*
then to *trust one.* We see it so expressed in the Articles of our Creed;
Credimus in Deum, we beleeve *in God,* and *in Christ,* and *in the
Holy Ghost;* And then *Credimus Ecclesiam Catholicam,* we beleeve
²⁷⁰ the Catholique Church. We will beleeve an honest man, that he will
doe as he sayes, we beleeve God much more, that he will performe his
promises; we will trust God, that he will doe as he sayes; But then,
Iob will *trust in God,* That though God have not spoken to his soule
as yet, though he have not interessed him in his promises, and in his
Covenant, (for *Iob* is not conceived to be *within the Covenant* made
by God to his people) yet he will *trust in him,* that in his due time,
he will visit him, and will apply him those mercies, and those means,
which no man, that had interest in them, can doubt, or distrust. And
therefore *Iob* professes his trust in God, in that word, which hath in
²⁸⁰ the use thereof in *Scriptures,* ordinarily three acceptations; The word
יחל   is *Jakal,* and *Jakal* signifies *Expectavit Deum,* his eye, his expectation
was upon nothing but God; And then it signifies *speravit,* he *Hoped*

for him, As he looked for nothing else, so he doubted not of him; And then it is *Moratus est,* As he was sure of him, so he prescribed him not a time, but humbly attended his leasure, and received his temporall, or spirituall blessings thankefully, whensoever it should be his pleasure to afford them.

First then, *Expectavit,* He *trusted in him,* that is, he trusted in *nothing but him.* For, beloved, as we have in the Schooles, a short and
290 a round way, to prove that the world was made of *nothing,* which is, onely to aske that man, who will need deny the world to be made of nothing, of *what* it was made; and, if he could find a preexistent matter, of which he thought the world was made, yet we must aske him againe, of *what,* that preexistent matter was made, and so upwards stil, till at last it must necessarily come to *nothing:* so we must aske that man, that will not be of *Iobs* mind, to *trust* in God, in what he would trust; would he trust in his *riches?* who shall preserve them to him? The *Law?* Then he trusts in the Law. But who shall preserve the Law? The *King?* Then his trust is in him. And who shall pre-
300 serve *him?* Almighty God; and therefore his trust must be at last in *him. To what nation is their God come so neere to them as the Lord our God is come neare unto us? what nation hath lawes, and ordinances, so righteous, as we have?* Moses sayd *this historically* of the *Iew,* and *prophetically* of *us;* Tis true, we are governed by a peaceable, and a just law; *Moses* his prophecy is fulfilled upon us, and so is *Esays* too, *Reges nutricii, Kings shall be thy nursing fathers;* It is true to us, The *law* is preserved to us, by a just, and a peacefull *prince;* but how often have the sinnes of the people, and their unthankfulnesse especially, induc'd new *lawes,* and new *princes?* The prince, and the law, are the
310 two most reverend, and most safe things, that man can rely upon; but yet (in other nations at least) sacred, and secular story declares, that for the iniquity of the people the *law* hath been perverted by *princes,* and for the sinne of the people, the *prince* hath been subverted by *God.* Howsoever there may be some collaterall, and transitory trust in by things, the radicall, the fundamentall trust, is onely in *God.*

Iob trusted in him, that is, in nothing but him: but then, *speravit,* he hoped for something at his hands; none can *give* but God; but God will give to none that doe not *hope* for it, and that doe not

Expectavit

Deut. 4.
[7, 8]

49.23

Speravit

[Exod. 16
and Numb.
11]

320 expresse their hope, by asking, by prayer; God scatters not his blessings, as Princes doe money, in *Donatives* at *Coronations* or *Triumphes,* without respect upon whom they shall fall. God rained downe *Manna* and *Quailes,* plentifully, abundantly; but he knew to what hand every bird, and every graine belonged. To trust in nothing else, is but halfe way; it is but a stupid neglecting of all; It is an ill affection to say, I look for nothing at the worlds hands, nor at Gods neither. God onely hath all, and God hath made us capable of all his gifts; and therefore we must neither hope for them, any where else, nor give over our hope of them, from him, by intermitting our
330 *prayers,* or our *industry* in a lawfull calling; for we are bound to suck at those breasts which God puts out to us, and to draw at those springs, which flow from him to us; and *prayer,* and *industry,* are these *breasts,* and these *springs;* and whatsoever we have by them, we have from him. *Expectavit, Job* trusted not in the *meanes,* as in the *fountaine,* but yet *speravit,* he doubted not, but God, who is the *fountaine,* would, by those meanes, derive his blessings, temporall and spirituall, upon him.

Rom. 8.24

  Hee Hoped; now *Hope* is onely, or principally of invisible things, for *Hope that is seen, is not hope,* says the Apostle. And therefore,
340 though we may hope for *temporall* things, for health, wealth, strength, and liberty, and victory where Gods enemies oppresse the Church, and for execution of laws, where Gods enemies undermine the Church; (for, whatsoever we may *pray* for, we may *hope* for, and all those temporall blessings are prayed for, by Christs appointment,

[Mat. 6.11]

in that petition, *Give us this day our daily bread*) yet our *Hope* is principally directed upon the *invisible* part, and invisible office of those visible and temporall things; which is, that by them, we may be the better able to performe religious duties to God, and duties of assistance to the world. When I expect a *friend,* I may go up to a
350 window, and wish I might see a *Coach,* or up to a Cliffe, and wish I might see a *ship,* but it is because I hope, that that friend is in that Coach, or that ship: so I wish, and pray, and labour for temporall things, because I hope that my soule shall be edified, and my salvation established, and God glorified by my having them: And therefore every Christian hope being especially upon spirituall things, is properly, and purposely grounded, upon these stones; that it be *spes*

veniæ, a hope of *pardon,* for that which is past, and then *spes gratiæ,*
a hope of *Grace,* to establish me in that state with God, in which, his
pardon hath placed mee, and lastly *spes gloriæ,* a hope that this
360 *pardon,* and this *grace,* shall lead me to that everlasting *glory,* which
shall admit no night, no eclipse, no cloud.

    First, for the first object of this hope, *pardon,* we are to consider   *Spes veniæ*
sinne, in two aspects, two apprehensions; as sinne is an *injury,* a
treason, yea a wound to *God;* And then as sinne is a *Calamity,* a
misery fallen inevitably upon *man.* Consider it the first way, and
there is no hope of pardon. *Nec talem Deum tuum putes, qualis nec
tu debes esse,* is excellently said by Saint *Augustine:* never imagine
any other quality to be in *Christ,* then such, as thou, as a *Christian,*
art bound to have in thy selfe. And, if a Snake have stung me, must
370 I take up that Snake, and put it into my bosome? If so poore a snake,
so poore a worme as I, have stung my Maker, have crucified my Redeemer, shall he therefore, therefore take me into his bosome, into his
wounds, and save me, and glorifie me? No, if I look upon *sinne,* in
that line, in that angle, as it is a wound to God, I shall come to that
of *Cain, Major iniquitas, my sinne is greater, then can be forgiven,*   [Gen. 4.13]
and to that of *Judas, Peccavi tradens, I have sinned in betraying the*   [Mat. 27.4]
innocent bloud, that is, in *Crucifying* him againe, who was crucified
for me, in betraying his righteous bloud, as much, by my unworthy
receiving, as *Judas* did, in an unjust *delivering* of it. But if I look upon
380 sinne, as sinne is now, the misery and calamity of *man,* the greater
the misery appears, the more hope of pardon I have; *Abyssus*   Psal. 42.7
Abyssum, as *David* speakes, *One Depth calls upon another;* Infinite
sinnes call for infinite mercy; and *where sinne did abound, grace,*   [Rom. 5.20]
and mercy shall much more. First *David* presents the greatnesse of
his sinnes, and then followes the *Miserere mei, have mercy upon me,*   [Psa. 51.1]
according to the greatnesse of thy mercy. Is there any *little mercy* in
God? Is not all his mercy *infinite,* that pardons a sinne done against
an infinite majesty? yes; but herein the greatnesse appeares to us, that
it delivers us from a great calamity. *Quia infirmus, Because I am*   [Psa. 6.2, 3]
390 *weake,* (borne weake, and subject to continuall infirmities) *Quia
ossa conturbata, Because my bones are troubled,* (my best repentances,
and resolutions are shaked) *Quia vexata anima,* because my soule is
in anguish, when after such resolutions, and repentances, and vowes,

I relapse into those sinnes, these miseries of his, were *Davids* inducements why God should pardon him, because it is thus with me, *have
mercy upon me.* And so God himselfe seemes to have had a
diverse, a two-fold apprehension of our sinnes, when he says, that

Gen. 6.5   because *all the imaginations of the thoughts of mans heart, were onely
evill continually, therefore he would spare none, he would destroy*

8.21   400 *all,* and after he says, *that because the imaginations of the thoughts of
mans heart, were evill from his youth, he would no more smite all
things living, as he had done;* for sinne, he would destroy them, and
yet for sinne, he would spare them: when we examine our sinnes,
and finde them to be out of *infirmity,* and not out of *rebellion,* we
may conclude Gods corrections, to be by way of *Medicin,* and not of
poyson, to be for our amendment, and not for our annihilation, and
in that case, there is *spes veniæ,* just hope of pardon.

Spes Gratiæ   Another degree of hope is, *spes gratiæ,* hope of *subsequent grace;*

Rom. 5.10   for, as Saint *Paul* builds his argument, *If when we were enemies, we*
410 *were reconciled to God, by the death of his Sonne, much more, being
reconciled, shall we be saved by his life:* in like manner, every sinner
may build his trust, and hope in God, *He that hath pardoned us, the
sinnes we have done, will much more assist us with his grace, that
we may be able to stand in that state with him, to which he hath
brought us.* He that succoured us, when there was nothing in us, but
his enemies, will much more send new supplies, when the town is
held for him, and by his friends. And this hope of *pardon,* for that
which is *past,* and of *grace* for the *present,* continues to the hope of

Spes Gloriæ   *glory* to *come:* of which glory we apprehend strong and effectuall
420 beames here, by conforming our selves, to that Gospell, which the

I Tim. 1.11   *Apostle* calls *the glorious Gospell of the blessed God;* and for the
consummation of this glory, we doe with patience abide for it, says

Rom. 8.25   the Apostle: which is the last of those three senses, in which we noted,
this word, in which *Job* expresses *his trust in God,* to be used in the
Scriptures, *Jakal, moratus est;* he did *trust* in *nothing else,* he did
trust in him, and then, he *staied his leasure.*

Moratus est   *Jacob* makes a solemne prayer to God, in *Genesis, 32. O God of
my Fathers, Abraham, and Isaac,* then he remembers God of his
promise, (Thou saydst unto me, returne, and I will doe thee good)
430 he tells him his *danger, (I feare my brother Esau, will come and smite*

me) he makes his *petition*, (*Deliver me from the hand of my brother*)
And yet, for all this, though he trusted in God, yet God infuses not
that confidence into him, as to goe on: He sent his present to his
brother, but himselfe *tarried there all night,* says the text. Yea, God
was so far, from giving him present meanes of deliverance, that he
made him worse able to deliver himselfe, he wrastled with him, and
lam'd him: but after all, in Gods appointed time, he and his brother
were reconciled. If thou pray to Almighty God, in temporall, in
spirituall calamities, if God doe not presently enlighten thine under-
440 standing in every *controversie of Religion,* in every *scruple of Conscience,* if he doe not rectifie thine *estate,* when it is decayed, thy *reputation,* when thou art reproached, yea if he wrastle with thee, and lame
thee, that is, bring all to a greater impotency, and improbability of
amendment then before, yet thou hast thy *Rule* from *Job,* thou hast thy
example from *Jacob,* that to *trust in God,* is not onely to trust in *nothing else,* nor onely to hope particularly, for *pardon,* for *grace,* for *glory*
from him, but it is to *stay* his leasure, for the outward, and inward
seales of all his mercies, and his benefits, which he shall, in his time, bestow upon thee. The *ambitious* man must stay, till he, whose office he
450 expects, be dead: the *Covetous* man must stay, till the *six moneths* be
run, before his *use* come in. Though thou have a religious ambition,
a holy covetousnesse even at Gods graces, thou must stay his time.
Os aperui, & attraxi, says *David, I opened my mouth, and panted,*   Psal.
because I loved thy Commandements; He loved them, and he longed   119.131
for them, yet he had not presently a full satisfaction. *Domine labia
mea aperies,* says he also, first, it must be the Lord that must *open*   [Psa. 51.15]
our lippes, in all our petitions; It must not be the anguish of the
calamity onely, nor the desire of that which thou prayest for onely,
that must open thy lippes, but the Lord, that is, the glory of God:
460 when the Lord hath opened thy lips in a rectified prayer, then followes the *Aperuit manus, the eyes of all things waite upon him, & he*   Psal.
gives them their meate in due season; he opens his hand, & filles every   145.[15,]16
living thing, at his good pleasure: Here's plentifull opening, and
filling, and filling *every* thing, but still *in due season,* and that due
season expressed, *At his pleasure:* for, as that is the *Nature* of every
thing, which God hath imprinted in it, so that is the *season* of every   Augustin.
thing, which God hath appointed for it. Thou wouldest not pray

for *harvest* at *Christmas;* seek not unseasonable comforts, out of
Musique, or Comedies, or Conversation, or Wine in thy distresses,
⁴⁷⁰ but seek it at the hand of God, and stay his leasure, for else thou doest
not trust in him.

2 Part   We have now passed over all those branches, which constituted our
first part, that which we called *Propositum,* what is the *purpose* and
resolution of a godly man, in *Job:* that he would not scatter his
thoughts in trusting upon *Creatures,* and yet he would not suffer
his thoughts to vanish and evaporate, he would rest them upon *something,* and not leave all to *fortune,* he would rest upon *God,* and yet
stay his time for the execution of his gracious purposes. There remaines yet, that which we call *præpositum,* in which we intended,
⁴⁸⁰ the foundation, and *ground* of that *purpose* and resolution; which
seems in *Job,* to have been, a debatement in himselfe, a contemplation
of all *dangers,* the worst was *death,* and yet, *Si occiderit, if I dye for
it,* and dye at his hands, *Though he kill me, yet will I trust in him.*
For when the children of God take that resolution, to suffer any
affliction, which God shall lay upon them, patiently, and cheerfully,
it must not be a sodaine, a rash, an undebated resolution, but they
must consider *why* they undertake it, and in whose strength, they
shall be able to do it: They must consider what they have *done* for
God, before they promise themselves the glory of *suffering* for him.

Gen. 11   ⁴⁹⁰ When they which enterprised the building of *Babel,* did no more
but say to one another, *Come let us make bricke, go to, let us build a
towre, whose top may reach to heaven,* how quickly they were *scat-*
Luke 14.28   *tered over the earth?* The way is, if you minde to build, to *sit downe
and count the cost;* if you purpose to *suffer* for Christ, to look to your
stock, your strength, and from whence it comes. The King that intends a war, in that Gospell, takes counsaile, whether he be able with
his *tenne thousand* to meet the enemy with *twenty thousand.* We are
too weake for our enemy; the world, the flesh, and the Devill, are
mustered against us; but yet, with our *ten thousand,* we may meet
⁵⁰⁰ their *twenty thousand,* if we have *put on Christ,* and be *armed* with
him, and his holy *patience,* and *constancy;* but from whom may we
derive an assurance, that we shall have that *armor,* that *patience,* that
constancy? First, a Christian must purpose to *Doe,* and then in cases
of *necessity,* to *suffer:* And give me leave to make this short note by

the way, no man shall *suffer* like a *Christian,* that hath *done* nothing
like a *Christian:* God shall thanke no man, for dying for him, and
his glory, that contributed nothing to his glory, in the actions of his
life: very hardly shall that man be a *Martyr* in a persecution, that did
not what he could, to keep off persecution.

510   Thus then *Job* comes first, to the *Si occiderit, If he should kill me;*
If Gods anger should proceed so far, as so far, it may proceed. Let no
man say in a *sicknesse,* or in any temporall calamity, this is the *worst;*
for a *worse* thing then that may fall: *five and thirty years* sicknesse may   [John 5.5,
fall upon thee; and, (as it is in that Gospell) *a worse thing* then that;   14]
Distraction, and *desperation* may fall upon thee: let no Church, no
State, in any distress say, this is the worst, for onely God knowes,
what is the worst, that God can doe to us. *Job* does not deny here, but
that this *Si occiderit,* if it come to a matter of *life,* it were another
manner of triall, then either the *si irruerent Sabæi,* if the *Sabæans*   [Job 1]
520 should come, and drive his Cattell, and slay his servants; more, then
the *si ignis caderet,* if the fire of God should fall from heaven, and
devoure all; more, then the *si ventus concuteret,* if the winde of the
wildernesse, should shake downe his house, and kill all his children.
The Devill in his malice saw, that if it came to matter of *life, Iob* was
like enough to be shaked in his faith; *Skin for skin, and all that ever*   [Job 2.4]
a man hath will he give for his life. God foresaw that, in his gracious
providence too; and therefore he took that clause out of *Satans* Commission, and inserted his *veruntamen animam ejus serva,* medle not
with his life. The love of this life, which is *naturall* to us, and im-
530 printed by God in us, is not *sinfull: Few and evill have the days of*   [Gen. 47.9]
my pilgrimage been, says *Iacob* to *Pharaoh:* though they had been
evill, (which makes our days seem long) and though he were no
young man, when he said so, yet the days which he had past, he
thought *few,* and desired more. When *Eliah* was fled into the wildernesse, and that in passion, and vehemence he said to God, *Sufficit*   [1 Kings
Domine, tolle animam meam, It is enough o Lord, now take away   19.4]
my life, if he had been heartily, thoroughly weary of his life, he
needed not to have *fled* from *Iesabel,* for he *fled* but to *save his life.*
The *Apostle* had a *Cupio dissolvi,* a desire to be dissolved; but yet a   [Philip.
540 love to his brethren corrected that desire, and made him finde that   1.23]
it was far better for him to live. Our Saviour himselfe, when it came

[Mat.
26.39]
to the pinch, and to the agony, had a *Transeat Calix*, a *naturall* declining of death. The naturall love of our naturall life is not *ill:* It is ill, in many cases, *not to love this life:* to expose it to unnecessary dangers, is alwayes ill; and there are overtures to as great sinnes, in *hating* this life, as in loving it; and therefore *Jobs* first consideration is, *si occiderit,* if *he should kill me,* if I thought he would kill me, this were enough to put me from trusting in any.

But *Jobs* consideration went farther, then to the *si occideret,* 550 *Though he should kill me,* for it comes to an absolute assurance that God *will* kill him; for so it is in the Originall, *Ecce occidet, Behold, I see he will kill me;* I have, I can have no hope of life, at his hands. Tis all our cases; *Adam* might have liv'd, if he would, but *I cannot.* God hath placed an *Ecce,* a marke of my death, upon every thing living, that I can set mine eye upon; every thing is a remembrancer, every thing is a Judge upon me, and pronounces, I *must* dye. The whole frame of the world is mortall, *Heaven and Earth passe away:*
[Mat.
24.35]
Heb. 9.27
Job 7.7
Iam. 4.14
and upon us all, there is a irrecoverable Decree past, *statutum est, It is appointed to all men, that they shall once dye.* But when? quickly; 560 If thou looke up into the aire, *remember that thy life is but a winde,* If thou see a cloud in the aire, aske St. *James* his question, *what is your life?* and give St. *James* his answer, *It is a vapour that appeareth and vanisheth away.* If thou behold a *Tree,* then *Job* gives thee a comparison of thy selfe; A *Tree* is an *embleme* of thy selfe; nay a Tree is the *originall,* thou art but the *copy,* thou art not so good as it: for,
Iob 14.7
There is hope of a tree (as you reade there) *if the roote wax old, if the stock be dead, if it be cut down, yet by the sent of the waters, it will bud, but man is sick, and dyeth, and where is he?* he shall not wake againe, till heaven be no more. Looke upon the *water,* and we 570 are as that, and as that spilt upon the ground: Looke to the *earth,* and we are not like that, but we are earth it self: At our Tables we feed upon the dead, and in the Temple we tread upon the dead: and when we meet in a Church, God hath made many *echoes,* many testimonies of our death, in the walls, and in the windowes, and he onely knowes, whether he will not make another testimony of our mortality, of the youngest amongst us, before we part, and make the very *place of our buriall,* our *deathbed. Jobs* contemplation went so far; not onely to a *Si occideret,* to a possibility that he *might* dye,

but to an *Ecce occidet,* to an assurance that he *must* dye; I know
580 there is an infalliblenesse in the Decree, an inevitablenesse in nature,
an inexorablenesse in God, I must dye. And the word beares a third
interpretation beyond this; for *si occiderit,* is not onely, *if he should
kill me,* as he *may,* if he *will,* and it may be he will; nor onely, *that I
am sure he will kill me,* I know I *must* dye, but the word may very
well be also, *though he have killed me.* So that *Jobs* resolution that
he will trust in God, is grounded upon all these considerations, That
there is exercise of our hope in God, *before* death, *in* the agony of
death, and *after* death. First, in our good dayes, and in the time of
health, Memorare novissima, sayes the wise man, we must remember   [Ecclus.
590 our end, our death. But that we cannot forget, every thing presents   7.40 in
that to us; But his counsell there, is, *in omnibus operibus,* In all thine   Vulg.; 7.36
undertakings, in all thine actions, remember *thine end;* when thou   in A.V.]
art in any worldly work, for advancing thy *state,* remember thy
naturall death, but especially when thou art in a *sinfull* worke, for
satisfying thy *lusts,* remember thy *spirituall death:* Be afraid of this
death, and thou wilt never feare the other: Thou wilt rather sigh with
David, My soule hath too long dwelt with him that hateth peace: Psal. 120.6
Thou wilt be glad when a *bodily death* may deliver thee from all
farther danger of a *spirituall death:* And thou wilt be ashamed of
600 that imputation, which is layd upon worldly men, by St. *Cyprian, Ad
nostros navigamus, & ventos contrarios optamus,* we pretend to be
sayling homewards, and yet we desire to have the winde against us;
we are travelling to the heavenly *Jerusalem,* and yet we are loath to
come thither. Here then is the use of our *hope before* death, that this
life shall be a gallery into a better roome, and deliver us over to a better
Country: for, *if in this life onely we have hope in Christ, we are of*   I Cor. 15.19
all men the most miserable.

Secondly, *in the agony of death;* when the Sessions are come, and
that as a prisoner may looke from that Tower, and see the Judge that
610 must condemne him to morrow, come in to night; so we lye upon
our death-bed, and apprehend a present judgement to be given upon
us, when, if we will not *pleade* to the Indictment, if we will stand
mute, and have nothing to say to God, we are condemned already,
condemned in our silence; and if we do plead, we have no plea, but
guilty; nothing to say, but to confesse all the Indictment against our

selves; when the flesh is too weake, as that it can performe no office, and yet would faine stay here, when the soule is laden with more sins then she can bear, and yet would faine contract more; in this agony, there is this use of our *hope,* that as God shall then, when our bodily

[Gen. 3.19]

⁶²⁰ eares are deaf, whisper to our soules, and say, *Memento homo, Remember, consider man, that thou art but dust,* and art *now returning into dust,* so we, in our hearts, when our bodily tongues are speech-

[Job] 10.[9]

lesse, may then say to God, as it is in *Job, Memento quæso, Remember thou also, I beseech thee, O God, that it is thou that hast made me as clay, and that it is thou that bringest me to that state againe;* and therefore come thou, and looke to thine owne worke; come and *let thy servant depart in peace, in* having *seen his salvation.* My hope *before* death is, that this life is the *way;* my hope *at* death is, that my death shall be *a doore* into a better state.

⁶³⁰ Lastly, the use of our *hope,* is *after* death, that God by his promise, hath made himself my debter, till he restore my body to me againe, in the resurrection: My body hath sinned, and he hath not redeemed a sinner, he hath not saved a sinner, except he have redeemed and saved my body, as well as my soule. To those soules that lye under the Altar and solicite God, for the resurrection, in the Revelation, God

6.11

sayes, *That they should rest for a little season, untill their fellow-servants, and their brethren, that should be killed, even as they were, were fulfilled.* All that while, while that number is fulfilling, is our hope exercised after our death. And therefore the bodies of the Saints

⁶⁴⁰ of God, which have been Temples of the Holy Ghost, when the soule is gone out of them, are not to be neglected, as a *sheath* that had lost the *knife,* as a *shell* that had spent the *kernell;* but as the Godhead did not depart from the dead body of Christ Jesus, then when that body lay dead in the grave, so the power of God, and the merit of Christ Jesus, doth not depart from the body of man, but his blood lives in our ashes, and shall in his appointed time, awaken this body againe, to an everlasting glory.

Since therefore *Job* had, and *we* have this assurance *before* we dye, *when* we dye, *after* we are dead, it is upon good reason, that he did,

⁶⁵⁰ and we do trust in God, *though he should* kill us, *when he doth* kill us, *after he hath* killed us. Especially since it is *Ille, He* who is spoken

Deut. 32.39

of before, he *that kills, and gives life,* he that *wounds, and makes whole againe.* God executes by what way it pleases him; condemned persons cannot chuse the manner of their death; whether God kill by *sicknesse,* by *age,* by the hand of the *law,* by the malice of *man, si ille,* as long as we can see that it is he, he that is *Shaddai, Vastator, & Restaurator,* the *destroyer,* and the *repairer,* howsoever *he kill,* yet *he gives life too,* howsoever he *wound,* yet he *heales too,* howsoever he lock us into our graves now, yet he hath the keys of hell, and death, 660 and shall in his time, extend that voyce to us all, *Lazare veni foras,* [Joh. 11.43] come forth of your putrefaction, to incorruptible glory. Amen.

Number 9.

A Lent-Sermon
Preached before the King, at White-Hall,
February 16, 1620 [1620/21].

I TIM. 3.16. *AND WITHOUT CONTROVERSIE, GREAT IS THE MYSTERY OF GODLINESS: GOD WAS MANIFEST IN THE FLESH, JUSTIFIED IN THE SPIRIT, SEEN OF ANGELS, PREACHED UNTO THE GENTILES, BELIEVED ON IN THE WORLD, RECEIVED UP INTO GLORY.*

---

2 Reg. 20.9
Josh. 10.12

THIS IS no Text for an Houre-glasse: if God would afford me *Ezekias* signe, *Ut revertatur umbra,* that the shadow might go backward upon the Dial; or *Joshuah's* signe, *Ut sistat Sol,* that the Sun might stand still all the day, this were text enough to employ all the day, and all the dayes of our life. The *Lent,* which we begin now, is a full Tythe of the year; but the houre which we begin now, is not a full tythe of this day, and therefore we should not grudge all that: But payment of Tythes is growne matter of controversie; and we, by our Text, are directed onely upon matter with-

10 out controversie: *And without controversie, &c.*

Here is the compass, that the essential Word of God, the Son of God, *Christ Jesus,* went: He was God, *humbled in the flesh;* he was Man, *received into glory.* Here is the compasse that the written Word of God, *went,* the Bible; that begun in *Moses,* in darknesse, in the *Chaos;* and it ends in Saint *John,* in clearnesse, in a Revelation. Here is the compass of all time, as time was distributed in the Creation,

[Gen. 1.5]

Vespere & mane; darknesse, and then light: the Evening and the Morning made the Day; Mystery and Manifestation make the Text.

206

The Doctrine of the present Season, is Mortification, Humiliation;
²⁰ and the experience of the present Place, where we stand now in
Court, is, that the glory of the persons, in whose presence we stand,
occasions Humility in us; the more glorious *they* are, the humbler
we are; and therefore to consider Christ, as he is *received into glory,*
is as much the way of our Humiliation and Mortification, as to consider him in his Passion, in his exinanition: At least, how small
account should we make of those things which we suffer for Christ
in this world, when we see in this Text, that in the describing the
History of Christ from his Incarnation to his Ascension, the Holy
Ghost pretermits, never mentions, never seems to consider the Pas-
³⁰ sion of Christ; as though all that he had suffered for man, were
nothing in respect of that he would suffer, if the justice of God had
required any heavier satisfaction.

The Text then is a sufficient Instruction to *Timothy,* to whom this
Epistle is sent, and to us, to whom it is sent too, that thereby we
might know how to behave our selves in the House of God, which
is the Church of God, the pillar and ground of Truth; as is said in
the verse immediately before the Text, and to which the Text hath
relation: we know how to behave our selves in the Church, if we
know in the Text that such a *Mystery of godlinesse* there is, and
⁴⁰ know what it is. Our parts therefore, are but two; Mystery and Manifestation. In the first, the Apostle proceeds thus: First, he recom-
mends to us such Doctrine as is without controversie: and truly there
is enough of that to save any soule, that hath not a minde to wrangle
it selfe into Hell. And then he sayes, that this Godlinesse, though it
be without controversie, yet it is a Mystery, a Secret; not present, not
obvious, not discernable with every eye: It is a Mystery, and a great
Mystery; not the greatest, but yet great, that is, great enough; he
that knowes that, needs no more. And then, for the second part,
which is the manifestation of the Mystery, we shall look upon that
⁵⁰ by all those beams, which shine out in this Text, *Ab ortu ad meridiem,*
from Christs East to his Noon, from his first *manifesting in the flesh,*
to his *receiving into glory.*

First then, he proposes Doctrine without controversie: for, *Quod
simpliciter prædicatur, credendum; quod subtiliter disputatur, in-
telligendum est.* That which Christ hath plainly delivered, is the

Part 1
Augustine

exercise of my Faith; that which other men have curiously disputed, is the exercise of my understanding: If I understand not their curious disputations, perchance I shall not be esteemed in this world; but if I believe not Christs plain Doctrine, I am sure I shall not be saved
60 in the next. It is true, that Christ reprehends them often, *Quia non intellexerunt,* but what? *Scripturas, legem:* because they understood not the Scriptures, which they were bound to believe. It is some negligence not to read a Proclamation from the King; it is a contempt, to transgresse it; but to deny the power from which it is derived, is treason. Not to labour to understand the Scriptures, is to slight God; but not to believe them, is to give God the lye: he makes God a lyer, if he believe not the Record that God gave of his Son. When I come to heaven, I shall not need to ask of S. *John*'s Angel, nor of his Elders, *Ubi Prophetæ, ubi Apostoli, ubi Evangelistæ;*
70 where are the Prophets, where are the Evangelists, where are the Apostles? for, I am sure I shall see them there: But perchance I may be put to ask S. *Paul*'s question, *Ubi Scribæ? ubi Sapientes?* where are the Scribes? where are the Wise men? where are the Disputers of the world? perchance I may misse a great many of them there. It is the Text that saves us; the interlineary glosses, and the marginal notes, and the *variæ lectiones,* controversies and perplexities, undo us: the Will, the Testament of God, enriches us; the Schedules, the Codicils of men, begger us: because the Serpent was subtiller then any, he would dispute and comment upon Gods Law, and so de-
80 ceiv'd by his subtilty. The Word of God is *Biblia,* it is not *Bibliotheca;* a Book, a Bible, not a Library. And all that book is not written in *Balthazars* character, in a *Mene, Tekel, Upharsim,* that we must call in Astrologers, and Chaldeans, and Southsayers, to interpret it. That which was written so, as that it could not be understood, was written, sayes the text there, with the fingers of mans hand; It is the hand of man that induces obscurities; the hand of God hath written so, as a man may runne, and read; walk in the duties of his calling here, and attend the salvation of his soul too. He that believes Christ, and *Mahomet,* indifferently, hath not proposed the right end: he
90 that believes the Word of God, and traditions, indifferently, hath not proposed the right way. In any Conveyance, if any thing be interlin'd, the interlining must be as well testified, and have the same witnesses

Marginal notes: 1 John 5.10 · 1 Cor. 1.20 · Gen. 3.1 · 2 Cor. 11.3 · Dan. 5.25 · v. 5 · [Hab. 2.2]

upon the Endorsment, as the conveyance it self had. When there are traditions in the Church (as declaratory traditions there are) they must have the same witnesses, they must be grounded upon the Word of God: for there onely is truth without controversie. *Pilate* ask'd Christ, *Quid veritas,* what was truth; and he might have known, if he would have staid; but *exivit,* sayes the Text there, *He went out,* out to the Jewes; and there he could not finde it, there he never thought of it more. Ask of Christ speaking in his Word, there you shall know; produce the Record, the Scripture, and there is *Communis salus;* I wrote unto you of the common Salvation: What's that? *Semel tradita fides,* sayes that Apostle there: The Faith which was once delivered to the Saints: where *semel* is not *aliquando;* once, is not once upon a time, I cannot tell when; but *semel* is *simul,* once is at once: The Gospel was delivered all together, and not by Postscripts. Thus it is, If we go to the Record, to the Scripture: and thus it is, if we ask a Judge (I do not say, The Judge, but A Judge) for, the Fathers are a Judge; a Judge is a Judge, though there lie an appeal from him. And will not the Fathers say so too? *Quod ubique, quod semper;* that's common salvation, which hath bound the *Communion of Saints;* that which all Churches alwayes have thought and taught to be necessary to salvation. Ask the Record, ask that Judge, and it will be so; and it will be so, if you ask the Counsel on the other side. Ask the *Council of Trent* it self, and the Idolaters of that Council will not say, that our Church affirmes any Errour; neither can they say, that we leave any truth unaffirmed, which the Primitive Church affirm'd to be necessary to salvation. For those things which the Schoole hath drawn into disputation since, as their form is, in the beginning of every question, to say, *Videtur quod non,* one would think it were otherwise; if when they have said all, I return to the beginning again, *Videtur quod non,* I think it is otherwise still, must I be damned? The evidence for my salvation is my *Credo,* not their *Probo;* And if I must get Heaven by a Syllogism, my *Major* is *Credo in Deum Patrem, I believe in God the Father;* for, *Pater major,* the Father is greater then all: And my *Minor* shall be, *Credo in Deum Filium, I believe in God the Son, Qui exivit de patre,* he came from God; And my Conclusion, which must proceed from *Major & Minor,* shall be *Credo in Spiritum Sanctum, I believe in the Holy Ghost,*

John 18.38

Jude 1.3

John 10.29

13.3

130 who proceeds from Father and Son: And this Syllogisme brought me into the Militant Church in my Baptisme, and this will carry me into the Triumphant, in my Transmigration; for, doctrine of Salvation is matter without controversie.

Myster.

But yet, as clear as it is, it is a Mystery, a Secret; not that I cannot see it, but that I cannot see it with any eyes that I can bring: not with the eye of Nature: *Flesh and blood hath not revealed this unto thee,* sayes Christ to *Peter:* not with the eye of Learning; *Thou hast hid these things from the wise,* sayes Christ to his Father: not with the
• eye of State, that wheresoever I see a good Government, I should pre-
140 sume a good Religion; for, we do not admit the *Church of Rome,* and yet we doe admire the *Court of Rome:* nor with the eye of a private sence; for no prophecy of any Scripture; (that is, noe interpretation of any Scripture) for, *Quod non nisi instinctu Dei scitur, prophetia est;* that which I cannot understand by reason, but by especiall assistance from God, all that is Prophecy; no Scripture is of private interpretation. I see not this mystery by the eye of Nature, of Learning, of State, of mine own private sence; but I see it by the eye of the Church, by the light of Faith, that's true; but yet organically, instrumentally, by the eye of the Church. And this Church is that which pro-
150 poses to me all that is necessary to my salvation, in the Word, and seals all to me in the Sacraments. If another man see, or think he sees more then I; if by the help of his Optick glasses, or perchance but by his imagination, he see a star or two more in any constellation then I do; yet that starre becomes none of the constellation; it adds no limb, no member to the constellation, that was perfect before: so, if other men see that some additional and traditional things may adde to the dignity of the Church, let them say it conduces to the well-being, not to the very being; to the existence, not to the essence of the Church; for that's onely things necessary to salvation. And this mystery is, Faith in a
160 pure conscience: for that's the same thing that is called Godliness in this text: and it is to profess the Gospel of Christ Jesus sincerely, and intirely; to have a conscience testifying to himself, that he hath contributed nothing to the diminution of it, that he labours to live by it, that he hopes to die in it, that he feares not to die for it. This is *Mysterium, opertum, & apertum,* hid from those that are lost, but manifested to his Saints.

Mat. 16.17

Mat. 11.25

2 Pet. 1.20

Gregory

1 Tim. 3.9

2 Cor. 4.3

Col. 1.26

It is a Mystery, and a great Mystery; that's next: not that there
is not a greater; for the Mystery of Iniquity is greater then the Mystery of Godliness: Compare Creeds to Creeds, and the new Creed
170 of the *Trent Council,* is greater by many Articles then the *Apostles
Creed* is. Compare Oathes to Oathes; and *Berengarius* old Oath in
the Roman Church, that he must sweare to the *Frangitur & teritur,*
that he broke the flesh of Christ with his teeth, and ground it with
his jawes; and the new Oath of the *Council of Trent,* that he must
sweare that all those subtill Schoole-points, determined there, in
which a man might have believed the contrary a few dayes before,
and yet have been a good Roman Catholick too, are true, and true
de fide; so true, as that he cannot be saved now, except he believe
them to be so: the *Berengarians* Oath, and the *Trent*-oath, have much
180 more difficulty in them, then to swear, that King *James* is lawfull
King in all his Dominions, and therefore exempt from all forreign
jurisdiction over him. There is a Mystery of Iniquity, declared in a
Creed of Iniquity, and in an Oath of Iniquity, greater then the Mystery of Godliness: but yet this is great, that is, great enough; he needs
no more, that hath this, faith with a pure conscience: he need not
go up to heaven for more, not to a Vice-god, to an infallible Bishop
of *Rome;* he need not go over-sea for more, sayes *Moses* there; not
to the hills, beyond-sea, nor to the lake beyond-sea: for God hath
given him his station in a Church, where this Mystery is sufficiently
190 declared and explicated. The Mystery of Iniquity may be great, for
it hath wrought a great while. *Jam operatur,* sayes the Apostle in his
time; the Mystery of iniquity doth already work, and it is likely to
work still: It is but a little while since we saw it work under ground,
in the vault. But if (as hath been lately, royally, and religiously intimated to us all) their insolency have so far infatuated them, as to think
themselves at an end of their work, and promise themselves a holy-day,
our assurance is in this, *Pater operatur adhuc, & ego operor,* sayes
Christ: My Father works yet, and I work: and if amongst us the Father work, and the Son work; for all the vain hopes of some, and the
200 vain feares of others, the *Mystery of godliness* will stand and grow.

Now, how far this Mystery, this great Mystery, this Mystery without controversie is revealed in this Text, we are to look by the severall
beames thereof; of which, the first is, *Manifestatus in carne, God*

Magnum

Deut. 30.12

2 Thes. 2.7

In Parliam.

Joh. 5.17

Part 2

Psal. 19.1

was manifested in the flesh. Cœli enarrant, sayes *David, The heavens declare the glory of God;* and that should be the harmony of the Spheares. *Invisibilia conspiciuntur,* sayes Saint *Paul, Invisible things of God are seen in the visible;* and that should be the prospect of this world. The knowledge of God was manifested often in the Prophets; he foretold, therefore he foresaw. His Wisdome was manifested ²¹⁰ often, in frustrating all Councels of all *Achitophels* against him. And his power was manifested often: In the water; consider it at least in the Red sea, and in *Pharaoh,* if you will bring it no nearer home; And in the Fire, consider it at least in the fiery Furnace, if you will bring it no nearer home. His Knowledge, his Wisdome, his Power, his Mercy, his Justice, all his Attributes are alwayes manifested in all his works. But, *Deus in carne,* that the person of God, God himself, should be manifested, and manifested in our flesh, *Ineffabile omni sermoni, omni ignotum intelligentiæ, ipsi Angelorum primati non agnitum.* And if the Primate of the Angels, the highest order of ²²⁰ them that stand in Gods sight, know it not; if no understanding were able to conceive it, that had all the refinings and concoction, that study, and speculation, and zeal to be *vir desideriorum* (as the Angel said to *Daniel*) a man that desired to dwell upon the meditation of his God, could give; must not I, who always come with *Moses* uncircumcised lips, not to speak perswasively; and always with *Jeremies* defect, *Puer sum, nescio loqui,* not to speak plainly; come now with *Zachary*'s dumbness, not to speak at all in this Mystery? But hearkning to that which he who onely knew this Mystery, hath said, *Verbum Caro factum est, The word was made flesh;* And *Deus* ²³⁰ *manifestatus in carne,* God was manifested in the flesh; rest my self in his Word, and pray you in Christs stead to doe so too, in this, and all Mysteries of your Religion, to rest upon the onely Word of God: for in this particular, it is not mis-grounded, nor mis-collected by him that says, *Omnes pæne errores,* almost all Errours have proceeded out of this, that this great Mystery, that *God was manifested in the flesh, Aut non omnino, aut non sicuti est creditum;* is either not at all, or not aright believed. The Jews believe it not at all; and to them *Tertullian* sayes enough: Since out of their Prophets they confess, that when the *Messias* shall be manifested, they must for a ²⁴⁰ time suffer many calamities in this world; if their *Messias* should be

Rom. 1.20

Areopag.

[Dan. 10.11]

[John 1.14]

Fulgent.

Tertul.

manifested now (sayes he) what could they suffer? They say they must suffer banishment; *Et ubi dispersio gentis, quæ jam extorris?* sayes he, whither shall that Nation be banish'd, which is already in banishment and dispersion? *Redde statum Judæis,* let the Jews shew me a *State,* a *Kingdom,* a *Common-wealth,* a *Government, Magistrates, Judicatures, Merchandise,* and *Armies;* let them shew something to loose for a *Messias,* and then let them look for a *Messias.* The Jewes are within the *non omnino,* they believe not this Mystery at all: And then, for the *non sicut est,* for the not believing it aright, as the old Valentinians are renewed in the Anabaptists (for both deny that Christ took flesh of the Virgin) so the old Manichæans are not renewed, but exceeded in the Transubstantiators: for they said the body of Christ was left in one place, in the Sun; these say, it is upon as many Tables, and in as many Boxes as they will. But whether the manifestation of God in the flesh were referred to the Incarnation of Christ; or to his Declaration, when the wise men of the East came to see him at *Bethleem;* whether when it was done, or when it was declared to be done, hath admitted a question, because the Western Church hath call'd that day of their coming to him, the *Epiphany;* and *Epiphany* is Manifestation. Then therefore is God manifested to us, when, as these wise men offer'd their Myrrhe and Frankincense, we offer the Sacrifice of Prayer; and as they offer'd their Gold, we offer our temporall wealth for the glory of Christ Jesus: And when the love of him corrects in thee the intemperances of adorning thy flesh, of pampering thy flesh, of obeying thy flesh, then especially is this *Epiphany, God is manifested in the flesh,* in thy flesh.

Now, when he was *manifested in the flesh,* it behooved him to be *justified in the spirit;* for he came *in similitudinem carnis peccati:* they took him for a sinner, and they saw him converse with sinners: for any thing they could see, it might have been *Caro peccati,* sinfull flesh; and they saw enough to make them sure that it was *Caro mortis,* mortall flesh. Though he were *Panis de cœlo,* Bread from Heaven, yet himself was hungry; and though he were *fons perennis,* an everlasting spring, yet himself was thirsty; though he were *Deus totius consolationis,* the God of all comfort, yet his soul was heavy unto death; and though he were *Dominus vitæ,* the Lord of Life, yet

Justificat. in spirit. Rom. 8.3

2 Cor. 1.3

Death had dominion over him. When therefore *Christ was mani-*
fested in the flesh, flesh subject to Death, Death, which was the re-
280 ward of Sin; and would take upon him to forgive sins; it behooved
him to be extraordinarily justified, extraordinarily declared to the
world: and so he was; he was justified *in Spiritu,* in the Spirit; first,
in Spiritu Sancto, in the Spirit, in the Holy Ghost; both when the
Holy Ghost was sent to him, and when the Holy Ghost was sent by
him, from him. The Holy Ghost was sent to him in his Baptisme,
and he tarried upon him: Christ was not, a Christian is not justified
by one accesse, one visitation, one approach of the Holy Ghost; not
by one religious act: it is a permanency, a perseverance that justifies:

Gal. 3.3 　　that foolishness, and that fascination (as the Apostle calls it) that
290 Witchcraft which he imputes to the *Galatians,* is not so worn out,
but that there are foolish and bewitched *Galatians* still, that begun
in the Spirit, and will be made perfect in the Flesh; that receiv'd
their Christianity in one Church, and attend a confirmation, a better
state, in a worse. Christ was justified by the Holy Ghost, when the
Holy Ghost came to him: so he was, when he came from him, at
Pentecost, upon his Apostles; and then he came in Tongues, and
fiery Tongues. Christ was not, a Christian is not justified in silence,
but in declarations and open professions; in tongues: and not in dark
and ambiguous speeches, nor in faint and retractable speeches, but
300 in fiery tongues; fiery, that is, fervent; fiery, that is, clear. He was
justified so, *a Spiritu Sancto;* and so he was, *a Spiritu suo,* by his own
Spirit: not onely in that protestation of his, *Who can accuse me of*

[John 8.46] 　*any sin?* for S. *Paul* could say that he was unreproachable in the sight
of men, and yet he could not chuse but say, *Quorum ego maximus;*

[1 Tim. 　　that he was the greatest sinner of all men. I were a miserable man,
1.15] 　　if I could accuse Christ of no sin; if I could not prove all my sins his,
I were under a heavy condemnation. But that which we intend by his
being justified, *a spiritu suo,* by his own spirit, is, not by the testimony
that he gave of himself; but by that Spirit, that God-head, that dwelt
310 bodily in him, and declared him, and justified him in that high
power and practise of Miracles. When Christ came into this world,
as if he had come a day before any day, a day before *Moses* his *in*
principio, before there was any creature (for when Christ came,
there was no creature that could exercise any natural faculty in op-

position to his purposes) when Nature his Vicegerent gave up her
sword to his hands; when the Sea shut up her selfe like Marble, and
bore him; and the Earth opened her selfe like a book, to deliver out
her dead, to wait upon him; when the winds, in the midst of their
own roaring, could heare his voyce; and Death it self, in putrid and
320 corrupt carkases, could heare his voice; and when his own body,
whom his own soul had left and abandoned, was not abandoned by
this Spirit, by this Godhead (for the Deity departed not from the
dead body of Christ) then was Christ especially justified by this
Spirit, in whose power he raised himself from the dead; he was justified *in Spiritu Sancto,* and *in spiritu suo;* two witnesses were enough
for him. Adde a third for thy self, *& justificetur in Spiritu tuo,* let
him be justified in thy spirit: God is safe enough in himself, and yet
it was a good declaratory addition, that the Publicans justified God: Luke 7.29
Wisdom is safe enough of her self, and yet Wisdome is justified of Mat. 11.19
330 her children: Christ is sufficiently justified; but *justificetur in Spiritu
tuo,* in thy spirit. To say, If I consider the *Talmud,* Christ may as
well be the *Messias,* as any whom the Jews place their marks upon;
if I consider the *Alchoran,* Christ is like enough to be a better Prophet
then *Mahomet;* if I consider the Arguments of the *Arrians,* Christ
may be the Son of God for all that; if I consider the Church of *Rome,*
and ours, he is as likely to manifest himself in his own Word here,
as there in their word; to say but so, Christ may be God for any
thing I know: this is but to baile him, not to justifie him; not to
acquit him, but to put him over to the Sessions, to the great Sessions,
340 where he shall justifie himself; but none of them, who do not justifie
him, testifie for him, *in spiritu suo,* sincerely in their souls: nay, that's 1 Cor. 2.11
not enough: to justifie is an act of declaration; and no man knowes
what is in man, but the spirit of man: and therefore he that leaves
any outward thing undone, that belongs to his calling, for Christ,
is so far from having justified Christ, as that at the last day, he shall
meet his voice with them that cried *Crucifie him,* and with theirs
that cried, *Not Christ, but Barabbas:* if thou doubt in thy heart, if
thou disguise in thine actions, *non justificatur in spiritu tuo,* Christ
is not justified in thy spirit; and that's it which concernes thee most.
350 Christ had all this testimony and more, *Visus ab Angelis,* he was *Visus ab*
seen of Angels: which is, not onely visited by Angels, serv'd by An- *Angelis*

gels; waited upon by Angels: so he was, and he was so in every passage, in every step. An Angel told his mother, that he should be born: and an Angel told the Shepherds, that he was born; and that which directed the wise men of the East where to finde him, when he was born, is also believed by some of the Ancients, to have been an Angel in the likeness of a Star. When he was tempted by the Devil, Angels came and ministred to him, but the Devil had left him before; his own power, had dissipated his. In his Agony in the
360 Garden, an Angel came from heaven to strengthen him; but he had recovered before, and was come to his *Veruntamen, Not my will, but thine be done.* He told *Peter,* he could have more then twelve legions of Angels to assist him; but he would not have the assistance of his own sword: he denies not that which the Devil sayes, that the Angels had in charge, *that he should not dash his foot against a stone;* but they had an easie service of it; for his foot never dasht, never stumbled, never tripp'd in any way. As soon as any stone lay in his way, an Angel removed it: *He rolled away the stone from the sepulchre.* There the Angel testified to the women that sought him,
370 not onely that he was not there, (that was a poor comfort) but where he was: He is gone into *Galilee,* and there you shall finde him. There also the Angel testified to the men of *Galilee,* that look'd after him, not onely that he was gone up (that was but a poor comfort) but that he should come again. *The same Jesus shall so come as he went.* There in Heaven, they perform that service, whilest he stayes there, which they are call'd upon to do: *Let all the Angels of God worship him;* and in judgement, *when the Son of man shall come in his glory, all the holy Angels shall be with him:* in every point of that great compass, in every arch, in every section of that great circle, of which
380 no man knows the Diameter, how long it shall be from Christs first coming to his second, *visus ab Angelis,* he was seen, he was visited, he was waited upon by the Angels. But there is more intended in this, then so.

Christ was seen of the Angels, otherwise now, then ever before: something was reveal'd to the Angels themselves concerning Christ, which they knew not before; at least, not so as they knew it now. For, all the Angels do not alwayes know all things: if they had, there would have been no dissention, no strife, no difference between the

Margin references:

Mat. 4.11

Luke 22.43

Mat. 26.53

Mat. 4.6

Mat. 28.2

Acts 1.11

Heb. 1.6
Mat. 25.31

two Angels; the Angel of *Persia* would not have withstood the other
390 Angel 21 dayes; neither would have resisted Gods purpose, if both
had known it; S. *Dionyse*, who considers the names, and natures,
and places, and apprehensions of Angels, most of any, observes of
the highest orders of Angels, *Ordines supremi ad Jesu aspectum
hæsitabant;* the highest of the highest orders of Angels, were amaz'd
at Christs coming up in the Flesh; it was a new and unexpected
thing to see Christ come thither, in that manner. There they say with
amazement, *Quis iste? Who is this that cometh from Edom, with
dyed garments from Bozrah?* And Christ answers there, *Ego, it is I,
I that speak in righteousness, I that am mighty to save.* The Angels
400 reply, *Wherefore are thy garments red, like him that treadeth the
wine-press?* and Christ gives them satisfaction, *calcavi;* You mistake
not the matter, *I have trodden the wine-press;* and *calcavi solus, I
have trodden the wine-press alone, and of the people there was none
with me.* The Angels then knew not this, not all this, not all the
particulars of this; The mystery of Christs Incarnation for the Redemption of Man, the Angels knew in generall; for, it was *commune
quoddam principium;* it was the generall mark, to which all their
service, as they were ministring spirits, was directed. But for particulars, as amongst the Prophets, some of the later understood more then
410 the former (*I understand more then the ancients,* sayes *David*) and
the Apostles understood more then the Prophets, even of those things
which they had prophesied, (*this Mystery in other ages was not made
known, as it is now revealed unto the holy Apostles;*) so the Angels
are come to know some things of Christ, since Christ came, in another manner then before. And this may be that which S. *Paul* intends, when he sayes, that he was made a Minister of the Gospel,
*To the intent, that now, unto principalities and powers, in heavenly
places, might be known by the Church, the manifold wisdome of
God.* And S. *Peter* also speaking of the administration of the Church,
420 expresses it so, *That the Angels desire to look into it.* Which is not
onely that which S. *Augustine* sayes, *Innotuit a sæculis per Ecclesiam
Angelis,* That the Angels saw the mystery of the Christian Religion,
from before all beginnings, and that by the Church, *Quia ipsa Ecclesia illis, in Deo apparuit;* Because they saw in God the future
Church, from before all beginnings; but even in the propagation and

Dan. 10.13

Isa. 63.1

Psal.
119.100
Ephes. 3.3–5

Ephes. 3.10

1 Pet. 1.12
Aug.

administration of the Church, they see many things now, which distinctly, effectually, experimentally, as they do now, they could not see before. And so, to this purpose, *Visus in nobis,* Christ is seen by the Angels, in us and our conversation now. *Spectaculum sumus,* ⁴³⁰ sayes the Apostle; *We are made a spectacle to men and angels.* The word is there *Theatrum,* and so S. *Hierom* reads it: And therefore let us be careful to play those parts well, which even the *Angels* desire to see well acted. Let him that finds himself to be the honester man by thinking so, think in the name of God, that he hath a particular tutelar Angel, it will do him no harm to think so: And let him that thinks not so, yet think, that so far as conduces to the support of Gods children, and to the joy of the Angels themselves, and to the glory of God, the Angels do see mens particular actions: and then, if thou wouldst not sollicite a womans chastity, if her servant were ⁴⁴⁰ by to testifie it; nor calumniate an absent person in the Kings ear, if his friends were by to testifie it; if thou canst slumber in thy self, that main consideration, That the eye of God is always open, and always upon thee; yet have a little religious civility, and holy respect, even to those Angels that see thee: That those Angels which see Christ Jesus now, sate down in glory at the right hand of his Father; all sweat wip'd from his Browes, and all teares from his Eyes; all his Stripes heal'd, all his Blood stanch'd, all his Wounds shut up, and all his Beauty returned there; when they look down hither, to see the same Christ in thee, may not see him scourged again, wounded, ⁴⁵⁰ torn and mangled again, in thy blasphemings, nor crucified again in thy irreligious conversation: *Visus ab Angelis,* he was seen of the Angels, in himself, whilest he was here: and he is seen in his Saints upon earth, by Angels now; and shall be so to the end of the world: Which Saints he hath gathered from the Gentiles: which is the next branch; *Prædicatus gentibus,* he was preached to the Gentiles.

Mercy and truth meet together, says *David:* every where in Gods proceedings they meet together; but no where closer, then in calling the Gentiles. Jesus Christ was made a Minister of the Circumcision for the truth of God: wherein consisted that truth? *To confirm the* ⁴⁶⁰ *promises made unto the fathers,* says the Apostle there, and that's to the Jews: but was Christ a Minister of the Circumcision onely for that, onely for the truth? No: *Truth and Mercy meet together,* as it

1 Cor. 4.9
Hierom

Prædicat.
Gentib.
Psal. 85.10
Rom. 15.8

followes there; *and that the Gentiles might glorifie God for his* [Rom. 15.9]
mercy. The Jewes were a holy Nation; that was their addition; *Gens*
Sancta; but the addition of the Gentiles, was *peccatores,* sinners: *we* Gal. 2.15
are Jewes by nature, and not of the Gentiles, sinners, sayes S. *Paul:*
He that touch'd the Jewes, touch'd the apple of Gods eye; And for [Zech. 2.8]
their sakes, God rebuk'd Kings, and said, *Touch not mine Anoynted:* [Psal.
but upon the Gentiles, not onely dereliction, but indignation, and 105.14, 15]
470 consternation, and devastation, and extermination, every where interminated, inflicted every where, and every where multiplied: The
Jewes had all kinde of assurances and ties upon God; both Law, and
Custome; they both prescribed in God, and God had bound himself
to them by particular conveyances; by a conveyance written in their
flesh, in Circumcision; and the counterpane written in his flesh;
I have graven thy name in the palmes of my hands: But for the Gen- Isa. 49.[16]
tiles, they had none of these assurances: *When ye were without Christ* Eph. 2.12
(sayes the Apostle) *having no hope* (that is, no covenant to ground
a hope upon) *ye were without God in this world.* To contemplate
480 God himself, and not in Christ, is to be without God. And then, for
Christ to be preached to such as these, to make this Sun to set at
noon to the Jewes, and rise at midnight to the Antipodes, to the
Gentiles, this was such an abundant, such a superabundant mercy,
as might seem almost to be above the bargain, above the contract,
between Christ and his Father; more then was conditioned and decreed for the price of his Blood, and the reward of his Death: for
when God said, I will declare my decree; That is, what I intended
to give him, which is expressed thus, *I will set him my King upon* Psal. 2.[6]
my holy hill of Sion; which seemes to concern the Jewes onely: God
490 addes then, *Postula a me,* petition to me, make a new suit to me;
& dabo tibi gentes: I will give thee not onely the Jewes, but the Gen-
tiles for thine inheritance: And therefore *lætentur gentes,* sayes [Psal. 67.4;
David, Let the Gentiles rejoyce; and we in them, that Christ hath 66.5 in
asked us at his Fathers hand, and received us: And *Lætentur insulæ,* Vulg.]
sayes that Prophet too, *Let the Islands rejoyce;* and we in them, that Psal. 97.1
he hath raised us out of the Sea, out of the ocean sea, that over-flowed
all the world with ignorance; and out of the *Mediterranean* Sea, that
hath flowed into so many other lands; the sea of *Rome,* the sea of
Superstition.

⁵⁰⁰ There was then a great mercy in that, *Prædicatus gentibus,* that he
was preached to the Gentiles; but the great power is in the next,

Creditus
Mundo

Creditus mundo, that he was believed in the world. We have a Calling in our Church; that makes us Preachers: and we have Canons
in our Church; that makes us preach: and we bring a Duty, and finde
favour; that makes us preach here: There is a power here, that makes
bills of Preachers: But in whose power is it to make bills of Believers?

Heb. 11.6

Oportet accedentem credere, says S. *Paul, He that comes hither
should believe before he comes:* But, *Benedictus sis egrediens,* says

Deut. 28.6

Moses, God bless you with the power of believing, when you go from

[James]
1.22

⁵¹⁰ *hence.* Where S. *James* says, *You deceive your selves, if you be
hearers, and not doers,* how far do you deceive your selves, if you
come not half way, if you be hearers, and not believers? *Tiberius,*
who spoke all upon disguises, took it ill, if he were believed: he that
was crucified under *Tiberius,* who alwayes speaks clearly, takes it
worse, if he be not believed; for, he hath reduced all to the *Tantum-
modo crede,* onely believe, and thou art safe: if we take it higher or
lower; either above, in hearing onely, or below, in working onely,
we may misse. It is not enough to hear Sermons; it is not enough to
live a morall honest life; but take it in the midst, and that extends
⁵²⁰ to all; for there is no believing without hearing, nor working with-
out believing. Be pleased to consider this great work of believing,
in the matter, what it was that was to be believed: That that Jesus,
whose age they knew, must be antedated so far, as that they must
believe him to be elder then *Abraham:* That that Jesus, whose Father
and Mother, and Brothers and Sisters, they knew, must be believed
to be of another Family, and to have a Father in another place; and
yet he to be as old as his Father; And to have another proceeding
from him, and yet he to be no older then that person who proceeded
from him: That that Jesus, whom they knew to be that Carpenters
⁵³⁰ Son, and knew his work, must be believ'd to have set up a frame, that
reached to heaven, out of which no man could, and in which any man
might be saved: was it not as easie to believe, that those teares which
they saw upon his cheeks, were Pearles; that those drops of Blood,
which they saw upon his back, were Rubies: That that spittle, which
they saw upon his face, was ennamel: that those hands which they
saw buffet him, were reached out to place him in a Throne: And that

that Voyce which they heard cry, *Crucifige, Crucifie him,* was a *Vivat Rex, Long live Jesus of Nazareth King of the Jewes;* As to believe, that from that man, that *worm, and no man,* ingloriously traduced
540 as a Conjurer, ingloriously apprehended as a Thief, ingloriously executed as a Traytor; they should look for glory, and all glory, and everlasting glory? And from that melancholick man, who was never seen to laugh in all his life, and *whose soul was heavy unto death;* they should look for joy, and all joy, and everlasting joy: And for salvation, and everlasting salvation from him, who could not save himself from the Ignominy, from the Torment, from the Death of the Crosse? If any State, if any Convocation, if any wise Man had been to make a Religion, a Gospel; would he not have proposed a more probable, a more credible Gospel, to mans reason, then this? Be
550 pleased to consider it in the manner too: it must be believed by preaching, by *the foolishness of preaching,* sayes the Apostle; by a few men, that could give no strength to it; by ignorant men, that could give no reason for it; by poor men, that could give no pensions, nor preferments in it: That this should be believed, and believed thus, and believed by the world, the world that knew him not; *He was in the world, and the world knew him not:* the world that hated them, who would make them know him; *I have chosen you,* sayes Christ, *and therefore the world hateth you:* That then when *Mundus totus in maligno positus,* the world, and all the world, not onely was, but was
560 laid in malignity and opposition against Christ; That then the world, and all the world, the world of Ignorance, and the world of Pride, should believe the Gospel; that then the *Nicodemus,* the learned and the powerfull man of the world, should stand out no longer, but to that one Probleme, *Quomodo,* How can a man be born again that is old; and presently believe, that a man might be born again even at the last gasp: That then they which followed him, should stand no longer upon their *durus sermo,* that it was a hard saying, that they must *eat his Flesh,* and *drink his Blood,* and presently believe that there was no salvation, except they did eat and drink that Flesh and
570 Blood: That *Mary Magdelene,* who was not onely tempted (is there any that is not so?) but overcom with the temptations (and how many are so!) and possessed, and possessed with seven Devils, should presently hearken after the powerfull charm of the Gospel, and

[Psal. 22.6]

[Matt. 26.38]

[1 Cor. 1.21]

Joh. 1.10

15.19
1 Joh. 5.19

[Joh. 6.60]

presently believe that she should be welcom into his arms, after all her prostitutions: that the world, this world, all this world, should believe this, and believe it thus; This was the Apostles *Altitudo divitiarum,* the depth of the riches of Gods wisdom: And this is his *Longitudo,* and *Latitudo,* the breadth, and length, and heighth, and depth, which no man can comprehend. *Theudas* rose up, *dicens se* 580 *esse aliquem,* he said he was some body; and he prov'd no body. *Simon Magus* rose up, *Dicens se esse aliquem magnum,* saying, he was some great body; and he prov'd as little. Christ Jesus rose up, and said himself not to be some body, nor some great body; but that there was no body else, no other name given under Heaven, whereby we should be saved; and was believ'd. And therefore, if any man think to destroy this generall, by making himself a wofull instance to the contrary; Christ is not believ'd in all the world, for I never believ'd in Christ; so poore an objection, requires no more answer, but that that will still be true in the generall; Man is a reasonable 590 creature, though he be an unreasonable man.

Now when he was thus preached to the Gentiles, and thus believed in the world, that is, meanes thus established, for believing in him, he had done all that he had to do here, and therefore, *Receptus in gloria,* he was received into glory: He was received, assumed, taken; therefore he did not vanish away; he had no airy, no imaginary, no fantasticall body; he was true man: and then he was received, re-assumed, taken again, and so was in glory before; and therefore was true God. This which we are fain to call *glory,* is an inexpressible thing, and an incommunicable: *Surely I will not give my glory unto* 600 *another,* says God, in *Esay.* We finde great Titles attributed to, and assumed by Princes, both Spiritual and Temporal: *Celsitudo vestra, & vestra Majestas,* is daily given, and duly given amongst us: and *Sanctitas vestra, & vestra beatitudo,* is given amongst others. *Aben-Ezra,* and some other Rabbins mistake this matter so much, as to deny that any person in the Old Testament ever speakes of himself in the plural number, *Nos, We:* That's mistaken by them; for there are Examples. But it is more mistaken in practise, by the Generals, nay Provincials of some Orders of Fryars, when they sign and sub-scribe in form and stile of Princes, *Nos frater N., We Fryar N.* &c. 610 It is not hard to name some, that have taken to themselves the addi-

Rom. 11.33

Ephes. 3.18
Act. 5.36

[Act. 8.9]

Receptus in gloria

48.11

1 Reg. 12.9
& 22.3
2 Chro. 10.9
In libros
Porret. in
Mat. etc.

tion of *Divus* in their life-time; a stile so high, as that *Bellarmine*
denies that it appertains to any Saint in heaven: and yet these men
have canoniz'd themselves, without the consent of *Rome;* and yet
remain'd good Sons of that Mother too: We shall finde in ancient
stiles, that high addition, *Æternitas nostra, Our Eternity:* and not
onely in ancient, but in our own days, another equal to that, given
to a particular Cardinal, *Numen Vestrum, Your Godhead.* We find
a Letter in *Baronius,* to a Pope, from a King of *Britain* (and so
Baronius leaves it, and does not tell us which *Britain;* he could have
⁶²⁰ been content to have had it thought ours; but he that hath abridg'd
his Book, hath abridg'd his *Britain* too, there it is *Britania minor:*   Spondanus
But he was a King, and therefore had power, if he fill'd his place;
and wisdom too, if he answered his name; for his name was *Solomon*)
and this King we finde reduc'd to this lowness, as that he writes to
that Bishop, *Adrian* 2. in that stile, *Precor omnipotentiam Dignitatis*
vestræ: he gives him the Title of *God, Almighty.* But two or three
years before, he was far from it; then, when he writ, he plac'd his
own name above the Popes: but it is a slippery declination, if it be
not a precipitation, to come at all under him. Great Titles have been
⁶³⁰ taken, Ambition goes far; and great given, Flattery goes as far;
greater then this in the Text, perchance have; but it hath not fallen
within my narrow reading, and observation, that ever Prince took,
that ever subject gave this Title, *Gloria nostra,* or *vestra; May it*
please your Glory, or *It hath seem'd good to our Glory. Glory be to*
God on high; and glory to the Father, and to the Son, and to the Holy
Ghost, and no more. As long as that scurff, that leprosie sticks to
every thing in this world, *Vanitas Vanitatum, that all is vanity;* can   [Eccles. 1.2]
any glory in any thing of this world, be other then vain-glory? What
Title of Honour hath any man had in any State, in Court, that some
⁶⁴⁰ prison in that State hath not had men of that Title in it? Nay, what
Title hath any Heraulds Book, that *Lucifers* Book hath not? Or who
can be so great in this World, but that as great as he have perished
in the next? *As it is not good for men to eat much honey; so, for men*   Prov. 25.27
to search their own glory, is not glory. Crowns are the Emblems of
Glory; and Kings out of their abundant Greatness and Goodness,
derive and distribute Crowns to Persons of Title; and by those
Crowns, and those Titles, they are *Consanguinei Regis,* the Kings

Cousins. Christ Jesus is crowned with glory in Heaven, and he sheds down Coronets upon you; Honour, and Blessings here, that you ⁶⁵⁰ might be *Consanguinei Regis;* contract a spiritual Kindred with that King, and be *idem Spiritus cum Domino,* as inseparable from his Father, as he himself is. The glory of Gods Saints in Heaven, is not so much to have a Crown, as to lay down that Crown at the Feet of the Lamb. The glory of good men here upon earth, is not so much to have Honour, and Favour, and Fortune, as to employ those Beams of Glory, to his glory that gave them. In our poor calling, God hath given us grace; but *grace for grace,* as the Apostle saies, that is, grace to derive, and convey, and seal grace to you. To those of higher Rank, God hath given glory; and *glory for glory;* glory therefore to ⁶⁶⁰ glorifie him, in a care of his glory. And because he dwells *in luce inaccessibili,* in a glorious light which you cannot see here; glorifie him in that wherein you may see him, in that wherein he hath manifested himself; glorifie him in his glorious Gospel: employ your Beams of Glory, Honour, Favour, Fortune, in transmitting his Gospel in the same glory to your Children, as you receiv'd it from your Fathers: for in this consists this Mystery of Godliness, which is, Faith with a pure Conscience: And in this lies your best Evidence, That you are already co-assumed with Christ Jesus into glory, by having so laid an unremoveable hold upon that Kingdom which he hath ⁶⁷⁰ purchased for you, with the inestimable price of his incorruptible Blood. To which glorious Son of God, *&c.*

[Joh. 1.16]

[1 Tim. 6.16]

Number 10.

Preached at White-hall,
April 8. 1621.

PROV. 25.16. *HAST THOU FOUND HONEY? EAT*
SO MUCH AS IS SUFFICIENT FOR THEE, LEST
THOU BE FILLED THEREWITH, AND
VOMIT IT.

THERE IS a temporall unsatiablenesse of riches, and there is a spirituall unsatiablenesse of sin. The first Covetousnesse, that of riches, the Apostle cals *The roote of all evill,* but the second Covetousnesse, that of sin, is the fruit of all evill, for that is *The treasure of Gods wrath,* as the Apostle speaks, when he makes our former sins, the mother of future sins, and then our future sins the punishments of former. As though this World were too little to satisfie man, men are come to discover or imagine new worlds, severall worlds in every Planet; and as though our Fathers hereto-
10 fore, and we our selves too, had beene but dull and ignorant sinners, we thinke it belongs to us to perfect old inventions, and to sin in another height and excellency, then former times did, as though sin had had but a minority, and an infancy till now. Though the pride of the Prince of Tyrus were ever in some Tyrans, who sayes there, *I am a god, and sit in the seat of God, in the midst of the Seas, and am wiser then Daniel;* Yet there is a Sea above these seas, a power above this power, a spirituall pride above this temporall pride, one so much wiser then *Daniel,* as that he is as wise as the Holy Ghost. The world hath ever had levities and inconstancies, and the foole hath changed
20 as the Moone; the same men that have cryed *Hosanna,* are ready to cry *Crucifige;* but, as in *Iobs* Wife, in the same mouth, the same word was ambiguous, (whether it were *blesse God,* or *curse God,* out of

[1 Tim. 6.10]
[Rom. 2.5]

Ezek. 28.2

Ecclus. 27.11

[Job 2.9]

the word we cannot tell) so are the actions of men so ambiguous, as
that we cannot conclude upon them; men come to our Prayers here,
and pray in their hearts here in this place, that God would induce
another manner of Prayer into this place; and so pray in the Congregation, that God would not heare the prayers of the Congregation;
There hath alwaies beene ambiguity and equivocation in words, but
now in actions, and almost every action will admit a diverse sense.

Ezek.
16.[29]

30 And it was the Prophets complaint of old, *You have multiplied your*
fornications, and yet are not satisfied; but we wonder why the Prophet
should wonder at that, for the more we multiplie temporally or
spiritually, the lesse we are satisfied. Others have thought, that our
soules sinned before they came into the world, and that therefore they
are here as in a prison; but they are rather here, as in a Schoole; for,
if they had studied sin in another world before, they practise it here,
If they have practised it before, they teach it now, they lead and
induce others into sin.

But this consideration of our insatiablenesse in sin, in my purpose
40 I seposed for the end of this houre; But who knowes whether your
patience, that you will heare, or who knowes whether yours, or my
life, that you can heare, shall last to the end of this houre? and therefore it is an excusable anticipation, to have begun with this spirituall
covetousnesse of sin, though our first paiment be to be made in the
literall sense of the text, A reprehension, and in it, a Counsaile, against
our generall insatiablenesse of the temporall things of this world.
Hast thou found honey? eat so much as is sufficient for thee, lest thou
bee filled therewith, and vomit it.

Divisio

In which words, there being first a particular Compellation, *Tu,*
50 hast *thou* found it? it remembers thee, that there be a great many,
that have not found it, but lack that which thou aboundest in; And
Invenisti, thou hast not inherited it, nor merited it, thou hast but
found it; and for that which thou hast found, it is *Honey,* sweetness,
but it is but Honey, which easily becomes choler, and gall, and bitternesse. Such as it is, *Comede,* thou maist *eat* it, and eat it safely, it is
not unwholesome; but *Comede sufficientiam,* eat no more then is
sufficient; And in that, let not the servant measure himselfe by his
Master, nor the subject by the King, nor the private man by the
Magistrate, but *Comede sufficientiam tuam,* eat that which is sufficient

⁶⁰ *for thee,* for more then that will *fill* thee, over-fill thee; perchance not
so full as thou wouldst bee, yet certainly so full, as that there will bee
no roome in thee for better things; and then thou wilt *vomit,* nay
perchance thou must vomit, the malice and plots of others shall give
thee a vomit, And such a vomit shall bee *Evacuans,* an exinanition,
leave thee empty; and *Immundum,* an uncleannesse, leave thee in
scorne and contempt; and *Periculosum,* a danger, breake a veine, a
veine at the heart, breake thy heart it selfe, that thou shalt never
recover it. *Hast thou found honey? eat so much as is sufficient for
thee, lest thou be filled therewith, and vomit it.*

⁷⁰   First then, for that Compellation *Tu,* hast *thou* found it? It is a
word first of familiarity, and then a word of particularity. It is a
degree of familiarity, that God hath notified himselfe to us in severall
Persons; that hee hath come so neere to our comprehension, as to be
considered not onely as an universall, and infinite God, but as a
Father, and as a Sonne, and opened himselfe unto us in these Notions,
Tu Pater, Tu Fili, Thou O Father, and *Thou* O Sonne, have mercy
upon us. A Constable, or Beadle will not bee spoke to so, to be *thou'd,*
and any Person in the Trinity, the whole Trinity together is content
with it; Take God altogether, and at highest, *Tu altissimus, Thou*
⁸⁰ *Lord art most high for evermore;* Take him from before any beginning, *Tu à seculo, Thy throne is established of old, and thou art from
everlasting;* Take him from beyond all ending, *Tu autem permanes,
Thou art the same, and thy yeares shall have no end.*

    In which, we goe not about to condemne, or correct the civill
manner of giving different titles, to different ranks of men; but to
note the slipperiness of our times, where titles flow into one another,
and lose their distinctions; when as the Elements are condensed into
one another, ayre condensed into water, and that into earth, so an
obsequious flatterer, shall condense a yeoman into a Worshipfull
⁹⁰ person, and the Worshipfull into Honorable, and so that which duly
was intended for distinction, shall occasion confusion. But that which
we purpose, in noting this *Tu,* is rather the singularity, the particularity, then the familiarity; That the Holy Ghost in this collects Man,
abridges Man, summes up Man in an unity, in the consideration of
one, of himselfe. *Oportet hominem fieri unum,* Man must grow in
his consideration, till he be but one man, one individuall man. If he

Tu

Psal. 92.8

93.2
102.27

Clem. Alex.

consider himselfe *in Humanitate,* in the whole mankinde, a glorious creature, an immortall soule, he shall see this immortall soule, as well in Goats at the left hand, as in Sheepe at the right hand of Christ, at the Resurrection; Men on both sides: If he consider himselfe *in Qualitate,* in his quality, in his calling, he shall heare many then plead their *Prophetavimus,* we have prophecied, and their *Ejecimus,* we have exorcised, and their *Virtutes fecimus,* we have done wonders, and all in thy Name, and yet receive that answer, *Nunquam cognovi,* I doe not know you now, I never did know you. *Oportet unum fieri,* he must consider himselfe *in individuo,* that one man, not that man in nature, not that man in calling, but that man in actions. *Origen* makes this use of those words, as he found them, *Erat vir unus, There was one man,* (which was *Elkanah*) He addes, *Nomen ejus possessio Dei,* this one man, sayes he, was, in his Name, Gods possession; *Nam quem Dæmones possident, non unus sed multi,* for he whom the Devill possesses, is not one. The same sinner is not the same thing; still he clambers in his ambitious purposes, there he is an Eagle; and yet lies still groveling, and trodden upon at any greater mans threshold, there he is a worme. He swells to all that are under him, there he is a full Sea; and his dog that is above him, may wade over him, there he is a shallow, an empty River. In the compasse of a few dayes, he neighes like a horse in the rage of his lust over all the City, and groanes in a corner of the City, in an hospitall. A sinner is as many men, as he hath vices; he that is *Elkanah, Possessio Dei,* possessed by God, and in possession of God, he is *unus homo,* one and the same man. And when God calls upon man so particularly, he intends him some particular good. It is S. *Hieromes* note, That when God in the Scriptures speakes of divers things in the singular number, it is ever in things of grace; And it is S. *Augustins* note, that when he speaks of any one thing in the plurall Number, it is of heavy and sorrowfull things; as *Ieptha* was buryed *In civitatibus Gilead,* in the Cities, but he had but one grave; And so that is, they made *Aureos vitulos,* Golden Calves, when it was but one Calfe.

When Gods voyce comes to thee in this Text, in particular, *Tu, Hast thou found,* he would have thee remember, how many seeke and have sought, with teares, with sweat, with blood, and lacke that, that thou aboundest in. That whereas his Evidence to them whom he

[Mat. 25.33]
Mat. 7.22

Origen
Homil.
unica in
lib. reg.

Hieron.

Judg. 12.7

loves not, in the next world shall be, *Esurivi, I was hungry, and yee gave me no meate;* And his proceeding with them whom he loves not in this world, is, *Si esuriero, If I be hungry, I will not tell thee,* I will not awaken thee, not remember thy conscience, wherein thou mayest doe me a service; He does call upon thee in particular, and ask thee, *Nonne tu,* Hast thou not fortune enough, to let fall some
140 crums upon him that starves? and, *Nonne tu,* hast not thou favour enough, to shed some beams upon him that is frozen in disgrace? There is a squint eye, that lookes side-long; to looke upon riches, and honor, on the left hand, and long life here, on the right, is a squint eye. There is a squint eye, that lookes upwards and downwards; to looke after God and Mammon, is a squint eye. There are squint eyes, that looke upon one another; to looke upon ones own beauty, or wisedome, or power, is a squint eye. The direct looke is to looke inward upon thine own Conscience; Not with *Nabuchadnezzar, Is not this great Babylon, which I have built by the might of my power,*
150 *and for the honor of my Majesty?* But with *David, Quid retribuam?* for if thou looke upon them with a cleare eye, thou wilt see, that though thou hast them, thou hast but *found* them, which is our next step.

Now, if you have but *found* them, thou hast them but by chance, by contingency, by fortune. The Emperour *Leo,* he calls money found, *Dei beneficium,* It is a benefit derived from God; but the great Lawyer, *Triphonius,* calls it, *Donum fortunæ* too, An immediate gift of fortune. They consist well enough together, God and fortune. S. *Augustine* in his Retractations makes a conscience of hav-
160 ing named her too oft, lest other men should be scandalized; and so the Prophet complaines of that, (as the Vulgat reads it) *Ponitis mensam fortunæ,* You sacrifice to fortune, you make fortune a god; that you should not doe; but yet you should acknowledge that God hath such a servant, such an instrument, as fortune too. Gods ordinary working is by Nature, these causes must produce these effects; and that is his common Law; He goes sometimes above that, by Prerogative, and that is by miracle, and sometimes below that, as by custome, and that is fortune, that is contingency; Fortune is as far out of the ordinary way, as miracle; no man knows in Nature, in reason, why
170 such, or such persons grow great; but it falls out so often, as we do

Mat. 25.42

Psal. 50.12

Dan. 4.30

Invenisti
Co. l. 10

Pand.

Esa. 65.11

not call it miracle, and therefore rest in the Name of Fortune. We need not quarrell the words of the Poet, *Tu quamcunque Deus tibi fortunaverit horam, Grata sume manu,* Thanke God for any good fortune, since the Apostle sayes too, that *Godlinesse hath the promise of this life;* The godly man shall be fortunate, God will blesse him with good fortune here; but still it is fortune, and chance, in the sight and reason of man, and therefore he hath but found, whatsoever he hath in that kinde. It is intimated in the very word which we use for all worldly things; It is *Inventarium,* an Inventory; we found ¹⁸⁰ them here, and here our successors finde them, when we are gone from hence. *Iezabel* had an estimation of beauty, and she thought to have drawne the King with that beauty, but she found it, she found it in her box, and in her wardrope, she was not truly fayre. *Achitophel* had an estimation of wisedome in Counsell, I know not how he found it; he counselled by an example, which no man would follow, he hanged himselfe. Thou wilt not be drawne to confesse, that a Man that hath an office, is presently wiser then thou, or a man that is Knighted, presently valianter then thou. Men have preferment for those parts, which other men, equall to them in the same things, have ¹⁹⁰ not, and therefore they doe but finde them; And to things that are but found, what is our title? *Nisi reddantur, rapina est,* sayes the Law, If we restore not that which we finde, it is robbery. S. *Augustine* hath brought it nearer, *Qui alienum negat, si posset, tolleret,* He that confesseth not that which he hath found of another mans, if he durst, he would have taken it by force. For that which we have found in this world, our calling is the owner, our debts are the owner, our children are the owner; our lusts, our superfluities are no owners: of all the rest, God is the owner, and to this purpose, the poore is God.

S. *Augustine* puts a case to the point: He sayes when he was at ²⁰⁰ Milan, a poore Usher of a Grammar Schoole found a bag of money, 200 *Solidorum;* let it be but one hundreth pounds; he set up bills; the owner came, offered him his tithe, ten pounds; he would none; he pressed him to five, to three, to two; he would none: and then he that had lost it, in an honorable indignation, disclaimed it all; *Nihil perdidi,* sayes he, it is all your own, I lost nothing: *Quale certamen! Theatrum mundus, spectator Deus,* Out of importunity, he that found

[1 Tim. 4.8]

2 King. 9.30

Aug. Serm.
19.
de verb.
Apost.

it, tooke it all, and out of conscience, that it was not his, gave it all
to the poore.

 The things of this world we doe but finde, and of the things which
²¹⁰ we finde, we are but Stewards for others. This finding is not so meerly
casuall, as that it implies no manner of seeking; We must put our selves
into the way, into a calling. The word is *Matza,* and that word is
allowed us; but a word like it, is not allowed us; *Matza* is, but *Matzah*
is not; if there be an *H* added, an *H,* as it is an aspiration, a breathing,
a panting after the things of this world, or an Ache, as it is a paine,
that it make our bones ake, or our hearts ake, or our conscience ake,
it is a seeking, and a finding, not intended in this word. Our prosecu-
tion and seeking must be moderate, our title and interest is but a
finding; and what hath the most fortunate found? *Hony;* it is true,
²²⁰ but yet but *Hony.*

 That which *Solomon* may justly seeme to intend, especially by
Hony in this Text, is that which the Poets, and other Masters of
language, have called *Magnas amicitias,* and *Magnas Clientelas,* dependance, and interest, and favour in great persons. It appeares by the
next verse, which depends upon this, and paraphrases it; *Withdraw
thy foot from thy neighbours house.* Where that which we reade,
Withdraw, is in the Originall *Hokar,* which is *Fac pretiosum,* make
not thy selfe cheape, not vulgar, have some respect to thy selfe, to
thine own ingenuity, but principally to the other, to thy great friend:
²³⁰ be not importune and troublesome by any indiscreet assiduity, to
them who are possessed with businesse, though at some times they
descend to thee; This is this *Hony,* where thou hast accesse, yet doe
not push open every doore, fling up every hanging, but use thy favour
modestly.

 But in this *Hony* is wrapped up also all that is delightfull in this
life; and *Solomon* carries us often to that Comparison; In the Chapter
before this, for Wisedome; *My Sonne, eat thou Hony, because it is
good; so shall the knowledge of wisedome be to thy soule;* and in
the seaven and twentieth verse of this Chapter, he uses it for Glory;
²⁴⁰ *It is not good to eat much hony; so for men to search their own glory,
is not glory.* In the sixt Chapter of this booke, when *Solomon* had
sent us to the *Ant,* to learne wisedome, betweene the eight verse and

Matzah
Exuxit, vel
expressit

Mel

Ver. 13

27
Prov. 6

the ninth, he sends us to another schoole, to the *Bee: Vade ad Apem &*
disce quomodo operationem venerabilem facit, Goe to the Bee, and
learne how reverend and mysterious a worke she works. For, though

S. *Hierome* acknowledge, that in his time, this verse was not in the
Hebrew Text, yet it hath ever been in many Copies of the Septuagint,
and though it be now left out in the Complutense Bible, and that
which they call the Kings, yet it is in that still, which they value above

²⁵⁰ all, the Vatican. S. *Hierome* himselfe takes it into his exposition, and
other Fathers into theirs. So far therefore we may hearken to that
voyce, as to goe to the Bee, and learne to worke by that Creature.

Both S. *Basil,* and S. *Chrysostome* put this difference in that place,
between the labour of the Ant, and the Bee, That the Ants worke but
for themselves, the Bee for others: Though the Ants have a Common-
wealth of their own, yet those Fathers call their labour, but private
labour; because no other Common-wealths have benefit by their
labour, but their own. Direct thy labours in thy calling to the good
of the publique, and then thou art a civill, a morall Ant; but consider
²⁶⁰ also, That all that are of the houshold of the faithfull, and professe
the same truth of Religion, are part of this publique, and direct thy
labours, for the glory of Christ Jesus, amongst them too, and then
thou art a religious and a Christian Bee, and the fruit of thy labour
shall be *Hony*. The labour of the Ant is *sub Dio,* open, evident, manifest; The labour of the Bee is *sub Tecto,* in a house, in a hive; They
will doe good, and yet they will not be seene to doe it; they affect not
glory, nay, they avoyd it. For in experience, when some men curious
of naturall knowledge, have made their Hives of glasse, that by that
transparency, they might see the Bees manner of working, the Bees
²⁷⁰ have made it their first work to line that Glasse-hive, with a crust of
Wax, that they might work and not be discerned. It is a blessed
sincerity, to work as the Ant, professedly, openly; but because there
may be cases, when to doe so, would destroy the whole worke, though
there be a cloud and a curtaine betweene thee, and the eyes of men, yet
if thou doe them clearely in the sight of God, that he see his glory
advanced by thee, the fruit of thy labour shall be Honey.

Pliny names one *Aristomachum Solensem,* that spent threescore
yeares in the contemplation of Bees; our whole time for this exercise
is but threescore minutes; and therefore wee say no more of this, but

²⁸⁰ *Vade ad Apem,* practise the sedulity of the Bee, labour in thy calling, And the community of the Bee, beleeve that thou art called to assist others, And the secresie of the Bee, that the greatest, and most authorized spie see it not, to supplant it, And the purity of the Bee, that never settles upon any foule thing, that thou never take a foule way to a faire end, and the fruit of thy labour shall bee Hony; God shall give thee the sweetnesse of this world, honour, and ease, and plenty, and hee shall give thee thy honey-combe, with thy honey, that which preserves thy honey to thee, that is, a religious knowledge, that all this is but hony; And honey in the dew of the flowres, whence it
²⁹⁰ is drawne, is but *Cœli sudor,* a sweaty excrement of the heavens, and   Plin. *Siderum saliva,* the spettle, the fleame of the starres, and *Apum vomitus,* the casting, the vomit of the Bee. And though honey be the sweetest thing that wee doe take into the body, yet there it degenerates into gall, and proves the bitterest; And all this is honey in the Anti-type, in that which it signifies, in the temporall things of this world; In the temporall things of this world there is a bitternesse, in our use of them; But in his hand, and his purpose that gives them, they have impressions of sweetnesse; and so *Comede, Eat* thy honey, which is also a step farther.

³⁰⁰   Here is liberty for any man to eat Honey, if hee have found it, and   *Comede* *Ionathan* the Kings sonne found honey upon the ground, and did but dip his staffe in it, and put it to his mouth, and hee must die for it.   1 Sam. 14.24 Of forbidden honey the least dramme is poyson, how sweet soever any collaterall respect make it. But *Ionathan* knew not that it was forbidden by the King: Ignorance is no plea in any subject against the Kings lawes; and there is a King, in breach of whose lawes, no King, no Kings sonne can excuse themselves by ignorance, if they doe but dip their Scepter in forbidden honey, in any unlawfull delight in this world; For they doe, or they may know the unlawfulnesse of it. But
³¹⁰ for the honey which God allowes us, whether God give it in that plenty, *Terram fluentem,* that the land flow with milke and honey,   Exod. 3.8 nay *Torrentes mellis,* rivers and streames of honey, that great fortunes   Iob 20.17 flow into men, in this world; or whether God put us to suck honey out of the Rock, that that which we have, we digge, and plough, and   Deut. 32.13 thresh for, yet when thou hast found that, *Comede,* use it, enjoy it, eat it; *Hee that will not work, shall not eat;* He that shuts himselfe   2 Thes. 3.10

up in a Cloyster, till the honey finde him, till meat bee brought to him, should not eat.

Luk. 24.42   Christ himselfe ate Honey, but after his Resurrection; when his 320 body needed not refection; when our principall end in worldly things, is not for the body, nor for the world, but that we have had a spirituall resurrection, that we can see Gods love in them, and shew Gods glory by them, then *Invenisti,* thou hast found; (for *Invenire, est in rem venire, id est in usum*) to find a thing is to make the right use of it, and *Invenisti mel,* thou hast found Honey, that which God intends for sweetnesse, for necessities, conveniences, abundances, recreations, and delights; and therefore *Comede,* eat it, enjoy it; but to thee also belongs that Caveat, *Comede ad sufficientiam,* Eat but enough.

Festus

Suffi-
cientiam   330   That great Morall man *Seneca,* could see, that *Nihil agere,* to passe this life, and intend no Vocation, was very ill; and that *Aliud agere,* to professe a Vocation, and be busier in other mens callings, then his owne, was worse; but the *Super-agere,* to over-doe, to doe more then was required at his hands, he never brought into comparison, hee never suspected; and yet that is our most ordinary fault. That which hath been ordinarily given by our Physitians, by way of counsell, That we should rise with an appetite, hath been enough followed by worldly men; They alwayes lie downe, and alwayes rise up with an appetite to more, and more in this world. An Office is but an Anti-340 past, it gets them an appetite to another Office; and a title of Honour, but an Anti-past, a new stomach to a new Title. The danger is, that we cannot goe upward directly; If wee have a staire, to goe any height, it must be a winding staire; It is a compassing, a circum-venting, to rise: A Ladder is a straight Engin of it selfe, yet if we will rise by that, it must be set a slope; Though our meanes be direct in their owne nature, yet wee put them upon crooked wayes; It is but a poore rising, that any man can make in a direct line, and yet it is, *Ad sufficientiam,* high enough, for it is to heaven. Have yee seene a glasse blowne to a handsome competency, and with one breath more, 350 broke? I will not ask you, whether you have seene a competent beauty made worse, by an artificiall addition, because they have not thought it well enough before; you see it every day, and every where. If

Act. 14.12 *Paul* himselfe were here, whom for his Eloquence the Lystrians

called *Mercury,* hee could not perswade them to leave their *Mercury;* It will not easily be left; for how many of them that take it outwardly at first, come at last to take it inwardly? Since the saying of *Solomon, Be not over righteous,* admits many good senses, even in Morall vertues, and in religious duties too, which are naturally good, it is much more appliable in temporall things, which are naturally indif-
360 ferent; Bee not over faire, over witty, over sociable, over rich, over glorious; but let the measure be *Sufficientia tua, So much as is sufficient for thee.*

Eccles. 7.16

But where shall a man take measure of himselfe? At what age, or in what calling shall he say, This is sufficient for me? *Ieremy* says, *Puer sum, I am a child, and cannot speake at all;* S. *Paul* says, *Quando puer, When I was a child,* no bigger, *I spake like a child;* this was not *sufficientia sua,* sufficient for him; for since he was to be a man, he was to speak like a man: The same clothes doe not serve us throughout our lives, nay not the same bodies, nay not the same
370 vertues, so there is no certaine Gomer, no fixed Measure for worldly things, for every one to have. As *Clemens Alexandrinus* saith, *Eadem Drachma data Nauclero, est Naulum,* The same piece of Money given to a Water-man, is his Fare; *Publicano Vectigal,* given to a Farmer of Custome, it is Impost; *Mercatori pretium,* to a Merchant it is the price of his Ware; *Operario Merces, Mendico Eleemosyna,* To a Labourer it is Wages, to a Begger it is Almes; So on the other side, this which we call sufficiency, as it hath relation to divers states, hath a different measure. I think the rule will not be inconveniently given, if we say, That whatsoever the world doth justly looke for at our
380 hands, wee may justly look for at Gods hands: Those outward meanes, which are requisite for the performance of the duties of your calling to the world, arising from your birth, or arising from your place, you are to pray for, you are to labour for; For that is *Sufficientia tua,* so much is sufficient for you, and so much Honey you may eat; but eat no more, sayes the Text, *Ne satieris, Lest you be filled.*

Tuam

[Jer. 1.6]
[1 Cor. 13.11]

Clem. Alex.

Hee doth not say yet, lest thou bee satisfied; there is no great feare, nay there is no hope of that, that he will be satisfied. We know the receipt, the capacity of the ventricle, the stomach of man, how much it can hold; and wee know the receipt of all the receptacles of blood,
390 how much blood the body can have; so wee doe of all the other con-

Ne satieris

duits and cisterns of the body; But this infinite Hive of honey, this insatiable whirlpoole of the covetous mind, no Anatomy, no dissection hath discovered to us. When I looke into the larders, and cellars, and vaults, into the vessels of our body for drink, for blood, for urine, they are pottles, and gallons; when I looke into the furnaces of our spirits, the ventricles of the heart and of the braine, they are not thimbles; for spirituall things, the things of the next world, we have no roome; for temporall things, the things of this world, we have no bounds. How then shall this over-eater bee filled with his honey? So
400 filled, as that he can receive nothing else. More of the same honey hee can; Another Mannor, and another Church, is but another bit of meat, with another sauce to him; Another Office, and another way of Extortion, is but another garment, and another lace to him. But he is too full to receive any thing else; Christ comes to this Bethlem, (Bethlem which is *Domus panis*) this house of abundance, and there is no roome for Christ in this Inne; there are no crums for Christ under this table; There comes *Boanerges,* (*Boanerges,* that is, *filius Tonitrui,* the sonne of Thunder) and he thunders out the *Væ's,* the Comminations, the Judgements of God upon such as hee; but if
410 the Thunder spoile not his drink, he sees no harme in Thunder; As long as a Sermon is not a Sentence in the Starre-chamber, that a Sermon cannot fine and imprison him, hee hath no roome for any good effect of a Sermon. The Holy Ghost, the Spirit of Comfort comes to him, and offers him the consolation of the Gospel; but hee will die in his old religion, which is to sacrifice to his owne Nets, by which his portion is plenteous; he had rather have the God of the Old Testament, that payes in this world with milke and honey, then the God of the New Testament, that cals him into his Vineyard in this World, and payes him no wages till the next: one *Iupiter* is worth all
420 the three *Elohims,* or the three *Iehovahs* (if we may speake so) to him. *Iupiter* that can come in a showre of gold, outwaighs *Iehova,* that comes but in a showre of water, but in a sprinkling of water in Baptisme, and sels that water so deare, as that he will have showres of teares for it, nay showres of blood for it, when any Persecutor hath a mind to call for it. The voyce of God whom he hath contemned, and wounded, The voyce of the Preacher whom he hath derided, and impoverished, The voyce of the poore, of the Widow, of the

Orphans, of the prisoner, whom he hath oppressed, knocke at his doore, and would enter, but there is no roome for them, he is so full.
430 This is the great danger indeed that accompanies this fulnesse, but the danger that affects him more is that which is more literally in the text, *Evomet,* he shall be so filled as that he shall *vomit;* even that fulnesse, those temporall things which he had, he shall cast up.

It is not a vomiting for his ease, that he would vomit; but he shall vomit; he shall bee forced to vomit. *He hath swallowed downe riches, and he shall vomit them up againe; God shall cast them out of his belly;* But by what hand? whether by his right hand, by the true way of justice, or his left hand, by malice, under colour of justice, his money shall be his Antimony, his own riches shall be his vomit.
440 *Solomon* says, he saw *a sore evill under the Sun;* but if he had lived as long as the Sun, he might have seen it every course of the Sun, *Riches reserved to their owners for their own hurt;* Rich men perish, that should not have perished, or not so soone, or not so absolutely, if they had not beene rich. Their confidence in their riches provokes them to some unjustifiable actions, and their riches provoke others to a vehement persecution. And in this vomit of theirs, if we had time to doe so, we would consider first, The sordidnesse, and the contempt and scorne that this evacuated Man comes to in the world, when he hath had this vomit of all his honey; That because there
450 can be no vacuity, he shall be filled againe, but *Saturabitur ignominia, He shall be filled with shame for glory, and shamefull spuing shall be upon his glory. He magnified himselfe against the Lord, and therefore was made drunk, and shall wallow in his vomit, and be had in derision.* His honey was his soule, and that being vomited, he is now but a rotten and abhorred carkass; At best he was but a bag of money, and now he is but the bag it selfe, which scarce any man will stoop to take up: And as in a vomit in a bason, the Physitian is able to shew the world, what cold meat, and what raw meat, and what hard and indigestible meat he had eaten; So when such a person
460 comes by justice, or malice to this vomit, every man becomes a Physitian, every man brings Inditements, and evidence against him, and can shew all his falshoods, and all his extortions in particular.

In these particulars we would consider the scorne upon this vomit; and then the danger of it in these, That nothing weakens the eyes

Evomas
Iob 20.15

Eccles. 5.13

Habak. 2.16

Ier. 48.26

more then vomiting; when this worldly man hath lost his honey, he hath lost his sight; he was dimme sighted at beginning, when he could see nothing but worldly things, things nearest to him, but when he hath vomited them, he hath lost his spectacles; through his riches he saw some glimmering, some colour of comfort, now he sees no
470 comfort at all: And a greater danger in vomiting is, that often times it breakes a veine within, and that is most commonly incurable; This man that vomits without, bleeds within; his fortune is broke, and his heart is broke; and he bleeds better blood then his owne, he bleeds out the blood of Christ Jesus himselfe; the blood of Christ Jesus poured into him heretofore in the consolation of the Gospel, and in the Cup of Salvation in the Sacrament (for so much as concernes him) is but spilt upon the ground; as though his honey, his worldly greatnesse, were his Father, and Mother, and Wife, and Children, and Prince, and friends, and all, when that is lost by this vomit, he
480 mournes for all, in a sad and everlasting mourning, in such a disconsolate dejection of spirit as ends either in an utter inconsideration of God, or in a desperation of his mercies. This is that *Incipiam te*

Revel. 3.16 *evomere* (as the Vulgat reads it) in this vomit of worldly things, God does begin to vomit him out of his mouth; and then God does not returne to his vomit, but leaves this impatient patient to his impenitiblenesse. But we must not lanch into these wide Seas now, to consider the scorne, or the danger of this vomit, but rather draw into the harbor, and but repeat the text, transferred from this world to the next, from temporall to spirituall things.

Conclusio 490 Thus far we have beene *In melle,* In honey, upon honey; but now *Super mel,* above honey. The judgements of the Lord are *Dulcia præ*
Psal. 19.10 *melle, Sweeter then honey, and the honey combe;* And the judgements of the Lord are that, by which the Lord will judge us, and this world; it is his word. His word, the sincerity of the Gospel, the truth of his Religion is our honey and honey combe; our honey, and our waxe, our Covenant, and our Seale; we have him not, if we have not his truth, if we require other honey; and wee trust him not, if we require any other Seale, if we thinke the word of God needs the traditions of men. And *Invenisti tu,* Hath God manifested to thee the
500 truth of his Gospell? Blesse thou the Lord, praise him and magnifie him for ever, whose day-spring from on high hath visited thee, and

left so many Nations in darknesse, who shall never heare of Christ, till they heare himselfe, nor heare other voyce from him then, then the *Ite maledicti;* Pity them that have not this honey, and confesse for thy selfe, that though thou have it, thou hast but found it; couldst thou bespeake Christian Parents beforehand, and say, I will be borne of such Parents as shall give me a title to the Covenant, to Baptisme? or couldst thou procure Sureties, that should bind themselves for thee, at the entring into the Covenant in Baptisme? Thou foundest thy selfe in the Christian Church, and thou foundest meanes of salvation there; thou broughtest none hither, thou boughtest none here; the Title of S. *Andrew,* the first of the Apostles that came to Christ, was but that, *Invenimus Messiam, We have found the Messias.* It is onely Christ himselfe that sayes of himselfe, *Comedi mel meum, I have eat my honey,* his owne honey. We have no grace, no Gospel of our owne, we find it here.

Cant. 5.1

But since thou hast found it, *Comede, Eat it;* do not drinke the cup of Babylon, lest thou drink the cup of Gods wrath too: but make this Honey (Christs true Religion) thy meate; digest that, assimilate that, incorporate that: and let Christ himself, and his merit, be as thy soul; and let the cleere and outward profession of his truth, Religion, be as thy body: If thou give away that body, (be flattered out of thy Religion, or threatned out of thy Religion) If thou sell this body, (be bought and bribed out of thy Religion) If thou lend this body, (discontinue thy Religion for a yeare or two, to see how things will fall out) if thou have no body, thou shalt have no Resurrection, and the cleere and undisguised profession of the truth, is the body.

Eat therefore this honey *Ad sufficientiam;* so much as is enough. To beleeve implicitly as the Church beleeves, and know nothing, is not enough; know thy foundations, and who laid them; Other foundations can no man lay, then are laid, Christ Jesus; neither can other men lay those foundations otherwise then they are laid by the Apostles, but eat *Ad sufficientiam tuam,* that which is enough for thee, for so much knowledge is not required in thee in those things, as in them, whose profession it is to teach them; be content to leave a roome stil for the Apostles *Æmulamini charismata meliora,* desire better gifts; and ever think it a title of dignity which the Angel gave *Daniel,* to be *Vir desideriorum;* To have still some farther object of

[1 Cor. 3.11]

[1 Cor. 12.31]

thy desires. Do not thinke thou wantest all, because thou hast not all; 540 for at the great last day, we shall see more plead Catechismes for their salvation, then the great volumes of Controversies, more plead their pockets, then their Libraries. If S. *Paul* so great an Argosie held no more, but *Christum crucifixum,* what can thy Pinnace hold? Let humility be thy ballast, and necessary knowledge thy fraight: for there is an over-fulnesse of knowledge, which forces a vomit; a vomit of opprobrious and contumelious speeches, a belching and spitting of the name of Heretique and Schismatique, and a losse of charity for matters that are not of faith; and from this vomiting comes emptinesse,

Psal. 90.14

The more disputing, the lesse beleeving: but *Saturasti nos benignitate* 550 *tua, Domine, Thou hast satisfied us early with thy mercy,* Thou gavest us Christianity early, and thou gavest us the Reformation early: and therefore since in thee we have found this honey, let us so

Levit. 18.25

eat it, and so hold it, *That the land do not vomit her Inhabitants, nor spew us out,* as it spewed out the Nations that were before us, but

Exod. 20.12

that our dayes may be long in this land, which the Lord our God hath given us, and that *with the Ancient of dayes,* we may have a day without any night in that land, which his Son our Saviour hath purchased for us with the inestimable price of his incorruptible blood. To which glorious Son of God, &c.

Number 11.

Preached at a Mariage [the marriage of Mistress Margaret Washington at the church of St. Clement Danes, May 30, 1621].

HOSEA 2.19. *AND I WILL MARY THEE UNTO ME FOR EVER.*

THE WORD which is the hinge upon which all this Text turns, is *Erash,* and *Erash* signifies not onely a betrothing, as our later Translation hath it, but a mariage; And so it is used by David, *Deliver me my wife Michal whom I maried;* and so our former Translation had it, and so we accept it, and so shall handle it, *I will mary thee unto me for ever.* 2 Sam. 3.14

The first mariage that was made, God made, and he made it in Paradise: And of that mariage I have had the like occasion as this to speak before, in the presence of many honourable persons in this
10 company. The last mariage which shall be made, God shall make too, and in Paradise too; in the Kingdome of heaven: and at that mariage, I hope in him that shall make it, to meet, not some, but all this company. The mariage in this Text hath relation to both those mariages: It is it self the spirituall and mysticall mariage of Christ Jesus to the Church, and to every mariageable soule in the Church: And it hath a retrospect, it looks back to the first mariage; for to that the first word carries us, because from thence God takes his metaphor, and comparison, *sponsabo, I will mary;* And then it hath a prospect to the last mariage, for to that we are carried in the last word, *in æternum,*
20 *I will mary thee unto me for ever.* Be pleased therefore to give me leave in this exercise, to shift the scene thrice, and to present to your religious considerations three objects, three subjects: first, a secular mariage in Paradise; secondly, a spirituall mariage in the Church;

and thirdly, an eternall mariage in heaven. And in each of these three we shall present three circumstances; first the Persons, *Me* and *Tibi, I will mary thee;* And then the Action, *Sponsabo, I will mary thee;* And lastly the Term, *In æternum, I will mary thee to mee for ever.*

In the first acceptation then, in the first, the secular mariage in Paradise, the persons were *Adam* and *Eve:* Ever since they are He and She, man and woman: At first, by reason of necessity, without any such limitation, as now: And now without any other limitations, then such as are expressed in the Law of God: As the Apostles say in the first generall Councell, *We lay nothing upon you but things necessary,* so we call nothing *necessary* but that which is commanded by God. If in heaven I may have the place of a man that hath performed the Commandements of God, I will not change with him that thinks he hath done more then the Commandements of God enjoyned him. The rule of marriage for degrees and distance in blood, is the Law of God; but for conditions of men, there is no Rule at all given. When God had made *Adam* and *Eve* in Paradise, though there were foure rivers in Paradise, God did not place *Adam* in a Monastery on one side, and *Eve* in a Nunnery on the other, and so a River between them. They that build wals and cloysters to frustrate Gods institution of mariage, advance the Doctrine of Devils in forbidding mariage. The Devil hath advantages enow against us, in bringing men and women together: It was a strange and super-devilish invention, to give him a new advantage against us, by keeping men and women asunder, by forbidding mariage. Between the heresie of the Nicolaitans, that induced a community of women, any might take any; and the heresie of the Tatians that forbad all, none might take any, was a fair latitude. Between the opinion of the *Manichæan* hereticks, that thought women to be made by the Devil, and the *Colliridian* hereticks that sacrificed to a woman, as to God, there is a fair distance. Between the denying of them souls, which S. *Ambrose* is charged to have done, and giving them such souls, as that they may be Priests, as the *Peputian* hereticks did, is a faire way for a moderate man to walk in. To make them Gods is ungodly, and to make them Devils is devillish; To make them Mistresses is unmanly, and to make them servants is unnoble; To make them as God made them, wives, is godly and manly too. When in the Roman

(margin) 1 Part / Persons / Acts 15.28 / 1 Tim. 4.3

Church they dissolve mariage in naturall kindred, in degrees where God forbids it not, when they dissolve mariage upon spirituall kindred, because my Grandfather Christned that womans Father; when they dissolve mariage upon legall kindred, because my Grandfather adopted that womans Father: they separate those whom God hath joyned so farre, as to give them leave to joyn in lawfull mariage. When men have made vows to abstain from mariage, I would they would be content to try a little longer then they doe, whether they could keep that vow or no: And when men have consecrated them-
70 selves to the service of God in his Church, I would they would be content to try a little farther then they doe, whether they could abstain or no: But to dissolve mariage made after such a Vow, or after Orders, is still to separate those whom God hath not separated. The Persons are He and She, man and woman; they must be so much; he must be a man, she must be a woman; And they must be no more; not a brother and a sister, not an unckle and a neece; *Adduxit ad eum,* was the case between *Adam* and *Eve;* God brought them together; God will not bring me a precontracted person, he will not have me defraud another; nor God will not bring me a mis-
80 beleeving, a superstitious person, he will not have me drawn from himself: But let them be persons that God hath made, man and woman, and persons that God hath brought together, that is, not put asunder by any Law of his, and all such persons are capable of this first, this secular mariage.

In which our second Consideration is the Action, *Sponsabo;* where the Active is a kinde of Passive, *I will mary thee,* is, *I will be maried unto thee,* for we mary not our selves. They are somewhat hard driven in the Roman Church, when making mariage a Sacrament, and being prest by us with this question, If it be a Sacrament, who admin-
90 isters it, who is the Priest? They are fain to answer, the Bridegroom and the Bride, he and she are the Priest in that Sacrament. As mariage is a civill Contract, it must be done so in publick, as that it may have the testimony of men; As mariage is a religious Contract, it must be so done, as that it may have the benediction of the Priest: In a mariage without testimony of men they cannot claim any benefit by the Law; In a marriage without the benediction of the Priest they cannot claim any benefit of the Church: for how Matrimonially soever such

[Gen. 2.22]

Sponsabo

Bellar. de
Matrimo.
l. 1. c. 6

persons as have maried themselves may pretend to love, and live together, yet all that love, and all that life is but a regulated Adultery, it is not mariage.

In ustionem

Now this institution of mariage had three objects: first, *In ustionem*, it was given for a remedy against burning; And then, *In prolem*, for propagation, for children; And lastly, *In adjutorium*, for mutuall help. As we consider it the first way, *In ustionem*, every heating is not a burning; every naturall concupiscence does not require a mariage; nay every flaming is not a burning; though a man continue under the flame of carnall tentation, as long as S. *Paul* did, yet it needs

[2 Cor. 12.9]

not come presently to a *Sponsabo*, I will mary. God gave S. *Paul* other Physick, *Gratia mea sufficit*, grace to stand under that tentation; And S. *Paul* gave himself other Physick, *Contundo corpus*, convenient disciplines to tame his body. These will keep a man from

Ambrose

burning; for *Vri est desideriis vinci, desideria pati, illustris est, & perfecti;* To be overcome by our concupiscences, that is to burn, but to quench that fire by religious ways, that is a noble, that is a perfect work. When God at the first institution of mariage had this first use of mariage in his contemplation, that it should be a remedy against burning, God gave man the remedy, before he had the disease; for mariage was instituted in the state of innocency, when there was no inordinatenesse in the affections of man, and so no burning. But as God created Reubarb in the world, whose quality is to purge choler, before there was any choler to purge, so God according to his abundant forwardnesse to doe us good, created a remedy before the disease, which he foresaw comming, was come upon us. Let him then that takes his wife in this first and lowest sense, *In medicinam*, but as his Physick, yet make her his cordiall Physick, take her to his heart, and fill his heart with her, let her dwell there, and dwell there alone, and so they will be mutuall Antidotes and Preservatives to one another, against all forein tentations. And with this blessing, blesse thou, ô Lord, these whom thou hast brought hither for this blessing: make all the days of their life like this day unto them; and as thy mercies are new every morning, make them so to one another; And if they may not die together, sustain thou the survivor of them in that sad hour with this comfort, That he that died for them both, will bring them together again in his everlastingnesse.

The second use of mariage was *In prolificationem,* for children: And therefore as S. *Augustine* puts the case, To contract before, that they will have no children, makes it no mariage but an adultery: To deny themselves to one another, is as much against mariage as to give themselves to another. To hinder it by Physick, or any other practise; ¹⁴⁰ nay to hinder it so far, as by a deliberate wish, or prayer against children, consists not well with this second use of mariage. And yet in this second use, we doe not so much consider generation as re-generation; not so much procreation as education, nor propagation as transplantation of children. For this world might be filled full enough of children, though there were no mariage; but heaven could not be filled, nor the places of the fallen Angels supplied, without that care of childrens religious education, which from Parents in lawfull mariage they are likeliest to receive. How infinite, and how miserable a circle of sin doe we make, if as we sinned in our Parents loins before ¹⁵⁰ we were born, so we sin in our childrens actions when we are dead, by having given them, either example, or liberty of sinning. We have a fearfull commination from God upon a good man, upon *Eli,* for his not restraining the licentiousnesse of his sons; *I will doe a thing in Israel,* says God there, *at which every mans eares that heares it shall tingle:* And it was executed, *Eli* fell down and broke his neck. We have also a promise of consolation to women for children, *She shall be saved in Child-bearing,* says the Apostle; but as *Chrysostome* and others of the Ancients observe and interpret that place (which inter-pretation arises out of the very letter) it is, *Si permanserint,* not if she, ¹⁶⁰ but if they, if the children continue in faith, in charity, in holinesse, and sobriety: The salvation of the Parents hath so much relation to the childrens goodnesse, as that if they be ill by the Parents example, or indulgence, the Parents are as guilty as the children. Art thou afraid thy childe should be stung with a Snake, and wilt thou let him play with the old Serpent, in opening himself to all tentations? Art thou afraid to let him walk in an ill aire, and art thou content to let him stand in that pestilent aire that is made of nothing but oaths, and execrations of blasphemous mouths round about him? It is S. *Chrysostomes* complaint, *Perditionem magno pretio emunt; Salutem* ¹⁷⁰ *nec dono accipere volunt;* we pay dear for our childrens damnation, by paying at first for all their childish vanities, and then for their

In prolem.

1 Sam. 3.11

4.18
1 Tim. 2.15

sinfull insolencies at any rate; and we might have them saved, and our selves to the bargain, (which were a frugall way, and a debt well hedg'd in) for much lesse then ours, and their damnation stands us in. If you have a desire, says that blessed Father, to leave them certainly rich, *Deum iis relinque Debitorem,* Doe some such thing for Gods service, as you may leave God in their debt. He cannot break; his estate is inexhaustible; he will not break promise, nor break day;

[Exod. 20.6] [180] *He will shew mercy unto thousands in them that love him and keep his Commandements.* And here also may another showre of his benedictions fall upon them whom he hath prepared and presented Ps. 128.3 here; *Let the wife be as a fruitful Vine, and their children like Olive plants:* To thy glory, let the Parents expresse the love of Parents, and the children, to thy glory, the obedience of children, till they both loose that secular name of Parents and Children, and meet all alike, in one new name, all Saints in thy Kingdome, and fellow servants there.

In adjutorium   The third and last use in this institution of secular mariage, was, *In adjutorium,* for mutuall help. There is no state, no man in any [190] state, that needs not the help of others. Subjects need Kings, and if Kings doe not need their Subjects, they need alliances abroad, and they need Counsell at home. Even in Paradise, where the earth produced all things for life without labour, and the beasts submitted themselves to man, so that he had no outward enemy; And in the state of innocency in Paradise, where in man, all the affections submitted themselves to reason, so that he had no inward enemy, yet God in this abundant Paradise, and in this secure innocency of Paradise, even in the survey of his own works, saw, that though all that he had made was good, yet he had not made all good; he found thus much [200] defect in his own work, that man lacked a helper. Every body needs the help of others; and every good body does give some kinde of help to others. Even into the Ark it self, where God blessed them all with a powerfull and an immediate protection, God admitted onely such as were fitted to help one another, couples. In the Ark, which was the Type of our best condition in this life, there was not a single person. Christ saved once one theef at the last gasp, to shew that there may be late repentances; but in the Ark he saved none but maried persons, to shew, that he eases himself in making them helpers to one

another. And therefore when we come to the *Posui Deum adjutorium*
²¹⁰ *meum,* to rely upon God primarily for our Help, God comes to the
faciam tibi adjutorium, I will make thee a help like thy self: not   [Gen. 2.18]
always like in complexion, nor like in years, nor like in fortune, nor
like in birth, but like in minde, like in disposition, like in the love of
God, and of one another, or else there is no helper. It was no kinde of
help that *Davids* wife gave him, when she spoke by way of counsell,   [2 Sam.
but in truth, in scorn and derision, to draw him from a religious act,   6.14, 20]
as the dancing before the Ark, at that time was: It is no help for any
respect, to slacken the husband in his Religion. It was but a poor
help that *Nabals* wife was fain to give him by telling *David, Alas my*   [1 Sam.
²²⁰ *husband is but a foole, like his name, and what will you look for at a*   25.25]
fools hand? It is the worst help of all to raise a husband by dejecting
her self, to help her husband forward in this world, by forfeiting sin-
fully, and dishonourably, her own interest in the next. The husband
is the Helper in the nature of a foundation, to sustain and uphold
all; The wife in the nature of the roof, to cover imperfections and
weaknesses: The husband in the nature of the head from whence all
the sinews flow; The wife in the nature of the hands into which
those sinews flow, and enable them to doe their offices. The husband
helps as legges to her, she moves by his motion; The wife helps as a
²³⁰ staffe to him, he moves the better by her assistance. And let this
mutuall help be a part of our present benediction too; In all the ways
of fortune let his industry help her, and in all the crosses of fortune
let her patience help him; and in all emergent occasions and dangers   [Book of
spirituall, or temporall, *O God make speed to save them, O Lord,*   Common
make haste to help them.   Prayer]
    We have spoken of the persons, man and woman, him and her;   *In æternum*
And of the action, first as it is Physick, but cordiall Physick; and
then for children, but children to be made the children of God; and
lastly for help, but true help and mutuall help; There remains yet in
²⁴⁰ this secular mariage, the Term, how long, for ever, *I will mary thee*
for ever. Now though there be properly no eternity in this secular
mariage, nor in any thing in this world, (for eternity is onely that
which never had beginning, nor ever shall have end) yet we may
consider a kind of eternity, a kind of circle without beginning, without end, even in this secular mariage: for first, mariage should have

no beginning before mariage; no half-mariage, no lending away of the minde, in conditionall precontracts before, no lending away of the body in unchaste wantonnesse before. The body is the temple of the Holy Ghost; and when two bodies, by mariage are to be made one temple, the wife is not as the Chancell, reserv'd and shut up, and the man as the walks below, indifferent and at liberty for every passenger. God in his Temple looks for first fruits from both; that so on both sides, mariage should have such a degree of eternity, as to have had no beginning of mariage before mariage. It should have this degree of eternity too, this quality of a circle to have no interruption, no breaking in the way by unjust suspitions and jealousies. Where there is *Spiritus immunditiei,* as S. *Paul* calls it, a spirit of uncleannesse, there will necessarily be *Spiritus zelotypiæ,* as *Moses* cals it, a spirit of jealousie. But to raise the Devill in the power of the Devill, to call up one spirit by another spirit, by the spirit of jealousie and suspition, to induce the spirit of uncleannesse where it was not, if a man conjure up a Devill so, God knows who shall conjure it down again. As jealousie is a care and not a suspition, God is not ashamed to protest of himself that he is a jealous God. God commands that no idolatry be committed, *Thou shalt not bow down to a graven Image;* and before he accuses any man to have bowed down to a graven Image, before any Idolatry was committed, he tells them that he *is a jealous God;* God is jealous before there be any harm done. And God presents it as a curse, when he says, *My jealousie shall depart from thee, and I will be quiet, and no more angry;* that is, I will leave thee to thy self, and take no more care of thee. Jealousie that implies care, and honour, and counsell, and tendernesse, is rooted in God, for God is a jealous God, and his servants are jealous servants, as S. *Paul* professes of himself, *I am jealous over you with a godly jealousie.* But jealousie that implies diffidence and suspition, and accusation, is rooted in the Devil, for he is the *Accuser of the brethren.*

So then, this secular mariage should be *In æternum,* eternall, for ever, as to have no beginning before, and so too, as to have no jealous interruption by the way; for it is so eternall, as that it can have no end in this life: Those whom God hath joyned, no man, no Devill, can separate so, as that it shall not remain a mariage so far, as that if those separated persons will live together again, yet they shall not

[Num. 5.30]

Exod. 20.[4, 5]

Ezech. 16.42

2 Cor. 11.2

[Rev. 12.10]

be new maried; so farre, certainly, the band of mariage continues still. The Devil makes no mariages; He may have a hand in drawing conveyances; in the temporall conditions there may be practice, but the mariage is made by God in heaven. The Devil can break no mariages neither, though he can by sin break of all the good uses, and take away all the comforts of mariage. I pronounce not now whether Adultery dissolves mariage or no; It is *S. Augustines* wis-
290 dome to say, Where the Scripture is silent, let me be silent too: And I may goe lower then he, and say, Where the Church is silent, let me be silent too; and our Church is so far silent in this, as that it hath not said, That Adultery dissolves mariage. Perchance then it is not the death of mariage, but surely it is a deadly wound. We have Authors in the Romane Church that think *fornicationem non vagam,* that such an incontinent life as is limited to one certain person, is no deadly sin. But there is none even amongst them that diminish the crime of Adultery. *Habere quasi non haberes,* is Christs counsell, To have a wife as though thou hadst none, that is, for continency, and temper-
300 ance, and forbearance and abstinence upon some occasions: But *non habere quasi haberes,* is not so; not to have a wife, and yet have her, to have her that is anothers, this is the Devils counsell. Of that salutation of the Angel to the blessed Virgin *Mary, Blessed art thou amongst women,* we may make even this interpretation, not onely that she was blessed amongst women, that is, above women, but that she was *Benedicta,* blessed amongst women, that all women blest her, that no woman had occasion to curse her: And this is the eternity of this secular mariage as far as this world admits any eternity; that it should have no beginning before, no interruption of jealousie in the
310 way, no such approach towards dissolution, as that incontinency in all opinions, and in all Churches is agreed to be. And here also without any scruple of fear, or of suspition of the contrary, there is place for this benediction, upon this couple; Build, ô Lord, upon thine own foundations, in these two, and establish thy former graces with future; that no person ever complain of either of them, nor either of them of one another, and so he and she are maried *in æternum,* for ever.

We are now come in our order proposed at first, to our second Part; for all is said that I intended of the secular mariage. And of this second, the spirituall mariage, much needs not to be said: There

[1 Cor. 7.29]

[Luke 1.28]

2^d Part

320 is another Priest that contracts that, another Preacher that celebrates that, the Spirit of God to our spirit. And for the third mariage, the eternall mariage, it is a boldnesse to speak any thing of a thing so inexpressible as the joyes of heaven; it is a diminution of them to goe about to heighten them; it is a shadowing of them to goe about to lay any colours or lights upon them. But yet your patience may perchance last to a word of each of these three Circumstances, The Persons, the Actions, the Term, both in this spirituall, and in the eternall mariage.

Persons   First then, as in the former Part, the secular mariage, for the per-
330 sons there, we considered first *Adam* and *Eve,* and after every man and woman, and this couple in particular; so in this spirituall mariage we consider first Christ and his Church, for the Persons, but more particularly Christ and my soul. And can these persons meet? in such a distance, and in such a disparagement can these persons meet? the Son of God and the son of man? When I consider Christ to be *Germen Jehovæ,* the bud and blossome, the fruit and off-spring of Jehovah, Jehovah himself, and my self before he took me in hand,
[Psa. 2.9]   to be, not a Potters vessell of earth, but that earth of which the Potter might make a vessel if he would, and break it if he would
[Col. 1.16] 340 when he had made it: When I consider Christ to have been from before all beginnings, and to be still the Image of the Father, the same stamp upon the same metall, and my self a peece of rusty copper, in which those lines of the Image of God which were imprinted in me in my Creation are defaced and worn, and washed and burnt, and ground away, by my many, and many, and many sins: When I consider Christ in his Circle, in glory with his Father, before he came into this world, establishing a glorious Church when he was in this world, and glorifying that Church with that glory which himself had before, when he went out of this world; and then
350 consider my self in my circle, I came into this world washed in mine own tears, and either out of compunction for my self or compassion for others, I passe through this world as through a valley of tears, where tears settle and swell, and when I passe out of this world I leave their eyes whose hands close mine, full of tears too, can these persons, this Image of God, this God himself, this glorious God, and

this vessell of earth, this earth it self, this inglorious worm of the earth, meet without disparagement?

They doe meet and make a mariage; because I am not a body onely, but a body and soul, there is a mariage, and Christ maries me. As by 360 the Law a man might mary a captive woman in the Warres, if he shaved her head, and pared her nails, and changed her clothes: so my Saviour having fought for my soul, fought to blood, to death, to the death of the Crosse for her, having studied my soul so much, as to write all those Epistles which are in the New Testament to my soul, having presented my soule with his own picture, that I can see his face in all his temporall blessings, having shaved her head in abating her pride, and pared her nails in contracting her greedy desires, and changed her clothes not to fashion her self after this world, my soul being thus fitted by himself, Christ Jesus hath maried 370 my soul, maried her to all the three intendments mentioned in the secular mariage; first, *In ustionem,* against burning; That whether I burn my self in the fires of tentation, by exposing my self to occasions of tentation, or be reserved to be burnt by others in the fires of persecution and martyrdome, whether the fires of ambition, or envy, or lust, or the everlasting fires of hell offer at me in an apprehension of the judgements of God, yet as the Spirit of God shall wipe all tears from mine eyes, so the tears of Christ Jesus shall extinguish all fires in my heart, and so it is a mariage, *In ustionem,* a remedy against burning.

380 It is so too, *In prolificationem,* for children; first, *væ soli,* woe unto that single soul that is not maried to Christ; that is not come into the way of having issue by him, that is not incorporated in the Christian Church, and in the true Church, but is yet either in the wildernesse of Idolatry amongst the Gentiles, or in the Labyrinth of superstition amongst the Papists, *væ soli,* woe unto that single man that is not maried to Christ in the Sacraments of the Church; and *væ sterili,* woe unto them that are barren after this spirituall mariage, for that is a great curse in the Prophet *Jeremy, Scribe virum istum sterilem, write this man childlesse,* that implied all calamities upon him; And 390 assoon as Christ had laid that curse upon the Fig-tree, *Let no fruit grow upon thee for ever,* presently the whole tree withered; if no

Action
Deut. 21.12

In ustionem

In prolem.

Ier. 22.30

Mat. 21.19

fruit, no leaves neither, nor body left. To be incorporated in the body
of Christ Jesus, and bring forth no fruits worthy of that profession,
is a wofull state too. *Væ soli:* First, woe unto the Gentiles not maried
unto Christ; and *væ sterili,* woe unto inconsiderate Christians, that
think not upon their calling, that conceive not by Christ; but there

Mat. 24.19   is a *væ prægnanti* too, wo unto them that are with child, and are
never delivered; that have sometimes good conceptions, religious dispositions, holy desires to the advancement of Gods truth, but for
400 some collaterall respects dare not utter them, nor bring them to their
birth, to any effect. The purpose of his mariage to us, is to have
children by us: and this is his abundant and his present fecundity,
that working now, by me in you, in one instant he hath children in
me, and grand children by me. He hath maried me, *in ustionem,* and
in prolem, against burning, and for children; but can he have any
use of me, *in adjutorium,* for a helper? Surely, if I be able to feed
him, and clothe him, and harbour him, (and Christ would not
condemne men at the last day for not doing these, if man could not
doe them) I am able to help him too. Great persons can help him
410 over sea, convey the name of Christ where it hath not been preached
yet; and they can help him home again; restore his name, and his
truth where superstition with violence hath disseised him: And they
can help him at home, defend his truth there against all machinations
to displant and dispossesse him. Great men can help him thus; and
every man can help him to a better place in his own heart, and his
own actions, then he hath had there; and to be so helped in me, and
helped by me, to have his glory thereby advanced, Christ hath maried
my soul: And he hath maried it *in æternum,* for ever; which is the
third and last Circumstance in this spirituall, as it was in the secular
420 mariage.

In æternum   And here the *æternum* is enlarged; in the secular mariage it was
an eternity considered onely in this life; but this eternity is not begun
in this world, but from all eternity in the Book of life, in Gods
eternall Decree for my election, there Christ was maried to my soul.
Christ was never in minority, never under years; there was never any
time when he was not as ancient as the Ancient of Days, as old as his
Father. But when my soul was in a strange minority, infinite millions of millions of generations, before my soul was a soul, did Christ

mary my soul in his eternall Decree. So it was eternall, it had no
430 beginning. Neither doth he interrupt this by giving me any occasion
of jealousie by the way, but loves my soul as though there were no
other soul, and would have done and suffered all that he did for me
alone, if there had been no name but mine in the Book of life. And
as he hath maried me to him, *in æternum,* for ever, before all beginnings, and *in æternum,* for ever, without any interruptions, so I
know, that *whom he loves he loves to the end,* and that he hath given   [John 13.1]
me, not a presumptuous impossibility, but a modest infallibility, that
no sin of mine shall divorce or separate me from him; for, that which
ends the secular mariage, ends not the spirituall: not death, for my
440 death does not take me from that husband, but that husband being
by his Father preferr'd to higher titles, and greater glory in another
state, I doe but goe by death where he is become a King, to have my
part in that glory, and in those additions which he hath received
there. And this hath led us to our third and last mariage, our eternall
mariage in the triumphant Church.

And in this third mariage, the persons are, the Lamb and my soul;   3ᵈ Part
The mariage of the Lamb is come, and blessed are they that are   Persons
called to the mariage Supper of the Lamb, says S. *Iohn* speaking of our   Apoc.
state in the generall Resurrection. That Lamb who was *brought to*   19.7, 9
450 *the slaughter and opened not his mouth,* and I who have opened my   Esay 53.7
mouth and poured out imprecations and curses upon men, and execrations and blasphemies against God upon every occasion; That
Lamb who *was slain from the beginning,* and I who was slain by him   [Apoc.
who *was a murderer from the beginning;* That *Lamb which took*   13.8]
away the sins of the world, and I who brought more sins into the   [Joh. 8.44]
world, then any sacrifice but the blood of this Lamb could take away:
This Lamb and I (these are the Persons) shall meet and mary; there
is the Action.

This is not a clandestine mariage, not the private seal of Christ in   Action
460 the obsignation of his Spirit; and yet such a clandestine mariage is a
good mariage: Nor it is not such a Parish mariage, as when Christ
maried me to himself at my Baptisme, in a Church here; and yet
that mariage of a Christian soul to Christ in that Sacrament is a
blessed mariage: But this is a mariage in that great and glorious
Congregation, where all my sins shall be laid open to the eys of all

the world, where all the blessed Virgins shall see all my uncleannesse, and all the Martyrs see all my tergiversations, and all the Confessors see all my double dealings in Gods cause; where *Abraham* shall see my faithlesnesse in Gods promises; and *Job* my impatience in Gods 470 corrections; and *Lazarus* my hardness of heart in distributing Gods blessings to the poore; and those Virgins, and Martyrs, and Confessors, and *Abraham,* and *Job,* and *Lazarus,* and all that Congregation, shall look upon the Lamb and upon me, and upon one another, as though they would all forbid those banes, and say to one another, Will this Lamb have any thing to doe with this soule? and yet there and then this Lamb shall mary me, and mary me *In æternum,* for ever, which is our last circumstance.

In æternum   It is not well done to call it a circumstance, for the eternity is a great part of the essence of that mariage. Consider then how poore 480 and needy a thing, all the riches of this world, how flat and tastlesse a thing, all the pleasures of this world, how pallid, and faint and dilute a thing, all the honours of this world are, when the very Treasure, and Joy, and glory of heaven it self were unperfect, if it were not eternall, and my mariage shall be soe, *In æternum,* for ever.

The Angels were not maried so; they incurr'd an irreparable Divorce from God, and are separated for ever, and I shall be maried to him, *in æternum,* for ever. The Angels fell in love, when there was no object presented, before any thing was created; when there was nothing but God and themselves, they fell in love with them- 490 selves, and neglected God, and so fell *in æternum,* for ever. I shall see all the beauty, and all the glory of all the Saints of God, and love them all, and know that the Lamb loves them too, without jealousie, on his part, or theirs, or mine, and so be maried *in æternum,* for ever, without interruption, or diminution, or change of affections.

Apoc. 6.12   I shall see the Sunne black as sackcloth of hair, and the Moon become as blood, and the Starres fall as a Figge-tree casts her untimely Figges, and the heavens roll'd up together as a Scroll. I shall see a divorce between Princes and their Prerogatives, between nature and all her elements, between the spheres, and all their intelligences, between 500 matter it self, and all her forms, and my mariage shall be, *in æternum,* for ever. I shall see an end of faith, nothing to be beleeved that I doe not know; and an end of hope, nothing to be wisht that I doe not

enjoy, but no end of that love in which I am maried to the Lamb for ever. Yea, I shall see an end of some of the offices of the Lamb himself; Christ himself shall be no longer a Mediator, an Intercessor, an Advocate, and yet shall continue a Husband to my soul for ever. Where I shall be rich enough without Joynture, for my Husband cannot die; and wise enough without experience, for no new thing can happen there; and healthy enough without Physick, for no sick-
510 nesse can enter; and (which is by much the highest of all) safe enough without grace, for no tentation that needs particular grace, can attempt me. There, where the Angels, which cannot die, could not live, this very body which cannot choose but die, shall live, and live as long as that God of life that made it. Lighten our darkness, we beseech thee, ô Lord, that in thy light we may see light: Illustrate our understandings, kindle our affections, pour oyle to our zeale, that we may come to the mariage of this Lamb, and that this Lamb may come quickly to this mariage: And in the mean time bless these thy servants, with making this secular mariage a type of the spir-
520 ituall, and the spirituall an earnest of that eternall, which they and we, by thy mercy, shall have in the Kingdome which thy Son our Saviour hath purchased with the inestimable price of his incorruptible blood. To whom, etc.

Number 12.

Preached upon Trinity-Sunday.

---

2 COR. 1.3. *BLESSED BE GOD, EVEN THE FATHER OF OUR LORD IESUS CHRIST, THE FATHER OF MERCIES, AND THE GOD OF ALL COMFORT.*

THERE WAS never Army composed of so many severall Nations, the Towre of Babel it self, in the confusion of tongues, gave not so many severall sounds as are uttered and mustered against God, and his Religion. The Atheist denies God; for, though *David* call it a foolish thing to do so, (*The foole hath said it in his heart*) And though *David* speake it in the singular number, *The foole,* as though there were not many so very fooles, as *to say,* and *to say in their heart, There is no God,* yet some such fooles there are, that say it in their very heart, and have made shift to think so indeed; ¹⁰ But for such fools as say it in their actions, that is, that live as though there were no God, *Stultorum plena sunt omnia;* We have seen fooles in the Court, and fooles in the Cloister, fooles that take no calling, and fooles in all callings that can be taken, fooles that heare, and fooles that preach, fooles at generall Councells, and fooles at Councell-tables, *Stultorum plena sunt omnia,* such fooles as deny God, so far, as to leave him out, are not in *Davids* singular number, but super-abound in every profession: So that *Davids* manner of expressing it, is not so much singular, as though there were but one, or few such fooles, but emphaticall, because that foole, that any way ²⁰ denies God, is the foole, the veryest foole of all kinds of foolishnesse.

Now, as God himselfe, so his religion amongst us hath many enemies; Enemies that deny God, as Atheists; And enemies that multiply gods, that make many gods, as Idolaters; And enemies that deny those divers persons in the Godhead, which they should con-

[Psal. 14.1; 53.1]

fesse, The Trinity, as Jews and Turks: So in his Religion, and outward
worship, we have enemies that deny God his House, that deny us
any Church, any Sacrament, any Priesthood, any Salvation, as Papists;
And enemies that deny Gods house any furniture, any stuffe, any
beauty, any ornament, any order, as non-Conformitans; And enemies
³⁰ that are glad to see Gods house richly furnished for a while, that they
may come to the spoile thereof, as sacrilegious usurpers of Gods part.
But for Atheisticall enemies, I call not upon them here, to answer
me; Let them answer their own terrors, and horrors alone at midnight, and tell themselves whence that proceeds, if there be no God.
For Papisticall enemies, I call not upon them to answer me; Let
them answer our Laws as well as our Preaching, because theirs is a
religion mixt as well of Treason, as of Idolatry. For our refractary,
and schismaticall enemies, I call not upon them to answer me neither;
Let them answer the Church of God, in what nation, in what age
⁴⁰ was there ever seen a Church, of that form, that they have dreamt,
and beleeve their own dream? And for our sacrilegious enemies, let
them answer out of the body of Story, and give one example of
prosperity upon sacriledge.

But leaving all these to that which hath heretofore, or may hereafter be said of them, I have bent my meditations, for those dayes,
which this Terme will afford, upon that, which is the character and
mark of all Christians in generall, The Trinity, the three Persons
in one God; not by way of subtile disputation, as to persons that
doubted, but by way of godly declaration, as to persons disposed to
⁵⁰ make use of it; not as though I feared your faith needed it, nor as
though I hoped I could make your reason comprehend it, but because I presume, that the consideration of God the Father, and his
Power, and the sins directed against God, in that notion, as the
Father; and the consideration of God the Son, and his Wisedome, and
the sins against God, in that apprehension, the Son; and the consideration of God the Holy Ghost, and his Goodnesse, and the sins
against God, in that acceptation, may conduce, as much, at least, to
our edification, as any Doctrine, more controverted. And of the first
glorious person of this blessed Trinity, the Almighty Father, is this
⁶⁰ Text, *Blessed be God, &c.*

In these words, the Apostle having tasted, having been fed with   *Divisio*

the sense of the power, and of the mercies of God, in his gracious
deliverance, delivers a short Catechisme of all our duties: So short,
as that there is but one action, *Benedicamus, Let us blesse;* Nor but
one object to direct that blessing upon, *Benedicamus Deum, Let us
blesse God.* It is but one God, to exclude an Idolatrous multiplicity
of Gods, But it is one God notified and manifested to us, in a triplicity
of persons; of which, the first is literally expressed here, That he is
a *Father.* And him we consider *In Paternitate æterna,* As he is the
70 eternall Father, *Even the Father of our Lord Iesus Christ,* sayes our

[Rom. 8.15]

Text; And then *In Paternitate interna,* as we have *the Spirit of Adoption, by which we cry, Abba, Father;* As he is *Pater miserationum,
The Father of mercies;* And as he expresses these mercies, by the
seale and demonstration of comfort, as he is *the God of comfort,*
and *Totius consolationis, Of all comfort.* Receive the summe of this,
and all that arises from it, in this short Paraphrase; The duty required of a Christian, is *Blessing,* Praise, Thanksgiving; To whom?
To *God,* to God onely, to the onely God. There is but one; But this
one God is such a tree, as hath divers boughs to shadow and refresh
80 thee, divers branches to shed fruit upon thee, divers armes to spread
out, and reach, and imbrace thee. And here he visits thee as a *Father:*
From all eternity a *Father of Christ Iesus,* and now thy Father in
him, in that which thou needest most, *A Father of mercy,* when thou
wast in misery; And a *God of comfort,* when thou foundest no comfort in this world, And *a God of all comfort,* even of spirituall comfort, in the anguishes, and distresses of thy conscience. *Blessed bee
God, even the Father, &c.*

1 Part
Benedictus

First then, the duty which God, by this Apostle, requires of man,
is a duty arising out of that, which God hath wrought upon him:
90 It is not a consideration, a contemplation of God sitting in heaven,
but of God working upon the earth; not in the making of his eternall
Decree there, but in the execution of those Decrees here; not in saying, God knowes who are his, and therefore they cannot faile, but
in saying in a rectified conscience, God, by his ordinary marks, hath
let me know that I am his, and therefore I look to my wayes, that
I doe not fall. S. *Paul* out of a religious sense what God had done for
him, comes to this duty, to blesse him.

There is not a better Grammar to learne, then to learne how to

blesse God, and therefore it may be no levity, to use some Grammar
¹⁰⁰ termes herein. God blesses man *Dativè,* He gives good to him; man
blesses God *Optativè,* He wishes well to him; and he blesses him
Vocativè, He speaks well of him. For, though towards God, as well
as towards man, reall actions are called blessings, (so *Abigail* called
the present which she brought to *David, A blessing,* and so *Naaman*
called that which he offered to *Elisha, A blessing*) though reall sacrifices to God, and his cause, sacrifices of Almes, sacrifices of Armes,
sacrifices of Money, sacrifices of Sermons, advancing a good publique
cause, may come under the name of blessing, yet the word here,
Εὐλογία, is properly a blessing in speech, in discourse, in conference,
¹¹⁰ in words, in praise, in thanks. *The dead doe not praise thee,* says
David; The dead (men civilly dead, allegorically dead, dead and
buryed in an uselesse silence, in a Cloyster, or Colledge, may praise
God, but not in words of edification, as it is required here, and they
are but dead, and doe not praise God so; and *God is not the God of
the dead, but of the living,* of those that delight to praise and blesse
God, and to declare his goodnesse.

    We represent the Angels to our selves, and to the world with wings,
they are able to flie; and yet when *Iacob* saw them ascending and descending, even those winged Angels had a Ladder, they went by
¹²⁰ degrees: There is an immediate blessing of God, by the heart, but
God requires the tongue too, because that spreads and diffuses his
glory upon others too. *Calici benedictionis benedicimus,* sayes the
Apostle, *The cup which we blesse, is a cup of blessing;* When we
have blessed it, according to Christs holy institution, then it derives
holy blessings upon us; and when we blesse God according to his
Commandement, he blesses us according to his promise, and our
desire. When God imployed *Moses,* and when he imployed *Ieremy,*
Moses and *Ieremy* had no excuse, but the unreadinesse of their
tongues; he that hath a tongue disposed to Gods service, that will
¹³⁰ speak all he can, and dares speake all he should to the glory of God,
is fit for all. As S. *Iames* says, *The tongue is but a little member,
but boasteth great things;* so truly, as little as it is, it does great things
towards our salvation. The Son of God, is Λόγος, *verbum, The
word;* God made us with his word, and with our words we make
God so farre, as that we make up the mysticall body of Christ Jesus

1 Sam. 25.27

2 King. 5.15

[Psal. 115.17]

[Mat. 22.32]

Gen. 28.12

1 Cor. 10.16

Exod. 6.12
Ier. 1.6

Iames 3.5

with our prayers, with our whole liturgie, and we make the naturall body of Christ Jesus appliable to our soules, by the words of Consecration in the Sacrament, and our soules apprehensive, and capable of that body, by the word Preached. Blesse him therefore in speaking
¹⁴⁰ to him, in your prayers: Blesse him in speaking with him, in assenting, in answering that which he sayes to you in his word: And blesse him in speaking of him, in telling one another the good things that
Psal. 34.1 he hath done abundantly for you. *I will blesse the Lord at all times,* sayes *David.* Is it at all times, sayes S. *Augustine, Cum circumfluunt omnia,* at all times, when God blesses mee with temporall prosperity? *Cum minus nascuntur, cum nata dilabuntur,* sayes that Father, when thy gaine ceases for the present, when that that thou hadst formerly got, wasts and perishes, and threatens penury for the future, still blesse thou the Lord, *Quia ille dat, ille tollit, sed seipsum à bene-*
¹⁵⁰ *dicente se non tollit;* The Lord gives, and the Lord takes away, but the Lord never takes away himselfe from him that delights in blessing his name. Blesse, praise, speake; there is the duty, and we have done with that which was our first Part: And blesse thou God, which is our second Part, and a Part derived into many Branches. *Blessed be God, even, &c.*
2 Part
*Deum
solum* Here first we see the object of our praises, whom we must blesse, *Benedictus sit Deus,* God. First, *Solus Deus,* God onely, that is, God and not man, and then *Deus solus,* the onely God, that is God, and not many Gods. God onely, and not man; not that we may not blesse,
¹⁶⁰ and wish well to one another, for there is a blessing from God, be-
Gen. 12.3 longs to that, *Benedicam benedicentibus tibi,* sayes God to *Abraham, I will blesse them that blesse thee:* Neither is it that we may not blesse, that is, give due praise to one another; for as the vices and sins of great persons are not smothered in the Scriptures, so their vertues, and good deeds are published with praise. *Noahs* drunkennesse, and *Lots* incest is not disguised, *Iobs* righteousnesse and holy
Rom. 13.3 patience is not concealed neither; *Doe that which is good,* sayes the Apostle, *and thou shalt have praise for the same.* Neither is it that we may not blesse, that is, pray for one another, of what sort soever;
¹⁷⁰ for we are commanded to doe that, for our superiours; inferiours may blesse superiours too; Nor that wee should not blesse, that is, pray to one another, in petitioning and supplicating our superiours for

those things which are committed to their dispensation; for the im- Luke 18.5
portunate sutor, the widow, is not blamed in the Gospel for her
importunity to the Judge; It is true, the Judge is blamed, for withholding Justice, till importunity extorted it. But to blesse, by praise,
or prayer, the man without relation to God, that is, the man, and
not God in the man, to determine the glory in the person, without
contributing thereby to the glory of God, this is a manner of blessing
¹⁸⁰ accursed here, because blessing is radically, fundamentally, originally,
here reserved to God, to God onely, *Benedictus sit Deus, God be
blessed.*

For, properly, truly none is to be thus blessed by us, but he upon
whom we may depend and rely: and can we depend and rely upon
man? upon what man? upon Princes? As far as we can looke for
examples, round about us, in our next neighbours, and in France, and
in Spaine, and farther, we have seene in our age Kings discarded,
and wee have seen in some of them, the discarded cards taken in
againe, and win the game. Upon what man wilt thou rely? upon
¹⁹⁰ great persons in favour with Princes? Have we not seen often, that the
bed-chambers of Kings have back-doores into prisons, and that the end
of that greatnesse hath beene, but to have a greater Jury to condemne
them? wilt thou rely upon the Prophet, he can teach thee; or upon
thy Brother, he does love thee; or upon thy Son, he should love thee;
or the Wife of thy bosome, she will say she loves thee; or upon thy
Friend, he is as thine owne soule? yet *Moses* puts a case when thou Deut. 13
must depart from all these, not consent, no not conceale, not pardon,
no not reprieve, *Thou shalt surely kill him,* sayes *Moses,* even this
Prophet, this *Brother,* this *Son,* this *Wife* may encline thee *to the
²⁰⁰ service of other Gods;* Thou canst not rely, and therefore doe not
blesse, not with praise, not with prayer and dependance upon him,
That Prophet, by what name or title soever he be called; that
Brother, how willingly soever he divide the inheritance with thee;
that Son, how dutifull soever in civill things; that Wife, how carefull
soever of her owne honour, and thy children; that Friend, how free
soever of his favours, and of his secrets, that enclines thee to other
Gods, or to other service of the true God, then is true. Greatnesse is
not the object of this blessing, for Greatnesse is often eclipsed by the
way, and at last certainely extinguished in death, and swallowed in

²¹⁰ the grave. Goodnesse, as it is morall, is not the object of this blessing; but blesse God onely; God in the roote, in himselfe, or God exemplified, and manifested in godly men; blesse God in them, in whom he appeares, and in them who appeare for him, and so thou doest blesse *solum Deum,* God onely.

Deus solus   This thou must doe, Blesse God onely, not man, and then the onely God, not other gods. For, this was the wretched and penurious narrownesse to which the Gentiles were reduced, that being unable to consider God intirely, they broke God in pieces, and crumbled, and scattered God into as many severall gods, as there are Powers in God, ²²⁰ nay almost into as many severall gods, as there are Creatures from God; and more then that, as many gods as they could fancie or imagine in making Chimera's of their owne, for not onely that which was not God, but that which was not at all, was made a God. And then, as in narrow channels that cannot containe the water, the water over-flowes, and yet that water that does so over-flow, flies out and spreads to such a shallownesse, as will not beare a Boat to any use; so when by this narrownesse in the Gentiles, God had over-flowne this bank, this limitation of God in an unity, all the rest was too shallow to beare any such notion, any such consideration of God, as apper- ²³⁰ tained to him: They could not think him an Omnipotent God, when if one God would not, another would, nor an Infinite God, when they had appeales from one God to another; and without Omnipotence, and without Infinitenesse they could not truly conceive a God. They had cantoned a glorious Monarchy into petty States, that could not subsist of themselves, nor assist another, and so imagined a God for every state and every action, that a man must have applied himselfe to one God when he shipped, and when he landed to another, and if he travailed farther, change his God by the way, as often as he

Deut. 6.4   changed coynes, or post-horses. But, *Heare O Israel, the Lord thy God* ²⁴⁰ *is one God.* As though this were all that were to be heard, all that were to be learned, they are called to *heare,* and then there is no more said but that, *The Lord thy God is one God.*

There are men that will say and sweare, they do not meane to make God the Author of sin; but yet when they say, That God made man therefore, that he might have something to damne, and that he made him sin therefore, that he might have something to damne him

for, truly they come too neare making God the Author of sin, for
all their modest protestation of abstaining. So there are men that
will say and sweare, they do not meane to make Saints Gods; but yet
²⁵⁰ when they will aske the same things at Saints hands, which they do
at Gods, and in the same phrase and manner of expression, when
they will pray the Virgin *Mary* to assist her Son, nay to command
her Son, and make her a Chancellor to mitigate his common Law,
truly they come too neare making more Gods then one. And so do we
too, when we give particular sins dominion over us; *Quot vitia, tot
Deos recentes,* sayes *Hierom:* As the Apostle sayes *Covetousnesse is
Idolatry,* so, sayes that Father, is voluptuousnesse, and licentiousnesse,
and every habituall sin. *Non alienum* sayes God, *Thou shalt have no
other God but me,* But, *Quis similis,* sayes God too, *Who is like me?*
²⁶⁰ Hee will have nothing made like him, not made so like a God as they
make their Saints, nor made so like a God, as we make our sins. Wee
thinke one King Soveraigne enough, and one friend counsellor
enough, and one Wife helper enough, and he is strangely insatiable,
that thinks not one God, God enough: especially, since when thou
hast called this God what thou canst, he is more then thou hast said
of him. *Cum definitur, ipse sua definitione crescit;* When thou hast
defined him to be the God of justice, and tremblest, he is more then
that, he is the God of mercy too, and gives thee comfort. When thou
hast defined him to be all eye, He sees all thy sins, he is more then
²⁷⁰ that, he is all patience, and covers all thy sins. And though he be in
his nature incomprehensible, and inaccessible in his light, yet this is
his infinite largenesse, that being thus infinitely One, he hath manifested himselfe to us in three Persons, to be the more easily discerned
by us, and the more closely and effectually applied to us.

Now these notions that we have of God, as a Father, as a Son, as
a Holy Ghost, as a Spirit working in us, are so many handles by
which we may take hold of God, and so many breasts, by which we
may suck such a knowledge of God, as that by it wee may grow up
into him. And as wee cannot take hold of a torch by the light, but by
²⁸⁰ the staffe we may; so though we cannot take hold of God, as God,
who is incomprehensible, and inapprehensible, yet as a Father, as a
Son, as a Spirit, dwelling in us, we can. There is nothing in Nature
that can fully represent and bring home the notion of the Trinity to

[Col. 3.5]

[Exod. 20.3]

Hilar.

Trinitas

us. There is an elder booke in the World then the Scriptures; It is not well said, in the World, for it is the World it selfe, the whole booke of Creatures; And indeed the Scriptures are but a paraphrase, but a comment, but an illustration of that booke of Creatures. And therefore, though the Scriptures onely deliver us the doctrine of the Trinity, clearely, yet there are some impressions, some obumbrations 290 of it, in Nature too. Take but one in our selves, in the soule. The understanding of man (that is as the Father) begets discourse, ratiocination, and that is as the Son; and out of these two proceed conclusions, and that is as the Holy Ghost. Such as these there are many, many sprinkled in the Schoole, many scattered in the Fathers, but, God knowes, poore and faint expressions of the Trinity. But yet,

Tertul.　*Præmisit Deus naturam magistram, submissurus & prophetiam,* Though God meant to give us degrees in the University, that is, increase of knowledge in his Scriptures after, yet he gave us a pedagogy, he sent us to Schoole in Nature before; *Vt faciliùs credas* 300 *prophetiæ discipulus naturæ,* That comming out of that Schoole, thou mightest profit the better in that University, having well considered Nature, thou mightest be established in the Scriptures.

He is therefore inexcusable, that considers not God in the Creature, that comming into a faire Garden, sayes onely, Here is a good Gardiner, and not, Here is a good God; and when he sees any great change, sayes onely, This is a strange accident, and not, a strange Judgement. Hence is it, that in the books of the Platonique Philosophers, and in others, much ancienter then they, (if the books of *Hermes Trismegistus* and others, be as ancient as is pretended in 310 their behalfe) we finde as cleare expressing of the Trinity, as in the Old Testament, at least; And hence is it, that in the Talmud of the Jews, and in the Alcoran of the Turks, though they both oppose the Trinity, yet when they handle not that point, there fall often from them, as cleare confessions of the three Persons, as from any of the elder of those Philosophers, who were altogether dis-interested in that Controversie.

Aleus.　But because God is seene *Per creaturas, ut per speculum, per verbum ut per lucem,* In the creature, and in nature, but by reflection, In the Word, and in the Scriptures, directly, we rest in the knowledge 320 which we have of the plurality of the persons, in the Scriptures; And because we are not now in a Congregation that doubts it, nor in a place to multiply testimonies, we content our selves (being already possest with the beliefe thereof) with this illustration from the old Testament, That the name of our one God, is expressed in the plurall number, in that place, which we mentioned before, where it is said, *The Lord thy God is one God,* that is, *Elohim, unus Dii,* one Gods. And though as much as that seem to be said by God to *Moses, Eris Aaroni in Elohim, Thou shalt be as Gods to Aaron;* Yet that was because *Moses* was to represent God, all God, all the Persons in God, ₃₃₀ and therefore it might as well be spoken plurally of *Moses,* so, as of God. But because it is said, *Gods appeared unto Iacob;* And againe, *Dii Sancti ipse est, Hee is the Holy Gods;* And so also, *Vbi Deus factores mei? Where is God my Makers?* And God sayes of himselfe, *Faciamus hominem,* and *Factus est sicut unus ex nobis,* God sayes, *Let us make man,* and he sayes, *Man is become as one of us,* We imbrace humbly, and thankfully, and profitably, this, shall we call it *Effigiationem ansarum,* This making out of handles? Or *Protuberationem mammarum,* This swelling out of breasts? Or *Germinationem gemmarum,* This putting forth of buds, and blossomes, and ₃₄₀ fruits, by which we may apprehend, and see, and taste God himself, so as his wisedome hath chosen to communicate himself to us, in the notion and manifestation of divers persons? Of which in this Text, we lay hold on him, by the first handle, by the name of Father. *Blessed be God, even the Father, &c.*

Now we consider in God, a two-fold Paternity, a two-fold Fatherhood: One, as he is Father to others, another as to us. And the first is two-fold too: One essentially, by which he is a Father by Creation, and so the name of *Father* belongs to all the three Persons in the Trinity, for, *There is one God, and Father of all, who is above all,* ₃₅₀ *and through all, and in you all,* Which is spoken of God gathered into his Essence, and not diffused into persons. In which sense, the Son of God, Christ Jesus, is called Father, *Vnto us a Son is given, and his name shall be The Everlasting Father:* And to this Father, even to the Son of God, in this sense, are the faithfull made sons, *Son, be of good cheare, thy sins are forgiven thee,* sayes Christ to the Paralytique, And *Daughter, thy faith hath made thee whole,* sayes he to the woman with the bloody issue; Thus Christ is a Father;

Marginal references:

Deut. 6.4
Exod. 4.16

Gen. 35.7
Ios. 24.19
Iob 35.10

Gen. 1.26
3.22

Pater Essentialiter

Eph. 4.6

Esay 9.6

Mat. 9.2
Mark 5.34

And thus *Per filiationem vestigii,* By that impression of God, which is in the very beeing of every creature, God, that is, the whole Trinity,

Iob 38.28 ³⁶⁰ is the Father of every creature, as in *Iob, Quis pluviæ Pater? Hath the raine a Father? or who hath begotten the drops of dew?* And so in

Mal. 2.10 the Prophet, *Have we not all one Father? hath not one God created us?* But the second Paternity is more mysterious in it selfe, and more precious to us, as he is a Father, not by Creation, but by Generation, *Even the Father of our Lord Iesus Christ.*

Personaliter
Esay 53.8

Now, *Generationem istam quis enarrabit?* who shall declare this generation? who shall tell us how it was? who was there to see it? Since the first-borne of all creatures, the Angels, who are almost sixe thousand yeares old, (and much elder in the opinion of many of the ³⁷⁰ Fathers, who think the Angels to have been created long before the generall Creation) since, I say, these Angels are but in their swathing clouts, but in their cradle, in respect of this eternall generation, who was present? *Quis enarrabit?* who shall tell us how it was? who shall tell us when it was, when it was so long before any time was, as that, when time shall be no more, and that, after an end of time, wee shall have lived infinite millions of millions of generations in heaven, yet this generation of the Son of God, was as long before that immortall life, as that Immortality, and Everlastingnesse shall be after this life? It cannot be expressed, nor conceived how long our life shall be after, ³⁸⁰ nor how long this generation was before.

Nazian.

This is that Father, that hath a Son, and yet is no elder then that Son, for he is *à Patre,* but not *Post Patrem,* but so from the Father,

Biel as he is not after the Father: He hath from him *Principium Originale,* but not *Initiale,* A root from whence he sprung, but no springtime, when he sprung out of that root. *Blessed be God even the Father of our Lord Iesus Christ.* Wherefore blessed? *Quia potuit?* Because he could have a Son? *Non generavit potentia, sed natura;* God did not beget this Son because he had alwayes a power to doe so; for then, if this Son had ever been but *in Potentia,* onely in such a condition, as ³⁹⁰ that he might have been, then this had not been an eternall generation, for if there were a time, when only he might have been, at that time he was not. He is not blessed then because he could, is he blessed (that is, to be blessed by us) because he would beget this Son? *Non generavit voluntate, sed natura:* God did not beget this Son, then

when he would, that is, had a will to doe so, for, if his will determined
it, now I will doe it, then till that, there had been no Son, and so this
generation had not been eternall neither. But when it was, or how it
was, *Tu ratiocinare, ego mirer,* sayes S. *Augustine,* Let others discourse it, let me admire it; *Tu disputa, ego credam,* Let others dis-
400 pute it, let me beleeve it. And when all is done, you have done disputing, and I have done wondring, that that brings it nearer then
either, is this, That there is a Paternity, not by Creation, by which
Christ and the Holy Ghost are Fathers too, nor by generation, by
which God is, though inexpressibly, the Father even of our Lord
Jesus Christ, but by Adoption, as in Christ Jesus, he is Father of us
all, notified in the next appellation, *Pater miserationum, The Father
of mercies.*

    In this alone, we discerne the whole Trinity; here is the *Father,*   *Pater*
and here is *Mercy,* which mercy is in the Son; And the effect of this
410 mercy, is *the Spirit of Adoption, by which also we cry, Abba, Father*   Rom. 8.15
too. When Christ would pierce into his Father, and melt those bowels
of compassion, he enters with that word, *Abba, Father, All things are*   Mark 14.36
possible to thee; take away this Cup from me. When Christ apprehended an absence, a dereliction on Gods part, he cals not upon him
by this name, not *My Father,* but *My God, my God, why hast thou*   Mat. 27.46
forsaken me? But when he would incline him to mercy, mercy to
others, mercy to enemies, he comes in that name, wherein he could be
denied nothing, Father; *Father forgive them, they know not what*   Luke 23.34
they doe. He is *the Lord of Hosts;* There hee scatters us in thunder,
420 transports us in tempests, enwraps us in confusion, astonishes us with
stupefaction, and consternation; *The Lord of Hosts,* but yet *the
Father of mercies,* There he receives us into his own bowels, fills our
emptinesse, with the blood of his own Son, and incorporates us in
him; *The Lord of Hosts,* but *the Father of mercy.* Sometimes our
naturall Fathers die, before they can gather any state to leave us, but
he is the immortall Father, and all things that are, as soone as they
were, were his. Sometimes our naturall Fathers live to waste, and
dissipate that state which was left them, to be left us: but this is the
Father, out of whose hands, and possession nothing can be removed,
430 and who gives inestimably, and yet remaines inexhaustible. Sometimes our naturall Fathers live to need us, and to live upon us: but

this is that Father whom we need every minute, and requires nothing of us, but that poore rent of *Benedictus sit,* Blessed, praised, glorified be this Father.

*Misera-
tionum*
Psal. 59.17
Numb.
14.19
Psal. 51.1

Psal. 17.7
Psal. 31.21

Psal. 89.49
[Dan. 7.9,
13]
[Lam. 3.23]

⁴⁴⁰

⁴⁵⁰

⁴⁶⁰

This Father of mercies, of *mercies* in the plurall; *David* calls God, *Misericordiam suam,* His mercy; all at once: *God is the God of my mercy:* God is all ours, and all mercy. *Pardon this people,* sayes *Moses, Secundùm magnitudinem misericordiæ, According to the greatnesse of thy mercy.* Pardon me, sayes *David, Have mercy upon me, Secundùm multitudinem misericordiarum, According to the multitude of thy mercies:* His mercy, in largenesse, in number, extends over all; It was his mercy that we were made, and it is his mercy that we are not consumed. *David* calls his mercy, *Multiplicatam,* and *Mirificatam,* It is manifold, and it is marvellous, miraculous: *Shew thy marvellous loving kindnesse;* and therefore *David* in severall places, carries it *Super judicium,* above his judgements, *Super Cœlos,* above the heavens, *Super omnia opera,* above all his works. And for the multitude of his mercies, (for we are now upon the consideration of the plurality thereof, *Pater miserationum, Father of mercies*) put together that which *David* sayes, *Vbi misericordiæ tuæ antiquæ? Where are thy ancient mercies?* His mercy is as Ancient, as *the Ancient of dayes,* who is God himselfe, And that which another Prophet sayes, *Omni mane, His mercies are new every morning,* And put betweene these two, betweene Gods former, and his future mercies, his present mercy, in bringing thee this minute to the consideration of them, and thou hast found *Multiplicatam,* and *Mirificatam,* manifold, and wondrous mercy.

But carry thy thoughts upon these three Branches of his mercy, and it will be enough. First, that upon *Adams* fall, and all ours in him, he himselfe would think of such a way of mercy, as from *Adam,* to that man whom Christ shall finde alive at the last day, no man would ever have thought of, that is, that to shew mercy to his enemies, he would deliver his owne, his onely, his beloved Son, to shame, to torments, to death: That hee would plant *Germen Iehovæ in semine mulieris,* The blossome, the branch of God, in the seed of the woman: This mercy, in that first promise of that Messias, was such a mercy, as not onely none could have undertaken, but none could have imagined but God himselfe: And in this promise, we were conceived

In visceribus Patris, In the bowels of this Father of mercies. In these
470 bowels, in the womb of this promise we lay foure thousand yeares;
The blood with which we were fed then, was the blood of the
Sacrifices, and the quickning which we had there, was an inanimation, by the often refreshing of this promise of that Messias in the
Prophets. But *in the fulnesse of time,* that infallible promise came to
an actuall performance, *Christ came in the flesh,* and so, *Venimus
ad partum,* In his birth we were borne; and that was the second
mercy; in the promise, in the performance, he is *Pater miserationum,
Father of mercies.* And then there is a third mercy, as great, That he
having sent his Son, and having re-assumed him into heaven againe,
480 he hath sent his Holy Spirit to governe his Church, and so becomes
a Father to us, in that Adoption, in the application of Christ to us,
by the Holy Ghost; and this is that which is intended in the last
word, *Deus totius Consolationis, The God of all Comfort.*

[Gal. 4.4]

I may know that there is a Messias promised, and yet be without
comfort, in a fruitlesse expectation; The Jews are so in their dispersion. When the Jews will still post-date the commings of Christ, when
some of them say, There was no certaine time of his comming designed by the Prophets; And others, There was a time, but God for
their sins prorogued it; And others againe, God kept his word, the
490 Messiah did come when it was promised he should come, but for their
sins, he conceales himselfe from Manifestation; when the Jews will
postdate his first comming, and the Papists will antidate his second
comming, in a comming that cannot become him, That he comes,
even to his Saints in torment, before he comes in glory, That when
he comes to them at their dissolution, at their death, he comes not to
take them to Heaven, but to cast them into one part of hell, That the
best comfort which a good man can have at his death, is but Purgatory, *Miserable comforters are they all.* How faire a beame of the
joyes of Heaven is true comfort in this life? If I know the mercies of
500 God exhibited to others, and feele them not in my self, I am not of
Davids Church, not of his Quire, *I cannot sing of the mercies of God:*
I may see them, and I may sigh to see the mercies of God determined
in others, and not extended to me; but I cannot sing of the mercies
of God, if I find no mercy. But when I come to that, *Consolationes
tuæ lætificaverunt, In the multitude of my thoughts within me, thy*

Consolatio

[Job 16.2]

Psal. 89.1

Psal. 94.19

comforts delight my soule, then the true Comforter is descended upon
me, and the *Holy Ghost* hath *over-shadowed* me, and all that shall
be *borne* of me, and *proceed* from me, shall be *holy. Blessed are they*

Mat. 5.4   *that mourne,* sayes Christ: But the blessednesse is not in the mourn-
510 ing, but because *they shall be comforted.* Blessed am I in the sense of
my sins, and in the sorrow for them, but blessed therefore, because this
sorrow leads me to my reconciliation to God, and the consolation of
his Spirit. Whereas, if I sinke in this sorrow, in this dejection of
spirit, though it were Wine in the beginning, it is lees, and tartar in
the end; Inordinate sorrow growes into sinfull melancholy, and that
melancholy, into an irrecoverable desperation. The Wise-men of the
East, by a lesse light, found a greater, by a Star, they found the Son
of glory, Christ Jesus: But by darknesse, nothing: By the beames of
comfort in this life, we come to the body of the Sun, by the Rivers, to
520 the Ocean, by the cheerefulnesse of heart here, to the brightnesse, to
the fulnesse of joy hereafter. For, beloved, Salvation it selfe being so
often presented to us in the names of Glory, and of Joy, we cannot
thinke that the way to that glory is a sordid life affected here, an
obscure, a beggarly, a negligent abandoning of all wayes of preferment, or riches, or estimation in this World, for the glory of Heaven
shines downe in these beames hither; Neither can men thinke, that
the way to the joyes of Heaven, is a joylesse severenesse, a rigid
austerity; for as God loves a cheerefull giver, so he loves a cheerefull
taker, that takes hold of his mercies and his comforts with a cheerefull
530 heart, not onely without grudging, that they are no more, but without
jealousie and suspition that they are not so much, or not enough.

Deus   But they must be his comforts that we take in, Gods comforts. For,
to this purpose, the Apostle varies the phrase; It was *The Father of*
mercies; To represent to us gentlenesse, kindnesse, favour, it was
enough to bring it in the name of *Father;* But this *Comfort,* a power
to erect and settle a tottering, a dejected soule, an overthrowne, a
bruised, a broken, a troden, a ground, a battered, an evaporated, an
annihilated spirit, this is an act of such might, as requires the assurance, the presence of God. God knows, all men receive not comforts,
540 when other men think they do, nor are all things comforts to them,
which we present, and meane should be so. Your Father may leave
you his inheritance, and little knowes he the little comfort you have

in this, because it is not left to you, but to those Creditors to whom you have engaged it. Your Wife is officious to you in your sicknesse, and little knowes she, that even that officiousnesse of hers then, and that kindnesse, aggravates that discomfort, which lyes upon thy soul, for those injuries which thou hadst formerly multiplied against her, in the bosome of strange women. Except the God of comfort give it, in that seale, in peace of conscience, *Nec intus, nec subtus, nec circa* 550 *te occurrit consolatio,* sayes S. *Bernard; Non subtus,* not from below thee, from the reverence and acclamation of thy inferiours; *Non circa,* not from about thee, when all places, all preferments are within thy reach, so that thou maist lay thy hand, and set thy foote where thou wilt; *Non intus,* not from within thee, though thou have an inward testimony of a morall constancy, in all afflictions that can fall, yet not from below thee, not from about thee, not from within thee, but from above must come thy comfort, or it is mistaken. S. *Chrysostome* notes, and *Areopagita* had noted it before him, *Ex beneficiis acceptis nomina Deo affingimus,* We give God names ac-560 cording to the nature of the benefits which he hath given us: So when God had given *David* victory in the wars, by the exercise of his power, then *Fortitudo mea,* and *firmamentum, The Lord is my Rock, and my Castle:* When God discovered the plots and practises of his enemies to him, then *Dominus illuminatio, The Lord is my light, and my salvation.* So whensoever thou takest in any comfort, be sure that thou have it from him that can give it; for this God is *Deus totius consolationis, The God of all comfort.*

    Preciosa divina consolatio, nec omnino tribuitur admittentibus alienam: The comforts of God are of a precious nature, and they lose 570 their value, by being mingled with baser comforts, as gold does with allay. Sometimes we make up a summe of gold, with silver, but does any man binde up farthing tokens, with a bag of gold? Spirituall comforts which have alwayes Gods stampe upon them, are his gold, and temporall comforts, when they have his stampe upon them, are his silver, but comforts of our owne coyning, are counterfait, are copper. Because I am weary of solitarinesse, I will seeke company, and my company shall be, to make my body the body of a harlot: Because I am drousie, I will be kept awake, with the obscenities and scurrilities of a Comedy, or the drums and ejulations of a Tragedy: I will

Psal. 18.2

27.1

Totius
Bernard

⁵⁸⁰ smother and suffocate sorrow, with hill upon hill, course after course
at a voluptuous feast, and drown sorrow in excesse of Wine, and
call that sickness, health; and all this is no comfort, for *God is the
God of all comfort,* and this is not of God. We cannot say with any

Gen. 27.38   colour, as *Esau* said to *Iacob, Hast thou but one blessing, my Father?*
for he is the God of all blessings, and hath given every one of us,
many more then one. But yet Christ hath given us an abridgement,

Luke 10.42   *Vnum est necessarium,* there is but one onely thing necessary, And
David, in Christ, tooke knowledge of that before, when he said,
Vnum petii, One thing have I desired of the Lord, What is that one

Psal. 27.4   ⁵⁹⁰ thing? All in one; *That I may dwell in the house of the Lord* (not
be a stranger from his Covenant) *all the dayes of my life,* (not dis-
seised, not excommunicate out of that house) *To behold the beauty
of the Lord,* (not the beauty of the place only) but to *inquire in his
Temple,* (by the advancement and advantage of outward things, to
finde out him) And so I shall have true comforts, outward, and
inward, because in both, I shall finde him, who is the God of all
comfort.

Gen. 37.35   *Iacob* thought he had lost *Ioseph* his Son, *And all his Sons, and all
his Daughters rose up to comfort him, Et noluit consolationem,* sayes
⁶⁰⁰ the Text, *He would not be comforted,* because he thought him dead.

Mat. 2.18   *Rachel wept for her children and would not be comforted, because
they were not.* But what aylest thou? Is there any thing of which
thou canst say, It is not? perchance it is, but thou hast it not: If thou
hast him, that hath it, thou hast it. Hast thou not wealth, but poverty
rather, not honour, but contempt rather, not health, but daily sum-

Bernard   mons of Death rather yet? *Non omnia possidet, cui omnia cooperan-
tur in bonum,* If thy poverty, thy disgrace, thy sicknesse have brought
thee the nearer to God, thou hast all those things, which thou thinkest
thou wantest, because thou hast the best use of them. *All things are*

1 Cor. 3.23   ⁶¹⁰ *yours,* sayes the Apostle; why? by what title? *For you are Christs, and
Christ is Gods.* Carry back your comfort to the root, and bring that
comfort to the fruit, and confesse, that God who is both, is *the God
of all comfort.* Follow God in the execution of this good purpose
upon thee, to thy Vocation, and heare him, who hath left East, and
West, and North, and South, in their dimnesse, and dumnesse, and
deafnesse, and hath called thee to a participation of himselfe in his

Church. Go on with him to thy justification, That when in the congregation one sits at thy right hand, and beleeves but historically (It
may be as true which is said of Christ, as of *William* the Conquerour,
⁶²⁰ and as of *Iulius Cæsar*) and another at thy left hand, and beleeves
Christ but civilly, (It was a Religion well invented, and keeps people
well in order) and thou betweene them beleevest it to salvation in
an applying faith; proceed a step farther, to feele this fire burning
out, thy faith declared in works, thy justification growne into sanctification, And then thou wilt be upon the last staire of all, That
great day of thy glorification will breake out even in this life, and
either in the possessing of the good things of this world, thou shalt
see the glory, and in possessing the comforts of this World, see the
joy of Heaven, or else, (which is another of his wayes) in the want
⁶³⁰ of all these, thou shalt have more comfort then others have, or perchance, then thou shouldest have in the possessing of them: for he
is *the God of all comfort,* and of all the wayes of comfort; And
therefore, *Blessed be God, even the Father, &c.*

Number 13.

Preached upon Trinity-Sunday.

---

1 PET. 1.17. *AND IF YE CALL ON THE FATHER, WHO WITHOUT RESPECT OF PERSONS JUDGETH ACCORDING TO EVERY MANS WORKS, PASSE THE TIME OF YOUR SOJOURNING HERE IN FEARE.*

YOU MAY remember, that I proposed to exercise your devotions and religious meditations in these exercises, with words which might present to you, first the severall persons in the Trinity, and the benefits which we receive, in receiving God in those distinct notions of Father, Son, and holy Ghost; And then with other words which might present those sins, and the danger of those sins which are most particularly opposed against those severall persons. Of the first, concerning the person of the Father, we spoke last, and of the other, concerning sins against the Father, these words will occasion
10 us to speak now.

Psal. 51.1   It is well noted upon those words of *David, Have mercy upon me, O God,* that the word is *Elohim,* which is *Gods* in the plurall, *Have mercy upon me, O Gods:* for *David,* though he conceived not divers Gods, yet he knew three divers persons in that one God, and he knew that by that sin which he lamented in that Psalme, that *peccatum complicatum,* that manifold sin, that sin that enwrapped so many sins, he had offended all those three persons. For whereas we consider principally in the Father, *Potestatem,* Power, and in the Son *Sapientiam,* Wisdome, and in the holy Ghost *Bonitatem,* Good-
20 nesse, *David* had sinned against the Father, in his notion, *In potestate,*

[2 Sam.   in abusing his power, and kingly authority, to a mischievous and
11.14–17]   bloody end in the murder of *Vriah:* And he had sinned against the

274

Son, in his notion, *In sapientia,* in depraving and detorting true wisdome into craft and treachery: And he had sinned against the holy
Ghost in his notion, *In bonitate,* when he would not be content with
the goodnesse and piety of *Vriah,* who refused to take the eases of
his owne house, and the pleasure of his wifes bosome, as long as God
himselfe in his army lodged in Tents, and stood in the face of the
Enemy. Sins against the Father then, we consider especially to be
30 such as are *In potestate,* Either in a neglect of Gods Power over us,
or in an abuse of that power which we have from God over others;
and of one branch of that power, particularly of Judgement, is this
Text principally intended, *If ye call on the Father, who without respect of persons judgeth, &c.*

   In the words we shall insist but upon two parts, First, A Counsaile,   *Divisio*
which in the Apostles mouth is a commandement; And then a
Reason, an inducement, which in the Apostles mouth is a forcible, an
unresistible argument. The Counsell, that is, The commandement, is,
If ye call on the Father, feare him, stand in feare of him; And the
40 reason, that is, the Argument, is, The name of *Father* implyes a great
power over you, therefore feare him; And amongst other powers, a
power of *judging* you, of calling you to an account, therefore feare
him: In which Judgement, this Judge *accepts no persons,* but judges
his sons as his servants, and therefore feare him: And then, he judges,
not upon words, outward professions, but upon *works,* actions,
according to every mans works, and therefore feare him: And then
as on his part he shall certainly call you to judgement when you goe
hence, so on your part, certainly it cannot be long before you goe
hence, for your time is but a *sojourning here,* it is not a dwelling,
50 And yet it is a *sojourning here,* it is not a posting, a gliding through
the world, but such a stay, as upon it our everlasting dwelling depends; And therefore that we may make up this circle, and end as
we begun, with the feare of God, *passe that time,* that is, all that
time, *in fear;* In fear of neglecting and undervaluing, or of over-
tempting that great power which is in the Father, And in feare of
abusing those limmes, and branches, and beames of that power which
he hath communicated to thee, in giving thee power and authority
any way over others; for these, To neglect the power of the Father,
or To abuse that power which the Father hath given thee over others,

60 are sinnes against the Father, who is power. *If ye call on the Father, &c.*

1 Part

First then, for the first part, the Counsell, *Si invocatis, If ye call on the Father, In timore,* Doe it *in feare,* The Counsell hath not a voluntary Condition, and arbitrary in our selves annexed to it; If you call, then feare, does not import, If you doe not call, you need not feare; It does not import, That if you professe a particular forme of Religion, you are bound to obey that Church, but if you doe not, but have fancied a religion to your selfe without precedent, Or a way to salvation without any particular religion, Or a way out of the world without any salvation or damnation, but a going out like a candle, 70 if you can think thus you need not feare, This is not the meaning of this *If* in this place, *If you call on the Father, &c.* But this *If* implyes a wonder, an impossibility, that any man should deny God to be the Father: If the author, the inventer of any thing usefull for this life be called the father of that invention, by the holy Ghost himselfe,

Gen. 4.20

Iabal was the father of such as dwell in Tents, and Iubal his brother the father of Musique, And so *Horace* calls *Ennius* the *father* of one kind of Poeme: how absolutely is God our Father, who (may I say?) invented us, made us, found us out in the depths, and darknesse of

Iam. 1.17

nothing at all? He is *Pater,* and *Pater luminum, Father,* and *Father* 80 *of lights,* of all kinds of lights, *Lux lucifica,* as S. *Augustine* expresses it, The light from which all the lights which we have, whether of nature, or grace, or glory, have their emanation. Take these *Lights* of which God is said to be *the Father,* to be the Angels, (so some of

2 Cor. 11.14

the Fathers take it, and so S. *Paul* calls them *Angels of light;* And so *Nazianzen* calls them *Secundos splendores primi splendoris administros,* second lights that serve the first light) Or take these *Lights* of which God is said to be *the Father* to be the Ministers of the Gospel, the Angels of the Church, (so some Fathers take them too, and

Mat. 5.14

so Christ sayes to them, in the Apostles, *You are the light of the* 90 *world*) Or take these *Lights* to be those faithfull servants of God, who have received an illustration in themselves, and a coruscation towards others, who by having lived in the presence of God, in the

[Joh. 5.35]

houshold of his faithfull, in the true Church, are become, as *Iohn Baptist* was, *burning and shining lamps,* (as S. *Paul* sayes of the

Phil. 2.15

faithfull, *You shine as lights in this world,* And as *Moses* had contracted a glorious shining in his face, by his conversation with God)

Or take this *light* to be a fainter light then that, (and yet that which
S. *Iames* doth most literally intend in that place) The light of naturall understanding, That which *Plinie* calls *serenitatem animi,* when
the mind of man, dis-encumbred of all Eclipses, and all clouds of
passion, or inordinate love of earthly things, is enlightned so far, as
to discerne God in nature; Or take this *light* to be but the light of a
shadow, (for *umbræ non sunt tenebræ, sed densior lux,* shadows
are not darknesses, shadows are but a grosser kind of light) Take it
to be that shadow, that designe, that delineation, that obumbration
of God, which the creatures of God exhibit to us, that which *Plinie*
calls *Cœli lætitiam,* when the heavens, and all that they imbrace, in
an opennesse and cheerefulnesse of countenance, manifest God unto
us; Take these *Lights* of which S. *Iames* speaks, in any apprehension,
any way, Angels of heaven who are ministring spirits, Angels of
the Church, who are spirituall Ministers, Take it for the light of
faith from hearing, the light of reason from discoursing, or the light
flowing from the creature to us, by contemplation, and observation
of nature, Every way, by every light we see, that he is *Pater luminum,*
the Father of lights; all these lights are from him, and by all these
lights we see that he is A Father, and Our Father.

So that as the Apostle uses this phrase in another place, *Si opertum*
Euangelium, If the Gospel be hid, with wonder and admiration, Is
it possible, can it be that this Gospel should be hid? So it is here, *Si*
invocatis, If ye call God Father, that is, as it is certaine you doe, as it
is impossible but you should, because you cannot ascribe to any but
him, your Being, your preservation in that Being, your exaltation
in that Being to a well-Being, in the possession of all temporall, and
spirituall conveniencies, And then there is thus much more force in
this particle *Si, If,* which is (as you have seene) *Si concessionis, non*
dubitationis, an *If* that implyes a confession and acknowledgement,
not a hesitation or a doubt, That it is also *Si progressionis, Si con-*
clusionis, an *If* that carryes you farther, and that concludes you at
last, *If* you doe it, that is, *Since* you do it, *Since you do call God*
Father, since you have passed that act of Recognition, since not onely
by having been produced by nature, but by having beene regenerated
by the Gospel, you confesse God to bee your Father, and your Father
in his Son, in Christ Jesus: Since you make that profession, *Of his*

2 Cor. 4.3

Iames 1.18

owne will begate he us, with the word of Truth, If you call him Father, since you call him Father, thus, goe on farther, *Timete,* Feare him; *If yee call him Father, feare him, &c.*

Timete

Now, for this *feare of God,* which is *the beginning of wisedome,* and the end of wisedome too, we are a little too wise, at least, too subtile, sometimes in distinguishing too narrowly between a filiall
140 feare, and a servile feare, as though this filiall feare were nothing but a reverend love of God, as he is good, and not a doubt and suspition of incurring those evils, that are punishments, or that produce pun-

Prov. 8.13   ishments. *The feare of the Lord is to hate evill,* It is a holy detestation of that evill which is *Malum culpæ,* The evill of sin, and it is a holy trembling under a tender apprehension of that other evill, which we call *Malum pœnæ,* The evill of punishment for sin. God presents to us the joyes of heaven often to draw us, and as often the torments

Origen   of hell to avert us. *Origen* sayes aright, As *Abraham* had two sons, one of a Bond-woman, another of a Free, but yet both sons of *Abra-*
150 *ham;* so God is served by two feares, and the later feare, the feare of future torment, is not the perfect feare, but yet even that feare is the

Chrysost.   servant, and instrument of God too. *Quis tam insensatus;* Who can so absolutely devest all sense, *Qui non fluctuante Civitate, imminente naufragio,* But that when the whole City is in a combustion and commotion, or when the Ship that he is in, strikes desperately and irrecoverably upon a rock, hee is otherwise affected toward God then, then when every day, in a quietnesse and calme of holy affections, he heares a Sermon? *Gehennæ timor* (sayes the same Father) *regni nos affert coronam,* Even the feare of hell gets us heaven. Upon

Gen. 15.12   160 *Abraham* there fell *A horrour of great darknesse,* And *Moses hid*
Exod. 3.6   *his face, for he was afraid to look upon God.* And that way, towards
Esay 66.2   that dejected look, does God bend his countenance; *Vpon this man will I look, even to him that is poore, and of a contrite spirit, and trembleth at my word.* As there are both impressions in security, vitious and vertuous, good and bad, so there are both in feare also. There is a wicked security in the wicked, by which they make shift to put off all Providence in God, and to think God like themselves, indifferent what becomes of this world; There is an ill security in the godly, when for the time, in their prosperity, they grow ill hus-

Psal. 30.6   170 bands of Gods graces, and negligent of his mercies; *In my prosperity* (sayes *David* himself, of himself) *I said, I shall not be moved.* And there is a security of the faithfull, a constant perswasion, grounded upon those marks, which God, in his Word, hath set upon that state, *That neither height, nor depth, nor any creature shall separate us from God:* But yet this security is never discharged of that feare, which he that said that, had in himselfe, *I keep under my body, lest when I have preached to others, I my self should be a cast-away;* And which he perswades others, how safe soever they were, *Work out your salvation with feare and trembling,* And, *Let him that* ¹⁸⁰ *thinketh he standeth, take heed lest he fall.*

      [Rom. 8.39]
      1 Cor. 9.27
      Phil. 2.12
      1 Cor. 10.12

As then there is a vitious, an evill security; and that holy security which is good, is not without feare: so there is no feare of God, though it have some servility, (so farre, as servility imports but a feare of punishment) but it is good. For, *Timor est amor inchoativus,* The love of God begins in feare, and then *Amor est timor consummatus,* The feare of God ends in love; which *David* intends when he sayes, *Rejoyce with trembling;* Conceive no such feare as excludes spirituall joy, conceive no such assurance, as excludes an humble and reverentiall feare. There is a feare of God too narrow, when we thinke ¹⁹⁰ every naturall crosse, every worldly accident to be a judgement of God, and a testimony of his indignation, which the Poet (not altogether in an ill sense) calls a disease of the soule, *Quo morbo mentem concusse? timore deorum;* He imagines a man may be sick of the feare of God, that is, not distinguish between naturall accidents, and immediate judgements of God; between ordinary declarations of his power, and extraordinary declarations of his anger. There is also a feare of God too large, too farre extended, when for a false feare of offending God, I dare not offend those men, who pretend to come in his name, and so captivate my conscience to the traditions ²⁰⁰ and inventions of men, as to the word, and law of God. And there is a feare of God conceived, which never quickens, but putrifies in the womb before inanimation; the feare and trembling of the Devill, and men whom he possesses, desperate of the mercies of God. But there is a feare acceptable to God, and yet hath in it, a trembling, a horrour, a consternation, an astonishment, an apprehension of Gods dereliction for a time. The Law was given in thundring, and lightning, and the people were afraid. How proceeds *Moses* with them?

      August.

      Psal. 2.11

      Exod. 20.20

Feare not, saies he, *for God is come to prove you, that his feare might be before your faces.* Here is a *feare not,* that is, feare not with de-
²¹⁰ spaire, nor with diffidence, but yet therefore, That you may feare the Law; for, in this place, the very *Law* it selfe (which is given to direct them) is called *feare;* As in another place, God himselfe is

Gen. 31.53
called *feare,* (as he is in other places called *love* too) *Iacob swore by the Feare of his Father Isaac;* that is, by him whom his Father *Isaac* feared, as the Chalde Paraphrase rightly expresses it.

Briefly, this is the difference between Fearfulnesse, and Feare, (for so we are fain to call *Timiditatem* and *Timorem*) Timidity, Fearful-nesse, is a fear, where no cause of fear is; and there is no cause of feare, where man and man onely threatens on one side, and God

Esay 41.14
²²⁰ commands on the other: *Feare not, thou worme of Iacob, I will help thee, saith the Lord thy redeemer, the Holy one of Israel. Moses*

Heb. 11.23
Parents had overcome this fearfulnesse: *They hid him,* says the Text, *Et non metuerunt Edictum Regis, They feared not the Procla-mation of the King,* Because it was directly, and evidently, and un-disputably against the manifest will of God. Queen *Esther* had over-come this fearfulnesse; she had fasted, and prayed, and used all pre-scribed and all possible meanes, and then she entred the Kings Chamber, against the Proclamation, with that necessary resolution,

Esther 4.16
Si peream, peream, If I perish, I perish; Not upon a disobedient, not
²³⁰ upon a desperate undertaking, but in a rectified conscience, and well established opinion, that either that Law was not intended to forbid her, who was his Wife, or that the King was not rightly informed, in that bloody command, which he had given for the execution of all her Countrymen. And for those who doe not overcome this fear-fulnesse, that is, that feare where no cause of feare is, (and there is no cause of feare, where Gods cause is by godly wayes promoved, though we doe not alwayes discern the wayes, by which this is done) for those men that frame imaginary feares to themselves, to the with-drawing or discouraging of others in the service of God, we see where

Apoc. 21.8
²⁴⁰ such men are ranked by the Holy Ghost, when S. *Iohn* sayes, *The unbeleeving, the murderer, the whore-monger, the sorcerer, the idolater, shall have their portion in the lake of brimstone, which is the second death:* We see who leads them all into this irrecoverable precipitation, The fearfull, that is, he that beleeves not God in his

promises, that distrusts God in his owne cause, as soone as he seemes
to open us to any danger; or distrusts Gods instruments, as soone as
they goe another way, then he would have them goe. To end this,
there is no love of God without feare, no Law of God, no God himselfe without feare; And here, as in very many other places of Scrip-
²⁵⁰ ture, the feare of God is our whole Religion, the whole service of
God; for here, Feare him, includes Worship him, reverence him, obey
him. Which Counsell or Commandement, though it need no reason,
no argument, yet the Apostle does pursue with an argument, and
that constitutes our second Part.

Now the Apostles arguments grow out of a double root; One argu- 2 Part
ment is drawne from God, another from man. From God, thus implied, If God be a Father, feare him, for naturally we acknowledge
the power of a Father to be great over his children, and consequently
the reverent feare of the children great towards him. The Father
²⁶⁰ had *Potestatem vitæ & necis,* A power over the life of his child, he
might have killed his childe; but that the child should kill his Father,
it never entred into the provision of any Law, and it was long before
it fell into the suspition of any Law-maker. *Romulus* in his Laws,
called every man-slaughter *Parricidium,* because it was *Paris occisio,*
He had killed a man, a Peere, a creature equall to himselfe; but for
Parricide in the later sense, when *Parricide* is *Patricide,* the killing
of a Father, it came not into the jealousie of *Romulus* Law, not into
the heart or hand of any man there in sixe hundred yeares after:
Cum lege cœperunt, & facinus pœna monstravit, sayes their Morall Seneca
²⁷⁰ man: That sin began not, till the Law forbad it, and only the punishment ordained for it, shewed that there might be such a thing. *He* Exod. 21.17
that curseth Father or Mother, shall surely dye, sayes *Moses;* And he Deut. 21.18
that is but *stubborne* towards them, shall *dye* too. The dutifull love
of children to Parents is so rooted in nature, that *Demosthenes* says,
it is against the impressions and against the Law of nature, for any
child ever to love that man, that hath done execution upon his Father,
though by way of Justice: And this naturall Obligation is not conditioned with the limitations of a good or a bad Father, *Natura te non* Epictetus
bono patri, sed patri conciliavit, sayes that little great Philosopher,
²⁸⁰ Nature hath not bound thee to thy father, as hee is a good Father,
but meerely as he is thy Father.

Now for the power of Fathers over their children, by the Law of
Nations, that is, the generall practise of Civill States, the Father had
power upon the life of his child; It fell away by discontinuance, in a
great part, and after was abrogated by particular Laws, but yet, by
a connivence admitted in some cases too. For, as in Nature man is
Microcosmus, a little World, so in nature, a family is a little State, a
little Commonwealth, and what power the Magistrate hath in that,
the Father hath in this. *Ipsum regnum suapte natura imperium est*
290 *paternum,* The power of a King, if it be kept within the bounds of
the nature of that Office, is onely to be a Father to his people: And,
Gratius est nomen pietatis, quam potestatis, Authority is presented
in a more acceptable name, when I am called a Father, then when I
am called a Master; and therefore, sayes *Seneca,* our Ancestors
mollified it thus, *Vt invidiam Dominis, contumeliam servis detra-*
herent, That there might accrue no envy to the Master for so great
a title, nor contempt upon the servant for so low a title, they called
the Master *Patremfamilias,* The Father of a houshould, and they called
the servants, *familiares,* parts and pieces of the family. So that in the
300 name of *Father* they understand all power; and the first Law that
passed amongst the Romans against Parricides, was *Contra inter-*
fectores Patrum & Dominorum; They were made equall, Fathers
and Soveraignes: And in the Law of God it selfe, *Honour thy Father,*
wee see all the honour, and feare, and reverence that belongs to the
Magistrate, is conveyed in that name, in that person, the Father is
all; as in the State of that people, before they came to be settled,
both the Civill part of the Government, and the Spirituall part,
was all in the Father, that Father was King and Priest over all that
family.

310   Present God to thy self then as a Father, and thou wilt feare him;
and take knowledg, that the Son might not sue the Father; Enter no
action against God why he made thee not richer, nor wiser, nor
fairer; no, nor why he elects, or refuses, without respect of good or
bad works; But take knowledge too, that when by the Law, the
Father might punish the Son with death, he might not kill his Son
before he was passed three yeares in age, before hee was come to some
demonstration of an ill, and rebellious nature, and disposition: Whatsoever God may doe of his absolute Power, beleeve that he will not

Aristot.

Tertul.

L. Pompeia

[Exod.
20.12]

execute that power upon thee to thy condemnation, till thine actuall
³²⁰ sins have made thee incapable of his love: What he may do, dispute
not, but be sure he will do thee no harme if thou feare him, as a
Father.

Now to bring that nearer to you, which principally we intended, *Sacerdotalis*
which is, the consideration and precaution of those sins, which vio-
late this Power of God, notified in this name of *Father,* we consider
a threefold emanation or exercise of Power in this Father, by occasion
of a threefold repeating of this part of the Text, in the Scripture. The
words are waighty, alwayes at the bottome; for we have these words
in the last of the Prophets, in *Malachie,* and in the last of the Euan-
³³⁰ gelists, in *Iohn,* And here in this Apostle, we have them of the last
Judgement. In *Malachi* he sayes, *A Son honoureth his Father, if then* Mal. 1.6
I be a Father, where is my honour? This God speaks there to the
Priest, to the Levite; for, the Tribe of *Levi,* had before, (as *Moses* Exod. 32.29
bade them) consecrated their hands to God, and punished by a
zealous execution, the Idolatry of the golden Calfe; and for this service, God fastned the Priesthood upon them. But when they came in
Malachies time, to connive at Idolatry it selfe, God, who was himselfe
the roote of the Priesthood, and had trusted them with it, and they
had abused that trust, and the Priesthood, Then when the *Prophet* Hose. 9.7
³⁴⁰ was become a *foole,* and the *spirituall Man, mad,* or (as S. *Hierom*
reads it) *Arreptitius,* that is, possessed by others, God first of all
turnes upon the Priest himselfe, rebukes the Priest, interminates his
judgement upon the Priest, for God is our high Priest. And therefore feare this Father in that notion, in that apprehension, as a Priest,
as thy high Priest, that refuses or receives thy sacrifices, as he finds
them conditioned; and if he looke narrowly, is able to finde some
spot in thy purest Lambe, some sin in thy holiest action, some devia-
tion in thy prayer, some ostentation in thine almes, some vaine glory
in thy Preaching, some hypocrisie in thy hearing, some concealing
³⁵⁰ in thy confessions, some reservation in thy restitutions, some relapses
in thy reconciliations: since thou callest him Father, feare him as thy
high Priest: So the words have their force in *Malachie,* and they
appertaine *Ad potestatem Sacerdotalem,* To the power of the Priest,
despise not that.

And then, in the second place, which is in S. *Iohn,* Christ sayes, *Civilis*

Iohn 8.42 *If God were your Father, you would love me:* And this Christ
speakes to the Pharisees, and to them, not as Sectaries in Religion,
but as to persons in Authority, and command in the State, as to
Iohn 19.11 Rulers, to Governours, to Magistrates: So Christ sayes to *Pilate, Thou*
360 *couldst have no power at all against me, except it were given thee*
Rom. 13.1 *from above:* And so S. *Paul, There is no power but of God, The*
powers that be, be ordained of God. Christ then charges the Pharisees,
that they having the secular Power in their hands, they went about
to kill him, when he was doing the will of his Father, who is the
roote, as of Priesthood, so of all Civill power, and Magistracy also.
Feare this Father then, as the Civill Sword, the Sword of Justice is
in his hand. He can open thee to the malicious prosecutions of adversaries, and submit thee to the penalties of those Lawes, which, in
truth, thou hast never transgressed: Thy Fathers, thy Grandfathers
370 have sinned against him, and thou hast been but reprieved for two
sessions, for two generations, and now maiest come to execution.
Thou hast sinned thy selfe, and hast repented, and hast had thy pardon sealed in the Sacrament; but thy pardon was clogged with an
Ita quòd se bene gerat, Thou wast bound to the peace by that pardon,
and hast broken that peace since, in a relapse, and so fallest under
execution for thine old sins: God cuts off men by unsearchable wayes
and meanes; and therefore feare this Father as a Soveraigne, as a
Magistrate, for that use this word in S. *Iohn* may have.

Iudiciaria   In *Malachie* we consider him in his supreme spirituall power, and
380 in S. *Iohn* in his supreme temporall power; And in this Text, this
Father is presented in a power, which includes both, in a judiciary
power, as a Judge, as our Judge, our Judge at the last day, beyond
all Appeale; And (as this Apostle S. *Peter*, is said by *Clement,* who
is said to have beene his successor at Rome, to have said) *Quis peccare*
poterit, &c. Who could commit any sin at any time, if at all times he
had his eye fixed upon this last Judgement? We have seene purses
cut at the Sessions, and at Executions, but the Cutpurse did not see
the Judge looke upon him: we see men sin over those sins to day,
for which Judgement was inflicted but yesterday, but surely they
Rom. 2.5   390 doe not see then that the Judge sees them. *Thou treasurest up wrath,*
says the Apostle, *against the day of wrath, and revelation of the*
judgement of God: There is no Revelation of the day of Judgement,

no sense of any such day, till the very day it selfe overtake him, and swallow him. Represent God to thy selfe as such a Judge, as S. *Chrysostome* sayes, That whosoever considers him so, as that Judge, and that day, as a day of irrevocable judgement, *Gehennæ pœnam tolerare malit, quàm adverso Deo stare,* He will even think it an ease to be thrown down into hell out of the presence of God, rather then to stand long in the presence, and stand under the indignation of [Mat. 25.41]
400 that incensed Judge: The *Ite maledicti* will be lesse then the *Surgite* [Eph. 5.14]
qui dormitis. And there is the miserable perplexity, *Latere impossible,* Bernard
Apparere intolerabile, To be hid from this Judge is impossible, and to appeare before him, intolerable: for he comes invested with those two flames of confusion, (which are our two next branches in the Text) first, He respects no persons, Then, He judges according to workes: *Without respect of persons, &c.*

Nine or ten severall times it is repeated in the Scriptures, and, I *Acceptor*
thinke, no one intire proposition so often, *That God is no accepter* *personarum*
of persons. It is spoken by *Moses,* that they who are conversant in [Deut.
410 the Law might see it, and spoken in the Chronicles, that they might 10.17]
see it who are conversant in State-affaires, and spoken in *Iob,* that men [Job 34.19]
in afflictions might not mis-imagine a partiality in God: It is spoken to
the Gentiles, by the Apostle of the Gentiles, S. *Paul,* severally; To the [Rom. 2.11;
Romanes, to the Galatians, to the Ephesians, to the Colossians: And Gal. 2.6]
spoken by the chiefe Apostle, S. *Peter,* both in a private Sermon in [Acts 10.34]
Cornelius his house, and now in this Catholique Epistle written to
all the world, that all the world, and all the inhabitants thereof might
know, *That God is no accepter of persons:* And lest all this should
not be all, it is spoken twice in the Apocryphall books; and though
420 we know not assuredly by whom, yet we know to whom, To all that
exercise any judiciary power under God, it belongs to know, *That*
God is no accepter of persons. In divers of those places, this also is
added, *Nor receiver of Rewards;* whether that be added as an equall
thing, That it is as great a sin to accept persons, as to accept rewards,
Or as a concomitancy, they goe together, He that will accept persons,
will accept rewards, Or as an Identity, It is the same thing to accept
persons, and to accept rewards, because the preferment which I looke
for from a person in place, is as much a reward, as money from a
person rich in treasure; whether of these it be, I dispute not: Clearly

⁴³⁰ there is a Bribery in my love to another, and in my feare of another
there is a Bribery too: There is a bribery in a poore mans teares, if
that decline me from justice, as well as in the rich mans Plate, and
Hangings, and Coach, and Horses.

Let no man therefore think to present his complexion to God for
an excuse, and say, My choler with which my constitution abounded,
and which I could not remedy, enclined me to wrath, and so to bloud;
My Melancholy enclined me to sadnesse, and so to Desperation, as
though thy sins were medicinall sins, sins to vent humors. Let no
man say, I am continent enough all the yeare, but the spring works
⁴⁴⁰ upon me, and inflames my concupiscencies, as though thy sins were
seasonable and anniversary sins. Make not thy Calling the occasion
of thy sin, as though thy sin were a Mysterie, and an Occupation;
Nor thy place, thy station, thy office the occasion of thy sin, as though
thy sin were an Heir-loome, or furniture, or fixed to the freehold of
that place: for this one proposition, *God is no accepter of persons,*
is so often repeated, that all circumstances of Dispositions, and Callings, and time, and place might be involved in it. *Nulla discretio*
personarum, sed morum; God discernes not, that is, distinguishes
not Persons, but Actions, for, *He judgeth according to every mans*
⁴⁵⁰ *works,* which is our next Branch.

Now this judging according to works, excludes not the heart, nor
the heart of the heart, the soule of the soule, Faith. God requires the
heart, *My sonne give me thy heart;* He will have it, but he will have
it by gift; and those Deeds of Gift must be testified; and the testimony of the heart is in the hand, the testimony of faith is in works.
If one give me a timber tree for my house, I know not whether the
root be mine or no, whether I may stub it by that gift: but if he give
me a fruit tree for mine Orchard, he intends me the root too; for
else I cannot transplant it, nor receive fruit by it: God judges accord-
⁴⁶⁰ ing to *the worke,* that is, Root and fruit, faith and worke; That is
the worke; And then he judges according unto *Thy worke;* The
works of Other men, the Actions and the Passions of the blessed
Martyrs, and Saints in the Primitive Church, works of Supererogation are not thy works. It were a strange pretence to health, that
when thy Physitian had prescribed thee a bitter potion, and came
for an account how it had wrought upon thee, thou shouldst say,

Ambros.

Opera

[Prov.
23.26]

My brother hath taken twice as much as you prescribed for me, but
I tooke none, Or if he ordained six ounces of bloud to be taken from
thee, to say, My Grandfather bled twelve. God shall judge according
⁴⁷⁰ to *The worke,* that is, The nature of the worke, and according to
Thy worke, The propriety of the worke: Thee, who art a Protestant,
he shall judge by thine owne worke, and not by S. *Stephens,* or
S. *Peters;* and thee, who art a Papist, he shall judge by thine owne
worke, and not by S. *Campians,* or S. *Garnets,* as meritorious as thou
thinkest them. And therefore if God be thy Father, and in that title
have soveraigne power over thee, A power spirituall, as High-priest
of thy soule, that discernes thy sacrifices; A power Civill, and drawes
the sword of Justice against thee, when he will; A power judiciary,
and judges without accepting persons, and without error in appre-
⁴⁸⁰ hending thy works, If he be a Father thus, feare him, for these are
the reasons of feare, on his part, and then feare him, for this reason
on thy part, That this time which thou art to stay here, first, is But
a sojourning, it is no more, but yet it is a sojourning, it is no lesse,
Passe the time of your sojourning here, &c.

　　When there is a long time to the Assises, there may be some hope   *Incolatus*
of taking off, or of smothering Evidence, or working upon the Judge,
or preparing for a pardon: Or if it were a great booty, a great possession which we had gotten, even that might buy out our peace. But
this world is no such thing, neither for the extent that we have in it,
⁴⁹⁰ It is but little that the greatest hath, nor for the time that we have
in it; In both respects it is but a *sojourning,* it is but a *pilgrimage,*
says *Iacob,* And *But the dayes of my pilgrimage;* Every one of them   Gen. 47.9
quickly at an end, and all of them quickly reckoned. *Here we have*   Heb. 13.14
no continuing City; first, no City, no such large being, and then no
continuing at all, it is but a sojourning. The word in the Text is
παροικίας, we have but a parish, we are but parishioners in this
world, and they that labour to purchase whole shires, usurp more
then their portion; and yet what is a great Shire in a little Map?
Here we are but *Viatores,* Passengers, way-faring men; This life is
⁵⁰⁰ but the high-way, and thou canst not build thy hopes here; Nay, to
be buried in the high way is no good marke; and therefore bury not
thy selfe, thy labours, thy affections upon this world. What the Prophet
sayes to thy Saviour, (*O the hope of Israel, the Saviour thereof in*   Ier. 14.8

time of trouble, why shouldest thou be a stranger in the land, and as
a wayfaring man, that turnes aside to tarry for a night?) say thou
to thy soule, Since thou are a stranger in the land, a wayfaring man,

Mic. 2.10   turned aside to tarry for a night, since the night is past, *Arise and*
depart, for here is not thy rest; prepare for another place, and *feare*
him whom thou callest *Father,* and who is shortly to be thy *Iudge;*
510 for here thou art no more then a *sojourner;* but yet remember withall
that thou art so much, Thou art a *sojourner.*

Incolatus   This life is not a Parenthesis, a Parenthesis that belongs not to
the sense, a Parenthesis that might be left out, as well as put in. More
depends upon this life then so: upon every minute of this life, depend millions of yeares in the next, and I shall be glorified eternally,
or eternally lost, for my good or ill use of Gods grace offered to me
this houre. Therefore where the Apostle sayes of this life, *Peregrina-*

2 Cor. 5.6   *mur à Domino, We are absent from the Lord,* yet he sayes, *We are*
at home in the body: This world is so much our home, as that he
520 that is not at home now, he that hath not his conversation in heaven
here, shall never get home. And therefore even in this Text, our
former Translation calls it *Dwelling;* That which we reade now,
passe the time of your sojourning, we did reade then, *passe the time*
of your dwelling; for this, where we are now, is the suburb of the
great City, the porch of the triumphant Church, and the Grange, or
Country house of the same Landlord, belonging to his heavenly
Palace, in the heavenly Jerusalem. Be it but a sojourning, yet thou
must pay God something for thy sojourning, pay God his rent of
praise and prayer; And be it but a sojourning, yet thou art bound to
530 it for a time; Though thou sigh with *David, Heu mihi, quia pro-*

Psal. 120.5   *longatus incolatus,* woe is me that I sojourne so long here, Though
the miseries of thy life make thy life seeme long, yet thou must stay
out that time, which he, who tooke thee in, appointed, and by no
practice, no not so much as by a deliberate wish, or unconditioned
prayer, seeke to be delivered of it: Because thy time here is such a
sojourning as is quickly at an end, and yet such a sojourning as is
never at an end, (for our endlesse state depends upon this) fear him,
who shall so certainly, and so soone be a just Judge of it; feare him,
in abstaining from those sinnes which are directed upon his power;
540 which are, principally, (as we intimated at the beginning, and with

which we shall make an end) first, The negligence of his power upon thee, And then, the abuse of his power communicated to thee over others.

First then, the sin directed against the Father, whom wee consider to be the roote and center of all power, is, when as some men have thought the soule of man to be nothing but a resultance of the temperament and constitution of the body of man, and no infusion from God, so they thinke that power, by which the world is governed, is but a resultance of the consent, and the tacite voice of the people, who 550 are content, for their ease to bee so governed, and no particular Ordinance of God: It is an undervaluing, a false conception, a misapprehension of those beames of power, which God from himself sheds upon those, whom himselfe cals Gods in this World. We sin then against the Father, when we undervalue God in his Priest. God hath made no step in that perverse way of the Roman Church, to prefer, so as they doe, the Priest before the King; yet, speaking in two severall places, of the dignity of his people, first, as Jews, then as Christians, he sayes in one place, They shall be *a Kingdome,* and *a Kingdome of Priests;* and he sayes in the other, They shall be 560 *Sacerdotium,* and *Regale Sacerdotium, Priests,* and *royall Priests:* In one place, *the King,* in the other, *the Priest* mentioned first, and in both places, both involved in one another: The blessings from both are so great, as that the Holy Ghost expresses them by one another mutually. When God commands his people to bee numbred in every Tribe, one moves this question, Why in all other Tribes he numbred but from twenty yeares upward, and in the Tribe of *Levi* from a moneth upward? *Agnosce sacerdos,* sayes he, *quanti te Deus tuus fecerit,* Take knowledge, thou who art the Priest of the high God, what a value God hath set upon thee, that whereas he takes other 570 servants for other affaires, when they are men, fit to doe him service, he took thee to the Priesthood in thy cradle, in thine infancie. How much more then, when the Priest is not *Sacerdos infans,* A Priest that cannot or does not speake; but continues watchfull in meditating, and assiduous in uttering, powerfully, and yet modestly, the things that concerne your salvation, ought you to abstaine from violating the power of God the Father, in dis-esteeming his power thus planted in the Priest?

Negligentia

Exod. 19.6

1 Pet. 2.9

Num. 1
Oleaster

Civilis

So also doe we sin against the Father, the roote of power, in con-
ceiving amisse of the power of the Civill Magistrate: Whether where
580 God is pleased to represent his unity, in one Person, in a King; or to
expresse it in a plurality of persons, in divers Governours, When God

[Prov. 8.15]

says, *Per me Reges regnant, By me Kings raigne;* There the *Per,* is
not a Permission, but a Commission, It is not, That they raigne by
my Sufferance, but they raigne by mine Ordinance. A King is not a
King, because he is a good King, nor leaves being a King, as soone as

Rom. 13.5

he leaves being good. All is well summed by the Apostle, *You must
needs be subject, not only for wrath, but also for conscience sake.*

Iudiciaria

But then the greatest danger of sinning against the Father, in this
notion of power, is, if you conceive not aright of his Judiciary power,
590 of that judgement, which he executes, not by Priests, nor by Kings
upon earth, but by his owne Son Christ Jesus in heaven. For, not to
be astonished at the Contemplation of that judgement, where there
shall be Information, Examination, Publication, Hearing, Judgement,
and Execution in a minute; where they that never beleeved, till they
heard me, may be taken in, and I that Preached and wrought their
salvation, may be left out; where those wounds which my Saviour
received upon earth, for me, shall be shut up against me, and those
wounds which my blasphemies have made in his glorified body, shall
bleed out indignation, upon sight of me, the murtherer, not to think
600 upon, not to tremble at this judgement, is the highest sin against the
Father, and his power, in the undervaluing of it.

Abusus

But there is a sin against this power too, in abusing that portion of
that power, which God hath deposited in thee. Art thou a Priest, and
expectest the reverence due to that holy calling? Be holy in that

Ambr. Ep. 6
ad Iren.

calling. *Quomodo potest observari à populo, qui nihil habet secretum
à populo?* How can the people reverence him, whom they see to be
but just one of them? *Quid in te miretur, si sua in te recognoscit?* If
they finde no more in thee, then in one another, what should they
admire in thee? *Si quæ in se erubescit, in te, quem reverendum*
610 *arbitratur, offendit?* If they discerne those infirmities in thee, which
they are ashamed of in themselves, where is there any object, any
subject, any exercise of their reverence? Art thou great in Civill

Psal. 52.1

Power? *Quid gloriaris in malo, quia potens es? Why boastest thou thy
selfe in mischiefe, O mighty man?* Hast thou a great body therefore,

because thou shouldest stand heavy upon thine own feet, and make them ake? Or a great power therefore, because thou shouldest oppresse them that are under thee? use thy power justly, and call it the voyce of allegeance when the people say to thee, as to *Iosua, All that* *thou commandest us, we will doe, and whither soever thou sendest us,* ⁶²⁰ *we will goe:* Abuse that power to oppression, and thou canst not call that the voyce of sedition, in which, *Peter* and the other Apostles joyned together, *We ought to obey God rather then man.* Hast thou any judiciall place in this world? here there belongs more feare then in the rest: Some things God hath done in Christ as a Priest in this world, some things as a King; But when Christ should have been a Judge in civill causes, he declined that, he would not divide the Inheritance, and in criminall causes he did so too, he would not condemne the Adulteresse. So that for thy example in judgement, thou art referred to that which is not come yet, to that, to which thou ⁶³⁰ must come, The last, the everlasting judgement. Waigh thine affections there, and then, and think there stands before thee now, a prisoner so affected, as thou shalt be then. Waigh the mercy of thy Judge then, and think there is such mercy required in thy judgement now. Be but able to say, God be such to me at the last day, as I am to his people this day, and for that dayes justice in thy publique calling, God may be pleased to cover many sins of infirmity. And so you have all that we intended in this exercise to present unto you, The first person of the Trinity, God the Father, in his Attribute of power, Almighty, and those sins, which, as farre as this Text leads us, are ⁶⁴⁰ directed upon him in that notion of *Father.* The next day the Son will rise.

Jos. 1.16

Acts 5.29

[Luke 12.13]
[John 8.11]

Number 14.

Preached upon Trinity-Sunday.

---

1 Cor. 16.22. *IF ANY MAN LOVE NOT THE LORD IESUS CHRIST, LET HIM BE ANATHEMA, MARANATHA.*

CHRIST is not defined, not designed by any name, by any word so often, as by that very word, *The Word, Sermo,* Speech. In man there are three kinds of speech; *Sermo innatus,* That inward speech, which the thought of man reflecting upon it selfe produces within, He thinks something; And then *Sermo illatus,* A speech of inference, that speech which is occasioned in him by outward things, from which he drawes conclusions, and determins; And lastly, *Sermo prolatus,* That speech by which he manifests himselfe to other men. We consider also three kindes of speech in God; and
¹⁰ Christ is all three. There is *Sermo innatus,* His eternall, his naturall word, which God produced out of himselfe, which is the generation of the second Person in the Trinity; And then there is *Sermo illatus,* His word occasioned by the fall of *Adam,* which is his Decree of sending Christ, as a Redeemer; And there is also *Sermo prolatus,* His speech of manifestation and application of Christ, which are his Scriptures. The first word is Christ, the second, the Decree, is for Christ, the third, the Scripture, is of Christ. Let the word be Christ, so he is God; Let the word be for Christ, for his comming hither, so he is man; Let the word be of Christ, so the Scriptures make this God
²⁰ and man ours. Now *If* in all these, if in any of these apprehensions, *any man love not the Lord Iesus Christ, let him be Anathema, Maranatha.*

Divisio　　By most of those, who, from the perversenesse of Heretiques, have taken occasion to prove the Deity of Christ, this text hath been cited; and therefore I take it now, when in my course proposed, I am to

speak of the second Person in the Trinity; but, (as I said of the first
Person, the Father) not as in the Schoole, but in the Church, not in
a Chaire, but in a Pulpit, not to a Congregation that required proofe,
in a thing doubted, but edification, upon a foundation received; not
30 as though any of us would dispute, whether Jesus Christ were the
Lord, but that all of us would joyne in that Excommunication, *If any
man love not the Lord Iesus Christ, let him be, &c.* Let this then be
the frame that this exercise shall stand upon. We have three parts;
The person upon whom our Religious worship is to be directed, *The
Lord Iesus Christ:* And secondly, we have the expression and the
limitation of that worship, as farre as it is expressed here, *Love the
Lord Iesus Christ:* And lastly, we have the imprecation upon them
that doe not, If any man doe not, let him be *Anathema, Maranatha.*
In the first we have *Verbum naturale, verbum innatum,* As he is the
40 essentiall word, *The Lord,* a name proper only to God; And then
Verbum conceptum, verbum illatum, Gods Decree upon consideration of mans misery, that Christ should be a Redeemer, for to that
intent he is *Christus,* Anointed to that purpose; And lastly, *Verbum
prolatum, verbum manifestatum,* That this *Christ* becomes *Iesus,*
That this Decree is executed, that this person thus anointed for this
office, is become an actuall Saviour; So the *Lord* is made *Christ,* and
Christ is made *Iesus.* In the second Part we shall finde another argument for his Deity, for there is such a *love* required towards the *Lord
Iesus Christ,* as appertaines to God onely; And lastly, we shall have
50 the indeterminable, and indispensable excommunication of them,
who though they pretend to *love the Lord,* (God in an universall
notion) yet doe not *love the Lord Iesus Christ,* God, in this apprehension of a Saviour; and, *If any man love not, &c.*

First then, in the first branch of the first part, in that name of our
Saviour, *The Lord,* we apprehend the eternall Word of God, the
Son of God, the second Person in the Trinity: for, He is *Persona
producta,* Begotten by another, and therefore cannot be the first; And
he is *Persona spirans,* a Person out of whom, with the Father, another
Person, that is, the Holy Ghost proceeds, and therefore cannot be the
60 last Person, and there are but three, and so he necessarily the second.
Shall we hope to comprehend this by reason? *Quid magni haberet
Dei generatio, si angustiis intellectus tui comprehenderetur?* How

1 Part
Dominus

Nazian.

Idem

*Ex Scrip-
turis*

Mat. 3. ult.
Heb. 1.8

Apoc. 1.8

22.16

Acts 20.28

1 Iohn 5.20

small a thing were this mystery of Heaven, if it could be shut in, in so narrow a piece of the earth, as thy heart? *Qui tuam ipsius generationem vel in totum nescis, vel dicere sit pudor,* Thou that knowest nothing of thine owne begetting, or art ashamed to speake that little that thou doest know of it, wilt not thou be ashamed to offer to expresse the eternall generation of the Son of God? It is true, *De modo,* How it was done, our reason cannot, but *De facto,* that it was ⁷⁰ done, our reason may be satisfied. We beleeve nothing with a morall faith, till something have wrought upon our reason, and vanquished that, and made it assent and subscribe. Our divine faith requires evidence too, and hath it abundantly; for, the works of God are not so good evidence to my reason, as the Word of God is to my faith; The Sun shining is not so good a proofe that it is day, as the Word of God, the Scripture is, that that which is commanded there, is a duty. The roote of our beliefe that Christ is God, is in the Scriptures, but wee consider it spread into three branches, ¹The evident Word it selfe, that Christ is God; ²The reall declaration thereof in his manifold ⁸⁰ Miracles; ³The conclusions that arise to our understanding, thus illumined by the Scriptures, thus established by his miracles.

In every mouth, in every pen of the Scriptures, that delivers any truth, the Holy Ghost speaks, and therefore whatsoever is said by any there, is the testimony of the Holy Ghost, for the Deity of Christ. And from the Father we have this testimony, that he is his Son, *This is my beloved Son,* And this testimony that his Son is God, *Vnto his Son he saith, Thy Throne, O God, is for ever and ever.* The Holy Ghost testifies, and his Father, and himselfe; and his testimony is true, *I am Alpha and Omega, the beginning, and the ending, saith* ⁹⁰ *the Lord, which is, which was, and which is to come, the Almighty.* Hee testifies with his Father; and then, their Angels and his Apostles testifie with him, *I Iesus have sent mine Angels, to testifie unto you these things in the Church, That I am the Roote, and the Off-spring of David,* not the off-spring onely, but the roote too, and therefore was before *David.* God and his Angels in Heaven testifie it, And visible Angels upon earth, his Apostles, *God hath purchased his Church, with his owne blood,* sayes S. *Paul;* He who shed his blood for his Church, was God; and no false God, no mortall God, as the gods of the Nations were, but, *This is the true God, and eternall life;*

¹⁰⁰ and then, no small God, no particular God, as the Gods of the Nations were too, but, *We looke for the glorious appearing of our great God, our Saviour Christ Iesus:* God, that is, God in all the Persons, Angels, that is, Angels in all their acceptations, Angels of Heaven, Angels of the Church, Angels excommunicate from both, the fallen Angels, Devils themselves, testifie his Godhead, *Vncleane Spirits fell downe before him, and cryed, Thou art the Sonne of God.*

This is the testimony of his Word; the testimony of his Works, are his Miracles. That his Apostles did Miracles in his name, was a testimony of his Deity. *His name, through faith in his Name, hath* ¹¹⁰ *made this man strong,* sayes S. *Peter,* at the raysing of the Creeple. But that he did Miracles in his own Name, by his own Power, is a nearer testimony; *Blessed be the Lord God of Israel,* sayes *David, Qui facit Mirabilia solus, Which doth his Miracles alone,* without deriving power from any other, or without using an other instrument for his Power. For, *Mutare naturam, nisi qui Dominus naturæ est, non potest:* Whosoever is able to change the course of nature, is the Lord of nature; And he that is so, made it; and he that made it, that created it, is God. Nay, *Plus est,* it is more to change the course of Nature, then to make it; for, in the Creation, there was no reluctation ¹²⁰ of the Creature, for there was no Creature, but to divert Nature out of her setled course, is a conquest upon a resisting adversary, and power-full in a prescription. The *Recedat Mare, Let the Sea go back,* and the *Sistat Sol, Let the Sun stand still,* met with some kinde of opposition in Nature, but in the *Fiat Mare,* and *Fiat Sol, Let there be a Sea, and a Sun,* God met with no opposition, no Nature, he met with nothing. And therefore, *Interrogemus Miracula, quid nobis de Christo loquantur,* Let us aske his Miracles, and they will make us understand Christ; *Habent enim si intelligantur, linguam suam,* If wee understand them, that is, If wee would understand them, they ¹³⁰ speake loud enough, and plaine enough. In his Miraculous birth of a Virgin, In his Miraculous disputation with Doctors at twelve yeares of age, in his fasting, in his invisibility, in his walking upon the Sea, in his re-assuming his body in the Resurrection, Christ spoke, in him-selfe, in the language of Miracles. So also had they a loud and a plaine voyce, in other men; In his Miraculous curing the sick, raising the dead, dispossessing the Devill, Christ spoke, in other men, in the

Tit. 2.13

Mar. 3.11

Miracula

Acts 3.16

Psal. 72.18

Epipha.

Tertul.

[Exod. 14.21]
[Josh. 10.12]
August.

language of Miracles. And he did so also, as in himselfe, and in other men, so in other things; In the miraculous change of Water into Wine, in the drying up of the Fig-tree, In feeding five thousand with
¹⁴⁰ five loaves, in shutting up the Sun in darknesse, and opening the graves of the Dead to light, in bringing plenty of Fish to the Net, and in putting money into the mouth of a Fish at the Angle, Christ spoke in all these Creatures, in the language of Miracles. So the Scriptures testifie of his Deity, and so doe his Miracles, and so doe those Conclusions which arise from thence, though we consider but that one, which is expressed in this part of the Text, that he is *the Lord, If any love not the Lord, &c.*

Dominus   We reason thus, God gives not his glory to others, and his glory is in his Essentiall Name, and in his Attributes; and to whomsoever
¹⁵⁰ he gives them, because they cannot be given from God, he who hath them, is God. Of these, none is so peculiar to him, as the name of *Iehova;* the name, which for reverence, the Jews forbore to sound, and in the room therof ever sounded, *Adonai,* and *Adonai,* is *Dominus,* the name of this Text, *The Lord;* Christ by being the Lord thus, is Jehovah, and if Jehovah, God. It is *Tertullians* observation, *Et si Pater sit, & dicatur Dominus, & Filius sit, & dicatur Deus,* That though the Father be the Lord, and be called the Lord, and though the Son be God, and be called God, yet, sayes he, the manner of the Holy Ghost in the New Testament, is, to call *the Father God,* and
¹⁶⁰ *the Son the Lord.* He is Lord with the Father, as he was Con-creator, his Collegue in the Creation; But for that Dominion and Lordship
[Isa. 63.3]   which he hath by his Purchase, by his Passion, *Calcavit solus, He trod the Wine-presse alone,* not onely no man, but no Person of the Trinity, redeemed us, by suffering for us, but he. For the ordinary appellation of *Lord* in the New Testament, which is Κύριος, it is but a name of Civility, not onely no name implying Divine worship, but not implying any distinction of ranke or degree amongst men. *Mary Magdalen* speaks of Christ, and speakes to the Gardiner, (as she thought) and both in one and the same word; it is Κύριος, *Dominus,*
Iohn 20.15 ¹⁷⁰ *Lord,* to both: when she sayes, *They have taken away my Lord,* meaning Christ, and when she saies to the Gardiner, *Sir, if thou hast borne him hence,* it is the same word too. But all that reaches not to
1 Cor. 12.3   the style of this Text, *The Lord,* for here *The Lord,* is God; And *no*

man can say, that Iesus is the Lord, but by the Holy Ghost. All that
was written in the Scriptures, all that was established by Miracles,
all that is deduced by reason, conduces to this, determines in this,
That every tongue should confesse, that Iesus Christ is the Lord; in
which essentiall name, the name of his nature, he is first proposed,
as the object of our love.

180   Now this *Lord,* Lord for ever, is become that which he was not for
ever, (otherwise then in a secondary consideration) that is, *Christ,*
which implies a person prepared, and fitted, and anointed to a peculiar
Office in this World. And can the Lord, the ever-living Lord, the Son
of God, the onely Son of God, God himselfe have any preferment? preferment by an Office in this World? Was it a preferment to *Dionysius,*
who was before in that height over men, to become a schoole-master
over boyes? Were it a preferment to the Kings Son, to be made gover-
nour over a Bee-hive, or over-seer over an Ant-hill? And men, nay
Mankinde is no more, not that, not a Bee-hive, not an Ant-hill, com-
190 pared to this Person, who being *the Lord,* would become *Christ.* As he
was *the Lord,* we considered him as God, and that there is a God, naturall reason can comprehend; As he is *Christ,* we consider him God and
Man, and such a Person, naturall reason (not rooted in the Scriptures,
not illustrated by the Scriptures) cannot comprehend; Man will much
easilier beleeve *the Lord,* that is, God, then *Christ,* that is, God and
Man in one Person.

   Christ then is the style, the title of his Office; *Non Nomen, sed
Appellatio, Christ* is not his Name, but his Addition. *Vnctus signifi-
catur,* sayes he, *& unctus non magis nomen, quam vestitus, calceatus;*
200 *Christ* signifies but anointed, and anointed is no more a Name, then
apparelled, or shod, is a name: So, as hee was apparelled in our flesh,
and his apparell dyed red in his owne blood, so as he was shod to
tread the Wine-presse for us, So he was *Christ.* That it is *Nomen
Sacramenti,* as S. *Augustine* cals it, A mystery, is easily agreed to:
for all the mysteries of all the Religions in the World, are but Milke
in respect of this Bone, but Catechismes in respect of this Schoole-
point, but Alphabets in respect of this hard Style, God and Man in
one person. That it is *Nomen Sacramenti,* as *Augustine* says, is easie;
but that it is *Nuncupatio potestatis,* as *Lactantius* cals it, is somewhat
210 strange, that it is an office of power, a title of honour: for the Creator

[Phil. 2.11]

Christus

Tertul.

to become a Creature, and the Lord of life the object of death, nay the seat of death, in whom death did sojourn three dayes, can *Lactantius* call this a declaration of power? is this *Nuncupatio potestatis,* a title of honour? Beloved, he does, and he may; for it was so: for, it was an Annointing; *Christus* is *unctus;* and unction was the Consecration of Priests, *Thou shalt take the annointing Oyle,* *and powre it upon his head.* The Mitre (as you may see there) was upon his head then; but then there was a Crowne upon the Mitre; There is a power above the Priest, the regall power; not above the 220 function of the Priest, but above the person of the Priest; But Unction was the Consecration of Kings too; *Samuel saluted Saul with a kisse,* *and all the people shouted, and sayd, God save the King;* but, *Is it* *not,* sayes *Samuel, because the Lord hath annointed thee, to be cap-* *taine over his inheritance?* Kings were above Priests; and in extraordinary cases, God raysed Prophets above Kings; for there is no ordinary power above them: But Unction was the Consecration of these Prophets too; *Elisha* was *annointed* to be *Prophet* in *Elias* roome; and such a Prophet as should have use of the Sword: *Him* *that scapes the Sword of Hazael,* (*Hazael* was King of Syria) *shall* 230 *the Sword of Iehu slay, and him that scapes the Sword of Iehu (Iehu* was King of Israel) *shall the Sword of Elisha slay.* In all these, in Priests who were above the people, in Kings, who (in matter of Government) were above the Priests, in Prophets, who (in those limited cases expressed by God, and for that time, wherein God gave them that extraordinary employment) were above Kings, The Unction imprinted their Consecration, they were all *Christs,* and in them all, thereby, was that *Nuncupatio potestatis,* which *Lactantius* mentions; Unction, Annointing was an addition and title of honour: Much more in our *Christ,* who alone was all three; *A Priest after the* 240 *Order of Melchizedek; A King set upon the holy hill of Sion;* And a *Prophet, The Lord thy God will rayse up a Prophet, unto him shall* *yee harken:* And besides all this threefold Unction, *Humanitas uncta* *Divinitate;* He had all the unctions that all the other had, and this, which none other had; In him the Humanity was Consecrated, anointed with the Divinity it selfe.

So then, *unio unctio,* The hypostaticall union of the Godhead to the humane nature, in his Conception, made him *Christ:* for, *oleo*

Exod. 29.7

1 Sam. 10.1
and 24

1 Reg.
19.16, 17

Psal.
110.[4]
[109 *F* as in
Vulg.]
Psal. 2.6
Deut.
18.[15]

Nazian.
Cyrill.

lætitiæ perfusus in unione, Then, in that union of the two natures,
did God annoint him with the oyle of gladnes above his fellows. There   Psal. 45.7
²⁵⁰ was an addition, something gained, something to be glad of; and, to
him, as he was God, *The Lord,* so nothing could be added; If he were
glad above his fellows, it was in that respect wherein he had fellows,
and as God, as *The Lord,* he had none; so that still, as he was made
Man, he became this *Christ.* In which his being made Man, if we
should not consider the last and principall purpose, which was to
redeem man, if we leave out his part, yet it were object inough for
our wonder, and subject inough for our praise and thankesgiving, to
consider the dignity, that the nature of man received in that union,
wherin this *Lord* was thus made this *Christ,* for, the Godhead did not
²⁶⁰ swallow up the manhood; but man, that nature remained still; The
greater kingdom did not swallow the lesse, but the lesse had that
great addition, which it had not before, and retained the dignities and
priviledges which it had before too. *Christus est nomen personæ, non*   Damasc.
naturæ, The name of *Christ* denotes one person, but not one nature:
neither is Christ so composed of those two natures, as a man is composed of Elements; for man is thereby made a third thing, and is not
now any of those Elements; you cannot call mans body fire or ayre,
or earth or water, though all foure be in his composition: But Christ
is so made of God and Man, as that he is Man still, for all the glory
²⁷⁰ of the Deity, and God still, for all the infirmity of the manhood:
Divinum miraculis lucet, humanum contumeliis afficitur: In this one   Idem
Christ, both appear; The Godhead bursts out, as the Sun out of a
cloud, and shines forth gloriously in miracles, even the raysing of the
dead, and the humane nature is submitted to contempt and to torment, even to the admitting of death in his own bosome; *sed tamen*   Idem
ipsius sunt tum miracula, tum supplicia, but still, both he that rayses
the dead, and he that dyes himself, is one Christ, his is the glory of
the Miracles, and the contempt and torment is his too. This is that
mysterious person, who is *singularis,* and yet not *individuus; singu-*
²⁸⁰ *laris,* There never was, never shall be any such, but we cannot call
him Individuall, as every other particular man is, because *Christitatis*   Idem
non est Genus, there is no genus nor species of Christs; it is not a
name, which, so (as the name belongs to our Christ, that is, by being
annointed with the divine nature) can be communicated to any other,

as the name of Man, may to every Individuall Man. Christ is not that *Spectrum,* that *Damascene* speaks of, nor that *Electrum* that *Tertullian* speakes of: not *Spectrum,* so as that the two natures should but imaginarily be united, and only to amaze and astonish us, that we could not tell what to call it, what to make of it, a spectre, an appari-

290 tion, a phantasma, for he was a Reall person. Neither was he *Tertullians Electrum,* a third metall made of two other metals, but a person so made of God and Man, as that, in that person, God and Man, are in their natures still distinguished. He is *Germen Davidis,* in one Prophet, The branch, the Off-spring of *David;* And he is *Germen Iehovæ,* The Branch, the Off-spring of God, of the Lord, in another: When this *Germen Davidis,* the Sonne of Man would do miracles, then he was *Germen Iehovæ,* he reflected to that stock into which the Humanity was engrafted, to his Godhead; And when this *Germen Iehovæ,* the Son of God, would indure humane miseries, he reflected

300 to that stock, to that humanity, in which he had invested, and incorporated himself. This person, this *Christ dyed for our sins,* says S. *Paul;* but says he, He dyed *according to the Scriptures; Non sine onere pronunciat Christum mortuum;* The Apostle thought it a hard, a heavy, an incredible thing to say that this person, this Christ, this Man and God, was dead, And therefore, *Vt duritiam molliret, & scandalum auditoris everteret,* That he might mollifie the hardnes of that saying, and defend the hearer from being scandalized with that saying, *Adjecit, secundùm scripturas,* He adds this, Christ is dead, *according to the Scriptures:* If the Scriptures had not told us

310 that Christ should die, and told us againe, that Christ did die, it were hard to conceive, how this person, in whom the Godhead dwelt bodily, should be submitted to death. But therein principally is he *Christus,* as he was capable of dying. As he was *Verbum naturale,* and *innatum,* The naturall and essentiall word of God, He hath his first name in the text, He is *the Lord:* As he is *verbum illatum,* and *Conceptum,* A person upon whom there is a Decree and a Commission, that he shall be a person capable to redeem Man by death, he hath this second name in the text, He is *Christ;* As he is *The Lord,* he cannot die; As he is *Christ* (under the Decree) he cannot chuse

320 but die; But as he is *Iesus,* He is dead already, and that is his other, his third, his last name in this Text, *If any man love not &c.*

Iere. 23.5

Isa. 4.2

1 Cor. 15.3
Tertul.

We have inverted a little, the order of these names, or titles in the Text; because the Name of *Christ,* is in the order of nature, before the name of *Iesus,* as the Commission is before the Execution of the Commission. And, in other places of Scripture, to let us see, how both the capacity of doing it, and the actuall doing of it, belongs onely to this person, the Holy Ghost seems to convey a spirituall delight to us, in turning and transposing the Names every way; sometimes *Iesus* alone, and *Christ* alone, sometimes *Iesus Christ,* and sometimes
330 *Christ Iesus,* that every way we might be sure of him. Now we consider him, as *Iesus,* a reall, an actuall Saviour. And this was his Name; The Angel said to his Mother, *Thou shalt call his name Iesus, for he shall save his people;* And we say to you, Call upon this name *Iesus,* for he hath saved his people; for, *Now there is no condemnation to them that are in Christ Iesus:* As he was *verbum conceptum,* and *illatum,* The word which the Trinity uttered amongst themselves, so he was decreed to come in that place, *The Lord of the vineyard* (that is, Almighty God seeing the misery of Man, to be otherwise irremediable) *The Lord of the vineyard said, what shall I doe? I will*
340 *send my beloved Sonne; it may be, they will reverence him when they see him.* But did they reverence him, when they saw him? This sending made him *Christ,* a person, whom, though the Sonne of God, they might see: They did see him; but then, says that Gospell, *they drew him out and killed him.* And this he knew before he came, and yet came, and herein was *Iesus,* a reall, an actuall, a zealous Saviour, even of them that slew him: And in this (with piety and reverence) we may be bold to say, that even the Son of God, was *filius prodigus,* that powred out his blood even for his Enemies; but rather in that acclamation of the prodigall childs Father, *This my sonne was dead,*
350 *and is alive againe, he was lost, and is found.* For, but for this desire of our salvation, why should he who was *the Lord,* be ambitious of that Name, the name of *Iesus,* which was not *Tam expectabile apud Iudæos nomen,* no such name as was in any especiall estimation amongst the *Iews:* for, we see in *Iosephus,* divers men of that name, of no great honour, of no good conversation. But because the name implyes salvation, *Iosua,* who had another name before, *Cum in hujus sacramenti imagine parabatur,* when he was prepared as a Type of this *Iesus,* to be a Saviour, a Deliverer of the people, *Etiam nomi-*

Iesus

[Mat. 1.21]

Rom. 8.1

Luk. 20.13

[Luke 15.24]

Tertull.

Idem

nis Dominici inauguratus est figura, & Iesus cognominatus, then he
360 was canonized with that name of salvation, and called *Iosua,* which
is *Iesus.*

The Lord then, the Son of God, had a *Sitio* in heaven, as well as
upon the Crosse; He thirsted our salvation there; and in the midst of
the fellowship of the Father from whom he came, and of the Holy
Ghost, who came from him and the Father, and all the Angels, who
came (by a lower way) from them all, he desired the conversation
of Man, for Mans sake; He that was God *The Lord,* became *Christ,*
a man, and he that was *Christ,* became *Iesus,* no man, a dead man,
to save man: To save man, all wayes, in all his parts, And to save all
370 men, in all parts of the world: To save his soule from hell, where
we should have felt pains, and yet been dead, then when we felt
them; and seen horrid spectacles, and yet been in darknes and blind-
nes, then when we saw them; And suffered unsufferable torments,
and yet have told over innumerable ages in suffering them: To save
this soule from that hell, and to fill that capacity which it hath, and
give it a capacity which it hath not, to comprehend the joyes and
glory of Heaven, this *Christ* became *Iesus.* To save this body from
the condemnation of everlasting corruption, where the wormes that
we breed are our betters, because they have a life, where the dust of
380 dead Kings is blowne into the street, and the dust of the street blowne
into the River, and the muddy River tumbled into the Sea, and the
Sea remaunded into all the veynes and channels of the earth; to save
this body from everlasting dissolution, dispersion, dissipation, and
to make it in a glorious Resurrection, not onely a Temple of the holy
Ghost, but a Companion of the holy Ghost in the kingdome of
heaven, This *Christ* became this *Iesus.* To save this man, body and
soule together, from the punishments due to his former sinnes, and
to save him from falling into future sinnes by the assistance of his
Word preached, and his Sacraments administred in the Church,
390 which he purchased by his bloud, is this person, The *Lord,* the *Christ,*
become this *Iesus,* this Saviour. To save so, All wayes, In soule, in
body, in both; And also to save all men. For, to exclude others from
that Kingdome, is a tyrannie, an usurpation; and to exclude thy selfe,
is a sinfull, and a rebellious melancholy. But as melancholy in the
body is the hardest humour to be purged, so is the melancholy in the

soule, the distrust of thy salvation too. Flashes of presumption a calamity will quench, but clouds of desperation calamities thicken upon
us; But even in this inordinate dejection thou exaltest thy self above
God, and makest thy worst better then his best, thy sins larger then
⁴⁰⁰ his mercy. Christ hath a Greek name, and an Hebrew name; *Christ*
is Greeke, Iesus is Hebrew; He had commission to save all nations,
and he hath saved all; Thou givest him another Hebrew name, and
another Greek, when thou makest his name *Abaddon,* and *Apollyon,*   Apoc. 9.11
a Destroyer; when thou wilt not apprehend him as a Saviour, and
love him so; which is our second Part, in our order proposed at first,
If any man love not, &c.

In the former part, we found it to be one argument for the Deitie   2 Part
of Christ, That he was *Iehovah, The Lord;* we have another here,
That this great branch, nay this very root of all divine worship due
⁴¹⁰ to God, is required to be exhibited to this person, That is, *Love, If*   Cicero
any man love not, &c. If any man could see Vertue with his eye, he
would be in love with her: Christ Jesus hath beene seen so: *Quod*
vidimus, sayes the Apostle, *That which we have seene with our eyes,*   [1 John 1.1]
we preach to you, and therefore *If any man love not, &c.* If he love
him not with that love which implyes a Confession, that the Lord
Jesus is God, That is, if he love him not with all his heart, and all his
power: *What doth the Lord thy God require of thee? To love him*   Deut. 10.12
with all thy heart, and all thy soule. God forbids us not a love of the
Creature, proportionable to the good that that creature can doe us:
⁴²⁰ To love fire as it warms me, and meat as it feeds me, and a wife as
she helps me; But because God does all this, in all these severall
instruments, God alone is centrically, radically, directly to be loved,
and the creature with a love reflected, and derived from him; And
Christ to be loved with the love due to God himselfe: *He that loveth*   Mat. 10.37
father or mother, son or daughter more then me, is not worthy of me,
sayes Christ himselfe. If then we love him so, as we love God, intirely, we confesse him to be the *Lord;* And if we love him so, as he
hath loved us, we confesse him to be *Christ Iesus:* And we consider
his love to us (for the present) in these two demonstrations of it,
⁴³⁰ first *Dilexit in finem,* As he *loved,* so he *loved to the end;* And then   [John 13.1]
Posuit animam, Greater love there is not, then to die for one, and   [John 15.13]
he did that.

In finem

Our Saviour Christ forsooke not *Peter,* when *Peter* forsooke him:
because he loved him, he loved him to the end. Love thou Christ
to the end; To His end, and to Thy end. *Finem Domini vidistis,*

Iames 5.11

sayes S. *Iames, You have seene the end of the Lord;* That is, sayes
Augustine to what end the Lord came; His way was contempt and
misery, and his end was shame and death: Love him there. Thy love
is not required onely in the *Hosanna's* of Christ, when Christ is mag-
440 nified, and his Gospel advanced, and men preferred for loving it:
No, nor onely in the *Transfiguration* of Christ, when Christ appeares to thee in some particular beames, and manifestation of his
glory; but love him in his *Crucifigatur,* then when it is a scornfull
thing to love him, And love him in the *Nunquid & tu?* when thou

Iohn 18.25,
26

must passe that examination, *Wert not thou one of them?* And in the
Nonne ego te vidi? if witnesses come in against thee for the love of
Christ, love him when it is a suspicious thing, a dangerous thing to
love him; And love him not onely in spirituall transfigurations, when
he visits thy soule with glorious consolations, but even in his inward
450 eclipses, when he withholds his comforts, and withdrawes his cheerfulnesse, even when he makes as though he loved not thee, love him.
Love him, all the way, to his end, and to thy end too, to the laying
downe of thy life for him.

Mortificatio

Love him then in the laying downe of the pleasures of this life
for him, and love him in the laying downe of the life it selfe, if his
love need that testimony. Of the first case, of crucifying himselfe to

Epist. 39

the world, S. *Augustine* had occasion to say much to a young Gentle-
man, young, and noble, and rich, and (which is not, in such persons,
an ordinary tentation, but where it is, it is a shrewd one) as he was
460 young, and noble, and rich, so he was learned in other learnings,
and upon that strength withdrew, and kept off from Christ. It was
Licentius, to whom S. *Augustine* writes his 39. Epistle. He had sent
to S. *Augustine* a handsome Elegie of his making, in which *Poeme*
he had said as much of the vanity and deceivablenesse of this world,
as S. *Augustine* could have looked for, or, perchance, have said in a
Homily; And he ends his Elegy thus, *Hoc opus, ut jubeas,* All this
concerning this world I know already, Do you but tell me, doe you
command me, what I shall doe. *Iubebit Augustinus conservo suo?*
sayes that sensible and blessed Father: Shall I, shall *Augustine* com-

⁴⁷⁰ mand his fellow-servant? *Et non plangat potiùs frustra jubere Do-minum?* Must not *Augustine* rather lament that the Lord hath com-manded thee, and is not obeyed? Wouldst thou heare me? Canst thou pretend that? *Exaudi teipsum, Durissime, Immanissime, Sur-dissime;* Thou that art inexorable against the perswasions of thine owne soule, Hard against the tendernesse of thine owne heart, Deafe against the charmes of thine owne Verses, canst thou pretend a will-ingnesse to be led by me? *Quam animam, quod ingenium non licet immolare Deo nostro?* How well disposed a soule, how high pitched a wit is taken out of my hands, that I may not sacrifice that soule, ⁴⁸⁰ that I may not direct that wit upon our God, because, with all these good parts, thou turnest upon the pleasures of this world? *Mentiun-tur, moriuntur, in mortem trahunt:* Doe not speake out of wit, nor out of a love to elegant expressions, nor doe not speake in jest of the dangerous vanities of this world; *Mentiuntur,* they are false, they performe not their promises; *Moriuntur,* they are transitory, they stay not with thee; and *In mortem trahunt,* they dye, and they dye of the infection, and they transfuse the venome into thee, and thou dyest with them: *Non dicit verum, nisi veritas, & Christus veritas,* Nothing will deale truely with thee but the Truth it selfe, and onely ⁴⁹⁰ Christ Jesus is this Truth. He followes it thus much farther, *Si cali-cem aureum invenisses in terra,* If thou foundest a chalice of gold in the earth, so good a heart as thine would say, Surely this belongs to the Church, and surely thou wouldst give it to the Church: *Accepisti à Deo ingenium spiritualiter aureum,* God hath given thee a wit, an understanding, not of the gold of Ophir, but of the gold of the heavenly Jerusalem, *Et in illo, Satanæ propinas teipsum?* In that chalice once consecrated to God, wilt thou drink a health to the devill, and drink a health to him in thine owne bloud, in making thy wit, thy learning, thy good parts advance his kingdome? He ends all ⁵⁰⁰ thus, *Miserearis jam mei, si tibi viluisti,* If thou undervalue thy selfe, if thou thinke not thy selfe worth hearing, if thou follow not thine owne counsels, yet *miserearis mei,* Have mercy upon me, me, whose charge it is to bring others to heaven, me, who shall not bee received there, if I bring no body with mee; bee content to goe with me, that way, which by the inspiration of the holy Ghost I do shew, and that way, which by the conduct of the holy Ghost I would fain goe. All

bends to this, First, love Christ so far as to lay down the pleasures of this life for him, and so far, as to lay down the life it self for him.

Martyrium

Christ did so for thee: and his blessed Servants the Martyrs, in the Primitive Church, did so for him, and thee; for his glory, for thy example. Can there be any ill, any losse, in giving thy life for him? Is it not a part of the reward it selfe, the honour to suffer for him?

Mark 10.30

When Christ sayes, *Whosoever loses any thing for my sake, and the Gospels, he shall have a hundred fold in houses, and lands, with persecutions,* wee need not limit that clause of the Promise, (*with persecutions*) to be, That in the midst of persecutions, God will give us temporall blessings, but that in the midst of temporall blessings, God will give us persecutions; that it shall be a part of his mercy, to be delivered from the danger of being puffed up by those tem-porall abundances, by having a mixture of adversity and persecutions; and then, what ill, what losse, is there in laying downe this life for

Tertul.

him? *Quid hoc mali est, quod martyrialis mali, non habet timorem, pudorem, tergiversationem, pœnitentiam, deplorationem?* What kinde of evill is this, which when it came to the highest, *Ad malum martyriale,* to martyrdome, to death, did neither imprint in our holy predecessors in the Primitive Church, *Timorem,* any feare that it would come; nor *Tergiversationem,* any recanting lest it should come; nor *Pudorem,* any shame when it was come; nor *Pœnitentiam,* any repentance that they would suffer it to come; nor *Deplorationem,* any lamentation by their heires, and Executors, because they lost all, when it was come? *Quid mali?* What kinde of evill can I call this, in

Idem

laying down my life, for this Lord of life, *Cujus reus gaudet,* when those Martyrs called that guiltinesse a joy, *Cujus accusatio votum,* and the accusation a satisfaction, *Cujus pœna fœlicitas,* and the suffering perfect happinesse? Love thy neighbour as thy selfe, is the farthest of that Commandement; but love God above thy selfe; for, indeed, in doing so thou dost but love thy selfe still: Remember that thy soule is thy selfe; and as if that be lost, nothing is gained, so if that be gained, nothing is lost, whatsoever become of this life.

Dominus

Love him then, as he is presented to thee here; Love the *Lord,* love *Christ,* love *Iesus.* If when thou lookest upon him as the *Lord,* thou findest frowns and wrinkles in his face, apprehensions of him, as of a Judge, and occasions of feare, doe not run away from him, in that

apprehension; look upon him in that angle, in that line awhile, and that feare shall bring thee to love; and as he is *Lord,* thou shalt see him in the beauty and lovelinesse of his creatures, in the order and succession of causes, and effects, and in that harmony and musique of the peace between him, and thy soule: As he is *the Lord,* thou wilt feare him, but no man feares God truly, but that that feare ends
550 in love.

Love him as he is the *Lord,* that would have nothing perish, that he hath made; And love him as he is *Christ,* that hath made himselfe man too, that thou mightest not perish: Love him as the *Lord* that could shew mercy; and love him as *Christ,* who is that way of mercy, which the Lord hath chosen. Returne againe, and againe to that mysterious person, *Christ;* And let me tell you, that though the Fathers never forbore to call the blessed Virgin *Mary, Deiparam,* the Mother of God, yet in *Damascens* time, they would not admit that name, *Christiparam,* that she was the Mother of Christ: Not that there is
560 any reason to deny her that name now; but because then, that great Heretique, *Nestorius,* to avoid that name, in which the rest agreed, *Deiparam,* (for he thought not Christ to be God) invented a new name, *Christiparam:* Though it be true in it self, that that blessed Virgin is *Christipara,* yet because it was the invention of an Heretique, and a fundamentall Heretique, who though he thought Christ to be anointed by the Holy Ghost above his fellowes, yet did not beleeve him to be God, *Damascen,* and his Age, refused that addition to the blessed Virgin; So reverently were they affected, so jealously were they enamoured of that name, *Christ,* the name which
570 implyed his Unction, his Commission, the Decree, by which he was made a Person, able to redeeme thy soule: And in that contemplation, say with *Andrew,* to his brother *Peter, Invenimus Messiam; I have found the Messias;* I could finde no meanes of salvation in my selfe, nay, no such meanes to direct God upon, by my prayer, or by a wish, as hee hath taken; but God himselfe hath found a way, a *Messias;* His Son shall bee made man; And *Inveni Messiam,* I have found him, and found, that he, who by his Incarnation, was made able to save me, (so he was *Christ*) by his actuall passion, hath saved me, and so I love him as *Iesus.*
580 Christ loved *Stephen* all the way, for all the way *Stephen* was dis-

Christus

[John 1.41]

Iesus

posed to Christs glory, but in the agony of death (death suffered for

him) Christ expressed his love most, in opening the windowes, the curtaines of heaven it selfe, to see *Stephen* dye, and to shew himselfe to *Stephen*. I love my Saviour as he is *The Lord,* He that studies my salvation; And as *Christ,* made a person able to work my salvation; but when I see him in the third notion, *Iesus,* accomplishing my salvation, by an actuall death, I see those hands stretched out, that stretched out the heavens, and those feet racked, to which they that racked them are foot-stooles; I heare him, from whom his nearest

590 friends fled, pray for his enemies, and him, whom his Father forsooke, not forsake his brethren; I see him that cloathes this body with his creatures, or else it would wither, and cloathes this soule with his Righteousnesse, or else it would perish, hang naked upon

[Rev. 21.6] the Crosse; And him that hath, him that is, *the Fountaine of the water of life,* cry out, *He thirsts,* when that voyce overtakes me, in my

Lament. crosse wayes in the world, *Is it nothing to you, all you that passe by?*

1.12 *Behold, and see, if there be any sorrow, like unto my sorrow, which is done unto me, wherewith the Lord hath afflicted me, in the day of his fierce anger;* When I conceit, when I contemplate my Saviour

600 thus, I love the *Lord,* and there is a reverent adoration in that love, I love *Christ,* and there is a mysterious admiration in that love, but I love *Iesus,* and there is a tender compassion in that love, and I am content to suffer with him, and to suffer for him, rather then see any diminution of his glory, by my prevarication. And he that loves not thus, that loves not the Lord God, and God manifested in Christ, *Anathema, Maranatha,* which is our next, and our last Part.

3 Part   Whether this *Anathema* be denounced by the Apostle, by way of

Imprecatio Imprecation, that he wished it so, or pronounced by way of excommunication, That others should esteem them so, and avoid them, as

610 such persons, is sometimes debated amongst us in our books. If the Apostle say it by way of Imprecation, if it sound so, you are to remember first, That many things are spoken by the Prophets in the Scriptures, which sound as imprecations, as execrations, which are indeed but prophesies; They seeme to be spoken in the spirit of anger, when they are in truth, but in the spirit of prophesie. So, in very many places of the Psalmes, *David* seemes to wish heavy calamities upon his and Gods enemies, when it is but a declaration of those

judgements of God, which hee prophetically foresees to be imminent upon them: They seeme Imprecations, and are but Prophesies; and
[620] such, wee, who have not this Spirit of Prophesie, nor foresight of Gods wayes, may not venture upon. If they be truly Imprecations, you are to remember also, that the Prophets and Apostles had in them a power extraordinary, and in execution of that power, might doe that, which every private man may not doe: So the Prophets rebuked, so they punished Kings. So ªElizeus called in the Beares to devoure the boyes; And so ᵇElias called downe fire to devoure the Captaines; So S. Peter killed ᶜAnanias, and Sapphira with his word; And ᵈso S. Paul stroke Elymas the Sorcerer with blindnesse. But upon Imprecations of this kinde, wee as private men, or as publique
[630] persons, but limited by our Commission, may not adventure neither. But take the Prophets or the Apostles in their highest Authority, yet in an over-vehement zeale, they may have done some things some times not warrantable in themselves, many times many things, not to be imitated by us. In Moses his passionate vehemency, Dele me, If thou wilt not forgive them, blot me out of thy booke, And in the Apostles inconsiderate zeale to his brethren, Optabam Anathema esse, I could wish that my selfe were accursed from Christ; In Iames and Iohns impatience of their Masters being neglected by the Samaritans, when they drew from Christ that rebuke, You know not of what
[640] spirit you are; In these, and such as these, there may be something, wherein even these men cannot be excused, but very much wherein we may not follow them, nor doe as they did, nor say as they said. Since there is a possibility, a facility, a proclivity of erring herein, and so many conditions and circumstances required, to make an Imprecation just and lawfull, the best way is to forbeare them, or to be very sparing in them.

But we rather take this in the Text, to be an Excommunication denounced by the Apostle, then an Imprecation: So Christ himselfe, If he will not heare the Church, let him be to thee as a Heathen, or
[650] a Publican; That is, Have no conversation with him. So sayes the Apostle, speaking of an Angel, Anathema, If any man, if we our selves, if an Angel from heaven, preach any other Gospel, let him be accursed. Now the Excommunication is in the Anathema, and the aggravating thereof in the other words, Maranatha. The word Anath-

ª2 King. 2.24
ᵇ2 Kings 1
ᶜActs 5
ᵈActs 13.8

Exod. 32.32

Rom. 9.3

Luke 9.55

Excom- municatio
Mat. 18.17

Gal. 1.8

Just. Mart.

ema had two significations; They are expressed thus, *Quod Deo dicatum, Quod à Deo per vitium alienatum;* That which for some excellency in it, was separated from the use of man, to the service of God, or that which for some great fault in it, was separated from Chrysost.   God and man too. *Ab illo abstinebant tanquam Deo dicatum, Ab*
660 *hoc recedebant, tanquam à Deo abalienatum:* From the first kinde, men abstained, because they were consecrated to God, and from the other, because they were aliened from God; and in that last sense, irreligious men, such as love not the Lord Jesus Christ, are *Anathema,* aliened from God. Amongst the Druides, with the Heathen, they excommunicated Malefactors, and no man might relieve him in any necessity, no man might answer him in any action: And so amongst the Jews, the *Esseni,* who were in speciall estimation for sanctity, excommunicated irreligious persons, and the persons so excommunicated starved in the streets and fields. By the light of na-
670 ture, by the light of grace, we should separate our selves from irreligious, and from idolatrous persons; and that with that earnestnesse, which the Apostle expresses in the last words, *Maran Atha.*

Maran Atha   In the practise of the Primitive Church, by those Canons, which we call The Apostles Canons, and those which we call The penitentiall Canons, we see there were different penances inflicted upon different faults, and there were, very early, relaxations of penances, Indulgences; and there were reservations of cases; in some any Priest, in some a Bishop onely might dispense. It is so in our Church still; Impugners of the Supremacy are excommunicated, and not restored
680 but by the Archbishop: Impugners of the Common prayer Booke excommunicated too, but may bee restored by the Bishop of the place: Impugners of our Religion declared in the Articles, reserved to the Archbishop: Impugners of Ceremonies restored when they repent, and no Bishop named: Authors of Schisme reserved to the Archbishop; maintainers of Schismatiques, referred but to repentance; And so maintainers of Conventicles, to the Archbishop; maintainers of Constitutions made in Conventicles, to their repentance. There was ever, there is yet a reserving of certaine cases, and a relaxation or aggravating of Ecclesiasticall censures, for their waight, and
690 for their time: and, because *Not to love the Lord Iesus Christ* was

the greatest, the Apostle inflicts this heaviest Excommunication, *Maran Atha.*

The word seemes to be a Proverbiall word amongst the Jews after their returne, and vulgarly spoken by them, and so the Apostle takes it, out of common use of speech: *Maran,* is *Dominus, The Lord,* and *Atha* is *Venit, He comes:* Not so truly, in the very exactnesse of Hebrew rules, and terminations, but so amongst them then, when their language was much depraved: but, in ancienter times, we have the word *Mara* for *Dominus,* and the word *Atha* for *Venit;* And
700 so *Anathema, Maran Atha* will be, *Let him that loveth not the Lord Iesus Christ, be as an accursed person to you, even till the Lord come.* S. *Hierom* seems to understand this, *Dominus venit,* That the Lord is come; come already, come in the flesh; *Superfluum,* sayes he, *odiis pertinacibus contendere adversus eum, qui jam venit;* It is super-abundant perversnesse, to resist Christ now; Now that he hath ap-peared already, and established to himselfe a Kingdome in this world. And so S. *Chrysostome* seems to take it too; Christ is come already, sayes he, *Et jam nulla potest excusatio non diligentibus eum;* If any excuse could be pretended before, yet since Christ is come, none can
710 be: *Si opertum,* sayes the Apostle, *If our Gospel be hid now, it is hid from them who are lost;* that is, they are lost from whom it is hid. But that is not all, that is intended by the Apostle, in this place. It is not onely a censorious speech, It is a shame for them, and an inexcus-able thing in them, if they doe not love the Lord Jesus Christ, but it is a judiciary speech, thus much more, since they doe not love the Lord, *The Lord judge them when he comes;* I, sayes the Apostle, take away none of his mercy, when he comes, but I will have nothing to doe with them, till he comes; to me, he shall be *Anathema, Maran Atha,* separated from me, till then; then, the Lord who shews mercy
720 in minutes, do his will upon him. Our former Translation had it thus, *Let him be had in execration,* and *excommunicated till death;* In death, Lord have mercy upon him; till death, I will not live with him.

To end all, If a man love not the Lord, if he love not God, which is, which was, and which is to come, what will please him? whom will he love? If hee love the *Lord,* and love not *Christ,* and so love a God

Dan. 4.16
Deut. 33.2

[2 Cor. 4.3]

in generall, but lay no hold upon a particular way of his salvation, *Sine Christo, sine Deo,* sayes the Apostle to the Ephesians, when ye were *without Christ,* ye were *without God;* A non-Christian, is an 730 Atheist in that sense of the Apostle. If any man finde a *Christ,* a Saviour of the World, but finde not a *Iesus,* an actuall Saviour, that this Jesus hath saved him, *Who is a lyar,* sayes another Apostle, *but he that denieth that Iesus is the Christ?* And (as he sayes after) *Whosoever beleeveth that Iesus is the Christ, is borne of God.* From the presumptuous Atheist, that beleeves no God, from the reserved Atheist, that beleeves no God manifested in Christ, from the melancholique Atheist that beleeves no Jesus applied to him, from him of no Religion, from him of no Christian Religion, from him that erres fundamentally in the Christian Religion, the Apostle enjoynes a sepa- 740 ration, not till clouds of persecution come, and then joyne, not till beames of preferment come, and then joyne, not till Lawes may have beene slumbred some yeares, and then joyne, not till the parties grow somewhat neare an equality, and then joyne, but *Maran Atha, donec Dominus venit,* till the Lord come to his declaration in judgement, *If any man love not the Lord Iesus Christ, let him be accursed. Amen.*

Eph. 2.12

1 Iohn 2.22

5.1

Number 15.

Preached upon Trinity-Sunday.

PSAL. 2.12. *KISSE THE SON, LEST HE BE ANGRY.*

WHETHER we shall call it a repeating againe in us, of that which God had done before to Israel, or call it a performing of that in us, which God promised by way of Prophesie to Israel, that is certainly afforded to us by God, which is spoken by the Prophet of Israel, *God doth draw us with the cords of a man,* Hos. 11.4 *and with bands of love: with the cords of a man,* the man Christ Jesus, the Son of God, and *with the bands of love,* the band and seale of love, a holy kisse, *Kisse the Son, lest he be angry.* No man comes to God, except the Father draw him; The Father draws no man, but
10 by the Son; and the Son receives none, but by love, and this cement and glue, of a zealous and a reverentiall love, a holy kisse; *Kisse the Son, &c.*

The parts upon which, for the enlightning of your understandings, *Divisio* and assistance of your memories, we shall insist, are two: first our duty, then our danger; The first is an expression of love, *Kisse the Son;* the second is an impression of feare, *lest he be angry.* In the first we shall proceed thus: we shall consider first The object of this love, the Person, the second Person in the Trinity, *The Son;* The rather, because that consideration will cleare the Translation; for, in no one
20 place of Scripture, do Translations differ more, then in this Text; and the Roman Translation and ours differ so much, as that they have but *Apprehendite disciplinam, Embrace knowledge,* where we have, (as you heard) *Kisse the Son.* From the Person, *The Son,* we shall passe to the act, *Osculamini, Kisse the Son;* In which we shall see, That since this is an act, which licentious men have depraved, (carnal men doe it, and treacherous men doe it; *Iudas* (and not onely *Iudas*) have *betrayed* by a *kisse*) and yet God commands this, and expresses love in this. Every thing that hath, or may be abused, must

not therefore be abandoned; the turning of a thing out of the way,
30 is not a taking of that thing away, but good things deflected to ill
uses, by some, may be by others reduced to their first goodnesse. And
then in a third branch of this first part, we shall consider, and magnifie the goodnesse of God, that hath brought us into this distance,
that we may *Kisse the Son,* that the expressing of this love lies in our
hands, and that, whereas the love of the Church, in the Old Testament, even in the Canticle, went no farther but to the *Osculetur me,*

Cant. 1.2   *O that he would kisse me with the kisses of his mouth!* now, in the
Christian Church, and in the visitation of a Christian soule, he hath
invited us, enabled us to kisse him, for he is presentially amongst us:
40 And this will lead us to conclude that first part, with an earnest perswasion, and exhortation *to kisse the Son,* with all those affections,
which we shall there finde to be expressed in the Scriptures, in that

[Rom.   testimony of true love, *a holy kisse.* But then, lest that perswasion by
16.16]   love should not be effectuall, and powerfull enough to us, we shall
descend from that duty, to the danger, from love, to feare, *Lest he be
angry;* And therein see first, that God, who is love, can be angry;
And then, that this God who is angry here, is the Son of God, He
that hath done so much for us, and therefore in Justice may be angry;
He that is our Judge, and therefore in reason, we are to feare his
50 anger: And then, in a third branch, we shall see, how easily this anger
departs, a kisse removes it, Do it, lest he be angry; And then lastly,
we shall inquire, what does anger him; and there consider, That as
we attribute power to the Father, and so, sins against power (the
undervaluing of Gods power in the Magistrate over us, or the abusing
of Gods power, in our selves, over others) were sins against the
Father; so wisedome being the attribute of the Sonne, ignorance,
which is so far under wisedome, and curiosity, which carries us beyond wisedome, will be sinnes against the Sonne.

1 Part   Our first branch in our first part, directs us upon him, who is first
Persona, 60 and last, and yesterday and to day, and the same for ever; The Son
Filius   of God, *Osculamini filium, Kisse the Sonne.* Where the Translations
differ as much, as in any one passage. The Chalde paraphrase (which
is, for the most part, good evidence) and the translation of the Septuagint, (which adds much weight) and the currant of the Fathers
(which is of importance too) doe all reade this place, *Apprehendite*

disciplinam, Embrace knowledge, and not *Osculamini filium, Kisse the sonne.* Of the later men in the Roman Church, divers read it as we do, *Osculamini,* and some farther, *Amplectimini, Embrace the sonne.* Amongst the Jews, *Rabbi Solomon* reads it, *Armamini dis-*
70 *ciplina, Arme your selves with knowledge;* And another moderne man, reads it, *Osculamini pactum, Kisse the Covenant;* And, *Adorate frumentum, Adore the Corne,* and thereby carries it from the pacification of Christ in heaven, to the adoration of the bread in the Sacrament. Clearly, and without exception, even from *Bellarmine* himselfe, according to the Originall Hebrew, it ought to be read, as we reade it, *Kisse the Sonne.* Now very many, very learned, and very zealous men of our times, have been very vehement against that Translation of the Roman Church, though it be strengthned, by the Chalde, by the Septuagint, and by the Fathers, in this place. The reason of the
80 vehemence in this place, is not because that sense, which that translation presents, may not be admitted; no, nor that it does not reach home, to that which is intended in ours, *Kisse the Sonne:* for, since the doctrine of the Sonne of God, had been established in the verses before, to say now, *Apprehendite disciplinam,* lay hold upon that Doctrine; That doctrine which was delivered before, is, in effect the same thing, as, *Kisse the Sonne.* So *Luther,* when he takes, and follows that translation of that Church, sayes, *Nostra translatio, ad verbum, nihil est, ad sensum propriissima;* That translation, if we consider the very words only, is far from the Originall, but if we re-
90 gard the sense, it is most proper. And so also *Calvin* admits; Take it which way you will, *Idem manet sensus,* the sense is all one. And therefore another Author in the Reformation says, *In re dubia, malim vetustissimo interpreti credere,* since upon the whole matter it is doubtfull, or indifferent, I would not depart, sayes he, from that Translation, which is most ancient.

Pellican.

The case then being thus, that that sense may be admitted, and admitted so as that it establish the same doctrine that ours does, why are our late men so very vehement against it? Truly, upon very just reason: for, when those former reverent men were so moderate as
100 to admit that translation in this place; The Church of Rome, had not then put such a sanctity, such a reverence, such a singularity, and preheminence, and supremacy, such a *Noli me tangere,* upon

that Translation; It had the estimation then of a very reverend Translation, and compared with any other Translations, then the best. But when in the Councell of Trent they came to make it as Authenticall, to prefer it before the Originals themselves, to decide all matters of Controversie by it alone, and to make the doing so, matter of faith, and heresie, in any thing to depart from that Translation, then came these later men justly to charge it with those errors, wherein, by
[110] their own confessions, it hath departed from the Originall; Not that these men meant to discredit that Translation so, as that it should not still retain the estimation of a good and usefull Translation, but to avoyd that danger, that it should be made matter of faith, to be bound to one Translation; or that any Translation should be preferred before the Originall. And so truly it is, in many other things, besides the translation. They say S. *Peter* was at Rome; and all moderate men went along with them; S. *Peter* was at Rome. But when upon S. *Peters* personall being at Rome, they came to build their universall supremacy over all the Church, and so to erect matter of faith
[120] upon matter of fact, then later men came to deny, that it could be proved out of Scripture, that *Peter* was at Rome; So the Ancients spoke of many Sacraments, so they did of Purgatory, so they did of many things controverted now; when as they, then, never suspected that so impious a sense would have been put upon their words, nor those opinions and doctrines so mischievously advanced, as they have been since. If they would have let their translation have remained such a translation, we would not have declined it; since they will have all tryals made by it, we rather accept the Originall; and that is in this place, *Osculamini filium, Kisse the Son.*

Osculamini [130] The person then (which was our first Consideration) is the *Sonne;* The testimony of our love to this person, is this *kisse, Osculamini:* where we see, that God cals upon us, and enjoyns unto us, such an outward act, as hath been diversly depraved, and vitiated before amongst men. God gives no countenance to that distempered humor, to that distorted rule; It hath been ill used, and therefore it may not be used. Sacred and secular Stories abound with examples of the treacherous *kisse;* Let the Scriptures be our limits. *Ioabs* complement
2 Sam. 20.9 with *Amasa; Art thou in health, my brother?* ended in this; *He took*

him with the right hand, as to kisse him, and killed him. Enlarge
[140] your thoughts a little upon *Iudas* case; *Iudas* was of those, who had   Heb. 6.5
tasted of the word of God, and the powers of the world to come; He
had lived in the Conversation, in the Pædagogy, in the Discipline
of Christ; yet he sold Christ; and sold him at a low price, as every
man that is so unprovident, as to offer a thing to sale, shall do; and
he stayed not till they came to him, with, What will you take for
your Master? but he went to them, with, What will you give me for
Christ? yet Christ admits him, admits him to supper, and after all
this, cals him *friend;* for, after all this, Christ had done two, perchance three offices of a friend to *Iudas;* He washed his feet; and,
[150] perchance, he gave him the Sacrament with the rest; and by assigning the sop for a particular mark, he let him see, that he knew he was
a traytor, which might have been inough to have reclaimed him:
It did not; but he proceeded in his treason, and in the most mischievous and treacherous performing of it, to betray him with a kisse;
He gave them a signe, whomsoever I shall kisse, the same is he: Dat   Mat. 26.48
signum osculi, cum veneno Diaboli, sayes *Hierome,* He kisses with
a biting kisse, and conveys treason in a testimony of love. It is an
Apophthegme of *Luthers, Mali tyranni, hæretici pejores, falsi fratres*
pessimi: A persecutor is ill; but he that perswades me to any thing,
[160] which might submit me to the persecutors rage, is worse; but he
that hath perswaded me, and then betrays me, is worst of all. When
all that happens, when *a mans enemies are the men of his own house,*   Mic. 7.6
when *amongst our selves men arise, and draw away the Disciples,*   Act. 20.30
remember that *Iudas* defamed this kisse before, he kissed his Master,
and so betrayed him. *Homo sum, & inter homines vivo,* sayes S. *Au-*
gustine, I am but a man my selfe, and I look but for men to live
amongst; *Nec mihi arrogare audeo, meliorem domum meam, quam*
Arca Noah, I cannot hope to have my house clearer than *Noahs*
Arke, and there, in eight, there was one ill; nor then *Iacobs* house,
[170] and there the Sonne went up to the Fathers bed; nor then *Davids,*
and there the brother forced the sister; nor then Christs, and there
Iudas betrayed his Master, and with a kisse: which alone does so
aggravate the fact, as that for the atrocity and hainousnesse thereof,
three of the Evangelists remember that circumstance, *That he be-*   [Luke
trayed him with a kisse; and as though it might seeme impossible,   22.48]

incredible to man, that it could be so, S. *Iohn* pretermits that circumstance, That it was done with a kisse.

In *Ioabs* treachery, in *Iudas* treason, is the kisse defamed, and in the carnall and licentious abuse of it, it is every day depraved. They
180 mistake the matter much, that thinke all adultery is below the girdle: A man darts out an adultery with his eye, in a wanton look; and he wraps up adultery with his fingers, in a wanton letter; and he breaths in an adultery with his lips, in a wanton kisse. But though this act of love, be so defamed both wayes, by treachery, by licentiousnes, yet God chooses this Metaphore, he bids us *kisse the Sonne*. It is a true, and an usefull Rule, that ill men have been Types of Christ, and ill actions figures of good: Much more, may things not ill in themselves, though deflected and detorted to ill, be restored to good againe; and therfore doth God, in more then this one place, expect our love in a
190 kisse; for, if we be truly in love with him, it will be a holy and an acceptable Metaphore unto us, els it will have a carnall and a fastidious taste. *Frustra ad legendum amoris carmen, qui non amat, accedit:* He that comes to read *Solomons* Love-song, and loves not him upon whom that Song is directed, will rather endanger, then profit himselfe by that reading: *Non capit ignitum eloquium frigidum pectus:* A heart frozen and congealed with the love of this world, is not capable, not sensible of the fires of the holy Ghost; *Græcè loquentes non intelligit, qui Græcè non novit, & lingua amoris ei, qui non amat, barbara;* As Greek it selfe is barbarous to him that understands not
200 Greek, so is the language of love, and the kisse which the holy Ghost speaks of here, to him that always groveleth, and holds his face upon the earth.

Treachery often, but licentiousnesse more, hath depraved this seale of love; and yet, *Vt nos ad amplexus sacri amoris accendat, usque ad turpis amoris nostri verba se inclinat;* God stoops even to the words of our foule and unchast love, that thereby he might raise us to the heavenly love of himselfe, and his Son. *Cavendum, ne machina quæ ponitur ut levet, ipsa aggrevet:* Take thou heed, that that ladder, or that engine which God hath given to raise thee, doe not load thee,
210 oppresse thee, cast thee downe: Take heed lest those phrases of love and kisses which should raise thee to him, do not bury thee in the memory and contemplation of sinfull love, and of licentious kisses.

Hieron.
Ep. 131
G. Sanctius
2 Sam. 14
n. 29

Bernar.

Idem

Idem

Gregor.

Idem

Idem

Palea tegit frumentum; palea jumentorum, frumentum hominum:
There is corne under the chaffe; and though the chaffe and straw be
for cattell, there is corne for men too: There is a heavenly love, under
these ordinary phrases; the ordinary phrase belongs to ordinary men;
the heavenly love and the spirituall kisse, to them who affect an
union to God, and him whom he sent, his Son Christ Jesus. S. *Paul*
abhors not good and applyable sentences, because some secular Poets
220 had said them before; nor hath the Christian Church abhorred the
Temples of the Gentiles, because they were profaned before with
idolatrous sacrifices. I do not conceive how that Jesuit *Serarius* should

In Jos. 6.
q. 40

conceive any such great joy, as he sayes he did, when he came to a
Church-porch, and saw an old statue of *Iupiter,* and another of *Hercules,* holding two basins of holy water; when *Iupiter* and *Hercules*
were made to doe Christians such services, the Jesuit is over-joyed.
His *Iupiter* and his *Hercules* might well enough have been spared
in the Christian Church, but why some such things as have beene
abused in the Roman Church, may not be preserved in, or reduced to
230 their right use here, I conceive not; as well as (in a proportion) this
outward testimony of inward love, though defamed by treachery,
though depraved by licentiousnesse, is exacted at our hands by God
himselfe, towards his Son, *Kisse the Son, lest he be angry.*

*Propin-
quitas*

For all *Ioabs* and *Iudas* treason, and carnall lovers licentiousnesse,
kisse thou the Sonne, and be glad that the Sonne hath brought thee,
in the Christian Church, within that distance, as that thou mayest
kisse him. The nearest that the Synagogue, or that the Spouse of
Christ not yet married came to, was, *Osculetur me, Let him kisse me*

Cant. 1.2

with the kisses of his mouth. It was but a kissing of his hand, when
240 he reached them out their spirituall food by others; It was a mariage,
but a mariage by a proxie; The personall mariage, the consummation
of the mariage was in the comming of Christ, in establishing a reall
presence of himselfe in the Church. *Præcepta Dei oscula sunt,* sayes
Gregory; In every thing that God sayes to us, he kisses us; *Sed per
Prophetas & Ministros, alieno ore nos osculatur,* He kissed us by another mans mouth, when he spoke by the mouth of the Prophets;
but now that he speaks by his owne Son, it is by himselfe. Even his
servant *Moses* himself was *of uncircumcised lips,* and with the uncir-

Exod. 6.12
Esay 6.5

cumcised there was no mariage. Even his servant *Esay* was *of un-*

²⁵⁰ *cleane lips,* and with the uncleane there was no mariage: Even his

Jer. 1.6

servant *Ieremie* was *oris infantilis,* he was *a child and could not speake,* and with children, in infancie, there is no mariage: But in Christ, God hath abundantly performed that supply promised to

[Exod. 7.1]

Moses, there, *Aaron thy brother shall be thy Prophet;* Christ himselfe shall come and speake to thee, and returne and speak for thee: In

[Isa. 6.6–7]

Christ, the *Seraphim* hath brought that *live coale* from the *Altar,* and *touched Esayes lips,* and so spoken lively, and clearly to our soules;

[Jer. 46.28]

In Christ, God hath done that which he said to *Ieremy, Feare not, I am with thee;* for in this *Immanuel,* God and man, Christ Jesus, ²⁶⁰ God is with us.

      In *Eschines* mouth, when he repeated them, they say, even *Demosthenes* Orations were flat, and tastlesse things; Compare the Prophets with the Son, and even the promises of God, in them, are faint and

2 King. 4.34

dilute things. *Elishaes* staffe in the hand of *Gehazi* his servant, would not recover the Shunamites dead child; but when *Elisha* himselfe came, and put his mouth upon the childs mouth, that did: In the mouth of Christs former servants there was a preparation, but effect, and consummation in his owne mouth. In the Old Testament, at first, God kissed man, and so breathed the breath of life, and made ²⁷⁰ him a man; In the New Testament Christ kissed man, he breathed the breath of everlasting life, the holy Ghost, into his Apostles, and

Cant. 8.6

so made the man a blessed man. *Love is as strong as death;* As in death there is a transmigration of the soule, so in this spirituall love, and this expressing of it, by this kisse, there is a transfusion of the soule too: And as we find in *Gellius* a Poëm of *Platoes,* where he sayes, he knew one so extremely passionate, *Vt parùm affuit quin moreretur in osculo,* much more it is true in this heavenly union, expressed in this kisse, as S. *Ambrose* delivers it, *Per osculum adhæret anima Deo, et transfunditur spiritus osculantis,* In this kisse, where

Psal. 85.10

²⁸⁰ *Righteousnesse and peace have kissed each other,* In this person, where the Divine and the humane nature have kissed each other, In this Christian Church, where Grace and Sacraments, visible and invisible meanes of salvation, have kissed each other, *Love is as strong as death;* my soule is united to my Saviour, now in my life, as in death, and I am already made *one spirit with him:* and whatsoever death can doe, this kisse, this union can doe, that is, give me a present,

an immediate possession of the kingdome of heaven: And as the most mountainous parts of this kingdome are as well within the kingdome as a garden, so in the midst of the calamities and incommodities of
²⁹⁰ this life, I am still in the kingdome of heaven. In the Old Testament, it was but a contract, but *per verba de futuro, Sponsabo, I will marry thee;* but now that Christ is come, the *Bride-groome* is with us for ever, and the *children of the Bridechamber* cannot *mourne.*

Hos. 2.19
Mat. 9.15

Now, by this, we are slid into our fourth and last branch of our first part, The perswasion to come to this holy kisse, though defamed by treachery, though depraved by licentiousnesse, since God invites us to it, by so many good uses thereof in his Word. It is an imputation laid upon *Nero,* That *Neque adveniens, neque proficiscens,* That whether comming or going he never kissed any: And Christ himselfe
³⁰⁰ imputes it to *Simon,* as a neglect of him, That when he *came into his house,* he did not *kisse* him. This then was in use, first among kins-folks; *In illa simplicitate antiquorum, propinqui propinquos oscu-labantur:* In those innocent and harmlesse times, persons neare in bloud did kisse one another: And in that right, and not onely as a stranger, *Iacob kissed Rachel,* and told her how near of *kin* he was to her. There is no person so neare of kin to thee, as Christ Jesus: Christ Jesus thy Father as he created thee, and thy brother as he took thy nature: Thy Father as he provided an inheritance for thee, and thy brother as he divided this inheritance with thee, and as he dyed to
³¹⁰ give thee possession of that inheritance: He that is *Nutritius,* thy Foster-father who hath nursed thee in his house, in the Christian Church, and thy Twin-brother, so like thee, as that his Father, and thine in him, shall not know you from one another, but mingle your conditions so, as that he shall find thy sins in him, and his righteous-nesse in thee; *Osculamini Filium,* Kisse this Son as thy kinsman.

Exhortatio

Luke 7.45

August.

Gen. 29.11

This kisse was also in use, as *Symbolum subjectionis,* A recognition of soveraignty or power; *Pharaoh sayes to Ioseph, Thou shalt be over my house, and according to thy word shall all my people be ruled;* there the Originall is, *All my people shall kisse thy face.* This is the
³²⁰ Lord Paramount, the Soveraigne Lord of all, The Lord Jesus; *Iesus, at whose name every knee must bow, in heaven, in earth, and in hell; Iesus, into whose hands all power in heaven and in earth is given; Iesus,* who hath opened a way to our Appeal, from all powers upon

Gen. 41.40

Phil. 2.10

Mat. 28.18

Mat. 10.28

earth, *Fear not them which kill the body, but are not able to kill the soule; Iesus,* who is the *Lion* and the *Lambe* too, powerfull upon others, accessible unto thee; *Osculamini Filium,* Kisse this Son, as he is thy Soveraigne.

Gen. 31.55

It was in use likewise *In discessu,* friends parting kissed; *Laban rose up early in the morning, and kissed his sons and his daughters,*

Act. 20.37

330 *and departed:* And *at Pauls departing, they fell on his neck, and wept, and kissed him.* When thou departest to thy worldly businesses, to thy six dayes labour, kisse him, take leave of him, and remember that all that while thou art gone upon his errand, and though thou worke for thy family, and for thy posterity, yet thou workest in his vineyard, and dost his worke.

Gen. 33.4

They kissed too *In reditu; Esau ran to meet his brother, and fell on his neck and kissed him.* When thou returnest to his house, after thy six dayes labour, to celebrate his Sabbath, kisse him there, and be able to give him some good account, from Sabbath to Sabbath, from 340 week to week, of thy stewardship, and thou wilt never be bankrupt.

2 Sam. 14.33

They kissed in reconciliation; *David kissed Absalon.* If thou have not discharged thy stewardship well, Restore to man who is damnified therein, Confesse to God who hath suffered in that sin, Reconcile thy selfe to him, and kisse him in the Sacrament, in the seale of Reconciliation.

1 King.
19.18

They kissed in a religious reverence even of false gods; *I have, sayes God, seaven thousand knees that have not bowed unto Baal, and mouths that have not kissed him.* Let every one of us kisse the true God, in keeping his knees from bowing to a false, his lips from 350 assenting, his hands from subscribing to an Idolatrous worship. And, as they kissed *In Symbolum concordiæ,* (which was another use

Rom. 16.16

thereof; *Salute one another with a holy kisse*) upon which custome, *Iustin Martyr* sayes, *Osculum ante Eucharistiam,* before the Communion, the Congregation kissed, to testifie their unity in faith in him, to whom they were then Sacramentally to be united, as well as Spiritually, And *Tertullian* calls it *Osculum signaculum Orationis,* Because they ended their publique Prayers with that seale of unity and concord. Let every Congregation kisse him so; at every meeting to seale to him a new band, a new vow that they will never break, in 360 departing from any part of his true worship. And to that purpose kisse his feet, as *Mary Magdalen* did: *Speciosi pedes Euangeli-zantium;* Let his feet, his Ministers, in whom he comes, be acceptable unto you; and love that, upon which himselfe stands, The Ordinance which he hath established for your salvation.

Kisse the Son, that is, imbrace him, depend upon him all these wayes; As thy kinsman, As thy Soveraigne, At thy going, At thy comming; At thy Reconciliation, in the truth of religion in thy selfe, in a peaceable unity with the Church, in a reverent estimation of those men, and those meanes, whom he sends. Kisse him, and be not
370 ashamed of kissing him; It is that, which the Spouse desired, *I would kisse thee, & not be despised.* If thou be despised for loving Christ in his Gospel, remember that when *David* was thought base, for dancing before the Arke, his way was to be more base. If thou be thought frivolous for thrusting in at Service, in the fore-noone, bee more frivolous, and come againe in the after-noone: *Tanto major requies, quanto ab amore Iesu nulla requies:* The more thou troublest thy selfe, or art troubled by others for Christ, the more peace thou hast in Christ.

We descend now to our second Part, from the duty to the danger,
380 from the expressing of love to the impression of feare, *Kisse the Son, lest he be angry:* And first that anger and love, are not incompatible, that anger consists with love: God is immutable, and God is love, and yet God can be angry. God stops a little upon scorne, in the fourth verse of this Psalme, *When the Kings of the earth take counsell against his anointed, he laughs them to scorne, he hath them in dirision.* But it ends not in a jest; *He shall speake to them in his wrath, and vexe them in his sore displeasure;* And that is not all; *He shall breake them with a rod of iron, and dash them in pieces like a Potters vessell.*
390 *Lactantius* reprehends justly two errors, and proposes a godly middle way in the Doctrine of the anger of God. Some say, sayes he, that onely favour, and gentlenesse can be attributed to God, *Quia illæsibilis,* He himselfe cannot be hurt, and then why should he be angry? And this is, sayes he, *Favorabilis & popularis oratio,* It is a popular and an acceptable proposition, God cannot be angry, doe what you will, you cannot anger him, for he is all gentlenesse. Others, sayes *Lactantius,* take both anger, and gentlenesse from God, and say

he is affected neither way: And this is, sayes he well, *Constantior error,* An error that will better hold together, better consist in it selfe,
400 and be better stood to; for they are inseparable things; whosoever does love the good, does hate the bad: and therefore if there be no anger, there is no love in God; but that cannot be said. And therefore, sayes he, we must not argue thus, Because there is no anger in God, therefore there is no love; for that indeed would follow, if the first were true; But because there is love in God, therefore there is anger: And so he concludes thus, This is *Cardo Religionis,* This is the hinge upon which all Religion, all the Worship of God turnes and moves, *Si nihil præstat colenti non debetur cultus, nec metus si non irascitur non colenti;* If God gave me nothing for my love, I should not love
410 him, nor feare him if he were not angry at my displeasing him. It is argument enough against the Epicures, (against whom principally hee argues) *Si non curat, non habet potestatem:* If God take no care of humane actions, he hath no power; for it is impossible to thinke, that hee hath power, and uses it not; An idle God is as impossible an imagination, as an impotent God, or an ignorant God. Anger, as it is a passion that troubles, and disorders, and discomposes a man, so it is not in God, but anger as it is a sensible discerning of foes from friends, and of things that conduce, or disconduce to his glory, so it is in God. In a word, *Hilarie* hath expressed it well, *Pœna patientis,*
420 *ira decernentis,* Mans suffering is Gods anger; when God inflicts such punishments, as a King justly incensed would doe, then God is thus angry.

Filius   Now here, our case is heavier; It is not this Great, and Almighty, and Majesticall God, that may be angry; that is like enough; But even the *Son,* whom we must *kisse,* may be *angry:* It is not a person whom we consider meerly as God, but as man; Nay, not as man
[Psa. 22.6] neither, but *a worme, and no man,* and he may be angry, and angry to our ruine. But is it he? Is it the Son, that is intended here? Ask the Romane Translation, and it is not he: There it is, *Ne irascatur*
430 *Dominus, Lest the Lord be angry;* But the Record, the Originall will be against them: Though it were so, *The Lord,* it might be *He, the Sonne,* but it is not *the Lord,* but must necessarily bee *the Sonne;* The Son may, the Son will be angry with us. If he could be angry, why did he not shew it to the Devill that tempted him, to the Jews that

crucified him? God blesse us from such an anger, as works upon the Devill, in a desperate unsensiblenesse of any mercy, from any trade in that Sea, which environs the whole world, and makes all that, one Iland, where onely the Devill can be no Merchant, The bottomelesse Sea of his blood; And God blesse us from such an anger, as works
440 upon the Jews, in an obduration, and the punishment of it, a dispersion. Are ye sure *David* was not angry with *Shimei,* because he reprieved him for a time? Are ye sure the Son is not angry now, because ye perish not yet? Doe you not say, A fruit is perished, if it be bruised in one place? Is not your Religion perished, if Locusts and Eare-wigges have eaten into it, though they have not eaten it up? Is not your Religion perished, if irreligion and prophanenesse be entred into your manners, into your lives, though Religion have some motion in our ordinary meetings, and publique exercises here?

[2 Sam. 19.23]

The Son is *Caput,* and *Corpus,* as S. *Augustine* sayes often, Christ,
450 and the Church of Christ, are Christ; And, *Quis enumeret omnia, quibus corpus Christi irascitur?* sayes the same Father; Who can reckon how many wayes, this Christ, this body of Christ, the Church, is constrained to expresse anger? How many Excommunications, how many Censures, how many Suspensions, how many Irregularities, how many Penances, and Commutations of Penances, is the body of Christ, the Church, forced to inflict upon sinners? And how heavy would these be to us, if we did not waigh them with the waights of flesh in the Shambles, or of Iron in the Shop; if we did not consider them only in their temporall damage, how little an excommunication
460 took from us of our goods, or worldly substance, and not how much it shut up the ordinary and outward meanes of our salvation. When the anger of the Body, the Church, is thus heavy, what is the anger of the Head, of Christ himselfe, who is Judge in his owne cause? When an unjust judgement was executed upon him, how was the frame of nature shaked in Eclipses, in Earth-quakes, in renting of the Temple, and cleaving the Monuments of the dead: When his pleasure is to execute a just judgement upon a Nation, upon a Church, upon a Man, in the infatuation of Princes, in the recidivation of the Clergy, in the consternation of particular consciences, *Quis stabit?*
470 who shall be able to stand in that Judgement? *Kisse the Son lest he be angry;* But when he is angry, he will not kisse you, nor be kissed

by you, but *throw you into unquenchable fire,* if you be *cold,* and if you be *luke-warme, spit you out of his mouth,* remove you from the benefit and comfort of his Word.

This is the anger of God, that reaches to all the world; and the anger of the Son, that comes home to us; and all this is removed with this holy and spirituall kisse: *Osculamini Filium, Kisse the Son lest he be angry,* implies this, If ye kisse him, he will not bee angry. What this kisse is, we have seene all the way; It is to hang at his lips, for the Rule of our life, To depend upon his Word for our Religion, and to succour our selves, by the promises of his Gospel, in all our calamities, and not to provoke him to farther judgements, by a perverse and froward use of those judgements which he hath laid upon us: As it is, in this point towards man, it is towards God too; *Nihil mansuetudine violentius,* There is not so violent a thing as gentlenesse, so forcible, so powerfull upon man, or upon God. This is such a saying, as one would think he that said it, should be ready to retract, by the multiplicity of examples to the contrary every day. Such Rules as this, He that puts up one wrong invites and calls for another, will shake *Chrysostomes* Rule shrewdly, *Nihil mansuetudine violentius,* That no battery is so strong against an enemy, as gentlenesse. Say, if you will, *Nihil melius,* There is no better thing then gentlenesse, and we can make up that with a Comment, that is, nothing better for some purposes; Say, if you will, *Nihil frugalius,* There is not a thriftier thing then gentlenesse, It saves charges, to suffer, It is a more expensive thing to revenge then to suffer, whether we consider expense of soule, or body, or fortune; And, (by the way) that, which we use to adde in this account, opinion, reputation, that which we call Honour, is none of the Elements of which man is made; It may be the ayre, that the Bird flies in, It may be the water, that the Fish swimmes in, but it is none of the Elements that man is made of, for those are onely soule, and body, and fortune. Say also, if you will, *Nihil accommodatius,* Nothing conformes us more to our great patterne Christ Jesus, then mildnesse, then gentlenesse, for that is our lesson from him, *Discite à me, quia mitis, Learne of me, for I am meeke.*

All this *Chrysostome* might say; but will he say, *Nihil violentius,* There is not so violent, so forcible a thing as mildnesse? That there

[Rev. 3.16]

Osculum amovet

Chrysost.

[Mat. 11.29]

⁴⁸⁰

⁴⁹⁰

⁵⁰⁰

is no such Bullet, as a Pillow, no such Action, as Passion, no such
510 revenge, as suffering an injury? Yet, even this is true; Nothing de-
feats an anger so much as patience; nothing reproaches a chiding so
much as silence. *Reprehendis iratum? accusas indignationem?* sayes
that Father: Art thou sorry to see a man angry? *Cur magis irasci vis?*
Why dost thou adde thy anger to his? Why dost thou fuell his anger
with thine? *Quod igni aqua, hoc iræ mansuetudo,* As water works
upon fire, so would thy patience upon his anger. S. *Ambrose* hath
expressed it well too, *Hæc sunt arma justi, ut cedendo vincat;* This
is the warre of the righteous man, to conquer by yeelding. It was
Ezechiahs way; when *Rabshakeh* reviled, They held their peace,   Esay 36.21
520 (where, the very phrase affords us this note, That *silence* is called
holding of our peace, we continue our peace best by silence) *They
held their peace,* sayes that text, *and answered him not a word, for
the King had commanded them not to answer.* Why? S. *Hierom* tels
us why; *Ne ad majores blasphemias provocaret;* Lest the multiplying
of cholerique words amongst men, should have occasioned more
blasphemies against God. And as it is thus with man, with God it is
thus too; Nothing spends his judgements, and his corrections so
soone, as our patience, nothing kindles them, exasperates them so
much, as our frowardnesse, and murmuring. *Kisse the Son,* and he
530 will not be *angry;* If he be, kisse the rod, and he will be angry no
longer; love him lest hee be, feare him when hee is angry: The
preservative is easie, and so is the restorative too: The Balsamum of
this kisse is all; To suck spirituall milke out of the left breast, as well
as out of the right, To finde mercy in his judgements, reparation in
his ruines, feasts in his Lents, joy in his anger. But yet we have
reserved it for our last Consideration, what will make him angry:
what sins are especially directed upon the second Person, the Sonne
of God, and then wee have done all.

    Though those three Attributes of God, Power, and Wisedome, and   *Sapientia*
540 Goodnesse, be all three in all the three Persons of the Trinity, (for
they are all (as we say in the Schoole) *Co-omnipotentes,* they have all
a joynt-Almightinesse, a joynt-Wisdome, and a joynt-Goodnesse)
yet, because the Father is *Principium,* The roote of all, Independent,
not proceeding from any other, as both the other Persons do, and
Power, and Soveraignty best resembles that Independency, therefore

we attribute Power to the Father: And because the Son proceeds *Per modum intellectus,* (which is the phrase that passes through the Fathers, and the Schoole) That as our understanding proceeds from our reasonable soule, so the second Person, the Son, proceeds from
550 the Father, therefore we attribute Wisdome to the Son: And then, because the Holy Ghost is said to proceed *Per modum voluntatis,* That as our soule (as the roote) and our understanding, proceeding from that soule, produce our will, and the object of our will, is evermore *Bonum,* that which is good in our apprehension, therefore we attribute to the Holy Ghost, Goodnesse. And therefore *David* formes his prayer, in that manner, plurally, *Miserere mei Elohim,* Be mercifull unto me all, because in his sin upon *Vriah,* (which he laments in that Psalme) he had transgressed against all the three Persons, in all their Attributes, against the Power, and the Wisdome, and the Good-
560 nesse of God.

Psal. 51

That then which we consider principally in the Son, is Wisdome. And truly those very many things, which are spoken of Wisdome, in the Proverbs of *Solomon,* do, for the most part, hold in Christ: Christ is, for the most part, the Wisdome of that book. And for that book which is called altogether, The book of Wisdome, *Isidore* sayes, that a Rabbi of the Jews told him, That that book was heretofore in the Canonicall Scripture, and so received by the Jews; till after Christs Crucifying, when they observed, what evident testimonies there were in that book for Christ, they removed it from the Canon. This I
570 know, is not true; but I remember it therefore, because all assists us, to consider Wisdome in Christ, as that does also, That the greatest Temple of the Christians in Constantinople, was dedicated in that name, *Sophia,* to Wisdome; by implication to Christ. And in some apparitions, where the Son of God is said to have appeared, he cals himself by that name, *Sapientiam Dei.* He is Wisdome, therefore, because he reveales the Will of the Father to us; and therefore is no man wise, but he that knowes the Father in him. *Isidore* makes this difference *Inter sapientem, & prudentem,* that the first, The wise man, attends the next world, the last, The prudent man, but this world:
580 But wisdome, even heavenly wisdome, does not exclude that prudence, though the principall, or rather the ordinary object thereof, be this world. And therefore sins against the second Person, are sins

against Wisdome, in either extreame, either in affected and grosse ignorance, or in over-refined and sublimed curiosity.

As we place this Ignorance in Practicall things of this world, so it is Stupidity; and as we place it in Doctrinall things, of the next world, so Ignorance is Implicite Beliefe: And Curiosity, as we place it upon Practical things, is Craft, and upon Doctrinal things, Subtilty; And this Stupidity and this Implicite faith, and then this Craft, and this
590 Subtilty, are sins directed against the Son, who is true and onely Wisdome.

First then, A stupid and negligent passage through this world, as though thou wert no part of it, without embarking thy selfe in any calling; To crosse Gods purpose so much, as that, whereas he produced every thing out of nothing, to be something, thou wilt go so far back, towards nothing againe, as to be good for nothing, that when as our Lawes call a Calling, an Addition, thou wilt have no Addition, And when (as S. *Augustine* saies) *Musca Soli præferenda, quia vivit,* A Fly is a nobler Creature then the Sun, in this respect,
600 because a Fly hath life in it selfe, and the Sun hath none, so any Artificer is a better part of a State, then any retired or contemplative man that embraces no Calling, These chippings of the world, these fragmentary and incoherent men, trespasse against the Son, against the second Person, as he is Wisdome. And so doe they in doctrinall things, that swallow any particular religion, upon an implicite faith. When Christ declared a very forward knowledge, in the Temple, at twelve yeares, with the Doctors, yet he was there, *Audiens & interrogans,* He heard what they would say, and he moved questions, to heare what they could say; for, *Ejusdem scientiæ est, scire quid inter-*
610 *roges, quidve respondeas,* It is a testimony of as much knowledge to aske a pertinent question, as to give a pertinent answer. But never to have beene able to give answer, never to have asked question in matter of Religion, this is such an Implicitenesse, and indifferency, as transgresses against the Son of God, who is Wisdome.

It is so too, in the other extreame, Curiosity; And this, in Practicall things, is Craft, in Doctrinall, Subtilty. Craft, is properly and narrowly, To go towards good ends, by ill wayes: And though this be not so ill, as when neither ends, nor wayes be good, yet this is ill too. The Civilians use to say of the Canonists, and Casuists, That they

Stupiditas

Luke 2.46

Origen

Curiositas

⁶²⁰ consider nothing but *Crassam æquitatem,* fat Equity, downe-right Truths, things obvious and apprehensible by every naturall man: and to doe but so, to be but honest men, and no more, they thinke a diminution. To stay within the limits of a profession, within the limits of precedents, within the limits of time, is to over-active men contemptible; nothing is wisdome, till it be exalted to Craft, and got above other men. And so it is, with some, with many, in Doctrinall things too. To rest in Positive Divinity, and Articles confessed by all Churches, To be content with Salvation at last, and raise no estimation, no emulation, no opinion of singularity by the way, only to ⁶³⁰ edifie an Auditory, and not to amaze them, onely to bring them to an assent, and to a practise, and not to an admiration, This is but home-spun Divinity, but Country-learning, but Catechisticall doctrine. Let me know (say these high-flying men) what God meant to doe with man, before ever God meant to make man: I care not for that Law that *Moses* hath written; That every man can read; That he might have received from God, in one day; Let me know the Cabal, that which passed betweene God and him, in all the rest of the forty dayes. I care not for Gods revealed Will, his Acts of Parliament, his publique Proclamations, Let me know his Cabinet Counsailes, his ⁶⁴⁰ bosome, his pocket dispatches. Is there not another kinde of Predesti-nation, then that which is revealed in Scriptures, which seemes to be onely of those that beleeve in Christ? May not a man be saved, though he doe not, and may not a man bee damned, though he doe performe those Conditions, which seeme to make sure his salvation in the Scriptures? Beloved, our Countreyman *Holkot,* upon the booke of Wisdome, sayes well of this Wisdome, which we must seeke in the Booke of God: After he hath magnified it in his harmonious manner, (which was the style of that time) after he had said, *Cujus authore nihil sublimius,* That the Author of the Scripture was the highest ⁶⁵⁰ Author, for that was God, *Cujus tenore nihil solidius,* That the assurance of the Scripture was the safest foundation, for it was a Rock, *Cujus valore nihil locupletius,* That the riches of the Scripture was the best treasure, for it defrayed us in the next World, After he had pursued his way of Elegancy, and called it *Munimentum Majestatis,* That Majesty and Soveraignty it selfe was established by the Scriptures, and *Fundamentum firmitatis,* That all true constancy

was built upon that, and *Complementum potestatis,* That the exercise
of all power, was to be directed by that, he reserves the force of all
to the last, and contracts all to that, *Emolumentum proprietatis,* The
660 profit which I have, in appropriating the power and the wisdome of
the Scriptures to my selfe: All wisdome is nothing to me, if it be not
mine: and I have title to nothing, that is not conveyed to me, by God,
in his Scriptures; and in the wisdome manifested to me there, I rest.
I looke upon Gods Decrees, in the execution of those Decrees, and
I try whether I be within that Decree of Election, or no, by examining
my selfe, whether the marks of the Elect be upon me, or no, and so I
appropriate the wisdome of the Scripture to my selfe. A stupid negligence in the practicall things of this World, To do nothing; and an
implicite credulity in doctrinall things, To beleeve all; and so also, a
670 crafty preventing, and circumventing in the Practicall part; and a
subtile, and perplexing intricacy, in the Doctrinall part; The first on
this side, The other beyond, do both transgresse from that Wisdome
of God, which is the Sonne, and, in such a respect, are sins, especially
against the second Person in the Trinity.

Number 16.

Preached at Lincolns Inne.

COLOS. 1.24. *WHO NOW REJOYCE IN MY SUFFERINGS FOR YOU, AND FILL UP THAT WHICH IS BEHIND OF THE AFFLICTIONS OF CHRIST IN MY FLESH, FOR HIS BODIES SAKE WHICH IS THE CHURCH.*

WE ARE NOW to enter into the handling of the doctrine of Evangelicall counsailes; And these words have been ordinarily used by the writers of the Roman Church, for the defence of a point in controversie between them and us; which is a preparatory to that which hereafter is to be more fully handled upon another Text. Out of these words, they labour to establish works of supererogation, in which (they say) men doe or suffer more then was necessary for their owne salvation; and then the superfluity of those accrues to the Treasury of the Church, and by the Stewardship, and dispensation of the Church may be applied to other men living here, or suffering in Purgatory by way of satisfaction to Gods justice; But this is a doctrine which I have had occasion heretofore in this place to handle; And a doctrine which indeed deserves not the dignity to be too diligently disputed against; And as we will not stop upon the disproving of the doctrine, so we need not stay long, nor insist upon the vindicating of these words, from that wresting and detortion of theirs, in using them for the proofe of that doctrine. Because though at first, they presented them with great eagernesse and vehemence, and assurance, *Quicquid hæretici obstrepunt, illustris hic locus,* say the Heretiques what they can, this is a clear and evident place for that doctrine, yet another after him is a little more cautelous and reserv'd, *Negari non potest quin ita exponi possint,* it cannot be denied, but

Greg. de Valent.

Bellar.

332

that these words may admit such an exposition; And then another
more modified then both says, *Primò & propriè non id intendit*
Apostolus; the Apostle had no such purpose in his first and proper
intention to prove that doctrine in these words. *Sed innuitur ille*
sensus; qui etsi non genuinus, tamen à pari deduci potest: some such
sense (says that author) may be implied and intimated, because,
though it be not the true and naturall sense, yet by way of compari-
30 son, and convenience, such a meaning may be deduced. Generally
their difference in having any patronage for that corrupt doctrine out
of these words, appeares best in this, that if we consider their authors
who have written in controversies, we shall see that most of them
have laid hold upon these words for this doctrine; because they are
destitute of all Scriptures, and glad of any, that appear to any, any
whit that way inclinable; But if we consider those authors, who by
way of commentary and exposition (either before, or since the controversies have been stirred) have handled these words, we shall find
none of their owne authors of that kind, which by way of exposition
40 of these words doth deliver this to be the meaning of them, that
satisfaction may be made to the justice of God by the works of
supererogation of one man for another.

Cornel.
à Lapide

To come then to the words themselves in their true sense, and
interpretation, we shall find in them these two generall considerations. First, that to him that is become a new creature, a true
Christian, all old things are done away, and all things are made new:
As he hath a new birth, as he hath put on a new man, as he is going
towards a new *Jerusalem,* so hath he a new Philosophy, a new production, and generation of effects out of other causes, then before, he
50 finds light out of darknesse, fire out of water, life out of death, joy
out of afflictions; *Nunc gaudeo, now I rejoyce in my sufferings &c.*
And then in a second consideration he finds that this is not by miracle,
that he should hope for it but once, but he finds an expresse, and
certaine, and constant reason why it must necessarily be so, because I
fill up that which is behind of the afflictions of Christ &c. It is strange
that I should conceive joy out of affliction, but when I come to see the
reason that by that affliction, *I fill up the sufferings of Christ &c.* it
is not strange, it cannot chuse but be so. The parts then will be but
two, a proposition, and a reason; But in the first part it will be fit to

Divisio

⁶⁰ consider first, the person, not meerely who it is, but in what capacity, the Apostle conceives this joy; And secondly, the season, Now, for joy is not always seasonable, there is a time of mourning, but now rejoycing; And then in a third place we shall come to the affection it selfe, Joy, which when it is true, and truly placed, is the nearest representation of heaven it selfe to this world. From thence we shall descend to the production of this joy, from whence it is derived, and that is out of sufferings, for this phrase *in passionibus, in my suffer-ings,* is not in the middest of my sufferings, it is not that I have joy and comfort, though I suffer, but *in passionibus* is so in suffering, as ⁷⁰ that the very suffering is the subject of my joy, I had no joy, no occa-sion of joy, if I did not suffer. But then these sufferings which must occasion this joy, are thus conditioned, thus qualified in our text; That, first, it be *passio mea, my suffering,* and not a suffering cast by my occasion upon the whole Church, or upon other men; *mea,* it is determined and limited in my selfe, and *mea,* but not *pro me,* not for my selfe, not for mine owne transgressions, and violating of the law, but it is for others, *pro vobis,* says the Apostle, for out of that root springs the whole second part, why there appertaines a joy to such sufferings, which is that the suffering of Christ being yet, not un-⁸⁰ perfect, but unperfected, Christ having not yet suffered all, which he is to suffer to this purpose, for the gathering of his Church, I fill up that which remaines undone; And that *in Carne,* not onely in spirit and disposition, but really in my flesh; And all this not only for the making sure of mine own salvation, but for the establishing and edifying a Church, but yet, his Church; for men seduced, and seducers of men have their Churches too, and suffer for those Churches; but this is for his Church, and that Church of his which is properly *his body,* and that is the visible Church: and these will be the particu-lar branches of our two generall parts, the proposition, *Gaudeo in* ⁹⁰ *afflictionibus &c.* And the reason, *Quia adimpleo &c.*

1 Part
Ego
To beginne then with the first branch of the first part, The person; we are sure it was Saint *Paul,* who we are sure was an Apostle, for so he tells the *Colossians* in the beginning of the Epistle; *Paul an Apostle of Jesus Christ, by the will of God,* but yet he was not
Rom. 11.13
properly, peculiarly their Apostle, he was theirs as he was the Apostle of the *Gentiles;* but he was not theirs, as he was the Apostle of the

Corinthians; If I be not an Apostle to others (says he) *yet doubtlesse
I am to you;* for amongst the *Corinthians* he had laid the foundations
of a Church, *Are ye not my worke in the Lord?* (says he there) but
100 for the *Colossians,* he had never preached to them, never seen them;
Epaphras had laid the foundation amongst them; And *Archippus*
was working, now at the writing of this Epistle, upon the upper
buildings, as we may see in the Epistle it selfe; *Epaphras* had planted,
and *Archippus* watered; How entred *Paul?* First as an Apostle, he
had a generall jurisdiction, and superintendency over them, and over
all the *Gentiles,* and over all the Church; And then, as a man whose
miraculous conversion, and religious conversation, whose incessant
preaching, and whose constant suffering, had made famous, and
reverend over the whole Church of God, all that proceeded from him
110 had much authority, and power, in all places to which it was directed;
As himselfe says of *Andronicus* and *Junia* his kinsmen; that they
were *Nobiles in Apostolis,* Nobly spoken of amongst the Apostles,
so Saint *Paul* himselfe was *Nobilis Apostolus in Discipulis,* rever-
endly esteemed amongst all the Disciples, for a laborious Apostle;
Saint *Augustine* joyned his desire to have heard Saint *Paul* preach,
with his other two wishes, to have seen *Christ* in the flesh, and to
have seen *Rome* in her glory; And Saint *Chrysostome* admires
Rome, so much admired by others for other things, for this principally, that she had heard Saint *Paul* preach; And that, *Sicut corpus*
120 *magnum & validum, ita duos haberet illustres oculos,* as she was a
great and glorious body, so she had two great and glorious eyes; The
presence and the memories of Saint *Peter,* and Saint *Paul;* he writes
not to them then meerely as an Apostle, not in that capacity, for he
joines *Timothy* with himselfe at the beginning of the Epistle, who
was no Apostle, properly; though upon that occasion, of *Pauls* writing in his owne, and in *Timothies* name, Saint *Chrysostome* saies,
in a larger sense, *Ergo Timotheus Apostolus,* if *Timothy* be in commission with *Paul, Timothy* is an Apostle too: But Saint *Paul* by his
fame and estimation, having justly got a power and interest in them,
130 he cherishes that by this salutation, and he binds them the more to
accept his instructions, by giving them a part in all his persecutions,
and by letting them see, how much they were in his care, even in
that distance. A servile application of himselfe to the humors of

1 Cor. 9.1

Col. 1.7;
4.17

Rom. 16.7

August.

Chrysost.

Chrysost.

others, becomes not the Minister of God; It becomes him not to depart from his ingenuity, and freedome, to a servile humoring, but to be negligent of their opinion of him, with whom he is to converse, and upon whose conscience he is to worke, becomes him not neither. It is his doctrine that must beare him out; But if his discretion doe not make him acceptable too, his doctrine will have the weaker
140 roote; when Saint *Paul* and the *Colossians* thought well of one another, the work of God was likely to goe forward amongst them; And where it is not so, the work prospers not.

Nunc   This was then the person; *Paul,* as he had a calling, and an authority by the Apostleship, and *Paul* as he had made his calling, and authority, and Apostleship easy, and acceptable to them, by his wisedome and discreet behaviour towards them, and the whole Church. The season followes next, when he presents this doctrine to them, *Nunc Gaudeo,* now I rejoyce, and there is a *Nunc illi,* and a *Nunc illis* to be considered, one time it hath relation to Saint *Paul* himselfe,
150 and another that hath relation to the *Colossians.*

Illi   His time, the *Nunc illi,* was *nunc in vinculis,* now when he was in prison at *Rome,* for from thence he writ this Epistle; Ordinarily a prisoner is the lesse to be beleeved for his being in prison and in fetters, if he speak such things as conduce to his discharge of those fetters, or his deliverance from that imprisonment, it is likely enough that a prisoner will lye for such an advantage; But when Saint *Paul* being now a prisoner for the preaching of the Gospell, speaks still for the advancement of the Gospell, that he suffers for, and finds out another way of preaching it by letters and by epistles, when he opens
160 himselfe to more danger, to open to them more doctrine, then that was very credible which he spake, though in prison; There is in all
Irenæ.   his epistles *impetus Spiritus sancti,* as *Irenæus* says, a vehemence of
Chrysost.   the holy Ghost, but yet *amplius habent quæ è vinculis,* says St. *Chrysostome,* Those epistles which Saint *Paul* writ in prison, have more of this vehemency in them: a sentence written with a cole upon a wall by a close prisoner, affects us when we come to read it; Stolne letters, by which a prisoner adventers the losse of that liberty which he had, come therefore the more welcome, if they come. It is not always a bold and vehement reprehension of great persons, that is
170 argument enough of a good and a rectified zeale, for an intemperate

use of the liberty of the Gospell, and sometimes the impotency of a satyricall humor, makes men preach freely, and over-freely, offensively,
scandalously; and so exasperate the magistrate; God forbid that a man
should build a reputation of zeale, for having been called in question
for preaching of a Sermon; And then to think it wisdome, *redimere se*
quo queat minimo, to sinke againe and get off as good cheape as he
can; But when the malignity of others hath slandred his doctrine, or
their galled consciences make them kicke at his doctrine, then to proceed with a Christian magnanimity, and a spirituall Nobility in the
180 maintenance of that doctrine, to preferre then before the greatnesse of
their persons and before the greatnesse of his owne danger, the greatnesse of the glory of God, and the greatnesse of the losse which Gods
Church should suffer by his levity and prevarication: To edifie others
by his constancy, then when this building in apparence and likelyhood
must be raised upon his owne ruine, then was Saint *Pauls Nunc,* concerning himselfe, then was his season to plant and convey this doctrine
to these *Colossians,* when it was most dangerous for him to doe so.

   Now to consider this season and fitnesse as it concerned them, The
Nunc illis; It was then, when *Epaphras* had declared unto him their
190 love, and when upon so good testimony of their disposition, he had
a desire that they might be fulfilled with knowledge of Gods will in
all wisdome and spirituall understanding, as he says *verse* 9. when
he knew how farre they had proceeded in mysteries of the Christian
Religion, and that they had a spirituall hunger of more, then it was
seasonable to present to them this great point, that Christ had suffered throughly, sufficiently, aboundantly, for the reconciliation of
the whole world, and yet that there remained some sufferings, (and
those of Christ too) to be fulfilled, by us; That all was done, and
yet there remained more to be done; that after Christs *consummatum*
200 *est,* which was all the text, there should be an *Adimplendum est,*
interlined, that after Christ had fulfilled the Law, and the Prophets
by his sufferings, Saint *Paul* must fulfill the residue of Christs sufferings, was a doctrin unseasonably taught, till they had learnt much,
and shewed a desire to learn more; In the Primitive Church men of
ripe understandings were content to think two or three yeares well
spent in learning of Catechisms and rudiments of Christian Religion;
and the greatest Bishops were content to think that they discharged

Illis
[Col. 1.7, 8]

Gennadius

their duties well, if they catechized ignorant men in such rudiments, for we know from *Gennadius* an Ecclesiasticall author, that the ²¹⁰ Bishops of Greece, and of the Eastern Church, did use to con S. *Cyrils* sermons (made at Easter and some other Festivals) without book, and preached over those Sermons of his making, to Congregations of strong understandings, and so had more time for their Catechizing

Optatus

of others; *Optatus* thinks, that when Saint *Paul* says, *Ego plantavi, Apollos rigavit, I planted the faith, and Apollos watered,* he intended in those words, *Ego de pagano feci catechumenum, ille de catechumeno Christianum,* That Saint *Paul* took ignorant persons into his charge, to catechize them at first, and when they were instructed by

Tertull.

him, *Apollos* watered them with the water of Baptism; *Tertullian* ²²⁰ thought hee did young beginners in the knowledge of Christianity no wrong, when he called them *catulos infantiæ recentis, nec perfectis luminibus reptantes,* Young whelps which are not yet come to a perfect use of their eyes, in the mysteries of Religion. Now God hath delivered us in a great measure from this weaknesse in seeing, because we are catechized from our cradles, and from this penury in preaching, we need not preach others Sermons, nor feed upon cold meat, in Homilies, but wee are fallen upon such times too, as that men doe not thinke themselves Christians, except they can tell what God meant to doe with them before he meant they should bee Chris- ²³⁰ tians; for we can be intended to be Christians, but from Christ; and wee must needs seek a Predestination, without any relation to Christ; a decree in God for salvation, and damnation, before any decree for the reparation of mankind, by Christ. Every Common-placer will adventure to teach, and every artificer will pretend to understand the purpose, yea, and the order too, and method of Gods eternall and unrevealed decree; Saint *Paul* required a great deal more knowledge then these men use to bring, before he presented to them, a great deal lesse point of Doctrin then these men use to aske.

Gaudium

This was then the *Nunc illis* their season, when they had humbly ²⁴⁰ received so much of the knowledge of the fundamentall points of Religion, Saint *Paul* was willing to communicate more and more, stronger and stronger meat unto them; That which he presents here is, that which may seem least to appertain to a Christian, (that is Joy) because a Christian is a person that hath surrendred himself over to a sad and a serious, and a severe examination of all his actions, that all bee done to the glory of God; but for all this, this joy, true joy is truly, properly, onely belonging to a Christian; because this joy is the Testimony of a good conscience, that wee have received God, so as God hath manifested himself in Christ, and worshipt God, so God hath ordained, in a true Church. There are many *tesseræ externæ,* outward badges and marks, by which others may judge, and pronounce mee to bee a true Christian; But the *tessera interna,* the inward badge and marke, by which I know this in my selfe, is joy; The blessednesse of heaven it selfe, Salvation, and the fruits of Paradise, (that Paradise which cannot be expressed, cannot be comprehended) have yet got no other name in the subtilty of the Schools, nor in the fulnesse of the Scriptures, but to be called the joys of heaven; Essentiall blessednesse is called so, *Enter into thy Masters joy,* that is, into the Kingdome of heaven; and accidentall happinesse added to that essentiall happinesse is called so too: There is joy in heaven at the conversion of a sinner; and so in the *Revelation, Rejoyce ye heavens, and yee that dwell in them, for the accuser of our brethren is cast down;* There is now joy even in heaven, which was not there before; Certainly as that man shall never see the Father of Lights after this life, to whom the day never breaks in this life: As that man must never look to walk with the Lamb wheresoever he goes in heaven, that ranne away from the Lamb whensoever he came towards him, in this life; so he shall never possesse the joyes of heaven hereafter, that feels no joy here; There must be joy here, which *Tanquam Cellulæ mellis* (as Saint *Bernard* says in his mellifluous language) as the honey-comb walles in, and prepares, and preserves the honey, and is as a shell to that kernell; so there must bee a joy here, which must prepare and preserve the joys of heaven it self, and be as a shell of those joys. For heaven and salvation is not a Creation, but a Multiplication; it begins not when wee dye, but it increases and dilates it self infinitely then; Christ himself, when he was pleased to feed all that people in the wildernesse, he asks first, *Quot panes habetis, how many loafes have you?* and then multiplyed them abundantly, as conduced most to his glory; but some there was before. *When thou goest to receive that bread, of which whosoever eates shall never dye,* the bread of life in the Land of life, Christ shall

Marginal notes:

Matth. 25.21

Luke 15.7 and 10 12.10

Bernard

[Mat. 15.34]

consider what joy thou broughtest with thee out of this world, and
he shall extend and multiply that joy unexpressibly; but if thou carry
none from hence, thou shalt find none there. Hee that were to travell
into a far country, would study before, somewhat the map, and the
manners, and the language of the Country; Hee that looks for the
fulnesse of the joyes of heaven hereafter, will have a taste, an insight
in them before he goe: And as it is not enough for him that would
travail, to study any language indifferently (were it not an imperti-
²⁹⁰ nent thing for him that went to lye in France, to study Dutch?) So
if wee pretend to make the joys of heaven our residence, it is a madnesse to study the joys of the world; *The Kingdome of heaven is
righteousnesse, and peace, and joy in the Holy Ghost,* says Saint *Paul;*
And this Kingdome of heaven is *Intra nos,* says Christ, it is in us,
and it is joy that is in us; but every joy is not this Kingdome, and
therefore says the same Apostle, *Rejoyce in the Lord;* There is no
other true joy, none but that; But yet says he there, *Rejoyce, and
again, I say rejoice;* that is, both again we say it, again, and again we
call upon you to have this spirituall joy, for without this joy ye have
³⁰⁰ not the earnest of the Spirit; And it is *again rejoyce,* bring all the
joys ye have, to a second examination, and see if you can rejoyce in
them again; Have you rejoyced all day in Feasts, in Musickes, in
Conversations? well, at night you must be alone, hand to hand with
God. *Again, I say rejoyce,* sleep not, till you have tryed whether your
joy will hold out there too. Have you rejoyced in the contemplation
of those temporall blessings which God hath given you? 'tis well,
for you may do so: But yet again I say *Rejoyce;* call that joy to an
accompt, and see whether you can rejoyce again, in such a use of
those blessings, as he that gave them to you, requires of you. Have
³¹⁰ you rejoyced in your zeal of Gods service? that's a true rejoycing in
the Lord; But yet still rejoyce again, see that this joy be accompanyed
with another joy; that you have zeal with knowledge: *Rejoyce,* but
rejoyce again, refine your joy, purge away all drosse, and lees from
your joy, there is no false joy enters into heaven, but yet no sadnesse
neither.

There is a necessary sadnes in this life, but even in this life necessary only so, as Physick is necessary, *Tristitia data, ut peccata de-
leamus,* It is *Data,* a gift of God, a sadnes and sorrow infused by him,

Rom. 14.17

[Luke
17.21]
Phil. 4.4

Tristitia
Chrysost.

and not assumed by our selves upon the crosses of this world; And
³²⁰ so it is physick, and it is *Morbi illius peccati,* it is proper and peculiar
physick for that disease, for sinne; But, (as that Father pathetically
enlarges that consideration) *Remedium lippitudinis non tollit alios
morbos,* water for sore eyes, will not cure the tooth-ach, sorrow and
sadnesse which is prescribed for sinne, will not cure, should not be
applyed to the other infirmities and diseases of our humane condition; *Pecunia mulctatus est,* (says that Father still) *Doluit, non
emendavit,* A man hath a decree passed against him in a Court of
Justice, or lost a Ship by tempest, and hee hath griev'd for this, hath
this revers'd the decree, or repaired the shipwrack? *Filium amisit,*
³³⁰ *doluit, non resuscitavit.* His Son, his eldest Son, his onely Son, his
towardly Son is dead, and he hath grieved for this; hath this raised
his Son to life again? *Infirmatur ipse, doluit, abstulit morbum?* Himself is fallen into a consumption, and languishes, and grieves, but
doth that restore him? Why no, for sadnesse, and sorrow is not the
physick against decrees, and shipwracks, and consumptions, and
death: But then *Peccavit quis* (says he still) *& doluit? peccata delevit;*
Hath any man sinned against his God, and come to a true sorrow
for that sinne? *peccata delevit* he hath wash't away that sinne, from
his soule; for sorrow is good for nothing else, intended for nothing
³⁴⁰ else, but onely for our sinnes, out of which sadnesse first arose: And
then, considered so, this sadnesse is not truly, not properly sadnesse,
because it is not so intirely; There is health in the bitternesse of
physique; There is joy in the depth of this sadnesse; Saint *Basill*
inforces those words of the Apostle, 2 *Cor.* 6.10. *Quasi tristes, semper
autem gaudentes,* usefully to this point; *Tristitia nostra habet quasi,
gaudium non habet,* Our sorrow, says he, hath a limitation, a modifi-
cation, it is but as it were sorrow, and we cannot tell whether we may
call it sorrow or no, but our joy is perfect joy, because it is rooted in
an assurance: *Est in spe certa,* our hope of deliverance is in him that
³⁵⁰ never deceived any; for, says he then, our sadnesse passes away as a
dreame, *Et qui in somnium judicat, addit quasi, quasi dicebam, quasi
equitabam, quasi cogitabam,* he that tells his dreame, tells it still in
that phrase, me thought I spoke, me thought I went, and me thought
I thought, so all the sorrow of Gods children is but a *quasi tristes,*
because it determines in joy, and determines soon. To end this, be-

Concor. 2
in Psal. 48

cause there is a difference *inter delectationem & gaudium,* between
delight and joy (for delight is in sensuall things, and in beasts, as
well as in men, but joy is grounded in reason, and in reason rectified,
which is, conscience) therefore we are called to rejoyce againe; to try
360 whether our joy be true joy, and not onely a delight, and when it is
found to be a true joy, we say still rejoyce, that is, continue your
spirituall joy till it meet the eternall joy in the kingdome of heaven,
and grow up into one joy, but because sadnesse and sorrow have but
one use, and a determined and limited imployment, onely for sin,
we doe not say, be sorry, and again be sorry, but when you have been
truly sorry for your sinnes, when you have taken that spirituall
physique, beleeve your selfe to be well, accept the seale of the holy
Ghost, for the remission of your sins, in Christ Jesus, and come to
that health which that physique promises, peace of conscience.

In passio- 370   This joy then which Saint *Paul* found to be so essentiall, so neces-
nibus   sary for man, he found that God placed within mans reach; so neare
him as that God afforded man this joy where he least looked for it,
even in affliction; And of this joy in affliction, we may observe three
steps, three degrees; one is indeed but halfe a joy; and that the
Philosophers had; A second is a true joy, and that all Christians have;
but the third is an overflowing, and aboundant joy, to which the
Apostle was come, and to which by his example, hee would rouse
2 Cor. 7.4   others, that joy, of which himselfe speaks againe; *I am filled with
comfort and am exceeding joyfull, in all our tribulations;* The first
380 of these, which we call a halfe joy, is but an indolency, and a forced
unsensiblenesse of those miseries which were upon them; a searing
up, a stupefaction, is not of the senses, yet of the affections; That
resolution which some morall men had against misery, *Non facies
ut te dicam malam,* no misery should draw them to doe misery that
honour, as to call it misery; And, in respect of that extreme anguish
which out of an over tendernesse, ordinary men did suffer under the
calamities of this life, even this poore indolency and privation of
griefe, was a joy, but yet but a halfe joy; the second joy, which is a
true joy, but common to all Christians, is that assurance, which they
390 have in their tribulations, that God will give them the issue with
the temptation; not that they pretend not to feel that calamity, so the
Philosophers did, but that it shall not swallow them, this is naturall

to a Christian, he is not a Christian without this; Thinke it not 1 Pet. 4.12
strange, says the Apostle, as though some strange thing were come
unto you, (for we must accustome our selves to the expectation of
tribulation) but rejoyce, says he, and when his glory shall appeare,
yee shall be made glad and rejoyce; He bids us rejoyce, and yet all
that he promises, is but rejoycing at last, he bids us rejoyce, all the
way; though the consummate, and undeterminable joy come not till
400 the end, yet God hath set bounds to our tribulations, as to the sea,
and they shall not overflow us; But this perfect joy (to speake of
such degrees of perfection, as may be had in this life) this third joy,
the joy of this text, is not a collaterall joy, that stands by us in the
tribulation, and sustaines us, but it is a fundamentall joy, a radicall
joy, a viscerall, a gremiall joy, that arises out of the bosome and
wombe and bowels of the tribulation it selfe. It is not that I rejoyce,
though I be afflicted, but I rejoyce because I am afflicted; It is not
because I shall not sink in my calamity, and be buried in that valley,
but because my calamity raises me, and makes my valley a hill, and
410 gives me an eminency, and brings God and me nearer to one another,
then without that calamity I should have been, when I can depart
rejoycing, and that therefore, because I am counted worthy to suffer Acts 5.41
rebuke for the name of Christ, as the Apostles did, when I can feel
that pattern proposed to my joy, and to my tribulation, which Christ
gives, *Rejoyce and be glad, for so persecuted they the Prophets,* when Matth. 5.12
I can find that seale printed upon me, by my tribulation, If ye be 1 Pet. 4.14
railed on for the name of Christ, blessed are ye, for the spirit of God
and of glory resteth on you, that is, that affliction fixes the holy Ghost
upon me, which in prosperity, falls upon me but as Sun-beames;
420 Briefly if my soule have had that conference, that discourse with God,
that he hath declared to me his purpose in all my calamities, (as he
told *Ananias* that he had done to *Paul, he is a chosen vessell unto
me, for I will shew him how many things he must suffer for my sake)* Acts 9.16
If the light of Gods Spirit shew us the number, the force, the intent
of our tribulations, then is our soule come to that highest joy, which
she is capable of in this life, when as cold and dead water, when it
comes to the fire, hath a motion and dilatation and a bubling and a
kind of dancing in the vessell, so my soule, that lay asleep in prosperity, hath by this fire of Tribulation, a motion, a joy, an exaltation.

430   This is the highest degree of suffering; but this suffering hath this condition here, that it be *passio mea;* And this too, that it be *mea,* and not *pro me,* but *pro aliis:* that it be mine, and no bodies else, by my occasion; That it be mine without any fault of mine, that I be no cause that it fell upon me, and that I be no occasion, that it fall upon others. And first, it is not mine, if I borrow it; I can have no joy in the sufferings of Martyrs and other Saints of God, by way of applying their sufferings to me, by way of imitation and example I may, by way of application and satisfaction I cannot, borrowed sufferings are not my sufferings: They are not mine neither, if I steale
440 them, if I force them; If my intemperate, and scandalous zeal, or pretence of zeal, extort a chastisement from the State, if I exasperate the Magistrate and draw an affliction upon my self, this stoln suffering, this forced suffering is not *passio mea,* it is not mine, if it should

not be mine; *Natura cujusque rei est, quam Deus indidit,* That onely is the nature of every thing which God hath imprinted in it: That affliction onely is mine, which God hath appointed for me, and what

he hath appointed we may see by his exclusions: Let none of you suffer as a murtherer, or as a thief, or as an evill doer, or as a busiebody in other mens matters, (and that reaches far:) I am not *pos-*
450 *sessor bonæ fidei,* I come not to this suffering by a good title, I cannot call it mine; I may finde joy in it, that is, in the middest of it, I may finde comfort in the mercy of Christ, though I suffer as a malefactor; But there is no joy in the suffering it self, for it is not mine, it is not I, but my sinne, my breach of the law, my disobedience that suffers. It is not mine again, if it be not mine in particular, mine, and limited in me. To those sufferings that fall upon me for my conscience, or for the discharge of my duty, there belongs a joy, but when the whole Church is in persecution, and by my occasion especially, *or at all,* woe unto them, by whom the first offence comes; this is no joyfull
460 matter, and therefore *væ illis per quos scandalum,* they who by their ambition of preferment, or indulgence to their present ease, or indifferency how things fall out, or presumptuous confidence in Gods care, for looking well enough to his own, how little soever they doe, give way to the beginnings of superstition, in the times of persecution; when persecutions come, either they shall have no sufferings, that is, God shall suffer them to fall away, and refuse their testimony in his

cause, or they shall have no joy in their sufferings, because they shall
see this persecution is not theirs, it is not limited in them, but induced
by their prevarication upon the whole Church; And lastly, this suf-
470 fering is not mine, if I stretch it too far; if I over-value it, it is not
mine; A man forfeits his priviledge, by exceeding it; There is no joy
belongs to my suffering, if I place a merit in it; *Meum non est cujus
nomine nulla mihi superest actio,* says the Law; That's none of mine
for which I can bring no action; and what action can I bring against
God, for a reward of my merit? Have I given him any thing of mine?
Quid habeo quod non accepi? what have I that I received not from
him? Have I given him all his own? how came I to abound then,
and see him starve in the streets in his distressed members? Hath he
changed his blessings unto me into single mony? Hath he made me
480 rich by half pence and farthings; and yet have I done so much as
that for him? Have I suffered for his glory? Am not I *vas figuli,* a   [Jer. 19.11]
potters vessell, and that Potters vessel; and whose hand soever he
imploys, the hand of sicknesse, the hand of poverty, the hand of justice, the hand of malice, still it is his hand that breakes the vessell,
and this vessell which is his own; for, can any such vessell have a
propriety in it selfe, or bee any other bodies primarily then his, from
whom it hath the beeing? To recollect these, if I will have joy in
suffering it must be mine, mine, and not borrowed out of an imaginary treasure of the Church, from the works of others Supererogation:
490 mine, and not stollen or enforced by exasperating the Magistrate to
a persecution: mine by good title and not by suffering for breach of
the Law; mine in particular, and not a generall persecution upon the
Church by my occasion; And mine by a stranger title then all this,
mine by resignation, mine by disavowing it, mine by confessing that
it is none of mine; Till I acknowledge, that all my sufferings even
for Gods glory, are his works, and none of mine, they are none of
mine, and by that humility they become mine, and then I may rejoyce
in my sufferings.

Through all our sufferings then, there must passe an acknowledge-   *Pro vobis*
500 ment that we are unprofitable servants; towards God utterly unprofitable; So unprofitable to our selves, as that we can merit nothing by
our sufferings; but still we may and must have a purpose to profit
others by our constancy; it is *Pro vobis,* that Saint *Paul* says hee suf-

2 Cor. 12.15
1 Cor. 1.13

2 Cor. 1.6

Phil. 2.17

4.1

1 Thes. 2.19

fers for them, for their souls; *I will most gladly bestow, and be bestowed for your soules,* (says he.) But *Numquid Paulus crucifixus pro vobis,* was *Paul* crucified for you? is his own question; as he suffered for them here, so we may be bold to say he was crucified for them; that is, that by his crucifying and suffering, the benefit of Christs sufferings, and crucifying might be the more cheerfully em-⁵¹⁰braced by them, and the more effectually applyed to them; *Pro vobis,* is *Pro vestro commodo,* for your advantage, and to make you the more active in making sure your own salvation; *We are afflicted* (says he) *for your consolation;* that's first, that you might take comfort, and spirituall courage by our example, that God will no more forsake you, then he hath done us, and then, hee addes *salvation* too; for your consolation and salvation; for our sufferings beget this consolation; and then, this consolation facilitates your salvation; and then, when Saint *Paul* had that testimony in his own conscience, that his purpose in his sufferings, was *Pro illis,* to advantage Gods children, ⁵²⁰and then saw in his experience so good effect of it, as that it wrought, and begot faith in them, then the more his sufferings encreast, the more his joys encreast; Though (says he) I be offered up, upon the service, and sacrifice of your faith, I am glad and rejoyce with you all; And therefore hee calls the Philippians, who were converted by him, *Gaudium, & Coronam,* his Joy and his Crown; not onely a Crown, in that sense, as an auditory, a congregation that compasses the Preacher, was ordinarily called a Crown, *Corona.* (In which sense that Martyr *Cornelius* answered the Judge, when he was charged to have held intelligence, and to have received Letters from ⁵³⁰Saint *Cyprian* against the State, *Ego de Corona Domini,* (says he) from Gods Church, 'tis true, I have, but *Contra Rempublicam,* against the State, I have received no Letters.) But not onely in this sense, Saint *Paul* calls those whom he had converted, his Crown, his Crown, in the Church; but he cals them his Crown in heaven, *What is our hope, our joy, our Crown of rejoycing, are not even you it?* and where? *even in the presence of our Lord Jesus Christ at his coming,* says the Apostle; And therefore not to stand upon that contemplation of Saint *Gregories,* that at the Resurrection *Peter* shall lead up his converted Jewes, and *Paul* his converted Nations, and every ⁵⁴⁰Apostle his own Church; Since you, to whom God sends us, doe as well make up our Crown, as we doe yours, since your being wrought upon, and our working upon you conduce to both our Crowns, call you the labour, and diligence of your Pastors, (for that's all the suffering they are called to, till our sins together call in a persecution) call you their painfulnesse your Crown, and we shall call your applyablenesse to the Gospel, which we preach, our Crown, for both conduce to both; but especially childrens children, are the Crown of the Elders, says *Solomon:* If when we have begot you in Christ, by our preaching, you also beget others by your holy life and conversation, 550 you have added another generation unto us, and you have preached over our Sermons again, as fruitfully as we our selves; you shall be our Crown, and they shall be your Crowns, and Christ Jesus a Crown of everlasting glory to us all. Amen.

Pro. 17.6

Number 17.

Preached at Saint Pauls upon
Christmasse day, 1621.

JOHN 1.8. *HE WAS NOT THAT LIGHT, BUT WAS*
SENT TO BEAR WITNESSE OF THAT LIGHT.

IT IS AN injury common to all the Evangelists, (as *Irenæus* notes)
that all their *Gospels* were severally refused by one Sect of *Hereticks* or other. But it was proper to Saint *John* alone, to be refused
by a Sect, that admitted *all the* other three Evangelists, (as *Epiphanius* remembers) and refused onely Saint *John*. These were the
Alogiani, a limme and branch of the *Arians*, who being unable to
looke upon the glorious Splendour, the divine Glory, attributed by
Saint *John* to this *Logos*, (which gave them their name of *Alogiani*)
this *Word*, this *Christ*, not comprehending this *Mystery*, That *this*
[Joh. 1.1]   10 *Word was so with God, as that it was God;* they tooke a round way,
and often practised, to condemne all that they did not understand,
and therefore refuse the whole *Gospell*. Indeed his *whole Gospell* is
comprehended in the beginning thereof. In this *first Chapter* is contracted all that which is extensively spred, and dilated through the
whole Booke. For here is first, the *Foundation* of all, the *Divinitie*
of Christ, to the 15. verse. Secondly, the *Execution* of all, the *Offices*
of Christ, to the 35. verse. And then the *Effect*, the *Working*, the
Application of all, that is, who were to *Preach* all this, to the ends of
the world, the *calling of his Apostles,* to the end of the Chapter. For
20 the first, *Christs Divinity*, there is enough expressed in the very first
verse alone: for, there is his *Eternitie,* intimated in that word, *In*
principio, in the beginning. The first booke of the Bible, *Genesis,* and
the last booke, (that is, that which was *last written*) *this Gospell,*
begin both with this word, *In the beginning.* But the *last* beginning
was the *first,* if *Moses* beginning doe onely denote the *Creation,* which

was not 6000. yeares since, and Saint *Johns,* the *Eternity of Christ,*
which no Millions, multiplied by Millions, can calculate. And then,
as his *Eternitie,* so his *distinction of Persons,* is also specified in this
1. verse, when the *Word,* (that is, *Christ*) is said to have been *apud*
30 *Deum, with God.* For, therefore, (saith Saint *Basil*) did the *Holy
Ghost* rather choose to say *apud Deum,* then *in Deo, with God,* then
in God, ne auferendæ Hypostaseos occasionem daret, lest he should
give any occasion of denying the same *Nature,* in divers *Persons;*
for it doth more clearly notifie a distinction of Persons, to say, he was
with him, then to say, he was *in him;* for the severall Attributes of
God, (*Mercy* and *Justice,* and the rest) are *in God,* and yet they are
not distinct Persons. Lastly, there is also expressed in this 1. verse
Christs *Equality* with God, in that it is said, *& Verbum erat Deus,*
and *this Word was God.* As it was *in the beginning,* and therefore
40 *Eternall,* and as it was *with God,* and therefore a *distinct* Person, so
it was *God,* and therefore *equall* to the Father; which phrase doth
so vexe and anguish the *Arians,* that being disfurnished of all other
escapes, they corrupted the place, onely with a false interpunction,
and broke of the words, where they admitted no such pause; for, they
read it thus, *Verbum erat apud Deum;* (so far, well) *Et Deus erat.*
There they made their point; and then followed in another sentence:
Verbum hoc erat in principio, &c.

The first part then of this Chapter, (and indeed of the whole Gospell) is in that 1. verse the *manifestation* of his *Divine Nature,* in his
50 *Eternitie,* in the *distinction* of Persons, in the *equalitie* with the
Father. The second part of the Chapter layeth downe the *Office of
Christ,* his *Propheticall,* his *Priestly,* his *Royall Office.* For the first,
the Office of a *Prophet* consisting in three severall *exercises,* to *manifest* things *past,* to *foretell* things *to come,* and to *expound* things
present, Christ declared himself to be a Prophet in all these three: for,
for the first, he was not onely a *Verball,* but an *Actuall* manifester of
former *Prophecies,* for all the former Prophecies were accomplished
in his *Person,* and in his *deeds,* and *words,* in his *actions* and *Passion.*
For the second, his foretelling of *future* things, he foretold the state
60 *of the Church,* to the end of the world. And for the third (declaring
of *present things*) He told the *Samaritan woman,* so exquisitely, all
her own History, that she gave presently that attestation, *Sir, I see*   John 4.19

that thou art a Prophet: so his *Propheticall* Office, is plainly laid down. For his *second* Office, his *Priesthood,* that is expressed in the 36. verse, *Behold the Lambe of God;* for, in this, he was our *Priest,* that he was our *Sacrifice;* he was our *Priest,* in that he offered him-selfe for our sinnes. Lastly, his *Royall Office* was the *most naturall* to him of all the rest. The Office of a *Prophet* was *Naturall* to none; none was *born* a Prophet. Those who are called the *children of the*
70 *Prophets,* and the *sonnes of the Prophets,* are but the *Prophets Dis-ciples.* Though the Office of *Priesthood,* by being annexed to *one Tribe,* may (in some sense) be called *Naturall,* yet in Christ it could not be so, for he was not of that Tribe of *Levi:* so that he had no

[Psa. 110.4;
Heb. 6.20]

interest in the *legall Priesthood,* but *was a Priest according to the Order of Melchisedec.* But his Title to be *King,* was *naturall,* by *descent,* he was of the *bloud Royall,* and the nearest in succession; so that he, and onely he, had, *De Jure,* all the *three unctions* upon him. *David* had *two;* he was both a *Prophet,* and a *King;* he had those two capacities; *Melchisedec* had *two* too; he was both a *King* and a *Priest;*
80 he had two: Onely Christ had all *three,* both a *Prophet,* and *Priest,* and *King.*

In the third part of the Chapter, which is *the calling of foure of his Apostles,* we may observe that the first that was called, was not *Peter,* but *Andrew;* that there might be laid at first some interruption, some stop to their zealous fury, who will still force, and heap up every action which any way concerns Saint *Peter,* to the building up of his imaginary *primacy,* which primacy, they cared not though *Peter* wanted, if they could convey that primacy to his *Successor,* by any *other Title;* for which Successours sake it is, and not for Saint *Peters*
90 own, that they are so over diligent in advancing his *prerogative.* But, it was not *Peter,* that was called, but *Andrew.* In *Andrews* present and earnest application of himself to *Christ,* we may note, (and onely so) divers particulars, fit for use and imitation. In his first question, *Master, where dwellest thou?* there is not onely, (as *Cyrill* observes) a reverent ascribing to him *a power of instructing* in that compellation, *Master,* but a desire to have more time afforded to hearken to his instructions, *Where dwellest thou,* that I may dwell with thee? And as soon as ever he had taken in some good portion of knowledge *himselfe,* he conceives presently a desire to communicate his hap-

[100] pinesse with *others;* and he seeks his brother *Peter,* and tells him, *Invenimus Messiam, we have found the Messias;* which is, (as Saint *Chrysostome* notes) *vox quærentis:* In this, that he rejoyces in the finding of him, he testifies that he had sought him, and that he had continued in the expectation of a *Messias* before. *Invenit Messiam,* he had found the *Messias;* but, saith the Text, *Duxit ad Jesum,* he brought his brother the glorious newes of having found a *King,* the King of the Jewes, but he led him to *Jesus,* to a *Saviour;* that so, all kinds of happinesse, *temporall* and *spirituall,* might be intimated in this discovery of a *King,* and of a *Saviour;* What may not his servants [110] hope for at his hands, who is both those, a *King* and a *Saviour,* and hath *worldly* preferments, and the Glory of *Heaven in his power?*

Now, though the words of this Text, (*He was not that light, but was sent to beare witnesse of that light*) are placed in the first part of the Chapter, that which concernes *Christs Divine nature,* yet they belong, and they have a respect to all three; To his *Divine nature,* to his *Offices,* and to his *Calling of his Apostles:* For, first, *light* denotes his *Divine nature;* secondly, the testimony that is given of him by *John Baptist,* (of whom the words of our Text are spoken) declares him to be the *Messias,* and *Messias,* (which signifies *anointed*) in- [120] volves all his *Offices,* for his *three Offices,* are his *three vocations,* and thirdly, the Application of this testimony, given by *Iohn Baptist* here, by the *Apostles* and their *Successors* after, intimates or brings to our memory this their first *vocation,* in this Chapter. So that the Gospel of Saint *Iohn* containes all *Divinity,* this Chapter *all the Gospell,* and this Text all the *Chapter.* Therefore it is too large to goe through at this time; at this time we shall insist upon such branches as arise out of that consideration, *what, and who this light is,* (for, we shall finde it to be both a *personall light,* (it is *some body*) and, otherwise too, a *reall light,* (it is *some thing*) therefore we inquire, *what,* this light [130] is, (*what thing*) and *who* this light is, (*what person*) which *John Baptist* is denied to be. Hereafter we shall consider, *the Testimony* which is given of this light; in which part in due time, we shall handle, the *person* of the witnesse *John Baptist,* in whom we shall finde many considerable, and extraordinary circumstances: and then, his *Citation,* and calling to this testimony; and thirdly, the *testimony* it selfe that he gave: and lastly, *why any testimony* was requisite to so evident a thing as *light*. But the first part, *who*, and *what* this light is, belongs most properly to *this day*, and will fill that portion of the day, which is afforded us for this exercise. Proceed we therefore to that, ¹⁴⁰ *John Baptist* was not that light, *who was, what was?*

1 Part

Quis lux

　　　Though most expositors, as well ancient, as modern agree with one generall, and unanime consent, that *light* in this *verse* is intended and meant of *Christ*, Christ is this light, yet in some precedent and subsequent passages in this Chapter, I see other senses have been admitted of this word, *light*, then perchance those places will beare; certainly other then those places need: particularly in the *fourth verse* (*In it was life, and that life was the light of men*) there they understand *life*, to be nothing but this *naturall life* which we breath, and *light* to be onely that *naturall light, naturall reason*, which distinguishes us ¹⁵⁰ *men*, from other creatures. Now, it is true that they may have a pretence for some ground of this interpretation in antiquity it selfe, for, so says Saint *Cyrill, Filius Dei Creativè illuminat*, Christ doth enlighten us, in creating us. And so some others of the *Fathers*, and some of the *Schooles*, understand by that light *naturall Reason*, and that life, conservation in life. but this interpretation seemes to me subject to both these dangers, that it goes so farre, and yet reaches not home. So far, in wresting in *divers* senses into a word, which needs but *one*, and is of it selfe cleare enough, that is *light*, and yet reaches not home, for it reaches not to the *essentiall light*, which is ¹⁶⁰ *Christ Jesus*, nor to the *supernaturall light*, which is *Faith* and *Grace*, which seemes to have been the Evangelists principall scope, to declare the comming of *Christ*, (who is the *essentiall light*) and his purpose in comming, to raise and establish a Church, by *Faith* and *Grace*, which is the *supernaturall light:* For, as the holy Ghost himselfe

1 Ioh. 5.12

interprets *life* to be meant of Christ, (*He that hath the Sonne hath life*) so we may justly doe of *light* too, *he that sees* the Sonne, the *Sonne of God hath light*. For, light is never, (to my remembrance) found in any place of the Scripture, where it must necessarily signifie the light of nature, *naturall reason;* but wheresoever it is transferred ¹⁷⁰ from the naturall to a figurative sense, it takes a higher signification then *that;* either it signifies *Essentiall* light, Christ Jesus, (which answers our first question, *Quis lux, who is this light*, it is *Christ, personally*) or it signifies the *supernaturall light* of *Faith* and *Grace*,

(which answers our second question, *Quid lux, what is this light,* for
it is the *working of Christ,* by his Spirit, in his *Church,* in the infusion
of *Faith* and *Grace,* for *beliefe,* and *manners*) And therefore though
it be ever lawfull, and often times very usefull, for the raising and
exaltation of our devotion, and to present the plenty, and abundance
of the *holy Ghost* in the *Scriptures,* who satisfies us as with marrow,
¹⁸⁰ and with fatnesse, to induce the *diverse senses* that the Scriptures doe
admit, yet this may not be admitted, if there may be danger thereby,
to neglect or weaken the *literall sense* it selfe. For there is no necessity
of that *spirituall wantonnesse* of finding more then necessary senses;
for, the more *lights* there are, the more *shadows* are also cast by
those many lights. And, as it is true in religious duties, so is it in
interpretation of matters of Religion, *Necessarium & Satis conver-*
tuntur; when you have done that you ought to doe in your calling,
you have done enough; there are no such *Evangelicall counsailes,* as
should raise workes of *supererogation,* more then you are bound to
¹⁹⁰ doe, so when you have the *necessary sense,* that is the meaning of the
holy Ghost in that place, you have senses enow, and not till then,
though you have never so many, and never so delightfull.

Light therefore, is in all this Chapter fitliest understood of *Christ;*   *Illa lux*
who is noted here, with that distinctive article, *Illa lux, that light.*
For, *non sic dicitur lux, sicut lapis;* Christ is not so called *Light,* as he   Augustin.
is called a *Rock,* or a *Cornerstone;* not by a metaphore, but truly, and
properly. It is true that the Apostles are said to be *light,* and that with
an article, *the light;* but yet with a limitation and restriction, *the light*   Mat. 5.[14]
of the world, that is, set up to convey light to the world. It is true that
²⁰⁰ *John Baptist* himselfe was called *light,* and with large additions,
Lucerna ardens, a burning, and a shining lampe, to denote both his   Ioh. 5.[35]
owne *burning zeale,* and the *communicating* of this his light to others.
It is true, that *all the faithfull* are said to be *light in the Lord;* but all   Ephe. 5.[8]
this is but to signifie that they had been in darknesse before; they had
been beclouded, but were now illustrated; they were light, but light
by *reflexion,* by illustration of a greater light. And as in the first
creation, *vesper & mane dies unus, The evening and the morning*   [Gen. 1.5]
made the day, evening before *morning, darknesse* before *light,* so in
our *regeneration,* when wee are made *new Creatures,* the Spirit of
²¹⁰ God findes us in *naturall darknesse,* and by him we are made *light in*

the Lord. But Christ himselfe, and hee onely, is *Illa lux, vera lux;*
that light, the true light. Not so opposed to those other lights, as
though the *Apostles*, or *John Baptist*, or the *faithfull*, who are called
lights, were *false* lights; but that they were *weake* lights. But Christ
was *fons lucis*, the fountaine of all their light; light so, as no body else
was so; so, as that hee was nothing but light. Now, neither the
Apostles, nor *John Baptist*, nor the *Elect*, no nor the *virgin Mary*
(though wee should allow all that the *Roman Church* aske in her
behalfe) for the Roman Church is not yet come to that searednesse,
220 that obduratenesse, that impudency, as to pronounce that the *virgin*
Mary was *without originall sinne,* (though they have done many
shrewd acts towards it, to the prejudice of the contrary opinion) yet
none of these were so light, as they were nothing but light. *Moses*
himselfe who received and delivered the law, was not so; and to
intimate so much, there was an illustration, and irradiation upon *his*
face, but not so of *all his body*. Nay, *Christ Jesus* himselfe, who fulfilled the law, *as man,* was not so; which he also intimated in the
greatest degree of glorification which he accepted upon earth, which
Luke 9.29   was his *transfiguration,* for, though it be said in that, *That the fashion*
230 *of his Countenance was changed, and his garment was white, and*
Tertull.   *glistered,* yet, *lineamenta Petro agnoscibilia servavit,* hee kept that
former proportion of body, that *Peter* could know him by it. So that
this was not a glorifying of the body, and making it *thorough light;*
but hee suffered his *Divine nature* to appeare and shine thorough his
flesh, and not to swallow, or annihilate that flesh. All other men, by
occasion of this flesh, have darke *clouds,* yea *nights,* yea long and
frozen winter nights of *sinne,* and of the *works of darknesse*. Christ
was incapable of any such nights, or any such clouds, any approaches
towards *sinne;* but yet Christ admitted some *shadowes,* some such
240 degrees of *humane infirmity,* as by *them,* he was willing to show, that
the nature of man, in the best perfection thereof, is not *vera lux, tota*
lux, true light, all light, which he declared in that *Si possibile,* and
Mat. 26.39   that *Transeat calix, If it bee possible, let this cup passe;* words, to
which himselfe was pleased to allow so much of a retractation, and
a correction, *Veruntamen, yet Father,* whatsoever the sadnesse of my
soule have made mee say, *yet, not my will but thine be done; not*
mine, but thine; so that they were not altogether, *all one;* humane

infirmity made some difference. So that no one man, not Christ, (considered but so as man) was *tota lux,* all light, no cloud. No not *man-*
²⁵⁰ *kinde,* consider it *collectively,* can bee light so, as that there shall bee no darknesse. It was not so, when all mankind was in one *person,* in *Adam.* It is said sometimes in School, that *no man* can keep the commandements, yet *man, collectively,* may keep them. They intend no more herein, but that some one man may abstaine from doing any act against worshipping of *Images,* another from *stealing,* another from *adultery,* and others from others. But if it were possible to compose a man of such elements, as that the principallest vertues, and eminencies of all other men, should enter into his composition, and if there could bee found a man, as perfect in all particular vertues, as
²⁶⁰ *Moses* was in meeknesse, (who was a *meeke man, above all the men that were upon the earth*) yet this man would not bee *vera lux, tota lux,* true light, all light. *Moses* was not so *meeke,* but that hee *slew the Egyptian,* nor so meek, but that hee disputed and expostulated with *God* many times, passionately. Every man is so far from beeing *tota lux,* all light, as that he hath still *within him,* a darke vapor of *originall sinne,* and the cloud of *humane flesh without him.*

    Nay not onely no man, (for so we may consider him in the whole course of his life) but *no one act,* of the most perfect, and religious man in the world, though that act employ but halfe a minute in the
²⁷⁰ doing thereof, can bee *vera lux,* true light, all light, so perfect light, as that it may serve another, or thy selfe, for a lanthorne to his, or thy feet, or a light to his, or thy steps, so that hee or thou may thinke it enough to doe so still. For, another man may doe so good works, as it may justly work to thy shame, and confusion, and to the aggravating of thy condemnation, that thou livest not as well as *hee,* yet, it would not perchance serve thy turne, to live *but* so well; for, *to whom God gives more, of him he requires more.* No man hath *veram lucem,* true light, thorough light; no man hath *meridiem, Augem,* that high point that casts no shadow, because, besides *originall sinne,*
²⁸⁰ that ever smoakes up, and creates a soote in the soule, and besides *naturall infirmities,* which become sinnes, when wee consider *Grace,* no man does carry his good actions to that heighth as, by that grace, which God affords him, hee might doe. Slacker men have a declination even in their *mornings;* a *West* even in their *East;* coolings, and

Numb. 12. [3]

[Luke 12.48]

faintnesses and after-noones, as soon as they have any dawnings, any breake of day, any inchoation of any spirituall action or purpose. Others have some farther growth, and increasing, and are more diligent in the observation of spirituall duties; but yet they have not their *meridiem,* their *Augem,* their noon, their *south point,* no such
290 heighth, as that they might not have a higher, by that *grace* which they have received. In the best degree of our best actions, particularly in this service, which wee doe to God at this houre, if we brought with us hither a religious purpose to sanctifie this festivall, if wee answer to the callings of his most blessed Spirit, whilest wee are here, if wee carry away a detestation of our sinnes, and a holy purpose of amendment of life, this is a good degree of proficiency, and God bee blessed, if any of us all arrive to that degree; but yet, this is not *vera lux,* true light, all light; for, who amongst us can avoid the testimony of his conscience, that since he begun this present service to God, his
300 thoughts have not strayed upon *pleasures* and *vanities* or *profit,* and leapt the walls of this Church, yea, perchance within the walls of this flesh, which should bee the *Temple of the holy Ghost?* Besides, to become *vera lux, tota lux,* true light, thorough light, requires *perseverance* to the end. So that till our naturall light goe out, wee cannot say that wee have this light; for, as the darknesse of hell fire is, so this light of this heavenly fire, must bee everlasting. If ever it go cleane out, it was never throughly kindled, but kindled to our farther damnation; it was never *vera lux,* true light, for, as one office of the *law* is, but to show sinne, so all the *light of grace* may end in
310 this, to show me my desperate estate, from the abuse of grace. In all Philosophy there is not so darke a thing as *light;* As the sunne, which is *fons lucis naturalis,* the beginning of naturall light, is the most evident thing to bee seen, and yet the hardest to be looked upon, so is naturall light to our reason and understanding. Nothing clearer, for it is *clearnesse* it selfe, nothing darker, it is enwrapped in so many scruples. Nothing nearer, for it is round about us, nothing more remote, for wee know neither entrance, nor limits of it. Nothing more *easie,* for a child discerns it, nothing more *hard,* for no man understands it. It is apprehensible by *sense,* and not comprehensible by
320 *reason.* If wee winke, wee cannot chuse but see it, if we stare, wee know it never the better. No man is *yet* got so neare to the knowledge of the

qualities of light, as to know whether *light* it selfe be a *quality,* or a
substance. If then this *naturall light* be so darke to our naturall reason, if wee shall offer to pierce so far, into the light of this text, the
Essentiall light Christ Jesus, (in his nature, or but in his *offices*) or
the *supernaturall light* of *faith* and *grace,* (how far *faith* may be had,
and yet lost, and how far the *freewill* of man may concur and
cooperate with *grace,* and yet *still* remaine nothing in it selfe) if wee
search farther into these points, then the Scripture hath opened us a
330 way, how shall wee hope to unentangle, or extricate our selves? They
had a precious composition for *lamps,* amongst the *ancients,* reserved
especially for *Tombes,* which kept light for many hundreds of yeares;
we have had *in our age* experience, in some casuall openings of
ancient vaults, of finding such lights, as were kindled, (as appeared
by their inscriptions) *fifteen* or *sixteen hundred* yeares before; but,
as soon as that light comes to our light, it vanishes. So this *eternall,*
and this *supernaturall light, Christ* and *faith,* enlightens, warmes,
purges, and does all the profitable offices of *fire,* and *light,* if we keep
it in the right spheare, in the proper place, (that is, if wee consist in
340 *points necessary* to salvation, and *revealed* in the Scripture) but when
wee bring this light to the common light of *reason,* to our inferences,
and consequencies, it may be in danger to vanish it selfe, and perchance extinguish our reason too; we may search so far, and reason
so long of *faith* and *grace,* as that we may lose not onely *them,* but
even our reason too, and sooner become *mad* then *good.* Not that we
are bound to believe any thing *against reason,* that is, to believe, we
know not why. It is but a slacke opinion, it is not *Beliefe,* that is not
grounded upon reason. He that should come to a *Heathen man,* a
meere naturall man, uncatechized, uninstructed in the rudiments of
350 the Christian Religion, and should at first, without any preparation,
present him first with this necessitie; Thou shalt burn in fire and
brimstone eternally, except thou believe *a Trinitie of Persons, in an
unitie of one God,* Except thou believe the *Incarnation* of the second
Person of the Trinitie, the Sonne of God, Except thou believe that *a
Virgine had a Sonne,* and the same Sonne that God had, and that
God was Man too, and being the immortall God, yet died, he should
be so farre from working any spirituall cure upon this poore soule, as
that he should rather bring Christian Mysteries into scorne, then *him*

to a beliefe. For, that man, if you proceed so, Believe all, or you
360 burne in Hell, would finde an easie, an obvious way to escape all;
that is, first not to believe *Hell* it selfe, and then nothing could binde
him to believe the rest.

The *reason* therefore of Man, must first be satisfied; but the way
of such satisfaction must be *this,* to make him see, That this World,
a frame of so much harmony, so much concinnitie and conveniencie,
and such a correspondence, and subordination in the parts thereof,
must necessarily have had a workeman, for nothing can make it selfe:
That no such workeman would deliver over a frame, and worke, of
so much Majestie, to be governed by *Fortune,* casually, but would
370 still retain the Administration thereof in his owne hands: That if he
doe so, if he made the World, and *sustaine* it still by his watchfull
Providence, there belongeth a worship and service to him, for doing
so: That therefore he hath certainly revealed to man, what kinde of
worship, and service, shall be acceptable to him: That this manifestation of his Will, must be permanent, it must be *written,* there must
be a *Scripture,* which is his *Word* and his *Will:* And that therefore,
from that Scripture, from that Word of God, all Articles of our
Beliefe are to bee drawne.

If then his *Reason* confessing all this, aske farther proofe, how he
380 shall know that *these Scriptures* accepted by the Christian Church,
are the true Scriptures, let him bring any other Booke which pre-
tendeth to be the Word of God, into comparison with these; It is
true, we have not a *Demonstration;* not such an Evidence as that one
and two, are three, to prove these to be Scriptures of God; God hath
not proceeded in that manner, to drive our Reason into a pound, and
to force it by a peremptory necessitie to accept these for Scriptures, for
then, here had been no exercise of our *Will,* and our assent, if we
could not have resisted. But yet these Scriptures have so orderly, so
sweet, and so powerfull a working upon the reason, and the under-
390 standing, as if any third man, who were utterly discharged of all
preconceptions and anticipations in matter of Religion, one who were
altogether *neutrall,* disinteressed, unconcerned in either party, nothing towards a *Turke,* and as little toward a *Christian,* should heare
a *Christian* plead for his Bible, and a *Turke* for his Alcoran, and
should weigh the evidence of both; the Majesty of the *Style,* the

punctuall accomplishment of the *Prophecies,* the harmony and concurrence of the *foure Evangelists,* the consent and unanimity of the
Christian Church ever since, and many other such reasons, he would
be drawne to such an Historicall, such a Grammaticall, such a Logicall
400 beliefe of our Bible, as to preferre it before any other, that could be
pretended to be the Word of God. He would believe it, and he would
know *why* he did so. For let no man thinke that *God* hath given him
so much ease here, as to save him by believing he knoweth not what,
or why. *Knowledge* cannot save us, but we cannot be saved without
Knowledge; Faith is not on this side Knowledge, but beyond it; we
must necessarily come to *Knowledge* first, though we must not stay
at it, when we are come thither. For, a regenerate Christian, being
now a *new Creature,* hath also *a new facultie of Reason:* and so
believeth the Mysteries of Religion, out of another Reason, then as a
410 meere naturall Man, he believed naturall and morall things. He believeth them for their own sake, by *Faith,* though he take *Knowledge*
of them before, by that common Reason, and by those humane Arguments, which worke upon other men, in naturall or morall things.
Divers men may walke by the Sea side, and the same beames of the
Sunne giving light to them all, one gathereth by the benefit of that
light pebles, or speckled shells, for curious vanitie, and another
gathers precious Pearle, or medicinall Ambar, by the same light. So
the common light of reason illumins us all; but one imployes this
light upon the searching of impertinent vanities, another by a better
420 use of the same light, finds out the Mysteries of Religion; and when
he hath found them, loves them, not for the lights sake, but for the
naturall and true worth of the thing it self. Some men by the benefit
of this light of Reason, have found out things profitable and usefull
to the whole world; As in particular, *Printing,* by which the learning
of the whole world is communicable to one another, and our minds
and our inventions, our wits and compositions may trade and have
commerce together, and we may participate of one anothers understandings, as well as of our Clothes, and Wines, and Oyles, and other
Merchandize: So by the benefit of this light of reason, they have
430 found out *Artillery,* by which warres come to quicker ends then heretofore, and the great expence of bloud is avoyded: for the numbers of
men slain now, since the invention of Artillery, are much lesse then

before, when the sword was the executioner. Others, by the benefit
of this light have searched and found the secret corners of gaine, and
profit, wheresoever they lie. They have found wherein the weake-
nesse of another man consisteth, and made their profit of that, by
circumventing him in a bargain: They have found his riotous, and
wastefull inclination, and they have fed and fomented that disorder,
and kept open that leake, to their advantage, and the others ruine.
440 They have found where was the easiest, and most accessible way, to
sollicite the Chastitie of a woman, whether *Discourse, Musicke,* or
Presents, and according to that discovery, they have pursued *hers,* and
their own eternall destruction. By the benefit of this light, men see
through the darkest, and most impervious places, that are, that is,
Courts of Princes, and the greatest *Officers* in Courts; and can submit
themselves to second, and to advance the humours of men in great
place, and so make their profit of the weaknesses which they have
discovered in these great men. All the wayes, both of *Wisdome,* and
of *Craft* lie open to this light, this light of naturall reason: But when
450 they have gone all these wayes by the benefit of this light, they have
got no further, then to have walked by a tempestuous Sea, and to have
gathered pebles, and speckled cockle shells. Their light seems to be
great out of the same reason, that a Torch in a misty night, seemeth
greater then in a clear, because it hath kindled and inflamed much
thicke and grosse Ayre round about it. So the light and wisedome of
worldly men, seemeth great, because he hath kindled an admiration,
or an applause in Aiery flatterers, not because it is so in deed.

But, if thou canst take this light of reason that is in thee, this poore
snuffe, that is almost out in thee, thy faint and dimme knowledge of
460 God, that riseth out of this light of nature, if thou canst in those
embers, those cold ashes, finde out one small coale, and wilt take the
paines to kneell downe, and blow that coale with thy devout *Prayers,*
and light thee a *little candle,* (a *desire* to reade that Booke, which
they call the Scriptures, and the Gospell, and the Word of God;) If
with that little candle thou canst creep humbly into low and poore
places, if thou canst finde thy Saviour in a *Manger,* and in his
swathing clouts, in his humiliation, and blesse God for that beginning, if thou canst finde him flying into Egypt, and finde in thy
selfe a disposition to accompany him in a persecution, in a banish-

470 ment, if not a bodily banishment, a locall banishment, yet a *reall, a spirituall banishment,* a banishment from those sinnes, and that sinnefull conversation, which thou hast loved more then thy *Parents,* or *Countrey,* or thine owne body, which perchance thou hast consumed, and destroyed with that sinne; if thou canst finde him contenting and containing himselfe at home in his fathers house, and not breaking out, no not about the worke of our salvation, till the due time was come, when it was to be done. And if according to that example, thou canst contain thy selfe in that station and vocation in which God hath planted thee, and not, through a hasty and precipitate

480 *zeale,* breake out to an imaginary, and intempestive, and unseasonable *Reformation,* either in *Civill* or *Ecclesiasticall* businesse, which belong not to thee; if with this little poore light, these *first degrees* of *Knowledge* and *Faith,* thou canst follow him into the *Garden,* and gather up some of the droppes of his precious Bloud and sweat, which he shed for thy soule, if thou canst follow him to *Jerusalem,* and pick up some of those *teares,* which he shed upon that City, and upon thy soule; if thou canst follow him to the place of his scourging, and to his crucifying, and provide thee some of that balme, which must cure thy soule; if after all this, thou canst turne this little light inward, and canst

490 thereby discerne where thy diseases, and thy wounds, and thy corruptions are, and canst apply those teares, and blood and balme to them, (all this is, That if thou attend the light of naturall reason, and cherish that, and exalt that, so that that bring thee to a *love of the Scriptures,* and that *love to a beleefe* of the truth thereof, and that *historicall faith* to a *faith of application, of appropriation,* that as all those things were certainly done, so they were certainly done *for thee*) thou shalt never envy the lustre and glory of the great lights of worldly men, which are great by the infirmity of others, or by their own opinion, great because others think them great, or because they

500 think themselves so, but thou shalt finde, that howsoever they magnifie their lights, their wit, their learning, their industry, their fortune, their favour, and *sacrifice to their owne nets,* yet thou shalt see, that thou by thy small light hast gathered *Pearle* and *Amber,* and they by their great lights nothing but shels and pebles; they have determined the light of nature, upon the booke of nature, this world, and thou hast carried the light of nature higher, thy naturall reason,

Habak. 1.
[16]

and even *humane arguments,* have brought thee to reade the Scriptures, and to that *love,* God hath set to the seale of *faith.* Their light shall set at noone; even in their heighth, some heavy crosse shall cast
510 a damp upon their soule, and cut off all their succours, and devest them of all comforts, and thy light shall grow up, from a *faire hope,* to a modest assurance and *infallibility,* that that light shall never go out, nor the *works of darknesse,* nor the *Prince of darknesse* ever prevaile upon thee, but as thy light of *reason* is exalted by *faith* here, so thy light of *faith* shall be exalted into the light of *glory,* and fruition in the Kingdome of heaven. Before the sunne was made, there was *a light* which did that office of distinguishing night and day; but when the sunne was created, that did all the offices of the former light, and more. *Reason* is that first, and primogeniall light,
520 and goes no farther in a naturall man; but in a man regenerate by faith, that light does all that reason did, *and more;* and all his *Morall,* and *Civill,* and *Domestique,* and indifferent actions, (though they be never done *without Reason*) yet their principall scope, and marke is the glory of God, and though they seeme but *Morall,* or *Civill,* or *domestique,* yet they have a deeper tincture, a heavenly nature, a relation *to God,* in them.

The light in our Text then, is *essentially* and *personally Christ* himself, from *him* flowes the *supernaturall light* of *faith* and *grace,* here also intended; and because this light of *faith,* and *grace* flowing
530 from that fountaine of light Christ Jesus, works upon the light of *nature,* and *reason,* it may conduce to the raising of your devotions, if we do (without any long insisting upon the severall parts thereof) present to you some of those many and divers lights, which are in this world, and admit an application to this light in our Text, the *essentiall* light, *Christ Jesus;* and the *supernaturall* light, *faith* and *grace.*

*Lux
Essentiæ*

Of these lights we shall consider some few couples; and the first payre, *Lux Essentiæ,* and *Lux Gloriæ,* the light of the *Essence of God,* and the light of the *glory of his Saints.* And though the first of these,

[1 Cor.
13.12;
1 John 3.2]
1 Tim. 6.16

be that essentiall light, by which we shall *see God face to face, as he is,*
540 and the effluence and emanation of beams, from the face of God, which make that place *Heaven,* of which light it is said, *That God who onely hath Immortality, dwels in luce inaccessibili,* in the light that none can attaine to, yet by the light of faith, and grace in

sanctification, we may come to such a *participation* of that light of
Essence, or such a *reflection* of it in this world, that it shall be true of
us, which was said of those Ephesians, *You were once darknesse, but*   5.8
now are light in the Lord; he does not say *enlightned,* nor *lightsome,*
but *light* it self, light *essentially,* for *our conversation is in heaven;*   Phil. 3.20
And as God sayes of *Jerusalem,* and his blessings here in this world,
Calceavi te Ianthino, I have shod thee, with Badgers skinne, (some   Ezek. 16.10
translate it) (which the Antients take for some *precious* stuffe) that
is, I have enabled thee to tread upon all the most estimable things of
this world, (for as the Church it self is presented, so every true member of the Church is endowed, *Luna sub pedibus,* the Moone, and all   Apo. 12.1
under the Moone is under our feet, we tread upon this world, even
when we are trodden upon in it) so the *precious promises of Christ,*   2 Pet. 1.4
make us partakers of the Divine Nature, and the light of faith, makes
us the same *Spirit with the Lord;* And this is our participation of   1 Cor. 6.17
the light of essence, in this life. The next is the light of glory.
    This is that *Glorification* which we shall have at the last day, of   *Lux Gloriæ*
which glory, we consider a great part to be in that *Denudation,* that
manifestation of all to all; as, in this world, a great part of our inglorious servitude is in those disguises, and palliations, those colours,
and pretences of *publique good,* with which men of power and
authority apparell their oppressions of the poore; In this are we the
more miserable, that we cannot see *their ends,* that there is none of
this denudation, this laying open of our selves to one another, which
shall accompany that state of glory, where we shall see one anothers
bodies, and *soules, actions* and *thoughts.* And therefore, as if this
place were now that Tribunall of Christ Jesus, and this that day of
Judgement, and denudation, we must be here, as we shall be there,
content to stand *naked* before him; content that there be a discovery,
a revealing, a manifestation of all our sinnes, wrought upon us, at
least to our owne *consciences,* though not to the congregation; If we
will have glory, we must have this *denudation.* We must not be glad,
when our sins scape the *Preacher.* We must not say, (as though there
were a comfort in that) though he have hit such a mans *Adultery,*
and anothers *Ambition,* and anothers *extortion,* yet, for all his diligence, he hath missed *my sinne;* for, if thou wouldest faine have it
mist, thou wouldest faine hold it still. And then, why camest thou

hither? What camest thou for to *Church,* or to the *Sacrament?* Why doest thou delude God, with this *complementall visit,* to come to his house, if thou bring not with thee, a disposition to his honour, and his service? Camest thou onely to try whether God *knew* thy sinne, and could tell thee of it, by the Preacher? Alas, he knowes it infallibly; And, if he take no knowledge of his knowing it, to thy *conscience,* by the words of the Preacher, thy state is the more desperate. God sends us to preach *forgivenesse of sinnes;* where wee finde no sinne, we have no Commission to execute; How shall we finde your 590 sinnes? In the old sacrifices of the law, the Priest did not fetch the sacrifice from the herd, but he received it from him that brought it, and so sacrificed it for him. Doe thou therefore prevent the Preacher; Accuse thyselfe before he accuse thee; offer up thy sinne thy selfe; Bring it to the top of thy memory, and thy conscience, that he finding it there, may sacrifice it for thee; Tune the instrument, and it is the fitter for his hand. Remember thou thine own sins, first, and then every word that fals from the preachers lips shall be a drop of the

[Gen. 27.28;   *dew of heaven,* a dram of the *balme of Gilead,* a portion of the bloud

Jer. 8.22]   of thy Saviour, to wash away that sinne, so presented by thee to be 600 so sacrified by him; for, if thou onely of all the congregation finde that the preacher hath not touched *thee,* nor hit *thy sinnes,* know then, that thou wast not in his Commission for the *Remission* of sinnes, and be afraid, that thy conscience is either *gangrend,* and unsensible of all incisions, and *cauterizations,* that can be made by denouncing the *Judgements* of God, (which is as far as the preacher can goe) or that thy whole constitution, thy complexion, thy composition is sinne; the preacher cannot hit thy particular sinne, because thy whole life, and the whole body of thy actions is one continuall sin. As long as a man is alive, if there appeare any offence in 610 his breath, the physician will assigne it to some *one* corrupt *place,* his *lungs,* or *teeth,* or *stomach,* and thereupon apply convenient remedy thereunto. But if he be dead, and putrefied, no man askes *from whence that ill aire and offence comes,* because it proceeds from thy whole carcasse. So, as long as there is in you a *sense* of your sinnes, as long as we can touch the offended and wounded part, and be felt by you, you are not desperate, though you be froward, and impatient of our increpations. But when you *feele nothing,* whatsoever wee

say, your soule is in an *Hectique fever,* where the distemper is not
in any one humor, but in the whole substance; nay, your soule it selfe
620 is become a carcasse. This then is our first couple of these lights, by
our *Conversation in heaven* here, (that is, a watchfulnesse, that we
fall not into sinne) we have *lucem essentiæ,* possession and fruition
of heaven, and of the light of Gods presence; and then, if we doe,
by infirmity, fall into sinne, yet, by this *denudation* of our soules, this
manifestation of our sinnes to God by *confession,* and to that purpose,
a gladnesse when we heare our sinnes spoken of by the preacher, we
have *lumen gloriæ,* an inchoation of our glorified estate; and then,
an other couple of these lights, which we propose to be considered,
is *lumen fidei,* and *lumen naturæ,* the light of *faith,* and the light of
630 *nature.*

Of these two lights, *Faith* and *Grace,* first, and then *Nature* and
Reason, we said something before, but never too much, because contentious spirits have cast such clouds upon both these lights, that some
have said, *Nature* doth *all* alone, and others, that Nature hath *nothing*
to do at all, but all is *Grace:* we decline wranglings, that tend not to
edification, we say onely to our present purpose, (which is the operation of these severall couples of lights) that by this light of *Faith,* to
him which hath it, all that is involved in *Prophecies,* is clear, and
evident, as in a History already done; and all that is wrapped up in
640 *promises,* is his own already in *performance.* That man needs not goe
so high, for his assurance of a *Messias* and *Redeemer,* as to the first
promise made to him in *Adam,* nor for the limitation of the stock and
race from whence this *Messias* should come: so far as to the renewing
of this promise in *Abraham:* nor for the description of this *Messias*
who he should be, and of whom he should be born, as to *Esaias;* nor
to *Micheas,* for the *place;* nor for the *time* when he should accomplish all this, so far as to *Daniel;* no, nor so far, as to the *Evangelists*
themselves, for the History and the evidence, that all this that was
to be done in his behalf by the *Messias,* was done 1600. yeares since.
650 But he hath a whole *Bible,* and an abundant Library in his own heart,
and there by this light of *Faith,* (which is not onely a knowing, but
an applying, an *appropriating* of all to thy benefit) he hath a better
knowledge then all this, then either *Propheticall,* or *Evangelicall;*
for though both these be irrefragable, and infallible proofs of a Mes-

Lux fidei

Gen. 3.15

12.3
Esay 7.14
Mich. 5.2
Dan. 9.24

sias, (the Propheticall, that he *should*, the Evangelicall, that he *is* come) yet both these might but concern others: this light of Faith brings him home *to thee*. How sure so ever I be, that the *world* shall never perish by *water*, yet *I may* be drowned; and how sure so ever

[Joh. 1.29] that the *Lamb of God hath taken away the sinnes of the world*, I may
660 perish, without I have this *applicatory Faith*. And as he needs not looke back to *Esay*, nor *Abraham*, nor *Adam*, for the Messias, so neither needs he to looke forward. He needs not stay in expectation of the *Angels Trumpets*, to awaken the dead; he is not put to his

[Rev. 6.10] *usquequo Domine, How long, Lord, wilt thou defer our restitution?*
[Num. but he hath already *died the death of the righteous;* which is, to die
23.10] to sinne; He hath already had his *buriall*, by being *buried with Christ*
[Col. 2.12] *in Baptisme*, he hath had his *Resurrection* from sinne, his *Ascension* to holy purposes of amendment of life, and his *Judgement*, that is, *peace of Conscience*, sealed unto him, and so by this light of applying
670 Faith, he hath already apprehended an eternall possession of Gods eternall Kingdome. And the other light in this second couple is *Lux naturæ*, the light of Nature.

Lux Naturæ   This, though a fainter light, directs us to the other, *Nature to Faith:* and as by the quantitie in the light of the *Moone*, we know the position and distance of the *Sunne*, how far, or how neare the Sunne is to her, so by the working of the light of *Nature* in us, we may discern, (by the measure and virtue and heat of that) how near to the other greater light, the light of *Faith*, we stand. If we finde our *naturall faculties rectified*, so as that that *free will* which we have in
680 *Morall* and *Civill* actions, be bent upon the *externall duties* of *Religion*, (as every naturall man may, out of the use of that *free will*, come to Church, heare the Word preached, and believe it to be true) we may be sure, the other greater light is about us. If we be *cold* in them, in actuating, in exalting, in using our *naturall faculties* so farre, we shall be deprived of all light; we shall not see the *Invisible* God,

Rom. 1.20 in *visible things*, which Saint *Paul* makes so *inexcusable*, so unpardonable a thing, we shall not see the hand of God in all our *worldly crosses*, nor the seal of God in all our *worldly blessings;* we shall not see the face of God in his House, his presence here in the *Church*, nor
690 the mind of God in his *Gospell*, that his gracious purposes upon mankinde, extend so particularly, or reach so far, as to include us. I shall

heare in the Scripture his *Venite omnes, come all,* and yet I shall
thinke that his eye was not upon me, that his eye did not becken me
and I shall heare the *Deus vult omnes salvos, that God would save
all,* and yet I shall finde some perverse reason in my selfe, why it is
not likely that God will save *me.* I am commanded *scrutari Scripturas, to search the scriptures;* now, that is not to be able to *repeat* any
history of the Bible without booke, it is not to *ruffle* a Bible, and
upon any word to turne to the Chapter, and to the verse; but this is
700 *exquisita scrutatio,* the true searching of the Scriptures, to finde all
the *histories* to be *examples* to me, all the *prophecies* to induce a
Saviour for *me,* all the *Gospell* to apply Christ Jesus to *me.* Turne
over all the folds, and plaits of thine owne heart, and finde there the
infirmities, and waverings of thine *owne faith,* and an ability to say,
Lord, I beleeve, help mine unbeleefe, and then, though thou have no
Bible in thy hand, or though thou stand in a dark corner, nay though
thou canst not reade a letter, thou hast searched that Scripture, thou
hast turned to *Marke* 9. *ver.* 24. Turne thine eare to God, and heare
him turning to thee, and saying to thy soule, *I will marry thee to my*
710 *selfe for ever;* and thou hast searched that Scripture, and turned to
Hos. 2. *ver.* 19. Turne to thine owne *history,* thine *owne life,* and if
thou canst reade there, that thou hast endeavoured to turne thine
ignorance into *knowledge,* and thy knowledge into *Practice,* if thou
finde thy selfe to be an example of that rule of Christs, *If you know
these things, blessed are you, if you do them,* then thou hast searched
that Scripture, and turned to *Jo.* 13. *ver.* 17. This is *Scrutari Scripturas,
to search the Scriptures,* not as though thou wouldest make a *con-
cordance,* but an *application;* as thou wouldest search a *wardrobe,*
not to make an *Inventory* of it, but to finde in it something fit for
720 thy wearing. *John Baptist was not the light,* he was not Christ, *but
he bore witnesse of him.* The light of *faith,* in the highest exaltation
that can be had, in the *Elect,* here, is not that very *beatificall vision,*
which we shall have in heaven, but it beares witnesse of that light.
The light of *nature,* in the highest exaltation is not *faith,* but it *beares
witnesse* of it. The lights of *faith,* and of *nature,* are subordinate *John
Baptists: faith* beares me witnesse, that I have *Christ,* and the light of
nature, that is, the *exalting of my naturall faculties* towards *religious
uses,* beares me witnesse that I have *faith.* Onely that man, whose

[Isa. 55.1]

[1 Tim.2.4]

[Joh. 5.39]

conscience testifies to himself, and whose *actions* testifie to the world,
⁷³⁰ that he *does* what he *can,* can beleeve himself, or be beleeved by
others, that he hath the true light of faith.

And therefore, as the Apostle saith, *Quench not the Spirit,* I say
too, *Quench not the light of Nature,* suffer not *that* light to goe out;
study your *naturall faculties;* husband and improve them, and love
the *outward acts of Religion,* though an *Hypocrite,* and though a
naturall man may doe them. Certainly he that loves not the *Militant
Church,* hath but a faint faith in his interest in the *Triumphant.* He
that cares not though the *materiall Church* fall, I am afraid is falling
from the *spirituall.* For, can a man be sure to have his *money,* or his
⁷⁴⁰ *plate,* if his *house* be burnt? or to preserve his *faith,* if the *outward
exercises* of Religion faile? He that undervalues *outward things,* in
the religious service of God, though he begin at *ceremoniall* and
rituall things, will come quickly to call *Sacraments* but outward
things, and *Sermons,* and *publique prayers,* but outward things, in
contempt. As some *Platonique* Philosophers, did so over-refine Religion, and devotion, as to say, that nothing but the *first thoughts*
and *ebullitions* of a devout heart, were fit to serve God in. If it came
to any *outward action* of the body, *kneeling,* or lifting up of *hands,*
if it came to be but invested in our *words,* and so made a *Prayer,* nay
⁷⁵⁰ if it passed but a revolving, a turning in our inward thoughts, and
thereby were mingled with our *affections,* though *pious affections,*
yet, say they, it is not pure enough for a service to God; nothing but
the *first motions* of the heart is for him. Beloved, outward things
apparell God; and since God was content to take *a body,* let not us
leave him naked, nor ragged; but, as you will bestow not onely some
cost, but some *thoughts,* some *study,* how you will clothe your *children,* and how you will clothe your *servants,* so bestow both cost and
thoughts, thinke seriously, execute cheerfully in outward declarations,
that which becomes the dignity of him, who evacuated himselfe for
⁷⁶⁰ you. The *zeale of his house* needs not *eat you up,* no nor eat you out
of house and home; God asks not *that* at your hands. But, if you eat
one dish the lesse at your feasts for his house sake, if you spare somewhat for his reliefe, and his glory, you will not be the leaner, nor the
weaker, for that abstinence. *John Baptist* bore witnesse of the light,
outward things beare witnesse of your faith, the exalting of our *nat-*

urall faculties beare witnesse of the supernaturall. We do not compare the master and the servant, and yet we thank that servant that brings us to his master. We make a great difference between the *treasure* in the chest, and the *key* that opens it, yet we are glad to
770 have that key in our hands. The *bell* that cals me to *Church,* does not catechise me, nor preach to me, yet I observe the sound of that bell, because it brings me to *him* that does those offices to me. The light of *nature* is far from being enough; but, as a *candle* may kindle a *torch,* so into the faculties of nature, well imployed, God infuses *faith.* And this is our second couple of lights, the subordination of the light of *nature,* and the light of *faith.* And a third payre of lights of *attestation,* that beare witnesse to the light of our Text, is *Lux æternorum Corporum,* that light which the *Sunne* and *Moone,* and those glorious bodies give from heaven, and *lux incensionum,* that
780 light, which those things, that are naturally combustible, and apt to take fire, doe give upon earth; both these beare witnesse of this light, that is, admit an application to it. *For,* in the first of these, the glorious lights of heaven, we must take nothing for *stars,* that are *not stars;* nor make Astrological and fixed conclusions out of *meteors,* that are but transitory; they may be *Comets,* and *blazing starres,* and so portend much mischiefe, but they are none of those *æterna corpora,* they are not fixed stars, not stars of heaven. So is it also in the *Christian Church,* (which is the proper spheare in which the light of our text, *That light* the *essentiall light* Christ Jesus moves by that supernaturall
790 light of *faith* and *grace,* which is truly the *Intelligence* of that spheare, the Christian Church) As in the heavens the stars were created at once, with one *Fiat,* and then being so made, stars doe not beget new stars, so the *Christian doctrine necessary* to salvation, was delivered at once, that is, intirely in one spheare, in the body of the Scriptures. And then, as stars doe not beget stars, Articles of faith doe not beget Articles of faith; so, as that the *Councell of Trent* should be brought to bed of *a new Creed,* not conceived before by the *holy Ghost* in the Scriptures, and, (which is a monstrous birth) the child greater then the Father, as soon as it is borne, the new Creed of the *Councell of*
800 *Trent* to containe more Articles, then the old Creed of the Apostles did. Saint *Jude* writing of the *common salvation,* (as he calls it) (for, Saint *Jude,* it seems, knew no such *particular salvation,* as that it was

Lux æternorum corporum

verse 3

impossible for *any man* to have, salvation is *common salvation*) ex-
horts them to *contend earnestly for that faith, which was once delivered unto the Saints. Semel, once;* that is, *at once, semel, simul,
once altogether.* For this is also *Tertullians* note; that the rule of faith

is, that it be *una, immobilis, irreformabilis;* it must not be *deformed,*
it cannot be *Reformed;* it must not be mard, it cannot be mended;
whatsoever needs mending, and *reformation,* cannot be the rule of

⁸¹⁰ faith, says *Tertullian. Other foundation can no man lay then Christ;*
not onely no *better,* but no *other;* what other things soever are added
by men, enter not into the nature and condition of a foundation. The
additions, and traditions, and superedifications of the Roman Church,
they are not *lux æternorum corporum,* they are not fixed bodies, they
are not stars to direct us; they may be *meteors,* and so exercise our discourse, and Argumentation, they may raise controversies; And they
may be *Comets,* and so exercise our feares, and our jealousies, they
may raise *rebellions* and *Treasons,* but they are not fixed and glorious
bodies of heaven, they are not *stars.* Their *non-communions,* (for,
⁸²⁰ communions where there are no communicants, are no communions)
when they admit no bread at all, no wine at all, all is *transubstan-
tiated,* are no communions; their *semi-communions,* when they admit
the *bread* to be given, but *not the wine;* their *sesqui-communions,*
Bread and Wine to the taste, and to all other trialls of bread and
wine, and yet that bread and wine, the very body, and the very bloud
of Christ; their *quotidian miracles,* which destroy and contradict even
the nature of the miracle, to make miracles ordinary, and fixed, constant and certain; (for, as that is not a miracle which nature does, so
that's not a miracle which man can doe certainly, constantly, infal-
⁸³⁰ libly every day, and every day, every Priest can miraculously change
bread into the body of Christ, and besides they have certaine fixed
shops, and *Marts of miracles,* in one place a shop of miracles for
barrennesse, in another, a shop for the *tooth-ache*) To contract this,
their *occasionall Divinity,* doctrines to serve present occasions, that in
eighty eight, an Hereticall Prince must necessarily be excommunicated, and an Hereticall Prince excommunicated must necessarily
be deposed, but at another time it may be otherwise, and *conveniencies,* and *dispensations* may be admitted, these, and such as these,
traditionall, occasionall, Almanack Divinity, they may bee *Comets,*

⁸⁴⁰ they may be *Meteors,* they may raine bloud, and raine fire, and raine
hailestones, *hailstones as big as Talents,* (as it is in the Revelation)
milstones, to grinde the world by their oppressions, but they are not
lux æternorum corporum, the light of the stars and other heavenly
bodies, for, they were made *at once,* and diminish not, encrease not.
Fundamentall articles of faith, are always the same. And that's our
application of this *lux æternorum corporum,* the light of those heavenly bodies, to the light of our Text, Christ working in the Church.
　　Now, for the consideration of the other light in this third couple,
which is *lux incensionum,* the light of things, which take, and give
⁸⁵⁰ light here upon earth, if we reduce it to application and practise, and
contract it to one Instance, it will appeare that the *devotion* and *zeale*
of him, that is best affected, is, for the most part, in the disposition of
a *torch,* ⁺or a *knife,*⁺ ordained to take *fire,* and to give *light.* If it have
never been *lightned,* it does not easily take light, but it must be
bruised, and *beaten* first; if it have been lighted and put out, though
it cannot take fire *of it self,* yet it does easily conceive fire, if it be
presented within any convenient distance. Such also is the soule of
man towards the fires of the *zeale* of Gods glory, and *compassion* of
others misery. If there be any that *never* tooke this fire, that was never
⁸⁶⁰ affected with either of these, the glory of God, the miseries of other
men, can I hope to kindle him? It must be Gods worke to *bruise* and
beat him, with his rod of affliction, before he will take fire. *Paulus*
revelatione compulsus ad fidem, St. *Paul* was compelled to believe;
not the light which he saw, but the power which he felt wrought
upon him; not because that light shined from heaven, but because it
strooke him to the earth. *Agnoscimus Christum in Paulo prius co-*
gentem, deinde docentem; Christ begun not upon St. *Paul,* with
a *catechisme,* but with a *rod.* If therefore here be any in *Pauls* case,
that were never kindled before, Almighty God proceed the same way
⁸⁷⁰ with *them,* and come so neare to a friendship towards them, as to be
at enmity with them; to be so mercifull to them, as to seeme unmercifull; to be so well pleased, as to seeme angry; that so by inflicting
his *medicinall afflictions,* he may give them comfort by discomfort,
and life by death, and make them seeke his face, by turning his face
from them; and not to suffer them to continue in a stupid *inconsid-*
eration, and lamentable *senslesnesse* of their miserable condition, but

[Rev. 16.21]

*Lux incen-
sionum*

Hierom.

August.

bruise and *breake* them with his rod, that they may take fire. But for you, who have taken this fire before, that have been enlightned in both *Sacraments*, and in the *preaching* of the word; in the *meanes*, 880 and in some measure of *practise* of *holinesse* heretofore, if in not supplying *oyle* to your Lamps, which God by his ordinance had kindled in you, you have let this light go out by negligence or inconsideration, or that storms of *worldly calamities* have blowne it out, do but now at this instant call to minde, *what* sin of *yesterday,* or t'other day, or long ago, begun, and practised, and prevailed upon you, or *what future sinne,* what purpose of doing a sinne to night, or to morrow, possesses you; do but thinke seriously *what sinne,* or *what crosse* hath blown out that light, that grace, which was formerly in you, before that sinne, or that crosse invaded you, and turne your 890 soul, which hath been enlightned before, towards this fire which Gods Spirit blowes this minute, and you will conceive new fire, new zeale, new compassion. As this *Lux incensionum,* kindles easily, when it hath been kindled before, so the soule accustomed to the presence of God in *holy meditations,* though it fall asleep in some darke corner, in some *sinne of infirmity,* a while, yet, upon every holy occasion, it takes fire againe, and the meanest *Preacher* in the Church, shall worke more upon him, then the *foure Doctors* of the Church should be able to do, upon a person who had never been enlightned before, that is, never accustomed to the presence of God in his *private medi-* 900 *tations,* or in his *outward acts* of Religion. And this is our third couple of lights, that *beares witnesse,* that is, admit an application to the light of our Text; and then the fourth and last couple, which we consider, is *Lux Depuratarum Mixtionum,* the light and lustre of *precious stones,* and then *Lux Repercussionum,* the light of *Repercussion,* and *Reflexion,* when one body, though it have no light in it self, casts light upon other bodies.

Lux Depu-
ratarum
Mixtionum

In the application of the first of these lights, *Depuratarum Mixtionum, precious stones,* we shall onely apply their *making* and their *value.* Precious stones are first *drops of the dew* of heaven, and then 910 refined by the sunne of heaven. When by long lying they have exhal'd, and evaporated, and breathed out all their grosse matter, and received another concoction from the sunne, then they become precious in the eye, and estimation of men: so those *actions* of ours, that

shall be precious or acceptable in the eye of God, must at first have
been conceived from *heaven*, from the *word* of God, and then receive *another concoction*, by a holy *deliberation*, before we bring
those actions to *execution*, lest we may have mistaken the roote
thereof. Actions precious, or acceptable in Gods eye, must be *holy
purposes* in their beginning, and then *done in season;* the *Dove* must
920 lay the *egge*, and hatch the *bird;* the *holy Ghost* must infuse the
purpose, and *sit* upon it, and *overshadow* it, and mature and ripen it,
if it shall be precious in Gods eye. The *reformation of abuses* in *State*
or *Church*, is a holy purpose, there is that drop of the dew of heaven
in it; but if it be *unseasonably attempted*, and have not a farther concoction, then the *first motions of our owne zeale*, it becomes in-
effectuall. Stones precious in the estimation of men, begin with the
dew of Heaven, and proceed with the *sunne of Heaven;* Actions
precious in the acceptation of God, are purposes conceived by his
Spirit, and executed in his time *to his Glory*, not conceived out of
930 *Ambition*, nor executed out of *sedition*. And this is the application of
this *Lux depuratarum mixtionum*, of precious stones, out of their
making; we proposed another out of their *valuation*, which is this,
That whereas a Pearle or Diamond of such a bignesse, of so many
Carats, is so much worth, one that is twice as big, is ten times as much
worth. So, though God vouchsafe to value every good work thou
dost, yet as they grow greater he shall multiply his estimation of
them infinitely; When he hath prized at a high rate, the *chastitie* and
continency of thy *youth*, if thou adde to this, a *moderation* in thy
middle age, from *Ambition*, and in thy latter age from *covetousnesse*
940 and *indevotion*, there shall be no price in Gods treasure (not the last
drop of the blood of his Sonne) too deare for thee, no roome, no state
in his Kingdome (not a *Jointenancie* with his onely Sonne) too glorious for thee. This is one light in this Couple; The lustre of precious
stones: the other the last is *Lux Repercussionum*, The light of Repercussion, of Reflexion.

    This is, when Gods light cast upon us, reflecteth upon *other men
too*, from us; when God doth not onely accept our works for *our
selves*, but imploves those works of ours upon *other* men. And here
is a true, and a Divine *Supererogation;* which the *Devill*, (as he doth
950 all *Gods Actions*, which fall into his compasse) did mischievously

*Lux Reper-
cussionum*

counterfeit in the *Romane Church,* when he induced their Doctrine of *Supererogation,* that a man might do so much more then he was bound to do *for God,* as that *that superplusage* might *save* whom he would; and that if he did not direct them in his intention, upon any particular person, the *Bishop of Rome,* was generall *Administrator* to all men, and might bestow them where he would. But here is a true supererogation; not from *Man,* or *his Merit,* but *from God;* when our good works shall not onely profit *us,* that *do* them, but *others* that *see them* done; and when we by this light of *Repercus-*

Tertull.   960 *sion,* of *Reflexion,* shall be made *specula divinæ gloriæ, quæ accipiunt & reddunt,* such looking glasses as *receive* Gods face upon our selves, and *cast it upon others by a holy life,* and *exemplary conversation.*

Conclusio   To end all, we have no *warmth* in *our selves;* it is true, but Christ came even in the *winter:* we have *no light* in our selves; it is true, but he came even in the *night.* And now, I appeall to your own *Consciences,* and I aske you all, (not as a *Judge,* but as an *Assistant* to your Consciences, and *Amicus Curiæ,*) whether any man have made as good use of this light, as he might have done. Is there any man that in the compassing of his *sinne,* hath not met this light by the way,

Numb.   970 *Thou shouldest not do this?* Any man, that hath not onely as *Balaam*
22.22   did, met this light as an *Angell,* (that is, met *Heavenly inspirations* to avert him,) but that hath not *heard* as *Balaam* did, *his own Asse;* that is, those reasons that use to carry him, or those very *worldly respects* that use to carry him, dispute against that sinne, and tell him, not onely that there is more *soule* and more *heaven,* and more *salvation,* but more *body,* and more *health,* more *honour,* and more *reputation,* more *cost,* and more *money,* more *labour,* and more *danger* spent upon such a sinne, then would have carried him the right way?

Recapitu-   *They that sleep, sleep in the night, and they that are drunke, are*
latio   980 *drunke in the night.* But to you the *Day starre,* the *Sunne of Right-*
1 Thes. 5.7   *eousnesse,* the Sonne of God is risen this day. The day is but a little longer now, then at *shortest;* but a *little* it is. Be a little better now, then when you came, and mend a little at every coming, and in lesse then seaven *yeares apprentissage,* which your occupations cost you, you shall learn, not the Mysteries of your *twelve Companies,* but the Mysteries of the *twelve Tribes,* of the *twelve Apostles,* of their *twelve Articles,* whatsoever belongeth to the *promise,* to the performance,

to the *Imitation* of Christ Jesus. He, who is *Lux una*, light and *light alone*, and *Lux tota*, light and *all light*, shall also, by that light, which
⁹⁹⁰ he sheddeth from himselfe upon all his, the light *of Grace*, give you all these Attestations, all these witnesses of that his light; he shall give you *Lucem essentiæ*, (really, and essentially to be incorporated into him, to be made partakers of the Divine Nature, and the same Spirit with the Lord, by a Conversation in Heaven, here) and *lucem gloriæ*, (a gladnesse to give him glory in a *denudation* of your souls, and your sinnes, by humble *confession* to him, and a gladnesse to receive a denudation and manifestation of your selves to your selves, by his messenger, in his *medicinall* and *musicall increpations*, and a gladnesse to receive an inchoation of future glory, in the remission
¹⁰⁰⁰ of those sinnes.) He shall give you *lucem fidei*, (faithfull and unremovable possession of future things, in the present, and make your *hereafter, now*, in the fruition of God.) And *Lucem naturæ* (a love of the *outward beauty* of his house, and *outward testimonies* of this love, in inclining your *naturall faculties* to religious duties.) He shall give you *Lucem æternorum Corporum*, (a love to walk in the light of the stars of heaven, that never change, a love so perfect in the *fundamentall articles* of Religion, without impertinent additions.) And *Lucem incensionum*, (an aptnesse to take holy fire, by what hand, or *tongue*, or *pen* soever it be presented unto you, according to
¹⁰¹⁰ Gods Ordinance, though that light have formerly been suffered to go out in you.) He shall give you *Lucem depuratarum Mixtionum*, (the lustre of precious stones, made of the dew of heaven, and by the heat of heaven, that is, *actions* intended at first, and produced at last, *for his glory;* and every day multiply their value, in the sight of God, because thou shalt every day grow up from grace to grace.) And *Lucem Repercussionum*, (he shall make you able to reflect and cast this light upon others, to his glory, and their establishment.)

Lighten our darknesse, we beseech thee, O Lord, with all these lights; that in thy light we may see light; that in this Essentiall *light,*
¹⁰²⁰ *which is Christ, and in this* Supernaturall *light, which is grace, we may see all these, and all other beames of light, which may bring us to thee, and* him, *and that blessed Spirit which proceeds from both. Amen.*

Essentiæ

Gloriæ

Fidei

Naturæ

Æternorum Corporum

Incensionum Depuratarum Mixtionum

Repercussionum

Number 18.

Preached upon Candlemas Day.

Rom. 12.20. *THEREFORE IF THINE ENEMY HUNGER FEED HIM, IF HE THIRST GIVE HIM DRINK; FOR, IN SO DOING THOU SHALT HEAP COALES OF FIRE ON HIS HEAD.*

IT FALLS out, I know not how, but, I take it, from the instinct of the Holy Ghost, and from the Propheticall spirit residing in the Church of God, that those Scriptures which are appointed to be read in the Church, all these dayes, (for I take no other this Terme) doe evermore afford, and offer us Texts, that direct us to patience, as though these times had especial need of those instructions. And truly so they have; for though God have so farre spared us as yet, as to give us no exercise of patience in any afflictions, inflicted upon our selves, yet, as the heart akes if the head doe, nay, if the foote ake, the heart
¹⁰ akes too; so all that professe the name of Christ Jesus aright, making up but one body, we are but dead members of that body, if we be not affected with the distempers of the most remote parts thereof. That man sayes but faintly, that he is heart-whole, that is macerated with the Gout, or lacerated with the Stone; It is not a heart, but a stone growne into that forme, that feeles no paine, till the paine seize the very substance thereof. How much and how often S. *Paul* delights himselfe with that sociable syllable, *Syn, Con, Conregnare,* and *Con-*
2 Tim. 2.12   *vificare,* and *Consedere,* of Raigning together, and living, and quick-
Eph. 2.1, 6   ning together: As much also doth God delight in it, from us, when
²⁰ we expresse it in a Conformity, and Compunction, and Compassion, and Condolency, and (as it is but a little before the Text) *in weeping with them that weepe.* Our patience therefore being actually exercised in the miseries of our brethren round about us, and probably threatned in the aimes and plots of our adversaries upon us, though

376

I hunt not after them, yet I decline not such Texts, as may direct our thoughts upon duties of that kinde.

This Text does so; for the circle of this Epistle of S. *Paul,* this precious ring, being made of that golden Doctrine, That Justification is by faith, and being enameled with that beautifull Doctrine of good
30 works too, in which enameled Ring, as a precious stone in the midst thereof, there is set, the glorious Doctrine of our Election, by Gods eternall Predestination, our Text falls in that part, which concernes obedience, holy life, good works; which, when both the Doctrines, that of Justification by faith, and that of Predestination have suffered controversie, hath been by all sides embraced, and accepted; that there is no faith, which the Angels in heaven, or the Church upon earth, or our own consciences can take knowledge of, without good works. Of which good works, and the degrees of obedience, of patience, it is a great one, and a hard one that is enjoyned in this Text;
40 for whereas S. *Augustine* observes sixe degrees, sixe steps in our behaviour towards our enemies, whereof the first is *nolle lædere,* to be loth to hurt any man by way of provocation, not to begin; And a second, *nolle amplius quam læsus lædere,* That if another provoke him, yet what power soever he have, he would returne no more upon his enemy, then his enemy had cast upon him, he would not exceed in his revenge; And a third, *velle minus,* not to doe so much as he suffered, but in a lesse proportion, onely to shew some sense of the injury; and then another is, *nolle lædere licèt læsus,* to returne no revenge at all, though he have been provoked by an injury; And a
50 higher then that, *paratum se exhibere ut amplius lædatur,* to turne the other cheeke, when he is smitten, and open himselfe to farther injuries; That which is in this Text, is the sixt step, and the highest of all, *lædenti benefacere,* to doe good to him, of whom we have received evill, *If thine enemy hunger, to feed him, if he thirst, to give him drinke; for in so, &c.*

The Text is a building of stone, and that bound in with barres of Iron: fundamentall Doctrine, in point of manners, in it selfe, and yet buttressed, and established with reasons too, *therefore,* and *for;* Therefore feed thine enemy; For, in so doing, thou shalt heape coales.
60 This *therefore,* confirmes the precedent Doctrine, and this *For,* confirmes that confirmation

Divisio

But all the words of God are Yea, and Amen, and therefore we need not insist upon reasons, to ratifie or establish them. Our parts shall be but two; *Mandatum,* and *Emolumentum;* first the Commandement, (for we dare not call it by so indifferent a name, as an Euangelicall Counsell that we may choose whether we will doe or no; It is a Commandement, *doe good to thine enemy*) And secondly, the benefit that we receive by that benefit, *we heap coales upon his head.* Each part will have divers branches: for, in the Commande-
70 ment, we shall first looke upon the person, to which God directs us, *inimicus,* though he be an *enemy,* and *inimicus tuus,* though he be *thine enemy;* but yet it is but *tuus,* thine enemy; It is not simply *inimicus homo,* the Devill, nor *inimicus vester,* a spreading enemy, an enemy to the State, nor *inimicus Dei,* an enemy to Religion; And from the person, we shall passe to the duty, *Ciba,* and *Da aquam, feed,* and *give drink,* in which, all kindes of reliefes are implyed: But that is, *si esurierit, if he be hungry;* There is no wanton nor superfluous pampering of our enemy required, but so much as may preserve the man, and not nourish the enmity. In these considerations
80 we shall determine our first part; and our second in these; First, that God takes nothing from us, without recompence; nothing for nothing; he seales his Commandement with a powerfull reason, promise of reward: And then, the reward specified here, arises from the enemy himselfe; And that reward is, That *thou shalt cast coales of fire upon his head;* and *congeres, accumulabis, Thou shalt heap coales of fire upon him.*

1 Part
Mandatum
Peltanus

It is not ill said by a Jesuit, of these words, *Sententia magis Euangelica, quàm Mosaica;* This Text, that enjoynes benefits upon our enemies, is fitter for the Gospel, then for the Law, fitter for the new,
90 then for the old Testament; and yet it is *tam Mosaica, quam Euangelica,* to shew that it is Universall, Catholique, Morall Doctrine, appertaining to Jew, and Christian, and all, this Text is in the old Testament, as well as in the new. In the mouth of two witnesses is this truth established, in the mouth of a Prophet, and in the mouth
Prov. 25.21 of an Apostle, *Solomon* had said it before, and S. *Paul* sayes it here, *If thine enemy hunger, feed him, if he thirst, &c.*

Your *Senecaes* and your *Plutarchs* have taught you an art, how to make profit of enemies, because as flatterers dilate a man, and make

him live the more negligently, because he is sure of good interpreta-
[100] tions of his worst actions; So a mans enemies contract him, and shut
him up, and make him live the more watchfully, because he is sure
to be calumniated even in his best actions: But this is a lesson above
Seneca, and *Plutarch,* reserved for *Solomon,* and Saint *Paul,* to make
profit by conferring and placing benefits upon enemies: And that is
our first branch, *Though he be an enemy.*

S. *Augustine* cites, and approves that saying of the morall Philoso-   *Etsi*
pher, *Omnes odit, qui malos odit,* he that hates ill men, hates all men,   *inimicus*
for if a man will love none but honest men, where shall he finde any
exercise, any object of his love? So if a man will hold friendship with
[110] none, nor doe offices of society to none, but to good natur'd, and
gentle, and souple, and sociable men, he shall leave very necessary
businesses undone. The frowardest and perversest man may be good
ad hoc, for such or such a particular use. By good company and good
usage, that is, by being mingled with other simples, and ingredients,
the very flesh of a Viper, is made an Antidote: A Viper loses not his
place in Physick, because he is poyson; a Magistrate ceases not to be
a Magistrate, because he is an ill man; much lesse does a man cease
to be a man, and so to have a title to those duties, which are rooted in
nature, because he is of an ill disposition. *God makes his Sun to shine*   Mat. 5.45
[120] *upon the good, and upon the bad, and sendeth raine upon the just,*
and upon the unjust. God hath made of one bloud all mankinde: [Acts 17.26]
how unkindly then, how unmanly is it to draw bloud? We come too
soone to the name of enemy, and we carry it too farre: Plaintife and
Defendant in a matter of Trespasse, must be enemies: Disputers in
a Problematicall matter of Controversie, that concernes not foundations, must be enemies; And then all enmity must imply an irrecon-
cileablenesse, once enemies may never be friends againe: we come
too soone to the name, and we stand too long upon the thing; for
there are offices and duties even to an enemy; and that, though an
[130] enemy in as high a Degree, as the word imports here, *osor,* a hater,
and *osor tuus,* such an enemy as hates thee, which is our next Branch.

We use to say, that those benefits are longest remembred, which   *Tuus*
are publique, and common; and those injuries, which are private,
and personall: But truly in both, the private, and personall makes
the greatest impression. For, if a man have benefitted the publique,

with a Colledge, with an Hospitall, with any perpetuall endowment, yet he that comes after to receive the benefit of any such place, for the most part determines his thankfulnesse upon that person, who brought him thither, and reflects little upon the founder, or those that are descended from him. And so it is in injuries, and violences too, we hate men more for personall, then for nationall injuries; more, if he have taken my Ship, then if he have attempted my Country. We should be more sensible of the publique, but because private and personall things doe affect us most, the Commandement here goes to the particular; Though he be thine enemy, and hate thee. *If you love them that love you, and lend to them that pay you, what thanks have you?* Truly not much: *Publicans doe the same,* sayes S. *Matthew; Sinners doe the same,* sayes S. *Luke:* But *love you your enemies;* For, in the same place, where Christ puts all those cases, If a man have been *angry with his Brother,* If a man have said *Racha to his Brother,* if he have called *his Brother Foole,* he ends all with that, *Agree with thine adversary;* Though he be thine adversary, yet he is thy Brother. If he have damnified thee, calumniated thee, pardon him. If he have done that to another, thou hast no power to pardon him; Herein onely thou hast exercise of greatnesse and goodnesse too, If he be thine enemy, thou and thou onely canst pardon him; and herein onely thou hast a Supremacy, and a Prerogative to shew.

So far then, the text goes literally, do good to an enemy; to thine enemy; and literally, no farther: It does not say to a State, *Si Inimicus vester,* It does not binde us to favour, or further a publique enemy; It does not binde the Magistrate to favour Theeves and Murderers at land, nor Pirates at Sea, who are truly *Inimici nostri,* our enemies even as we are men, enemies to mankinde. It does not binde Societies and Corporations Ecclesiasticall or Civill, to sinke under such enemies, as would dissolve them or impaire them in their priviledges; for such are not onely *Inimici vestri,* but *Vestrorum,* enemies of you, and yours, of those that succeed you: And all men are bound to transferre their jurisdictions and priviledges, in the same integrity, in which they received them, without any prevarication. In such cases it is true, that Corporations have no soules, that is, they are not bound to such a tendernesse of conscience; for there are divers lawes in this

Luke 6.32

Mat. 5.22

Non vester

doctrine of patience, that binde particular men, that doe not binde
States and Societies, under those penalties.

Much lesse does the Commandment bind us to the *Inimicus homo,*
which is the devill, to farther him, by fuelling and advancing his tentations, by high dyet, wanton company, or licencious discourse; and
so, upon pretence of maintaining our health, or our cheerefulnesse,
invite occasions of sinne. S. *Hierome* tells us of one sense, in which
wee should favour that enemy, the devill, and that in this text, we
180 are commanded to doe so: *Benevolus est erga Diabolum,* saies he, he
is the devils best friend, that resists him; for by our yeelding to the
devils tentations, we submit him to greater torments, then, if he mist
of his purpose upon us, he should suffer. But betweene this enemy
and us, God himselfe hath set such an enmity, that, as no man may
separate those whom God hath joyned, so no man may joyne those
whom God hath separated; God created not this enmity in the devill;
he began it in himselfe; but God created an enmity in us, against
him; and, upon no collaterall conditions, may wee bee reconciled to
him, in admitting any of his superstitions.

190   It is not then *Inimicus vester,* the common enemy, the enemy of
the State; lesse, *Inimicus homo,* the spirituall enemy of Mankinde,
the devill; least of all, *Inimicus Dei,* they who oppose God, (so, as
God can be opposed) in his servants who professe his truth. *David*
durst not have put himselfe upon that issue with God, (*Doe not I
hate them, that hate thee?*) if hee had beene subject to that increpa-
tion, which the Prophet *Iehu* laid upon *Iehoshaphat, Shouldst thou
helpe the ungodly, and love them, that hate the Lord?* But *David*
had the testimony of his conscience, that *hee hated them, with a perfect hatred:* which, though it may admit that interpretation, that it is
200 *De perfectione virtutis,* that his perfect hatred, was a hatred becom-
ming a perfect man, a charitable hatred; yet it is *De perfectione in-
tentionis,* a perfect hatred is a vehement hatred, and so the Chalde
paraphrase expresses it, *Odio consummato,* a hatred to which nothing
can be added; *Odio religioso,* with a religious hatred; not onely that
religion may consist with it, but that Religion cannot subsist without it; a hatred that gives the tincture, and the stampe to Religion
it selfe. The imputation that lyes upon them, who doe not hate those

*Inimicus
homo*
Luk. 10.19

Gen. 3.15

Psal. 139.21

2 Chron.
19.2
[Psa.
139.22]

Hilar.

that hate God, is sufficiently expressed in S. *Gregory;* He saw how
little temporisers and worldly men, were moved with the word Im-
210 piety, and ungodlinesse, and therefore he waves that; He saw they
preferred the estimation of wisdome before and above piety, and
therefore hee saies not *Im'pium est,* but *stultum est, si illis placere
quærimus, quos non placere domino scimus:* It is a foolish thing,
to endeavour to be acceptable to them, who, in our own knowledge,
doe not endeavour to be acceptable to God.

But yet, Beloved, even in those enemies, that thus hate God, *Solo-*
Eccles. 3.8 *mons* rule hath place, *There is a time to hate, and a time to love.*
Though the person be the same, the affection may vary. As S. *Cyprian*
De singula-
rit. Cleric. saies, (if that booke be not rather *Origens,* then *Cyprians,* for it is
220 attributed to both) *Ama fœminas inter Sacra solennia,* Love a woman
at Church, (that is, love her comming to Church,) (though, as S. *Augustine* in his time did, we, in our times may complaine of wanton
meetings there) But *Odio habe in communione privata,* Hate, that
is, forbeare women in private conversation; so, for those that hate
God in the truth of his Gospell, and content themselves with an
Idolatrous Religion, we love them at Church, we would be glad to
see them here, and though they come not hither, wee love them so
far, as that we pray for them; and we love them in our studies so
far, as we may rectifie them by our labours; But wee hate them in
230 our Convocations, where wee oppose Canons against their Doctrines,
and we hate them in our Consultations, where we make lawes to
defend us from their malice, and we hate them in our bed-chambers,
where they make children Idolaters, and perchance make the children
themselves. We acknowledge with S. *Augustine, Perfectio odii est in
charitate,* the perfect hatred consists with charity, *Cum nec propter
vitia homines oderimus, nec vitia propter homines amemus;* when
the greatnesse of the men brings us not to love their religion, nor the
illnesse of their Religion, to hate the men. *Moses,* in that place, is
S. *Augustines* example, whom he proposes, *Orabat & occidebat,* he
240 prayed for the Idolaters, and he slew them; he hated, saies he, *Iniqui-
tatem, quam puniebat,* that sin which he punished, and he loved
Humanitatem, pro qua orabat, that nature, as they were men, for
whom he prayed: for, that, saies he, is *perfectum odium, quod facti
sunt diligere, quod fecerunt, odiisse,* to love them as they are creatures,

to hate them as they are Traytors. Thus much love is due to any
enemy, that if God be pleased to advance him, *De ejus profectu non
dejiciamur,* sayes S. *Gregory,* His advancement doe not deject us, to
a murmuring against God, or to a diffidence in God; And that when
God, in his time, shall cast him downe againe, *Congaudeamus justi-*
250 *tiæ Iudicis, condoleamus miseriæ pereuntis,* Wee may both congratu-
late the justice of God, and yet condole the misery of that person,
upon whom that judgement is justly fallen: for, though *Inimicus
vester,* the enemy that malignes the State, and *Inimicus Dei,* the
enemy that opposes our religion, be not so far within this text, as that
we are bound to feed them, or to doe them good; yet there are scarce
any enemies, with whom wee may not live peaceably, and to whom
we may not wish charitably.

We have done with all, which was intended and proposed of the   *Ciba*
person; we come to the duty expressed in this text, *Ciba, feed him,*
260 and *give him drinke.* Here, there might be use in noting the largenesse, the fulnesse, the abundance of the Gospell, above the law: Not
onely in that the blessings of God are presented in the Old Testament, in the name of Milke and Hony, and Oyle, and Wine, (all
temporall things) and in the New Testament, in the name of Joy,
and Glory, (things, in a manner spirituall,) But that also, in the Old
Testament, the best things are limited, and measured unto them; a
Gomer of Manna, and no more, for the best man, whereas for the   [Exod.
joy of the Gospell, we shall enter *In Gaudium Domini, Into our Mas-*   16.18]
ters Ioy, and be made partakers with Christ Jesus, of that *Ioy, for*   Mat. 25.21
270 *which he endured the Crosse;* And here, in this world, *Gaudium*   Heb. 12.2
meum erit, saies Christ, *My Ioy shall be in you;* in what measure?   Iohn 15.11
Implebitur, saies he, *Your Ioy shall be full;* How long? for ever;
Nemo tollet, your Ioy shall no man take from you. And such as the   Iohn 16.22
Joy is, such is the glory too: How precious? *Divitiæ Gloriæ, The*   Eph. 1.18
Riches of the Glory of his Inheritance; How much? *Pondus gloriæ,*   2 Cor. 4.17
A waight of glory; How long? *Immarcescibilis Corona, A crowne*   1 Pet. 5.4
of Glory, that never fadeth: We might, I say, take occasion of making
this comparison, betweene the Old, and the New Testament, out of
this Text, because this charity, enjoyned here, in this text, to our
280 enemy, in that place, from whence this text is taken, in the Proverbs,
is but *Lachem,* and *Maiim, Bread,* and *Water;* But here, in S. *Paul,*

it is in words of better signification, *feed him, give him drinke*. But indeed, the words, at the narrowest, (as it is but bread and water) signifie whatsoever is necessary for the reliefe of him, that stands in need. And if we be enjoyn'd so much to our enemy, how inexcusable are those *Datores cyminibiles* (as the Canonists call them) that give Mint, and Cummin for almes, a roote that their Hogs will not, a broth that their Dogs will not eate. Remember in thy charity, the times, and the proportions of thy Saviour; After his Death, in the

[John 19.34] 290 wound in his side, he poured out water, and bloud, which represented both Sacraments, and so was a bountifull Dole: provide in thy life, to doe good after thy death, and it shall be welcome, even in the eyes of God, then: But remember too, that this dole at his death, was not the first almes that he gave; his water was his white mony, and his blood was his gold, and he poured out both together in his agony, and severally in his weeping, and being scourged for thee. What proportion of reliefe is due to him, that is thy brother in Nature, thy brother in Nation, thy brother in Religion, if meate and drinke, and in that, whatsoever is necessary to his sustentation, bee due to thine enemy?

Si esurierit 300   But all this bountifull charity, is *Si esurierit, si sitit, If he be hungry, if he be thirsty.* To the King, who beares the care and the charge of the publique, wee are bound to give, *Antequam esuriat, Antequam sitiat,* before he be overtaken with dangerous, and dishonorable, and lesse remediable necessities: not onely substantiall wants, upon which our safety depends, but circumstantiall and ceremoniall wants, upon which his Dignity, and Majesty depends, are alwaies to bee, not onely supplied, but prevented. But our enemy must be in hunger, and thirst, that is, reduced to the state, as hee may not become our enemy againe, by that which we give, before wee are bound, by this text, to

310 give any thing. No doubt but the Church of Rome hungers still for the money of this land, upon which they fed so luxuriantly heretofore: and no doubt but those men, whom they shall at any time animate, will thirst for the blood of this land, which they have sought before; but this is not the hunger, and the thirst of the enemy, which we must feed: The Commandement goes not so far, as to feed that enemy, that may thereby be a more powerfull enemy; But yet, thus far, truly, it does goe, deny no office of civility, of peace, of commerce,

of charity to any, onely therefore, because hee hath beene heretofore an enemy.

³²⁰ There remaines nothing of those two branches, which constitute our first part, the person, that is, an enemy reduced to a better disposition; and the duty, that is, to relieve him, with things necessary for that state: And for the second part, we must stop upon those steps laid downe at first, of which the first was, That God takes nothing for nothing, he gives a Reward. When God tooke that great proportion of Sheep and Oxen out of his subjects goods in the State of Israel, for Sacrifice, that proportion, which would have kept divers Kings houses, and would have victualed divers navies, perchance no man could say, I have this, or this benefit, for this, or this Sacrifice; ³³⁰ but yet could any man say, God hath taken a Sacrifice for nothing? Where we have Peace, and Justice, and Protection, can any man say, he gives any thing for nothing? When God saies, *If I were hungry, I would not tell thee,* that's not intended, which *Tertullian* saies, *Scriptum est, Deus non esuriet nec sitiet,* It is written, God shall neither hunger nor thirst, (for, first, *Tertullians* memory failed him, there is no such sentence in all the Scripture, as he cites there; And then God does hunger and thirst, in this sense, in the members of his mysticall body,) neither is that onely intended in that place of the Psalme (though *Cassiodore* take it so) That if God in his poore ³⁴⁰ Saints, were hungry, he could provide them, without telling thee; but it is, If I were hungry, I need not tell thee; for, *The earth is the Lords, and the fulnesse thereof, and they that dwell therein.* God does not alwaies binde himselfe to declare his hunger, his thirst, his pressing occasions, to use the goods of his subjects, but as the Lord gives, so the Lord takes, where and when he will: But yet, as God transfuses a measure of this Right and power of taking, into them, of whom he hath said, you are Gods, so he transfuses this goodnesse too, which is in himselfe, that he takes nothing for nothing; He promises here a reward, and a reward arising from the enemy, which ³⁵⁰ puts a greater encouragement upon us, to doe it; *Super caput ejus, In so doing, thou shalt heape coales of fire on his head.*

God is the Lord of Hosts, and in this Text, he makes the seate of the warre in the enemies Country, and enriches his servants *Ex*

2 Part

[1 Kings 8.63]

Psal. 50.12

Psal. 24.1

[Psa. 82.6]

Ex Inimicis

manubiis, out of the spoyle of the enemy; *In caput ejus,* It shall fall upon his head. Though all men that go to the war, goe not upon those just reasons deliberated before in themselves, which are, the defence of a just cause, the obedience to a lawfull Commandment, yet of those that do goe without those conscientious deliberations, none goes therefore, because he may have roome in an Hospitall, or 360 reliefe by a pension, when he comes home lame, but because he may get something, by going into a fat country, and against a rich enemy; Though honour may seeme to feed upon blowes, and dangers, men goe cheerefully against an enemy, from whom something is to be got; for, profit is a good salve to knocks, a good Cere-cloth to bruises, and a good Balsamum to wounds. God therefore here raises the reward out of the enemy, feed him, and thou shalt gaine by it. But yet the profit that God promises by the enemy here, is rather that we shall gaine a soule, then any temporall gaine; rather that we shall make that enemy a better man, then that we shall make him a weaker 370 enemy: God respects his spirituall good, as we shall see in that phrase, which is our last branch, *Congeres carbones, Thou shalt heape coales of fire upon his head*

Carbones   It is true that S. *Chrysostome* (and not he alone) takes this phrase to imply a Revenge: that Gods judgements shall be the more vehement upon such ungratefull persons, *Et terrebuntur beneficiis,* the good turnes that thou hast done to them, shall be a scourge and a terror to their consciences. This sense is not inconvenient; but it is too narrow: The Holy Ghost hath taken so large a Metaphor, as implyes more then that. It implyes the divers offices, and effects of 380 fire; all this; That if he have any gold, any pure metall in him, this fire of this kindnesse will purge out the drosse, and there is a friend made. If he be nothing but straw and stubble, combustible still, still ready to take fire against thee, this fire which Gods breath shall blow, will consume him, and burn him out, and there is an enemy marred: If he have any tendernesse any way, this fire will mollifie him towards thee; *Nimis durus animus,* sayes S. *Augustine,* he is a very hard hearted man, *Qui si ultro dilectionem non vult impendere, etiam nolit rependere,* Who, though he will not requite thy love, yet will not acknowledge it. If he be waxe, he melts with this fire; and if he 390 be clay, he hardens with it, and then thou wilt arme thy selfe against

that pellet. Thus much good, God intends to the enemy, in this phrase, that it is *pia vindicta si resipiscant,* we have taken a blessed revenge upon our enemies, if our charitable applying of our selves to them, may bring them to apply themselves to God, and to glorifie him: *si benefaciendo cicuremus,* sayes S. *Hierome,* if we can tame a wilde beast by sitting up with him, and reduce an enemy by offices of friendship, it is well. So much good God intends him in this phrase, and so much good he intends us, that, *si non incendant,* if these coales do not purge him, *si non injiciant pudorem,* if they do
400 not kindle a shame in him, to have offended one that hath deserved so well, yet this fire gives thee light to see him clearely, and to run away from him, and to assure thee, that he, whom so many benefits cannot reconcile, is irreconcileable.

Origen

Aben Ezra
Levi
Gherson

*Textual Notes to the Sermons
in Volume III*

Notes to Sermon No. 1

[This is perhaps the worst printed of the many badly printed sermons in *XXVI Sermons*. We have not recorded in our notes a number of places where a single letter has failed to print in most copies, or where the division between words has been wrongly made, as in line 323, second part of sermon, where all the copies which we have seen read "werea cknowledgements" for "were acknowledgements." We have, however, recorded all the numerous changes in punctuation which we have been forced to make, for the punctuation of *F* is so bad that it cannot possibly reproduce Donne's original intention.

In *XXVI Sermons* this sermon is described in the Table of Contents as no. X, and in the body of the volume it is numbered throughout in the margin as "Serm. 10," occupying pages 129–152. But on p. 141 "Sermon 10" appears to end, part of the page being left blank, and on p. 142 there is a fresh heading, "The Second Sermon Preached at White-Hall upon Eccles. 5.12, & 13," and the text is repeated. There is, however, no separate number attached to this sermon, which we should expect to be "Sermon XI" if it were really a separate sermon, and in the Table of Contents at the beginning of *XXVI Sermons* it is included with the earlier part of the sermon as "Sermon X," there being no "Sermon IX," and "Sermon XI" being the sermon preached at Greenwich on April 30, 1615. In all copies of this Folio known to us (and also in all those recorded by Dr. Geoffrey Keynes in his *Bibliography of John Donne*) there is a sheet (sig. R) missing, and nos. 121–128 are missing in the pagination, while there is no sermon numbered as IX.

It might therefore be conjectured that for some reason (perhaps a question of copyright) a sermon which originally had been chosen to precede this had to be omitted, and that this was divided into two in order to make up the number XXVI which had already been announced as part of the title. The present volume of our edition was one of those allotted to George Potter as principal editor, and he left on record his opinion that the division of the sermon into two was the work of John Donne junior, who edited *XXVI Sermons,* or of the printer. There is, however, the possibility that Donne himself had divided into two what was originally one sermon, as he divided into two the single sermon which he preached on Matthew 4.18–20 at the Hague, December 19, 1619, when he was revising and "digesting" his notes in his sickness at his daughter's house in 1630.[1]

_____

[1] See Vol. II of the present edition, pp. 38–39, 269. Donne's heading to the first sermon runs thus: "At the Haghe Decemb. 19. 1619. I Preached upon this Text. Since in my sicknesse at Abrey-hatche in Essex, 1630, revising my short notes of that Sermon, I digested them into these two."

There he enlarged the sermon considerably, and added such notes as "For those [circumstances] that belong to the second part ... it would be an impertinent thing, to open them now, because I doe easily foresee, that this day we shall not come to that part."[2] Similarly in the present sermon he may have supplied the words "But that will not fall into this exercise" (line 174, first part of sermon, printed in the Folio as a separate paragraph).

We have thought it best to include this second heading in our text, while at the same time numbering the two parts as one sermon, thus following the example of the Folio. Though this may seem inconsistent, we are thus presenting all the evidence to the reader, leaving him to form his own judgement of how and why the division was made.]

LINE

Line ⎫
under ⎬ Ver. 12 and 13]
text ⎭

NOTE. This is the numbering of the Bishops' Bible and the Geneva, and also of the Vulgate, while in the King James version the numbering is 13 and 14. Since Donne was quoting his text from the Geneva Bible, he thought it necessary to give four sets of references.

6 *mg.* Hierome : Hierm. *F.*

13 wishes : wishes, *F*

18 *Moses,* : *Moses F*

29 love, this : love. This *F*

33 might] Final "t" has failed to print in most copies.

40 Emperor:) : Emperor: *F*

41 *soule?* : *soule; F*

47 Riches, : Riches; *F*

48 stones, : stones? *F*

52 Leaven : Laeven *F*

54 words; first, : words, first *F*

63 *mg.* Agg. 1.6 : Agg. 1.16 *F*

67 world. Least : world, least *F*

73–75 it (*Canticum Canticorum,* ... Songs; *Deus* ... gods; *Dominus* ... Lords; *Cœli* ... Heavens) *Edd. conj.* : it; *Canticum Canticorum;* ... Songs, *Deus* ... gods, *Dominus* ... Lords; *Cœli* ... Heavens, *F*

84–85 for though ... misled him, : (for though ... misled him,) *F*

89 *Man* ... *vanity* : Man ... vanity *F*

---

[2] Vol. II, No. 13, lines 53–57.

LINE

89   proceeds : proceeeds *F*

89–90 *surely,* that is, ... contradiction, : surely that is ... contradiction *F*

90   *every Man* : everyMan *F*

90   that is, ... exception, : that is ... exception; *F*

91   *in ... state* : in ... state *F*

91   *is ... vanity* : is ... vanity *F*

98   reposed : repose *F*

99   for] The "f" has failed to print in some copies.

102   he, and so may we : he and so may we, *F*

113 *mg.* *F* here has *I Cor.* 8.4, which is repeated below (rightly) for line 115. Here it is obviously an error for some other reference, probably *Deut.* 32.21, which reads: "Ipsi me provocaverunt in eo qui non erat Deus, et irritaverunt in vanitatibus suis."

123   *all nations ... nothing* : all nations ... nothing *F*

126   *they are all less then nothing* : they are all less then nothing *F*

127   *vanity* : vanity *F*

      NOTE. These three passages beginning *all nations, they are,* and *vanity* are all taken from *Isaiah* 40, and should be italicized to correspond with the previous quotation in line 121.

127   what's : whats *F*

127   *inane* : in ane *F*

127   that's : thats *F*

171   *evill.* There follows *Edd. conj.* : *evill.* And those riches perish by evil travail: and he begetteth a son; and in his hand is nothing. [New paragraph] There follows *F*

172   the riches perish. *And those Riches* Edd. conj. : the riches perish. *There is an evil sickness that I have seen under the Sun: Riches reserved to the owners thereof for their evil. And those Riches F*

173–174 *is nothing.* But : *is* nothing. [New paragraph] But *F*

182   St. *Hierom.*]

      NOTE. The reader naturally expects this to be the famous St. Jerome whom Donne quotes so often, but the quotation which follows is from a less-known writer, St. Eusebius Hieronymus, who wrote six books on the prophecies of Jeremiah. In his comment on *Jer.* 5.26 and 27 occurs the phrase "ut impleatur philosophorum illa sententia: omnis dives aut iniquus aut hæres iniqui" (*Corpus Scriptorum Ecclesiasticorum Latinorum,* LIX,

S. Euseb. Hieron. Opera (Sec. II, Pars I) *In Hieremiam Pro-phetam Libri Sex,* Liber Secundus, v. Reiter, Leipzig, 1913). The marginal reference "Epist. 160" must be wrong. The great St. Jerome wrote 154 epistles which have been preserved, but the phrase does not, apparently, occur in any of them.

190   nourishment, : nourishment; F

193–196   NOTE. The text of F 26 seems corrupt here. The words "they" and "either" have only "Rich" to which to refer. Perhaps the original wording was "He had rather we were Rich then Poor."

204   is in : in F

210   are reserved : arereserved F

212 *mg.*   Luke 6 : Luke 26 F

269   over-board : over board F

273   heart; : heart, F

279   riches, : riches; F

284 *mg.*   Psal. 136 : ver. 36 F

289   harm; That ... sickness. Now : harm. That ... sickness; Mow F

309   wash : washes F
    NOTE. Cf. "overcome and weigh" earlier in the same sentence.

319   rheum, thy : rheum: Thy F

321   did, : did. F

322   cure, : cure. F

323   turn, : turn. F

324   *I am* : I *am* F

332   letargy : leturgy F

333   Pleurisie, : Pleurisie; F

345   wonder : wounder F

347   *Pharaoh* : *Pharoah* F

347–350   people; ... people; ... people; : people. ... people. ... people. F

361   sinne *Edd.conj.* : time *F, Al*
    NOTE. The sense here demands "sin"; and there are examples in other sermons for which variant manuscript readings exist, of the misreading of "sinne" as "time," or vice versa.

368   name : name, F

371   it, : it; F

394   *pœnitebit* : *pœnetebit* F

396   *Basil*); : *Basil*) F

397   St. : St, F

398   *Solomon*   :   Solomon *F*
404   fool,   :   fool *F*
406   it   :   It *F*
415   declares   :   declares, *F*
428   *persequeris,*   :   *per sequeris. F*
428   *Saul, why*   :   *Saul why, F*
433   generally   :   generaly *F*
442   selves;   :   selves. *F*
443   seeds,   :   seeds; *F*
443–444   Apostle calls   :   Apostles calls *F*
460 *mg.*   Col. 2   :   Col. 29 *F*

Notes to second part of Sermon No. 1

3   *præda*   :   *prœda F*
25–26   All ways   :   Always *F*
28   together   :   to gether *F*
30–31   perish, ... nothing;   :   perish; ... nothing, *F*
34   it;   :   it, *F*
39   wicked, *The way ... perish*   :   wicked. The way ... perish *F*
41   surely   :   surly *F*
41   and   :   anp *F*
42   taken,   :   taken; *F*
58   us ... inheritance,   :   us, ... inheritance *F*
81 *mg.*   Lam.   :   Chron. *F*
88   *travail;*   :   *travail,; F*
91   *in*   :   in *F*
131   diffidence   :   diffidence, *F*
134   way   :   way, *F*

> NOTE. This sentence is somewhat confusing; but the text may nevertheless quite possibly be sound—God proceeding in the same way with both righteous and wicked, with the wicked because they do trust in their own riches, with the righteous lest they should so trust.

135   do,   :   do *F*
139   their   :   rheir *F*
146   principally   :   pricipally *F*
162   riches,]   *comma faint in F*
164   they   :   they, *F*
182   again.   :   again, *F*
198   it. Some   :   it; some *F*

LINE

200   rust : rust, *F*
NOTE. Cf. "a rust, a cancer at the heart" *post,* lines 206–207.
200   fil'd *F corr.* : fill'd *F originally*
200   off : of *F*
208   beginning, (the : beginning. (The *F*
210   history) : history.) *F*
213   calamities) ... silver, : calamities.) ... silver *F*
214   excesses) : excesses.) *F*
215   room; *Thesaurizasti iram,* thou : room. *Thesaurisasti iram.* Thou *F*
223   *Nisi F corr.* : *insi F originally*
223   *Dominus* : *Dominius F*
223   *custodierit,* : *custodierit. F*
226   travail, *Sed ... occupatione,* : travail. *Sed ... occupatione. F*
242–243   signification : signifigation *F*
246   travail : travail, *F*
247   *sudore* : *Sudore F*
250   travail, : travail; *F*
251   him : him, *F*
257–258   flesh; ... first, : flesh, ... first; *F*
261   afflictions; : afflictions, *F*
266   Why : *Why F*
267   after a *Domine* : after: *a domine F*
268 *mg.*   Lam. : Jam. *F*
270   is there, : is there,) *F*
273   finds : finds, *F*
283   *Son.* First : *Son;* first *F*
290   diminishes nothing : diminishes Nothing, *F*
293   *Barrenness Al* : *Barcenus F*
NOTE. The emendation of *Al* here seems to us sound, and so clearly required by the sense that it need hardly be called conjectural.
303 *mg.*   127.3 : 12.7.3. *F*
309   constitution : costitution *F*
314   this? : this. *F*
315–318   *Domino ... Deo* : *domino ... deo F*
318   which : wich *F*
328   man, : man; *F*
332   the faith, : the faith; *F*
335–336   Religion, ... children; : Religion; ... children, *F*

337   *vult,* : *vult: F*

340   heir, *Quærat ... Augustinum,* : heir. *Quærat ... Augusti-num F*

341   *Deo* : *deo F*

344   *fœderatio* : *fœderatio F*

355 *mg.*   Ecclus. 40.15 : Eccles. 40.13 *F*

360   man; : man. *F*

367   *Aurelius* : *Auretius F*

375   Howsoever : Howsoever, *F*

377 *mg.*   Ecclus. : Eccles. *F*

382   soon : soon, *F*

386   had) : had,) *F*

387   not his : not his, *F*

392   *disconsolatenes,* : *disconsolatenes; F*

393   seal, Absolution, : sea. Absolution, *F*

NOTE. We owe this emendation to Helen Gardner, who points out that "seal" is Donne's usual metaphor for the sacraments of the Church. The Book of Common Prayer allows the Anglican priest to receive confession from a sick person, and to give absolution, and Donne lays particular stress on this point in the sermon on *Psa.* 38.9 (Vol. II of our edition, Sermon 6, lines 590–610).

394   Ministers, comes : Ministers came *F*

NOTE. Alford found this passage hopeless and remarked, "It is thus in the text: I am quite unable to correct it satisfactorily"; but the whole passage is made intelligible by the emendation of "sea" to "seal" in line 393 above combined with this slight alteration.

397   fool : fool, *F*

398   the *Quæ parasti* : the, *Qua perasti F*

409   malice; ... though : malice, ... though, *F*

410   yet : yet, *F*

412   last; since though : last, since though, *F*

414–415   Conscience, ... die; : Conscience; ... die, *F*

417   hand; : hand, *F*

422   Maker, : Maker; *F*

Notes to Sermon No. 2

LINE

Title Preached ... 1620] At Whitehall, to yᵉ Kinge *D* : c4917
92g2 ıt 55hytehı66 [i.e., coram rege at Whytehall] *L* : *om.*
M, P, but *M* has note of place and date at end of sermon.

After ⎫
text ⎬ Being ... day] *om. L, M, P*
    ⎭

2–3 *Blessed is ... blessed is*] *Blessed are ... blessed are P*

2 *be*] *are P*

5 murmuring] murmurings *D, L, M*

7 saith] sayes *D, M*

10, ⎫
13, ⎬*Solomon*] Salomon *L*
15 ⎭

12 of heaven] in heaven *D, L, P*

15–16 *Solomon* represents by Wisedome] *Salomon* presents by wisedome *D, L, M* : Wisdome represents *P*

17 but a Christian wiseman] *om. D, L* : but allsoe a Christian
wiseman *P*

17 both] both his *L*

19 saith] saies *D, L, M, P* (and line 115)

26 hereafter] in heaven hereafter *D, L*

29 *licet D, L, M, P* : *licèt F*

30 saith] saies *D, L, M* (also line 71)

33 As then] And then as *D, L*

33 *sinistra beatitudo D, L, M, P* : *sinistrabeatitudo F*

34 *dextra* and] *Dextra et D, L* : *dextra & P*

36 seales and] *om. D, L*

40 is] the left interpretation is *P*

40 of these words] *om. P*

43 is not the] it is not the *D, L* : yet the *P*

44 is] (a right Interpretation) is *P*

54 truely] *om. D, L*

56 reflection] affliction *D, L*

58 it thus] us this *D, L*

60 yet, this] this yet *D, L*

61 Translators] translations *D*

61 Expositors] expositions *D, L*

64 *mg.* [1] *Interpretatio*] 1ᵃ Interpretatio *D, L, M, P*

72 *ad mercedem D, L, M, P* : *admercedem F*

LINE

72 he saith] he saies *D, L, M* : sayes *P*

77 chast] chaste hart *D, L*

78 and *D, L, M, P* : end *F*

84 away] *om. D, L, P*

86 Devill there] Devill, there is *D, L*

90 a man] the man *D, L* : them *P*

91–92 hee ... for him] *om. D, L*

94 make] be *D, L*

95 who ever] whosoever *D, L, P*

101 those] these *M, P*

106 *Hierome*] *Jerome D, L, M, P* (and elsewhere)

106 saith] saies *D, L, M, P*

108 the Father] his Father *D, L, P*

109 mystery] ministry *D, L*

115 properly] *om. D, L*

118 that] it *D, L*

121–123 for us ... necessary] *om. D, L*

125 *sperandum* : *speran/dum F*

129 onely are] are onlye *M*

130 things *D, L, M, P* : thing *F, Al*

131 *invito*] *invioto* (an Enimy can take it away against a mans will) *P*

132 any] an *D, L, P*

132 and] and a *D, L, P*

133 that that] that which *D, L, M* : that *P*

137 not worth the] not worth *D* : worth *L*

137 keeping.] keeping, and the spirituall blessings of a faithfull man are never lost totally; though he fall into sins of infirmity, though he fall into Scruples in [of *P*] matter [matters *M*] of faith, yet there is *Semen dei* in him, all is not lost *D, L, M, P* [*P* adds after *Semen dei* (the seede of God)]

NOTE. Evidently these words were in Donne's first draft, and he excised the whole passage when revising the sermon. See Vol. I of the present edition, pp. 69–70, note 44.

138 estate, : estate *F*

140 his Wife was] he had his wife *P*

143 pity] his pity *D, L*

149 Father] Author *D, L*

153 that is] that's *D, L, M, P*

159–161 that it ... doctrine] *om. D, L*

LINE

163–164 yet ... blessings] *om. D, L*

164 *mg.* Iudg. 20.16 : Iudg. 20.10 *F* : 10.16 *D, P* : *om. L*

166–167 considering] considering that *D, L*

169 works] markes *D, L*

169 correct that] correct the *D, L, P*

173 *dixerunt D, L, M, P* : *dixerint F, Al*

174 or *F corr. in errata, D, L, M, P* : for *F originally*

178 *falsa* and *vera*] *falsa et vera D, L* : *vera & falsa P*

178 *dextra* and] *dextra et D, L* : *dextra & P*

179–180 *Inchoativa* and] *Inchoativa et D, L* : *Inchoativa & P*

193 amongst ... amongst] among ... among *D, L, P*

195 whether] whether this *D, L* : whither *P*

196 plurall] plurall number *D, L, P*

201–202 with which ... Psalmes] that David begins his booke of Psalmes withal *P*

203 passes] passed *D, L, P*

206 blessednesse] blessings *D, L, P*

209–210 is never the better] *om. M*

214 blessednesse] blessings *D, L*

214 them who] those that *D, L*

222 uselesse blessings,] stolne blessings, for they belong truely to the servants of God *D, L, M, P*

NOTE. Evidently these words belong to Donne's first draft. See Vol. I of the present edition, pp. 69–70, n. 44.

231 *mg.* Mat. 19.29] Mat. 19.22 *D, L* : Mat. 21.29 *P, which places the reference opposite line* 233

235 a hundred] an hundred *M* : one hundred *D, L* : ten *P*

236 *Accipiet*] recipiet (he shall receive an hundredfolde) *P*

239 God repaired] if God repaid *D, L* : God repayed *P*

242 *mg.* Iohn 10.10 *D, L* : *om. F, M*

242 *sed ut D, L, P* : *sed F, M*

243 diverse] divers *M, P* : many *D, L*

244 to] unto *D, L, M, P*

245 *mg.* Iohn 10.9 : Iohn 9.10 *F* : 9 [i.e., v. 9] *D, L* : *om. M, P*

247 sap and] *om. D, L*

250 blessed] infallible *D, L, P* : an infallible *M*

252–253 his ... his] this ... this *D, L*

255 found] had found *M*

262 and] *om. D, L, P*

262 *Socrates* his time] Socrates tyme *D* : the time of Socrates *P*

LINE

265   in a Reformed Church]   *om. D, L*

267   a peace-preserver]   a preserver of Peace *P*

282   things]   blessings *M*

285   monosyllable *D, L*   :   monasyllable *F*   :   monasillable *M*

286   that is, so,]   *om. D, L*

287   they]   the People *P*

289   which are]   *om. D, L*   :   are *M*

292   *invasion*]   innovation *D, L*

316   very very]   very *L, M, P*

319   sayes]   saith *D, L, P*

327   St. *D, L, M, P*   :   See *F, Al*

327   a]   the *L*   :   *om. D*

330   *serenitas D, L, P*   :   *severitas F, Al*   :   *seneritas M*

333   *operarii pauci*]   *om. D, L*

334   workmen]   Laborers *P*

335   enow]   enough *P*   :   now *D, L*

335   gather; in that Homily he *Edd.*   :   gather, in that Homily; He
       F   :   gather. In that Homily he *P*   :   gather in that homilye,
       he *M*   :   gather in; in that Homilie hee *D, L*

337   *fœcundum*]   fœcundum (the earth was barren, and Gould was
       fruitfull) *P*

343   a way]   away *M, P*

343   a barrennesse]   barrennesse *D, L, P*

347   thine]   thy *D*   :   their *L*

348   for, for]   for *M*

351 *mg.*   *Sanitas D, L*   :   *om. F, M*

356   What is]   what's *D, L, M, P*

357   rebellions and]   *om. D, L*

357   shaking]   choking *D, L*

369   *Ezechias D, L, M*   :   *Ezekiah P*   :   *Hezekias F, Al*
       NOTE. *Ezechias*, the Vulgate form, is generally (though not
       always) used by Donne. A.V. has *Hezekiah*. The printer has
       probably tried to normalize.

373   blessings]   things *D, L*

375 *mg.*   *Populus*]   *om. D, L*   :   *In Quibus Personis P*

376   persons]   blessings *D, L*

379   does]   doth *M, P*

380   *man*]   man; it reaches to all the parties, all the faculties, all the
       actions of man *D, L*

382–383   *walke,* and *stand,* and *sit*]   sit, stand, walke *P*

387   meanes]   the meanes *M*
388   be come]   come *M, P*
388   get]   trade *D, L*
389   the people is not blessed]   *om. D, L*
389–390   yea, if ... blessed]   *om. M*
392–394   by *David* ... sayes]   *om. D, L*
396   beeing]   King *D, L*
398   supplied]   applied *D, L*
400   *are*]   *is M*
401   these blessings]   the blessinge *P*   :   these things *D, L*
403–407   If ... plenty]   *om. P*
411   that is]   thats *M, P*   :   that it is *D, L*
427   subjects]   Subject *M, P*
434 *mg.*   Mar.]   Math. *M*
447   *for*]   to *D, L*   :   *om. P*
450   there]   that there *D, L*
452   then]   *om. M, P*
453–456   And ... soule]   *om. P*
453   wee]   we can *D, L*
456   that]   it *D, L*
458   there is]   there's *D, M*
461–462   understanding his *D, L, M, P*   :   understanding, his *F*
463, 468   there is]   there's *D, L, M, P*
467   discerning]   desiring *D, L*
467   the purpose]   purpose *D, L, P*
469–472   he may ... soule]   *om. D, L*
474   the discerning]   his discerninge *P*   :   the desiring *D, L*
480   saith]   saies *D, L, M*
480 *mg.*   Psal. 112.2   :   Psal. 112.1 *F, L*
481   generation. Wherein is it expressed?]   generation wherein it is expressed *D, L, P*
482   *shall bee*]   is *D, L, P*
485   doth]   does *D, L, M*
490   the left to the]   thy left to [unto *P*] thy *M, P*
492   that]   who *M, P*
494   and in ... thine]   *om. L*
505–507   he is without ... Atheist.]   *om. D, L, P*
511   was no]   was a *D, L, P*
516, 519   saith]   saies *D, L, M, P* (also line 557)
534   and man. It is]   in man. It is *D*   :   in man, is *L*

LINE

534–535   a God ... *Deum*]   *om. D, L*

535   so]   that is *D, L*

537   or know ... notions]   *om. P*

541   gangrened]   gangrene *D, L*   :   gangred *M*

544   no]   not *M*

552–553   Christ Jesus]   Jesus Christ *D, L*

554   as ... as]   and ... and *D, L*

558   *Da*]   *om. D, L*

560   why doe wee call]   how is it *P*

564   a provident]   provident *D, L, M, P*

573   refection]   reflection *D, L*   :   perfection *P*

587 *mg.*   Esay 2. ult.]   *om. D, L, P*

593   least]   best *D, L*

594–595   gave us not onely a well-being in this life]   in this life not onely gave us a well being *D, L*

596   preferments]   preferment *D, L*

599   Physitians]   Phisitian *D, L*

600   began]   begunne *D, L*   :   beginne *P*

602 *mg.*   Esay 4.2]   2. *P*   :   *om. M*

611   blessednesse]   blessings *M*

616   includes]   included *D, L*

617–618   our ... of]   a ... in *D, L*

619   amongst   :   amonst *F*

621   made]   had *D, L*

624   those]   them *M*

628   thereby]   *om. D, L*

634   seed-corne]   seed corner *D, L, M*

638   let all us]   let us *D, L, P*

641   felt]   endur'd *D*   :   endure *L*

644   seales]   seale *D, L*

649   incorruptible]   immortall *D, L*

649   In]   To *D, L*

650   NOTE. After "&c." *M* adds "Finis of Doctor Dunns sermon preach'd at Whit-hall before the Kinge the thirtyeth of Aprill 1620." *P* adds "ffinis" on a separate line.

Notes to Sermon No. 3

[Eight of the sermons in this volume, Nos. 3, 4, 6, 7, 8, 11, 16, and 17, are printed from the Folio of 1649 (*Fifty Sermons*). This Folio is extremely inconsistent in its use of italics, and we have not attempted to correct all its aberrations. The guiding principle in all three Folios is that italics should be used for proper names, words of Latin, Greek, or Hebrew origin, and for quotations from the Bible or Prayer Book. If such quotations are given both in Latin and in English, the English version need not necessarily be in italics, though it often is so. In *F* 50 these italic quotations are often broken by the printing of one or two words in roman. The use of roman type in an italic sentence should properly denote one of two things: first, it denotes emphasis, just as an italic word does in a sentence printed in roman; or, secondly, it may mean that the word in roman is not part of the quotation, but has been supplied by the preacher. Neither of these reasons applies to such words in the present sermon as "that" in line 163, "and" in line 171, "the" in line 299, and we have therefore printed them in italic, so as not to break up the quotations, and have recorded the change in the following notes.

This Folio also uses italics for emphasis much more freely than either of the other two Folios, but we have hesitated to alter these, as we cannot be sure which of them were indicated by Donne in his manuscript. Similarly there is a plethora of commas in many places, but as we cannot know which of them Donne would have omitted, we have decided that where the sense is clear it is better to leave the text as we find it in the Folio, even though it may be overpunctuated in comparison with the text of the other Folios.]

LINE

71 *mg.* *Iudæi* : *Iudhi F*
75 *mg.* Numb. 16.32 : Numb. 16.31 *F*
77 *mg.* [Isa.] 26.19 (placed wrongly against line 76 in *F*)
80 *mg.* 14 (placed wrongly against line 77 in *F*)
83 *two* : two *F*
107 *I know ... againe, at the* : I know ... againe, at the *F*
109 *mg.* Luke 14.14 : Luke 14.12 *F*
153 *mg.* Nazianz. : Narianz. *F*
162 *mg.* Psal. 8.4 : Psal. 8.5 *F*
163 *that* : that *F*
171 *and* : and *F*
198 conservation : conservation, *F*
241 hard]
NOTE. This form (for *heard*) occurs from the fourteenth to the seventeenth century in English literature, and survived until the nineteenth in Scottish (see *N.E.D.*).

LINE

288 *mg.*	Acts 23.6	: Acts 15.5 *F*
299	*the God of Isaac*	: the *God of Isaac F*
303–304	*some ... contempt*	: some ... contempt *F*
310 *mg.*	John	: Mat. *F*
367 *mg.*	13	: 12 *F*
386	*Calvinists*)	: *Calvinists, F*
387–388	his [followers]	: his *F*

NOTE. A word seems to have been omitted here, and we have conjecturally supplied "followers."

472	That	: *That F*
497	heart.	: heart, *F*
570–572	*them*) ... named;	: *them; ...* named) *F*
624	grave	: grace *F*
632 *mg.*	Acts 1.7	: Acts 17. *F*
658	*resurrectionis*	: *resurecionis F*
685–687	body, ... consideration;	: body; ... consideration, *F*
697	done. You	: done, you *F*
703	it, this	: it: This *F*
719–720	when my ... death-bed	: *when my ... death-bed F*
720 *mg.*	Apoc. 10.6	: Apoc. 10.7 *F*
722	shall.	: shall: *F*
734	Creator;	: Creator, *F*
735	*Riddle; ...* Church,	: *Riddle, ...* Church; *F*
736–737	Church; ... riddle,	: Church, ... riddle; *F*
741	death?)	: death.) *F*
743	elected?)	: elected.) *F*
784	delights	

NOTE. This is grammatically correct, but it reads very awkwardly with "their ... them."

789	in	: in in *F*
815	breast?	: breast. *F*
816	months	: mouths *F*

Notes to Sermon No. 4

8	blood; this	: blood. This *F*
75	*and*	: and *F*
84–85	*now this ... that*	: *now* this ... that *F*
96	*resurrection*	: *resurrectien F*
117	two *Al*	: too *F*

147 *Melancthon*]
NOTE. The correct spelling is *Melanchthon,* but Donne invariably omits the first *"h."*

159 true : ture *F*

161 *addidit* : *ad didit F*

162 super-immitted]
NOTE. This form is not recorded by *N.E.D.,* which, however, records "immit" as a rare or obsolete word from Latin *immittere,* 'to send in' or 'introduce.' This form is therefore one of the many compounds in which the prefix "super" is added to a word of Latin origin.

167 *mg.* Exod. 34 : Exod. 23 *F*

182 *in particular* : in *particular F*

198 *lumen,* : *lumen; F*

216–218 then)? ... then)? : then.) ... then.) *F*

220 here? : here. *F*

275 is *Al* : in *F*

356 others. : others? *F*

370 1605. : 603. *F*

382 *Tayler;* (for : *Tayler;*) for *F*

402 But : but *F*

408 *præsentis* : *prææsentis F*

519 *for* : for *F*

520 *and hee ... God* : and hee ... God *F*

549 *Septuagint.* : *Septuagint: F*

554 have *Al* : that have *F*

565 *Reason* : *Roason F*

593 is welcome *Al* : his welcome *F*

612 *impenitiblenesse* : *impenitablenesse F*
NOTE. The *N.E.D.* does not recognize the spelling with *"a."* The only examples which it gives of this rare word are taken from other passages of Donne where the spelling is *impenitiblenesse.*

667 *and separated* : and *separated F*

Notes to Sermon No. 5

8 *mg.* Luk. 11.11 : Luk. 11.12 *F*

250 *mg.* Esay 9. [6]
NOTE. The reading here given is not that of the Hebrew, the

LINE

Vulgate, or the English versions, but is taken from the Septuagint, as Donne indicates.

337 Trinity : Trinty *F*

465 Feffees] feofees *Al*
NOTE. Alford's reading makes the meaning clearer, but as *N.E.D.* records "feffees" as a form found in the fifteenth and sixteenth centuries, we have retained the Folio reading.

477 *mg.* Iob 34 : Iob 32 *F*

593 man *F corr. in errata* : mad *F originally*

693 which : whch *F*

Notes to Sermon No. 6

26 *mg.* Exod. 2.12 : Exod. 2.11 *F*

29 *mg.* Mat. 23.2 : Mat. 23.1 *F*

44 accident : accdient *F*

92 uncharitablenes : uncharitabenes *F*

100 *offences.* Each : *offences.* each *F*

118 the first : the firrst *F*

148 *I will* : I *will F*

171–172 *was trobled* : *was* trobled *F*

186 *mg.* Mat. 27.53 : Mat. 27.33 *F*

212 she : he *F*

248 *mg.* verse 46 : verse 36 *F*

259 satisfaction : satisfiaction *F*

332 *Non obstante* : *Nonobstante F*

332 *Amen?* : *Amen. F*

413 un-offended, : un-offended *F*

426 *mg.* Gen. 19 : Gen. 29 *F*

428–429 *Ægypto* ... Egypt : *Egypto* ... Ægypt *F*

502 *mg.* Mat. 19.10 : Mat. 19.9 *F*

509 *mg.* [Job] 1.22 : 2.22 *F*

Notes to Sermon No. 7

24 *(scazein)*] σκάζειν *Al*
NOTE. Donne here transliterates the Greek word into Roman letters. The marks of parenthesis are merely a form of quotation; see P. Simpson, *Shakespearian Punctuation,* Oxford, 1911, pp. 94–95.

LINE

44 occasion; ... this, : occasion, ... this; *F*

54 godlinesse, ... me; : godliness; ... me, *F*

76 *Michol*] Michal *Al*

NOTE. Donne follows the spelling of the Vulgate here.

157 *Laws;* : *Laws, F*

230 *mg.* Mat. 24.24 : Mat. 24.23 *F*

231 way) : way, *F*

258 *Thessalonians;* : *Thes. F*

260 Apostles : A-/stles *F*

264 *mg.* verse 9 : verse 8 *F*

283 assoon] as soon *Al*

NOTE. The two words were commonly written as one from the fifteenth to the eighteenth century, both with and without a following "as" (*N.E.D.*)

368 some : some/some *F*

401–402 as he ... does : as he ... do *F* : as he ... doeth *Al*

407 *mg.* Iudg. : Iude *F*

523 interpretations : intepretations *F*

539 make : make, *F*

Notes to Sermon No. 8

22 possess *Al* : possesses *F*

51 *and feared ... and eschewed* : and *feared ...* and *eschewed F*

99 *Wormewod*

NOTE. *Al* corrects to *wormwood*, but "wormewod" is a good sixteenth-century form, the word having been altered from O.E. "wermod" (*N.E.D.*).

130 *and* : and *F*

136 *Shaddai.* For, first, this word signifies *Dishonor*, as the *Septuagint* translate it in the Proverbs, *He that* Dishonoreth his parents ... [19.26 in *mg.*]

NOTE. There is no agreement among scholars about the derivation and meaning of the word. The Latin rendering is always, as Donne has said above in lines 129–130, *Omnipotens*. But the word used in *Prov.* 19.26 (rendered "does violence to" in R.S.V.) is from an entirely different root. Donne, who is following an older interpretation, is therefore in error in saying that the first

LINE

meaning of *Shaddai* is "dishonor" or "do violence to." For this note and that on Sermon 18, line 281, we are indebted to the Rev. Dr. C. A. Simpson, Christ Church, Oxford.

189 worldly : wordly *F*

198 *and* : and *F*

210 so ever : to ever *F*

230 another : anothet *F*

266 Confidence : Confidenee *F*

267 *one.* We : *one.* we *F*

270 an honest : a honest *F*

301 *mg.* Deut. 4 : Deut. 14 *F*

315 by things (see *N.E.D.* on "by" as a prefix to nouns)

366 pardon. : pardon, *F*

395–396 *have mercy upon me* : have mercy upon me *F*

421 *of the* : of the *F*

429 *me,* : *me F*

497 his *tenne thousand* : his *tenne thousand F*

558 *It* : It *F*

561–562 *what is your life?* : what is your life? *F*

566–568 *if . . . stock . . . by . . . it will . . . but . . . and* : if . . . stock . . . by . . . it will . . . but . . . and *F*

597 *mg.* Psal. 120.6 : Psal. 120.5 *F*

638–639 is our hope : is our hopes *F*

660 *foras* : *for as F*

Notes to Sermon No. 9

Title A Lent-Sermon . . . 1620] Preached to yᵉ Kinge at Whitehall 16 Febr. 1620 *D* : The Second Sermon, Preached by John Donne Doᵗʳ: of Devinity and Dean of Paules *P*

Text *manifest*] manifested *D, L*

1 no] the *D, L*

2 *Ezekias D, L, M* : *Ezekiah's F*

3 *mg.* Josh. 10.12 *M* : Josh. 10.11 *F, D, L* : *om. P*

4 this] their *D, L*

7 this] *om. D, L, P*

8 matter] a matter *D, L*

10 *&c*] & /Text *M*

11–12 of God, : of God *F*

LINE

17–18 the Morning *D, L, M, P* : Morning *F*

20 where] wherein *D, L*

24 Humiliation and Mortification] Mortification and humiliation *P*

25 exinanition] examination *L, P* : *the first "i" has been crossed out, and "a" after "n" altered to "i" in D*

27 in the] in *M, P*

33 Note. New paragraph begins with "The Text" in *M*. Paragraph continued in *F*.

34 too] *om. D, L*

36 as is] as it is *D, L*

37 before the Text] before my text *D, L*

37 and to *D, L, M, P* : to *F*

41–42 the Apostle ... to us] *om. M*

50 in] of *D, L*

50 *meridiem D, L, M, P* : *Meridium F*

51 *the*] his *D, L*

54 *prædicatur D, P* : *predicatur F, M*

67 of] *om. D, L*

71 Apostles? : Apostles; *F*

76 *lectiones*] *Lectiones* (divers readinges) *P*

77 Will, the] will, and *D* : will and the *L*

79 *mg.* 2 Cor. 11.3 : 2 Cor. 2.3 *F* : Cor. 2.11 *with "3" opposite next line P* : *om. D, L*

82 *mg.* Dan. 5.25 *L, P* : Dan 5 *D, M* : *om. F*

83 Chaldeans *L, M, P* : Chaldæans *D* : Caldeans *F*

84 that it] *om. D, L*

85 *mg.* v. 5 *M* : vers. 5 *D, P* : *om. F, L*

87 so, as a *Edd.* : so, a *F* : soe that *P* : as a *D, L*

87 duties] Wayes *P*

89 proposed] purposed *D, L*

95 the same] some *D* : *om. L*

95 witnesses] witnes *D, L*

105 I ... when] *om. P*

107 we] I *D, L*

110 too] *om. M, P*

112 alwayes have] and all wayes have *P* : have alwaies *D, L*

114 and it will be so;] *om. D, L*

114–115 Counsel ... Ask the] *om. P*

116 not] *om. M*

116 any] an *D, L*

117 any truth unaffirmed] un-affyrmed any truth *P*

122 still, must *D, L, M* : still. Must *F*

125 *Patrem* : *patrem F*

127 *mg.* 13.3 *D, L. M* : *om. F*

130 Father and Son] the Father and the Sonne *L, M*

135 but ... it] *om. D, L*

136 *mg.* Mat. 16.17 : Mat. 16.16 *F, M* : Mark 16.16 *D, L* : Mat. 16.18 *P*

137 *mg.* Mat. 11.25 : 11.25 *M* : 2.25 *D, L* : Mathew 25 *P* : *om. F*

140–141 and yet ... *Rome*] *om. D, L*

142 (that is, noe interpretation of any Scripture) *D, L, M, P* : *om. F*

144 *mg.* Gregory *D, L, M* : sayes Gregory *P* [in text after "est"] : *om. F*

145 Prophecy; no : Prophecy.) No *F* : Prophesie. noe *L*

150 necessary : necessay *F*

153 see] sees *D, L*

153 in any constellation then I do] then I doe in any constellation *D, L*

154–155 no member] or member *D, L*

156 and] or *D, L, P*

157 conduces] conducts *D, L* : produces *P*

165 *mg.* 2 Cor.] 1 Cor. *D, L*

166–167 Saints. [New paragraph] It *D, L, M* : Saints: It is [paragraph continued] *F*

167 *mg.* *Magnum* [so placed in *D, L, M* : misplaced opposite line 168 in *F*] : *om. P*

171 *Berengarius M* : *Berengarius* his *P* : *Berengarians F, D, L*

172 &] and *M*

185 need] needs *D, L, P. M* has "needs" with "s" scratched through.

187 need] needs *D, L, P*

196 a] an *D, L*

203 *mg.* *P* supplies "*Manifestatus.*"

204 *mg.* Psal. 19.1 *P* : Psal. 19.2 *F, D, L* (Vulg. 18.2)

208 manifested often] often manifested *D, L, P*

209–210 manifested often] often manifested *D, L* : shewed often *P*

LINE

210–211   in frustrating ... often]   *om. D, L*

217 *mg.*   Areopag.]   *om. D, L, P*

218   *ipsi D, L, M* : *ipse F*

219   *agnitum*]   *agnitum* (unspekeable to any Tounge unknowne to all understandinge, not knowne to the very Primate of Angells) *P*

219   order *D, L, M, P* : orders *F*

221   concoction]   concoctions *D, L, M, P*

234   that]   who *D, L*

234   *pæne* : *pene F, D, L, M* : *Pæne P*

239–241   they ... manifested]   *om. D, L*

243   sayes he *D, L, M, P* : *om. F*

246   *Judicatures*]   *Judicature M, P* : *Judicatores D, L*

246   let them]   *om. M, P*

251   Virgin]   blessed Virgin *P*

252   Transubstantiators]   Transubstantiation *M*

254   they]   you *M*

255   the manifestation]   this manifestation *M, P*

261   these]   those *M, P*

265   of pampering ... obeying thy flesh]   *om. D, L*

268   *manifested*] justified *D, L*

273   he were]   himself was *D, L*

276 *mg.*   2 Cor. 1.3 *M, P* : 2 Cor. 13 *F, D, L*

282   in the Spirit]   *om. P*

289 *mg.*   Gal. 3.3 *D, L* : 3.3 *M* : *om. F*

289   calls it]   saies *D, L*

296–297   and fiery]   in fiery *D, L, P*

298–300   and not ... tongues]   *om. P*

299   in faint *D, L, M* : infinite *F, Al*

301   and so]   and *D, L*

306   prove]   approve *D, L*

306   his]   to be his *M, P*

311   this]   the *D, L, P*

314   no creature *D, L, M, P* : creatures *F*

319–320   and Death ... voice]   *om. P*

322   this ... this]   his ... his *D, L*

322   Deity]   godhead *P*

323   this]   his *D, L*

324   in whose power]   when *D, L*

325   *in Spiritu* : in *Spiritu F*

LINE

325   *suo*]   *suo* (in the Holy spiritt and his owne Spiritt) *P*

329 *mg.* Mat. 11.19 : Mat. 2.19 *F, D, L* : *om. M*

333   *Alchoran*] Alcoran *M, P* : Alchoron *D, L*

334   *Arrians*] Arians *P*
     NOTE. The incorrect form "Arrians" which is found in *F, D, L, M* is recognized by *N.E.D.* as a sixteenth- and seventeenth-century form.

336   himself] *om. D, L*

339   acquit *D, L, M, P* : quit *F, Al*

342 *mg.* 1 Cor. 2.11 *M, P* : 1 Cor. 2.2 *F, D, L*

343   in ... of] in a ... of a *M, P*

346   *Crucifie him*] *Crucifige D, L, M, P*

348   thine] thy *D, L, P*

350   and more *D, L, M, P* : more *F*

354   Shepherds M [not clear, owing to blot at end of word] *P* : Shepherd *F, D, L*

357 *mg.* Mat. 4.11 *M, P* : Mat. 4.2 *F, D, L*

358   to] unto *L, P*

361   was] *om. D, L*

366   it] this *D, L*

372   that ... him] *om. P*

373   but] *om. M, P*

374 *mg.* Acts 1.11 *M, P* : Acts 1.2 *F, D, L*

377 *mg.* Mat. 25.31 *M* : *om. F, D, L*

385   Christ] Christ himselfe *D, L*

388   no dissention] *om. M, P*

388   strife, no difference] difference, noe strife *D, L*

389 *mg.* Dan. 10.13 : Dan. 10 *F, D, M* [*L* has "13" inserted in a later hand]

395   and] an *M, P* : *om. D, L*

397   *this*] that *P* : *om. D, L*

400 *mg.* *P* supplies "verse 2"

402 *mg.* *P* supplies "verse 3"

402   *I have ... solus*] *om. P*

405   this; : this, *F*

405–406 of Christs ... Man] *om. P*

406   Man, the Angels knew *D, L, M* : Man: the Angels knew it *F* : Man, the Angels themselves knew *P*

409   later] latter *M, P* : later order *D, L*

410   *ancients*] antient *D, L*

LINE

412–413   (*this Mystery* ... *Apostles*) : (this Mystery ... Apostles) *F*

412 *mg.*   Ephes. 3.3–5 : Ephes. 3.6 *F, D, L, M*

413–414   *revealed* ... are]   *om. P*

421   *sæculis D, L, M* : *seculis F*

422   mystery]   mysteryes *M, P*

422   of the]   of *D, L, P*

429   and]   in *D, L*

431   reads]   read *M*

435   it will *D, L, M, P* : that will *F*

438   God, : God; *F*

440   an]   an innocent *M, P*

442–443   open, and always upon thee] upon thee open *D, L*

450   blasphemings]   blasphemyes *M, P*

455   *Prædicatus L, M, P* : *Predicatus F, D* [but *F, D* have "*Prædicat.*" in margin of line 456]

456   *meet*]   mett *D, L, P*

457   proceedings : proceedings, *F* : proceedings. *M*

459–460   *To confirm* ... *fathers* : to confirm ... fathers *F*

461   Christ]   he *M, P*

462   *meet*]   mett *D, L, P*

463–464   *and that* ... *mercy* : and that ... mercy *F*

464–465   *Gens Sancta*]   *om. M, P*

465–466   *we* ... *sinners* : we ... sinners *F* : *om. P*

472   assurances *D, L, M, P* : assurance *F*

473   had]   hath *D, L*

474   conveyances *D, L, M, P* : conveyance *F*

475   in Circumcision ... flesh]   *om. L*

477   these assurances *D, L, M, P* : this assurance *F*

477   ye *M, P* : *they F, D, L*

      NOTE. This is the reading of A.V. and is parallel to "*ye were*" in line 479.

478   *hope*]   helpe *D, L*

481   to make]   soe make *M*

487   said]   had sayde *M, P*

491   *I will give thee*]   *om. P*

491   *give thee not onely*]   *not onely give thee D, L*

492 *mg.*   Psal. 67.4 *Edd.*

      NOTE. Psal. 97.1 is placed here by *F* and *D, L, M*, but "*lætentur gentes*" is not found in that verse. We have moved "Psal. 97.1" to the margin of line 494, where it is the correct reference for

LINE

"*Lætentur insulæ,*" which is left without a reference in *F* and the MSS.

495   sayes that] sayes the *M*

496   out of the Sea]   *om. P*

500   *Prædicatus D, L, P*   :   *Predicatus F*   :   *contracted form in M*

502 *mg.*   *Mundo D, L, M, P*   :   *Mun./do F*

504   makes]   make *M, P*

506   is it]   it is *D, L*

507   sayes S. *Paul*]   *om. M*

508–509   sayes *Moses*]   *om. D, L*

510   *hence.* Where *Edd.*   :   *hence:* where *F*

511   *doers,* how *D, L*   :   *doers,* How *M*   :   *doers;* How *F*

513   were]   were not *L*   :   "were" *followed by* "not" *added above the line D*

514–515   takes]   tooke *M*

518   It ... Sermons]   *om. P*

519   a morall honest]   an honest morall *M, P*   :   in honest morall *D, L*

523–524   whose age ... Jesus]   *om. D, L*

523   antedated *M, P*   :   antidated *F*   :   *om. D, L*

523   so far]   *om. M*

525   Brothers and Sisters]   Kinsmen *P*

527   he]   *om. D, L*

528   who]   which *D, L, P*

529   That that]   that the *D, P*

529   that Carpenters]   the Carpenters *D, L*

530   work]   workes *M*

532   believe]   be believed *D, L*

535   ennamel]   enamell'd *D, L*

536   place]   sett *D, L*

537   *Crucifige*]   Crucifye *M, P*

538   As]   And *D, L*

539   *worm, ... man,*   :   worm, ... man, *F*

541   as a *D, L, M, P*   :   a *F*

548   a Gospel]   *om. P*

554   preferments]   preferment *D, L*

555–556   *He ... not*]   *om. P*

556   *world, and D, L, M, P*   :   *word, and F*

561   of Pride]   *om. D, L*

563   man]   men *D, L, P*

LINE

569–570   eat and drink that Flesh and Blood] eate and drinke that flesh, and that blood *M, D, L* [*L* omits "and drinke"] : eate that fflesh and drinke that bloude *P*

571   temptations] temptation *D, L*

572   and possessed,] *om. D, L*

573   charm] charmes *L, P*

576 *mg.*   Rom. 11.33] Rom. 2.23 *D, L*

580   he said] he saies *D, L* : sayinge *P*

583   not to be] to be, not *M, P*

586   generall] generally *D, L* : Universall *P*

594   received] receyved up *M*

596   received] *Receptus D, L, M, P*

598   inexpressible] unexpressible *M, P*

599 *mg.*   48] Esay 48 *M, P*

600   *Esay D, L, M, P* : *Isaiah F*

602   *Majestas*] *Maiestas* (your Highnesse and your Maiesty) *P*

602   amongst] among *D, L, P*

603   *vestra beatitudo*] *Beatitudo vestra* (your Highnesse and your blessednesse) *P*

605   Old : old *F*

609   *frater* N. *M, P* : *Frater F, Al*

611   *Bellarmine*] Bellarmine himselfe *P*

615   addition] stile *D, L*

615   *Æternitas D, L, M, P* : *Eternitas F*

616   own] *om. D, L*

619–620   have been] bee *D, L*

620   had] *om. D, L. M*

620   it thought] thought it *M*

621 *mg.*   *Spondanus M* : *Spondamus F* : *om. D, L, P*

624   this lowness] that lownesse *M*

629   him. Great : him: great *F*

633   gave] *om. M*

636   and no] and to noe *M, P*

637   *Vanitas D, L, M* : *Vanitas, F*

643   *As* : As *F*

643   *good for men* : *good M*

643   *much*] too much *D, L*

643–644   *so ... not glory* : so ... not glory *F*

651   *cum Domino*] *in Domino* (the same Spirrit in the Lord) *P*

LINE

659 glory therefore]   therefore *M*

660 *in luce*   :   in *luce F*

670 you]   us *M*

NOTE. After line 671, *M* adds "ffinis of Doc: Donns Sermon at White-hall before the Kinge yᵉ 16: ffebruary 1620?" *L* adds "coram 92ge" followed by "1620" scratched through ["92ge" stands for "rege"].

Notes to Sermon No. 10

103 exorcised *F corr. in errata*   :   exercised *F originally*

231 at some times *Al*   :   at sometimes *F*

291 spettle] spittle *Al*

NOTE. The forms "spattle" and "spettle" from O.E. *spatl, spætl,* are older than "spittle" and were common in the sixteenth and seventeenth centuries. See *N.E.D.*

300 liberty   :   libery *F*

305 forbidden   :   forbid-/ken *F*

319 *mg.* Luk. 24.42   :   Luk. 24.41 *F*

356 *mg.* Eccles. 7.16   :   Eccles. 7.17 *F*

367 sufficient   :   sufficienr *F*

440 *mg.* Eccles. 5.13   :   Eccles. 5.12 *F*

489 next   :   text *F*

501 on high   :   an high *F*

536 Apostles   :   Apostles, *F*

555 *mg.* Exod. 20.12   :   29 *F*

Notes to Sermon No. 11

[This sermon is found in *F* and *Q*, and in three MSS—*E, M,* and *P*. The text and punctuation of *F* are not so good as usual, and wherever *Q, E, M, P* agree against it we have adopted their reading in place of that of *F*. *M* and *P* have a large number of variants in which they stand alone, and some of these suggest that the manuscript which was the common source of *M, P,* may have represented an earlier draft by Donne, of which the text of *F, Q, E* may be a revision. On this point see the discussion of the text of *E* in this sermon in Vol. II, App. A, pp. 368–370. The text of *Q* has fewer blunders than usual, and its punctuation is smoother than that of *F,* but the Scriptural quotations have been altered to make them conform, generally, to the text of A.V. (see lines 154, 160, 391). Evidently the learned "corrector" of the Cambridge University Press disliked Donne's loose method of quoting sometimes from the Geneva version and sometimes (inaccurately) from memory. We have omitted nearly all the numerous variants in which P stands alone, and many of those in which E and M stand alone.]

LINE

Title *Preached at a Mariage F* : By M^r D^r D at ye mariage of M^{ris} Washington [inserted above by another hand in a black ink which stands out against the brownish ink of the original hand. This second hand, which appears to be almost contemporary with the first hand, has made a number of corrections in the sermon] E : The Fourth Sermon by John Donne Doctor of Devinity and Deane of Paules ... [On next page] Preached at St Clements at Mr Washingtons Mariage P

2 *Erash*] [Erach] M

3 later] latter M, P

3 mariage] marrying Q

5 accept] accept of M

8 And] *om. E*

9 persons] Personages P

19 *in*] *om. M, P*

26 *thee*] thee unto me M, P

26 And then ... *mary thee*] *om. E*

26 *thee*] *om. M, P*

27 *to*] unto M, P

28 *mg.* I Q : I^t F

29 *mg.* Persons] *om. Q*

29–30 He and She Q, M, P, : he and she F, E

31 limitations Q, M, P : limitation F, E
NOTE. The following "are" requires the plural.

33 *mg.* Acts. 15] Acts 5 M, P

40 at all given Q, M, P : given at all F, E

40–41 Paradise, though there were four rivers in Paradise Q, M, P : Paradise F, E

43 build Q, M, P : built F, E

44–45 forbidding] forbidding of Q

45 advantages] advantage M, P

45 against] over M, P

49 induced] induce M, P

52 *Manichæan Q* : Manichean F

LINE

53, 56   the *Colliridian* . . . the *Peputian* *Q, M, P* : your Colliridian
     . . . your Peputian *F, E*
     NOTE. It is clear that the MS which was the common source of
     F and *E* misread the contraction "yᵉ" as "yʳ" both here (twice)
     and in line 60 below.

53   a woman]   women *M, P*

57   moderate]   modest *M, P*

58   To]   soe to *M, P*

60   the *Q, M, P* : your *F, E*

61   dissolve *Q, M, P* : dissolved *F, E*

61   mariage]   marriages *Q, P*

62   spirituall *Q, E* : spitituall *F*

64–65   when . . . Father]   *om. M, P*

66   so farre, as to give them *Q, M, P* : so, as to give *F, E*

70   the service of]   *om. E*

72   mariage]   marriages *Q*

74   He and She *Q, M, P* : he and she *F, E*

77   case *Q, E* ["cause" with "u" blotted out], *M, P* : cause *F*

79   nor]   *om. Q*

83   such persons are]   such are persons *Q*

87   *unto*]   to *Q, M, P*

87   for . . . our selves *Q* : *for . . . our selves F*

90   is . . . Priest]   are . . . Preists *M, P*

95   testimony]   the testimony *M, P*

107   it]   he *M, P*

111   disciplines]   discipline *E, M, P*

112–113   for *Vri . . . perfecti*]   *om. M, P*

113–114   that is . . . that is . . . that is]   thats . . . thats . . . thats *E, M, P*

114   that fire *Q, E, M, P* : the fire *F*

115   first use]   ayme *M, P*

123   foresaw]   saw *M, P*

124   his wife *M, P, Q* : a wife *F, E*

126   dwell there, and]   *om. E, P*

127   to one *Q, E, M, P* : one to *F*

128   And]
     NOTE. *M* uses capital letters, and makes a new paragraph to
     mark off the prayer which follows. Also in lines 180, 230, 518,
     M uses the same procedure to mark off each prayer for the
     married couple.

138   to one another *Q, M, P* : to another *F, E* (but "one" has been
inserted above the line in a second hand)

139–140   it ... it] that ... that *Q*

139   other] *om. M*

141–142   use ... use] ayme ... ayme *M, P*

144   transplantation *M, P, Q* : transportation *F, E*

151   having given] giving *M, P*

152   from] of *M, P*

154   says] sayth *M, P*

154   *every mans eares*] *both the eares of everyone Q* (following
A.V.)

154   *heares*] *heareth Q* (following A.V.)

155   broke] brake *M, P*

156   promise of consolation *Q, M, P* : consolation *F, E*

159   arises] ariseth *M, P*

160   in charity, in] *and charitie, and Q* (following A.V.)

161   and] and in *M, P* : *with Q* (following A.V.)

167   in that] in the *M, P*

171   by paying at first] at first by paying *M, P*

172   sinfull] *om. M*

175   says] sayth *M, P*

188   use] ayme *M, P*

198   works *Q, M, P* : work *F, E*

199   yet he ... good] *om. E*

201   does] doth *M, P*

202–204   Ark it self ... Ark] Ark *P*

204   couples] *om. M* (blank left)

210   Help] helper *Q*

213   birth] beauty *M, P*

214   another, *Q, M, P* : another *F*

214   else] *om. M*

223   dishonourably, : dishonourably *F*

224   the Helper] a helper *M, P*

226   whence *Q, M, P* : whom *F*

231   present] *om. M, P*

237   cordiall Physick] Cordiall *M, P*

242   onely that *Q, M, P* : that onely *F, E*

246   half-mariage] half marriages *Q*

257   *immunditiei Q, E, P* : *immunditii F*

258   *zelotypiæ Q, E* : zelotipia *M* : zelotipie^c *P* : *velotypiæ
F*

LINE

266–267 and before ... Image]   *om. P*

268 there be *Q, E, M, P*   :   there is *F*

269 as]   for *M, P*

274 professes]   protests *M, P*

277 *In æternum Q*   :   in *æternum F*

278 too, as]   as *M*   :   our *P*

279 interruption]   interruptions *M, P*

286 by God in heaven]   in heaven by God *M, P*

287 uses]   aymes *M, P*

289 dissolves]   dissolve *M, P*

290 Where]   *When Q*

290–291 Where ... and say]   *om. M, P*

297 there is]   there are *Q*

297 diminish]   diminishes *M, P*

298 *haberes*]   *habere M, P*

299 for continency *Q, M, P*   :   continency *F, E*

300 abstinence *Q, M, P*   :   abstinency *F, E*

302 this is *Q, E, M, P*   :   that is *F*

302 Of that *Q, E, M, P*   :   That *F*

304 make even]   make ever *Q, E, M*   :   even make *P*

305 that she *Q, E, M, P*   :   this she *F*

305 was]   is *E*

306 *Benedicta,*]   *om. M, P*

308 world]   word *M, P*

314 foundations]   foundation *M, P*

316 in *æternum, Q*   :   in *æternum F*   :   *om. P*

317 now come]   come now *Q*

319 needs not to]   neede not *M, P*

322 speak]   say *P*   :   offer to say *Q, M*

323 inexpressible]   unexpressible *M, P*

324 to heighten ... goe about]   *om. E*

325 lights *Q, M, P*   :   light *F, E*

325 yet]   yet perchance *E*

326 each]   either *M, P*

327–328 the eternall]   this Eternall *M, P*

332 but more *Q, M, P*   :   and more *F*

334 these]   *om. Q, E, M*

336 bud and]   Budd and the *M*   :   budd, the *P*

340 from]   *om. M, P*

343 those]   the *M, P*

LINE

345   and many,] *om. E*

348   in this] in the *M, P*

350   consider] I consider *E*

350   washed in] washed with *M, P*

350–351   mine own *Q, M, P* : my own *F*

351   compunction] compassion *M*

354   leave] have *Q*

359   and soul] and a soul *M, P*

371   *In ustionem Q* : in *ustionem F*

372   fires] fyer *M, P*

375   offer] offer all *M, P*

376   wipe] wipe away *E, P*

378   in] from *M, P*

378   a remedy] *om. M*

380   too, *In prolificationem*] *In prolificationem* too *M, P*

383   yet either *Q, M, P* : yet *F, E*

384   in the] else in *M, P*

386   to Christ *Q, M, P* : unto Christ *F, E*

391   *upon thee*] *on thee henceforward Q* (following A.V.)

391–392   if no fruit, *Q, E, M, P* : no fruit, *F*

392   leaves *Q, M, P* : leafes *F, E*

394   *soli:* First, *Q, M, P* : *soli, F, E*

395   unto Christ] to Christ *Q, M*

397   too] *om. M, P*

398   have sometimes *Q, M, P* : have *F, E*

403   by me in you] in me by you *E*

406   use] ayme *M, P*

406   Surely] Sure *M, P*

408   man] men *M, P*

413   machinations] imaginations *M, P*

421 *mg.*   *In æternum*] *om. Q*

428–429   did … soul] *om. M*

434–435   beginnings] beginning *Q, P*

435   in] *om. M, P*

439   ends not] doth not end *Q*

440   does] doth *Q* : *om. P*

441   by his Father preferr'd] preferred by his Father *M, P*

449   who *Q, M, P* : that *F, E*

449   *brought to* : brought to *F*

450 *mg.*   53.7 *Q* : 53.4 *F* : *om. M, P*

LINE

453 who *was*] which was *Q*

453 I who was *Q, E, M, P* : was *F*

459 *mg.* Action] *om. Q*

461 Nor it is not] nor is it *Q*

462 at] in *M, P*

466 uncleannesse] uncleannesses *Q*

473–474 as though ... another] *om. P*

476 mary me, and mary me *In Q, M, P* : mary me, *In F, E*

478 the] *om. M, P*

481 pallid] piled *M, P*

483 Treasure] Treasures *M, P*

484 soe *Q, M, P* : too *F* : *E* has "too" which has been corrected above the line by the second hand to "soe."

494 affections] affection *M, P*

495 *mg.* Apoc. 6.12] Rev. 6.12, 13, 14 *Q*

495–497 the Sunne ... Scroll] *the Sunne ... Scroll Q*

497 see] *om. E originally, but inserted by the second hand at end of line*

499 the] *om. M, P*

499 intelligences, *Q* : intelligences; *F*

503 the Lamb] that Lambe *E, M*

510 enter] enter there *M*

514 Lighten] *M begins a new paragraph*

515 we beseech thee] *om. M*

520 and the spirituall] *om. E originally, but inserted above the line by the second hand*

523 *At the end of the sermon E adds* "Finis"; *M adds* "ffinis of a sermon preach'd at St Clements danes by D: Dunn at Mr Washingtons marriage."

Notes to Sermon No. 12

143 *mg.* Psal. 34.1 : Psal. 34.2 *F*

225 over-flow : over flow *F*

334–335 God sayes ... and he sayes : *God sayes ... and he sayes F*

415 *mg.* Mat. 27.46 : Mat. 27.37 *F*

418 *mg.* Luke 23.34 : Luke 23.24 *F*

440 *Secundùm* : *Secùndum F*

LINE

444 *mg.*	Psal. 31.21	:	Psal. 31.22 *F*
450 *mg.*	Psal. 89.49	:	Psal. 89.50 *F*
584 *mg.*	Gen. 27.38	:	Gen. 17.38 *F*

NOTE. There is a curious mistake in this line: "*Esau* said to *Iacob*." Esau said the words to his father Isaac, not to Jacob; but we have kept the reading of *F* since it may be due to a slip of memory on Donne's part.

Notes to Sermon No. 13

56	limmes	: limnes *F*	: limbs *Al*
75	*Iubal*	: *Tubal F*	
80	lights,	: lights. *F*	
162 *mg.*	Esay 66.2	: Esay 66.12 *F*	
313	no, nor	: no nor *F*	
447	*discretio*	: *descretio F*	
492 *mg.*	Gen. 47.9	: Gen. 47.6 *F*	
503 *mg.*	Ier. 14.8	: Ier. 14.7 *F*	
558 *mg.*	Exod.	: Esay *F*	
604	in that	: in in that *F*	
618 *mg.*	Jos. 1.16	: Jos. 1.17 *F*	
625	King;	: King, *F*	

Notes to Sermon No. 14

11–12	generation of	: generati-/of *F*
110	Creeple]	cripple *Al*

NOTE. The form "creeple" or "creple" is common in the sixteenth and seventeenth centuries. See *N.E.D.*

247	in his *Al*	: is his *F*
249 *mg.*	Psal. 45	: Psal. 95 *F*
389	Sacraments	: Sacrrments *F*
417 *mg.*	Deut. 10	: Levit. 10 *F*
474	inexorable	: inoxorable *F*
651 *mg.*	Gal. 1.8	: Gal. 1.9 *F*
696	*Atha*	: *Athan F*

Notes to Sermon No. 15

LINE

28   this. : this, *F*

37 *mg.*   Cant. 1.2 : Cant. 1.1 *F*

238 *mg.* Cant. 1.2 : Cant. 11.1 *F*

268   Testament, : Testament. *F*

298   *proficiscens* : *profisciscens F*

305 *mg.* Gen. 29.11 : Gen. 29.12 *F*

328 *mg.* Gen. 31.55 : Gen. 31.15 *F*

346 *mg.* 1 King : 2 King *F*

358   concord. : concord, *F*

420   Gods : God *F*

Notes to Sermon No. 16

1   now]   *om. M*

5   hereafter is]   is hereafter *M*

14   will]   need *D, L* : *om. M*

16   of these]   those *E*

16   detortion]   detorting *D, L*

18   great eagernesse and vehemence]   that vehemence and eager-
     nesse *D, L* : great vehemence and egernes *M, E*

25   had]   hath *D, L, M, E*

27–28 such sense (says that author) may be]   such may bee (saies
     that Author), may bee *D, L, M, E* [*D* reads "the Author"]

31   difference]   diffidence *M*

35   of any]   if anie *M*

39   their owne]   the *D* : their *L*

42   of one *D, L, M, E* : one *F*

43 *mg.* *Divisio*]   [placed later in *E*, opposite line 58, "The parts then"]

43   then]   *om. M*

44   these two *D, L, M, E* : two *F*

48   hath he]   he hath *D, L, M, E*

51   afflictions]   Affliction *M, E*

59–60 first part it...consider first]   first part, first, it...consider
     D, L, M, E

61   for]   soe *M*

63   rejoycing]   I reioyce *M, E*

65   to this]   in this *M, E*

LINE

67   phrase]   place *M*

69–70   suffering ... suffering]   sufferings ... sufferings *M*

72   our]   this *D, L*

73   *suffering*]   sufferings *M*

73   a suffering cast by]   as by *D, L*   :   cast by *M, E*

75–76   not for my]   nor for my *M*

76   not for mine]   for mine *M*   :   not for my *D*

76   transgressions]   transgressing *M, E*

77   it is]   *om. D, L, M, E*

78   part,   :   part *F*

79–80   unperfect]   perfect *D, L*   :   ——— [illegible] [?] perfitt *M*

80   unperfected]   unperfitt *M*

82   onely in]   only in my *D, L, E*

83–84   the making *D, L, M, E*   :   making *F*

86   and suffer ... Churches]   *om. D, L, M, E*

92   are sure was]   are as sure was *M, E*

93   tells the]   tells these *D, L, M, E*

95 *mg.*   Rom. 11.13   :   Rom. 11.12 *F, L*

97–98   *to others ... yet doubtless I am to you*   :   to others ... yet doubtless I am to you *F*

98   *to you*]   unto you *D, M, E*

101, 104   *Archippus*]   Aristippus *E*

103   may]   *om. D, L, M, E*

108   made]   made him *L*

114   esteemed]   esteemed of *E*

114   Apostle]   desciple *M*

118   admired by others for *D, M, E*   :   admired by other for *L*   :   admired for *F*

120   as]   and *D*   :   and as *L*

121   and]   and a *L, E*

121   had]   had had *E*

123   to them then]   then to them now *D, L, M, E*

123   Apostle,   :   Apostle *F*

123   not in that capacity]   *om. D, L, M, E*

126   and in]   and *M*

126   saies *D, L, M, E*   :   say *F*

127   larger]   large *D, L*

128–129   by his fame and estimation]   *om. D, L, M, E*

131   by giving ... persecutions]   *om. M*

133   distance.   :   distance; *F*

134   Minister *D, L* : ministers *F, M, E*

134–135   It becomes ... servile humoring] *om. D, L, M, E*

137   conscience] consciences *M*

140   roote; when *E* : roote, when *L* : root when; *F*

141–142   And where ... prospers not] *om. D, L, M, E*

145   and Apostleship] and the Apostleship *M*

145   easy, and acceptable *D, L, M, E* : acceptable *F*

146   discreet : descreet *F*

147   them, : them *F*

149   considered] remembered *L*

149   it] that *D, L, M, E*

153   his] *om. D, L*

154   speak] spake *D, L, M*

154   conduce] conduc'd *D, L*

155   from that] from the *M*

155   likely] like *L, M*

157   the preaching] preaching *D, L*

158   the Gospell] that Gospell *M, E*

161   spake] spoke *D, L, M, E*

162   *sancti D, L, M, E* : *Christi F*

163–164   St. *Chrysostome D, L, M, E* : *Chrisostome F*

164   writ] hath writ *D, L*

165   vehemency] vehemence *M, E*

168   the] if the *M, E*

168   come. : come; *F*

169   and] and a *D, M, E*

169   of great persons] *om. D, L, M, E*

170   and a rectified] *om. D, L, M, E*

170   for] soe *M*

173   and so ... magistrate] *om. D, L, M, E*

175   preaching of] *om. M, E*

176   *quo*] quam *D, L*

181   their *D, L, M, E* : the their *F*

181   and before the *D, L, M, E* : and the *F*

183   levity *L, E* : lenity *F*

187   when it ... doe so] *om. D, L, M, E*

187   so. : so *F*

188–189   them, ... *illis;* : them; ... *illis, F*

189 *mg.*   [Col. 1.7,8] : v. 8 *D, M* : *om. F*

189   declared : declrared *F*

198–199 done, ... done;   :   done; ... done, *F*

199 remained]   was *M, E*

200 which ... text]   *om. D, L, M*

201 interlined]   *om. D, L, M, E*

202 of]   by *E*

202 Christs]   his *D, L, M, E*

203 unseasonably]   which had bine unseasonably *M, E*

203 taught]   offered *M*

205 understandings]   understanding *M, E*

208 men]   persons *M, E*

209 *mg.* Gennadius *D, M, E*   :   *om. F*

209 for]   soe *M*

209 an Ecclesiasticall author]   *om. D, L, M, E*

210 Greece]   Girræ *D, L*   :   Girra *E*

210 and of the Eastern Church]   *om. D, L, M, E*

212–213 to Congregations ... understandings]   *om. D, L, M, E*

214 of others]   *om. D, L, M, E*

215 *watered*]   watered it *D, L, M*

216 *ille*]   *om. M*

218–219 by him]   soe by him *M*

220 in the knowledge of *D, L, M, E*   :   in *F*

222 are]   were *D, L, M*

223 a perfect use of]   *om. D, L*

225 because we ... cradles]   *om. D, L, M, E*

226–227 we need ... Homilies]   *om. D, L, M, E*

230 be intended]   intend *D, L*

233 Christ. Every   :   Christ, every *F*

235 and method]   *om. D, L, M, E*

236 decree]   decrees *E*

237–238 a great deal lesse *D, L*   :   a great deal, a lesse *F*

239 *mg.* *Gaudium*   :   *Gandium F*

240 so much of]   *om. D, L, M, E*

241 Religion,   :   Religion. *F*

242 and stronger]   *om. M*

243 that which may]   that that which may *M*   :   that that may *E*

245 a serious *D, L, M, E*   :   serious *F*

246 but for]   for *D, L, E*   :   soe *M*

246 true]   this true *L*

247–248 because this joy is]   in *D, L, M, E*

248–250 that wee have ... a true Church]   *om. D, L, M, E*

LINE

250 ordained, in a true Church. There : ordained: In a true
Church there *F*

253 this in] *om. D, L*

256 name] names *M*

259 that is,] *om. D, L, M, E*

261 *mg.* and 10] *om. D, L* [placed wrongly opposite line 259]

262 *mg.* 12.10 *M* : 2.10 *F* [placed wrongly opposite line 259]

263 now joy] new Joy *D, L*

265 after this life *D, L, M, E* : after this *F*

265 the day] that day *D, L, M, E*

266 wheresoever] whethersoever *M*

267 whensoever] whersoever *D, L, M, E*

268 came] ranne *M, E*

270 *Cellulæ*] cellula *D, L, M*

270–271 in his mellifluous language] *om. D, L, M, E*

272–273 and is as a shell ... joy here,] *om. D, L, M, E*

273 which] *om. D, L, M, E*

274 and be ... those joys] *om. D, L, M, E*

274 For] soe *M*

278 *loafes*] loaves *L*

278 *you*] yee *E*

279 there] then *M*

280 *receive D, L, M, E* : eat *F*

282 with thee out ... world] out ... world with thee *E*

285 a far] another *M, E*

288 in them] *om. E*

289 indifferently] *om. D, L, M, E*

289 (were it not] (it were *M, E*

290 went] means *E*

292 *mg.* 14.17 *M* : 14.7 *F, L*

292 the world] this world *M, E*

292 *The Kingdome of* : The Kingdome of *F*

294 *nos*] vos *D, L, M, E*

295 joy] that Joy *D, L, M, E*

295 but every joy is] but yet everie Joy that is in us is *D, L, M, E*

297–298 *and again* : and again *F*

299 joy] faith *E*

299 ye] wee *M*

300 *again rejoyce* : again *rejoyce F*

301–302 and see if ... them again] *om. D, L, M, E*

304   *Again*   :   Again *F*

308   a use]   an use *D, L, M, E*

309   that]   who *D, L, M, E*

316   even in this life]   *om. D, L, M, E*

316 *mg.*   *Tristitia*   :   *Tristitiæ F*

317 *mg.*   Chrysost.   :   Chrisost. *F*

318–319   a sadnes ... crosses of this world]   *om. D, L, M, E*

320   so it is]   so is *D, L, M*

321   for that]   for the *M*

321   disease,   :   disease *F*

326   that]   the *D, M*

328   tempest]   a tempest *D, L*

331   hath this *D, L, M, E*   :   hath he *F*

334   doth that *D, L, M, E*   :   doth it *F*

336   then]   *om. D, L, M, E*

339   sorrow]   sadnes *D, L, M, E*

340   first]   at first *M, E*

342   it]   that *M*

344   6.10.]   6. *D, E*   :   8 *altered to* 6 *L*

345   *gaudentes*   :   *gandentes F*

349   an]   *om. D*

350   for,   :   for *F*

350   then]   there *E*

351   *in somnium*   :   *insomnium F*

356   *inter*]   betweene *E*

359   conscience)   :   conscience(*F*

359   are]   are all *M*

361   to be a]   to be *D*

363   have]   hath *D, L, M, E*

371   mans]   his *D, L, M, E*

371   reach]   ranke *D, L*

372   him as that God]   him to present to him, as that *D, L*   :   him, God present to him, as that *M*   :   him, soe present to him, as that God *E*

374   halfe a]   a halfe *M, E*

374   the]   all the *L*

376   and]   and an *E*

376   which the]   which this *E*

377   rouse]   raise *D, L, M, E*

LINE

378 *mg.* 2 Cor. 7.4 : 2 Cor. 17.4 *M, E* : 1 Cor. 17.4 *F, L*

380 a halfe] halfe a *M*

381–382 a searing . . . of the affections] *om. D, L, M, E*

383–385 *Non facies . . .* call it misery] *om. L*

386 out of . . . tendernesse] *om. D, L, M, E*

386 the] the extreme *D, L*

388 but yet but a halfe] but halfe a *D, L* : but, but a halfe *M, E*

390 tribulations] tribulation *M*

391–392 not that they . . . swallow them] *om. D, L, M, E*

393 *mg.* 1 Peter 4.12 *E* : 1 Pet. 4.4 *M* : *om. F*

397–398 He bids . . . rejoycing at last] *om. D, L, M, E*

399 and : aud *F*

399 undeterminable *D, L, M, E* : determinable *F*

405 a gremiall] *om. D, L, M, E*

405 bosome and] *om. D, L, M, E*

411 then without . . . should have been] *om. D, L, M, E*

412 counted worthy *M, E* : contented worthy *D, L* : worthy *F*

415 *for so . . . Prophets* : for so . . . Prophets *F*

415 *persecuted they*] they persecuted *M, E*

422–423 *he is . . . me* : he is . . . me *F*

425 that] the *D, L*

427 a bubling and] *om. D, L, M, E*

439 neither] *om. D, L, M, E*

440 if I force them] *om. D, L, M, E*

444–445 onely is] is onely *D, L*

447 he hath] he had *L*

448 suffer] *om. D, L, M, E*

452 Christ] God *M, E*

452 though I suffer as a malefactor] *om. D, L, M, E*

453 But] that *M*

453 mine, it is not] mine that is, not *E*

454 the] *om. D, L, M, E*

456 fall] shall fall *D, L*

458–459 *or at . . .* comes] *om. D, L, M, E*

461 to] of *D, L*

463 how little soever they doe] *om. D, L, M, E*

465 shall] *om. D, L*

465 that is,] *om. D, L, M, E*

473   says the Law]   *om. D, L, M, E*
477   came]   come *E, L*
479   into *D, L, M, E*   :   in *F*
484   breakes the]   breakes this *D, L, M, E*
486   primarily]   *om. D, L, M, E*
488   an]   any *M*
489   Church,   :   Church; *F*
490   or enforced]   nor forced *D, L, M, E*
491   good]   a good *D, L, M, E*
491   for]   for a *L*
492   Law;   :   Law, *F*
493   my]   mine *E, L*
493   stranger]   stronger *D, L*
494   mine by disavowing it, mine by]   mine by [blank] mine by
      disavowing, mine by *L*   :   myne by disteaming it, myne by
      disavowing by *M*   :   mine by disclayming it, mine by dis-
      avowing it, mine by *E*
495   even *M, E*   :   are even *F, D, L*
504 *mg.*   2 Cor. 12.15 *L*   :   1 Cor. 12.15 *F, M, E*
505   *Numquid*]   Nunquid *D, L, M*
506   question;   :   question, *F*
512 *mg.*   2 Cor. 1.6   :   2 Cor. 1.16 *E, L*   :   1 Cor. 1.16 *F, M*
515   and then]   and *M*
516   and salvation]   *om. M*
516   sufferings beget]   suffering begets *D, L*
519   in his]   and his *D, L*
522 *mg.*   Phil. 2.17   :   Phil. 2.15 *M, E*   :   Psal. 2.17 *D, L*   :   *om. F*
525 *mg.*   4.1 *M*   :   *om. F*
525   *Coronam*]   Corona *D, L*
526   in that]   in the *M*
526   compasses]   compassed *E*
533   Saint]   doth Saint *M, E*   :   both St. *D, L*
533   calls]   call *M, E*
534   in the *D, L, M, E*   :   that is, his *F*
534 *mg.*   1 Thes. 2.19 *E*   :   1 Thes. 2.14 *M*   :   *om. F*
535   *even you*]   you even *E*
542   to both]   both to both *D, L, M, E*
547 *mg.*   Pro. 17.6 *D, L, M*   :   Pro. vi.6 *E*   :   *om. F*
552   Crowns]   Crown *E*

553 everlasting] eternall and everlastinge *E*
553 Amen.] Amen/3° Calend: Sextilis./ *L*
NOTE. This date in *L* is the date of transcription, and is in our reckoning August 30. Earlier sermons in *L* give the year of transcription as 1624.

Notes to Sermon No. 17

19 Chapter. For : Chapter: for *F*
30 *with* : with *F*
41 therefore : thereforre *F*
54 *expound* things : *expound* thing *F*
58 in his *deeds* : *inhis deeds F*
149 *light* : *life F*
201 *and* : and *F*
229 *mg.* Luke 9.29 : Luke 9.27 *F*
254–255 may abstaine from doing any act against worshipping of *Images, . . . stealing, . . .*]
NOTE. There seems to be some confusion here. Donne is enumerating several of the sins forbidden in the Decalogue—idolatry, stealing, adultery. Should we read "abstaine from any act of worshipping *Images*"? "Abstaine from any act against" is the opposite of what he apparently intends.
278, 289 *Augem*]
NOTE. *Auge*, from Old French *auge*, taken from the Arabic, is an astronomical term, now obsolete, denoting the "apogee" or "highest point of the apparent course of the sun, moon, or a planet" (*N.E.D.*).
425 communicable : communica-/cable *F*
596 first, : first *F*
632 because : be cause *F*
716 *ver.* 17. : *ver.* 14. *F*
853 a *torch,* †or a *knife,*†
NOTE. We have marked the words "or a *knife*" as a corruption of the text, because the words of the context "to take *fire,* and to give *light*" are quite inapplicable to a "knife." We suggest that the word required in place of "knife" may be "knitch," a word now obsolete except in dialect, but used from the fourteenth to the seventeenth century to denote a bundle of wood, flax, or hay tied together, or a faggot (see *N.E.D.*).

LINE

854 *lightned*]

NOTE. "Lighten" is here used to mean 'kindle,' a sense which is now obsolete, though it was common in the seventeenth century.

932 *making; ... valuation,* : *making, ... valuation; F*

937 infinitely; : infinitely, *F*

968 as good use ... as : a good use ... as *F*

979 *and* : and *F*

1021 *us* : *ut F*

Notes to Sermon No. 18

1 take it, : take it *F*

146 *mg.* Luk. 6.32 : Luk. 6.34 *F*

150 have said : haue said *F*

NOTE. It is unusual to find "haue" in *F*, published in 1640. The change took place about 1632/3 in publishers' houses.

195 *thee?*) : *thee*) *F*

273 *mg.* Iohn 16.22 : Iohn 16.21 *F*

281 *Lachem*, and *Maiim*]

NOTE. The usual vocalization of *Lachem* is *Lechem*. It is vocalized *Lachem* in *Prov.* 25.21, which Donne is quoting here, because it comes at the end of a clause, and its position causes a lengthening of the first vowel from *e* to *a*. The Septuagint omits both *Lachem* and *Maiim*, hence St. Paul's omission of the two words, on which Donne comments here.

358 conscientious : conscientiense *F*